Double Non-taxation and the Use of Hybrid Entities

Series on International Taxation

VOLUME 66

Series Editors

Introduction & Contents

The Series on International Taxation deals with a wide variety of topics in the global tax arena. The authors include many of the field's leading experts as well as talented newcomers. Their expert views and incisive commentary have proven highly useful to practitioners and academics alike.

Objective

The volumes published in this series are aimed at offering high-quality analytical information and practical solutions to international tax practitioners.

Readership

Practitioners, academics and policy makers in international tax law.

Frequency of Publication

2-3 new volumes published each year.

The titles published in this series are listed at the end of this volume.

Double Non-taxation and the Use of Hybrid Entities

Second Edition

Leopoldo Parada

Wolters Kluwer

Published by:
Kluwer Law International B.V.
PO Box 316
2400 AH Alphen aan den Rijn
The Netherlands
E-mail: lrs-sales@wolterskluwer.com
Website: www.wolterskluwer.com/en/solutions/kluwerlawinternational

Sold and distributed by:
Wolters Kluwer Legal & Regulatory U.S.
920 Links Avenue
Landisville, PA 17538
United States of America
E-mail: customer.service@wolterskluwer.com

ISBN 978-94-035-4666-7

e-Book: ISBN 978-94-035-4676-6
web-PDF: ISBN 978-94-035-4686-5

To my parents

Table of Contents

List of Figures

List of Abbreviations

AEDAF	Asociación Española de Asesores Fiscales
AG	Attorney General
AOE	Apple Operations Europe
AOI	Apple Operations International
APAs	Advanced Pricing Agreements
ASI	Apple Sales International
ATAD	Anti-Tax Avoidance Directive
ATP	Aggressive Tax Planning
AU	Austria
AUS	Australia
BE	Belgium
BEPS	Base Erosion and Profit Shifting
BFH	Bundesfinanzhof
BGBl	Bundesgesetzblatt
BOE	Boletín Oficial del Estado (Spain)
BR	Brazil
BTR	British Tax Review
CA	Canada
CARF	Brazilian Administrative Council of Tax Appeals
CbC Reporting	Country-by-Country Reporting
CCCTB	Common Consolidated Corporate Tax Base
CEN	Capital Export Neutrality
CFC(s)	Controlled Foreign Companies
CH	Switzerland
CIN	Capital Import Neutrality
CIT	Corporate Income Tax

CJEU	Court of Justice of the European Union
CON	Capital Ownership Neutrality
CRS	Common Reporting Standard
CTB	Check-the-Box
DE	Germany
DD	Double Deduction
DGT	Dirección General de Tributos
DK	Denmark
DLP	Kommanditselskaber
DNT	Double Non-Taxation
D/NI	Deduction/Non-Inclusion
DTC(s)	Double Tax Convention(s)
EATLP	European Association of Tax Law Professors
EBITDA	Earnings Before Interest, Taxes, Depreciation and Amortization
EBRD	European Bank for Reconstruction and Development
EC	European Community
ECOFIN	Economic and Financial Affairs Council
EEC	European Economic Community
EEA	European Economic Area
EEIG	European Economic Interest Grouping
E&P	Earnings and Profits
ES	Spain
EStG	Einkommensteutergesetz
EU	European Union
EUR	Euros
FATCA	Foreign Account Tax Compliance Act
FDI	Foreign Direct Investment
FE	Fundatio Europaea
FTC	Foreign Tax Credit
GAAP	Generally Accepted Accounting Principles
GAAR(s)	General Anti-Avoidance rule(s)
GmbH	Gesellschaft mit beschränkter Haftung
HMA	Hybrid Mismatch Arrangements
HMRC	Her Majesty's Revenue & Customs
IBFD	International Bureau of Fiscal Documentation
ICJ	International Court of Justice
IFA	International Fiscal Association
IFRS	International Financial Reporting Standards
IGA(s)	Intergovernmental Agreement(s)
IN	India

IP	Intellectual Property
I&R Directive	Interest and Royalty Directive
I.R.C.	Internal Revenue Code
IRS	Internal Revenue Service
JP	Japan
KStG	Körperschaftsteuergesetz
LLC(s)	Limited Liability Company(s)
LLP(s)	Limited Liability Partnership(s)
LOB	Limitation of Benefits
LU	Luxembourg
MAP	Mutual Agreement Procedure
MC	Model Convention
MCMAA	Multilateral Convention on Mutual Administrative Assistance in Tax Matters
MERCOSUR	Mercado Común del Sur
MLI	Multilateral Instrument
MNE(s)	Multinationals
MS	Member State(s)
NID	Notional Interest Deduction
NL	The Netherlands
NYU	New York University
OECD	Organization for Economic Co-operation and Development
OECD Model	Organization for Economic Co-operation and Development Model Convention
OJ	Official Journal
PCIJ	Permanent Court of International Justice
PE	Permanent Establishment
PL	Poland
PPT	Principal Purpose Test
PSD	Parent-Subsidiary Directive
R&D	Research and Development
SAAR(s)	Specific Anti-Avoidance rule(s)
Sàrl	Société à responsabilité limitée
SAT	State Administration of Taxation
SCE	Societas Cooperativa Europaea
SE	Societas Europaea
Sec.	Section
SICAV	Société d'Investissement à Capital Variable
Spanish NRITL	Spanish Non-Residents Income Tax Law
SPV	Special Purpose Vehicle
STR	Special Tax Regime

T.C.	Tax Court
TIEA(s)	Tax Information Exchange Agreement(s)
Treas. Regs.	Treasury Regulations
TFEU	Treaty on Functioning of the European Union
UK	United Kingdom
UN	United Nations
US	United States
USCo	United States Corporation
US Model	United States Model Convention
USP	United States Partnership
VAT	Value Added Tax
VCLT	Vienna Convention on the Law of Treaties
WHT	Withholding Tax
WTO	World Trade Organization

Preface to the Second Edition

The second edition of this book, titled 'Hybrid Entities and Double Non-Taxation', provides a fresh, updated, and innovative perspective regarding the analysis of double non-taxation and the use (and misuse) of hybrid entities within the international context, considering both a domestic and a tax treaty perspective.

Following its predecessor edition in 2018, this book maintains a critical approach regarding the OECD recommendations on hybrids (*linking rules*) as well as its implementation into legislation, arguing for an alternative solution that is better informed under the policy principles of simplicity, coherence and administrability, and which is completely agnostic of the double non-taxation outcome. Most notably, the alternative proposal elaborated in this book, and which the author denominates 'reactive coordination rule', claims for coordination in the tax characterisation of entities following the characterisation given in the 'home country' of the entity under analysis, that is, the country where that entity is legally and formally organised.

The alternative approach presented in this book does not attempt to be a perfect solution, let alone an unbeatable one, but rather serves as a guide to re-orientate the tax policy discussion to what really matters regarding hybrid entity mismatches.

This holds particular significance during periods when the tax policy debate appears to begin with a focus on pragmatism and widely accepted concepts.

Acknowledgements

I want to express my heartfelt gratitude to my colleagues at the University of Leeds and the Centre for Business Law and Practice (CBLP) for their unwavering support in preparing this second edition. Special thanks to Prof Dr Peter Whelan, former CBLP Director, who generously allowed me to have a research assistant for this project, and to Prof Dr Rita de la Feria, my esteemed colleague in the realm of tax law, whose friendship and support have been invaluable.

I also extend my thanks to present and past colleagues at Leeds who have consistently encouraged and supported my academic endeavours. Among them, Prof Dr Pinar Akman, Dr Virag Blazsek, Dr Carrie Bradshaw, Dr Suren Gomtsyan (LSE), Dr Colin Mackie, Pedro Magalhães Batista, Dr Karina Patricio Ferreira Lima, Prof Dr Conor O'Reilly, Dr Alvaro Pereira (Georgia State University), Prof Dr Ilias Trispiotis, Dr Ilaria Zavoli, and Dr Qi (George) Zhou.

My gratitude also extends to my global network of tax professionals, academics, and friends who have played a significant role in promoting my academic work worldwide. Whether through sharing my ideas, inviting me to speak at conferences and guest lectures, or supporting the publication of my work, their contributions have been invaluable. I would like to offer special thanks to Prof Hugh Ault (Boston College), Prof Alice G Abreu (Temple University), Ms Melani Astuti (BKF Indonesia), Dr Andrés Báez Moreno (Universidad Carlos III de Madrid/Max Planck Munich), Philip Baker OBE, KC (University of Oxford), Dr Eduardo Baistrocchi (LSE), Prof Dr Gianluigi Bizioli (University of Bergamo), Dr Dominic de Cogan (University of Cambridge), Prof Dr Ana Paula Dourado (University of Lisboa), Prof Dr Alfredo García Prats (University of Valencia), Dr Ricardo García Antón (Tilburg University), Dr Mario Grandinetti (University of Turin), Emeritus Prof Judith Freedman (University of Oxford), Prof Dr Werner Haslehner (University of Luxembourg), Prof Mindy Herzfeld (University of Florida), Dr Svetislav Kostic (University of Belgrade), Dr Félix Martinez Laguna (Universidad Autónoma de Madrid), Prof Leandra Lederman (Indiana University Bloomington), Dr Michael McGowan (King's College of London), Prof Ruth Mason (University of Virginia), Prof Toshiko Miyamoto (Ritsumeikan University Kyoto), Dr Aitor Navarro (Universidad Carlos III de Madrid/Max Planck Munich), Prof Noam

Noked (Chinese University of Hong Kong), Vincent Ooi (Singapore Management University), Prof Dr Germaine Rekwest (University of Curaçao/Ministry of Finance), Dr Luisa Scarcella (International Chamber of Commerce), Prof Daniel Shaviro (NYU), Prof Dr Wolfgang Schön (Max Planck Munich), Dr Rita Szudoczky (WU Vienna), Prof Justin Tan (National University of Singapore), Prof Christine Tjen (University of Indonesia), Prof Dr Marta Villar Ezcurra (CEU San Pablo), Prof Dr John Vella (University of Oxford), Dr Joanna Wheeler (IBFD), Prof Masao Yoshimura (Hitotsubashi University Tokyo), and Dr Yige Zu (Durham University).

Lastly, I want to express my appreciation to Ms. Rui Ci Lee, a former law student at Leeds, for her invaluable research assistance in this second edition. I am also thankful to all others, both known and unknown, who have directly or indirectly contributed to the success of this project. Your support has been truly indispensable, and I am deeply grateful.

Introduction

The topics of double non-taxation (hereinafter, 'DNT') and the use of hybrid entities have been on the agenda of the international tax community for a long time.[1] Nevertheless, their analysis acquires particular importance in our days when transformations within the tax world have achieved a speed and perhaps also an international commitment not witnessed before.[2]

1. In 1999, e.g., the OECD launched the *Partnership Report*, which subsequently inspired the inclusion of Article 23(4) in the 2000 OECD Model. *See* OECD, *The Application of the OECD Model Tax Convention to Partnerships*, Issues in International Taxation No. 6, OECD Publishing, Paris, 1999. During 2010, the OECD also launched the *OECD Report on Addressing Task Risks Involving Bank Losses*, which paid special attention in the situations when the same tax loss is relieved in more than one country as a result of the differences in tax treatment between jurisdictions. Subsequently, in 2011, the OECD launched the *Report on Corporate Loss Utilization through Aggressive Tax Planning*, which recommended countries to consider introducing restrictions on the multiple uses of the same loss to the extent they are concerned with the results of DNT and tax deferral. *See* OECD, *Corporate Loss Utilization Through Aggressive Tax Planning*, OECD Publishing, Paris, 2011. Likewise, DNT was the central point of discussion in the International Fiscal Association (IFA) Congress in 2004 and hybrid entities was recently discussed in the version of the year 2014 of the same forum. *See* in this regard: Cahiers de droit fiscal international – Vol. 89a, *Double Non-taxation*, (IFA 2004) and Cahiers de droit fiscal international Vol. 99B, *Qualification of Taxable Entities and Tax Treaty Protection* (IFA 2014).
2. This can be particularly seen in the OECD Base Erosion and Profit Shifting Project (BEPS project). *See* OECD, *Addressing Base Erosion and Profit Shifting*, OECD Publishing, Paris, 2013 and OECD, *Action Plan on Base Erosion and Profit Shifting*, OECD Publishing, Paris, 2013. However, more recently we could also *see* how the international tax community has experienced even a more accelerated evolution, which is reflected in the OECD two-pillar approach adopted after BEPS (sometimes referred as BEPS 2.0) with the purpose of dealing with issues of redistribution of MNEs profits worldwide and the establishment of a minimum effective corporate income tax rate, respectively. For more information on the OECD Pillar 1, *see*, OECD, *Statement on a Two-Pillar Solution to Address the Tax Challenges Arising from the Digitalisation of the Economy* (OECD Publishing, 8 October 2021). *See also* OECD, *Statement on a Two-Pillar Solution to Address the Tax Challenges Arising from the Digitalisation of the Economy* (OECD Publishing, 1 July 2021). For a preliminary analysis on the OECD Pillar 1, *see, e.g.*, L. Parada, *The Unified Approach Under Pillar 1: An Early Analysis*, 96 Tax Notes Int'l 11 (2019). *See also*, A. Navarro, 'The Allocation of Taxing Rights under Pillar One of the OECD Proposal', in: F. Hasse and G Kofler (eds), *The Oxford Handbook of International Tax Law* (Oxford University Press, 2023). For more information on the OECD Pillar 2 (global minimum tax), *see* OECD, *Challenges Arising from the Digitalisation of the*

The international tax community, or the majority of it, has been generally sceptic regarding both the DNT outcome and the use of hybrid entities. The DNT outcome, on the one hand, supposes the complete absence of taxation, and as such, it seems to be as unfair or undesirable as its counterpart: double taxation. This idea has been largely reinforced under the academic postulate that income should be taxed at least once in any cross-border transaction.[3] Hybrid entities, on the other hand, have been criticised for being an open door for creating advantages with differences among country tax systems, which might be exploited in order to duplicate tax benefits and to minimise overall tax burdens.[4] Nonetheless, neither the international need to tax every single cross-border transaction at least once nor the differences in the tax characterisation of entities have been proved to be *a priori* a true concern.[5] In spite of the above, the influence of the current international tax reforms, and perhaps also the simplification offered in the use of notions given by granted, has created the perfect scenario for the

---

Economy: Commentary to the Global Anti-Base Erosion Model Rules (Pillar Two) (OECD Publishing 2022). *See also, e.g.*, M. Devereux et al, *The OECD Global Anti-Base Erosion Proposal*, Oxford University Centre for Business Taxation (2020). More recently, *see* J. Englisch, *GloBE Rules and Tax Competition*, Intertax 48(12) (2022) DOI: 10.54648/taxi2022086.

3. A further analysis at *infra* Chapter 1, s. 3.
4. For some authors this is a problem called *'cross-border tax arbitrage'* or *'international tax arbitrage'* and occurs when a taxpayer is involved in a transaction or set up a business structure to take advantage of differences among country tax systems with the goal of exploiting such differences in order to duplicate tax benefits and to minimize his overall tax burden. Therefore, inconsistent characterisation of income or entities among the countries might, e.g., give rise to tax arbitrage opportunities. Supporting the academic concept of tax arbitrage *see, e.g.*, L. Dell'Anese, *Tax Arbitrage and the Changing Structure of International Tax Law*, Egea, Milan, 2006. *See also* R. Avi-Yonah, *Tax Competition, Tax Arbitrage and the International Tax Regime*, 61 Bull. Int'l Taxn. 4 (2007), Journals IBFD; T. Rosembuj, *International Tax Arbitrage*, 39 Intertax 4 (2011) DOI: 10.54648/taxi2011019; J. Prebble, *Exploiting Form in Avoidance by International Tax Arbitrage–Arguments Towards a Unifying Hypothesis of Taxation Law*, 17 Asia-Pac. Tax Bull. 1 (2011), Journals IBFD. Nevertheless, the concept of international tax arbitrage is arguable, mostly when dealing with situations when taxpayers legitimately arrange their affairs to achieve DNT, using the uncoordinated tax rules among jurisdictions. In this opinion *see, e.g.*, H.D. Rosenbloom, *Cross-Border Arbitrage: The Good, The Bad and the Ugly*, 85 Taxes – The Tax Mag. 116 (2007). Accordingly, the concept of tax arbitrage is still unable to explain how, e.g., differences in the characterisation of entities or the corporate residence give rise to arbitrage, whilst differences in tax rates not. For a further analysis on this subject, *see* M. Kane, *Strategy and Cooperation in International Responses to International Tax Arbitrage*, 53 Emory L.J. 89 (2004). *See also*, J. Roin, *Taxation Without Coordination*, 31 J. Leg. Stud. 1, Part 2 (2002); D. Ring, *One Nation Among Many: Policy Implications of Cross-Border Tax Arbitrage*, 44 B.C. L. Rev. 1 (2002); T. Gresik, *The Taxing Task of Taxing Transnationals*, 39 J. Econ. Lit. 3 (2001); T. Edgar, *Corporate Income Tax Coordination as a Response to International Tax Competition and International Tax Arbitrage*, 51 Can. Tax J. 3 (2003).
5. For example, the OECD BEPS Action Plan states: 'No or low taxation *is not per se a cause of concern*, but it becomes so when it is associated with practices that artificially segregate taxable income from the activities that generate it.' (Emphasis added). *See* OECD (2013), *supra* n. 2, p. 10. In contrast, Action 11 seems to get back to the original idea that DNT is indeed the evil, regardless of the element of artificiality in a cross-border transaction, when it says: 'single taxation in cross-border transactions is indeed one of the principal aims of the project both in cases when the interaction of different tax rules leads to such an outcome or when the outcome arises from the shifting of profits from the jurisdictions where the activities creating that profits took place.' *Ibid.*, with regard to the disparities in the tax characterisation of entities, they seem to be the result of sovereign tax policy decisions, representing the general rule and not the exception in the international tax practice. *Infra* Chapter 3.

appearance of even more pragmatic approaches that simply combine both elements, i.e., the DNT outcome and the disparities derived from the different tax characterisation of entities, into one single target, which ought to be counteracted.[6] This idea seems to convince many, and it is sometimes difficult to argue against due to its pragmatism and complex construction. Nonetheless, it should not be encased as unquestionable at all.

In this vertiginous path of international tax changes, therefore, this work adopts a different approach, taking the time to discover to which extent the DNT outcome and the use of hybrid entities are (if they were once) interconnected elements that should serve each other in the design of domestic and tax treaty anti-hybrid provisions, or whether a re-orientated debate as regards to the use of hybrid entities might be proposed. This task is not superfluous because only once these issues have been properly clarified will it be possible to seriously determine whether or not the positions adopted and solutions proposed up to this date shall be supported, improved or simply discarded.

1 OBJECT AND PURPOSE

The object and purpose of this study are to analyse the interaction between the DNT outcome and the use of hybrid entities within the international context, including the application of tax treaties. For this purpose, this work considers the following research questions:

(1) Is there necessarily an interconnection between the use of hybrid and reverse hybrid entities and the DNT outcome? Should the rules targeting the use (or misuse) of hybrid and reverse hybrid entities be designed based exclusively on the DNT outcome?
(2) Is there an alternative approach to deal more directly with the use (or misuse) of disparities in the characterisation of entities for tax purposes, which does not consider the DNT outcome, or should the current *consequentialist approach* prevail?

Likewise, this work starts from the following hypotheses, which will be proved or disproved during the development of this work:

(a) The sole result of a D/NI outcome, i.e., DNT, should not be considered per se a matter of concern in any cross-border transaction. Likewise, the use of the DNT outcome as an immediate proxy to determine the existence of practices

6. OECD, *Neutralizing the Effects of Hybrid Mismatch Arrangements, Action 2-2015 Final Report*, OECD Publishing, Paris, 2015. In 2012, the OECD also produced a *Report on Hybrid Mismatch Arrangements*, which reviewed domestic anti-abuse norms responding to various potentially abusive practices and concluded that they were successful in combating such practices, recommending these solutions to the problem of hybrid mismatch arrangements from a unilateral perspective. OECD, *Report on Hybrid Mismatch Arrangements*, OECD Publishing, Paris, 2012. The concept of HMA is analysed in *infra* Chapter 5.

that might be considered abusive when they derive exclusively from the use of hybrids or reverse hybrid entities should be prevented.

(b) *Linking rules*, i.e., rules matching deductions with the respective inclusion of income in the other country, as the ones proposed within the OECD BEPS Action Plan 2, have the risk of setting up strong presumptions of abusive practices by the sole reason that the outcome of DNT has been achieved. Likewise, these rules are highly complex to administer, and they do not target the core issue with respect to hybrids and reverse hybrid entities, i.e., the different tax characterisation of entities. An alternative should thus be evaluated.

(c) Rules regulating the use of *transparent entities* at the level of tax treaties to prevent access to the benefits of a bilateral tax treaty by third countries out of that treaty are, in principle, recommendable. Nevertheless, the inclusion of Article 1(2) within the OECD Model, resembling Article 1(6) US Model, might generate important issues with respect to developing countries, mostly considering that these countries generally rely on source taxation. Similar concerns are shared as regards Article 3(1) MLI, which mirrors Article 1(2) of the OECD Model. Alternative solutions, including domestic ones, should be analysed.

2 SCOPE

This work refers exclusively to the study of the cases in which a DNT outcome derives exclusively from the different characterisation of the same entity by two different jurisdictions, i.e., when a different characterisation of the same entity results in a D/NI outcome. Therefore, this study will not refer to cases of 'double deduction' (DD) included within the OECD BEPS Action Plan 2 and will not analyse the cases of 'dual resident mismatches' either, as those cases refer neither to the characterisation of entities, such as the case of dual resident mismatches, nor they involve the DNT outcome, such as in the case of hybrid and reverse hybrid structures whose outcome is a DD.

Accordingly, this study will exclude the cases of DNT derived from the use of hybrid financial instruments, i.e., when the same financial instrument is qualified differently by two jurisdictions, that is, as debt in one jurisdiction whilst equity in the other.[7] This exclusion is justified by two reasons. First, hybrid entities and hybrid instruments are two different problems. Whilst the former supposes the different characterisation of an entity by two different jurisdictions, the latter implies a different characterisation of the payment (income) made by one taxpayer to the other. The above, however, does not mean to recognise that many transactions can, in practice, involve both a hybrid payment and a hybrid entity at the same time. Second, the exclusion has the purpose of simplifying the analysis of DNT as an outcome derived

7. For a complete study about this specific topic, *see*, *e.g.*, J. Bundgaard, *Hybrid Financial Instruments in International Tax Law*, Wolters Kluwer, BV, The Netherlands, 2017.

exclusively from the use of hybrid entities and to enable a better understanding of the nature of the issues involved. In the same order of ideas, the study will not refer to the cases concerning 'hybrid transfers', namely, arrangements to transfer a financial instrument where the laws of two jurisdictions differ on whether the transferor or the transferee has the ownership of the payments on the underlying asset, e.g., re-purchase (REPO) or securities lending transactions.[8]

Finally, this work will not include the cases of the so-called hybrid PE mismatches, i.e., when two jurisdictions disagree on whether a business activity is being carried out through a PE or not. The reasons for this last exclusion are twofold. First, PEs are not strictly entities or separate entities, regardless that they can be part of an entity. Second, the 'mismatch' in this case arises with respect to the existence (or not) of a PE, i.e., a legal fiction in itself created to tax the profits of a business (branch) when there was enough economic presence in a territory, and not with respect to the existence or not of an 'entity' due to its different characterisation in two countries. This is also perhaps the reason why the OECD also opted for elaborating a separate report on this matter.[9] Considering the justifications for the exclusion of 'PE mismatches' from this work, any references to the potential application of the proposed *reactive coordination rule* (*see* Chapter 6) to these situations will also be omitted.

3 METHODOLOGY

This work has opted for an analysis not strictly linked to any specific tax jurisdiction, which, in principle, might not necessarily follow the traditional paths for research in law, which normally use as a starting point the specific provisions of a given jurisdiction. However, the methodology chosen in this case finds its justification in two main reasons. First, it is given by the nature of the concepts under analysis, i.e., DNT and hybrid entities. Both issues represent problems that not only involve the interaction of different jurisdictions, i.e., international tax law issues that are not limited to a particular State but also the application of supranational law, such as EU law and tax treaty law. To this extent, it is more accurate to situate all these issues under analysis within an international context rather than to limit their scope to the laws of a given country, which would inevitably restrict the results of this work. Second, a more agnostic analysis, i.e., not strictly linked to a specific jurisdiction, allows this author to carry out a deeper study into the foundations of the concepts in abstract, absent of the specific limitations of domestic tax legislation, which might finally allow the

8. OECD (2015), *supra* n. 6, p. 26.
9. As well confirmed by the OECD: 'Branch mismatch arrangements are not 'hybrid' in the sense that they are not the result of differences in the tax treatment or characterisation of an instrument or entity.' *See* OECD, *Public Discussion Draft: BEPS Action 2 Branch Mismatch Structures*, OECD Publishing, Paris, 2016. Accordingly, all the examples involving hybrid entities and reverse hybrid entities within the OECD BEPS Action 2 assume that there is no PE in the country of establishment of the entity once this is considered as transparent in the country of the investors. *See also*, OECD, *Neutralizing the Effects of Branch Mismatch Arrangements, Action 2: Inclusive Framework on BEPS*, OECD Publishing, Paris, 2017.

elaboration of solutions applicable to a generality of cases. As such, therefore, this research work may properly be considered as an *international tax law* work.

The above, however, does not mean that the author completely renounces referring to the laws of specific tax jurisdictions either as a way of example or to support the analysis of the specific subjects treated during the development of this work. In this regard, it is important to note that the selection of the countries whose domestic legislations, including domestic jurisprudence, are used or analysed has not been randomly made. On the contrary, it strictly follows the path given by the nature of the general topics under analysis, i.e., DNT and hybrid entities, and the manner in which this research work has finally been structured. In this sense, for example, the author has chosen to carry out a more extensive analysis of the rules to characterise foreign entities for tax purposes in the United States of America (Check-the-box rules or CTB) in Chapter 3. This analysis is justified by the importance of these rules to generate hybrid and reverse hybrid entities in the international context, as well as a unique example in the world of an elective system of characterisation of foreign entities for tax purposes. Likewise, the *Spanish Income Attribution Regime* is analysed in Chapter 3 to provide a concrete example of coordination in the characterisation of foreign entities, even though such a coordinated outcome is the result of an administrative practice of the Spanish tax authority (DGT), which does not necessarily have a proper foundation within the strict text of the law. Similarly, the Danish law is analysed in Chapter 3 as another important example of coordination to solve issues regarding both hybrids and reverse hybrid entities. Indeed, the Danish rules appear as a reaction to the use (or misuse) of the CTB rules in the United States and have served as an orientation to the EU ATAD II, dealing with HMA with third countries outside the EU. All the other references to specific tax jurisdictions are used according to the specific subjects analysed during this work. In this regard, e.g., Chapter 1 refers to the tax credit and LOB clauses within the United States tax system as regards the discussion on the existence of an international principle that would oblige to pay taxes in at least one State in cases of cross-border transactions, known in literature as the *single tax principle*. Both specific provisions are used as part of the pros and cons arguments to prove or disprove its existence, and therefore, they may rarely be omitted. Another example can be found in the use of the German tax law to exemplify the use of *switch-over clauses* within tax treaties or the reference to tax treaty overrides in Chapter 2. Accordingly, some examples of solutions to deal with the dichotomy between Article 1(2) OECD Model and the *beneficial ownership* requirement of Articles 10, 11 and 12 OECD Model are taken from the treaties between Poland/United States and Canada/United States as it can be noted in Chapter 4. All of the above ratifies the international tax law character of this research work and justifies the use of tax laws and jurisprudence of different countries as the development of the work requires.

The apparent unsystematic analysis of EU tax law might also be a cause of concern from a traditional scholarly point of view. However, the analysis of EU tax law follows the consistent methodology adopted for this work, and it is analysed as part of the whole international context at various points throughout the work, as necessary. That is the reason, for instance, why some references to EU tax law first appear in Chapter 1 as part of the non-legal notion of *Aggressive Tax Planning* (ATP), in particular, because of the 'EU notion' of ATP given by the EU Commission. Similarly, EU tax law is used as part of the analysis of the concept of *Special Tax Regimes* (STR), included as part of the OECD BEPS Action Plan 6, and analysed in Chapter 2 because it might indeed generate concerns under primary and secondary EU tax law. In Chapter 3, a reference to EU tax law is again made to exemplify the evolution in the treatment of HMA within the EU. This evolution is certainly interesting because of the most recent developments within the EU to deal with HMA, most notably in the context of the EU ATAD I and II. Finally, it appears as part of the analysis of the OECD *linking rules* in Chapter 5 and its compatibility with EU primary and secondary law. The use of EU tax law to test the efficacy of *linking rules* finds its justification for two main reasons: first, because the notion of *discrimination* elaborated within the Court of Justice of the European Union (CJEU), when compared, e.g., to the one of Article 24 OECD Model, might lead to different results; second, because the EU has been particularly committed in the implementation of the OECD BEPS measures, including those related to HMA. This situation has been materialised in the EU ATAD I, which opted for including the OECD *linking rules* to deal with hybrids (both with regard to entities and financial instruments), and its subsequent amendment, also known as EU ATAD II. This demonstrates, indeed, a consistent methodological analysis of EU tax law.

A more agnostic analysis not restricted to any specific jurisdiction also has special relevance with respect to the study of the concepts of DNT and the use of hybrid entities within the tax treaty context. Although tax treaties represent a singular world, the use of tax treaty models, especially the widespread use of the OECD Model, might be helpful in extracting general conclusions applicable to the generality of tax treaties using similar provisions. Chapter 2, for example, analyses some specific provisions of the OECD Model, which at first glance might be interpreted in a manner of preventing DNT. However, a closer look demonstrates that they are far from being interpreted considering this broad tax policy goal. Similarly, Chapter 4 deals with the analysis of Article 1(6) US Model, which, regardless of not being included in all the treaties signed by the United States, may be compared with the proposed Article 1(2) OECD Model with the purpose of extracting general conclusions with respect to the use of hybrid and reverse hybrids entities in the context of tax treaties. In particular, the use of case studies in Chapter 4 to explain the consequences of both the application of Article 1(6) US Model and Article 1(2) OECD Model is justified in the subsequent analysis of the same case studies used for the purpose of analysing the proposal of Chapter 6. This creates a harmonic point of comparison, even though the proposal of this book is not intended to be implemented in the exclusive context of tax treaties.

Finally, there is another important reason to prefer an analysis not restricted to any specific jurisdiction. This work proposes an alternative approach (i.e., the *reactive coordination rule*) to deal with hybrid and reverse hybrid entities, which not only deviates from the OECD *linking rules* but also has the characteristic of being designed without considering a specific jurisdiction in mind. These attributes give the proposed rule the advantage of being a rule that, in principle, might be implemented in any jurisdiction, keeping in mind that hybrid entities are an international concern not restricted to a specific State. Accordingly, the proposal itself is based on some fundamental ideas. First, it attempts to be a simple rule that avoids the complex set of domestic *linking rules* recommended by the OECD and which may also serve as a viable and more administrable alternative. Second, it attempts to focus on the true issue involving the use of hybrid and reverse hybrid entities, i.e., the disparate characterisation of entities by two or more jurisdictions, proposing an alternative that is not based upon the outcomes of the hybrid transactions, particularly the DNT outcome. Third, it attempts to be a rule that might also provide more consistent results in the application of tax treaties, especially regarding Article 1(2) OECD Model and Article 3(1) MLI. The above might be intuitively understood since once coordination in the characterisation of entities has been achieved, the conflicts within tax treaties disappear, and the application of Article 1(2) OECD Model is restricted only to those cases in which two Contracting States consider an entity as fiscally transparent, which will occur exclusively when the entity is given a tax transparent treatment in its country of legal organisation. All these outcomes are further analysed in Chapter 6.

4 STRUCTURE OF THE WORK

This work is divided into three parts.

Part One refers to the study of the DNT outcome. This part of the study comprises two Chapters. Chapter 1 attempts to demonstrate that the DNT outcome should not be considered per se as a cause for concern in any cross-border transaction. This chapter also includes arguments against the supporters of the idea that an international tax law principle exists to obligate that income is taxed at least once in a cross-border transaction. Accordingly, by analysing the traditional legal concepts of tax evasion and tax avoidance, the chapter attempts to demonstrate that DNT should not be confused with these concepts that may distort its nature. The analysis in abstract of the notion of DNT will allow us to prevent an *a priori* negative perception of it, reinforcing its nature of a simple outcome. Chapter 2 analyses the concept of double non-taxation in light of the application of bilateral tax treaties. Taking some provisions of the OECD Model and some examples of tax treaty clauses, this chapter aims to demonstrate that no provisions within tax treaties adopt the general tax policy goal of preventing DNT. The above does not mean to recognise that under some circumstances, tax treaties might indeed prevent DNT, such as the case when *subject-to-tax* or *switch-over clauses* are expressly introduced within a tax treaty. However, these situations are as exceptional as when some provisions are introduced within tax treaties regardless of the DNT outcome, e.g., *tax sparing* or *matching credits*.

Part Two turns the discussion to the second main subject of this work: *hybrid entities*. This part of the study also comprises two chapters. Chapter 3 refers to some key concepts that are necessary to circumscribe the subsequent analysis of *hybrid entities* and *reverse hybrids*. This chapter also includes a general analysis of the different existing methods to characterise foreign entities for tax purposes around the world to demonstrate that no characterisation system prevails over the other and that there is no completely inviolable method of characterisation of entities at all. Similarly, it provides a detailed analysis of the US. CTB system is the largest and most famous 'elective system' to characterise entities for tax purposes, reserving the taxpayers the exclusive right to determine when a foreign entity will be taxable or not and also addressing the previous characterisation system used in the United States, i.e., the *Kintner* test. Accordingly, it analyses the cases of tax planning opportunities derived from the CTB election, specifically with reference to the avoidance of Subpart F income (CFC rule) and the inappropriate use of foreign tax credit, demonstrating that the elective characteristic of the CTB system is more apparent than real, and when compared, for example, with a resemblance or comparable system of characterisation, there is practically no difference in terms of the possibilities to predict a desired characterisation of entities. Finally, the chapter addresses three concrete examples of coordination in the tax characterisation of foreign entities around the world: Spain, Denmark and the attempted coordination stated in the original proposal of EU ATAD and the inclusion of Article 9a in the EU ATAD II, dealing with cases of payments made to reverse hybrid entities. These examples attempt to demonstrate that coordination in the characterisation of entities is not only a utopian academic idea, but it can also be an effective manner to deal with hybrids and reverse hybrid entities, also serving as an anteroom to the general proposal of this work. Chapter 4, on the other hand, deals with the use of hybrid entities and the entitlement to tax treaty benefits. For this purpose, the chapter briefly refers to the general rules regarding the entitlement to tax treaty benefits with respect to entities and analyses the principles established within the OECD Partnership Report with regard to conflicts of allocation of income. Accordingly, it provides a detailed analysis of Article 1(6) US Model, which is the first positive recognition of the principles stated in the OECD Partnership Report, subsequently materialised in Article 1(2) OECD Model, which is also analysed in this chapter. Together with a general analysis of the wording of the provisions in the US and OECD Model, the chapter also provides specific illustrations with respect to their application, which are divided into two groups: (i) strict bilateral cases, and (ii) triangular cases. Similarly, with regard to Article 1(6) US Model, it also provides some examples where the interplay between Article 1(6) US Model and other tax treaty and domestic provisions is either not entirely clear or is simply conflictive. The above includes the interplay with the concept of *beneficial owner* in Articles 10, 11 and 12 US Model; the US '*saving clause*', the US CTB regulations, and I.R.C. section 894(c). Moreover, with regard to Article 1(2) OECD Model, it also addresses some specific issues referred to its application, which include the interplay with the concept of *beneficial owner*, the *saving clause* and the double taxation relief, particularly considering the OECD BEPS Action 6 as well as the negative impact that Article 1(2) OECD Model may have for developing countries. Finally, the analysis and conclusions with regard to Article 1(2) OECD Model are extended to Article 3(1) of the MLI, which replicates the text of Article 1(2) OECD Model. Further analysis is also provided with regard to Article 3(3) and Article 11 MLI, which corresponds to the simplified and detailed '*saving clause*' version introduced within the MLI. Accordingly, this analysis is complemented by the study of Article 3(2) and Article 5 – Option C MLI, dealing with the impact of the saving clause and issues of double taxation relief.

Finally, Part Three analyses how both the DNT outcome and hybrid entities, analysed in Parts One and Two of this work, interact together as part of the notion of '*hybrid mismatch arrangements*' (HMA). For this purpose, Chapter 5 first analyses the notion of HMA and criticises its confusing and limited construction. It is also argued in this chapter that the attempt to connect disparities derived from different characterisations of the same entity by two different jurisdictions and the DNT outcome might ultimately create presumptions of abusive practices. Likewise, this chapter aims to demonstrate that the deficient construction of the notion of HMA is replicated in the elaboration of the remedies proposed to counteract them, i.e., '*linking rules*'. For this purpose, the chapter reinforces some issues of compatibility between *linking rules* and tax treaties and EU Law, respectively. Against this attempted interconnection between the use of hybrid and reverse hybrid entities and the DNT outcome, which has originated a complex set of rules to be implemented at both domestic and tax treaty levels and whose true efficacy is still an incognito, Chapter 6 proposes a different alternative denominated *reactive coordination rule*. The proposal aims to be a domestic alternative to coordinate the characterisation of entities according to the legal characterisation of the entity in the *home country*, i.e., the country where the entity, whose characterisation is under debate, is formally and legally organised. Accordingly, the proposal is based upon three specific tax policy aims, namely simplicity, coherence and administrability. The first part of the chapter describes the mechanics of the proposal, including its scope of application and the policy objectives. Likewise, it explains the functioning of the proposal using specific illustrations for this purpose, also illustrating its advantages and disadvantages. It finally provides a comparison between the effects of the proposed rule and other existing rules addressing the same path of coordination to clearly set up common points and deviations that ultimately make the proposed rule preferable. The second part of the chapter analyses the implications of the domestic *reactive coordination rule* within tax treaties. As recognised in Chapter 4, the inclusion of a new Article 1(2) OECD Model (and Article 3(1) MLI) solves many issues regarding the proper allocation of tax treaty benefits when tax-transparent entities are involved. However, this article is far from being a fair solution for developing (source) countries. This issue could, nevertheless, be mitigated in the hypothetical that the domestic *reactive coordination rule* is applied worldwide. Indeed, if that occurs, the scope of application of Article 1(2) OECD Model will be automatically reduced, providing more consistent tax treaty outcomes and indirectly enhancing the position of source countries in those cases where the pure application of Article 1(2) OECD Model would yield unfair results. Yet, the proposal does not attempt to be either a perfect solution or an unbeatable one but rather serves as a guide to re-orientate the discussion to what really matters in the debate regarding hybrid entity mismatches, especially during times when pragmatism and unprincipled approaches appear to lead the preferences. Chapter 7 finally summarises the main findings of this work.

PART I Double Non-taxation: Delimiting the Boundaries of a Stigmatised Concept

CHAPTER 1

Double Non-taxation: A Conceptual Analysis

1 INTRODUCTION

The use of the notion of Double Non-taxation (DNT)[10] has acquired considerable prominence during the last years. The appearance in the media of public tax cases concerning multinational corporations, such as Apple[11], Amazon[12], Fiat[13], Starbucks[14] and McDonald's[15], just to mention some of them, using sophisticated tax structures to reduce or eliminate taxation, including the role of activists promoting 'tax justice' and

10. Some authors use the term '*white income*' as equivalent to DNT. Nevertheless, this term might create certain confusion with other new notions that have also appeared in the international tax arena, such as the notion of '*stateless income*'. This latter, however, is certainly not a synonymous of DNT. Therefore, for the sake of clarity, I will only refer to the classic term of DNT as the complete absence of taxation in an international transaction. For the explanation of the term '*stateless income*', *see infra* s. 2.2. As an example of commentators using the term '*white income*' as an interchangeable concept with DNT *see, e.g.*, W. Haslehner, *Double Taxation Relief, Transfer Pricing Adjustments and State Aid Law* in: I. Richelle, W. Schön and E. Traversa (eds) *State Aid Law and Business Taxation*, Springer, Heidelberg (2016).
11. *See, e.g.*, US: US Senate Permanent Subcommittee on Investigations of the Committee on Homeland Security and Government Affairs, Hearing on Offshore Profit Shifting and the US Tax Code – Part 2, Apple Inc. (2013). *See also, e.g.*, A. Ting, *The Politics of BEPS – Apple's International Tax Structure and the US Attitude Towards BEPS*, 69 Bull. Intl. Taxn. 6/7 (2015), Journals IBFD; L. Sheppard, *Apple's Tax Magic*, Worldwide Tax Daily (26 May 2013).
12. *See, e.g.*, J. Martin, *Amazon Fighting IRS Over Cost-Sharing Agreements*, Tax Analyst, Featured Articles, posted online on 21 January 2013.
13. *See, e.g.*, T. Ciro and B. Mascitelli, *Machinations in the Global Automotive Industry: The Fiat and Chrysler Deal Examined*, 12 Derivs. & Fin. Instrums. 2 (2010), Journals IBFD. *See also*, L. Ambagtsheer-Pakarinen, *Commission*, 56 Eur. Taxn. 1 (2016), Journals IBFD.
14. *See, e.g.*, H. van den Hurk, *Starbucks Versus the People*, 68 Bull. Intl. Taxn. 1 (2014), Journals IBFD. *See also*, C. Allison, *How Starbucks Lost Its Social License – and Paid 20 Million pounds to Get it Back*, 71 Tax Notes Int'l 7, 637 (2013).
15. *See, e.g.*, EU: European Commission Press Release, *State aid: Commission Opens Formal Investigation into Luxembourg's Tax Treatment of McDonald's* (3 December 2015).

'fairness',[16] has certainly created an interesting scenario to debate or re-debate about a notion that seems to be understood *a priori* as something negative. The recent work of the Organisation for Economic Co-operation and Development (OECD), the 2013 BEPS project, has not only reaffirmed this negative idea of what double non-taxation is, but it has gone further and provided specific measures that countries should follow to counteract its undesirable effects.[17]

Nevertheless, a proper debate could not start from the basis of notions given by granted. On the contrary, within the debate on DNT, it is important to go one step back and ask whether we really have certainty about what we are debating. Do we know what DNT is? Is it correct to use this notion as an interchangeable one with some illegal or undesirable concepts, such as tax evasion or tax avoidance? Where is the limit? Is there a general prohibition under international law by which taxpayers are not permitted to legitimately pursue a DNT outcome in cross-border transactions?

This chapter provides an analysis in abstract of DNT aiming to answer those questions and to demonstrate that the notion of DNT should be neither regarded per se as a cause of concern in any cross-border business nor confused with other illegal or undesirable activities, such as tax evasion or tax avoidance. Equally undesirable is the use of 'non-legal notions' or pseudo-legal concepts created to justify international limits to cross-border tax planning. Particularly important is the notion of '*aggressive tax planning*' (ATP), whose *consequentialist approach*, which is based exclusively upon the outcome of DNT instead of traditional elements of economic substance or artificiality, may jeopardise even more the understanding of the notion of DNT. The chapter also argues against the belief, supported by some international tax scholars and defended even as an 'international tax principle', that income should be taxed at least once in any cross-border transaction, as one of the main responsible for the ambiguity of a notion whose nature is that of a simple outcome.

Section 2 summarises the traditional understanding of the notion of DNT in the international tax doctrine. Section 3 analyses the '*single tax principle*' (or the belief that income should be taxed at least once in cross-border transactions) and its negative influence on the understanding of the notion of DNT. Section 4 analyses in brief the traditional concepts of tax evasion and tax avoidance, reinforcing the idea that DNT should not be assimilated to any of these undesirable activities, whose limits are normally established by law. Section 5 attempts to demonstrate that the *consequentialist approach* adopted within the pseudo-category of ATP may also negatively influence the understanding of the notion of DNT, creating an artificial limit (not legal) for those transactions in which legitimate tax planning took place. Section 6 provides some final remarks.

16. In this regard, one of the biggest 'think tank' tax activist is the Tax Justice Network. The organisation has a wide network around the world, including North America, Latin America, Asia and Europe. More information about the Tax Justice Network at www.taxjustice.net.
17. OECD (2013), *supra* n. 2.

2 THE TRADITIONAL ATTEMPTS TO EXPLAIN AN AMBIGUOUS CONCEPT

The several traditional attempts to explain the notion of DNT are ambiguous. Whilst some scholars have been inclined to describe it as the simple reverse effect of double taxation or the absence of exercising sovereign taxing rights, others have included subjective elements, namely intentionality, to differentiate between objectionable and non-objectionable double non-taxation. There are also those who have simply opted to consider it as a per se undesirable and illegitimate outcome. Following these ambiguous developments, the author revisits the main attempts to explain the notion and summarises them as follows: (1) double non-taxation as the reverse side of double taxation; (2) double non-taxation, under-taxation and *stateless income*; (3) double non-taxation as an intended or unintended outcome; and (4) double non-taxation as a per se undesirable outcome.

2.1 Double Non-taxation as the Reverse Side of Double Taxation

Strictly speaking, DNT arises exactly in the reverse situation of double taxation.[18] This is to say, whilst double taxation implies that income is taxed twice or multiple times in a cross-border situation, double non-taxation supposes the complete absence of taxation in similar scenarios. In other words, DNT is the result of an uncoordinated exercise of taxing powers by different tax authorities, each of which provides different criteria, territorial, personal, and material, to establish a link between the taxable base and the taxing authority to ultimately justify the tax claim.[19]

Scholars have historically distinguished between two types of double taxation: juridical and economic. *Juridical double taxation* implies the imposition of identical or

18. In this sense, e.g., S. Pulido, *Avoidance of Double Non-taxation in Portugal* in: M. Lang (ed.) *Avoidance of Double Non-taxation*, Linde, Vienna (2003), p. 284; M. Ullah, *Avoidance of Double Non-Taxation in the United Kingdom* in: M. Lang (ed.) *Avoidance of Double Non-Taxation*, Linde, Vienna, (2003), p. 427; A. Verstraeten, *Double (Non)Taxation in VAT and Direct Taxes: Which Tax Is Better for Developing Countries?* in: M. Lang, P. Melz and E. Krostoffersson (eds) *Value Added Tax and Direct Taxation: Similarities and Differences*, IBFD (2009), p. 374; G. Bizioli, *Comparative Analysis of the Causes of Double (Non-) Taxation in the Income and VAT/GST Contexts* in: M. Lang, P. Melz and E. Krostoffersson (eds) *Value Added Tax and Direct Taxation: Similarities and Differences*, IBFD, Amsterdam (2009), p. 400. In the field of indirect taxation, specifically on VAT, some authors have considered that double non-taxation arises: '[W]hen no country has imposed the relevant tax on the relevant subject matter, which is therefore effectively 'tax-free' in the sense that there is no tax burden to pass on to consumers.' *See, e.g.*, R. Millar, *Intentional and Unintentional Double Non-Taxation* in: M. Lang, P. Melz and E: Kristofferson (eds) *Value Added Tax and Direct Taxation: Similarities and Differences*, IBFD (2009), p. 417. Also in this position, e.g., S. Menuchin and N. Baram, *Israel* in: Cahiers de droit fiscal international – Vol. 89a, *Double Non-taxation* (IFA 2004), p. 439.
19. E. Traversa and C. Hellepute, *Double (Non-) Taxation in VAT and Direct Taxes: How to Achieve Some Convergence Within a Summa Divisio? A European Perspective* in: M. Lang, P. Melz and E: Kristofferson (eds) *Value Added Tax and Direct Taxation: Similarities and Differences*, IBFD (2009), p. 340. Double taxation normally occurs because most states tax their residents on their worldwide income irrespective of whether the income derives from their country of residence or from abroad. *See also*, M. Rasmussen, *International Double Taxation*, Wolters Kluwer, New York, 2011.

similar taxes in two (or more) states on the same taxpayer with respect to the same taxable income, capital or event.[20] For example, a dividend payment received by a shareholder who is a non-resident in the state of the payer company (source state) will normally be subject to a WHT in that state, whilst the same dividend payment will also be included as income in the State of residence of the shareholder. In other words, the same shareholder is taxed twice on the same income (dividends). In contrast, *economic double taxation* occurs when two different persons are taxable in respect of the same income or capital.[21] For instance, when income is received according to the law of one state by a partnership treated as a taxable entity in that state, whilst the other state considers the same partnership as tax transparent and attributes the income directly to the partners liable to tax in its territory. In this order of ideas, if DNT is simply the reverse side of double taxation, then DNT will occur when a taxpayer engaged in an international transaction is not subject to any tax on behalf of the countries that have the right to tax.[22] In other words, as double taxation arises from the exercise of sovereign taxing rights of two or more countries, double non-taxation is a consequence of the opposite, and it occurs when no country exercises its sovereign taxing rights, either because the country of residence decides to exempt an item of foreign source income and the source country also decides not to tax such an income or because the DTC in force assigns taxing rights to either the source or resident country, but the assigned country simply does not exercise these taxing rights.[23]

The understanding of DNT as the reverse effect of double taxation does not imply, however, that this should be automatically considered an undesirable outcome. Indeed, neither the elimination of double taxation nor the avoidance of DNT are sacred principles of international tax law. On the one hand, the former idea confuses between how much taxes should be levied and how many times. From a legal point of view, however, both questions should not deserve the same attention. There should be concern about how much taxes are levied, mostly considering that taxes should, in any case, become confiscatory, but the same attention should not be paid to how many times these taxes are levied.[24] After all, many taxpayers should be indifferent if they are taxed once at a rate of 35% rather than thirty-five times at a rate of 1%. On the other hand, the latter idea (the prevention of DNT) simply disregards the nature of the concept, whose desirability (or not) will depend exclusively upon the agreement of two

20. A. Rust in: Reimer and Rust (eds) *Klaus Vogel on Double Taxation Conventions*, 4th edn Kluwer Law International, Alphen aan den Rijn (2015), Article 23 at m.no. 1. For a deeper analysis of the phenomenon of juridical double taxation *see, e.g.*, M. Pires, *International Juridical Double Taxation of Income*, Kluwer Law and Taxation Publishers, Boston, 1989.
21. Rust, *supra* n. 20, at m.no. 2. *See also*, M. Lang, *Introduction to the Law of Double Taxation Conventions*, 2nd ed., Linde, Vienna, 2013, pp. 29-30.
22. Verstraeten, *supra* n. 18.
23. *Ibid.*, p. 378.
24. Accordingly, in some cases the relief of double taxation seems not to be a problem at all, as it happens with developing countries or transition economies. As residents of these countries are expected to receive less income from foreign sources, the relief of double taxation is, in fact, not a priority. *See* R. Vann, *Chapter 18: International Aspects of Income Tax* in: V. Thuronyi (ed.) *Tax Law Design and Drafting*, Vol. II, International Monetary Fund, Washington USA (1998), p. 37.

jurisdictions.[25] In fact, there is no evidence that international law imposes any obligation on the countries to relieve double taxation or to prevent DNT in the absence of such agreements. As provided by Vogel: 'Double taxation, resulting from the interaction of the domestic laws of two (or more) States, will be consistent with international law as long as each individual legislation is consistent with international law.'[26] The above simply reinforces what the PCIJ stated in the *Lotus* case (1927) in terms that it is not prohibited under international law; it is indeed permitted.[27] In other words, in the absence of an international norm prohibiting either double taxation or DNT, one should conclude that both are generally permitted or tolerated outcomes.

2.2 Double Non-taxation: Under-Taxation and *Stateless Income*

In another attempt to explain the concept of DNT, some scholars have not only included the complete absence of taxation but also the cases of low taxation or under-taxation, even if they were achieved by a legitimate tax strategy.[28] However, putting in equal footing DNT and under-taxation deviate from the nature of the concept of DNT, which is, in essence, the absolute absence of taxation either by the disparities in domestic laws, the application of a tax treaty provision, or the simple decision of a state not to exercise its taxing rights.

The distinction between DNT and under-taxation can be easily illustrated using Apple's international tax structure as an example.[29] The tax structure of Apple is simple when compared with other international tax structures. Apple Inc., a US Corp, owns 100% of the stock in Apple Operations International (AOI), which subsequently owns 100% of the stock in Apple Operations Europe (AOE) and subsequently owns 100% of

25. This can easily be seen in the case of countries that, e.g., within a tax treaty, include a *subject-to-tax* or *switch-over clause* to counteract the effects of DNT. In such cases, there is no doubt that the outcome of DNT is indeed an undesired outcome. For a further analysis on the use of *subject-to-tax* and *switch-over clauses*, *see infra* Chapter 2, ss 4.2.1 and 4.2.2.
26. K. Vogel and A. Rust in: Reimer and Rust (eds) *Klaus Vogel on Double Taxation Conventions*, 4th edn, Kluwer Law International, Alphen aan den Rijn (2015), Introduction at m. no. 11.
27. The Lotus case of 1927 referred to a collision occurred in high seas between a French vessel (SS Lotus) and a Turkish vessel (Boz-Kourt) and which involved the application by Turkey of criminal law against both the French and Turkish officers on watch of the vessels. France alleged that the SS Lotus was using the French flag. Therefore, it should be assimilated to French territory and Turkey would have no jurisdiction to carry out criminal proceedings against the French captain of the SS Lotus. Accordingly, it was a common practice during that time that countries would avoid applying any of such criminal proceedings outside the territory. Denying the French request, the Permanent Court of International Justice, i.e., the judicial branch of the League of Nations, precedent of the United Nations, sustained: 'Even if the rarity of the judicial decisions to be found among the reported cases were sufficient to prove in point of fact the circumstances alleged by the Agent for the French Government, it would merely show that States had often, in practice, abstained from instituting criminal proceedings, and not that they recognized themselves as being obliged to do so [...].' International: *The case of the S.S. 'Lotus,'* Collection of Judgments, Publications of the Permanent Court of International Justice, Series A-No. 10, 7 September 1927, p. 28.
28. Even though the aim of any tax planning is to legitimately achieve DNT. *Infra* s. 4.2.1.
29. For a deeper analysis upon the Apple's tax structure, *see* A. Ting, *iTax–Apple's International Tax Structure and the Double Non-Taxation Issue,* BTR 1 (2014).

the stock in Apple Sales International (ASI).[30] These last three companies are incorporated in Ireland. However, AOI and ASI have their effective management and control in the United States.[31] AOI basically acts as a holding company for many group companies involved in overseas operations, receiving dividends from its subsidiaries.[32] ASI engages unrelated contract manufacturers in China to assemble the products and sells the final ones to distribution subsidiaries in Europe and Asia.[33] Consequently, ASI entered into a 'cost sharing agreement' with the ultimate parent company, Apple Inc., under which it possesses the economic rights to Apple's intellectual property, whilst the legal ownership of that property remains with Apple Inc. in the United States.[34] Finally, Apple derives over 60% of its income from foreign jurisdictions,[35] paying an effective tax rate lower than the statutory 12.5% of corporate tax rate in Ireland. As per Apple's international tax structure, it is possible to figure out clearly that whilst the outcome of DNT derives exclusively from the disparities in the domestic concepts of corporate tax residence,[36] the one of under-taxation derives from the legitimate use of

30. *Ibid.*, at 42-46.
31. *Ibid.*
32. *Ibid.*
33. *Ibid.*
34. A *cost-sharing agreement* is a regime introduced during the early 1990s and whose idea was that when a US multinational starts a new R&D project, it can enter into an agreement with its offshore subsidiaries to share the cost of development. If the project is finally a success, they also share the profits derived from it. *Ibid.*, at 47. The primary tax benefit from entering into a cost sharing agreement is that all participants to such agreement will be considered the owner of their respective interest in the intangible created, thereby preluding the application of the general transfer pricing rules related to the transfer of intangible property. Accordingly, if the participants enter into a *qualified cost sharing agreement*, i.e., a written agreement under which the participants agree to share the costs of developing intangibles proportionally to their relative shares of reasonable benefits from the individual exploitation of their assigned interest in the intangibles, the IRS is precluded from making transfer pricing adjustments (arm's length adjustments under s. IRC 482), unless it is strictly necessary to make each participant's share of intangible development costs equal to its share or reasonable anticipated benefits. *See* M. Levey and S. Wrappe, *Transfer Pricing: Rules, Compliance and Controversy*, 3rd ed., Wolters Kluwer Business, Chicago, 2010, pp. 137-138, para. 460.
35. This issue does not necessarily mean profit shifting. On the contrary, it could perfectly represent the successful business position of the group overseas.
36. According to US tax law, a corporation is resident when it is incorporated in the United States. Conversely, in Ireland the residency of a corporation is determined in accordance to the place of effective management and control. Therefore, AOI and ASI, both incorporated in Ireland and managed and controlled in the United States, were neither resident in the United States nor in Ireland, then there was no link to trigger taxation in any place. *See* Ting, *supra* n. 29, at 4-45. However, it is important to note that the Irish law was modified in 1999, also introducing the place of incorporation as an alternative to determine the residence of companies in Ireland. Yet, such option operated except in those cases in which the company operated in Ireland through a branch and it was ultimately controlled by a person in a country with a tax treaty in place with Ireland. The United States was one of these countries. Therefore, the place of management and control kept being the main rule for determining residence of companies in the Irish-US context. *See* R. Mason and S. Daly, *State Aid: The General Court Decision in Apple*, 99 Tax Notes Int'l 1317 (2020) (explaining the details of the Apple structure in the context of the EU General Court decision on state aid). For more on the EU tax law issues involving Apple, *see*, for example, L. Parada, *Between Apple and Oranges: The EU General Court's Decision in the 'Apple Case'*, EC Tax Rev. 2 (2021). *See* also, C. Peters, *Critical Analysis of the General Court's 'EU Arm's Length Tool': Beware of the Reflexivity of Transfer Pricing Law!*, EC Tax Rev. 1 (2022) DOI: 10.54648/ecta2022004.

a cost-sharing agreement between Apple Inc. and its subsidiary ASI, a regime introduced in the early 1990s in the United States.

Finally, it is worth referring to the cases where under-taxation or DNT might be achieved through the shifting of profits from high to low-tax jurisdictions made by multinationals around the world. This phenomenon that involves the shifting of income within a multinational tax group to reduce or completely avoid taxation has been denominated by some authors as '*stateless income*'.[37] Kleinbard defines *stateless income* as 'the income derived for tax purposes by a multinational group from business activities in a country other than the domicile of the group's ultimate parent company, but which is subject to tax only in a jurisdiction that is not the location of the customers of the factors of the production through which the income was derived, and is not the domicile of the group's parent company'.[38] In other words, *stateless income* implies 'the movement of taxable income within a multinational group from high to low-taxed source countries without shifting the location of externally supplied capital or activities involving third parties'.[39] Therefore, it involves the application of a series of international tax norms, including, e.g., the recognition of separate tax persons, transfer pricing rules, the treatment of income as debt or equity, etc., whose outcome might be or not non-taxation altogether. Hence, *stateless income* is a more complex construction whose treatment exceeds the purpose of this work; however, what it is interesting to point out here is that it does not necessarily mean to be a concept equivalent to DNT, even though such outcome might sometimes be achieved.[40]

2.3 Double Non-taxation as an Intended or Unintended Outcome

For a part of the international tax doctrine, DNT may also be divided into two sub-categories: intended (or voluntary) and unintended (or involuntary) DNT.[41] Intended DNT, on the one hand, would exist when every country that has the right to impose the relevant tax on a particular subject matter has agreed that no tax should be imposed upon that subject matter or the countries have agreed on which of them

37. E. Kleinbard, *Stateless Income*, 11 Fla. Tax Rev. 699 (2011).
38. *Ibid.*, p. 701.
39. *Ibid.*, p. 703.
40. For further references on this topic *see, e.g.*, E. Kleinbard, *The Lessons of Stateless Income*, 65 Tax L. Rev. 99 (2011); E. Kleinbard, *Stateless Income's Challenge to Tax Policy*, USC Center in Law, Economics and Organization, Research Paper No. C11-8, USC Legal Studies Research Paper No. 11-13 (2011); E. Kleinbard, *Through a Latte, Darkly: Starbucks's Stateless Income Planning*, 139 Tax Notes 13 (2013), pp. 1515-1535; K. Carey, *Stateless Income's Agency Problem: Are Multinationals Acting in the Best Interest of Shareholders Through the Creation of Stateless Income?* (14 May 2012), full text available on SSRN.
41. More recently, some authors have also made use of the notion of '*unintended double non-taxation*' to explain the modern pseudo-legal notion of '*aggressive tax planning*' (ATP). *See, e.g.*, P. Pistone, *La Planificación Fiscal Agresiva y las Categorías Conceptuales del Derecho Tributario Global*, Revista Española de Derecho Financiero 170, Abril-Junio 2016, pp. 109-151. Pistone argues that *unintended double non-taxation* would be a constitutive element of this pseudo-legal notion of ATP jointly with the exploitation of disparities among jurisdictions to obtain a tax advantage and the desalination between the place of origin of the income and the place where taxes on that income are actually paid. For a further analysis on the concept of ATP in connection with the DNT outcome, *see infra* s. 5.

should exercise the jurisdiction to tax a particular subject matter, but the relevant country has decided not to exercise that jurisdiction, either because it has chosen not to impose a tax of that type or simply not to tax that subject matter, or because the country has no effective ways to enforce the tax.[42] Unintended DNT, on the other hand, would be represented by the cases in which 'more than one country could impose the relevant tax on a particular subject matter, but none of them has done so because each of them is of the view that another has the (or a superior) jurisdiction to impose the tax'.[43] This could happen if the relevant countries disagree about the underlying principles that determine who has the jurisdiction to tax and they both take the position that they do not have it, or they agree on the underlying principles but interpret them differently, either in their laws or in the interpretations of the law made by courts, taxpayers and/or the tax administration.[44] In other words, unintended double non-taxation would be the case when the DNT outcome was not the result originally aimed by the states. Some authors have expressly reinforced the idea that the intentional element within the notion of unintended DNT refers exclusively to the 'intention of the states'[45] rather than the intention of the taxpayers, regardless of the ambiguity of the notion of intention of states itself. Yet, excluding this intentionality element, the taxpayers' intention makes sense since the taxpayers' intention in a cross-border transaction will always be to reduce their costs, namely taxes, if possible, to zero.[46] An interpretation of *a contrario sensu* will simply not recognise the reality of the cross-border transactions and the legitimate use of tax planning structures either.[47]

The whole idea of using a subjective element, i.e., *intentionality*, to explain the notion of DNT is, however, not only debatable but also very precarious from an argumentative point of view. First, it might give rise to many ad hoc interpretations of

42. Millar, *supra* n. 18, pp. 418-419. The intentional DNT is normally related with the stimulation of certain activities in both countries, having usually an economic-political character. *See* Lang, *supra* n. 21. *See also*, Bizioli, *supra* n. 18, p. 402.
43. Millar, *supra* n. 18, p. 428.
44. *Ibid.*
45. Pistone, e.g., when referring to *unintended double non-taxation* as an element of the notion of ATP, clearly states that the former excludes the intention of the taxpayers. In the original Spanish text, it can be read as follows: '*En este sentido, este tercer elemento viene comúnmente definido como "doble no imposición involuntaria" sin que esta expresión implique una reconstrucción de los aspectos subjetivos relativos a la planificación fiscal agresiva realizada por el contribuyente.*' [In this regard, this third element comes normally defined as unintended 'double non-taxation', but without implying that this expression means a subjective reconstruction of the subjective elements of aggressive tax planning made by the taxpayer] (author's translation). *See* Pistone, *supra* n. 41, p. 123.
46. Some authors, however, argue that unintended DNT would be the result of the improper use of domestic tax laws, tax treaty law or Community Law, being thus an undesirable effect in cross-border transactions. *See, e.g.*, Bizioli, *supra* n. 18. In a similar position, *see* J. Almudi, *Avoidance of Double Non-Taxation in Spain* in: M. Lang (ed.) *Avoidance of Double Non-Taxation*, Linde, Vienna (2003), p. 341; Ullah, *supra* n. 18; D. Gutmann, *Avoidance of Double Non-Taxation in France* in: M. Lang (ed.) *Avoidance of Double Non-Taxation*, Linde, Vienna (2003), p. 87. This notion becomes closer to the intention of the taxpayers, at least when referring to the 'improper use' of the domestic laws, treaties or EU Law. In these cases, the improper use of a tax treaty, for example, will be determined by objective and subjective factors, including the 'purpose' or 'principal purpose' of a transaction, which might be an indirect reference to the taxpayers' subjective intention.
47. *Infra* s. 4.2.1.

what the 'intention of the states' actually means and how it should be expressed. For example, someone could argue that the intention of the states needs to be established literally within the domestic laws of the states or within specific bilateral tax treaty provisions. In other words, no interpretation of the reasoning of the policymakers should be relevant to interpret whether two states intended or not to achieve DNT with respect to a certain item of income, being the express wording of the law the primary and unique source of intentionality.[48] However, others could legitimately argue that in the absence of a literal reference, the intention of the state could be tacitly obtained from somewhere else, e.g., legislation discussion meetings or treaty negotiation acts, opening the door for random tax policy interpretations that could finally jeopardise the taxpayers' legal certainty. Second, and more importantly, the argument forgets the complex problems of political malfunction that involve the law-making process both on a domestic and a global basis.[49] Indeed, the 'intention of the law' (or the politicians making the law) is most of the time influenced by external actors, e.g., multinationals, which directly or indirectly manipulate the final outcomes of a tax reform.[50] The above does not only include a direct lobby within the domestic law-making process, which is normally regulated and publicly known but also an indirect influential participation of these actors within the various international tax networks, such as the same OECD forum.[51] In this order of ideas, framing DNT based on the legislators' intent is incapable of truly controlling the taxpayers' behaviours because it is indeed very difficult to distinguish a pure 'intention of the states' in most of the cases, adding more difficulties to the always problematic holistic approach of determining legislative intent.

It is, therefore, my opinion that the use of subjective elements, such as *intentionality*, to explain the outcome of double non-taxation should be simply discarded or, alternatively, be used only when such an 'intention' is no other than the express

48. Pistone seems to follow this path when he argues that each limitation to the legitimate right to minimise the taxpayer's tax burden must be established within specific rules. Otherwise, the principle of legality (civil law countries) or the rule of law (common law) would be violated. Pistone, *supra* n. 41, p. 127 (n. 43).
49. A. Christians, *Avoidance, Evasion and Taxpayer Morality*, 44 Wash. U. J. L. & Pol'y 39 (2014), pp. 49-50. The UK government, e.g., has criticised the role of the Big Four accounting firms for initially aiding draft anti-avoidance legislation, and then abuse their position by finding ways to do exactly what the legislation intended to stop. *See also, e.g.*, J. Martin, *UK Lawmakers Lambaste Big 4 Accounting Firms*, 69 Tax Notes Int'l 6 (2013), pp. 518-519. In this latter article is provided the example of how a big four assisted in the drafting of the UK patent box legislation to latter on advice clients on how to use the law to avoid tax. Similar examples are provided with the drafting of CFC rules. *See also*, J. Martin, *Lawmakers Seek New Code of Conduct for Tax Accountants*, 70 Tax Notes Int'l 6, 519-520 (2013).
50. Christians, *supra* n. 49. In this opinion as well, Essers argues: 'The choices in the field of international tax law have to be made, explained and justified by responsible politicians and policymakers. But before those decisions are taken, many of these stakeholders in the international tax arena will do their best to influence and convince these politicians and policymakers.' P. Essers, *International Tax Justice Between Machiavelli and Habermas*, 68 Bull. Int'l Taxn. 2 (2014), Journals IBFD, p. 54.
51. Christians states that multinational companies play an important marketing role ('native advertising') presented as journalism, academic research or even the participation in international networks, being the most notable case the OECD where the access to lawmakers is perhaps held in an informal and unobservable way. Christians, *supra* n. 49.

wording of the domestic laws or tax treaties dealing specifically with cases of DNT.[52] In all other cases, its use should be simply avoided for the sake of clarity and legal certainty.

2.4 Double Non-taxation as a Per Se Undesirable Outcome

There are finally those who simply identify double non-taxation as an outcome per se negative, constituting a pervasive reality in the world of cross-border investment and commercial activity, whose opportunities can derive either from tax treaties, the differences of domestic laws or the failure to report income to the appropriate jurisdiction.[53]

3 DOUBLE NON-TAXATION AND THE *SINGLE TAX PRINCIPLE*

Perhaps one of the main reasons for the ambiguity in the concept of double non-taxation is derived from the influence of the so-called *single tax principle* or the assumption that income should be taxed once (and no more than once) in any cross-border transaction. This section attempts to demonstrate that beyond the debate regarding the simplistic construction of the single tax principle,[54] its *downside*

52. For example, when tax treaties include either *subject-to-tax* or *switch-over clauses* to prevent DNT, or when they include *tax sparing* and *matching credit clauses* in a clear tolerance of the DNT outcome. For a further analysis *tax sparing* and *matching credit clauses* within tax treaties, *see infra* Chapter 2, s. 4.2. Taking also the 'intentions' expressed within the wording of domestic laws or tax treaties, some authors have attempted to create new categories to explain the difference between intended and unintended DNT. Most notably, Martinez Laguna distinguishes between '*proper DNT*' and '*twice non-taxation*'. The former notion, on one hand, would represent the agreement of the parties within a tax treaty, being intended DNT in this case, e.g., when tax sparing or matching credit clauses are included and unintended DNT when, e.g., subject-to-tax and switch-over clauses are introduced. This latter notion relates to the parallel exercise of sovereignties by two States. In this case, Martinez Laguna argues that it is not possible to ascertain intentions in this context of uncoordinated exercises of sovereignty, being therefore this one the more precise notion used in the international debate and referred as 'unintended DNT'. *See* F. Martinez Laguna, *Abuse and Aggressive Tax Planning: Between OECD and EU Initiatives–The Dividing Line between Intended and Unintended Double Non-Taxation*, 9 World Tax J. 2 (2017), Journals IBFD. In my view, however, the categorisation proposed by Martinez Laguna is not only very complex to follow, but also it seems to serve the simple purpose of justifying another pseudo-legal notion that will be further analysed in this work, and whose legal validity is more than arguable, namely the notion of ATP. Indeed, it is Martinez Laguna himself who recognises this when he says: 'Unintended twice non-taxation is part of the concept of aggressive tax planning. Aggressive tax planning is reflected in all of the different measures implemented in domestic and treaty law tackling non-acceptable (unintended) outcomes from a state perspective in advance.' *Ibid.*, para. 6. For an analysis of the concept of ATP and its connection to DNT, *see infra* s. 5.
53. *See, e.g.*, D. Ring, *United States* in: Cahiers de droit fiscal international – Vol. 89a, *Double Non-taxation* (IFA 2004), p. 725.
54. Daniel Shaviro, for example, criticises the simplistic construction of the '*single tax principle*' when he says: 'Tax treaties generally require that the signatories eliminate "double taxation" [...] The treaties also commonly seek to address "fiscal evasion" [understood by some commentators as the avoidance of "double non-taxation"] [...] Put the two concern together and you arguably have a "single tax principle" [...].' D. Shaviro, *The Two Faces of the Single Tax Principle*, New York University Law and Economics Working Papers, Paper 419 (2015), p. 1.

departure, as named by some scholars,[55] i.e., the avoidance of DNT, cannot be supported either under the traditional argument of the use of the tax credit method to relieve double taxation or under the more recent ones that involves a misinterpretation of the Limitation of Benefits (LOB) provision within the US Model. Moreover, it raises some normative concerns regarding a modern idea of single taxation, also known in the tax literature as 'full taxation'.[56]

3.1 Historical Background

In 1998, H. D. Rosenbloom delivered an important lecture on international tax arbitrage, i.e., whether exploiting differences between the tax systems of two jurisdictions to minimise the taxes paid could be considered a problem, and if so, whether something could be done without a centralised international tax organisation.[57] Rosenbloom's thesis exposed by then was that international tax arbitrage would be the natural response of the taxpayers to the normal differences that exist between the tax systems around the world.[58] These differences would be the result of sovereign decisions that consider the legal, economic and political aims of a determined tax system. Therefore, they should not represent a problem, or at least an appropriate explanation for why they could be a problem should be given other than appealing to the existence of an 'international tax system'.[59] Rosenbloom's reaction was motivated by a statement about international tax policy emanated from the US Senate Finance Committee in 1986, in which the Committee, in reference to the discussion about dual residence companies, referred to the international tax system. The statement was as follows: 'The committee does not believe that the United States Senate wittingly agreed to an international tax system where taxpayers making cross-border investments, and only those taxpayers, could reduce or eliminate their U.S. corporate tax through self-help and gain an advantage over U.S. persons who make similar investments.'[60]

Contrary to Rosenbloom's position, Avi-Yonah supported the antagonist idea.[61] This is the existence of an international tax system (that he prefers to call an

55. *Ibid.*
56. *See infra* s. 3.3 for a full analysis.
57. Even though Reuven Avi-Yonah also made already a reference to the 'international tax regime' in 1997, the academic debate regarding its existence started with The David R. Tillinghast Lecture on International Tax Arbitrage and the 'International Tax Regime' held at NYU in 1998. *See*, H.D. Rosenbloom, *The David R. Tillinghast Lecture: International Tax Arbitrage and the 'International Tax System,'* 53 Tax L. Rev. 137 (2000). *See also*, R. Avi-Yonah, *International Taxation of Electronic Commerce*, 52 Tax L. Rev. 507 (1997).
58. Rosenbloom, *supra* n. 4, p. 116.
59. *Ibid.*, p. 166. Also, in line with Rosenbloom's argument *see, e.g.*, J. Roin, *Competition and Evasion: Another Perspective on International Tax Competition*, 89 Geo. L. J. 543 (2001); M. Graetz, *The David R. Tillinghast Lecture, Taxing International Income: Inadequate Principles, Outdated Concepts and Unsatisfactory Policies*, 54 Tax L. Rev. 261 (2001), M. Kane, *supra* n. 4.
60. S. Rep. No. 99-313, p. 422 (1986) in: Rosenbloom, *supra* n. 57, p. 137.
61. In support of his thesis, Avi-Yonah provides a question based upon the hypothetical case that a developing country or transition economy decided to adopt an income tax for first time: how free would this country be to write its international tax rules if it wishes to attract foreign investment?

'international tax regime'), which would rest basically in the bilateral tax treaty network and in domestic tax laws of the major trading nations and which would form part of customary international law.[62] The pillars of this regime would be two basic principles that underline it: the *single tax principle*, which implies that income in a cross-border transaction should be taxed once (no more and not less), and the *benefits principle,* which means that active business income must be taxed primarily at source and passive investment income primarily at residence.[63] The comfortable idea of recognising such a regime would directly imply that countries would not be free to adopt any international tax rules they please but rather should operate under the rules of this regime, disregarding a basic premise in taxation, which is that taxing and spending are still a matter of domestic tax policy.[64] In particular, the recognition of a *single tax principle* would drive us to an early conclusion that both double taxation and DNT must be equally eliminated, mitigated or at least prevented.

3.2 The Downside Departure of the *Single Tax Principle*

As already stressed, the single tax principle states that cross-border income should be taxed once, that is, not more and not less than once, at the rate determined by the benefits principle.[65] Therefore, the single tax principle would include both the traditional tax policy aim of avoiding double taxation as well as the avoidance of double non-taxation. Some tax scholars refer to these effects as the *'upside departure'* and *'downside departure'* of the single tax principle.[66] Both sides of the principle are built under the assumption that all countries would like to maintain both a personal and a corporate income tax, justifying the single tax principle from a theoretical and practical

He argues that the freedom of this country and most of the countries around the world to adopt international tax rules is severely constrained, even before entering a tax treaty, by the need to adapt to generally accepted principles of international taxation. *See* R. Avi-Yonah, *International Tax as International Law: An analysis of the International Tax Regime*, Cambridge University Press, New York, 2007, pp. 3-4. *See also*, R. Avi-Yonah, *Commentary (Response to article by H. David Rosenbloom), 53* Tax L. Rev. 167 (2000).

62. Avi-Yonah, *supra* n. 57.
63. The benefit principle provides that the residence jurisdiction would have the primary right to tax passive income (investment), whilst the source jurisdiction would have the primary right to tax active income (business). *See* Avi-Yonah (2007), *supra* n. 61, pp. 8-13. Although the benefit principle has been proved since long time not to explain in a very convincing manner the development of the modern digital economy, only recently Avi-Yonah has recognised its obsolescence arguing that, at least 'temporarily', this principle (pillar of the 'international tax regime') should be re-evaluated and be understood in a complete opposite way. As stated by Avi-Yonah: 'Most of the current issues can be solved if we taxed passive income primarily at source and active income primarily at residence.' *See* R. Avi-Yonah, *The International Tax Regime: A Centennial Reconsideration,* Glob. Tax'n. (2016).
64. Other international tax scholars have also supported the idea of the existence of an international tax regime. *See, e.g.*, H. Ault, *The importance of International Cooperation in Forging Tax Policy,* 26 Brook. J. Int'l L. 1693 (2001); H. Ault, *Some Reflections on the OECD and the Sources of International Tax Principles*, 70 Tax Notes Int'l 12 (2013) DOI: 10.2139/ssrn.2287834. Y. Brauner, *An International Tax Regime in Crystallization*, 56 Tax L. Rev. 259 (2003); Y. Brauner, *Integration in an Integrated World,* 2 N.Y.U. J. L. & Bus. 51 (2005); Dell' Anese, *supra* n. 4.
65. Avi-Yonah (2007), *supra* n. 61, p. 9.
66. Shaviro, *supra* n. 54.

point of view.[67] On the one hand, the upside departure of the single tax principle would help us to avoid income derived from cross-border transactions being taxed more heavily than domestically.[68] Indeed, double taxation leads to tax rates that can be extremely high and tend to disincentive international investment. The downside departure, on the other hand, would help to avoid cross-border income being under-taxed or not taxed at all, violating both the horizontal and vertical equity when compared to the higher rates imposed at the domestic level, also avoiding an erosion of the national tax base.[69] In other words, both the outcomes of double taxation and DNT would be naturally forbidden by the existence of a supreme principle recognised under international tax law that obliges to eliminate or mitigate these outcomes.

Scholars supporting the existence of a principle of single taxation have traditionally argued based on the extended tax treaty network around the world and, specifically, the use of the tax credit method to relieve double taxation rather than the exemption method. More recently, however, some scholars have also come up with some new arguments involving the interpretation of the 1981 LOB provision in the US Model. These arguments are subsequently analysed.

3.2.1 The Tax Credit Method to Ensure Single Taxation

Countries around the world tend to relieve double taxation, either unilaterally or bilaterally, mainly by two different manners, namely granting an exemption upon the foreign income received by a resident taxpayer, no matter the taxation of that income in the other country, or granting a credit upon the foreign taxes paid in the foreign country.[70] In other words, unlike the exemption method, the focus of the tax credit is

67. Avi-Yonah (2007), *supra* n. 61.
68. *Ibid.*
69. *Ibid.*
70. The use of credit or exemption relates to the classic economic arguments regarding tax neutrality, which has been largely discussed in the literature, and which promote different forms of efficiency. On the one hand, *capital export neutrality* (CEN) is an economic standard holding that taxation should be a neutral factor in a taxpayer's choice between carrying on economic activity in the taxpayer's residence country or in a foreign country. It is given effect in its purest form when the taxpayer's residence country taxes each resident's worldwide income as it is earned and provides the resident with an unlimited credit for foreign income taxes imposed on that income. In other words, it ensures that taxpayers face the same rate of tax on the return to capital irrespective of the country where the capital is deployed. On the other hand, *capital import neutrality* (CIN) ensures that taxpayers face the same rate of tax on the return to capital deployed in a given jurisdiction irrespective of the jurisdiction in which the taxpayer is resident. In other words, it ensures that local and foreign capital competes on equal foots in a determined country. Some authors also refer to a third type of neutrality called *national neutrality* (NN), which consists in providing relief of double taxation giving the taxpayer a deduction for the foreign taxes paid, the same way a deduction is granted for other costs. This type of neutrality would make investors indifferent between the pre-tax return on domestic investments and the return on foreign investments after paying foreign taxes. *See* D. Weisbach, *The Use of Neutralities in International Tax Policy*, 68 Nat'l Tax J. 635 (2015). In addition to the traditional discussion between CEN and CIN, some authors have developed the concept of *capital ownership neutrality* (CON), which means, in simple terms, that the world welfare is maximised if the identities of capital owners are unaffected by tax rate differences. *See* M. Desai and J. Hines, Evaluating International Tax Reform, 56 Nat'l Tax J. 487 (2003). *See also*, M. Desai and

on the amount of taxes effectively paid in the other country.[71] Therefore, the credit method would implicitly pursue the object of ensuring that the income is taxed at least in one country when a cross-border transaction takes place.[72] This assumption is, in principle, correct. As the foreign tax credit is granted on a dollar-by-dollar basis, no credit is allowed when there is no income tax paid in the source country.[73] The above could drive us to a preliminary conclusion that income will be taxed at least once. However, there is no proof that the real aim of the tax credit method is indeed to ensure single taxation. On the contrary, historical arguments in the design of the tax credit method (specifically in the US), as well as examples of tax treaty practice, should bring us to a totally different conclusion. Let me take the example of the US Foreign Tax Credit.[74]

The US Foreign Tax Credit proposal came into play right after the end of the First World War.[75] At that time, countries in Europe needed money for reconstruction and

---

J. Hines Jr., *Old Rules and New Realities: Corporate Tax Policy in a Global Setting*, 57 Nat'l Tax J. 937 (2004). The usual policy recommendation to achieve CON is for countries to adopt territorial tax systems, namely, not to tax business income earned in some countries. Indeed, the CON has been advanced as the basis of a policy reform in the United States to move toward a territorial tax system. For a critical analysis on the concept of CON, *see* Kleinbard (Tax Law Rev. 2011), *supra* n. 40. For Kleinbard, the CON principle assumes that the source country taxation is fully capitalised into prices of firms operating in that source country as well as they [MNEs] face a constant after-tax rate of return everywhere in the world, and suffer the same tax burden everywhere, when taxes include both implicit and explicit taxes. He argues that what he calls 'stateless income tax planning' vitiates the plausibility of this assumption. *Ibid.*, p. 100. As he states: 'Without the full capitalization of source country taxes in firms valuations, reliance on the CON principle to recommend that the United States adopt a territorial tax system reduces to a plea for a 'competitive' international tax framework, by which is meant a system no less generous than those available to firms domiciled in other countries. But that plea, in turn, is little different in practice from a call for trade export subsidies or the like, and strangely ignores the competitiveness of domestic operations.' *Ibid.*, p. 101. Kleinbard's work is added to the existing work of Grubert and Altshuler, who have also criticised the economic efficiency arguments for territorial tax systems. *See, e.g.*, H. Grubert and R. Altshuler, *Corporate Taxes in the World Economy: Reforming Taxation of Cross-Border Income*, Working Papers, Department of Economics, Rutgers, the State University of New Jersey No. 2006, 26 (2006).

71. This is because, if taxes are not effectively paid in the other country, then no credit is granted. Perhaps the exception to that are the clauses of *tax sparing* introduced within some tax treaties. A further analysis on this matter is carried on at *infra* Chapter 2, s. 4.1.1.
72. Avi-Yonah argues that T.S. Adams, the designer of the US tax credit system, implicitly recognised the existence of a principle of single taxation when he stated as follows: 'the state which with a fine regards for the rights if the taxpayers takes pains to relieve double taxation, may fairly take measures to ensure that the person or property pays at least one tax.' *See* T.S. Adams, *Interstate and International Double Taxation* in: Roswell Magill (ed.) Lectures *on Taxation* (1932), 101, cited in: Avi-Yonah, *Who Invented the Single Tax Principle? An Essay on the History of U.S. Treaty Policy*, 59 N.Y.L. Sch. L. Rev. 309 (2014), p. 313.
73. In contrast, the exemption method (at least in its purest form) applies no matter what happens in the source country. Indeed, if the income is by any reason not taxed in the source country, the exemption is granted anyway in the residence country. *See, e.g.*, the application of Article 23A of the OECD Model.
74. This example is not random. The Unites States was indeed the pioneer country introducing a tax credit system to relieve double taxation. Likewise, it is the design of the US Foreign Tax Credit normally used by the supporters of the single tax principle to argue in its favour. For an analysis on the history of the US FTC, *see* M. Graetz and M. O'Hear, *The 'Original Intent' of U.S. International Taxation*, 46 Duke Law J. 1021 (1997).
75. *Ibid.*, p. 1051.

increased their tax rates accordingly.[76] This phenomenon was extended even beyond Europe and implied that American investors were inevitably subject to tax outside the United States. In other words, the original design of the foreign tax credit system in the United States did not consider whether foreign countries would tax or not the income of American investors abroad because, in fact, the historic context was completely the opposite: countries after the war wanted to get revenues through taxation, thus the main idea in designing the tax credit relief was to avoid the potential double or multiple taxation that American investors might suffer, which reveals that the original aim of the credit method was not ensuring single taxation, but simply avoiding double or multiple taxation.[77]

The above brings us to the second important historical factor in the design of the US Foreign Tax Credit, which is related to the lack of competitiveness of American businesses abroad precisely derived from the potential double or multiple taxation to which they were exposed. As stated by Carroll: 'The American credit system is ideal for a wealthy nation that desires to encourage the expansion of its foreign trade, and is willing to afford relief from double taxation to its citizens or residents [...]. The United States says, in effect, to its citizens – go abroad and trade. If you have to pay tax on your earnings in foreign countries, show me your bill and I will give you relief [...].'[78] This concern about competition was also presented by T.S. Adams in his tax treaty work: '[Legislation authorizing U.S. negotiation of tax treaties] will enable the businessmen [sic] of those foreign countries which have benefit of conventions or treaties of this kind protecting them from the burden of international double taxation.' Therefore, unlike an instrument to ensure that income in a cross-border transaction must be taxed at least once, the history behind the US foreign tax credit (1918) demonstrates that it was primarily conceived as a tool to promote competitiveness of American businesses abroad to avoid the unfair result of taxing twice the income derived from these businesses. In other words, the single and unavoidable taxation abroad was simply the result of the historic moment in which the foreign tax credit came into life, but it was neither a purpose nor a condition for the implementation of the foreign credit system. To think otherwise would simply distort the history behind the origin of the foreign tax credit.

There are also strong tax treaty practice arguments to reject the idea that the tax credit method to relieve double taxation would serve the purpose of ensuring single taxation. It is undeniable that, in most cases, the tax credit is granted in the resident country to the extent that taxes have been effectively paid in the source country. Nevertheless, this outcome is indeed far from accomplishing with an international tax

76. As provided by Graetz and O'Hear: 'A variety of American economic and diplomatic interests required that a substantial quantity of American capital be channelled to rebuild post-war Europe. The United States was owed billion dollars by allied governments for wartime loans; somehow Europe would need access to American dollars to pay off this debt.' *Ibid.*

77. 'Americans wanted smaller government, lower taxes, and fewer international entanglements.' *Ibid.*, p. 1052.

78. M. Carroll, *The Double Taxation Conference* (3 September 1927), 28-29, unpublished manuscript available at T.S. Adam Papers, Yale University, Box 16, September 1927 folder, cited in: *Ibid.*, p. 1050.

law principle. The above can easily be seen in the use of *tax-sparing* and *matching credit clauses*. In these cases, the tax credit is granted regardless of the amount of taxes paid in the source country, working indeed as a notional tax credit. Accordingly, and despite the rejection of these clauses at the OECD level and by the US tax treaty practice, these clauses are negotiated and used by important economies in the world, including, for example, Brazil, in order to safeguard their own tax incentive policies.[79]

Moreover, if single taxation is going to be ensured by the tax credit method, or whether this is proof of the existence of the single tax principle, one should simply conclude that this is, in fact, a very inefficient system to achieve that purpose. Indeed, if income is not taxed in the source country and never repatriated to the resident country, it is clear that a DNT outcome will be achieved, but it is impossible, under that scenario, to ensure single taxation.[80] In simple words, the tax credit method complies with the primary role of mitigating double taxation and sometimes indirectly achieving the outcome of ensuring single taxation. However, this latter result depends exclusively on the ultimate repatriation of the income to the resident country. In the absence of this, the argument that the tax credit method ensures single taxation seems to be more an altruistic idea rather than a real outcome in practice.

3.2.2 The Agnosticism of the Exemption Method

As already stressed, the main difference between the exemption and credit method to relieve double taxation is that the former looks exclusively at the income, exempting foreign source income no matter the taxes paid abroad.[81] This special feature of the

79. More regarding the discussion on tax sparing and matching credits at *infra* Chapter 2, ss 4.1.1 and 4.1.2.
80. The above can be illustrated in the following example: if a US Corporation incorporates a subsidiary in a low-tax jurisdiction and it generates income exempt from taxation or taxed at a very low rate in that country, the result, i.e., deferral of US taxation, will be an exemption or at least something very similar to an exemption at the residence country, because foreign subsidiaries are not taxed in the United States so long as they do not repatriate dividends to the US parent company. A foreign subsidiary is not regarded as a US person even if wholly owned by a US person. *See* US: I.R.C. s. 7701(a)(5). When the subsidiary makes a distribution to the parent company, the parent will use the foreign income taxes the subsidiary paid to offset the tax liability imposed by repatriation. *See* US: I.R.C. s. 902(a).
81. This principle applies both in the case of '*full exemption*' and '*exemption with progression*' recognised in the OECD Model. In both cases the residence state has the right to tax exclusively the amount of domestic source income, exempting the amount of foreign source income received. The only difference is that in the case of exemption with progression, the amount of foreign source income is considered to determine the tax rate applicable in the residence state, which could finally imply a lower amount of taxes relieved in comparison with the full exemption. The above can be illustrated in the following example. If a resident of State A has USD 100,000 of worldwide income (USD 80,000 domestic and USD 20,000 from country B), and country A normally taxes USD 100,000 at a rate of 35% and USD 80,000 at a rate of 30%, then applying the exemption with progression, the resident of State A will be subject to 35% on the amount of USD 80,000 of foreign source income (USD 28,000), whilst if the full exemption were applied, he would be subject to 30% on the same USD 80,000 (USD 24,000). There will be a difference of USD 4,000 in relief between both methods, although the principle of exempting the foreign source income always will apply. *See* OECD Commentary on Articles 23A and 23B concerning the methods for elimination of double taxation, paras 18 and 19.

exemption method makes it completely ineffective to ensure single taxation because unless countries decide to include specific provisions to maintain a single taxation status, i.e., either a *subject to tax* or a *switch-over clause*, the DNT outcome will inevitably arise.[82] In other words, the exemption method is totally agnostic with respect to the aim of ensuring single taxation, or which is the same, avoiding DNT.

The general agnosticism of the exemption method to prevent DNT is recognised at the OECD level as an efficient element when compared with the credit method, thus making the election of the former prevail over the latter in relieving double taxation.[83] Indeed, as the exemption method does not require the residence state to undertake investigations upon the actual taxation in the source state and whether or not the right to tax is, in effect, exercised in this latter state, it is normally regarded as the most effective one.[84] This idea of absolute exemption is, nevertheless, partially mitigated when the outcome of DNT arises.[85] Paragraph 35 of the 2017 OECD Commentaries on Article 23A and 23B OECD Model states: 'Occasionally, negotiating States may find it reasonable in certain circumstances, in order to avoid double non-taxation, to make an

---

82. *Infra* Chapter 2, ss 4.2.1 and 4.2.2.
83. This statement is only focused on the simplicity of the exemption method used to relieve double taxation and it avoids the economic discussion on why countries could opt for one method instead of the other due to economic efficiency or equity reasons. This discussion refers to the economic notions of CEN and CIN neutrality. As already stressed in this chapter (*supra* n. 70), the former means that the investor should pay the same total tax, whether he receives an investment income from foreign or domestic sources. The latter means that capital funds originated in various countries should compete in equal feet in the capital market of any country. *See* K. Vogel, *Worldwide v. Source Taxation of Income – A Review and Re-evaluation of Arguments (Part II)*, 10 Intertax 310-311 (1988). Vogel observes that CEN thus supposes a worldwide taxation income with the use of foreign tax credit, whilst CIN implies a source-based taxation system with the use of the exemption method to relieve double taxation. *Ibid. See also*, Weisbach, *supra* n. 70. The literature has shown preference for CEN. *See, e.g.*, C. McLure Jr., *Substituting Consumption-Based Direct Taxation for Income Taxes as the International Norm*, 45 Natl. Tax J. 145 (1992). Vogel also mentions Richard Musgrave and Bernard Snoy in this position. *See* R. Musgrave, *Criteria for Foreign Tax Credit in: Taxation and Operations Abroad, Symposium* (1960), and B. Snoy, *Taxes on Direct Investment Income in the EEC, A Legal and Economic Analysis* (1975), both cited in: Vogel, *ibid*. Nevertheless, the preference for CEN has also been challenged. *See, e.g.*, L. Mutén, *Some Topical Issues Concerning International Double Taxation* in: S. Cnossen (ed.) *Comparative Tax Studies. Essays in Honor of Richard Goode* (1983), cited in: K. Vogel, *Taxation of Cross-Border Income, Harmonization, and Tax Neutrality under European Law* in: K. Vogel (ed.) *Taxation of Cross-Border Income, Harmonization, and Tax Neutrality under European Law* (1994), p. 24, and re-cited in: D. Pinto, *Exclusive Source or Residence-Based Taxation–Is a New and Simpler World Tax Order Possible?*, 61 Bull. Intl. Taxn. 7 (2007), Journals IBFD, p. 286 (n. 77). It has also been argued that the debate about capital export or import neutrality is less relevant in a globalised world. *See, e.g.*, D. Frisch, *The Economics of International Tax Policy: Some Old and New Approaches*, 47 Tax Notes 5 (1990). Similarly, considering both scenarios, namely an international world with exclusive residence-based taxation and one with exclusive source-based taxation, it is difficult to agree that any of them can exclusively be implemented internationally. Pinto, *Ibid.*, p. 291. For an interesting analysis about the notion of neutrality and EU Law, *see* W. Schön, *Neutrality and Territoriality – Competing or Converging Concepts in European Tax Law?*, 69 Bull Intl. Taxn. 4/5 (2015), Journals IBFD. For the alternative notion of *capital ownership neutrality* (CON), *see* Desai and Hines, *supra* n. 70. *See also*, Desai and Hines Jr., *supra* n. 70.
84. OECD Commentary on Articles 23A and 23B concerning the methods for elimination of double taxation, para. 34.
85. *Ibid.*, para. 35.

exception to the absolute obligation on the State of residence to give exemption [...]. Such may be the case where no tax on specific items of income or capital is provided under the domestic laws of the State of source, or tax is not effectively collected owing to special circumstances such as the set-off of losses, a mistake, or the statutory time limit having expired.'[86] Similar concerns on DNT actually motivated the modification of the OECD Commentaries on Article 23A OECD in the 2000 and the 2008 update version of the OECD Model, although, as we will see later on in this work, none of these modifications was enough to solve all the situations of DNT that they originally pretended.[87] Yet, regardless of these concerns, the OECD Commentaries recognise that the faculty of implementing the exemption method remains still within the context of domestic laws.[88] The above implies that the obligation to give an exemption to relieve double taxation might still be absolute if the countries desire to, regardless of the concerns about DNT explained above. More importantly, the wording of the Article 23A OECD Model still suggests that the residence State shall exempt the income or capital received by one of its residents to the extent that this income '*may be*' taxed in the State of source. In a nutshell, no effective or actual taxation is required in the source State in order to trigger the application of the exemption in the residence state.[89]

Despite the agnosticism of the exemption method to prevent DNT, this is still the preferred method to relieve double taxation among many countries, including, e.g., the whole of continental Europe.[90] The above responds to a series of factors, e.g., the capital import neutrality (CIN) tendency among European countries and the long-standing domestic tax law traditions giving preference to this method to relieve double taxation rather than the credit method. As explained by Schön: 'From an economic standpoint, both features of "tax neutrality" [capital import and capital export neutrality (CEN)] have their merits. It is a long-standing tradition to which many European states have submitted, and it is also sound fiscal policy to set up a tax system according to the idea of "capital import neutrality".'[91] Likewise, the European Commission's proposal for a CCCTB reinforces the primacy of the exemption method at the EU level.

86. *Ibid.*
87. *See infra* Chapter 2, ss 3.3 and 3.4.
88. OECD Commentary on Articles 23A and 23B concerning the methods for elimination of double taxation, para. 35.
89. This issue is further analysed in this work, where some examples are provided in order to demonstrate the substantial difference when Contracting States actually desire that income 'is taxed' or 'subject-to-tax,' and when this 'may be taxed.' *See infra* Chapter 2, s. 4.2.1.
90. The preference of the exemption method in Europe has been largely discussed in the European tax literature. *See, e.g.*, W. Schön, *Tax Competition in Europe – The National Perspective*, 42 Eur. Taxn. 12 (2002), Journals IBFD, p. 495. *See also*, J. Avery Jones, *Avoiding Double Taxation: Credit Versus Exemption – The Origins*, 66 Bull. Intl. Taxn. 2 (2012), Journals IBFD; M. Helminen, *The Problem of Double Non-Taxation in the European Union – To What Extent Could This Be Resolved Through a Multilateral EU Tax Treaty Based on the Nordic Convention?*, 53 Eur. Taxn. 7 (2013), Journals IBFD, p. 309; G. Maisto, *Credit Versus Exemption under Domestic Tax Law and Treaties* in: M. Lang et al., (eds) *Tax Treaties: Building Bridges Between Law and Economics*, IBFD, Amsterdam (2010), s. 2.
91. Schön, *supra* n. 83.

This proposal foresees unconditional exemption for distributions coming from companies outside the group, with the *switch-over clause* and a CFC rule only applying to distributions from subsidiaries that are resident outside the EU.[92]

Therefore, it is difficult for this author to agree with the existence of an international tax law principle that prevents DNT in cross-border situations when, indeed, neither the credit nor the exemption methods are fully effective in ensuring single taxation. Whilst the effectiveness of the credit method to ensure single taxation will depend exclusively on the ultimate repatriation of profits, the exemption method is completely agnostic in preventing DNT. Accordingly, when countries must decide among the two methods to relieve double taxation, there is a certain tendency to opt for the simplicity of the exemption method rather than the complexity of the credit method. The above, however, does not mean that countries might achieve an agreement to prevent double non-taxation introducing, e.g., *subject-to-tax* or *switch-over clauses* within their tax treaties. Nevertheless, this would be, in any case, a proof of the existence of an international tax law principle, but rather the simple result of an ad hoc tax treaty negotiation.[93]

3.2.3 *New Voices in Defence of the* Single Tax Principle

The conceptual evidence presented thus far does not give space for the recognition of single taxation as an international principle aimed at preventing DNT. Nevertheless, new voices have arisen and insisted on it. Specifically, some scholars have recently argued that the original introduction of a LOB provision in the 1981 US Model would be an argument strong enough to sustain the recognition of a principle of single taxation in cross-border transactions.[94]

3.2.3.1 The 1981 LOB Provision: US Model

The original design of the LOB provision under the US Model provided that the benefits of a reduced WHT under a treaty would not be applicable to non-publicly traded corporations residing in the treaty partner unless more than 75% of the shares of that corporation are owned by individual residents and the income is not paid out to residents of third countries.[95] In addition, paragraph 3 of Article 16 of the 1981 Tax Treaty Model provided that treaty benefits would not apply to corporations subject to

92. G. Kofler, *Indirect Credit Versus Exemption: Double Taxation Relief for Intercompany Distributions*, 66 Bull. Intl. Taxn. 2 (2012), Journals IBFD, p. 89. For an analysis on the CCTB proposal *see, e.g.*, L. Cerioni, *The Commission's Proposal for a CCCTB Directive: Analysis and Comment*, 65 Bull. Intl. Taxn. 9 (2011), Journals IBFD. *See also*, J. Barenfeld, *A Common Consolidated Corporate Tax Base in the European Union – A Beauty or a Beast in the Quest for Tax Simplicity*, 61 Bull. Intl. Taxn. 7 (2007), Journals IBFD.
93. A further analysis can be found at *infra* Chapter 2, ss 4.2.1 and 4.2.2.
94. Avi-Yonah, *supra* n. 72, pp. 313-318.
95. US: United States Model Income Tax Convention of 16 June 1981, Article 16(1).

a significantly lower tax in their country of residence.[96] The interpretation of paragraph 3 of Article 16 is that the reduction of WHT at source is contingent on the taxation at residence, regardless of the ownership of the recipient of the income.[97]

Although the above interpretation is not completely wrong, it is certainly not based on the idea of a principle of single taxation but rather on the legitimate interest of the source country, which restricts its taxation rights by granting a reduced WHT under a tax treaty, to coordinate this restriction with similar taxation in the residence country. Otherwise, there would be no interest for the source country to restrict itself from taxing a determined item of income. This also reaffirms the original intention of the LOB provisions, which is to limit the access of third parties to a treaty between two countries from which they are not residents[98] and not the avoidance of either double taxation or DNT.

Furthermore, there are other reasons that reinforce the idea that the contingency included in the original 1981 LOB provision had nothing to do with the recognition of a principle of single taxation. First, the original LOB provision in the 1981 US Model was not applicable to partnerships, which are currently recognised as persons under the most recent US Models, and therefore, being able to receive the benefits of a treaty. Therefore, it is difficult to conceive the application of a principle of single taxation applicable only to tax treaty cases in which a corporation or trust was involved.[99] Second, a tax treaty model is neither a negotiated treaty nor an ideal world of taxation.[100] Indeed, LOB provisions are subject to several modifications during the

---

96. Article 16(3) stated: 'Any relief from tax provided by a Contracting State to a resident of the other Contracting State under the Convention shall be inapplicable to the extent that, under the law in force in that other Contracting State, the income to which the relief relates bears significantly lower tax than similar income arising within that other State derived by residents of that other State.' US: United States Model Income Tax Convention of 16 June 1981, Article 16(3).
97. Avi-Yonah, *supra* n. 72, p. 317.
98. *See, e.g.*, N. Bammens and L. De Broe, *Treaty Shopping and Avoidance of Abuse in Tax Treaties: Building Bridges Between Law and Economics*, M. Lang et al. eds, IBFD, Amsterdam 2010, Online Books IBFD.
99. However, this argument lacks importance today with the suggestion to include partnerships within the scope of the LOB made by Rosenbloom in 1983 and further considered in the 1996 and 2006 United States Model Income Tax Conventions. As argued by Rosenbloom: 'Partnerships, on the other hand, are not themselves taxpayers in the United States or in many other countries, although they are generally regarded as 'persons' under recent US tax treaties, with their residence dependent on that of the treaty partners. Because treaty benefits are thus available to partnerships as such, and because corporations and trusts can serve as partners, partnerships should be included within the limitation as well - if only to preclude their use to avoid a limitation of benefits applicable to corporations and trusts. Moreover, because there are numerous entities in the world whose statuses as corporations, trusts, or partnerships may not be so clear, treaty drafter may find it convenient to speak in terms of 'all persons other than individuals'. Use of this phrase will obviate interpretative problems, and it is difficult to see how any possible over inclusion could be harmful.' H.D. Rosenbloom, *Tax Treaty Abuse: Policies and Issues*, 15 Law & Pol'y Int'l Bus. 763, 811-812 (1983). *See* the reference to 'persons other than individuals' included in Article 22(2)(f) of the United States Model Income Tax Convention of 20 September 1996 and Article 22(2)(e) of the United States Model Income Tax Convention of 15 November 2006.
100. As Rosenbloom explains: '[A] taxpayer may reject a treaty and its content and invoke its rights under domestic law [...].' Rosenbloom, *supra* n. 57, p. 164.

negotiation process and even sometimes not included.[101] Then, it would be difficult to recognise a principle of single taxation applicable only in those cases in which either the LOB provision was finally included in the negotiated treaty, or it was included exactly as it was designed in the treaty model.

Moreover, the subsequent elimination of paragraph 3 and the inclusion of a 'base erosion test' in the 1996 and 2006 Models reaffirms the idea that the LOB provisions have (and had) nothing to do with assuring single taxation. Article 22(2)(f)(ii) of the US Model establishes: 'A resident of a Contracting State shall be entitled to all the benefits of this Convention if the resident is: [...] (f) a person other than an individual, if: (ii) less than 50 percent of the person's gross income for the taxable year is paid or accrued, directly or indirectly, to persons who are not residents of either Contracting State (unless the payment is attributable to a permanent establishment situated in either State), in the form of payments that are deductible for income tax purposes in the person's State of residence.'[102] In other words, payments made to any resident of either Contracting State, as well as payments made to PEs, will not be considered base eroding payments.[103] Then, under the 1996 US Model, it was perfectly possible that a US partnership would pay a deductible payment to a resident of the other Contracting State, where that payment was not taxable, without considering that payment as base eroding.[104] Accordingly, Article 22(2)(f)(ii) of the 2006 US Model more or less maintained the wording of the 1996 version. This is to say, in case a person other than an individual (a partnership) made deductible payments that represent less than 50% of its gross income to non-residents of either Contracting State, these payments would be considered as base eroding.[105] However, these payments do not include arm's length payments in the ordinary course of business for services or tangible property.[106] This last inclusion reduces the scope of application of the LOB provision because it expressly excludes payments to non-residents of the treaty to the extent that these payments were made on an arm's length basis and in the ordinary course of business

101. Although it is a policy of the United States to include a LOB provision into its tax treaties, there are cases in which this provision has not been included. For example, the treaties between the United States and Greece, Hungary, Pakistan, Philippines, Poland and Romania do not include a LOB provision. *See* R. Avi-Yonah and O. Halabi, *US Treaty Anti-Avoidance Rules: An Overview and Assessment*, 66 Bull. Intl. Taxn. 4/5 (2012), Journals IBFD, p. 238.
102. US: United States Model Income Tax Convention of 20 September 1996, Article 22(2)(f)(ii).
103. US: Technical Explanation of the United States Model Income Tax Convention of 20 September 1996, Article 22.
104. To the extent that the recipients do not themselves base erode to non-residents. *Ibid.*
105. Article 22(2)(f)(ii) of the 2006 United States Model Income Tax Convention states: 'A resident of a Contracting State shall be a qualified person for a taxable year if the resident is:[...] (f) a person other than an individual, if: (ii) less than 50 percent of the person's gross income for the taxable year, as determined in the person's State of residence, is paid or accrued, directly or indirectly, to persons who are not residents of either Contracting State entitled to the benefits of this Convention under subparagraph a), subparagraph b), clause i) of subparagraph c), or subparagraph d) of this paragraph in the form of payments that are deductible for purposes of the taxes covered by this Convention in the person's State of residence (but not including arm's length payments in the ordinary course of business for services or tangible property).' *See* US: United States Model Income Tax Convention of 15 November 2006, Article 22(2)(f)(ii). *See also*, US: Technical Explanation of the United States Model Income Tax Convention of 15 November, 2006, Article 22.
106. *Ibid.*

for services or tangibles. This also increases the likelihood that certain arm's length deductible payments made from a treaty resident to another resident (or even a non-resident) are excluded from taxation in the hands of the recipient. This issue, however, would, in any case, demonstrate that the final target of the LOB provision is to ensure the single taxation of cross-border payments.

3.2.3.2 The 2016 LOB Provision: US Model

A separate reference should be made with respect to the new Article 22 of the 2016 US Model.[107] The new base erosion test includes deductible payments made to residents of either Contracting State that benefit from a '*Special Tax Regime*' (hereinafter, 'STR') in their Contracting State of residence with respect to the deductible payments.[108] For this purpose, the new Article 3(1) will consider an STR as 'any statute, legislation, or administrative practice in a Contracting State with respect to a tax described in Article 2 (Taxes Covered) that meet all of the following conditions: [...]'.[109] Likewise, the definition includes a list of cases where any legislation or regulation of administrative practice shall not be considered an STR.[110] Conversely to the 1996 and 2006 US Models,

107. US: United States Model Income Tax Convention of 17 February 2016, Article 22. *See also*, US: Proposed Limitation on Benefits Article, Select Draft Provisions of the US Model Income Tax Convention of 20 May 2015.

108. *Ibid.*

109. US: Proposed Treaty Rules Addressing '*Special Tax Regimes,*' Select Draft Provisions of the US Model Income Tax Convention, 20 May 2015. It is also important to remark that the definition of STR includes as administrative practice a 'ruling practice.' This is to say, for example, if a taxpayer obtains a ruling providing that its foreign source interest income will be subject to a low rate of taxation in the State of residence, and that rate is lower than the normal rate that applies to foreign source interest income received by residents of that State, the administrative practice under which the ruling is obtained will be considered an STR. *See* US: Technical Explanation for Definition of '*Special Tax Regime,*' Select Draft Provisions of the US Model Income Tax Convention of 20 May 2015, p. 2. It is convenient to note that up to the date this work was concluded, no technical explanations of the 2016 US Model had been made available. However, it is expected that the Select Draft Provisions of the US Model Income Tax Convention of 20 May 2015 are replicated in the final technical explanations. Indeed, more recently, the reference to special tax regimes in the LOB provision can be seen in the 2022 US/Croatia tax treaty. US: Convention Between the Government of the United States of America and the Government of the Republic of Croatia for the Avoidance of Double Taxation and the Prevention of Tax Evasion with respect to Taxes on Income, 7 December 2022, Article 22.

110. The draft of the new Article 3(1) of the US Model states: '[...] However, the term shall not include any legislation, regulation or administrative practice: i) the application of which does not disproportionately benefit interest, royalties or other income, or any combination thereof; ii) that, with regard to royalties, satisfies a substantial activity requirement; iii) that implements the principles of Article 7 (Business Profits) or Article 9 (Associated Enterprises); iv) that applies principally to persons that exclusively promote religious, charitable, scientific, artistic, cultural or educational activities; v) that applies principally to persons substantially all of the activity of which is to provide or administer pension or retirement benefits; vi) that facilitates investment in entities that are marketed primarily to retail investors, are widely-held, that hold real property (immovable property), a diversified portfolio of securities, or any combination thereof, and that are subject to investor-protection regulation in the Contracting State in which the investment entity is established; or vii) that the Contracting States have agreed shall not constitute a special tax regime because it does not result in a low effective rate of taxation.' *Ibid.*

the proposal of amendment includes deductible payments made to a treaty resident subject to a STR in the hands of the recipient, including low or zero tax jurisdictions. Practically speaking, the wording of the 2015 proposal of amendment is quite similar to that of paragraph 3, Article 16 of the 1981 US model. Therefore, and even though the wording of the norm seems to be exogenous to the original purpose of a LOB provision, this author argues again that the source country has a legitimate interest in coordinating a restriction to tax an item of income, provided a treaty is in force, with the corresponding taxation of that income at residence. This legitimate interest to coherently comply with the allocation of taxing powers made by a tax treaty does not have anything to do with a principle of single taxation that governs cross-border transactions. Instead, it responds to a rational concern of the source country that restricts its taxing powers when a tax treaty is negotiated and finally comes into play.

3.3 *Full Taxation*: A Modern Version of the *Single Tax Principle*

A special note should be made regarding a modern approach to the single-taxation paradigm, that is, the idea of 'full taxation'.[111] As originally suggested by Ruth Mason, the recent developments in international tax law, particularly the OECD BEPS project,[112] would reflect and effectuate an international norm[113] that would suggest that all a company's income should be taxed in places where it has real business activities.[114] In other words, the notion of *full taxation* would not deviate from the unsatisfactory idea of preventing DNT, but it would rather confirm it and disguise it behind a new conceptual denomination that also aims to tax business profits somewhere, no matter where.[115]

Mason's observation is rhetorically attractive. After all, it aims to explain with a less precise and more intuitive denomination the historical frustration behind the recognition of a single tax principle in international tax law. However, one must be

111. R. Mason, *The Transformation of International Tax*, 114(3) Am. J. Int'l Law 353 (2020) (who originally proposed the concept of 'full taxation' in the international tax literature).
112. *See* OECD (2013), *supra* n. 2.
113. Mason does not use the term 'international norm' in a strict legal sense. However, if analysed in a strict legal sense, it is evident that full taxation is far from constituting an international norm in the strict international law sense. *See* L. Parada, *Full Taxation: The Single Tax Emperor's New Clothes*, 24(2) Fl. Tax Rev. 771-783 (2021).
114. *Ibid.*, at 370. Other supporters of the idea of full taxation are, for example, N. Noked, *Defense of Primary Taxing Rights* 40 Va. Tax Rev. 341 (2020) (arguing for a 'defensive primary taxing right tax' which would follow the full taxation approach proposed by Ruth Mason); S. Moyal, *Back to Basics: Rethinking Normative Principles in International Tax*, 73 Tax Lawyer 1 (2019) (arguing for a broader interpretation of single taxation in order to set a minimum effective tax rate), and I. Grinberg, *The New International Tax Diplomacy*, 102 The Georgetown Law Journal 1137 (2016) (who stresses the influence of BEPS in the shaping of the international tax governance).
115. Mason, *supra* n. 111, at 372 (arguing that 'because states already faithfully adhered to the no-double-tax norm, growing acceptance of full taxation as a goal of international tax brings states closer to implementing Avi-Yonah's 'single-tax principle', which requires income to be taxed exactly once, no more and no less').

cautious about endorsing this conceptual observation blindly, especially from a normative perspective.[116]

As I have argued in the tax literature already, the idea of full taxation explains where income should be taxed, but it does it entirely divorced from a specific distributive rule.[117] In other words, full taxation is presented as completely agnostic regarding *where* income should be taxed, demanding only that taxing rights flow to states in which multinationals have real factors of production and real activities.[118] This makes the concept not only indeterminate and closer to the prevention of abuse but also certainly different from the original intent of single taxation.[119] Similarly, the indeterminism surrounding the idea of full taxation also creates the risk that countries may ultimately consider it legitimate to allocate revenues somewhere (no matter where), imposing taxation just for the sake of it.[120] This can be particularly sensitive in times when taxes seem to be the preferred tax policy tool to solve any global issue.[121]

116. For a normative criticism of the concept of full taxation, *see* Parada, *supra* n. 113.
117. *Ibid.*, p. 749.
118. Mason also recognises the indeterminism of the concept of full taxation in her work. *See* Mason, *supra* n. 111, pp. 385-88.
119. For example, Avi-Yonah, when he explains the 'international tax system', he argues not only that income in any cross-border taxation should be taxed once, but indeed he proposes specifically that active business income is taxed primarily at source and passive investment income is taxed primarily at residence. Avi-Yonah (2007), *supra* n. 61, pp. 8-13. Less than ten years later, however, Avi-Yonah also recognises the obsolescence of its own distributive rule. *See* Avi-Yonah (2016), *supra* n. 63.
120. Parada, *supra* n. 113, p. 752.
121. A good example is the taxation of big tech MNEs and the proliferation of digital services taxes (DSTs) in Europe. *Ibid.*, pp. 753-54. The debate on DSTs in Europe was first part of a proposal for directive, which did not meet the unanimity of all Member States to be approved as law. This failure pushed European countries to implement unilateral DSTs resembling the characteristics of the failed European directive. *See* European Commission, *Proposal for a Council Directive on the common system of a digital services tax on revenues resulting from the provision of certain digital services*, COM (2018) 148 final (3 March 2018). Unilateral DSTs have also been rightfully criticised for being discriminatory. In this regard, se R. Mason and L. Parada, *Digital Battlefront in the Tax Wars*, 92 Tax Notes Int'l 12, (2018). *See also*, Daniel Bunn, *A Summary of Criticisms of the EU Digital Tax* (Tax Foundation) (22 October 2018). More recently, R. Mason and L. Parada, *The Legality of Digital Taxes in Europe*, 40 Va. Tax Rev. 175 (2020). For the analysis of compatibility of DSTs and tax treaties, as well as their potential double taxation issues that are generated, *see, e.g.*, R. Ismer and C. Jescheck, *Taxes on Digital Services and the Substantive Scope of Application of Tax Treaties: Pushing the Boundaries of Article 2 of the OECD Model*, 46 Intertax 6/7 (2018); A. Martín Jiménez, *BEPS, the Digital(ized) Economy and the Taxation of Services and Royalties*, 46 Intertax 8/9 (2018) DOI: 10.54648/taxi2018067; A. Martín Jiménez, *Controversial Issues About the Concept of Tax in Income and Capital Tax Treaties and the post-BEPS World*, in *Tax Treaties After the BEPS Project: A tribute to Jacques Sasseville* (B. Arnold and A. Parollini (eds) (Canadian Tax Foundation 2018); D. Hohenwarter, G. Kofler, G. Mayr and J. Sinnig, *Qualification of the Digital Service Tax Under Tax Treaties*, 47 Intertax 2 (2019) DOI: 10.54648/taxi2019013, and G. Kofler and J. Sinnig, Equalization Taxes and the 2 (2019). For a defence on unIntertax 2 (2019). For a defence on unilateral DSTs, *see, e.g.*, W. Cui, *The Digital Services Tax: A Conceptual Defense*, Tax L. Rev. 73 (2019) (arguing that the DST would allow location-specific rent earned by digital platforms to be captured by the countries in which such rent arises). *See also*, Young Ran (Christine) Kim, *Digital Services Tax: A Cross-Border Variation of the Consumption Tax Debate*, 71(1) Al. L. Rev. (2020) (arguing that the DST would be a consumption tax, and that with certain modifications, could be a good solution for the tax challenges of the digital economy).

Nevertheless, full taxation is not only problematic because of its indeterminate character. Indeed, two other characteristics make the concept equally worrisome from a normative perspective. First, full taxation, unlike single taxation, appears as an overinclusive concept, which does not only include the prevention of DNT in its original form (i.e., the complete absence of taxation) but also the prevention of profit shifting, tax avoidance, tax evasion, tax loopholes, and even the still unclear notion of aggressive tax planning (ATP).[122] This does not only increase uncertainty from a conceptual point of view but also risks that countries may be tempted to use the notion of full taxation as a proxy for determining the existence of abusive practices, concluding *a priori* that any outcome that is not close to *full taxation* may imply that a whole transaction is qualified as abusive.[123] Second, *full taxation* also proves to be very instrumentalist,[124] serving the sole purpose of justifying provisions that operate under the premise that if one country does not impose taxation, another country must automatically act, pulling the 'tax trigger' without any principled guidance that truly supports this pragmatic approach other than the idea that all a company's income should be taxed once, and somewhere.[125] This premise is precisely what sustains the policy design of anti-hybrid rules[126] and, more recently, a proposal to achieve a minimum effective corporate income tax rate globally.[127]

It is difficult not to agree with Mason's observations on the OECD BEPS project. However, this is far from proving the existence of an international principle of single taxation. Indeed, and as argued somewhere else as well, full taxation, as a modern construction of the single taxation paradigm, may raise more serious normative concerns than the simple idea of taxing no more and not less than once.[128] Therefore, from a tax policy perspective, it should be carefully and restrictively considered.[129]

---

122. Parada, *supra* n. 113, p. 757. For the concept of ATP, *see infra* s. 5.2 of this chapter.
123. It is evident that there is not a general and horizontal concept of abuse of law, and different elements may be considered for this analysis. For example, under EU law the concept of abuse is clearly influenced by the element of artificiality, as the doctrine of the Court of Justice of the European Union (CJEU) has stated in *Cadbury Schweppes*, which makes it rather restrictive. *See Cadbury Schweppes Overseas Ltd v. CIR (Cadbury Schweppes)* (C-196/04) EU:C:2006:544. For literature on abuse of law, *see* various commentators in: *Prohibition of Abuse of Law, A New General Principle of Law?*, R. de la Feria and S. Vogenauer (eds) (Hart Publishing, 2011). *See also*, R. de la Feria, *Prohibition of Abuse of (Community) Law: The Creation of a New General Principle of EC Law through Tax*, 45 Com. Mkt. L. Rev. 395 (2008) DOI: 10.54648/cola2008027.
124. 'Instrumentalism is the view of law as merely a technique or a means to implement policy goals. To the instrumentalist, law is no more than just a particular technique. It is a product of policy that is used in order to implement policy, in particular to achieve economic and social ends such as economic growth and employment'. H. Gribnau, *Legislative Instrumentalism vs. Legal Principles in Tax Law*, International Tax Law Review 3 (2012), p. 18.
125. Mason, *supra* n. 111, pp. 385-388 (referring to these types of provisions as 'fiscal fail-safe rules'). Anti-hybrid rules analysed in this book (Chapter 5) should be considered as an example of fiscal-fail safe rules as per Mason's categorisation.
126. For a critical analysis of the OECD linking rules (anti-hybrid rules), *see infra* Chapter 5 of this book.
127. OECD (2022), *supra* n. 2. *See also*, Devereux et al (2020), and Englisch (2022), *supra* n. 2.
128. For a complete analysis and normative criticism of the notion of full taxation, *see* Parada, *supra* n. 113.
129. *Ibid.*

4 DOUBLE NON-TAXATION AND TAX EVASION/TAX AVOIDANCE

This section turns now to briefly revisit both the legal concepts of tax evasion and tax avoidance in order to demonstrate that DNT cannot be homologated (or confused) with any of those concepts. Likewise, it provides a critical analysis of the non-legal notion of ATP, a modern pseudo-category used within the OECD BEPS Project[130] and analysed by some scholars on equal footing with the legal concepts of tax evasion and avoidance.[131] This Section ultimately intends to demonstrate the negative impact derived from the use of non-legal concepts within the legal debate on DNT.

4.1 Tax Evasion in a Nutshell

Tax evasion and tax avoidance are eminently domestic legal concepts[132], and beyond the linguistic differences in the use of the terms,[133] there is substantial consensus on their meanings.[134]

---

130. The OECD refers twenty-two times to the concept of ATP just in the OECD BEPS Report from 2013. *See*, OECD (2013), *supra* n. 2. However, the OECD already referred to the concept of ATP in its 2011 report focused on transparency and the design of better tools for assessing tax compliance risks. *See* OECD (2011), *supra* n. 1.
131. Pistone, even though recognising the legal uncertainty behind the concept of ATP proposes a systematic analysis of this non-legal concept, referring to it as a 'new conceptual category of global tax law.' Pistone, *supra* n. 41, pp. 109-151.
132. The fact that they are domestic legal concepts does not prevent us from recognising that tax evasion and tax avoidance can have consequences beyond domestic borders. Indeed, a major problem for domestic tax jurisdictions is the fact that taxpayers hide offshore assets, failing to declare them, and in some cases, failing to pay the taxes due on the income derived from those assets. Likewise, and although tax avoidance is not an international notion, it is worth to briefly refer to the concept of tax avoidance (or 'tax abuse') elaborated by the jurisprudence of the CJEU in the case of *Halifax* and *Cadbury Schweppes*, both ruled in 2006. In *Halifax*, the CJEU provided that an abusive practice exists if certain transactions aimed to obtain a tax advantage contrary to the purpose of the law and this aim, i.e., obtaining the tax advantage, is indeed an essential aim. In *Cadbury Schweppes*, which referred to direct taxation matters only, the CJEU set up the limits on what kind of anti-avoidance measures might be justified in order to restrict the fundamental freedoms within the European Union. In this regard, the CJEU was clear in providing that only 'wholly artificial arrangements,' which do not reflect economic reality, may be targeted. In both cases, the CJEU set up important boundaries of what should be a matter of concern and what should be not, preventing therefore Member States to go beyond those limits to justify restrictive tax measures, which might ultimately affect the functioning of the European internal market. The above does not mean to recognise that a uniform concept of tax abuse exists under EU law, but some important patterns of a harmonised concept might be recognised. *See* EU: Judgment in *Halifax plc., Leeds Permanent Development Services Ltd., County Wide Property Investments Ltd. v. Commissioners of Custom and Excise*, C-255/02, ECLI:EU:C:2006:121, hereinafter '*Halifax* case' and EU: Judgment in *Cadbury Schweppes and Cadbury Schweppes Overseas Ltd v. Commissioners of Inland Revenue*, C-196/04, EU:C:2006:544, hereinafter '*Cadbury Schweppes* case'.
133. For example, the English term 'tax evasion' is synonymous of 'tax fraud', and it can be translated into German as '*Steuerhinterziehung*', into French as '*fraude fiscal*', into Spanish as '*evasión fiscal*' and into Portuguese as '*evasao fiscal*'. Conversely, the term 'tax avoidance' is translated into French as 'évasion fiscale', into German as 'Steuerumgehung', into Spanish as 'elusión fiscal' and into Portuguese as 'elusão fiscal'. *See* C. Alves, *Preventing Tax Avoidance: Is There Convergence in the Way Countries Counter Tax Avoidance?*, 67 Bull. Intl. Taxn. 7 (2013), Journals IBFD, p. 348.
134. *Ibid.*

In many countries, tax evasion represents fraudulent conduct from the taxpayer that is aimed at causing an illegal reduction in the amount of taxes to be paid. It generally involves a wilful conduct of the taxpayer and the respective lack of information by the authorities, which ends up in a reduction of the final tax assessment. This conduct is normally described in the law, and it is sanctioned, although the effective sanctions depend on the possibilities and the will of the specific government to prevent these patently illegal and objectionable behaviours. Therefore, in simple terms, tax evasion is no more than a question of governance failure in collecting taxes due to a lack of information. As well explained by Richard Vann: '[T]he prevention of fiscal evasion primarily refers to cases where taxpayers fraudulently conceal income in an international setting and rely on the inability of tax administrations to obtain information from abroad.'[135] This means that tax evasion is per se an illegal conduct, normally described and sanctioned by law, and which has to be with the intentions of a taxpayer to fraudulently hide his assets/income from the tax authorities, achieving, in those cases, most probably, double or multiple non-taxation. This latter outcome, however, is not necessarily a precondition for the existence of tax evasion situations. In other words, the fact that a taxpayer achieves DNT in a cross-border transaction is not a presumption that he is evading taxes. In most cases, this outcome will certainly be promoted or saved by the legislation involved in the transaction, and it will respond to specific incentives aimed at promoting the growth of a specific sector or the whole economy of a country.[136] Therefore, what is sanctioned in those cases of tax evasion is not that a taxpayer finally achieved non-taxation altogether in a cross-border transaction but rather that he unlawfully concealed assets from the tax authorities in order to reduce his final tax burden.

4.1.1 Tax Evasion Versus Tax Fraud

Although most of the countries do not draw a line to separate both tax evasion and tax fraud, there are countries that clearly distinguish among them. Perhaps the most interesting example is Switzerland, where tax evasion constitutes a wilful or negligent behaviour of the taxpayer that causes a predisposition to improperly omit or to make an incomplete final assessment.[137] Therefore, the offender, by action or omission, obtains an unjustified tax advantage, causing a deficit in the community.[138] The causal connection between the behaviour of the offender and the deficit in the community is

135. Vann, *supra* n. 24.
136. This can be seen in the use of tax incentives around the world, especially with respect to the research and development of intangibles with the IP Boxes regimes and the like. Accordingly, within the tax treaty context, countries normally negotiate the inclusion of clauses that safeguard the success of those incentives, namely *tax sparing* clauses. *See infra* Chapter 2, s. 4.1.1.
137. CH: Article 175 of the DBG (Federal Law on Direct Federal Tax) of 14 December 1990 and Article 56 of the StHG (Federal Law on Harmonization of Direct Taxes of the Cantons and Municipalities) of 14 December 1990.
138. *Ibid.*

necessary to consider the action or omission as tax evasion.[139] In contrast, tax fraud supposes that a person forges, fakes or uses false certifications to deceive third persons for purposes of tax evasion.[140] Conversely to tax evasion, the deficit in the community is not required.[141] Thus, both behaviours are sanctioned, although in a different manner.

The distinction between tax fraud and tax evasion in Switzerland has important consequences at the tax treaty level as well.[142] For example, the 1996 tax treaty between Switzerland and the United States (currently in force) grants exchange of information under Article 26 only in case of 'tax fraud or the like'.[143] This is to say, according to paragraph 10 of the Protocol, when the taxpayer has engaged in fraudulent conduct that causes or is intended to cause an illegal and substantial reduction in the amount of tax paid to a Contracting State.[144] In other words, exchange of information is not granted in cases of mere tax evasion.[145] Nevertheless, the above situation could change with the entry in force of the 2009 Protocol, which eliminates the reference to 'tax fraud and the like' and introduces a major information clause. Once the Protocol is ratified, it will be applied retroactively since 23 September 2009,

139. *Ibid.*
140. CH: Article 186 of the DBG and Article 59 of the StHG.
141. *Ibid.*
142. *See, e.g.*, CH: Decision of the Swiss Federal Administrative Court [Bundesverwaltungsgericht] A-737/2012 of 5 April 2012. In a more recent decision of 6 January 2014, the Swiss Federal Administrative Court [*Bundesverwaltungsgericht*] overturned a previous decision of the Swiss Federal Tax Administration granting administrative assistance to the IRS in disclosing some bank account data of American clients. The distinction between tax fraud and tax evasion was one of the main reasons provided by the Court to explain the denial to exchange information in this case. For more information about this Court decision, *see* CH: Press release, Media Relations A-5390/2013 and A-5540/2013, Swiss Federal Administrative Court, St. Gallen (8 January 2014). *See also* the official German text and an unofficial English translation in: CH: *X. v. Federal Tax Administration, A-5390/2013, Swiss Federal Administrative Court* [Bundesverwaltungsgericht], 6 January 2014 (ed. P. Baker), 17 ITLR, Lexis Nexis, London (2014). *See also*, L. Parada, *Intergovernmental Agreements and the Implementation of FATCA in Europe*, 7 World Tax J. 2 (2015), Journals IBFD, pp. 232-235. *See also*, L. Parada, *Lessons Learned from the Swiss Julius Baer Case*, 74 Tax Notes Int'l 13 (2014); S. Ronco, *Scambio di informazioni tra Stati Uniti e Svizzera: il caso Julius Baer*, Rassegna Tributaria 6 (2014), pp. 1332-1353.
143. CH/US: Convention between the United States of America and the Swiss Confederation for the avoidance of double taxation and the prevention of fiscal evasion with respect to taxes on income, signed at Washington on 2 October 1996 as amended by the Protocol signed on 2 October 1996, Article 26(1).
144. CH/US: Technical Explanations of the Convention between the United States of America and the Swiss Confederation for the avoidance of double taxation and the prevention of fiscal evasion with respect to taxes on income, signed at Washington on 2 October 1996 as amended by the Protocol signed on 2 October 1996.
145. For more information why Switzerland does not grant administrative assistance in a case of simple nondisclosure or tax evasion *see, e.g.*, M. Desax, *The Swiss Perspective of Information Exchange*, 58 Tax Notes Int'l 12, 955-957 (2010). For more information about the Swiss bank secrecy law and its coordination with tax treaties *see, e.g.*, G. Braidi and L. Cousinou, *Swiss Banking Secrecy: A Heaven of Peace in Distress for US Taxpayers*, 2 Quid? Fribourg L. Rev. 7-10 (2014).

the date of the signature of the Protocol.[146] However, the approval of the 2009 Protocol is still on hold in the US Senate.[147]

4.1.2 *The Reactions to Tax Evasion*

As explained above, tax evasion is basically a lack of information problem[148] and not a DNT problem. Governments, in cases of tax evasion, are unable to track taxpayers who intentionally hide their income, mostly offshore, resulting in a failure to collect taxes. That is why the natural reaction against tax evasion is exchange of information, namely, to extend the channels by which countries can cooperate to achieve appropriate levels of transparency that prevent taxpayers from hiding assets or income.

A global tendency towards tax transparency has been evidenced in the recent efforts made by countries to increase the levels of exchange of information, which is added to the old measures normally used to combat offshore tax evasion.[149] One major unilateral example is the 2010 FATCA legislation in the United States,[150] which, beyond the criticism of its extraterritoriality and the conflicts with other jurisdictions, has opened the door to developing more effective international instruments to exchange information between jurisdictions. An example of the above is the OECD/G-20 Global Standard on Automatic Exchange of Financial Account Information released in February 2014 (Common Reporting Standard or CRS),[151] which is based on the FATCA Intergovernmental Agreement (IGA) Model 1A.[152] Other global efforts have attended

146. CH/US: Protocol 2009 amending the Convention between the United States and the Swiss Confederation for the avoidance of double taxation with respect to taxes on income signed at Washington on 2 October 1996, Swiss Federal Gazette (27 November 2010), p. 224, Article 5(2).
147. The reason is that US Senator Rand Paul argues that the Protocol gives the IRS too much power to investigate noncriminal behaviours. *See* L. Shepard, *Don't Ask, Don't Tell: Swiss Behavioral Patterns*, 66 Tax Notes Int'l 1, 8 (2012).
148. Vann, *supra* n. 24.
149. Countries also combat offshore tax evasion through voluntary disclosure amnesties. These initiatives are generally successful, but they have limitations. For example, taxpayers can perceive unfairness and anticipate further amnesties, reducing the level of revenues collected by the governments. *See*, for example, L. Lederman, *The Use of Voluntary Disclosure Initiatives in the Battles Against Offshore Tax Evasion*, 57 Vill. L. Rev. 499, 519 (2012) DOI: 10.2139/ssrn.1993323. *See also*, C. Boise, *Breaking Open Offshore Piggybanks: Deferral and the Utility of Amnesty*, 14 Geo. Mason L. Rev. 667, 707 (2007).
150. US: Hiring Incentives to Restore Employment Act, Pub. L. No. 111-147, 124 Stat. 71 (2010). *See also*, US: Proposed FATCA Regulations (2012) and Final FATCA Regulations (2014), both available at www.irs.gov. For further information regarding the discussions about FATCA *see, e.g.*, A. Mahboob, *FATCA and the Fat Cats: Foreign Pass-through Payments and the Blocker Problem*, 71 Tax Notes Int'l 12 (2013); J. Arora et al., *U.S. releases Final FATCA Regs*, 69 Tax Notes Int'l 4 (2013); P. Carman, *Final FATCA Regulations Provide Certainty, Flexibility*, 15 Derivs. & Fin. Instrums. 2 (2013), Journals IBFD; V. Hammer, *US Update*, 66 Bull. Intl. Taxn. 6 (2012), Journals IBFD; W. Cui, *Passthru Payments and the Fantastic World of FATCA*, 13 Derivs. & Fin. Instrums. 4 (2011), Journals IBFD; Parada (2015), *supra* n. 142.
151. OECD, *Standard for Automatic Exchange of Financial Account Information: Common Reporting Standard*, OECD Publishing, Paris, 2014.
152. As provided in the OECD CRS: 'The Common Reporting Standard, with a view to maximizing efficiency and reducing costs for financial institutions draws extensively on the intergovernmental approach to implementing FATCA.' *Ibid. See also*, L. Sheppard, *Machiavellian Pragmatism in Tax Enforcement*, 77 Tax Notes Int'l 11, 927 (2015). *See also*, M. Stewart, *Transnational*

more to the disclosure of corporate taxpayers' information, such as the mandatory disclosure rules under the OECD BEPS Action 12[153] and the imposition on taxpayers to disclose their affairs before or after the lodgement of tax returns.[154] Similarly, the issuance of the MCMAA[155] and the CbCR[156] have contributed to increasing the power of the tax authorities to exchange information in a cooperative manner.[157]

This tax transparency path can also be found within the European Union since the establishment of the EU Saving Tax Directive (Council Directive 2003/48/EC).[158] This directive obliges financial institutions to report the identity of the EU residents who receive interest payments and to exchange it on an annual basis with the respective residence country.[159] More recently, the adoption by the European Commission of the Council Directive 2014/107/EU[160] and the Council Directive

---

Tax Information Exchange Networks: Steps Towards a Globalized, Legitimate Tax Administration, 4 World Tax J. 2 (2012), Journals IBFD, p. 169. It is important to clarify that there are two versions of the Intergovernmental Agreement Model 1: (i) the reciprocal version (Model 1A), which provides for the United States to exchange information currently collected on accounts held in US financial institutions by residents of treaty partner countries (either by bilateral tax treaties or TIEAs), and includes a policy commitment to pursue regulations and support legislation that would provide for equivalent levels of exchange by the United States; and (ii) the non-reciprocal version (Model 1B), where no reciprocal exchange of information takes place. *See* Parada (2015), *supra* n. 142, p. 204. *See also*, F. A. García Prats, *Los Nuevos Estándares Internacionales de Intercambio de Información: FATCA o el fin del Secreto Bancario* in *Intercambio de Información, Blanqueo de Capitales y Lucha contra el Fraude Fiscal* (Dir. F.A. García Prats), Instituto de Estudios Fiscales, Madrid (2014), pp. 205-206.

153. OECD, *Mandatory Disclosure Rules, Action 12–2015 Final Report*, OECD Publishing, Paris, 2015.
154. For example, in the case of disclose before lodgement of tax returns, through the issuance of rulings or voluntary administrative procedures, e.g., APAs. Accordingly, by exchanging information through DTCs or TIEAs after lodgement of tax returns.
155. OECD/EU (2011): Convention on Mutual Administrative Assistance in Tax Matter of 1 June 2011.
156. OECD, *Transfer Pricing Documentation and Country-by-Country Reporting, Action 13–2015 Final Report*, OECD Publishing, Paris, 2015.
157. M. Dirkis, *The 'Lyon's Mouth' post-box: A Comparative Review of the Limitations on the use by Revenue Authorities of Leaked and Stolen Information*, Working Paper University of Sydney, presented at the Tax Research Conference organized by the Ross Parson Centre for Commercial, Corporate and Taxation Law (Sydney) and the Max Planck Institute for Tax Law and Public Finance (Munich), 28-29 November 2016, p. 1.
158. EU: Council Directive 2003/48/EC of 3 June 2003 on Taxation of Saving Income in the Form on Interest Payments, OJ L157 (2003) as amended through 2006. As FATCA, the EU Saving Tax Directive pursues the combat against tax evasion imposing due diligence requirements on financial institutions. However, and contrary to FATCA, it is limited only to private individual who receive interests (not including entities) and it concerns only financial institutions located in Europe. *See* L. Cavelti, *Automatic Information Exchange Versus the WHT Regime Globalization and Increasing Sovereignty Conflicts in International Taxation*, 5 World Tax J. 2 (2013), Journals IBFD, p. 191 and I. Grinberg, *Taxing Capital Income in Emerging Countries: Will FATCA Open the Door?*, 5 World Tax J. 3 (2013), Journals IBFD, p. 337.
159. Among the characteristics of the EU Saving Tax Directive is that it provides a '*transitional WHT regime*' which works as a relief for those EU countries that still possess strict bank secrecy policies. Nonetheless, the effectiveness of the transitional WHT regime has been eliminated with the subsequent developments upon transparency. *See* Parada (2015), *supra* n. 142, p. 218.
160. EU: Council Directive 2014/107/EU of 9 December 2014 amending Directive 2011/16/EU as regards mandatory automatic exchange of information in the field of taxation, OJ L359 (2014).

2018/822/EU[161], amending the Directive 2011/16/EU on Administrative Cooperation in the Field of Taxation,[162] and extending the mandatory automatic exchange of information in accordance with the new OECD/G-20 global standards for automatic exchange of information added to the proposal of a Council Directive in order to repeal the EU Saving Tax Directive (Council Directive 2003/48/EC),[163] simply demonstrate that idea of setting up one unique standard for automatic exchange of information within the EU. Moreover, probably one of the most symbolic achievements in the last years at the EU level is, without doubt, the EU-Switzerland Tax Transparency Agreement of 2015.[164] The new EU-Switzerland tax transparency agreement is fully consistent with the OECD/G20 global standard for the automatic exchange of information, and it should not only improve the Member States' abilities to track down and tackle tax evaders, but it should also act as a deterrent against hiding income and assets abroad to evade taxes.[165]

Despite the importance of these global achievements towards tax transparency and exchange of information, one should not forget the importance of maintaining a proper balance between the protection of taxpayers' rights and the public interest in combating tax evasion. This is to say, there is a natural limitation in the fight against tax evasion, which is the protection of taxpayers' rights.[166] The above is particularly relevant when referring to how to gather information to start, for example, a civil or criminal proceeding against tax evasion and which type of information can be finally used in Court. Indeed, as we have witnessed during the last years, there are some publicly known cases in which information has been unlawfully obtained, either because it was leaked or stolen, and finally used by the tax authorities to start a tax evasion proceeding.[167] Unfortunately, there is not a unanimous position on this matter,

161. EU: Council Directive 2018/822/EU of 25 May 2018 amending Directive 2011/16/EU as regards mandatory automatic exchange of information in the field of taxation in relation to reportable cross-border arrangements, OJ L139 (2018) (also known as 'DAC6').
162. EU: Council Directive 2011/16/EU of 15 February 2011 on administrative cooperation in the field of taxation and repealing Directive 77/799/EEC, OJ L64 (2011).
163. EU: Proposal for a Council Directive repealing Council Directive 2003/48/EC, COM (2015) 129 final, 18 March 2015.
164. *See* EU: European Commission Press Release IP/15/5043, *Fighting tax evasion: EU and Switzerland sign historic tax transparency agreement*, 27 May 2015. *See also*, R. Höltschi, *Automatischer Informationsaustausch, Schweiz und EU unterzeichnen AIA*, Neue Zürcher Zeitung (27 May 2015).
165. Parada (2015), *supra* n. 142, pp. 219-220.
166. For different analyses upon the protection of taxpayers' rights in a world in which automatic exchange of information seems to be the final aim *see*, *e.g.*, P. Baker, *Some Recent Decisions of the European Court of Human Rights in Tax Matters*, 55 Eur. Taxn. 2/3 (2015), Journals IBFD; J. Calderón Carrero and A. Quintas Seara, *The Taxpayer's Right of Defense in Cross-Border Exchange of Information Procedures*, 68 Bull. Int'l. Taxn. 9 (2014), Journals IBFD; R. Desax, *Practical Protection of Fundamental Rights of Taxpayers*, 69 Bull. Int'l Taxn. 4/5 (2015), Journals IBFD; N. Serim, *Taxpayers' Rights–The Turkish Model*, 48 Eur. Taxn. 4 (2008), Journals IBFD; R. Camacho Palma, *An Overview of the Protection of Taxpayer Rights in Portugal*, 50 Eur. Taxn. 1 (2010), Journals IBFD, and M. de Zeeuw, *The Formulation of Taxpayer Rights and Obligations in a Developing Country*, 14 Asia-Pacific Tax Bull. 1 (2008), Journals IBFD. More recently, *see* J. Kokott and P. Pistone, *Taxpayers in International Law: International Minimum Standards for the Protection of Taxpayers' Rights* (Bloomsbury 2022).
167. Perhaps the most famous cases of stolen information are: (1) the 'LGT Kieber papers', where a former employee of the LGT Bank in Lichtenstein, stole information, put into a CD, and

and national Courts around the world have generated inconsistent precedents. In Germany, for example, there is a tendency to accept the use of leaked and stolen information without limitations, which might certainly jeopardise basic taxpayers' rights, such as the right to defence.[168] This tendency, however, has been mitigated by recent decisions, at least with regard to criminal matters.[169] France, on the other hand, seems to adopt a more restrictive position regarding the use of this type of information in Court.[170] This position was strengthened in 2010 and 2011 when the Civil Supreme Court stated that it is fundamental that a judge verifies that the information provided to the tax authorities is lawfully obtained without being distracted by economic considerations that prevent him from judging in accordance with the fundamental principles that govern the legitimacy of his actions.[171] Similarly, in Switzerland, the Federal Administrative Court has recently stated in a case regarding exchange of information under Article 28 of the Switzerland-France tax treaty (exchange of information) that Switzerland is not allowed to give any administrative assistance if the request for administrative assistance is based on stolen data.[172] Accordingly, the CJEU has just

---

subsequently sold it to the German tax authorities; (2) The 'Falciani list', where Mr. Hervé Falciani, a former employee of the HSBC in Geneva, stole information of around 130,000 customers and sold it to different EU Governments. *See* Dirkis, *supra* n. 157, pp. 8-13.

168. The German Federal Constitutional Court, in a case of stolen information by former employee of LGT Bank in Lichtenstein and subsequently sold to the German tax authorities, stated that it did not affect the fundamental right of privacy being thus not against the German Federal Constitution. *See* DE: BVerfG Beschl. v. 9 November 2010 [2 BvR 2101/09] – DStR 2010, 2512. *See also*, S. Soong Johnston, *State Court Rejects Challenge Against Use of Stolen Bank Data*, 73 Tax Notes Int'l 9 (2014) and K. Parillo, *German Court Permit Use of Stolen Data in Tax Probes*, 60 Tax Notes Int'l 10, 725 (2010).

169. DE: VGH Urteil v. 24 February 2014 [VGH B 26/13] Steuk 2014, 106. In this case, the Land Constitutional Court of Rhineland-Palatinate [*Rheinlandpfalz*] ruled against the arguments of a taxpayer who was trying to prevent the access of the tax authorities to register his house in suspicion of tax evasion. The information was contained in a CD with stolen data, and which was sold to five different governments. The Court sustained that the informant acted at his own initiative. Therefore, those acts were not attributable to the State and they did not infringe the right to a fair trial. However, what is interesting to highlight is that the Court confirmed that the acquisition of data media for purposes of criminal prosecution is indeed admissible only insofar as the public authorities do not systematically encourage the committing of crimes. This position does not only differ from the one sustained by the German Federal Supreme Court in 2010, but also opens the door to provide certain limitations in the use of stolen data, at least with respect to criminal proceedings.

170. For example, in 2011 the Court of Appeal in Paris [Court d'Appel de Paris] denied the French tax authorities the entrance in the house of a taxpayer to search for information related to a potential tax fraud case. J. Delaurière and C. Prest, *French Tax Authorities Lose Battle on Stolen Data*, 62 Tax Notes Int'l 3, 176 (2011). At that time, the French authorities tried to get the authorisation based on the information stolen by an employee of HSBC with respect to customers with bank accounts in Switzerland. *See*, Parada (2015), *supra* n. 142, pp. 212-215. *See also*, Dirkis, *supra* n. 157, s. 2.2.2.

171. The Supreme Civil Court strengthened this position in 2011 arguing: '[...] the economic considerations cannot be ignored by the judge, such considerations shall not distract the judge from his obligation to judge in accordance with the fundamental principles which govern the legitimacy of his action.' Delaurière and Prest, *supra* n. 170. The considerations of the Court were made under the basis of Article 6(1) of the European Rights Convention and the duty of loyalty. *Ibid*. *See also*, Parada (2015), *supra* n. 142, p. 213.

172. CH: Federal Administrative Court [*Bundesverwaltungsgericht*–BVGer], Urteil A-6843/2014 of 15 September 2015. *See also*, CH: Bundesverwaltungsgericht: Medienmitteilung v. 24 September 2015, *Keine Amtshilfe bei gestohlenen Daten*, Urteil A-6843/2014 v. 15 September 2015.

confirmed in the *Sabou* case the domestic law monopoly in the protection of taxpayers' rights.[173] In this case, the Czech Supreme Court stopped the proceedings between the Czech tax authorities and Mr Sabou and referred to the CJEU for a preliminary ruling. Among the inquiries, the Czech Supreme Court stated: '[A]re the tax authorities in the requested MS obliged, when providing information in accordance with the Directive 77/799/EEC (mutual assistance between MS), to observe a certain minimum content of their answer, so that it is clear from what sources and by what method the requested tax authorities have obtained the information provided? May the taxpayer challenge the correctness of the information thus provided, e.g., on grounds of procedural defects of the proceedings in the requested State?'[174] The CJEU established that the directive did not govern any of these questions and that they must be addressed only at a domestic level.[175] However, the AG's opinion was that in order to use the info in the requesting MS, the requested MS is obliged to provide 'adequate statements' about the inquiries conducted and upon which the information is based. This statement, in the author's opinion, brings a small chance to further improve the protection of the taxpayers' rights beyond MS's domestic laws.

To sum up, the reactions against tax evasion are given by the increase of the levels of transparency and cooperation in the exchange of information among countries. These reactions, however, cannot be implemented at any cost and should not prevent governments from providing the necessary safeguards for the fundamental taxpayers' rights, even beyond the national boundaries of domestic laws, as it has been done so far. This could be made, for example, through the use of tax treaties, TIEAs, or any other international instrument that may serve this purpose.[176]

4.2 Tax Avoidance in a Nutshell

Unlike tax evasion, tax avoidance has nothing to do with illegal or fraudulent behaviours aimed at hiding assets/income.[177] On the contrary, tax avoidance seems to

173. EU: Judgment in *Sabou v. The Czech Republic*, Case C-276/12, ECLI:EU:C:2013:678.
174. *Ibid.*, para. 22.
175. The Court specifically stated: 'It must be observed that Directive 77/799 does not address the taxpayer's right to challenge the accuracy of the information conveyed, and it does not impose any particular obligation with regard to the content of the information conveyed. In those circumstances, only national laws can lay down the relevant rules. The taxpayer may challenge the information concerning him conveyed to the tax authorities of the requesting Member State in accordance with the rules and procedures applicable in the Member State in question. The answer to the third question is therefore that Directive 77/799 does not govern the question of the circumstances in which the taxpayer may challenge the accuracy of the information conveyed by the requested Member State, and it does not impose any particular obligation with regard to the content of the information conveyed.' *Ibid.*, paras 48, 49 and 50.
176. I has already provided a similar argument in the context of 'Intergovernmental Agreements (IGAs)' and the implementation of FATCA. Considering the nature of these agreements, they could also be utilised to regulate the use of information unlawfully obtained avoiding misinterpretations and contradictory results, and contributing to the protection of the taxpayers' rights. *See* Parada (2015), *supra* n. 142, pp. 212-215. In a similar direction with respect to the protection of taxpayers' rights, *see* Calderón Carrero and Quintas Seara, *supra* n. 166.
177. 'In the case of tax avoidance, all facts are disclosed: the taxpayer tries to take advantage of a legal rule by interpreting it in the most favorable way from his point of view.' *See*, Essers, *supra* n. 50, p. 58.

be more a natural taxpayer's reaction to the imperfect design of domestic tax rules, which are finally used by him to reduce his tax burden, if possible, to zero. In this regard, tax avoidance is closer to being an issue of interpretation of the laws rather than an issue related to the lack of information. Indeed, in tax avoidance cases, taxpayers will often refer to the literal wording of the law or a treaty to support certain tax arrangements. If the outcome of the arrangement is against the object and purpose of the law, and the taxpayer was mainly motivated by tax reasons to get involved in such an arrangement, the tax judge might deny the outcome of such arrangement.[178] The above does not mean that transparency might not contribute to solving tax avoidance problems, but it will not be enough because information is not the core of the issue.

Tax avoidance, unlike tax evasion, is, however, not *a priori* objectionable.[179] This will depend exclusively upon the level of tolerance given in a specific jurisdiction, which is normally limited by the use of GAARs or SAARs at a domestic level.[180] In the United States, for example, it has been largely accepted that a taxpayer can arrange his businesses in order to pay as low taxes as possible or to defer their payment.[181] A similar doctrine of tolerance can be found under English common law.[182] The practical problem is, of course, that on many occasions, it is difficult, if not impossible, to distinguish the line between what is objectionable and what is not. This difficulty, however, should not prevent governments and policymakers from setting up the boundaries of tax avoidance, and the ones between this latter and tax evasion, strictly based upon the rule of law, avoiding the inclusion of non-legal standards to inflict legal sanctions.[183]

178. *Ibid.*
179. The reproach in the case of tax evasion comes directly from the fact that this is indeed an illegal conduct. However, it is also true that any source of law may potentially produce unintended corrupting effects. *See*, L. Pasculli and S. MacLennan, *'The Producers' of Tax Abuse: The Corrupting Effects of Tax Law and Tax Reliefs in the U.K. Film Industry*, 85:101 Law and Contemporary Problems (2022). In the same order of ideas, some commentators have stressed the problems related to the natural malleability of the law, creating opportunities for tax avoidance. *See*, for example, K. Pistor, *The Code of Capital: How the Law Creates Wealth and Inequality* (Princeton University Press, 2019).
180. *Infra* s. 4.2.2.
181. For example, in *Helvering v. Gregory*, it is stated that: 'Any one may so arrange his affairs that his taxes shall be as low as possible; he is not bound to choose that pattern which will best pay the Treasury; there is not even a patriotic duty to increase one's taxes.' US: *Helvering v. Gregory*, 69 F.2d 809, 810 (2d Cir. 1934). Another example is the well-known tolerance in the United States to accept the deferral on Subpart F income through the use of the 'Check-the-box' (CTB) regulations that allow the taxpayer to choose the tax treatment for US tax purposes of foreign entities not considered per se as Corporations. For a further analysis upon the US CTB regulations, *see infra* Chapter 3, s. 4.
182. In *Duke of Westminster v. IRC*, Baron Thomas Tomlin said: 'Every man is entitled if he can to order his affairs so as that the tax attaching under the appropriate Acts is less than it otherwise would be. If he succeeds in ordering them so as to secure this result, then, however unappreciative the Commissioners of Inland Revenue or his fellow taxpayers may be of his ingenuity, he cannot be compelled to pay an increased tax.' UK: *Duke of Westminster v. IRC*, [1936] 19 D.T.C. 490, 520 (Can.). Some commentators attribute to this doctrine the responsibility of creating a tax avoidance industry in the UK. *See*, Pasculli and MacLennan, *supra* n. 179, p. 123.
183. *Infra* s. 4.2.2. *See also*, *infra* s. 5 as regards to the concept of ATP.

As to DNT, it is not possible to argue that this outcome is a necessary condition for the occurrence of tax avoidance. In some cases, for instance, the reduction in the taxpayer's burden might be interpreted as the simple capacity to access tax benefits not originally available or to simply improve a business position. An example of the above could be the case of a corporate taxpayer subject to an interest limitation rule that prevents him from borrowing enough money from a related lender outside his residence country. Let us also assume that the domestic interest limitation rule is designed in such a way that it leaves open the application of transfer pricing rules as a carve-out clause, although not expressly stated within the law. In this case, nothing would prevent the taxpayer from proving that its interest payments meet the arm's length standard to escape the application of the interest limitation rule. Therefore, the use of this gap in the law has nothing to do with achieving DNT and responds exclusively to the desire to avoid a rule that limits his capacity to borrow money from abroad. In other cases, even when the outcome of DNT is clearly the final aim, such aim may be completely legitimated by law and would not constitute an objectionable tax avoidance situation. Therefore, whatever the source of the non-taxation outcome is, that is, legitimate or illegitimate tax avoidance, it is clear that this remains as an outcome, not representing in itself a proxy or a presumption of reproachable taxpayers' conduct.

4.2.1 *Tax Avoidance and International Tax Planning*

As slightly pointed out before, international tax planning is just the natural behaviour of an entrepreneur to optimise his costs,[184] being, therefore, a type of avoidance that is legitimated by law. The above could be arguable at an individual level.[185] However, there is no doubt about it at the corporate level, where the persons called to manage a company are legally bound to be involved in tax planning structures to minimise the company's costs. This obligation might be well interpreted within the context of the duty of loyalty or the duty of care that directors of a company have with the shareholders or investors of the entity. As explained by Schön: 'As dividends are paid out of profits, which have been subject to corporate income tax, the interest of the shareholders goes for the after-tax profit rather than for the pre-tax profit [...] This makes the minimization of the corporate tax burden an integral part of the managers' duty of care [...]. Therefore, they – i.e. the directors themselves – are legally bound to

184. This is also a fact expressly recognised within the OECD. *See* OECD, *International Tax Avoidance and Evasion, Double Taxation Conventions and the Use of Conduit Companies*, Issues in International Taxation No. 1, OECD Publishing, Paris, 1987, p. 11.

185. For example, there could always be exceptional cases of taxpayers whose level of social compromise brings them to pay as many taxes as possible, even twice. For an interesting economic analysis on how patriotism might moderate the incentives to avoid taxes, *see* B. Geys and K. Konrad, *Patriotism and Taxation*, Working Paper of the Max Planck Institute for Tax Law and Public Finance No. 2016-11 (2016).

engage in tax strategies.'[186] Therefore, unlike an individual taxpayer, the management body of a company must respond to the profit expectations of the shareholders and must fulfil this duty involving tax strategies that allow the company to maximise its profits.[187]

The outcome of DNT is, therefore, not only a possible and accepted one in the context of international tax planning but also, in most cases, a demonstration of a successful tax strategy aimed at reducing the company's costs. Since taxes are economic costs, any cross-border tax planning will be aimed at least to avoid double taxation, i.e., duplicated costs, or to achieve DNT, i.e., the optimisation of the overall tax liability to maximise profits. In other words, a taxpayer will always try to avoid paying taxes twice and will always try paying as close as possible to zero.[188] This conclusion, however, does not mean to recognise that the boundaries of what is legitimate tax planning today might vary as per the specific tax policies of a jurisdiction in the future, eventually affecting the whole tax planning strategy and, indirectly, the legitimacy of the DNT aim. Yet, this variation in the legal boundaries does not imply that the DNT outcome will become a presumption of illegal or illegitimate conduct, although it is evident that the new legal framework will make it more difficult to achieve such outcome.[189]

4.2.2 The Reactions to Tax Avoidance

Generally speaking, countries follow different approaches to draw the line between objectionable and non-objectionable tax avoidance, using, in most cases, the elements of economic substance and artificiality as a proxy to determine the presence of abusive transactions. As explained by Garcia Prats, it is possible to distinguish at least three main groups of anti-avoidance measures: (a) countries that use a sham/simulation concept instead of specific or general anti-avoidance measures, either by statute or by Court; (b) countries using GAARs, which may differ from country to country, SAARs (or TAARs), such as CFC rules or limitations in the deductibility of certain foreign payments, and (c) countries using law theories elaborated by Courts.[190] Among this last group, it is also possible to distinguish three main theories. First, step transaction or *Ramsay* doctrine, which advocates for the recognition of a series of transactions as a single one.[191]Subsequently, these step transactions are disregarded for tax purposes,

186. W. Schön, *Tax and Corporate Governance: A legal Approach* in: W. Schön (ed.) *Tax and Corporate Governance*, MPI Studies on Intellectual Property, Competition and Tax Law, Springer, Heidelberg (2008), p. 46.
187. *Ibid.*, p. 47.
188. R. Eicke, *Tax Planning with Holding Companies – Repatriation of U.S. Profits from Europe*, Kluwer Law International, BV, The Netherlands, 2009, pp. 11-21.
189. However, these new boundaries do not refer to the public perception of what is morally right or wrong, but rather to specific rules aimed to reduce the scope of tax planning strategies. The above reaffirms the idea of avoiding the use of pseudo-legal concepts to set up those boundaries, including the notion of ATP. *See infra* s. 5.
190. F.A. Garcia Prats, *The 'Abuse of Tax Law': Prospects and Analysis* in: G. Bizioli (ed.) *Essays in International and European Tax Law*, Jovene Editore, Napoli (2010), pp. 58-61.
191. *Ibid.*

and they are taxed as a unified transaction.[192] Second, business purpose, according to which transactions should be characterised according to their substance.[193] This is to say, distinguishing between transactions with valid business purposes and artificial ones designed exclusively to avoid taxes.[194] Third, and finally, economic substance, which does not relate to the purpose of a transaction but to its effects.[195] The basic premise of this theory is that a court may deny the tax benefits resulting from a transaction if this transaction itself lacks any economic benefit other than tax saving.[196]

Whatever path is taken to draw the line between objectionable and non-objectionable tax avoidance, it is important that this is made from the rule of law,[197] excluding arguments of morality or justice.[198] Following this path will benefit both taxpayers and governments. On the one hand, taxpayers can certainly rely on the legal certainty required to carry out their businesses. In other words, they can be aware before engaging in any tax avoidance scheme of the expected behaviours and, therefore, whether certain transactions can be disregarded. On the other hand, governments can impose more effective punishments for the cases in which the limits of legitimate tax avoidance are contravened, moving the tax system to a more coherent and consistent application.[199] More importantly, there will be a lower chance of confusion between tax evasion, which is an illegal behaviour, and tax avoidance, which can be considered a legitimate or illegitimate conduct depending on the level of tolerance established by the law of a specific jurisdiction, and ultimately, DNT, which is always legitimate tax planning purpose.[200]

---

192. J. Soled, *Use of Judicial Doctrines in Resolving Transfer Tax Controversies*, 42 Bos. College L. Rev. 3, 587 (2001).
193. Garcia Prats, *supra* n. 190.
194. P. Lampreave, *An Assessment of the Anti-Tax Avoidance Doctrines in the United States and the European Union*, 66 Bull. Intl. Taxn. 3, 155 (2012), Journals IBFD.
195. Garcia Prats, *supra* n. 190.
196. *Ibid.*, p. 154.
197. Although this concept belongs specifically to the common law tradition, I use it also as a synonymous of the *principle of legality* used in many civil law countries. In simple words, law should provide the boundaries between legitimate and illegitimate tax avoidance.
198. This issue is deeply analysed by A. Christians, who states: 'The idea that taxpayer behavior must be managed by law, rather than social sanction, rests fundamentally on the premise that tax policy can move toward greater coherence over time if the public persistently demands a means of monitoring lawmaking.' *See* Christians, *supra* n. 49, p. 59. Christians also argues that the turn to morality, rather than law, to delineate what is legal or illegal is indeed counterproductive to pursue a coherent tax policy in the long term and it can also have grave consequences for the future of tax policy on a global scale. *Ibid.*, pp. 39-40. *See also*, *e.g.*, A. Christians, *Tax Activists and the Global Movement for Development through Transparency in Tax*, in: M. Stewart and Y. Brauner (eds) *Law and Development*, Edward Elgar Publishing, Cheltenham/Northampton (2013), p. 288.
199. Christians, *supra* n. 49, p. 55.
200. For some commentators, however, DNT might consider a trigger to either avoidance or evasion conducts. This could be concluded seeing the legal system in its entirety, even beyond tax law, as a criminogenic environment that creates opportunities for what one could call a 'systemic abuse'. For more on the crossing paths between criminological theories and tax law, *see*, *e.g.*, Pasculli and MacLennan, *supra* n. 179. *See also*, L. Lederman, *The Fraud Triangle and Tax Evasion*, 106 Iowa L. Rev. 1153 (2021); R. de la Feria, *Tax Fraud and Selective Law Enforcement*, 47 J.L. & Soc'y 240 (2020).

5 DOUBLE NON-TAXATION AND '*AGGRESSIVE TAX PLANNING*'

Contrary to the idea stressed in section 4 that only law should set up the boundaries between legitimate and illegitimate tax planning (objectionable tax avoidance), we have recently witnessed the appearance of a non-legal category in the debate, namely the notion of ATP.[201] This Section aims to emphasise how the *consequentialist approach* observed in the ambiguous notion of ATP, which focuses only on the results of a transaction - i.e., DNT or low taxation - might negatively impact the proper understanding of the DNT outcome and indirectly affect the delineation of the traditional boundaries between legitimate and illegitimate tax avoidance, ultimately contributing to increasing the level of legal uncertainty for taxpayers.[202]

5.1 The Notion of ATP in Brief

ATP is a non-legal notion developed by the OECD within the context of the BEPS Project,[203] which, although lacking a consistent definition,[204] seems to have a very clear and instrumental purpose, namely to reduce the scope of (legal) tax planning and to set up new ethical standards for taxpayers to prevent abusive practices. The above can be especially noted, for example, in Action 12 of the OECD BEPS Action Plan,[205] where the notion of ATP is used to recognise tax planning structures that comply with the wording of the law but not with its spirit.[206] In other words, the notion of ATP would attempt to explain the loopholes and inconsistencies in cross-border transactions that involve the application of different domestic tax systems, aiming to create a more coherent framework. In this order of ideas, and at least *a priori*, this vague notion

201. The expression ATP is nevertheless not new. It was originated in the United States where it was used in reference to structures that were designed against the spirit or purpose of regulations. *See* J. Calderón Carrero and A. Quintas Seara, *The Concept of 'Aggressive Tax Planning' Launched by the OECD and the EU Commission in the BEPS Era: Redefining the Border Between Legitimate and Illegitimate Tax Planning*, 44 Intertax 3, 209 (2016) DOI: 10.54648/taxi2016015.
202. Therefore, this section does not attempt to provide an exhaustive analysis of the notion of ATP in the context of abuse of law. For this purpose, *see*, for example, A.P. Dourado, *Aggressive Tax Planning in EU Law and in the Light of BEPS: The EC Recommendation on Aggressive Tax Planning and BEPS Action 2 and 6*, 43 Intertax 1 (2015) DOI: 10.54648/taxi2015004; F.A. García Prats, *Los límities a la planificación fiscal agresiva y el abuso de las normas tributaries*, at AEDAF, X Congreso Tributario. La Justicia: ¿Garantía del Estado de Derecho? AEDAF, 2015; Pistone, *supra* n. 41; Calderón Carrero and Quintas Seara, *supra* n. 201; C. Fuest et al., *Profit Shifting and 'Aggressive' Tax Planning by Multinationals Firms: Issues and Options for Reform*, 5 World Tax J. 3 (2013), Journals IBFD; P. Piantavigna, *Tax Abuse and Aggressive Tax Planning in the BEPS Era: How EU Law and the OECD Are Establishing a Unifying Conceptual Framework in International Tax Law, Despite Linguistic Discrepancies*, 9 World Tax J. 1 (2017), Journals IBFD.
203. However, the OECD already referred to the notion of aggressive tax planning in its 2011 Report. *See* OECD (2011), *supra* n. 1.
204. This is not entirely true for the case of the concept of ATP in the EU law context. *See infra* s. 5.2 of this chapter.
205. OECD (2015), *supra* n. 153.
206. Calderón Carrero and Quintas Seara, *supra* n. 201, p. 210.

seems to serve more the purpose of being a guiding principle rather than a rule that should generally be applied.[207]

5.2 The EU Notion of ATP: A *Consequentialist Approach*

A broader understanding of the notion of ATP can be, however, found in the EU Commission Recommendation on ATP launched in 2012.[208] According to the EU Commission, '[a]ggressive tax planning consists of taking advantage of the technicalities of a tax system or of the mismatches between two or more tax systems for the purpose of reducing tax liability'.[209] The EU Commission also establishes that the consequences of these ATP schemes normally include the outcome of double deduction, i.e., when the same loss is deducted both in the State of source and residence, and the outcome of DNT, i.e., when income that is not taxed in the source state is also exempt in the residence state.[210] Therefore, as per the EU understanding, any operation whose purpose is to achieve DNT would be included within the notion of ATP, including, for example, non-artificial transactions with a pure (legal) tax purpose.

This broader understanding of ATP is confirmed by some tax scholars who explain it as a '[C]onceptual category of the global Tax Law, consisting in the exploitation of the disparities between tax systems with the purpose of obtaining tax advantages, which would have not been otherwise available.'[211] These commentators propose a systematic study of the notion as if we were referring to a true legal concept, which would include at least three elements: (a) the exploitation of the legal disparities between tax systems in order to obtain a tax advantage; (b) the desalination between the source of the income and where taxes are actually paid, and (c) the DNT outcome as a result not originally intended by the States. Only the simultaneous concurrence of these elements would allow classifying a cross-border tax planning structure as ATP.[212]

The '*consequentialist approach*',[213] however, or the fact that a tax planning structure will be regarded as aggressive or not based on the results of a specific transaction (i.e., DNT or low taxation), adopted by the EU Commission and also

207. This conclusion is important because it allows us to argue that in any case the notion of ATP can be used as synonymous of tax avoidance and reaffirms the idea that the notion of ATP is a non-legal category in itself. As provided by Calderón Carrero and Quintas Seara: '[T]he new concept of aggressive tax planning does not aim to be a type of overriding principle to be applied generally (like a 'soft law GAAR'), nor does it aim to constitute a 'rule of teleological interpretation' of the regulatory language, but its purpose may lie more in bringing about a change in the way the new international taxation system is understood [...].' *Ibid.* On the other hand, if the final aim were to establish a general rule that contemplates the new ATP category, i.e., a positive rule (hard law), it would be practically impossible to distinguish between this ATP category and a simple GAAR, generally applied by countries to counteract abusive practices. *Ibid.* On a different opinion, *see* Piantavigna, *supra* n. 202.
208. EU: European Commission Recommendation of 6 December 2012 on aggressive tax planning, COM (2012), 8806 final.
209. *Ibid.*
210. *Ibid.*
211. Pistone, *supra* n. 41, p. 117.
212. *Ibid.*
213. Calderón Carrero and Quintas Seara, *supra* n. 201, p. 220. The authors refer indistinctly to 'consequentialist standard' and 'quantitative standard'.

assumed by some tax scholars, might have serious negative effects. The most evident one is that it may turn the understanding of the concept of tax avoidance, traditionally linked to the lack of economic substance or artificiality of a cross-border transaction, into the elimination of DNT. This approach disregards all the other complexities that involve a cross-border transaction, such as the legality and the methods used in it, ultimately contributing to stigmatising even more the DNT outcome. For some authors, however, these effects are mitigated since the DNT outcome is relevant only when the states did not originally 'intend' this outcome.[214] Nevertheless, as stated in section 2.3 of this chapter, assuming that the 'intention of the States' can be obtained purely without considering the influence of political malfunctions simply implies not recognising the reality in the law-making process. Indeed, the influence of external actors in the law-making process does not only consider the direct lobby of multinationals but also the participation of these and other actors in international tax networks, including the OECD.[215] Therefore, the 'intention of the States' as to aim or not DNT should only be relevant when it is expressly stated in the wording of the law or the treaty, not giving space to subjective interpretations. Unfortunately, a clear tendency, on the contrary, can be seen in the participation of the media in the debate regarding tax evasion and tax avoidance, providing a general confusion of legal concepts, which, of course, includes an *a priori* rejection of the DNT outcome. In 2012, for example, James Henry, an American tax justice activist, said: 'Both evasion and avoidance have the same impact on the rest of us, which is, our tax burdens are greater because the truly rich are not paying their fair share: they are able to put their money abroad, *and basically are able to take advantage of a system that allows a double non-taxation. And that is a real problem* (emphasis added).'[216] The above can riskily drive us to conceive the notion of DNT as a per se pervasive reality in the world of cross-border investments and commercial activity, disregarding its legal validity as part of a legitimate tax planning strategy. The consequentialist approach to the notion of ATP, therefore, starts from a wrong and not demonstrated premise, which is that income derived from a cross-border transaction should be taxed somewhere. This idea, as already stressed in this chapter, has validity neither as a principle of international tax law nor as customary law.[217]

214. Pistone, *supra* n. 41, pp. 123-125.
215. Christians, *supra* n. 49. More recently, we have witnessed this in the context of the recent international tax reforms. *See*, for example, Emma Agyemang and Nic Fildes, *OECD pressed Australia to drop plan to reveal where multinational pay tax*, Financial Times, 7 July 2023. *See also*, Marc Bou Mansour, OECD breaks silence on lobbying – Tax Justice Network Response, Press Office, 9 July 2023.
216. *Ibid.*, p. 52.
217. Garcia Prats states that such a premise [single taxation] can be accepted only if a norm in each of the States (or at least one of them) establishes it. In absence of such a norm, the sole acceptance of the idea of single taxation would produce the nonsense result that States could unilaterally declare the exemption of some income, but when such an income had an international origin or destiny, this exemption would be nullified. *See* García Prats, *supra* n. 168, p. 125. The original Spanish text says: '*Dicha premisa solo puede resultar aceptable si existe una norma tributaria en cada una–o al menos en alguna– de las jurisdicciones afectadas que así lo establezca, de conformidad con los presupuestos de derecho interno que legitiman el*

Another effect, although not directly derived from the consequentialist approach but from the 'academic construction' of the notion of ATP itself, is the assumption that 'disparities' among legislation used by taxpayers to reduce their tax burden is an *a priori* evil element of the international tax system, or at least a proxy to determine abusive practices. As noted before in this work, however, disparities in the design of domestic tax laws are indeed the general rule and not the exception, and when countries want to restrict the potential abuse of these disparities, they normally do that from the rule of law and not from grey non-legal categories.[218] Similarly, the desalination between the source of the income and where taxes are actually paid may be a valid element to consider regarding the notion of ATP. However, its determination sometimes becomes very complex, if not impossible to determine. A clear example of the above is the case of hybrid entities.[219] In this situation, there is no such desalination between the source of the income or the place where activities are rendered and the place where taxes are paid (at least not that evident). The issue, in most of these cases, as we will see further on in this work, is reduced to the uncoordinated rules to characterise foreign entities among various jurisdictions, which might result in a DNT outcome. Therefore, one could validly conclude that if all the elements of the notion of ATP may simultaneously concur to classify a transaction or tax structure as ATP, the absence of any of these desalination elements in the case of hybrid entities may drive us to the opposite conclusion.[220]

As a result, the notion of ATP seems to be not only unclear and consequentialist but also very risky to implement without negative legal and tax policy consequences. First, it puts at risk the principle of legality in international transactions, contributing to increasing the level of uncertainty for taxpayers and situating the discussion on tax avoidance closer to moral arguments rather than legal ones. Second, it negatively affects the proper understanding of the DNT outcome. Both consequences should (and can) certainly be avoided.

6 FINAL REMARKS

Double non-taxation is an outcome that implies the complete absence of taxation in two or more jurisdictions. This simple understanding is, however, normally tergiversated in different manners, confusing the outcome of the transaction, i.e., DNT, with the intentions of the taxpayers or the intentions of the states, producing more confusing results that derive in an *a priori* negative perception of a notion that should, in principle, be understood as a simple outcome.

---

nacimiento de la obligación tributaria respectiva.' More recently, *see* Parada, *supra* n. 113 (analysing the concept of 'full taxation' and its recognition as an international norm).

218. As states by Rosenbloom: 'Countries differ in regard to the many rules of law that make up any system of taxation.' *See* Rosenbloom, *supra* n. 57, p. 140.
219. For the full analysis of hybrid entities, *see infra* Chapter 3 of this book.
220. According to Pistone, only the simultaneous concurrence of the three elements described in his work would allow classifying a cross-border transaction as ATP. Pistone, *supra* n. 41, p. 117. Therefore, the absence of any of these elements would make the category useless in the case of hybrid entities.

The negative perception of the DNT outcome has its very first origin in the wrong belief that income should be taxed at least once in any cross-border transaction. Commentators supporting this idea generally argue using the credit method to relieve double taxation as an example. However, as demonstrated in this chapter, ensuring single taxation using the credit method is very limited in practice and certainly not enough to conclude the existence of a general tax policy or even a tax principle aimed at ensuring single taxation. Indeed, and practically speaking, this outcome will always depend on the repatriation of income; that is, if income is finally not repatriated, there is no single taxation to be ensured. Accordingly, the historic antecedents of the origin of the credit method failed to demonstrate that the method was created to ensure single taxation. Regardless of the above, new voices still claim the existence of such a tax principle based basically upon the wording of the US LOB provision (1981), interpreted in a manner that the reduction of WHT at source is contingent on the taxation at residence. In my view, however, this rule has nothing to do with the application of any principle of taxation (or single taxation) but rather with the legitimate interest of the source country, which restricts its taxation rights through reduced WHTs under a tax treaty, to coordinate this restriction with similar taxation in the residence country.[221] Nothing really changes either with the appearance of a new concept – *full taxation* – that aims to revendicate the existence of a single tax principle in international tax law. As noted already, such concept may ultimately be more dangerous from a normative perspective than the pure idea of taxing at least once.

The understanding of DNT as a simple outcome in cross-border transactions is not superfluous. Indeed, it is especially relevant with respect to the negative consequences that could arise from a tax policy perspective if the concept goes beyond that simple understanding. First, conceiving DNT beyond a simple outcome could increase the risk of homologating it with other traditional and undesired legal consequences, such as tax evasion or tax avoidance, ultimately affecting legitimate transactions whose aim is precisely to reduce taxation. Second, it could indirectly grant recognition to pseudo-legal concepts, such as the concept of ATP, whose *consequentialist approach* has only contributed to increasing the level of legal uncertainty among taxpayers. The above does not mean to recognise that the DNT outcome may be achieved through tax evasion or illegitimate tax avoidance. In contrast, it simply means that DNT should not be regarded as a proxy for any of these legally sanctioned actions. Third, the understanding of DNT beyond a simple outcome may derive from the incoherent design of domestic rules that use the DNT outcome and its core feature. The above has already been demonstrated in the OECD Action Plan 2 ('*linking rules*'), an issue that will be further analysed in this work.

As a result, this chapter concludes that the boundaries of the notion of DNT should remain within its nature of a simple outcome, absent of subjective interpretations, not being therefore regarded per se as a cause of concern. This idea will at least govern the remaining part of this work.

221. A further analysis on the double non-taxation outcome and bilateral tax treaties can be seen in *infra* Chapter 2.

CHAPTER 2

Double Non-taxation and Bilateral Tax Treaties

1 INTRODUCTION

Tax treaties have historically been associated with the object and purpose of preventing or alleviating double taxation.[222] They also seek to address fiscal or tax evasion, a problem related to the asymmetries of information and the governance failure in collecting taxes,[223] but that some scholars have also interpreted as including a broader tax policy goal: the avoidance of double non-taxation.[224] This tendency has become

222. Nevertheless, and although an analysis of double taxation as an object and purpose of the tax treaties is out of the scope of this work, it is important to highlight here that the capacity of the tax treaties to prevent or mitigate double taxation is also very limited. Under the OECD Model, e.g., only persons *'liable to tax'* have access to the treaty relief of double taxation. Likewise, the relief is granted only regarding the taxes covered by the treaty, i.e., taxes on income and capital, and more rarely inheritance and gift taxes and it is only contemplated for the so-called *juridical double taxation*. However, *'economic double taxation'*, i.e., when a same element of income or the same economic transaction is subject to the same type of tax in the hands of two or more different taxpayers, it is not included in the treaty relief. *See* M. Lang, *General Report* in: Cahiers de droit fiscal international - Vol. 89a, *Double Non-taxation* (IFA 2004), pp. 78-81. Likewise, other tax scholars have interestingly argued that the prevention of double taxation would be more an apparent objective of the tax treaties than a real one at the time countries sit down and negotiate them. *See* T. Dagan, *The Tax Treaty Myth*, 32 N.Y.U. J. Int'l L. Pol. 939 (2000). Dagan argues that the idea that tax treaties exist primarily to alleviate double taxation would have its origin in a false premise that countries would not be able to do so in absence of them. However, most of the countries include in their domestic laws either the exemption or the credit method. Accordingly, in some cases the relief of double taxation seems not to be a problem at all, as it happens with developing countries or transition economies. As residents of these countries are expected to receive less income from foreign sources, the relief of double taxation is indeed not a priority. *See* Vann, *supra* n. 24. In a similar analysis, involving developing countries, *see*, e.g., J. Braun and M. Zagler, *An Economic Perspective on Double Tax Treaties with(in) Developing Countries*, 6 World Tax J. (2014), Journals IBFD.
223. *Supra* Chapter 1, s. 4.1.
224. *See, e.g.*, Ault (2013), *supra* n. 64; Avi-Yonah, *supra* n. 72.

particularly evident after the 1999 OECD Partnership Report[225] and the inclusion of Article 23(4) in the 2000 OECD Model, achieving perhaps its maturity in the OECD BEPS Action Plan 6.[226]

This chapter attempts to demonstrate that the prevention of double non-taxation is still an exogenous element of tax treaties. This is to say, unless some specific provisions have been included within the tax treaties to ensure single taxation, these instruments should not be interpreted in light of the broad tax policy goal of avoiding DNT. This conclusion, however, should not be understood as if the outcome of DNT was a desired and general tax treaty outcome either. In fact, in the same order of ideas, and as it will be demonstrated further on, unless some specific provisions are directly introduced into tax treaties, e.g., *tax sparing* or *matching credits*, the DNT outcome will be equally exceptional. The above simply reinforces the idea already stressed in Chapter 1, which is that DNT is indeed a simple outcome whose impact (negative or positive) will depend on the transaction and the countries involved. Section 2 of this chapter analyses the rules of interpretation of tax treaties contained in the Vienna Convention of the Law of Treaties (VCLT)[227] and the role that the OECD Model and its Commentaries have for interpretative purposes. Section 3 focuses on the analysis of specific provisions of the OECD Model, commonly included in tax treaties and which, at first glance, might be interpreted as ensuring single taxation. However, a closer look at them should bring us to a different conclusion. Section 4 studies specific provisions included within tax treaties that either tolerate the outcome of DNT, such as *tax sparing* and *matching credits* or prevent its occurrence, such as the case of *subject-to-tax* and *switch-over clauses*. The above has the purpose of emphasising the exceptionality of both the occurrence and the avoidance of DNT within the tax treaty context. Section 5 analyses the impact of some OECD proposals contained in Action 6 and refers to the outcome of DNT, namely (1) a modification of the title of the OECD Model including a reference to tax evasion and tax avoidance; (2) a recommendation of a preamble, which includes that tax treaties cannot create opportunities for non-taxation or reduced taxation through tax evasion or tax avoidance; and (3) the inclusion of the concept of *'Special Tax Regimes'* (STR). Section 6 provides some final remarks.

2 INTERPRETATION OF TAX TREATIES

There are two elements that should be considered when analysing the interpretation of tax treaties. The first relates to the object of interpretation. In this regard, the interpretation of a tax treaty supposes the establishment of the true meaning of a validly concluded or negotiated treaty and not an abstract MC, regardless of the

225. OECD (1999), *supra* n. 1.

226. For the OECD Action 6, *see* OECD, *Preventing the Granting of Treaty Benefits in Inappropriate Circumstances*, Action 6 – 2015 Final Report, OECD Publishing, Paris, 2015. For the OECD 'BEPS Project,' *see* OECD (2013), *supra* n. 2. For a preliminary evaluation of the OECD BEPS Project, *see, e.g.*, Y. Brauner, *BEPS: An Interim Evaluation*, 6 World Tax J. 1 (2014), Journals IBFD, p. 10.

227. UN: Vienna Convention on the Law of Treaties ['VCLT'] of 23 May 1969, United Nations, Treaty Series, Vol. 1155, I-18232, p. 331.

practical importance that an MC can have in the interpretative process.[228] In this order of ideas, a tax treaty should be understood as a legal transaction, like a private contract under domestic law, by which the contracting parties establish mutual obligations and rights and whose law-creating character derives from the application of the international law rule of *pacta sunt servanda*.[229] The second element refers to the specific tools used to interpret a tax treaty. Indeed, tax treaties like domestic law are interpreted in accordance with specific rules provided for that reason and which are contained in Articles 31, 32 and 33 of the VCLT. Whilst Article 31 refers to the general rules of interpretation, Article 32 deals specifically with preparatory work, and Article 33 is concerned with the interpretation of the treaties in multiple languages.[230] As follows, the author will analyse each one of these rules separately.

2.1 General Rule of Interpretation

Whilst Article 31(1) of the VCLT establishes the general rule of interpretation, Articles 31(2), (3) and (4) elaborate on the general rule specifying what the context of a treaty is and which kind of materials should be considered along with the context, including the fact that, if appropriate, a term of the treaty may be given a special meaning rather than its ordinary one.[231] Article 31(1) of the VCLT states: 'A treaty shall be interpreted in good faith in accordance with the ordinary meaning to be given to the terms of the treaty in their context and in the light of its object and purpose.'[232] The above means that the text of the treaty, i.e., the 'ordinary meaning' of the 'terms', the wording of the entire agreement in its context, and the object and purpose of it, are relevant elements to consider for interpretative purposes.

The *ordinary meaning of the terms* of the treaty refers to the technical language internationally developed and used in certain specialised areas, such as tax law, and does not mean everyday usage.[233] The text of the treaty is generally understood as an independent source of interpretation, which means that the text of the treaty prevails over other ways of interpretation (e.g., the context or the object and purpose), perhaps under the assumption that there is no better place to reflect the intention of the parties

228. G. Schwarzenberger, *A Manual of International Law*, 5th ed., Steven & Sons Limited, London, 1967, p. 164.
229. As provided by Kelsen: '[T]he treaty has a law-applying and at the same time a law-creating character. It has a law-applying character because every conclusion of a treaty is the application of the rule of general international law *pacta sunt servanda*; it has a law-creating function because every treaty constitutes obligations and rights that, prior to the conclusion of the treaty, had not yet existed, obligations and rights which come into existence by the treaty.' H. Kelsen, *Principles of International Tax Law*, 2nd ed., Holt, Rinehart &Winston Inc., New York, 1967, p. 456.
230. The analysis of Article 33 of the VCLT is a matter that exceeds the concern of this chapter. Therefore, I will focus exclusively on Articles 31 and 32. However, for a full analysis of this topic, *see*, for example, G. Maisto (ed.), *Multilingual Texts and Interpretation of Tax Treaties and EC Tax Law*, Amsterdam, IBFD, 2005.
231. B. Arnold, *The Interpretation of Tax Treaties: Myth and Reality*, 64 Bull Intl. Taxn. 1 (2010), Journals IBFD, p. 5.
232. Article 31(1) of the VCLT.
233. Vogel and Rust, *supra* n. 26, Introduction at m.no. 84.

than the text of the treaty itself. This position, whose purpose is to achieve certainty in the interpretation of tax treaties, reducing, therefore, the scope of subjectivity, has been not only the position undertaken by the International Law Commission, the Institute of International Law and the jurisprudence of the International Court of Justice[234] but also a commonly recognised practice among the States.[235]

Unlike the ordinary meaning of the terms of a treaty, the *object and purpose*, is an integral expression,[236] which does not refer to the intention of the Contracting States but to the objective aim of the treaty reflected by the treaty as a whole.[237] This does not imply that the intention of the Contracting States is absolutely useless, but it will only be relevant to the extent it has been expressed in the text of the treaty.[238] As provided by Article 31(4) VCLT, the parties may attribute a 'special meaning' to a term of the treaty, which will thus reflect the intention of the Contracting States.[239] However, what is not acceptable is that an interpretation intends to presume what the parties wanted, even if the strict interpretation of the wording carries out a non-logical result.[240] In other words, the purpose shall influence the interpretation in a manner of giving light of the terms of the treaty, but it will be subordinated to the text of the treaty and it will not constitute an independent mean of interpretation.[241] This approach by which the text of the treaty must be the dominant consideration has been criticised by some authors, because indeed Article 31 of the VCLT does not establish any clear weight that should be given either to the text, the context or the purpose of a treaty.[242] In other words, nothing would prevent a judge or other interpreter, e.g., to conclude that a treaty provision is reasonably clear that it must be applied without regard to the context and purpose, or in contrast, that the purpose of a treaty justify an interpretation,

234. I. Brownlie, *Principles of Public International Law*, 4th ed., Clarendon Press, Oxford, 1990, p. 627.
235. In Germany, e.g., the Federal Fiscal Court [*Bundesfinanzhof*] did not allow an interpretation against the wording of the treaty. DE: 1965 BStBl III 258 (BFH 1965) cited in C. Heber and C. Sternberg, *Chapter 6: Germany* in: R. van Brederode and R. Krever (eds) *Legal Interpretation of Tax Law*, Kluwer Law International BV, The Netherlands (2014), p. 185. Accordingly, in France, e.g., the Conseil d' État does not only give more relevance to the literal interpretation, but it provides that the literal interpretation should be applied even if it deprives the taxpayer from a legitimate advantage or if it grants an advantage to the taxpayer that was not foreseen by the negotiators of the treaty. *See* D. Gutmann, *Tax Treaty Interpretation in France* in: M. Lang (ed.) *Tax Treaty Interpretation*, Linde, Vienna, 2001, p. 109.
236. Vogel and Rust, *supra* n. 26, Introduction at m.no. 85.
237. *Ibid.*, Introduction at m. no. 82.
238. *Ibid.*, Introduction at m. no. 83.
239. Article 31(4) of the VCLT states: 'A special meaning shall be given to a term if it is established that the parties so intended.'
240. In France, e.g., the Conseil d' État decided in 2000 to grant a French resident a tax credit with respect to the WHT paid on the interest derived from Italian State bonds. It turned out later that, derived from the literal interpretation of Article 22 of the 1958 France-Italian Income Tax Treaty, the tax credit granted was higher than the amount of foreign taxes effectively paid in Italy, contradicting the spirit of the convention. Regardless of the above, the interpretation prevailed. *See* FR: CE, 3rd and 8th s.-s., 24 May 2000, req. no. 209 699 et rec. no. 209 891, CRCAM *Normand (Concl.), DF* no. 48, 2000, comm. 943, concl. Touvet cited in: Gutmann, *supra* n. 235, p. 110.
241. Vogel and Rust, *supra* n. 26, Introduction at m.no. 83.
242. Arnold, *supra* n. 231, pp. 5-6.

stretching the words of a treaty or even ignoring them.[243] Arnold considers that this amplitude might not be necessarily harmful and it could help the interpretative role of the judiciary.[244] After all, the work of the judges is essentially subjective and it could be improved if there are less strict rules of interpretation.[245] Likewise, he stresses that taxpayers and tax advisors generally prefer a literal interpretation due to a self-motivated interest, considering that they normally plan around or take undue advantage of rules read literally.[246] Nonetheless, Arnold does not offer sufficient argument either to disregard certainty as a value itself in the interpretative process or to assume that a literal interpretation must necessarily help a misconduct of taxpayers.

The mandate to interpret a tax treaty *in light of its object and purpose* also supposes that both authorities and courts of the Contracting States apply a consistent interpretation. This is to say, both Contracting States should seek the treaty interpretation that is most likely to be accepted in both States, also known as 'common interpretation'.[247] This does not mean that a State must simply accept the case law of the other State without reviewing it, but to research and evaluate his reasoning.[248] This reasoning has been taken to the extreme of considering that a common interpretation means to achieve a similar result using a similar method of interpretation. The aim seems to be that both countries give the same meaning to a tax treaty, avoiding a different interpretation that could lead to situations of double taxation or DNT. Nevertheless, it is obvious that the common interpretation is concerned with the result of the interpretation and not with the method of interpretation used.[249] Accordingly,

243. In *Thiel v. Federal Commissioner of Taxation,* the Australian Court clearly endorsed a 'purposive' approach to the interpretation of the treaties. *See* AUS: *Thiel v. Federal Commissioner of Taxation* [1990] HCA 37; 171 CLR 338, cited in: R. Krever and P. Mellor, *Chapter 2: Australia* in: R. van Brederode and R. Krever (eds) *Legal Interpretation of Tax Law,* Kluwer Law International BV, The Netherlands (2014), p. 42. Similarly, in the famous *Glaxo case* in Japan, the Supreme Court did not only attend the text of Article 7 of the Japan-Singapore Income Tax Treaty to consider that the application of the Japan's CFC rules were not prohibited or restricted, but included a whole examination of the CFC rules and their compatibility with the object and purpose of the treaty. The Court found that the CFC contained various exemptions for genuine activities and also a tax credit if the CFC rule was triggered. As the Japan's CFC rules were regarded as reasonable as well, the Court concluded that it did not impede Singapore's taxation according to Article 7 of the Japan-Singapore Income Tax Treaty. *See* JP: Supreme Court, 29 October 2009, Glaxo, Minshu, Vol. 63 No. 8, 1881 cited in: Y. Masui, *Chapter 9: Japan* in: R. van Brederode and R. Krever R. van Brederode and R. Krever (eds) *Legal Interpretation of Tax Law,* Kluwer Law International BV, The Netherlands (2014), p. 257.
244. Arnold, *supra* n. 231, pp. 5-6.
245. *Ibid.*
246. *Ibid.*, p. 7.
247. Vogel and Rust, *supra* n. 26, Introduction at m.no. 90 and m.no. 92.
248. *Ibid.*, Introduction at m.no. 90. Likewise, Masui recognises the influence that foreign court cases had in the *Glaxo case* in Japan (e.g., the *Schneider Electric* case decided by the French Conseil d' État), regardless none of these cases were formally cited in the decision of the Supreme Court of Japan, which is nevertheless a generalised practice, that is, Courts in Japan never cite foreign tax cases in tax decisions. *See* Masui, *supra* n. 243, p. 258. *See also*, FR: Conseil d' État, 28 June 2002, Case No. 232276, *Schneider Electric,* RJF 10/02, no. 1080. For an analysis of the case, *see, e.g.*, P. Dibout, *L'inapplicabilité de l'article 209 B du CGI face à la convention fiscal franco-suisse du septembre 1966,* 36 Revue de Droit Fiscal (2000), pp. 1133-1141.
249. Arnold, *supra* n. 231, p. 11.

nothing can guarantee that the use of the same method of interpretation will produce the same result.[250]

With respect to the *context* of the treaties, it should be noted that it includes any related completed document made in connection to the treaty, including notes and letters exchanged when the treaty was signed.[251] It also includes the preamble of the treaty. However, any 'accompanying materials', i.e., materials created during the negotiation of a treaty, supporting documents, position papers, etc., may only be referred to as a supplementary source and inasmuch they confirm the interpretation made under Article 31 of the VCLT or in case of doubts.[252] Nevertheless, 'technical explanations', like the ones normally released by the US Treasury Department after the negotiation of a tax treaty by the United States, or any other type of explanation post-negotiation is regarded neither as part of the context of the treaty nor as accompanying materials, and they thus cannot be used for interpretation purposes.[253]

Finally, some brief remarks must be made regarding the term *good faith*, which is normally read in conjunction with the rest of Article 31(1) of the VCLT without any special connotation,[254] although it is one of the cornerstones of public international law.[255]

Article 31(1) VCLT mandates that a tax treaty shall be interpreted in *good faith* according to the ordinary meaning, the context and the object and purpose of a treaty. This Article does not give any hints as to what *good faith* means.[256] However, for the majority of scholars, *good faith* in the interpretation of tax treaties means that a treaty must be interpreted honestly, fairly and reasonably and in accordance with the common interpretation of the parties as expressed or implied in the tax treaty.[257] The most important manifestation of good faith is, in fact, the general rule of international law, '*pacta sunt servanda*' codified in Article 26 VCLT,[258] an interpretation that is reaffirmed by the jurisprudence of the ICJ.[259] This element of 'reasonableness' applies

250. *Ibid.*
251. Vogel and Rust, *supra* n. 26, Introduction at m.no. 85.
252. *Ibid.*, Introduction at m.no. 86.
253. *Ibid.*
254. *See, e.g.*, K. Vogel and R. Prokisch, *General Report* in: Cahiers de droit fiscal international – Vol. LXXVIIa, *Interpretation of Double Taxation Conventions* (IFA 1993), pp. 55-85.
255. *See* L. De Broe, *International Tax Planning and Prevention of Abuse*, Doctoral Series IBFD, Vol. 14, Amsterdam (2008), p. 240. *See also*, K. Olenik, *Tax Treaties and the Recourse to Historical Interpretation under the Vienna Convention on the Law of Treaties* in: T. Ecker and G. Ressler (eds) *History of Tax Treaties. The Relevance of the OECD Documents for the Interpretation of Tax Treaties*, Linde, Vienna (2011), p. 69.
256. N. Shelton, *Interpretation and Application of Tax Treaties*, Lexis Nexis, London, 2004, p. 167.
257. *Ibid.*, p. 242. *See also*, F. Engelen, *Interpretation of Tax Treaties under International Law*, Doctoral Series No. 7, IBFD (2005), pp. 131-132.
258. Article 26 of the VCLT states: 'Every treaty in force is binding upon the parties to it and must be performed by them in *good faith* (emphasis added).'
259. In the 1997 *Gabcikovo-Nagymaros case*, the ICJ stated: 'This latter element [good faith], in the Court's view, implies that [...] it is the purpose of the Treaty, and the intention of the parties concluding it, which should prevail over its literal application. The principle of good faith obliges the parties to apply it in a reasonable way and in such a manner that its purpose can be realized.' *See* International: *Case Concerning the Gabcikovo-Nagymaros Project (Hungary/Slovakia)*, Judgment of 25 September 1997, ICJ Reports 1997, p. 76. *See also* a reference to the case in: De Broe, *supra* n. 255, p. 241. The Commentary on Article 31 of the

to the entire process of interpretation, although it finds its limitations in the creation of new obligations which are no longer covered either by the wording of the treaty or the intention of the parties.[260] Therefore, the principle should act only in a way to clear up ambiguous wording in a treaty and not to create new obligations. In other words, it works only as a principle, lending contours.[261]

2.2 Supplementary Means of Interpretation

Article 32 of the VCLT represents an attempt to limit the use or influence of supplementary materials, especially *preparatory work*, that are considered less authentic than the one provided in Article 31.[262] In fact, at the Vienna Convention's conclusion, the United States proposed to remove the apparent hierarchy of sources between Articles 31 and 32 and proposed to combine both articles, giving, therefore, more scope to preparatory work and the circumstances in which the treaty was concluded.[263] This proposal received little support.[264] In contrast, the distinction was justified since the elements of interpretation in Article 31 relate to an agreement between the parties at the time when or after it receives authentic expression in the text, whilst preparatory work, e.g., did not have the same authentic character.[265]

According to Article 32 of the VCLT, supplementary materials can be considered basically in three circumstances: (a) to confirm the meaning resulting from the application of Article 31; (b) where, after applying Article 31, the meaning of the provisions at issue is still ambiguous or obscure; and (c) where the application of Article 31 leads to a result which is manifestly absurd or unreasonable.[266] Nevertheless, the structure of Article 32 is not exempt from criticism. First, unless the interpretation of Article 31 leads to an ambiguous, obscure, absurd or unreasonable result, the application of Article 32 will generally be dismissed. This is because the remaining alternative would be to use the supplementary material to confirm the interpretation of Article 31, but what if that interpretation is not confirmed? There is no manner to resort to Article 32 unless there is an ambiguous, obscure, absurd or unreasonable interpretation under Article 31. Therefore, an unambiguous, clear, not absurd and reasonable interpretation of a provision of a tax treaty according to Article 31, which is not confirmed under the preparatory work of Article 32, will anyway be acceptable. Second, the distinction between supplementary materials and other more authentic materials is not always clear. This is especially relevant in the case of the OECD

VCLT also sustains that good faith 'flows directly from the rule *pacta sunt servanda*'. *See* United Nations, *Yearbook of the International Law Commission, Vol.* II, New York, 1967, p. 221, s. 12.

260. S. Reinhold, *Good Faith in International Law*, Bonn Research Paper on International Law, Paper No. 2 (2013), p. 20.
261. *Ibid.*
262. Arnold, *supra* n. 231, p. 7.
263. Brownlie, *supra* n. 234, p. 628.
264. *Ibid.*
265. *Ibid.*
266. Article 32 of the VCLT.

Commentaries on the OECD Model and its value as preliminary work, an issue that will be analysed in more detail in the subsequent section of this chapter.

2.3 The Interpretative Role of the OECD Model and Its Commentaries

The legal basis for reference to the OECD Model and its Commentaries as an aid to interpreting a specific tax treaty is far from being settled. If we strictly analyse the rules of interpretation of Article 31 of the VCLT explained in the Section above, we might conclude that the Commentaries do not fit into any of these categories. After all, Commentaries on an MC are not made in connection with a negotiated tax treaty, which is indeed a unique legal instrument.[267] Likewise, it is arguable if they could be considered as supplementary means of interpretation under Article 32 of the VCLT because the OECD Model and its Commentaries are neither an instrument made in connection with the conclusion of a treaty nor *preparatory work* used or produced in connection to an individual tax treaty.[268] An alternative, however, to overcome these formal constraints and the bridge created between Articles 31 and 32 of the VCLT could be through the use of Article 31(4) of the VCLT.[269] As proposed by Ault, the terms contained in the OECD Commentaries could be regarded as a special meaning when interpreting the provisions of a tax treaty, which can be especially relevant in the case of OECD member countries.[270] As such, the OECD Commentaries would represent a sort of 'default rule', which would reflect the intention of the Contracting States.[271] In accordance with this interpretation, it would be presumed that OECD member countries wanted to convey the meaning intended in the OECD Model and its Commentaries,[272] being this meaning considered as a *special meaning* according to Article 31(4) of the VCLT.[273] This conclusion should not discard the possibility of the States making reservations or observations to the Commentaries.[274] A similar presumption would

267. *See*, P. Baker, *Double Taxation Conventions*, Sweet & Maxwell, London, 2014, p. E-13. *See also*, H.D. Rosenbloom, *Current Developments in regard to Tax Treaties*, 40 N.Y.U. Inst. on Fed. Tax'n §31 (1982).
268. Supporting the view that the OECD Commentaries cannot be regarded as preparatory work, *see, e.g.*, E. Reimer, *Tax Treaty Interpretation in Germany* in: M. Lang (ed.) *Tax Treaty Interpretation*, Linde, Vienna (2001), p. 135. Reimer argues that German case law and legal theory do not consider the OECD Commentaries either as a genuine source of international law (thus being regarded as not binding documents) or as preparatory work as per Article 32 of the VCLT. Conversely, in *Thiel v. Federal Commissioner of Taxation* in Australia, there is a clear reference to the OECD Commentaries as 'supplementary means of interpretation' for the purposes of Article 32 of the VCLT. *See* Krever and Mellor, *supra* n. 243, p. 42.
269. For the complete analysis, *see* H. Ault, *The Role of the OECD Commentaries in the Interpretation of Tax Treaties*, Intertax 4 (1994), pp. 144-148 DOI: 10.54648/taxi1994023.
270. *Ibid.*, p. 147.
271. *Ibid.*
272. *Ibid.*
273. *Ibid.*, p. 146. *See also*, Vogel and Rust, *supra* n. 26, Introduction at m.no. 101.
274. Vogel and Rust, *supra* n. 26, Introduction at m.no. 103. Reimer, on the contrary, is very critical on this matter, because he considers that the ordinary meaning under Article 31(1) of the VCLT cannot depend on the lack of such observations. Thus, the issue is to understand that the ordinary terms of a treaty, as the terms used by the OECD, would imply a sort of pre-legal understanding, i.e., some sort of everyday meaning of the words used by a treaty. Likewise,

arise if the text of the OECD Model is not adopted literally, but a formulation is chosen that permits an interpretation according to the OECD Model or if the text of the provision is identical to the OECD Model, but a related provision that differs from it suggests a different interpretation.[275]

Giving the OECD Commentaries a special meaning carries out two important consequences. First, the possibility of relying on the OECD Commentaries as a sort of 'official interpretation' (OECD countries) or at least as an important official guidance of interpretation (non-OECD members). Second, the possibility of recognising the OECD Commentaries as a certain binding character, mostly for OECD members.

As for the first consequence, there are almost no doubts regarding the important guidance that the OECD Commentaries have in solving tax treaty cases in practice for both OECD and non-OECD members. An interesting example from non-OECD members can be found in the famous cases of *Eagle I* (2006) and *Eagle II* (2008) regarding the application of Brazilian CFC rules and the compatibility with Articles 7 and 10 of the Brazil-Spain Income Tax Treaty.[276] In this case law, the Brazilian Courts emphasised the role of the OECD Commentaries as a 'useful tool to help in the interpretation [of tax treaties]' and of 'great assistance in the application and interpretation of the conventions and, in particular, in the settlement of any disputes'.[277] This issue has special importance, considering that Brazilian Courts normally refer neither to the VCLT nor to the OECD Commentaries when solving tax treaty cases.[278] Also, one should consider that Brazil has been through a long process to become a member of the OECD. The above, however, does not imply that the OECD Model and its Commentaries have a very limited importance with respect to non-OECD countries.[279] The weight given to the Commentaries will, nevertheless, depend on a case-by-case analysis.[280]

Article 31(4) of the VCLT (special meaning) is not a reliable source either. It requires a consensus between the Contracting parties and a mere observation (unilateral act) would not qualify for that. *See* Reimer, *supra* n. 268.

275. Vogel and Rust, *supra* n. 26, Introduction at m.no. 101. *See also*, Ault, *supra* n. 269.
276. Brazil: Brazilian Administrative Council of Tax Appeals, Judgment No. 101-95.802 – *Eagle I* – and Brazilian Administrative Council of Tax Appeals, Judgment No. 101-97.070 – *Eagle II*. For a further reference to *Eagle I* case law *see, e.g.*, A. Júnior, *Caso Eagle 1: Interpretação das Normas Brasileiras de Tributação de Lucros e Rendimentos oriundos do exterior pelo CARF* in: L. Freitas de Moraes e Castro and A. Ribeiro (eds) *Tributação Internacional: análise de casos*, MP Editora, São Paulo (2010), pp. 259-278. For a further reference to the *Eagle II* case law in Brazil *see, e.g.*, L. Freitas de Moraes e Castro, *Brazilian CFC Rules: Background and Status After Eagle II Case*, 18 Latin America Law & Business Report 3 (2010); R. Da Silveira, *Case Eagle II: Tributação de auferidos no exterior em virtude de participação societária* in: L. Freitas de Moraes e Castro and A. Ribeiro (eds) *Tributação Internacional: análise de casos*, MP Editora, São Paulo (2010), pp. 279-304. *See also*, L. Parada, *A Comparative Analysis of CFC Regimes in Latin America*, 68 Tax Notes Int'l 10, 968-971 (2012).
277. L. Schoueri, *Chapter 3: Brazil* in: R. van Brederode and R. Krever (eds) *Legal Interpretation of Tax Law*, Kluwer Law International BV, The Netherlands, 2014, p. 69.
278. *Ibid.*
279. Vogel and Rust state that the OECD Model and its commentaries are less important, although not irrelevant. The above can be seen, e.g., in the similitude between the UN Model used by developing countries and the OECD Model. Vogel and Rust, *supra* n. 26, Introduction at m.no. 104.
280. *Ibid.*

Nevertheless, the practical value that the OECD Commentaries can have for interpretative purposes should not bring us, at least not immediately, to conclude that they must be regarded as legally binding documents. In other words, the presumption that OECD countries wanted to convey the meaning of the OECD Model, being that meaning either ordinary or special, does not grant per se a binding character to the OECD Commentaries.[281] There is no doubt that a binding character of the OECD Commentaries might positively help in providing a coherent and perhaps more uniform interpretation of tax treaties, mostly among OECD members. However, there is no evidence that proves their binding nature either upon OECD Members States or upon non-OECD Members States.[282] On the contrary, the nonbinding character of the OECD Commentaries is specifically ratified within the text of the OECD Model, when paragraph 3 of its introductory Chapter provides: 'Member countries, when concluding or revising bilateral conventions *should* conform to this Model Convention as interpreted by the Commentaries [...]' (emphasis added).[283] Accordingly, paragraph 29 remarks the auxiliary character of the commentaries and its nonbinding nature when it establishes: 'Although the Commentaries are not designed to be annexed in any manner to the conventions signed by the Member countries, which unlike the Model are legally binding international instruments, they can nevertheless be of great

281. R. Prokisch, *Fragen der Auslegung von Doppelbesteuerungsabkommen*, 4 SWI 52 (1994).
282. D. Ward et al. state: 'There is no consensus concerning the application of Articles 31 and 32 of the VCLT as regards to the OECD commentaries. This undoubtedly arises because the commentaries in the OECD Model are, as we discuss below, not intended to be binding and are unique as they do not relate to an actual treaty but to a Model treaty, which also is non-binding.' D. Ward et al., *The Interpretation of Income Tax Treaties with Particular Reference to the commentaries on the OECD Model*, IBFD, Amsterdam, 2005, p. 18. Likewise, e.g., Pijl states: 'The Commentary cannot be considered to be a binding source of international law. It is a legally non-binding document, which has no bearing on the State as a whole, and only creates a moral obligation for the executive.' *See* H. Pijl, *The OECD Commentary As a Source of International Law and the Role of the Judiciary*, 46 Eur. Taxn. 5 (2006), Journals IBFD, p. 224. Also, Engelen, although supporting a theory that the OECD members and parties of a treaty would be bound by conduct to interpret and apply a treaty in accordance with the commentaries, recognises that the commentaries 'as such' are not binding on the OECD member countries when he says: '[W]hether the Commentaries *as such* are legally binding on the OECD members countries, I fully endorse Mr. Ward's view that it should be answered in the negative.' F. Engelen, *Some Observations on the Legal Status of the Commentaries on the OECD Model*, 60 Bull. Intl. Taxn. 3 (2006), Journals IBFD, p. 105. Regarding non-OECD members, it is evident that the commentaries are 'less important.' *See* Vogel and Rust, *supra* n. 26, Introduction at m.no. 104. Conversely, Baker considers that the OECD commentaries can be relevant, even for non-OECD members, when is clear that the specific treaty has been concluded based on the OECD Model. *See* P. Baker, *supra* n. 267, p. E-19. West also analyses the relevance of the OECD Commentaries in those cases in which a treaty or a protocol expressly referred to them as an interpretational rule. Although, he recognises that this would not change the nonbinding nature of the Commentaries, it could certainly help as a 'soft law' tool to resolve constitutional conflicts that can appear in case the Commentaries are used as an ambulatory interpretation rule. For a further analysis, *see* C. West, *References to the OECD Commentaries in Tax Treaties: A Steady March from 'Soft' Law to 'Hard' Law?*, 9 World Tax J. 1 (2017), Journals IBFD. More recently, *see* A. Navarro, *International Tax Soft Law Instruments: The Futility of the Static v. Dynamic Interpretation Debate*, 48 Intertax 10 (2020) DOI: 10.54648/taxi2020086 (who analyses whether the Commentaries have a privileged value over other equally non-binding texts in the context of the interpretation process of tax treaties).
283. OECD Model Tax Convention and Commentaries (2014), Para. 3, Introductory Chapter.

assistance in the application and interpretation of the conventions and, in particular, in the settlement of any disputes.'[284] Likewise, the Recommendation of the OECD Council concerning the MC (1997) simply provided a 'recommendation' to the member countries to conform to the MC and that the tax administrations follow the commentaries when interpreting the OECD Model, but in any case, it settles an obligation to do so. Therefore, the OECD Commentaries can create only a moral or 'soft' obligation for these countries in order to follow them for interpretative reasons, but in any case, they are bound to do so.[285] This conclusion also has special relevance to discard the idea that due to the widespread acceptance of the OECD Model and its Commentaries, they can constitute a sort of customary international tax law.[286]

Some authors have, however, insisted on supporting the binding nature of the OECD Commentaries and their interpretative value based on the international public law doctrines of acquiescence and estoppel.[287] The Encyclopaedia of Public International Law defines *acquiescence* as 'the proposition of binding effect resulting from passivity and inaction with respect to foreign claims which, according to the general practice of States, usually call for protest in order to assert, preserve of safeguard rights'.[288] Thus, acquiescence, which finds expression in the adage '*qui tacet consentire videtur si loqui debuisset ac potuisset*', means the act of implying consent to a certain

284. *Ibid.*, para. 29, Introductory Chapter.
285. The interpretational use of the OECD commentaries cannot be considered as State practice either. They could constitute State practice in one moment, but this issue will depend on the subsequent judicial practice. *See* Pijl, *supra* n. 282, p. 220.
286. A full analysis on this matter certainly exceeds the purpose of this chapter. However, it is worth mentioning that the formation of customary law implies the concurrence of two constitutive elements: State practice or *usus* and *opinio juris*. Whilst the former implies that a number of States contribute, actively or passively, towards the customary international rules, the latter supposes the conviction of a State that it follows certain practice accepted as law. *See* International: Statute of the International Court of Justice, Article 38(1)(b). Therefore, even if the OECD Commentaries are generally used and accepted for interpretation purposes, their nonbinding nature would imply the absence of *opinio juris*, i.e., a necessary element for the formation of customary law. The importance of the *opinio juris* in the formation of customary law has been widely recognised by the international public law doctrines as well as for the jurisprudence of the International Court of Justice (ICJ). *See, e.g.*, Brownlie, *supra* n. 234; B. Lepard B., *The Necessity of Opinio Juris in the Formation of Customary International Law*, Discussion Paper for Panel on 'Does Customary International Law Need *Opinio Juris?*' pp. 2-4; M. Mendelson, *The Subjective Element in Customary International Law*, 66 Brit. Y.B. Int'l L. 1, 208 (1995); F. Parisi, *The Formation of Customary Law*, George Mason Law & Economics Research Paper No. 01-06, p. 5, available at SSRN. Conversely, however, in 2000 the International Law Association (ILA) elaborated a concept of customary international law excluding the element *opinio juris*. The report declared that a rule of customary law 'is one which is created and sustained by the constant and uniform practice of States and other subjects of international law in or impinging upon their international legal relations, in circumstances which give rise to a legitimate expectation of similar conduct in the future.' *See* International Law Association, *Statement of Principles Applicable to the Formation of General Customary International Law*, adopted by Resolution No. 16/2000, London Conference, 2000, s. 1(i), p. 8.
287. Engelen, *supra* n. 282.
288. J.P. Müller and T. Cottier, *Acquiescence* in: R. Bernhardt (ed.) *Encyclopedia of Public International Law*, Volume I (1992), p. 14.

fact by remaining silent.[289] On the other side, the principle of *estoppel*, very similar to the Roman law principles of *non licet venire contra factum proprium* and *allegans contraria non audiendus est*, attends to the effect that a person who represents a fact to another who in turn alters his position in reasonable reliance on such representation may not deny that the fact exists.[290] In other words, under the principle of estoppel, a party is not permitted to take upon a legal position that is in contradiction with its own previous representations or conduct when another party has been led to assume obligations towards or attribute rights to the former party in reliance upon such representations or conducts. For example, if State A relies on the conduct of State B, this latter State is precluded from acting contrary to its representation. If State B acts contrary to this representation, it is acting without good faith and contrary to international law.[291] Thus, both acquiescence and estoppel are principles based on *good faith*,[292] although they differ in the components of time and reliance.[293] Whilst acquiescence is passivity in relation to a right of another State to the extent that good faith affords the passivity the character of consent, estoppel hinges on previous presentations.[294] In this order of ideas, if OECD (and non-OECD) countries have not made an observation on the interpretation of the provisions of the OECD Model as set out in the commentaries when concluding or revising a tax treaty, it would mean that the countries have acquiesced in that interpretation and it becomes legally binding, being a sort of tacit agreement to interpret the provisions of the treaty as per the OECD Model and its Commentaries.[295] Accordingly, if there are any doubts as to the parties' acceptance of the OECD Commentaries, the countries are estopped or precluded from denying such acceptance.[296]

The application of the doctrines of acquiescence and estoppel, as explained above, seems to be inappropriate to justify a binding character of the OECD Commentaries, mostly considering their contradictory results.[297] Indeed, if the principle of acquiescence were applied, it would force countries that did not make observations to the Commentaries to tacitly accept the effects of their interpretation, recognising a sort of official interpretation that might, in fact, jeopardise the rule of *pacta sunt servanda*. This conclusion would contradict the international tax treaty practice, which demonstrates that OECD members do not always enter an observation when they disagree with the OECD Commentaries,[298] but sometimes, these observations are simply not

289. *Ibid.*, p. 106. The I.C.J. has recognised the principle of acquiescence in, e.g., International: *Case Concerning the Delimitation of the Maritime Boundary in the Gulf of Maine Area (Canada v. United States of America)* (Merits), Judgment of 12 October 1984, I.C.J. Rep 305.
290. Engelen, *supra* n. 82, p. 106.
291. Reinhold, *supra* n. 260, pp. 13-14.
292. *Supra* s. 2.1.
293. *Ibid.*
294. *Ibid.*
295. Engelen, *supra* n. 282, p. 109.
296. *Ibid.*, p. 106.
297. This issue has been extensively analysed somewhere else. For this purpose, *see* Pijl, *supra* n. 282.
298. Ward et al. provide the example of para. 7 of Article 1 of the 1977 OECD Model. The text of para. 7 which, although recognising that taxpayers have the possibility of exploiting tax differences between States, left the door open to include domestic laws to counteract potential abusive

required. The latter situation can be easily demonstrated through the history of the MCs and its Commentaries. In fact, many times, the OECD Commentaries have been modified to include the predominant opinion of the OECD members, which means that in those cases, the OECD members departed from the Commentaries, but no observation was needed.[299] The above conclusion does not diminish the value of the OECD Commentaries in the interpretative process but simply reaffirms that they cannot be considered legally binding documents.[300]

Similar concerns should exist with respect to the application of the principle of estoppel to justify the binding character of the OECD Commentaries. If two countries agree on a tax treaty based on the OECD Model and its Commentaries, which both have accepted, they would be precluded from denying such acceptance, even if such acceptance comes in a tacit manner, e.g., if the tax treaty follows exactly the provisions of the Model Convention. Nevertheless, one should not confuse the existence of a soft obligation derived from the OECD Commentaries as an interpretation of the OECD Model with the real rights and obligation derived from the negotiated tax treaty itself and based on the international law rule of *pacta sunt servanda.* Could the parties be really precluded from denying the acceptance of the OECD Commentaries when, in fact, this document never created legal rights or obligations to the parties? To justify the binding character of the OECD Commentaries based on the principle of estoppel seems to go too far, mostly considering its restrictive application in the field of international public law.

A few words should be finally said regarding the different versions in time of the OECD Commentaries and their use for interpretation purposes. The majority of international tax scholars agree that the version of the OECD Model and its Commentaries at the time of the conclusion of a tax treaty is the only one that can be considered for interpretation purposes.[301] This implies that further changes[302] to the OECD Commentaries should not affect the interpretation of a specific tax treaty concluded before those changes entered into force. This approach is particularly relevant considering that the OECD Commentaries can represent the ordinary meaning of a treaty between two OECD members under Article 31(1) of the VCLT or, at least, they could

situations, i.e., anti-abuse rules. Despite the dissenting views regarding the fact that anti-abuse rules should be confirmed in the treaty texts (the majority opinion argued that no reference in the treaty should be made), no observations were made after the 1992 OECD Commentaries that expressly recognised the majority opinion in para. 24 of Article 1. Ward et al., *supra* n. 282, pp. 49-50.

299. *Ibid.*, p. 51.

300. *Ibid.*

301. Vogel and Rust, *supra* n. 26, Introduction at m.no. 105. *See also*, M. Lang, *supra* n. 21, p. 50. In contrast, *see, e.g.*, Navarro, *supra* n. 282, who argues that the version of the Commentaries that should prevail is the one containing the most adequate interpretative outcome in accordance with the possible meanings of the terminology of the rule being interpreted, its context, and its purpose. Therefore, the distinction between what version of the Commentaries should be used would be simply futile.

302. But not all changes of the OECD Commentaries will have legal effects. For example, a change in the language to make the English or French more alike will have no legal significance. *See* Vogel and Rust, *supra* n. 26, Introduction at m.no. 106.

convey a special meaning under Article 31(4) of the VCLT.[303] This conclusion has logic since the only version to which the negotiator of a tax treaty had access was the one existing at the time of the conclusion of a tax treaty.

2.4 The Reference to Domestic Law: Article 3(2) of the OECD Model

Article 3(2) of the OECD Model provides a general rule of interpretation that allows referring to domestic law in case any *term*[304] is not defined in a tax treaty unless the context otherwise requires.[305] The reference to the domestic law of the Contracting States (known as *lex fori*) has logic since a tax treaty is negotiated with the domestic laws of the Contracting States in mind, and tax treaties exist in order to coordinate these two tax jurisdictions, limiting their taxing powers by the treaty.[306] Accordingly, it also provides practical advantages because it prevents the overloading of tax treaties with definitions that would render its application difficult,[307] as well as increases legal certainty.[308] However, one should also recognise that Article 3(2) contradicts the primary goal of a 'common interpretation' of tax treaties, also increasing the possibilities of different interpretations and qualification conflicts.

Generally, Article 3(2) of the OECD Model is applied with certain limitations. First, it only covers the interpretation of the *terms* used in a tax treaty.[309] Therefore, the provision does not apply to use principles of domestic law in the interpretation of tax treaties or to clarify unclear passages of a treaty itself.[310] Furthermore, according to

303. Ault also coincides with this static view when he says: 'A later-arising special meaning would be hard to conceive. Thus at least with respect to some terms, if the Commentaries are to be used, it must be on a static basis.' Ault, *supra* n. 269, p. 148.
304. The use of 'term' should be interpreted in a manner wider than just 'words'. At least this should be justified in fact that many times the governing language of a treaty is not the one of the domestic laws, and even in some cases it is a third language, commonly English, that takes precedent. In this latter case, as argued by Avery Jones, 'a third language will never be found in either State's domestic laws', and so the 'term' must be wider than just words. *See* J. Avery Jones, *The Interaction Between Tax Treaty Provisions and Domestic Law* in: G. Maisto (ed.) *Tax Treaties and Domestic Law*, EC and International Tax Law Series Vol. 2, IBFD (2006), p. 134.
305. Article 3(2) of the 2014 OECD MODEL was modified in 1995 and according to the 2014 OECD Model, it provides: 'As regards the application of the Convention at any time by a Contracting State, any term not defined therein shall, unless the context otherwise requires, have the meaning that it has at that time under the law of that State for the purposes of the taxes to which the Convention applies, any meaning under the applicable tax laws of that State prevailing over a meaning given to the term under other laws of that State.'
306. Arnold, *supra* n. 231, p. 9.
307. Instead, taxpayers, administrative authorities and courts can keep the meaning of a term as it is already known in domestic law. *See* Vogel and Prokisch, *supra* n. 254, p. 77.
308. As provided by Avery Jones: 'Article 3(2) was a brilliant solution. The result is that in any case where the treaty relieves a category of income from tax, the relief corresponds exactly with the internal law taxing provision. This is far more important than that the treaty category of income has the same scope in each State; the internal law charging provisions are most unlikely to be the same either. Indeed, the result of relying on internal law definitions is superior to the treaty containing a definition of a type of income, which may well be different from the internal law definition used for taxing the income.' *See* Avery Jones, *supra* n. 304, p. 125.
309. A. Rust in: Reimer and Rust (eds) *Klaus Vogel on Double Taxation Conventions*, 4th edn (2015), Article 3(2) at m.no. 111.
310. *Ibid.*.

Article 3(2) of the OECD Model, it is possible to conclude that if the terms of the treaty have no particular or established legal meaning under domestic laws or a term is used in private law only, then the resort to domestic law would not be possible.[311] It is also important to note that Article 3(2) of the OECD Model refers exclusively to the meaning of the terms that the Contracting State applying the treaty gives at the moment the treaty is applied and not when this is concluded.[312] Second, the provision only refers to the law of those taxes covered by the convention, excluding thus any reference to private or tax law regarding taxes not included, e.g., VAT. Likewise, it is clear that when a term has a meaning for tax law purposes, whilst a different one for another field of law, the former prevails.[313]

The reference to domestic law is conditioned by the expression, *unless the context otherwise requires*, used in Article 3(2) of the OECD Model, which means that the *renvoi* to the domestic law under Article 3(2) is limited by the interpretation derived from the context of the treaty. In this regard, one should not consider the term *context* in the same manner as it is used for purposes of Article 31(2) of the VCLT. Indeed, the function of the term *context* is completely different in the two provisions.[314] For many authors, the use of *context* under Article 3(2) of the OECD Model has a wider meaning than the one in Article 31(2) of the VCLT, which helps avoid the inappropriate use of domestic law definitions.[315] As provided by Helminen, the context under Article 3(2) of the OECD Model clearly indicates situations in which the contextual meaning should prevail over the *lex fori* meaning as per Article 3(2) of the OECD Model,[316] even though one should stress that it is not possible to extract from the reading of the Article 3(2) any kind of preference or hierarchy for interpretation from the context.[317] Therefore, the term context should be widely interpreted to include any materials that indicate that the *lex fori* meaning is not consistent.[318] The case law *Padmore v. IRC* in the United Kingdom is a good example of the application of the above.[319] The issue in this case was that the treaty between the UK and Jersey defined the term 'person', including any 'body of persons, corporate or not corporate'. However, English law expressly excluded Partnerships from the concept of a 'body of persons'. The Court concluded that

311. In *Thiel v. Federal Commissioner of Taxation*, e.g., the High Court of Australia rejected an interpretation of both the terms 'enterprise' and 'profits' because these terms did not have any particular or established meaning under Australian domestic law. *See Thiel v. Federal Commissioner of Taxation*, cited in: Krever and Mellor, *supra* n. 243. A similar reasoning can be found in the Dutch case *Hoge Raad*, where the Supreme Court said that Article 3(2) of the OECD Model could not be applied to interpret a term that is not used in a similar context under the domestic law. *See* NL: Decision of the Dutch Supreme Court *Hoge Raad*, 1 December 2006, BNB 2007/75-79 cited in: A. Bosman, *Casualty under Tax Treaties*, 44 Intertax 5, 393 (2016) DOI: 10.54648/taxi2016031.
312. Rust, *supra* n. 309.
313. *Ibid.*
314. Vogel and Prokisch, *supra* n. 254, p. 82.
315. J. Avery Jones, *United Kingdom* in: Cahiers de droit fiscal international Vol. LXXVIIa, Interpretation of Double Taxation Conventions (IFA 1993), p. 610.
316. M. Helminen, *Tax Treaty Interpretation in Finland* in: M. Lang (ed.) *Tax Treaty Interpretation*, Linde, Vienna (2001), pp. 84-86.
317. Rust, *supra* n. 309, Article 3(2) at m.no. 121.
318. *Ibid. See also*, Helminen, *supra* n. 316.
319. UK: *Padmore v. IRC* [1989] STC 493.

the context required that the internal law be not used because the context required otherwise.[320] Likewise, in the *Estate of Burghardt v. Commissioner*, regarding the US-Italy Estate Tax Treaty, the Court ruled that as neither the IRC nor the Treasury Regulations use the term 'specific exemption' in the Estate Tax Area, the term should be interpreted in the context of the treaty and not by other rules of domestic law.[321]

Some tax scholars have interpreted Article 3(2) of the OECD Model in a way by which this provision should be applied only to the extent that no other solution can be derived from the tax treaty itself.[322] Lang explains this restrictive interpretation with the example of the concept of 'business profits' under Article 7 of the OECD Model. He states that the fact this term is not defined anywhere in the OECD Model does not mean that one should resort immediately to domestic law in order to get the answer.[323] On the contrary, based on the systematic, theological and historical factors of the treaty, one should arrive at the conclusion that the concept of business profits applies to income from activities that are not services of where there is a significant capital expenditure.[324] Nevertheless, Lang's arguments seem to be not that convincing, mostly considering the wording of Article 3(2) of the OECD Model. Indeed, as noted already, the reference to domestic law is limited by the expression '*unless the context otherwise requires*' and not '*unless the context yields no other, or absolutely no other, interpretation*'.[325] Therefore, not every single interpretation from the context should give rise to a divergence with Article 3(2) of the OECD Model, but only those based on relatively strong arguments.[326] This also confirms what I have already stressed in this work, which is that there is no priority for interpretation from the context, at least not one that can be inferred from the wording of Article 3(2). Yet, one should recognise that the fewer cases where domestic law is used to interpret treaty terms, the greater the probability that both States will try hard to interpret the treaty in its context, trying to achieve a common understanding, which could also reduce the chances, e.g., for qualification conflicts.[327]

To sum up, therefore, Article 3(2) of the OECD Model establishes the following order for interpretation of terms used in the tax treaties: (1) a special definition in the tax treaty will be applied; (2) if no special definition exists, then the domestic law of the Contracting State applying the treaty (*lex fori*) must be applied to the extent it relates to the taxes covered by the treaty and only if the context otherwise requires; (3) if the interpretation from the context is strong enough, this should be used instead, although

320. J. Avery Jones, *Tax Treaty Interpretation in the United Kingdom* in: M. Lang (ed.) *Tax Treaty Interpretation*, Linde, Vienna (2001), p. 369.
321. US: US Tax Court of 11 April 1983, No. 20766-81, *Estate of Burghardt v. Commissioner*, 80 T.C. 705 (1983).
322. Rust disagrees with this conclusion when he states: 'It is, on the other hand, itself a special rule of interpretation in relation to the general rules contained in the VCLT governing the interpretation of DTCs, as such, it takes precedence over those general rules.' Rust, *supra* n. 309.
323. Lang, *supra* n. 21, p. 45.
324. *Ibid.*
325. Rust, *supra* n. 309, Article 3(2) at m.no. 122.
326. *Ibid.*
327. M. Lang, *2008 OECD Model: Conflicts of Qualification and Double Non-Taxation*, 63 Bull. Intl. Taxn. 5 (2009), Journals IBFD, p. 206.

the resorting to the context is not automatic and it should be measured among with the alternative interpretations; (4) if the context does not provide for a different interpretation, the general rules of interpretation should be applied.[328]

3 DOUBLE NON-TAXATION AND THE OECD MODEL AND ITS COMMENTARIES

As already noted, the OECD Model is not an object of interpretation itself.[329] Nevertheless, it might be useful to analyse some of its provisions, normally included in tax treaties, which, at first glance, might be interpreted in a manner of preventing DNT. This perception, however, may easily disappear when a closer look at these provisions is taken and an interpretation, as per the rules analysed in section 2, is applied. As follows, I offer an analysis of the following OECD Model provisions: (a) The term '*liable to tax*' of Article 4(1) OECD Model; (b) the concept of *beneficial owner*; (c) the Article 23A(1), and (d) the Article 23A(4) OECD Model.

3.1 The Interpretation of the Term *'Liable to Tax'*

Article 4(1) OECD Model establishes that a resident, for purposes of a tax treaty, means any person who, under the law of that State, is '*liable to tax*' therein by reason of his domicile, residence, place of management or any other criterion of a similar nature.[330] The meaning of the term *liable to tax* is, however, highly disputed. On one side, tax scholars interpret the term as including a person who is subject to actual taxation in the residence state. This idea would support the assumption that tax treaties ensure single taxation or, which is the same, that they aim to avoid DNT. On the other side, commentators attribute to it the meaning of a person who is just subject to full taxation (i.e., worldwide taxation), even though taxes might be effectively applied or not in that State. This latter interpretation, in my view, seems to be more in accordance with both the wording of the OECD Commentaries and the tax treaty practice. Some observations can be made to support this idea.

At first glance, the basic function of tax treaties is to allocate taxing rights but not to ensure that those rights are effectively exercised.[331] Indeed, there are no mechanisms within the OECD Model to carry out such a task unless specific provisions have been

328. Rust, *supra* n. 309, Article 3(2) at m. nos 125 and 126.
329. *Supra* s. 2.
330. Article 4 of the OECD Model Convention.
331. The above position has been repeatedly supported by the international jurisprudence. For example, in 2001, a decision of the *Cour Administrative in Luxembourg* sustained that: '[A] tax treaty is a bilateral instrument limiting each contracting state's right to tax by attributing the taxation right to one of the two contracting states. This limitation is, in principle, permanent and cannot be changed by one of the contracting states on the basis of the argument that the other contracting state does not make use of its taxation right.' *See* LU: Cour adm., 27 juillet 2011, n° 28115C du role.

included during the bilateral negotiation of a tax treaty.[332] In other words, once the treaty has allocated the exclusive right to tax certain items of income or capital to a Contracting State, that State keeps the right to exercise or not such right, not being even necessary for the concurrence of double taxation for residents to claim treaty benefits. Such interpretation could, e.g., lead to an acceptable outcome of DNT because it is a conscious decision of the Contracting State whether or not they enter into a tax treaty that leaves open the possibility of DNT.[333] As an example of the tax treaty practice, it is well-known that Belgium does not tax capital gains realised neither by individuals nor by corporations.[334] If a State decides to enter into a tax treaty with Belgium or any other country having a similar practice and includes a provision such as Article 13(5) OECD Model, it is reasonable to expect that that State has examined or has at least been informed regarding this domestic practice.[335] Therefore, if that State insists on concluding the treaty without any reservation that allows him to preserve its taxing rights in case income is not effectively taxed in Belgium, or, for example, both countries do not include any specific provision to ensure single taxation, one should simply conclude that DNT is a tolerated outcome. This fact does not contradict the object and purpose of the negotiated tax treaty. On the contrary, States normally enter into tax treaties with other States reputed as low-tax countries, and they still decide to unconditionally forgive their taxing rights over income not taxed or low-taxed in those States.[336]

Accordingly, it is often understood that a person *liable to tax* is one who, by reason of various criteria (i.e., residence, domicile, etc.), is subject to '*comprehensive taxation*'.[337] Although the OECD Commentaries do not provide a definition of what *comprehensive taxation* means, they recognise that in many States, a person is considered liable to comprehensive taxation even if that State does not impose taxes effectively.[338] This would be the case of, e.g., pension funds, charities and other organisations that might be exempted from taxation if they meet all the requirements of the specific domestic law for that purpose but who are still subject to tax laws in that Contracting State.[339] It can also be the case of any person whose income is below the taxable minimum or who makes use of losses or allowances to reduce tax assessment.[340] If one interprets the term *liable to tax* in a way to ensure effective or single

332. Article 4(1)(b) of the 1989 tax treaty between India and the United States establishes, e.g., that the residence of partnerships, estates and trusts depends on their being *subject to tax* (actual taxation) either in their hands or in the hands of their partners. *See* Tax Convention between the Government of the United States of America and the Government of the Republic of India of 1 January 1991, Article 4(1)(b).
333. R. Ismer and K. Riemer in: Reimer and Rust (eds) *Klaus Vogel on Double Taxation Conventions*, 4th edn (2015), Article 4 at m.no. 19.
334. De Broe, *supra* n. 255, p. 359.
335. *Ibid.*
336. *See, e.g.*, A. Martin Jiménez, *Domestic-Anti Abuse Rules and Double Taxation Treaties: A Spanish Perspective – Part I*, 56 Bull. Intl. Taxn. 11, 542-553 (2002).
337. OECD Commentary on Article 4 concerning the definition of resident, paras 8 and 8.6.
338. OECD Commentary on Article 4 concerning the definition of resident, para. 8.6.
339. *Ibid.*
340. De Broe, *supra* n. 255, p. 358.

taxation, all those persons would be immediately excluded from the treaty protection.[341] Thus, being subject to *comprehensive taxation* does not mean being subject to taxes in the other country. This conclusion is indeed supported in the wording of Article 4(1) OECD Model, which requires that a person is 'liable' and not 'subject' to tax.[342] Whilst the first expression is commonly used to refer to potential taxation, the latter is used to ensure actual taxation.[343] Explained in a different manner, the concept of '*liable to tax*' comprehends taxation and exemption, whilst the concept of '*subject to tax*' does not include exemption but only situations of effective taxation and others in which there is no effective taxation due to deductions and reductions in the calculation of the tax liabilities.[344]

The distinction between the concepts of '*liable to tax*' and '*subject to tax*' is well illustrated in the '*Weiser* case' that involved the application of the UK-Israel tax treaty.[345] In brief, the case referred to a resident of Israel who received pension income from the UK. He claimed that this pension income was exempt from taxes in the UK because the income was derived by a resident of Israel, subject thus to tax in that country. After the taxpayer's claim was refused by the HMRC on the ground that the pensions were not '*subject to tax*' in Israel, he appealed to the First-tier Tribunal, which not only confirmed the position of the HMRC but also reaffirmed the clear distinction between both expressions.[346] The First-tier Tribunal sustained that the taxpayer confused the expressions '*subject to tax*' and '*liable to tax*' as employed in tax treaties.[347] '*Liable to tax*', on the one hand, requires only an abstract liability to taxation; namely, a Contracting State might exercise its right to tax the income in question, being irrelevant whether or not that State finally exercises its right to tax and whether or not an amount of tax becomes payable. '*Subject to tax*', on the other hand, requires income to be actually included in the computation of the individual's taxable income, resulting in a tax payable subject to deductions for allowances, reliefs, etc. This clear distinction has also been repeated in the tax treaty practice of other countries. In China, e.g., the term '*liable to tax*' is interpreted by the SAT, which has the general power to interpret tax legislation and tax treaties, and which is rarely

341. *Ibid.*
342. Ismer and Riemer, *supra* n. 333, Article 4 at m.no. 26.
343. *Ibid.*
344. Pulido, *supra* n. 18, p. 291.
345. UK: FTT, 10 August 2012, *Paul Weiser v. Commissioner for Her Majesty's Revenue and Customs*, [2012] UKFTT 501 (TC), [2012] SFTD 1381, Tax Treaty Case Law IBFD. *See also*, B. Cleave, *The Weiser Case: UK Pension Income Not Subject to Tax in Israel under the Israel-United Kingdom Income Tax Treaty (1962)*, 67 Bull. Intl. Taxn. 6 (2013), Journals IBFD.
346. *Ibid.*, p. 280.
347. Judge Berner referred to the emblematic cases of *Bayfine UK* (2011) and *Smallwood* (2010) for the principles to be applied in this case. *Ibid.*, For the full text of the cases, *see* UK: CA, 23 March 2011, *Bayfine UK v. Commissioner for H M Revenue and Customs*, [2011] EWCA Civ 304, Tax Treaty Case Law IBFD and UK: CA, 8 July 2010, *Smallwood (Trevor Smallwood and Mary Caroline Smallwood, Trustees of the Trevor Smallwood Trust) v. Commissioners for the H M Revenue and Customs*, [2010] EWCA Civ 778, Tax Treaty Case Law IBFD. *See also*, B. Cleave, *The Bayfine Case, Elaborate Tax Avoidance Scheme Using Tax Treaty Fails in Court of Appeal of England and Wales*, 65 Bull. Intl. Taxn. 11 (2011), Journals IBFD, and B. Cleave, *The Smallwood Case: Dual Residence of Trustees*, 65 Bull. Intl. Taxn. 8 (2011), Journals IBFD.

contradicted by courts, as having the legal obligation to pay tax on a comprehensive basis, but not actual payment of tax.[348]

Another issue that is normally disregarded in the analysis of the expression *'liable tax'* refers to the fact that it is up to the Contracting States, according to their domestic laws, to determine the connecting factors that will trigger taxation and the requirements under which these factors (i.e., domicile; residence; place of management, etc.) will be applied.[349] In other words, it finally depends on each Contracting State to lay down the conditions under which a person will be regarded as 'resident' for purposes of a tax treaty and, therefore, subject to comprehensive taxation. The above can certainly derive different results. In France, e.g., the definition of residence is exceptionally modified in certain cases to ensure single taxation. Under Article 4B(2) of the French Tax Code, civil servants who perform their duties abroad are deemed to have their domicile in France, despite not being residents, to the extent they are not subject to unlimited liability in the foreign country where they perform their activities.[350] In the United States, some deviations from the OECD Model can be recognised, such as the inclusion of 'citizenship' as one of the factors to determine residence in the case of individuals or the 'place of incorporation' as a residence determination factor in the case of corporations. Accordingly, and perhaps the most notable extension of the concept of residence, is the inclusion of a LOB provision, which basically limits the benefits of the treaty to bona fide residents, namely, taxpayers with strong connections with the treaty partner and not only residents as per the domestic law of that State.[351] Since the concept of resident for tax treaty purposes might thus be restricted or extended as per the countries' domestic laws desire, it seems to be incorrect to argue that always the avoidance of DNT is safeguarded in the tax treaty context.

3.2 The Concept of *Beneficial Owner* as a Meaning to Prevent DNT

Like the concept of *'liable to tax'* analysed before, there is an easy temptation to interpret the concept of *'beneficial owner'* used in Articles 10, 11 and 12 OECD Model as to prevent DNT. Although this concept has been profoundly studied in the international tax literature, and it is certainly not my intention to emulate the results of those studies here, some brief observations regarding its interpretation are still required.[352]

---

348. J. Li, *The Great Fiscal Wall of China: Tax Treaties and Their Role in Defining and Defending China's Tax Base*, 66 Bull. Intl. Taxn. 9 (2012), Journals IBFD, pp. 455-456.
349. OECD Commentary on Article 4 concerning the definition of resident, para. 4.
350. Gutmann, *supra* n. 235, p. 97.
351. Y. Brauner, *Chapter 23: United States* in: G. Maisto (ed.) *Residence of Companies under Tax Treaties and EC Law*, EC and International Tax Law Series Vol. 5, IBFD, Amsterdam (2009), pp. 876-877.
352. With regard to the literature about the meaning of the concept of *beneficial owner*, *see*, *e.g.*, C. du Toit, *Beneficial Ownership of Royalties in Bilateral Tax Treaties*, IBFD, Amsterdam (1999); R. Fraser and J. Oliver, *Beneficial Ownership: HMRC's Draft Guidance on Interpretation of the Indofood Decision*, BTR 1 (2007); J. Bernstein, *Beneficial Ownership: An International Perspective*, 45 Tax Notes Int'l 12 (2007); P. Baker, *The United Nations Model Double Taxation Convention Between Developed and Developing Countries: Possible Extension of the Beneficial*

The concept of '*beneficial owner*' or '*bénéficiare effectif*' (French translation)[353] was first and officially introduced in the 1977 OECD Model[354] and made reference to the limitation that payments of dividends, interests or royalties (Articles 10, 11 and 12 OECD Model), normally subject to a reduced WHT at source, must be 'beneficially owned' by a resident of the other Contracting State.[355] The historical reason behind this concept is to prevent treaty shopping through the imposition of conduit companies by third-state residents in order to claim treaty benefits not otherwise available to them,[356] and it was included for the very first time in the 1966 Protocol of the 1945 US-UK tax treaty.[357] The original intent of this provision, according to its design under English law, was actually to distinguish between the legal owner and the non-beneficial owner for the title given on the sale of land.[358] The same distinction was made in the law of equity between the legal ownership of the trustee and the equitable, or beneficial, ownership of the beneficiary.[359] Not surprisingly, however, the term has no equivalence in most civil law countries, where a split of ownership is not known, at least not to the extent recognised in common law countries.[360] Indeed, civil law countries, apart

---

Owner Concept in: Committee of Experts on International Cooperation in Tax Matters: Fourth Session, Geneva (20-24 October 2008); A. Martín Jiménez, *Beneficial Ownership: Current Trends*, 2 World Tax J. (2010), Journals IBFD; M. Lang et. al. (eds), *Beneficial Ownership: Recent Trends*, IBFD, Amsterdam, 2013. For a historic evolution and academic discussions regarding the concept of *beneficial owner* in different jurisdictions, *see also* A. Meindl-Ringler, *Beneficial Owner in International Tax Law*, Kluwer Law International, Alphen aan den Rijn, 2016. More recently, *see* Błazej Kuźniacki, *Beneficial Ownership in International Taxation*, Edward Elgar, 2022. *See also*, Pablo Hernández González-Barreda, *Beneficial Owner in Tax Law and Tax Treaties*, Bloomsbury Publishing, 2021.

353. Some authors argue that the French official translation of the term is more accurate than the English expression because the emphasis is not put on the person's ownership of the income, but rather on whether this person really benefits from the income. *See, e.g.*, P. Pistone, *Italy: Beneficial Ownership as Anti-Abuse Provision in International Taxation* in: M. Lang et.al. (eds) *Beneficial Ownership: Recent Trends*, IBFD, Amsterdam (2013), p. 184. The above, in view of others, could also be an indication that civil law countries represented at the OECD did not want to use the common law concept of *beneficial ownership* when they negotiate tax treaties, because this concept is indeed closer to the person's ownership of the income. *See*, De Broe, *supra* n. 255, p. 680.
354. However, the first time that was introduced in an OECD draft was in 1974. *See* R. Ng, *The Concept of Beneficial Owner* in: T. Ecker and G. Ressler (eds) *History of Tax Treaties. The Relevance of the OECD Documents for the Interpretation of Tax Treaties*, Linde, Vienna (2011), p. 514. Ng also provides some other examples of tax treaties that included the term '*beneficial owner*', even before its official introduction in the OECD Model. In this regard, e.g., the 1968 UK-the Netherlands treaty; the 1968 Ireland-France treaty; the 1969 Australia-Japan treaty and the 1975 UK-Spain treaty. *Ibid.*, p. 515.
355. R. Vann, *Beneficial Ownership: What Does History (and Maybe Policy) Tell Us* in: M. Lang et.al. (eds) *Beneficial Ownership: Recent Trends*, IBFD, Amsterdam (2013), p. 281.
356. De Broe explains that both the 1977 OECD Model Commentaries and the 1986 OECD Conduit Companies Report indicate that the term is used as an anti-avoidance device against treaty shopping using conduit companies by third-States residents. *See* De Broe, *supra* n. 255, pp. 654 and 664. *See also*, OECD (1987), *supra* n. 184. *See also*, E. Kemmeren in: Reimer and Rust (eds) *Klaus Vogel on Double Taxation Conventions*, 4th edn (2015), Pre Articles 10-12 at m.no. 21.
357. For a complete historic analysis, *see* R. Vann, *supra* n. 355, p. 275. *See also*, Ng, *supra* n. 354.
358. J. Avery Jones et al., *The Origin of the Concepts and Expressions Used in the OECD Model and Their Adoption by States*, 60 Bull. Int'l. Taxn. 6 (2006), Journals IBFD, p. 246.
359. *Ibid.*
360. De Broe, *supra* n. 255, p. 663.

from a few exceptions,[361] do not use the term *'beneficial owner'* in their domestic laws.[362] The interpretation of the term *'beneficial owner'* presents many troubles because it is not a defined concept at the tax treaty level unless some references in the OECD Commentaries on Articles 10, 11 and 12 OECD Model are made.[363] The interpretation thus could actually take two routes: (i) a domestic interpretation, derived by the application of Article 3(2) OECD Model; or (ii) an autonomous interpretation, derived by the tax treaties themselves.

The interpretation according to Article 3(2) OECD Model, on the one hand, and as already stressed somewhere else in this work, allows resorting to domestic law in case any term is not defined in a tax treaty unless the context of the treaty otherwise requires.[364] But even if the context requires otherwise, there is no rule in Article 3(2) OECD Model that allows us to conclude *a priori* that the interpretation based on the context of the treaty should have priority.[365] However, one should bear in mind that the fewer the application of Article 3(2) OECD Model, the greater the probability that both States achieve a common interpretation, which is one of the final aims of the interpretation of tax treaties.[366] There are, however, additional reasons to support this line of argumentation. In the first place, the concept of *'beneficial owner'* has no

361. The Netherlands is, for example, an exception. Article 4(3) of the 1965 Dividend WHT Act; Article 25 of the 1969 Corporate Income Tax Act and Article 9.2 of the 2001 Individual Income Tax Act defines the concept in a negative manner. In this regard, *see* H. Pijl, *Beneficial Ownership and Second Tier Beneficial Owners in Tax Treaties of the Netherlands,* 31 Intertax 10, 353 (2003) DOI: 10.54648/taxi2003067. By other side, there are also common law countries where, even though including references to the term *beneficial owner* in their domestic laws, the concept lacks importance, at least in light of its main purpose, which is to combat treaty shopping. This is the case, e.g., of the United States where the courts have somehow abandoned the concept as a meaningful weapon against treaty shopping. This is especially evident in the *Aiken Industries* case (1971). *See* US: USTC, 5 August 1971, *Aiken Industries Inc. v. Commissioner of Internal Revenue*, 56 T.C. 925. In this case, the US court was able to deny treaty relief in absence of a *beneficial owner* provision. For a complete analysis of the case, *see* Y. Brauner, *Beneficial Owner In and Outside US Tax Treaties* in: M. Lang et.al. (eds) *Beneficial Ownership: Recent Trends*, IBFD, Amsterdam (2013), pp. 143-166. *See also*, De Broe, *supra* n. 255, pp. 423-430.
362. *See*, W. Eynatten, K. De Haen and N. Hostyn, *The Concept of 'Beneficial Owner' under Belgian Tax Law: Legal Interpretation is Maintained*, 31 Intertax 12, 523 (2003) DOI: 10.54648/taxi2003092. *See also*, De Broe, *supra* n. 255, p. 663.
363. Most of the references in the 2014 OECD Commentaries intend to clarify the interaction between a reduced WHT in the State of source, granted by a tax treaty, and the income derived from dividend, interest or royalties, which is received by intermediaries in the State of residence. In this sense, e.g., para. 12 of the 2014 Commentaries on Article 10 states: 'The requirement of beneficial ownership was introduced in paragraph 2 of Article 10 to clarify the meaning of the words 'paid ... to a resident' as they are used in paragraph 1 of the Article.' Likewise, para. 4 of the 2014 Commentaries on Article 12 provides: 'The requirement of beneficial owner was introduced in paragraph 1 of Article 12 to clarify how the Article applies in relation to payments made to intermediaries.' Indeed, since 1977 that this requirement was introduced to make clear that agents and nominees are not to be regarded as beneficial owners. *See* De Broe, *supra* n. 255, p. 656. However, none of these references is indeed a definition of the concept. *See* Eynatten, De Haen and Hostyn, *supra* n. 362. In fact, the information why the OECD introduced the *beneficial owner* requirement is still confidential. *See*, du Toit, *supra* n. 352, p. 179.
364. *Supra* s. 2.4.
365. Rust, *supra* n. 309, Article 3(2) at m.no. 121.
366. Vogel and Rust, *supra* n. 26, Introduction at m. nos 90 and 92.

counterpart in civil law countries.[367] The above makes it difficult for those countries to come up with an interpretation based on a concept that does not exist under their legislation.[368] In the second place, the history behind the notion of '*beneficial owner*' tells us that this was introduced to avoid treaty shopping. Therefore, a uniform interpretation seems to be more in line with this aim. Otherwise, there would be a clear risk that its ordinary meaning goes beyond its tax treaty use, ending up perhaps in cases of treaty override, which is especially clear in the case of countries that use the term *beneficial owner* as an anti-avoidance provision.[369] Furthermore, a domestic interpretation of the concept could also lead to inappropriate results, suggesting that an autonomous treaty meaning makes more sense. De Broe explains this situation well from the perspective of Belgian law, although its implications can also be extrapolated to any other civil law country. The term 'beneficial owner' is recognised neither under Belgian private law nor under Belgian tax law. Thus, many authors simply apply the equivalent concept of '*legal ownership*' under the Belgian Civil Code. In simple words, the '*beneficial owner*' would be either the person holding the legal title or another right in rem, e.g., *usufruct*.[370] Such interpretation, as expected, leads to the inappropriate result that a fiduciary owner or a nominee holding the legal title to the assets and collecting income from such property in his own name but on behalf of the principal is characterised as the beneficial owner and thus, is entitled to tax treaty benefits.[371] Similar inappropriate tax treaty results have been produced in the past due to the absence of equivalent concepts in common and civil law countries.[372] However, for

367. Civil law countries do not split ownership, at least not to the extent recognised in common law countries. De Broe, *supra* n. 255, p. 663.
368. Even though in those cases in which there is no meaning for the term under income tax law, but under other domestic laws, such meaning should only be used in those cases in which this is relevant for tax purposes. This has been widely recognised in the comparative jurisprudence. *See, e.g.*, the cases of *Thiel v. Federal Commissioner of Taxation* (Australia) and *Hoge Raad* (The Netherlands), referred at *supra* n. 243 and *supra* n. 311, respectively.
369. The US rules on conduit entities are an example of the above. *See* US: Treas. Reg. s. 1.881-3 et seq. These regulations empower the district director to disregard the participation of a conduit entity in a conduit financing arrangement if the taxpayer engages in such an arrangement pursuant to a tax avoidance plan. There is no reference to *beneficial owner* in the regulations, which rely more on domestic anti-abuse doctrines, such as *substance over form*, rather than the treaty concept. De Broe, *supra* n. 255, p. 670. Nevertheless, this is not surprising considering the little relevance of the concept of *beneficial owner* in the United States. Brauner, *supra* n. 361.
370. The legal concept of '*usufruct*' (from Latin 'usus fructus'), recognised in civil law countries, grants a person a limited right in rem to use something (usufruct holder). However, the full ownership remains in the hands of another person who has the legal title. *Ibid.*
371. De Broe, *supra* n. 255, pp. 668-669.
372. An example is the civil law concept of 'Commissionaire', which is recognised in civil law countries, but interpreted as if it were a simple 'undisclosed agency' (common law concept) for purposes of the application of Article 5(6) of the OECD Model. As the 'indirect representation' does not have counterpart in common law countries, all the commissionaires are treated as binding the principal in common law countries. However, in civil law countries, the commissionaire acts on behalf of the principal, but in his own name. Thus, the principal is not a party in the contracts with the customers and only relates to the commissionaire being therefore not bound, unless specific domestic law provisions provide the opposite. For tax treaty purposes, the above means that a 'commissionaire' will always be regarded as a PE in a common law country, whilst it will not be such in civil law countries, unless provided otherwise. The interpretation of the concepts of Commissionaire lead in the past to contradictory results in the

some authors, it is unobjectionable today that the term 'beneficial owner' is an international term, and a domestic meaning is only relevant inasmuch as this is consistent with the OECD Commentaries. That would be confirmed in the 2011 and 2012 OECD discussion draft papers on the concept of '*beneficial owner*' and the wording of the 2014 OECD Model, which suggests a contextual meaning without reference to any 'technical meaning that it could have had under the domestic law of the specific country [...]'.[373]

The treaty meaning of the term '*beneficial owner*', on the other hand, could be understood in three different manners: (i) the domestic meaning in common law jurisdictions imported to the OECD Model;[374] (ii) the meaning of the OECD Commentaries;[375] or (iii) the '*beneficial owner*' considered as the person to whom the income is attributed under the tax law of the residence and/or source State. This last alternative deserves special attention because the idea of considering the term '*beneficial owner*' as the person to whom income is attributed sets up a meaning of the concept beyond a simple anti-avoidance device,[376] driving some scholars to argue that the concept of '*beneficial owner*' would actually ensure that income is '*subject to tax*' in the State of residence, underlying the idea that the term '*beneficial owner*' would, in the end, help to prevent the outcome of DNT.[377]

---

famous *Zimmer* and *Dell* cases in France and Norway respectively. For a deeper analysis on this topic, *see* J. Avery Jones and D. Ward, *Agents as Permanent Establishments under the OECD Model Tax Convention*, 1 BTR 346 (1993). *See also, e.g.*, L. Parada, *Agents v. Commissionaires: A Comparison in light of the OECD Model Convention*, 72 Tax Notes Int'l 1 (2013).

373. *See* Kemmeren, *supra* n. 356, Pre Articles 10-12 at m.no. 31. *See also*, OECD, *Clarification of the Meaning of 'Beneficial Owner' in the OECD Model Convention. Discussion Draft*, OECD Publishing, Paris, 2011; OECD, *OECD Model Tax Convention: Revised Proposals Concerning the Meaning of 'Beneficial Owner' in Art. 10, 11 and 12*, OECD Publishing, Paris, 2012.

374. In this opinion, du Toit argues that there is a strong presumption that the term '*beneficial owner*' would have been included within the OECD Model adopting its meaning from domestic common law countries. du Toit' s argument is sustained in two main precedents. First, the drafter of the OECD Model opted for this term instead of alternatives, such as '*final recipient*', '*economic owner*' or '*beneficially entitled*'. Second, the term was used before its introduction within the OECD Model, and even after that there were no observations to the term, as it would have been expected from civil law countries. *See* du Toit, *supra* n. 352, pp. 178-179. In a critical opinion on this theory, De Broe argues that it is unrealistic to think in two civil law countries negotiating a treaty and intending to incorporate a common law concept, which is indeed exogenous to their legislation. Accordingly, De Broe states that there is no evidence in the OECD materials suggesting that the drafters wanted to incorporate the common law the meaning of the concept of beneficial owner. De Broe, *supra* n. 255, pp. 676-680.

375. On this matter, it is publicly known that the OECD Commentaries only describe in a negative fashion manner the persons who are not going to be considered as beneficial owners. Such a description comes from the 1977 OECD Model, and it is reinforced in the 1986 OECD Conduit Companies Report. De Broe, *supra* n. 255, pp. 680-690.

376. In this opinion *see, e.g.*, B. Arnold, *Tax Treaties and Tax Avoidance: The 2003 Revisions to the Commentary to the OECD Model*, 58 Bull. Intl. Taxn. 6 (2004), Journals IBFD. Arnold states that the beneficial ownership requirement in the Articles 10, 11 and 12 is more a fundamental rule of taxation rather than an anti-avoidance rule.

377. Oliver, e.g., explains his position as follows: 'The question that arises for purposes of defining the beneficial owner of the payment is whether the recipient of the payment is subject to tax on that payment in the resident country, not simply subject to tax or liable to tax generally, but subject to tax on that payment.' *See* J.D. Oliver et al., *Beneficial Owner*, 54 Bull. Int. Taxn. 7 (2000), Journals IBFD, p. 322.

The interpretation of the term '*beneficial owner*' as the person to whom income is attributed makes sense. Juridical double taxation, the main object and purpose of tax treaties,[378] could only arise if the income is attributed to a 'taxpayer' of the other Contracting State. Thus, the fact that the source State gives relief from double taxation only in those cases in which the income is attributed to a person who is a resident of the other State is certainly convincing. Similar suggestions might be extracted from the 1999 OECD Partnership Report with respect to transparent entities and access to treaty benefits when it states that the determination of the *beneficial owner* will be made by looking at the treatment of the entity in the country of residence of the taxpayer claiming the treaty benefits.[379] Nevertheless, there are several reasons to discard that such an interpretation necessarily means that the person to whom the income is attributed must be the person '*subject to tax*' in the State of residence, or which is the same, that the terms '*beneficial owner*' and '*subject to tax*' are equivalent ones. First, and as it has been already stressed, the term was officially introduced in the 1966 Protocol of the 1945 US-UK tax treaty with the idea of replacing the '*subject-to-tax*' clause contained in that specific treaty, under which the source country would deny benefits under Articles 10, 11 and 12 if the recipient of the income was not subject to tax in the residence country.[380] Thus, it would be at least contradictory to interpret the term '*beneficial owner*' in a manner of ensuring single taxation through a '*subject-to-tax*' requirement in the residence state when the concept precisely aimed to replace an original provision aiming to accomplish that target. Similarly, the original provision implied to exclude, for example, charities and pension funds from the reduced WHT granted by the treaty because they were actually exempt from taxation in the country of residence. However, this exclusion could only be regarded as a '*subjective subject-to-tax criterion*', as some authors refer to,[381] but in any case, it implies the requirement of effective taxation, i.e., an '*objective subject-to-tax criterion*'.[382]

Second, when revisiting the process of review of the 1963 OECD Model, it is possible to see that the OECD began asking delegates to identify some problems in the

378. With respect to the limitation of tax treaties to relieve all cases of juridical double taxation and economic double taxation, *see* the references in *supra* n. 196.
379. However, neither the OECD Partnership Report nor Article 1(2) OECD Model properly considers the interplay with the concept of *beneficial owner*. This issue is specifically analysed at *infra* Chapter 4, s. 3.3.2.3, regarding the OECD Partnership Report and s. 5.3.1, regarding Article 1(2) OECD Model.
380. *See* Vann, *supra* n. 355, and Ng, *supra* n. 354.
381. *See, e.g.*, M. Distaso and R. Russo, *The EC Interest and Royalty Directive- A Comment*, 44 Eur. Taxn. 4 (2004), Journals IBFD. *See also*, B. Terra and P. Wattel, *European Tax Law*, 6th ed., Kluwer Law International BV, The Netherlands, 2012.
382. A similar requirement is found, e.g., in the definition of qualified companies in the EU Interest and Royalty Directive, where a company must be '*subject*' to one of the specific listed corporate taxes, without being exempt. This requirement, however, seems to be rather clear in excluding companies that are '*subjectively exempt*' and does not mean any form of effective taxation of the interest or royalty income. *See* J. López Roriguez and G. Kofler, *Beneficial Ownership and EU Law* in: M. Lang et.al. (eds) *Beneficial Ownership: Recent Trends*, IBFD, Amsterdam (2013), p. 223.

draft document.[383] The UK delegation proposed the inclusion of a '*subject to tax*' clause as a way to solve the defective drafting of Articles 10, 11 and 12. The UK delegates observed: 'If a "subject to tax" test is not included in these Articles we think that the drafting is defective [...].'[384] However, in 1967, the Fiscal Committee created the Working Party No. 27, consisting of Luxembourg, France, and the Netherlands, dealing with the redrafting of the interest and royalties articles, which rapidly clarified that the real UK intent was indeed to propose either a '*subject to tax clause*', under which the source country would renounce its taxing rights inasmuch the resident country taxed the income or that Articles 10, 11 and 12 were to be applied only if they were paid to the '*beneficial owner*' of the income.[385] The above emphasises the different meanings of both concepts, a fact that was reaffirmed in the Working Party No. 1 of the Committee on Fiscal Affairs on Double Taxation, Working Group No. 23 (Germany-Belgium), where referring to Article 10 OECD Model, it recommended the second solution, i.e., the inclusion of the *beneficial owner's* concept rather than a '*subject-to-tax*' requirement.[386] Furthermore, the absence of correlation between the terms '*beneficial owner*' and '*subject-to-tax*' is also reaffirmed in the 2014 Commentaries on Article 12 OECD Model. The Commentaries emphasise that it is not specified whether the application or not of the exemption in the State of source should be conditional upon the royalties being subject to tax in the residence state.[387] In fact, they provided that those issues could be settled during the bilateral negotiation.[388] Thus, it is possible that the Contracting States agree during the negotiation of a tax treaty to the specific inclusion of a '*subject-to-tax clause*' within the treaty, but in any case, the requirement of subjecting to (effective) taxation of the income in the residence state should be considered as an ordinary interpretation of the concept of beneficial owner.

383. OECD, *Observations of Member Countries on Difficulties Raised by the OECD Draft Convention on Income and Capital*, Fiscal Committee TFD/FC/216, Paris, 1967, available at www.taxtreatieshistory.org.
384. Vann, *supra* n. 355, p. 282. *See also*, OECD (1967), *supra* n. 383, p. 14. According to Avery Jones, the uncertainty created by the United Kingdom, suggesting that a '*subject-to-tax*' test was required, or alternatively that there should be a beneficial owner requirement, attended to the interpretation of specific domestic rules which existed during the time of the discussion draft in 1967, but that no longer existed at the implementation of the '*beneficial owner*' provision in the 1977 OECD Model. In other words, the inclusion of the provision was indeed not necessary. For a full analysis, *see* Avery Jones, *supra* n. 320, pp. 333-339.
385. 'The United Kingdom Delegation considers that as they stand Articles 10, 11 and 12 are defective in that they would apply to dividends, interests and royalties paid to an agent or a nominee with a legal right to the income. To remedy this situation, it proposes either that a "subject to tax clause" be introduced, under which the country of source would give up its right to tax only if the country of residence taxed the income, or else that these Articles be made to apply only to income paid to the "beneficial owner".' *See* OECD, *Working Party No. 27 of the Fiscal Committee (Luxembourg-France-The Netherlands), Report on suggested amendments to Articles 11 and 12 of the Draft Convention, Relating to Interest and Royalties Respectively*, FC/WP27(70)1, Paris, 1970, p. 13, available at www.taxtreatieshistory.org.
386. OECD, *Working Party No. 1 of the Committee on Fiscal Affairs on Double Taxation, Working Group No. 23 (Germany-Belgium), Revision of Article 10 of the 1963 Model Convention and Commentary Thereon*, CFA/WP1(73)2, Paris, 1973, available at www.taxtreatieshistory.org. *See also*, Ng, *supra* n. 354, p. 523.
387. OECD Commentary on Article 12 concerning the taxation of royalties, para. 6.
388. *Ibid.*

3.3 Conflicts of Qualification and DNT: The New Interpretation of Article 23A(1) OECD Model

A third provision that might be interpreted as preventing DNT is related to what is known in doctrine as *conflicts of qualification*. A *conflict of qualification* arises when a tax treaty contains terms from domestic law that are understood in their respective meanings by the residence or source State or that can be interpreted in an independent or autonomous manner.[389] These *qualification conflicts* originated, *inter alia*, due to the interaction of Article 3(2) OECD Model and the normal disparities between the domestic systems of the Contracting States, and they can derive either in double taxation or DNT.[390] For example, in this case, two States characterise differently the same item of income or the same entity.[391] With regard to DNT, it might arise because of the application of Article 23A OECD Model (exemption method) when two Contracting States, due to differences in their domestic laws, apply different provisions of the tax treaty in such a way that the source State considers itself prevented from taxing the income at issue whilst the residence State, in application of another distributive rule, considers that the source State has the right to tax the income and therefore exempts the income under Article 23A(1) OECD Model.[392] The OECD Model and its Commentaries deal specifically with these cases in paragraphs 32 et seq. of the OECD Commentary on Article 23A and 23B of the OECD Model.

The OECD approach, originated in the Partnership Report of 1999[393] and included in the 2000 OECD Commentaries (updated in 2008) on Article 23A and 23B OECD Model, suggests that the phrase '*in accordance with the provisions of this Convention, may be taxed*', included in those Articles, should also be interpreted in relation to possible cases of DNT arisen due to the application of Article 23A.[394] This is to say, the

389. Vogel and Prokisch, *supra* n. 254, p. 82.
390. *Ibid.*, *See also*, C. Marchgraber, *Conflicts of Qualification and Interpretation: How Should Developing Countries React?*, 44 Intertax 4, 307 (2016) DOI: 10.54648/taxi2016023.
391. *See* the example of para. 32.4 of the OECD Commentary on Article 23A and Article 23B concerning the methods for elimination of double taxation, referred to the conflict derived from the different qualification of the same entity for tax purposes. These conflicts, however, are not strictly related to the different characterisation of entities (like conflicts of allocation of income), but rather to the discrepancies with regard to the nature of an item of income. For the analysis of hybrid entities and the entitlement to tax treaty benefits, *see infra* Chapter 4.
392. OECD Commentary on Article 23A and Article 23B concerning the methods for elimination of double taxation, para. 32.6. *See also*, R. Sudoczky, *Double Taxation Relief, Transfer Pricing Adjustments and State Aid Law: Comments* in: I. Richelle, E. Traversa and W. Schön (eds) *State Aid Law and Business Taxation*, Springer, Heidelberg (2016), p. 169.
393. Article 23A(1) OECD Model states: 'Where a resident of a Contracting State derives income or owns capital which, in accordance with the provisions of this Convention, *may be taxed* in the other Contracting States [...].'
394. OECD Commentary on Article 23A and Article 23B concerning the methods for elimination of double taxation, para. 32.6. With respect to the avoidance of double taxation, the phrase '*in accordance with the provisions of this Convention*' is interpreted by the OECD Commentaries as requiring the residence state to grant relief from double taxation (through exemption or credit) in case of conflicts of qualification resulting from differences in domestic law. In these cases, the residence state is bound by the qualification of the source state. OECD Commentary on Article 23A and Article 23B concerning the methods for elimination of double taxation, para. 32.3. *See also*, Lang, *supra* n. 327, p. 204.

OECD proposes that the residence state is not obliged to exempt an item of income or capital if the source state considers itself prevented from taxing that item of income or capital, which would otherwise *have had the right to tax*, if the residence state considers, in the application of another distributive rule, that the source state *has the right to tax* the income, and therefore, exempts the income as per Article 23A OECD Model.[395] Therefore, DNT might be avoided by means of the interpretation of Articles 23A(1) and 23B(1) OECD Model.[396] The 2008 update of the OECD Model extends this approach even to the cases where the source state refrains from levying tax under its domestic law but would have been prevented anyway by the treaty, understood in light of its domestic law.[397] In simple words, the application of the OECD approach would go beyond the different qualifications of the same treaty rule.[398]

The conclusion that the new OECD interpretation of Article 23A(1) OECD Model effectively counteracts cases of DNT when a conflict of qualification is involved, *ergo* constituting a sort of indication that the avoidance of DNT might be regarded as an object and purpose of the tax treaties, is certainly not precise and it can be subject to a serious criticism. First, Article 23A(1) OECD Model is applicable only if the income '*may be taxed*' in the State of source.[399] A person '*may be taxed*' in the State of source '*in accordance with the provisions of this Convention*' only if the tax treaty does not prevent the State from doing so.[400] Therefore, whether or not the tax was indeed levied in the source state is absolutely irrelevant.[401] A different interpretation should simply derive absurd results. As accurately explained by Lang: '[...] the same approach should be followed in the mirror situation [the exercise of taxing rights]. If the source state, under its domestic interpretation of the treaty terms can exercise taxing rights but refrain from doing so domestically, the income still "may be taxed" in "accordance with the provisions of the Convention". Therefore, a resident state that, under its domestic law interpretation, takes the position that the income falls under a different allocation rule and that therefore it may also exercise taxing rights should be prevented from doing so since the income 'may be taxed' in the other state'.[402] Second, there are qualification conflicts to which Article 23A(1) OECD Model is simply not applicable. Therefore, in those cases, DNT should be a tolerated outcome. Vogel explains that tax treaties contain two types of distributive rules: complete and open.[403] Complete distributive rules are those that, whilst maintaining the taxation by one of the Contracting States, exclude the other Contracting States from taxing the item of income

395. A. Rust, *The New Approach to Qualification Conflicts Has Its Limits*, 57 Bull. Intl. Taxn. 2 (2003), Journals IBFD, p. 45. The original 2000 version used the phrase 'have taxed' instead of 'have had the right to tax' and the phrase 'to tax' instead of 'to have the right to tax'. *See* Lang, *supra* n. 327.
396. Marchgraber, *supra* n. 390, p. 309.
397. Lang, *supra* n. 327.
398. *Ibid.*
399. *Ibid.*
400. *Ibid.*
401. *Ibid.*
402. *Ibid.*
403. K. Vogel, *Conflicts of Qualification: The Discussion is Not Finished*, 57 Bull. Intl. Taxn. 2 (2003), Journals IBFD, p. 43.

in question. They can be normally distinguished by the use of the words '*shall be taxable only*', e.g., Article 7(1) when it provides that the profits of an enterprise that is not regarded as a PE in the source state shall be taxable only in the State of residence, or Article 8(1) OECD Model that provides that the profits from the operation of ships or aircraft in international traffic shall be taxable only in the State where the place of effective management of the enterprise is situated;[404] or Article 19(1)(a) when, according to the interpretation of the State of residence, the taxpayer receives a salary from the other Contracting State and becomes a resident solely for the purpose of rendering a service.[405] The distributive rules might be considered as a *lex specialis* to Article 23 and be applicable at least side-by-side.[406] On the other hand, open distributive rules are those which maintain the taxation by one of the Contracting States. However, they do not determine whether and how the income in question will be taxed by the taxpayer's residence state. They normally use the words '*may be taxed*', e.g., Article 7(1), when it provides that income received through a PE in the State of source *may be* taxed by that State. Contrary to the complete distributive rules, these rules must be completed by Article 23 OECD Model. Furthermore, the distinction between '*shall be taxable only*' and '*may be taxed*' is not accidental, and it is indeed a standard pattern of tax treaties, observed by the OECD Model and by all the treaties following it.[407]

Following Vogel's classification of the tax treaty provisions, one could conclude that Article 23A(1) OECD Model is not effective in solving cases of DNT in cases where the residence state applies a complete distributive rule that allows only the State of source to tax the income.[408] Indeed, Article 23A(1) OECD Model does not impose an additional obligation on the State of residence to exempt the income (Article 23 OECD Model might be applied).[409] Likewise, the obligation to exempt the income contained in the distributive rule is still in force because Article 23A(1) cannot lift the State of residence from that obligation. In other words, the source state's qualification is not binding on the residence state.[410] Thus, if the source state believes that it is prevented from taxing the income, this income remains untaxed in both residence and source, and Article 23A(1) will not be of help.[411]

Moreover, tax treaties not only contain distributive rules, but they also have non-distributive rules, e.g., rules determining the territorial and personal scope of the treaty, the taxes to which it applies, the definition of treaty terms, etc. All these provisions use terms taken from domestic laws of the Contracting States. Therefore,

---

404. *Ibid.*
405. Rust, *supra* n. 395, p. 49. Also, Article 20 OECD Model can be a good example when a student or business apprentice becomes a resident of the State in which he is studying or training. *See* J. Avery Jones, *Conflicts of Qualification: Comments on Prof. Vogel's and Alexander Rust's Articles*, 57 Bull. Intl. Taxn. 5 (2003), Journals IBFD, p. 184.
406. Rust, *supra* n. 395.
407. *Ibid.*
408. Vogel, *supra* n. 403, pp. 42-43.
409. *Ibid.*
410. *Ibid.*, p. 50.
411. This does not mean that a different solution can be followed, e.g., the application of Article 25 OECD Model (Mutual Agreement Procedure). *See* OECD Commentary on Article 23A and Article 23B concerning the methods for elimination of double taxation, para. 32.5. In this opinion, *see* Avery Jones, *supra* n. 405.

conflicts of qualification might also arise.[412] Vogel explains how unsolved DNT cases also remain in the case of non-distributive rules, despite the new interpretation of Article 23A and 23B OECD Model, in the following example: 'An independent singer who is a citizen of Austria alternates between performing in Austria and in Germany. He has a permanent contract with an opera company in Germany, committing him to a certain number of appearances each year. During the taxable year in question, he had, in addition, some separate engagements in Austria. In both states, he lives in hotels. On several occasions, he stayed part of the day in Austria and part in Germany. Therefore, the aggregate of his stays in each of the two states was more than six months. He received dividends and interest from portfolios in a third country. Both Austria and Germany want to tax these receipts.'[413] The issue in this case is that both countries would allege unlimited tax liability (worldwide taxation). Germany would argue that a stay of more than six months constitutes a *habitual abode*, whilst Austria would say that, under Austrian law, he is a resident, although he does not have a habitual abode. Austria and Germany will prefer to exclude the application and Articles 10 and 11 of the OECD Model and to apply Article 21 (other income), which grants exclusive taxation to the resident state. For that purpose, however, the singer should also be considered a resident for tax treaty purposes. The tiebreaker rule of Article 4(2)(b) OECD Model establishes that if the taxpayer does not have a permanent home available in either State (he was living in hotels), the residency will be that of his *habitual abode*, a term that should be interpreted in accordance with the domestic laws.[414] Article 4(2)(b) OECD Model does not contemplate the time necessary to be considered *habitual*, and it just says that the time must be *sufficient*. Thus, a resort to domestic law in accordance with Article 3(2) OECD Model is needed. For Austrian law purposes, there was no habitual abode; therefore, his habitual abode would be in Germany. For German tax purposes, however, the habitual abode implies the fact of staying more than six months, which means that under German domestic law, the singer has a habitual abode in both countries. This would imply that according to the tiebreaker rule of Article 4(2) OECD Model, the citizenship of the singer would prevail (he is Austrian). Germany thus cannot tax either, being the result no other than DNT. Vogel's example can be criticised because it does not include the possibility of a MAP to resolve the dual residency problem.[415] However, beyond this legitimate criticism, the example illustrates very well that when a term exists in domestic law and is used in a tax treaty context, qualification conflicts might arise, and they cannot be solved by application of Article 23A(1) or 23B(1) OECD Model, at least not in cases of non-distributive rules.

Some final words should be said regarding the tax policy implications of the new interpretation of Article 23A(1) OECD Model upon developing countries or emergent

412. Although Vogel recognises that, as these conflicts do not refer to types of income, a varying qualification does not lead to double taxation and very rarely to DNT. Vogel, *supra* n. 403, pp. 42-43.

413. *Ibid.*, p. 42 at 'Case 2'.

414. Vogel, however, recognises that this is controversial, and there are tax scholars who consider that the term *habitual abode* has an autonomous interpretation. *Ibid.*

415. Avery Jones, *supra* n. 405, p. 186.

economies. Despite the fact that Article 23 UN Model recently included the OECD Commentaries of paragraphs 32.1-32.7, it is still not clear why developing countries should agree to accept the OECD's interpretation that the residence state always taxes in the case of a conflict of qualification leading to DNT (or low taxation as well).[416] More important is the wording of the updated 2008 OECD Model, which states that the residence state should not be obliged to apply the exemption method if the source state, in light of its domestic law, interprets the provision of the treaty as precluding it from taxing an item of income or capital, which would not have taxed under its domestic law anyway. If such an interpretation is adopted, tax incentives normally granted by developing countries to attract FDI might be totally nullified if the exemption method is finally not applied in the residence state.[417]

3.4 Conflicts of Interpretation and DNT: Article 23A(4) OECD Model

As noted before, the OECD interpretation of Article 23A(1) OECD Model does not mitigate all the cases of DNT being its effects rather limited to the qualifications resulting from disparities between the domestic tax systems of the Contracting States. Indeed, if, e.g., DNT arises from the varying evaluation of the facts or the diverging interpretation of a treaty provision (known as 'conflicts of interpretation'), Article 23A(1) OECD Model is absolutely ineffective in ensuring single taxation.[418] Considering the above, the OECD included Article 23A(4) in the OECD Model in order to deal specifically with those cases of DNT resulting from the different interpretations of a provision of the Model Convention or the facts of a case.[419]

As per Article 23A(4), '[t]he provisions of paragraph 1 shall not apply to income derived or capital owned by a resident of a Contracting State where the other Contracting State applies the provisions of this Convention to exempt such income or capital from tax or applies the provisions of paragraph 2 of Article 10 or 11 to such income'. Therefore, under the OECD approach, the residence state shall not be obliged to grant an exemption if the source state interprets the facts of a case or the provisions of the Convention in such a way that it considers itself fully or partially restricted from taxing an item of income or capital, whilst the residence state adopts a different interpretation of the facts or the provisions of the Convention, considering that the same item of income or capital should be taxed in the source state, which thus would lead to apply the exemption.[420] In this order of ideas, the effect of Article 23A(4) OECD

416. For an extended analysis, *see* Marchgraber, *supra* n. 390.
417. Developing countries have similar incentives to negotiate 'tax-sparing' clauses with tax credit countries, because despite the tax incentive in the host country, if a credit is not granted in home country (investor), the incentive can be nullified. *See* a further analysis on *tax-sparing clauses* at *infra* s. 4.1.1.
418. Marchgraber, *supra* n. 390, p. 312.
419. OECD Commentary on Article 23A and Article 23B concerning the methods for elimination of double taxation, para. 56.1.
420. OECD Commentary on Article 23A and Article 23B concerning the methods for elimination of double taxation, para. 56.1.

Model is identical to a 'switch-over clause'.[421] The OECD also emphasises that these cases where Article 23A(4) OECD Model applies should be distinguished from those 'where the qualification of an item of income under the domestic law of the source state interacts with the provisions of the Convention to preclude that State from taxing an item of income or capital in circumstances where the qualification of an item under domestic law of the residence state would not have had the same result'.[422]

Regardless of the above, the truth is that Article 23A(4) OECD Model is not completely effective in solving all the cases of DNT derived from a conflict of interpretation. According to the OECD Commentaries, if the source state considers that it *may tax* an item of income or capital in accordance with the OECD Model, but no tax is actually payable on that income or capital because of domestic law, DNT shall be an unavoidable outcome.[423] In such a case, the residence state must apply the exemption method because the exemption at source does not result from the Convention but rather from the domestic law of the source state, and a tax treaty cannot take away that domestic exemption.[424] This conclusion is also corroborated by paragraph 34 of the Commentary on Article 23A and 23B OECD Model, which establishes that the residence state must exempt the item of income or capital which, in accordance with the Convention, *may be taxed* by the source state, regardless of whether or not the right to tax is in effect exercised by the source state.[425]

4 DOUBLE NON-TAXATION AND SPECIFIC TAX TREATY PROVISIONS

This Section now turns to analyse some examples of the tax treaty practice in which, through the inclusion of specific provisions within the tax treaties, the outcome of DNT is either tolerated or prevented. Nevertheless, whatever path is followed, it is worth highlighting that the use of these provisions appears to be exceptional, and it responds to specific tax policy reasons. The above simply emphasises that neither the outcome of DNT nor its prevention is indeed an object and purpose of the tax treaties unless the Contracting States have expressly decided otherwise.

4.1 DNT as an Outcome Tolerated by Tax Treaties

There can be many examples in which tax treaties tolerate the outcome of DNT.[426] However, hereby will refer exclusively to the cases of *tax-sparing* and *matching-credit*

421. *Infra* s. 4.2.2.
422. OECD Commentary on Article 23A and Article 23B concerning the methods for elimination of double taxation, para. 56.3.
423. OECD Commentary on Article 23A and Article 23B concerning the methods for elimination of double taxation, para. 56.2.
424. *Ibid.*
425. OECD Commentary on Article 23A and Article 23B concerning the methods for elimination of double taxation, para. 34.
426. In some cases, it would even be possible to affirm that the outcome of DNT is directly pursued. This is, for example, the case of income derived from research activities from teachers or

clauses, commonly used by developing countries or emergent economies to attract FDI. In these cases, and due to more important policy reasons, countries are simply indifferent when facing the outcome of DNT.

4.1.1 Tax Sparing

Many countries, especially developing countries, provide a series of tax incentives, including, e.g., tax holidays or reduced corporate tax rates, to attract FDI.[427] The success of these tax incentives, however, does not depend entirely on the exclusive policy in the country hosting the investment. In fact, in most cases, the success of the tax incentive will also depend upon the taxation of the income derived from that investment in the investors' home country and the subsequent relief of the potential double taxation generated. In this regard, if the investors' home country uses the exemption method to relieve double taxation, there will generally be no effects upon the tax incentive provided by the host country inasmuch the exemption method applies, disregarding the amount of taxes paid in the investment's host country, which is indeed the general rule.[428] However, if the home country applies the exemption only to the extent the source State has a minimum level of taxation, then the tax incentive is neutralised.[429] Similarly, if the home country applies the tax credit method to relieve double taxation, the effect of the tax incentive is again nullified.[430] This is because the tax credit method generally applies only with respect to the taxes effectively paid in the foreign country. To avoid such a result, host countries normally negotiate the inclusion of *tax-sparing clauses* that enable the investors to obtain a tax credit in their home

professors. An example is the Article 21 of the 1971 France-Portugal Tax Treaty, which exempts in both Contracting States the income received by a professor or a teacher who is a resident of a Contracting State and who is moving to the other states for a maximum of two years. *See* Gutmann, *supra* n. 46, p. 90.

427. One reasonable explanation with regard to the importance of attracting FDI in developing countries can be found in the change of paradigm of many countries of Central and Eastern Europe and Latin America after the 1970s. The political movement from socialism to market economy, followed by the trend towards a freer flow or investment capital, and specially, the process of privatisations can be seen as a clear reason of that. Indeed, previously, many of these countries were very suspicious regarding FDI, which was seen as a form of post-colonialism or dollar-imperialism. *See* A. Easson, *Tax Incentives for Foreign Direct Investment, Part I: Recent Trends and Countertrends*, 55 Bull. Intl. Taxn. 7 (2001), Journals IBFD, p. 267. More recently, and in the context of the OECD Global Minimum Corporate Income Tax Rate or Pillar 2, *see* A. Navarro, *Jurisdiction Not to Tax, Tax Sparing Clauses, and the OECD Minimum Taxation (GloBE) Proposal*, Nordic Tax Law Journal 1 (2021) DOI: 10.2478/ntaxj-2021-0004.

428. Generally, the exemption method should apply in this manner, without paying attention to the taxes paid in the other country, contrary to the tax credit that is generally granted in a 'dollar-by-dollar' basis. For a comparative analysis between the credit and exemption methods as international mechanisms used to relief double taxation *see, e.g.*, G. Maisto, *supra* n. 90. *See also*, G. Kofler, *supra* n. 92. The simplicity of the exemption method, when compared to the credit method, have made it the preferred method to relieve double taxation among continental European countries, fitting better the objectives of the internal market. In this regard, *see, e.g.*, W. Schön, *supra* n. 83. *See also*, M. Helminen, *supra* n. 90.

429. Although the OECD Commentaries use a different expression: '[...] the incentive granted by a State of source *may be* reduced [...] (emphasis added)'. *See* OECD Commentary on Article 23A and Article 23B concerning the methods for elimination of double taxation, para. 72.

430. *Ibid.*

country upon the taxes that they should have paid in the host country in the absence of the tax incentive. As expected, in some cases, the absence of taxation in the host country due to a specific tax incentive added to the application of the credit method upon a statutory tax (not effectively paid) in the home country may derive in DNT.[431] The result of DNT, in this case, is an accepted outcome that guarantees the success of the tax incentive in the host country and, ultimately, helps to promote investment and economic growth in developing countries.[432]

Some tax scholars have, nevertheless, openly criticised the exaggerated importance given to *tax-sparing clauses*.[433] They basically argue that tax sparing is a problem only when the investor invests through a branch in the host country because if he does it through a subsidiary, the residence country (home country) will generally not impose taxes on the profits generated by the subsidiary and the dividends received from the subsidiary will be exempt in the home country due to the participation exemption.[434] Then, if the developed country also exempts the profits of the foreign branch, there would not be a problem at all.[435] Accordingly, other scholars sustain that tax-sparing clauses can constitute a clear infringement of the non-discrimination principle recognised in Article 24 OECD Model and other supranational legislation, such as EU Law.[436] A similar criticism can be found in the *OECD Report on Tax Sparing*,

431. Although this is only true in those cases in which the tax incentive attends to a reduction in the tax rates that affect the investment or simply in a tax holiday. Other tax incentives do not attend to the direct payment of taxes, e.g., in the case of an accelerated depreciation granted.

432. L. Schoueri, *Tax Sparing: uma reconsideração da reconsideração* in: R. Mariz de Oliveira at al. (eds) *Direito Tributário Atual*, Dialética/IBDT (2011), pp. 93-108. *See also, e.g.*, A. Celine, R. Desbordes and J. Mucchielli, *Do Tax Sparing Agreements Contribute to the Attraction of FDI in Developing Countries*, 14 Intl. Tax and Pub. Fin. 5 (2007); J. Amico, *Brazil: Developing and Implementing Tax Treaty Policy: The Tax Sparing Clause*, 43 Bull. Intl. Fisc. Doc. 8/9 (1989).

433. In a complete analysis regarding base erosion in developing countries, *see* H. Ault and B. Arnold, *Protecting the Tax Base of Developing Countries: An Overview*, Paper on Selected Topics in Protecting the Tax Base of Developing Countries (UN), Draft Paper No. 1, United Nations, New York (2013), p. 32.

434. *Ibid*. The statement of these authors is correct, although it disregards that one of the major capital exporter countries in the world, i.e., the United States, does not apply the participation exemption, but rather the tax credit upon profits repatriated. Thus, it could rarely be argued that a developing country, which has important tax incentives to attract FDI, is indifferent in the negotiation of a treaty with the United States. Accordingly, the United States has also firmly rejected the inclusion of tax-sparing clauses within its tax treaties, despite the fact that the tax treaty between the United States and Pakistan was indeed the first one to include such a provision in 1957, although finally rejected by the US Senate. Previously, in 1953, it was also discussed in the report of the British Royal Commission, which recommended the adoption of tax-sparing clauses to aid British investment abroad. The proposal was finally rejected in 1957. *See* OECD, *Tax Sparing – A Reconsideration*, OECD Publishing, Paris, 1997, p. R (14)-10 and 11.

435. This critic, however, is not entirely precise, because it does not consider the role of CFC rules around the world, and whose strength is recommended in the latest OECD BEPS Action 3, as an effective manner to tax the undistributed profits of a subsidiary established in the host country. This can be especially true when CFC rules apply to both active and passive income, e.g., in Brazil. *See* references at *supra* n. 276.

436. This is because *tax-sparing* clauses involve a worse treatment for residents' domestic investors than foreign investors. Likewise, it could also be argued that they infringe the principle of tax neutrality (CEN), although it is not less valid to consider that the different treatment between residents and non-residents is justified by the public policy goal of encouraging investment in lesser-developed countries. For a further analysis, *see* R. Mason, *Tax Discrimination and Capital Neutrality*, 2 World Tax J. 2 (2010), Journals IBFD, p. 136.

which also makes equivalent the concepts of tax sparing and matching credits.[437] The main point of criticism stated in the report was that tax-sparing and matching-credit clauses had a very limited influence on foreign investor decisions, opening new possibilities for tax evasion and other types of abuse.[438] Likewise, the OECD Commentaries on Article 23A and 23B, concerning the methods for elimination of double taxation, sustain that tax-sparing provisions constitute a departure from those articles,[439] being thus a reproduction of the principles summarised in the OECD Report on Tax Sparing, which remain unchanged until today.[440]

Nonetheless, and beyond the criticism that can exist with respect to the effectiveness and efficiency of tax-sparing clauses, it is undeniable that they still represent an important tax policy tool for developing countries, and only a few countries are prepared to take the risk of unilaterally withdrawing these clauses from their tax treaties.[441] In a nutshell, unless all developing countries decide to withdraw these provisions at once, the incentive to keep them is still higher.[442] The outcome of DNT will thus remain an acceptable one in those treaties which, although exceptionally, still include *tax-sparing clauses*.

4.1.2 Matching Tax Credits

Unlike the similitude with *tax-sparing clauses*, the matching credit clauses have nothing to do with tax incentives or any other kind of subsidy provided by the source country.[443]

Generally speaking, a *matching-credit* provision implies that the residence State will credit a fixed amount of tax on certain items of income ('notional tax') derived from the source State, regardless of whether or not those items were subject to effective taxation in that State.[444] The tax credit granted will be normally higher than the one

437. For a critical analysis on this matter, *see* V. Arruda and A. Trindade, *Tax Sparing and Matching Credit: From An Unclear Concept to An Uncertain Regime*, 67 Bull. Intl. Taxn. 8 (2013), Journals IBFD.
438. OECD (1997), *supra* n. 434, p. R(14)-19 to 24.
439. OECD Commentary on Article 23A and Article 23B concerning the methods for elimination of double taxation, para. 74.
440. Arruda and Trindade, *supra* n. 437, p. 399.
441. Easson, *supra* n. 427, p. 273. However, from a practical point of view, as many tax-sparing provisions are subject to a limited period of time, most of them have already elapsed. This implies that the practical significance of the provisions has decreased. Nevertheless, this does not mean that developing countries have stopped using them as a tool to attract investment, as it is the case of many countries part of the MERCOSUR. For an analysis on the economic influence of tax sparing and matching credits, *see, e.g.*, C. Forcada, *The Economic Effect of Taxation on the Flow of Software Copyright Royalties in MERCOSUR*, 65 Bull. Intl. Taxn. 7 (2011), Journals IBFD.
442. This is illustrated as the classic economic theory known as the 'prisoner's dilemma.' *See* Easson, *supra* n. 427.
443. The OECD, however, mixes both the concepts of tax sparing and matching credits in its Report on Tax Sparing. *See* OECD (1997), *supra* n. 434.
444. The predetermination in the tax treaty of the exact amount of credit to be granted by the State of residence makes the difference between a *matching credit* and a *tax-sparing* provision because whilst the former contains this predetermination, the latter responds exclusively to a

actually paid or withheld in the source country, even higher than the one provided by the specific tax treaty. If the notional tax allowed as a credit is equal to the tax at residence, then a full exemption will be granted. In other words, the outcome of DNT will again be an inevitable consequence of the *matching credit* provision in the tax treaty.

4.2 DNT as an Outcome Specifically Avoided by Tax Treaties

Contrary to the cases of *tax sparing* and *matching credits* where the countries directly tolerate the outcome of DNT, sometimes tax treaties attempt to prevent an item of income from remaining untaxed in both the residence and source State, affecting thus the country which, due to the tax treaty, limited its rights to tax a specific income. For this purpose, the Contracting States normally negotiate the inclusion within their tax treaties of either *subject-to-tax* or *switch-over* provisions. Nevertheless, the use of these provisions is exceptional and sometimes is subject to justified criticism, both derived from their ambiguous interpretation as well as from some tax policy concerns.

4.2.1 Subject-to-Tax Clauses

As noted already, one of the options for those countries that decide to grant tax treaty benefits only in situations where the item of income in question is taxed in the other Contracting State is through the inclusion within their tax treaties of specific provisions known as '*subject to tax clauses*'. Although the wording of *subject-to-tax clauses* can vary from country to country and sometimes from tax treaty to tax treaty within the same country, they all have the same aim in common, which is to ensure single taxation either in the residence or source state.[445]

The OECD Commentaries recognise the possibility of including *subject-to-tax* provisions within tax treaties as an exception to the absolute obligation of the State of

---

specific tax incentive in the source country which, due to this fact, does not exercise its taxing rights. *See* Arruda and Trindade, *supra* n. 437, p. 400. *See also*, L. Freitas de Moraes e Castro, *Brazil's Anti-Treaty Shopping Measures: Current and Future Developments regarding Beneficial Ownership and Limitation on Benefits Clauses in Tax Treaties*, 65 Bull. Intl. Taxn. 12 (2011), Journals IBFD, p. 662 (n. 6).

445. In Austria, e.g., some tax treaties include a *subject-to-tax* clause to ensure taxation in Austria as the source country. An example of the above can be found in the Article 15(2) of the Australia-Austria tax treaty, where besides the requirement of the 183 days, the country of employment (source state) is prevented from exercising its taxing rights with respect to income from dependent services only to the extent the income is or will be subject to tax in the residence state. Similar provisions can be found in the Article 20(1) of the tax treaty Austria-Malaysia, the Article 12(3) of the former tax treaty Canada-Austria, or Article 13 of the treaty Austria-UK and Austria-Switzerland. *See* M. Achatz, B. Gröhs and R. Weninger, *Taxation of Non-resident Individuals in Austria*, 58 Bull. Intl. Taxn. 11 (2004), Journals IBFD, p. 529. Germany also includes these clauses in some of its treaties. For example, Article 23(3) of the German-New Zealand tax treaty (1978) and Article 23(1) of the German-UK tax treaty (2010). However, the inclusion of *subject-to-tax clauses* should not be considered as a general German treaty policy. *See* J. Lüdicke, *Exemption and Tax Credit in German Tax Treaties – Policy and Reality* in: P. Baker and C. Bobbett (eds) *Tax Policy Math, Essays in Honor of John F. Avery Jones*, IBFD, Amsterdam (2010), p. 292.

residence to relieve double taxation through the exemption method in cases where the other Contracting State does not tax the respective item of income.[446] Those cases could arise when no taxes are applied in the State of source with respect to the specific item of income or capital, or the taxes are not effectively collected due to, e.g., a set off of losses, an expiration of the statutory time limit, or a simple mistake.[447] Nevertheless, the application of *subject-to-tax clauses* is not absent of interpretation problems, mostly derived from their varied wording in different countries and the absence of common rules at the level of the OECD Model. For example, whilst some countries might consider that 'subject to tax' is equivalent to 'liable to tax' (i.e., being subject to taxation in a jurisdiction, regardless of whether taxes are finally paid), other countries could simply consider that 'subject to tax' is indeed a synonym of effective taxation. However, effective taxation does not always imply 'to be taxed', but sometimes could be regarded as the simple act of 'being subject to a tax regime'. In most of the cases, the absence of domestic jurisprudence increases the uncertain results. The above can be seen, e.g., in the case of the *subject-to-tax provision* contained in Article 22(1)(a) of the German-Luxembourg tax treaty.[448] This clause targets situations in which income remains wholly or partially untaxed in Luxembourg, as Luxembourg does not or cannot exercise its taxing rights under the tax treaty due to its domestic rules.[449] The treaty, therefore, grants the exemption to relieve double taxation in Germany only in those cases of income sourced in Luxembourg, which is 'effectively taxed' *('tatsächlich besteuert')* in Luxembourg.[450] Nevertheless, it is not entirely clear in Luxembourg what 'effective taxation' means for purposes of the tax treaty, as there is no administrative guidance or case law that might help in clarifying this term. Another practical application of the above can be found, e.g., in the Belgian tax treaty practice.[451] Belgian tax treaties generally include in Article 23 the exemption method as a relief of double taxation. In the case of some tax treaties,[452] however, the expression 'may be taxed', normally used in Article 23 OECD Model, is substituted by the expression 'is taxed'.[453] In parallel, when interpreting the treaty relief provision and the expression 'is taxed', the Belgian tax authority has been inclined to apply a domestic doctrine known as '*exemption vaut impôt*', which means that the wording 'is taxed' is interpreted as being

446. OECD Commentary on Article 23A and Article 23B concerning the methods for elimination of double taxation, para. 35.
447. *Ibid.*
448. Convention between the Federal Republic of Germany and The Grand Duchy of Luxembourg for the avoidance of double taxation of 23 April 2012 (which replaced the treaty of 1958), Article 22(1)(a).
449. F. Jacob and A. Hagena, *The Germany-Luxembourg Income and Capital Tax Treaty (2012)*, 66 Bull. Intl. Taxn. 10 (2012), Journals IBFD, p. 537.
450. *Ibid.*
451. N. Bammens, *Subject-to-Tax Clauses in Belgian Tax Treaties – 'Exemption Vaut Impôt' Doctrine Rejected Again in Case Law*, 68 Bull. Intl. Taxn. 8 (2014), Journals IBFD, p. 432. *See also*, L. De Broe and N. Bammens, *Interpretation of Subject-to-Tax Clauses in Belgium's Tax Treaties: Critical Analysis of the 'exemption vaut impôt' Doctrine*, 63 Bull. Intl. Taxn. 2 (2009), Journals IBFD.
452. For example, the treaties with Estonia, Greece, Latvia, Lithuania and the United States. *See* De Broe and Bammens, *supra* n. 451, p. 69.
453. Bammens, *supra* n. 451.

'*subject to a tax regime in the source country*' and not necessarily '*to be subject to effective taxation*' in the source state.[454] The Belgian jurisprudence has been quite contradictory on this matter. The Brussels Court of Appeal, e.g., in the *Sidro* case in 1970, ruled that the condition of Article 23 of the Belgian-Canada tax treaty should be interpreted as 'effective taxation'.[455] However, the Belgian Supreme Court ruled later on in favour of the taxpayer and provided that the requirement of being taxed abroad is not subject to any condition based on the nature, form or amount of the foreign tax.[456] In other words, it is enough to be subject to a tax regime in the source State, even though no taxes are finally assessed. In a recent decision ('*Mons Court* case') of 2014,[457] however, the *Tribunal de Première Instance de Mons* turned back and reaffirmed that the expression 'is taxed' should be interpreted as requiring effective taxation in the source State and denying the application of the '*exemption vaut impôt*' doctrine.[458] As per the *Tribunal de Première Instance de Mons*'s decision, the First-tier Tribunal (Tax Chamber) in the UK, during the *Weiser* case in 2012, set up a clear distinction between '*liable to tax*' and '*subject to tax*'.[459] In the decision, it was stated that whilst '*liable to tax*' is a term normally used in reference to a taxpayer that falls within the scope of a state's taxation in general, '*subject to tax*' is used in relation to the chargeability of a specific item of income.[460] In other words, the term '*subject to tax*' requires that income be actually within the charge to tax in the sense of being included in the computation of the taxpayer's taxable income, with the result of a tax being paid.[461] In other cases, it is doubtful whether or not a *subject-to-tax provision* is indeed a 'subject-to-tax requirement'. Such is the case of Germany, which includes a '*general subject to tax clause*' in some of its tax treaties, known as '*Regress clauses* or *Rückfallklauses*'.[462] An example can be found in the wording of Article 23(3) of the 1981 German-Canada tax treaty, which reads as follows: 'For purposes of this Article, profits, income or gains of a resident of a Contracting State shall be deemed to arise from sources in the other

454. *Ibid.*
455. The case concerned *Sidro*, a Belgian company, was the majority shareholder of a Canadian company. During the 1960s, *Sidro* sold its shares in the Canadian subsidiary, realizing a capital gain. However, no taxes were charged on that capital gain in Canada. Accordingly, Belgium's unilateral relief provided for a reduced tax rate on income earned and taxed abroad. The Court of Appeals in Brussels held that the reduced rate could not be applied, because the capital gains were not 'effectively taxed abroad.' *See* De Broe and Bammens, *supra* n. 451, p. 68. *See also*, Belgium: Brussels Court of Appeals, 28 May 1969, *Rev. Fisc.* 81 (1970).
456. *Ibid.*
457. Belgium: Mons., 11 September 2013, No. 11/1078/A.
458. The case, referred to the application of Article 23(2)(a) of the Belgium-Lithuania tax treaty (1998), concerned a Belgian resident who worked as a consultant in Lithuania for the EBRD. According to Lithuanian domestic law, the remuneration received by the Belgian resident was taxable in Lithuania, but the Framework Agreement between Lithuania and the EBRD required Lithuania to exempt it. The taxpayer, relying in the '*exemption vaut impôt*' doctrine, argued that Belgium should exempt the remuneration even though this has not been subject to tax in Lithuania, because of the Framework Agreement. *See* Bammens, *supra* n. 451, pp. 432-433.
459. *See* the reference to the *Weiser* case law at *supra* n. 345.
460. Cleave, *supra* n. 345, p. 282.
461. *Ibid.*, p. 281.
462. H. Chen, *Interpretation of Subject-to-Tax Clauses* in: M. Schilcher and P. Weninger (eds) *Fundamental Issues and Practical Problems in Tax Treaty Interpretation*, Linde, Vienna (2008), pp. 379-380.

Contracting State if they are taxed in that other Contracting State in accordance with this Agreement.'[463] The BFH, however, has been clear in sustaining that such clauses do not constitute *subject-to-tax clauses.*[464]

Other problems associated with the use of *subject-to-tax* clauses refer to the evident contradiction between *subject-to-tax clauses* and the pure application of the exemption method to relieve double taxation.[465] As I have argued before in this work, the exemption method, unlike the credit method to relieve double taxation, should be applied regardless of the consideration of the taxation of the income in the other country.[466] This simplicity is, in fact, one of the main reasons for countries to opt for the exemption rather than the credit method to relieve double taxation, and it is also one of the reasons for its justified success in continental Europe, where it is the preferred method.[467] This is why some authors have recommended that unless some particular reasons inspired in the other Contracting States' tax system motivate the inclusion of *subject-to-tax clauses*, a good tax treaty policy should indeed refrain from doing that.[468]

An issue of particular interest in the whole study of *subject-to-tax clauses* is how some countries have opted for introducing these clauses onto domestic laws, overriding the tax treaty provisions that refer to the application of the exemption method. This is the case of Germany, e.g., which in 2004 introduced a treaty override provision under which income from employment is only treaty exempt insofar as the taxpayer gives evidence that this has been taxed or that the other State waived its right to tax.[469] Subsequently, in 2007, it introduced a second domestic rule by which the tax treaty exemption is denied if the income is not taxed in the other country by reason of a domestic law that forbids that State to tax the income for the sole reason that the taxpayer is not liable to unlimited taxation, because of his residence, habitual abode (domicile), place of management, seat or any other similar criterion.[470] In parallel, and

463. Agreement between Canada and the Federal Republic of Germany for the avoidance of Double Taxation with respect to Taxes on Income and certain others of 17 July 1981 (also 'German-Canada Tax Treaty'), Article 23(3).
464. DE: BFH 17.02.2003.1 R 14/02. BStBl II 2004, referred to Article 23(3) of the German-Canada Tax Treaty.
465. Likewise, one could also argue that the economic idea behind the application of the exemption method (CIN) is violated by the use of these subject-to-tax clauses. Nevertheless, this analysis certainly exceeds the purpose of this chapter and this whole work.
466. OECD Commentary on Article 23A and 23B concerning the methods for elimination of double taxation, para. 34.
467. *See, e.g.*, Schön, *supra* n. 89.
468. *See* Lüdicke, *supra* n. 445, p. 296.
469. DE: s. 50d(8) of the Income Tax Act ['*Einkommensteutergesetz* – EStG']. According to Lüdicke, this provision is also inconsistent with a long-standing unilateral exemption policy of certain employee income derived from Germany's non-tax treaty partners. *See* Lüdicke, *supra* n. 445, p. 294. Interestingly, however, in a decision of 15 December 2015, the Federal Constitutional Court (BVerfG – *Bundesverfasungsgericht*) held that s. 50d(8) of the Income Tax Act is absolutely compatible with the German Constitution, despite the fact of overriding tax treaty law. *See* DE: BVerfG, Beschl. 15.12.2015 – 2 BvL 1/2, URL: http://www.bverfg.de/e/ls20151215_2bvl000112.html.
470. DE: s. 50d(9), No. 2 of the Income Tax Act ['*Einkommensteutergesetz* – EStG']. This domestic rule was introduced as a reaction to the jurisprudence of the German Federal Tax Court [*Bundesfinanzhof* (BFH)], specifically to the landmark decision of 17 December 2003 regarding the application of the 1981 Canada-Germany tax treaty, according to which relevant provisions

most importantly, a further treaty override provision was introduced in German law, with retroactive effect in this case, according to which a treaty exemption is not granted inasmuch the other State applies the treaty in a way that income is not taxed or it is taxed at a very reduced rate.[471] For some authors, however, this latter provision works in practice more as a *switch-over clause* rather than a *subject-to-tax clause.*[472] Needless to say, tax treaty override represents a real threat to legal certainty.[473]

Finally, it is worth assuming the question of whether a *general subject-to-tax clause* to prevent DNT shall be included in the OECD Model. Such type of provision can be found, e.g., in Article 26(2) of the Nordic Tax Convention, although its application is limited. According to Article 26(2), if the treaty attributes the right to tax to any income or property to the source State, and that State, according to its domestic law, does not subject entirely such income or property to tax liability, that income not included in the tax liability shall be taxable only in the residence State. This provision, however, does not apply to qualification or interpretation conflicts. It does not apply in case of disagreements between the Contracting States on the facts and circumstances of a case or on the interpretation of the Convention. In other words, it deals very well with cases of DNT caused by national laws, but it does not, however, for cases of DNT derived by the application of the treaty in a situation of classification conflict. It is undeniable that such a clause could make things easier in terms of avoiding ambiguous interpretations of tax treaties, at least with respect to the avoidance of DNT.[474] However, it is not surprising that no discussion was carried out during (or after) the major tax revolution started with the BEPS Project in 2013. It is, therefore, my view that inasmuch no general *subject-to-tax provision* comes into play, the use of *subject-to-tax-clauses*, and subsequently the idea of ensuring single taxation as a tax treaty aim, will remain very exceptional.

---

contained in the treaty should not be interpreted such that they allow Germany to tax only items of income that are not subject to tax in the other Sate. This provision is triggered in cases where income that would be taxed in the hands of residents of the source state, it is exempt for non-residents, either by application of a treaty or domestic law. However, it excludes general domestic tax exemptions applicable to both residents and non-residents. *See* R. Resch, *The New German Unilateral Switch-Over and Subject-to-Tax Rule*, 47 Eur. Taxn. 10 (2007), Journals IBFD, p. 480.

471. DE: s. 50d(9), No. 1 of the Income Tax Act ['*Einkommensteutergesetz* – EStG']. This provision only applies in a tax treaty context. Therefore, it is not triggered because of any tax exemption of the domestic laws of the Contracting States. *Ibid.*

472. *Ibid.*

473. The OECD addressed the problem of treaty override in its 1989 report, in which it recommended member countries to avoid enacting any legislation that is intended to have effects that contradict international treaty obligations. *See* OECD, *Tax Treaty Override*, OECD Publishing, Paris, 1989. For an analysis on the debate with respect to treaty override in Germany *see, e.g.*, A. Perdelwitz, *Treaty Override – Revival of the Debate over the Constitutionality of Domestic Treaty Override Provisions in Germany*, 53 Eur. Taxn. 9/Special Issue (2013), Journals IBFD, p. 445.

474. Chen, *supra* n. 462, pp. 383-384.

4.2.2 Switch-Over Clauses

Switch-over clauses are another way by which countries may ensure that income does not remain untaxed, preventing DNT from arising. Most notably, these clauses allow a State to switch from the exemption method to the credit method in cases where DNT arises.[475] As per the *subject-to-tax clauses*, the design and use of the *switch-over clauses* vary from country to country, although they all have in common the aim of avoiding that income remains untaxed because of the application of the exemption method to relieve double taxation.[476]

The inclusion of *switch-over clauses* within tax treaties is, however, not always an acceptable tax policy, and it can become irrelevant under certain circumstances. This is especially true if the same 'switch-over' effect can be achieved under other provisions in the OECD Model, e.g., under the OECD interpretation of Article 23A(4) OECD Model. As already stressed during this chapter, the OECD approach on this matter is that the residence state shall not be obliged to grant the exemption method if the source state interprets the facts of a case or the provisions of the Convention in such a way that it considers itself fully or partially restricted from taxing a specific item of income or capital.[477] This is exactly the same effect that could be achieved through a *switch-over provision*. Likewise, the use of switch-over clauses is redundant in cases where a *subject-to-tax clause* was already included within the same tax treaty. Having in mind the aim of preventing DNT, it is certainly impossible to imagine the practical function of a *switch-over clause* when an item of income was already taxed due to the proper application of a *subject-to-tax clause*.

The spread use of switch-over clauses can also generate special tax treaty concerns when domestic *switch-over clauses* are introduced within domestic laws overriding tax treaty obligations.[478] This problem could be even exacerbated if a massive treaty override practice is implicitly encouraged by specific legislative projects at a supranational level. An example of the above can be materially found in the original text of the Anti-Tax Avoidance Directive (ATAD) in Europe, which was issued at the beginning of 2016. In brief, the European Directive was part of a whole Anti-Tax

475. Lang, *supra* n. 21, p. 129.

476. Germany, e.g., has used *switch-over clauses* in its tax treaties since the 1980s. The original intention of them was to avoid double taxation and DNT, although later the clauses were restricted to the aim of eliminating DNT. The switch from the exemption to the credit method applies if in the Contracting States items of income or capital are placed under different provisions or attributed to different persons, and inasmuch the conflict cannot be solved before through an MAP, and if, as a result of the difference in placement or attribution, the relevance income or capital would remain untaxed or taxed lower than without this conflict. Thus, in theory, the application of the clause depends on the (un)successful prior MAP, although this requirement has been overridden by the application of domestic provisions included in 2007, which made the MAP requirement useless. *See* Lüdicke, *supra* n. 445, p. 291. For an example of the German tax treaty practice of including switch-over clauses, *see, e.g.*, Article 23(1)(e)(aa) of the Germany-United Kingdom tax treaty (2010) or Article 24(1) of the Germany-Singapore tax treaty (2004).

477. *Supra* s. 3.4. *See also*, OECD Commentary on Article 23A and Article 23B concerning the methods for elimination of double taxation, para. 56.1.

478. The issue of tax treaty override and the Constitutional concerns derived from it has been largely discussed in Germany. *See, e.g.*, Lüdicke, *supra* n. 445; Perdelwitz, *supra* n. 473.

Avoidance Package that intended to address a number of issues connected to the implementation of the OECD BEPS Project. Among the provisions proposed was the inclusion of a *switch-over clause* (Article 6)[479] that would allow an MS to refrain from the application of the exemption method to relieve double taxation in cases where the taxpayer receives profit distributions or proceeds from a disposal of shares held in an entity located in a third country (not MS) regarded as low-tax jurisdiction.[480] Beyond the criticisms stressed somewhere else by commentators regarding the limitation in the use of the exemption method to relieve double taxation and the comparison between statutory corporate tax rates to trigger the application of this article,[481] the promotion of a massive treaty override was indeed a major fact, especially because of the prevalence of EU Law over treaty commitments, at least regarding tax treaties signed after 1 January 1958.[482] Fortunately, the final text of the EU directive was modified, and indeed, it does not include a *switch-over* provision anymore. This decision seems to be more in line with the whole OECD BEPS project, which has never included a literal *switch-over clause*[483] and which ultimately aims to tax income where profits are sourced or the value is created.[484]

It is interesting to note that even considering the undesirable effects of *switch-over clauses* described above, and regardless of the inclusion of Article 23A(4) in the OECD Model, some countries insist on the use of these clauses to avoid DNT. The above, in the author's view, is not only a recognition that Article 23A(4) OECD Model is not completely effective in solving all situations of DNT derived from conflicts of interpretation but also a demonstration that countries understand that without the explicit inclusion of these type of clauses, DNT cannot be implicitly understood as an aim or purpose of the tax treaties themselves, remaining therefore as an exception within the tax treaty practice.

479. The original text of Article 6(1) reads as follows: 'Member States shall not exempt a taxpayer from tax on foreign income which the taxpayer received as a profit distribution from an equity in a third country or as proceeds from the disposal of shares held in an entity in a third country or as income from a permanent establishment situated in a third country […].'

480. The determination of a low-tax jurisdiction criterion is made based on a comparison between both the corporate statutory tax rates of the State of the subsidiary and the State of the taxpayer. If the profits or proceeds were subject to a statutory corporate tax rate lower than 40% of the statutory tax rate that would have been charged under the applicable corporate tax system in the MS of the taxpayer. *Ibid.*

481. *See* A. Navarro, L. Parada and P. Schwarz, *The Proposal for an EU Anti-avoidance Directive: Some Preliminary Thoughts*, 25 EC Tax Rev. 3 (2016).

482. Because of Article 351 TFEU, tax treaties signed before 1 January 1958 would prevail over EU Law. For the prevalence of EU Law over tax treaty commitments, *see* EU: Judgment in *Costa v. E.N.E.L.*, C-6/64, EU:C:1964:66.

483. Indirectly, however, we could argue that the defensive rule promoted under the OECD BEPS Action 2 has a similar effect than a *switch-over clause*. Indeed, as we will see further on in this work, this rule obligates a country to deny an exemption in the receiving country of the payment if the income received was deducted in the payor country. *See infra* Chapter 5.

484. The concept of 'value creation' has been, however, subject to criticism by important scholars, basically because of its lack of consistency with the traditional application of the arm's length standard. *See, e.g.*, W. Schön, *Transfer Pricing Issues of BEPS in the Light of EU Law*, 3 British Tax Rev. 417 (2015) and Y. Brauner, *supra* n. 226.

5 THE IMPACT OF THE OECD BEPS ACTION 6 PROPOSAL

The OECD has proposed a modification of the OECD Model, which might include expressly the avoidance of DNT as an object and purpose of the tax treaties. This proposal has been issued by the 2013 OECD BEPS Action Plan 6,[485] and it is ratified and explained in detail in the subsequent 2014 deliverables[486] as well as in the 2015 final report.[487] It is also ratified in the wording of the recently released draft of the 2017 update to the OECD Model.[488] When finally introduced, these changes might directly impact the interpretation of tax treaties as per the rules of Article 31 of the VCLT already analysed in section 2 of this chapter.

The OECD proposal can be divided into three main amendments concerning the outcome of DNT. First, a modification of the title of the OECD Model, including a reference to tax evasion and tax avoidance. Second, a recommendation of a preamble, which includes that tax treaties cannot create opportunities for non-taxation or reduced taxation through tax evasion or tax avoidance, and third, the inclusion of the concept of STR. All of them are separately analysed in the following subsections.

5.1 Modification of the Title of the OECD Model

The first modification introduced by the OECD BEPS Action Plan 6 was to replace the current title of the OECD Model with the following: 'Convention between (State A) and (State B) for the elimination of double taxation with respect to taxes on income and on capital and the prevention of tax evasion and avoidance.'[489]

Although this modification is part of the 2013 OECD BEPS Action Plan, it is, in fact, not a novel feature in the OECD Model. Specifically, in 2003, paragraph 7 of the OECD Commentaries on Article 1 was already modified in order to include such a reference to tax evasion and tax avoidance. Paragraph 7 reads now as follows: '[...] It is also a purpose of tax conventions to prevent tax avoidance and evasion'.[490] Accordingly, the OECD Model 2014 provides that States that wish to include in the title a reference to either the avoidance of double taxation or both the avoidance of double taxation and the prevention of fiscal evasion may do so.[491] Therefore, the real impact of this modification with regard to the question of whether tax treaties aim or not to prevent DNT is practically zero. First, it refers to two concepts (tax evasion and tax

485. *Ibid.*
486. OECD, *Preventing the Granting of Treaty Benefits in Inappropriate Circumstances*, OECD/G20 Base Erosion and Profit Shifting Project, OECD Publishing, Paris, 2014.
487. OECD (2015), *supra* n. 226.
488. OECD, *Draft Contents of the 2017 Update to the OECD Model Convention*, OECD Publishing, Paris, 2017. *See also*, OECD, *Draft Contents of the 2017 Update to the OECD Model Convention, Comments received on the 11 July public release*, OECD Publishing, Paris, 2017a.
489. *Ibid.*, p. 91. The current title of the OECD Model 2014 says: 'Convention between (State A) and (State B) with respect to taxes on income and capital,' without any reference to double non-taxation. The wording is ratified in the draft contents of the 2017 update to the OECD Model. OECD (2017), *supra* n. 488.
490. OECD Commentary on Article 1 concerning the persons covered by the Convention, para. 7.
491. Title of the 2014 OECD Model Tax Convention, n. 1.

avoidance) that are not equivalent to the outcome of DNT and whose scope is already included within Article 26 (new Article 27) OECD Model.[492] As I have argued already in this work, fiscal or tax evasion is, in fact, an aim of tax treaties recognised in Article 26 of the OECD Model (new Article 27) regarding the exchange of information, and which refers to problems of governance failure in collecting taxes due to a lack of information.[493] However, tax evasion has nothing to do with ensuring single taxation or avoiding DNT. Likewise, tax avoidance supposes that a taxpayer can use legal alternatives available or can create new ones to reduce its tax burden as low as possible, not being an illegal behaviour. Therefore, this behaviour of the taxpayer will be considered objectionable or not depending on the level of tolerance in a determined jurisdiction and the effect on the public revenues.[494] Second, the absence of a direct reference to DNT in the title allows me to conclude that an interpretation that tax treaties aim to prevent DNT should be simply discarded. If that aim wanted to be included, there is nothing that prevents its explicit inclusion in the title of the OECD Model.

5.2 The Inclusion of a Recommended Preamble in the OECD Model

Jointly with a modification in the title of the OECD Model, the OECD Model recommends a preamble that includes expressly that tax treaties are not intended to 'create opportunities for non-taxation or reduced taxation through tax evasion or tax avoidance (including through treaty-shopping arrangements aimed at obtaining reliefs provided in this Convention for the indirect benefit of residents of third States)'.[495] The modification of the preamble is accompanied by an inclusion of paragraph 16.1 in the Introduction, which says: "The changes made expressly recognize that the purpose of the Convention are not limited to the elimination of double taxation and that the Contracting States do not intend the provisions of the Convention to create opportunities for non-taxation or reduced taxation through tax evasion and avoidance.'[496] The above, if finally included within a negotiated treaty,[497] might have an immediate

492. *Supra* Chapter 1, s. 4.
493. *Ibid.*
494. *Supra* Chapter 1, s. 4.2.
495. OECD (2015), *supra* n. 226, p. 92. A similar wording was included in the revised preamble of the 2016 US Model, which states: 'The Government of the United States of America and the Government of [...], intending to conclude a Convention for the elimination of double taxation with respect to taxes on income without creating opportunities for non-taxation or reduced taxation through tax evasion or avoidance (including through treaty-shopping arrangements aimed to obtain reliefs provided in this Convention for the indirect benefit of residents of third states), have agreed as follows:' United States Model Income Tax Convention (2016), front page. *See also* the same wording in the recently released draft contents of the 2017 update to the OECD Model. OECD (2017), *supra* n. 488.
496. OECD (2015), *supra* n. 226, p. 93.
497. The literal wording of this proposed preamble (and title) has already been used in the new tax treaty between Germany and Australia, which says: 'Australia and the Federal Republic of Germany, Desiring to further develop their economic relationship and to enhance their cooperation in tax matters, Intending to conclude an Agreement for the elimination of double taxation with respect to taxes on income and on capital *without creating opportunities for*

impact on the interpretation of tax treaties since the preamble of tax treaties is part of their context and, therefore, a fundamental part of their interpretation.[498]

Nevertheless, the wording of the preamble at stake is open to criticism both in form and in substance. First, the proposed preamble includes not only cases of DNT but also cases of 'reduced taxation', whatever reduced taxation means for this purpose. The above might create serious problems of interpretation. First, it is not clear which references should be used to compare tax systems to determine that a level of 'reduced taxation' has been achieved. For example, one might compare using statutory tax rates or 'effective tax rates' or, perhaps, a pre-elaborated OECD table might determine the 'minimum' of taxation required by a country. Second, and as it has been stressed before in this work, DNT and reduced taxation (under-taxation) should not be regarded as equivalent concepts because, in fact, they represent two different outcomes.[499] Whilst the former implies a complete absence of taxation, the latter supposes that at least a minimum level of taxation was achieved. Thus, the item of income in question was taxed at least once. However, when put together (non-taxation and reduced taxation), we confuse again the nature of DNT, creating an *a priori* negative perception of it.[500]

Second, it has been intrinsically suggested in the wording of the proposed preamble that only the cases of DNT derived strictly from cases of tax evasion or tax avoidance should be a matter of concern.[501] Hence, one should conclude that in all of those cases in which the outcome of DNT has been generated neither through fraudulent conduct from the taxpayer that it is aimed to cause an illegal reduction in the amount of tax to be paid nor through an objectionable, but not illegal conduct aimed to reduce the taxpayer's tax burden, the outcome of DNT is not to be regarded as a cause of concern at all. This intrinsic limitation is remarkable because it recognises that DNT is not, per se, problematic. However, it might generate new problems of interpretation because both the concepts of tax evasion and tax avoidance are eminently domestic concepts, and as such, their boundaries are not homogeneous for all countries.[502] As already stressed in Chapter 1, tax evasion is generally recognised as an illegal conduct among countries. However, tax avoidance is not. Therefore, the level of tolerance to tax avoidance, i.e., the limits imposed by domestic anti-avoidance provisions, in each country will certainly determine the extent to which the preamble of the treaty

---

non-taxation or reduced taxation through tax evasion or avoidance (including through treaty-shopping arrangements aimed at obtaining reliefs provided in this Agreement for the indirect benefit of residents of third States [...].' (emphasis added). *See* Agreement between Australia and the Federal Republic of Germany for the Elimination of Double Taxation with respect to Taxes on Income and on Capital and the Prevention of Fiscal Evasion and Avoidance of 11 November 2015, p. 2.

498. Article 31(1) of the VCLT.
499. *Supra* Chapter 1, s. 2.2.
500. *Ibid.*
501. The use of the word 'through' instead of 'for example' or 'among others' in the proposed Preamble clearly suggests a narrow interpretation. The preamble states that tax treaties are not intended 'to create opportunities for non-taxation or reduced taxation *through* tax evasion or tax avoidance [...]'. *See* OECD (2015), *supra* n. 226.
502. *Supra* Chapter 1, s. 4.

contributes to its interpretation. In other words, the concept of tax avoidance can be interpreted autonomously, and it will always require a reference to domestic law.

Third, and finally, this author considers that the wording of the proposed preamble certainly exceeds the mandate of the G-20 when the BEPS Project was launched. If recalled, the BEPS Action Plan stated: 'No or low taxation is not per se a cause of concern, but it becomes so when it is associated with practices that artificially segregate taxable income from the activities that generate it.'[503] This is to say, tax treaty entitlement is conditioned to substance and economic functionality, i.e., activities that contribute to value creation or active trade or business, etc. Therefore, taxpayers should not be seen as abusing a treaty where genuine businesses are set up, even if non-taxation derived from the application of that treaty is the result of those businesses. As already stressed in this work, DNT can indeed be an acceptable result within a tax treaty context, provided that non-artificial arrangements are observed.[504]

5.3 The New Concept of *'Special Tax Regime (STR)'*

The OECD BEPS Action 6 also includes a proposal, not originally introduced in the 2014 draft,[505] addressing what is called Special Tax Regimes (STR).[506] Under the proposal, the treaty benefits related to interest (Article 11 OECD Model), royalties (Article 12 OECD Model) and other income (Article 21 OECD Model) would be denied in case of persons that are subject to an STR with respect to these particular items of income.[507] For this purpose, an STR with respect to an item of income or profits 'means any legislation, regulation or administrative practice that provides a preferential effective rate of taxation to such income or profit, including through reductions in the tax rate or the tax base [...]'.[508] Several exclusions from the special tax regime status are also provided for any legislation, regulation or administrative practice that, e.g., is designed to prevent double taxation or that implements the principles of Article 7 or Article 9 OECD Model, among others.[509] The proposal also includes the respective modification in Articles 11, 12 and 21 OECD Model in order to entitle the source state to tax these

503. OECD (2013), *supra* n. 2, p. 10.
504. A similar view was provided in the Revised Public Discussion Draft on Action 6. *See* OECD, *Comments Received on Revised Public Discussion Draft, Follow-up Work on BEPS Action 6: Prevent Treaty Abuse*, OECD Publishing, Paris, 2015, pp. 100-101.
505. OECD (2014), *supra* n. 486.
506. OECD (2015), *supra* n. 226, pp. 96-98.
507. *Ibid.*
508. *Ibid.*, p. 96.
509. The 2015 Final Draft states: 'However, the term shall not include any legislation, regulation or administrative practice: (i) the application of which does not disproportionately benefit interest, royalties or other income, or any combination thereof; (ii) except with regard to financing income, that satisfies a substantial activity requirement; (iii) that is designed to prevent double taxation; (iv) that implements the principles of Article 7 (Business Profits) or Article 9 (Associated Enterprises); (v) that applies to persons which exclusively promote religious, charitable, scientific, artistic, cultural or educational activities; (vi) that applies to persons substantially all of the activity of which is to provide or administer pension or retirement benefits; (vii) that facilitates investment in widely-held entities that hold real property (immovable property), a diversified portfolio of securities, or any combination thereof, and that are subject to investor-protection regulation in the Contracting State in which

types of income, beneficially owned by a resident of the other Contracting State, if such resident is subject to an STR at any time during the taxable period in which the income is paid, as well as a treaty rule to deal with the future changes in Contracting States' domestic laws.[510]

Unsurprisingly, the STR proposal of BEPS Action 6, originally tabled by the US delegate to the Working Party, mirrors the draft of the 2016 US Model, which includes a similar concept in Article 3(1).[511] Unlike the OECD proposal, however, the draft of the US Model is accompanied by a more detailed Technical Explanation draft, from which it is possible to determine that the tax policy behind its introduction is no other than to mitigate the generation of DNT in instances where tax treaties are abused in combination with tax regimes that offer especially beneficial tax status. As provided in the Preamble of the of the 2016 US Model: 'Consistent with the G20-OECD Base Erosion and Profit Shifting (BEPS) initiative, the STR provisions are intended to mitigate instances of double non-taxation whereby a taxpayer uses provisions in the tax treaty, combined with STR, to pay no or very low tax in either treaty country.'[512] This intention is later reaffirmed in the same text when it states: 'It is inappropriate for tax treaties to reduce US statutory withholding rates on deductible US source payments when the related income is subject to no or very little tax.'[513] However, and although not expressly recognised in the 2015 Final Report on Action 6, it was perhaps the existence of STR related to the transfer of intellectual property rights from one country to a lower-tax jurisdiction and the resulting granting treaty benefits to base-eroding payments (i.e., 'IP Boxes'), the real aim behind this proposal.[514]

5.3.1 *A Critical View upon the Concept of STR*

There is no doubt that the aim of the concept of STR is to prevent DNT in cases where it derives from the use of these regimes. Some deficiencies in the design of the rule,

the investment entity is established; or (viii) that the Contracting States have agreed shall not constitute a special tax regime because it does not result in a low effective rate of taxation.' *Ibid.*, p. 97.

510. *Ibid.*, p. 98.
511. US Model Tax Convention (2016), Article 3(1).
512. Preamble to US Model Income Tax Convention of 17 February 2016, p. 2.
513. *Ibid.*
514. The analysis of the 'IP Box regimes' certainly exceeds the purpose of this work. However, for further and detailed analysis on this subject *see, e.g.*, R. Danon, *General Report* in: Cahiers de droit fiscal international Vol. 100A – *Tax Incentives for R&D* (IFA 2015), pp. 17-56; E. Traversa, *Tax Incentives and Territoriality Within the European Union: Balancing the Internal Market with the Tax Sovereignty of Member States*, 6 World Tax J. 3 (2014), Journals IBFD; P. Palazzi, *Taxation and Innovation*, OECD Taxation Working Paper No. 9, OECD Publishing, Paris, 2011; I. Zammit, *Centralized Intellectual Property Business Models – Tax Implications of EU Patent Box Regimes*, 69 Bull Intl. Taxn. 9 (2015), Journals IBFD; Å. Hansson and C. Brokelind, *Tax Incentives, Tax Expenditures Theories in R&D: The Case of Sweden*, 6 World Tax J. 2 (2014), Journals IBFD; R. Matteotti and P. Roth, *Tax Incentives on Research and Development*, Archives de droit fiscal Suisse May/June 2015, Special issue IFA Basel 2015, available at www.asa.online, acceded on 11 January 2017; M. Soler and E. Gil, *Encouraging Research and Development (and Innovation) in the Spanish Tax System*, 70 Bull. Intl. Taxn. 8 (2016), Journals IBFD. For a comprehensive study of IP box regimes in Europe, *see* P. Schwarz, *IP Box Regime im Europäischen Steuerrecht*, Nomos Verlagsgesellschaft, 2017.

however, still leave serious doubts regarding its capability to achieve its aim and open the door for criticism. In this order of ideas, it can be first argued that the scope of application of the STR rule is very broad and subjective. On the one hand, it is broad if we consider that under the OECD proposal, the STR rule applies to both related and unrelated transactions, even though the information available as to whether a tax regime is special or not is not equally available in both situations. For example, it is expected that both taxpayers and tax authorities will require detailed information about a taxpayer in the other Contracting States. This information can easily be obtained in case of related parties; however, it is possible to imagine some important limitations in the case of unrelated ones. Likewise, it is more likely that loan or royalty transactions made with the purpose of wrongfully acceding to the benefits of a treaty be carried out between related rather than unrelated parties. Hence, I do not see any strong reason to extend the application of the STR rule to unrelated parties.[515] On the other hand, it is subjective since there is no objective benchmark as to what a tax regime should be compared with. For example, should a tax regime be regarded as special with respect to another just because the former contains different tax depreciation rules or different rules for claiming financial expense? What if a tax regime contains special features included in a comprehensive way within the tax regime as a whole? Is that also 'special' for purposes of the STR rule? The proposed paragraph 15.2 of the introduction of the 2017 OECD Model is, unfortunately, helpless to provide some clarity. This paragraph only contains a general statement which provides as follows: 'States should also consider whether there are elements of another State's tax system that could increase the risk of non-taxation, which may include tax advantages that are ring-fenced from the domestic economy.'[516] Nevertheless, it is still unclear what a 'tax advantage' means for this purpose. A reference could be made, however, to the US Model, which provides some more objective criteria. One of the requirements for a statute, regulation or administrative practice to be regarded as an STR is that it 'is generally expected to result in a *rate of taxation* that is less than the lesser of: (A) 15%; or (B) 60% of the general statutory rate of company tax applicable in the other Contracting State'.[517] This objective criterion can certainly help improve the design of the STR rule, but more importantly, avoid taxpayers and tax authorities from adopting conflicting positions with respect to the concept of STR.

Accordingly, it is not entirely clear to which extent an 'administrative practice' can become an STR. In other words, it is clear that the term STR includes the ruling practice of a State (perhaps the only real motive of this rule), although a ruling practice can vary a lot from country to country. Some insights might, however, be extracted again from the US Model Technical Explanation's draft, which provides an illustrative example on this matter. The example states as follows: '[I]f a taxpayer obtains a ruling

515. *Ibid.* The scope of the STR was already narrowed in the 2016 US Model, where the rule applies only to related-party interest payments, royalty payments and guarantee fee payments within the scope of Article 21 US Model. A similar modification should be made with respect to the OECD proposal.
516. Paragraph 15.2 of the Introduction of the 2017 OECD Model. *See* OECD (2015), *supra* n. 226, pp. 94-95.
517. US Model Income Tax Convention (2016), Article 3(1)(iii).

providing that its foreign source interest income will be subject to a low rate of taxation in the residence State, and that rate is lower than the rate that generally would apply to foreign source interest income received by residents of that State, the administrative practice under which the ruling is obtained is a special tax regime.'[518] Although the example is clear, providing that a ruling will be included as administrative practice, it is still not evident from that example if both private and public rulings will be equally considered.

Moreover, within the list of exceptions of legislation, regulations or administrative practices that should not be regarded as STR, there is an exception by which any legislation, regulation or administrative practice 'designed to prevent double taxation' is not considered an STR. Following this order of ideas, if a taxpayer obtains a ruling in State X, which grants the application of a domestic exemption to relieve double taxation with respect to foreign-sourced interest coming from State Z and which is beneficially owned by a resident in country Y, that ruling should not be regarded as an STR, for purposes of the application of the treaty between State Y and State X, because it aims to prevent double taxation. Subsequently, if State Y does not tax the interest either,[519] the DNT outcome remains an acceptable one. A similar conclusion can be achieved if that rule is introduced by statute or any other regulation. This effect could, however, be neutralised by the parallel proposal in the BEPS Action 6 that intends to make a tax treaty responsive to certain future changes in a country's domestic tax laws.[520] Under this proposal, if at any time after signing the Convention, either of the Contracting State provides an exemption from the taxation to resident companies or resident individuals for substantially all foreign source income (including interest and royalties), the provisions of Articles 10, 11, 12 and 21 OECD Model may cease to have effect.[521] For this purpose, a Contracting State may notify the other Contracting State through diplomatic channels that it will cease to apply the abovementioned provisions, which will have effect for both Contracting States.[522]

Finally, it is important to highlight that under the application of the STR rule with respect to Articles 11, 12 and 21 OECD Model, it is still up to the source State, to which the final taxing rights are assigned in those cases, to decide whether to tax those items of income. As provided, e.g., in the modification of Article 11 OECD Model, and repeated in the proposed modifications of Articles 12 and 21 OECD Model: 'Interest arising in a Contracting State and beneficially owned by a resident of the other Contracting State *may be* taxed in the first-mentioned Contracting State [...]' (emphasis added).[523] In simple words, the application of the new STR rule should not be interpreted as a '*subject-to-tax*' provision or the like.[524] On the contrary, considering the

518. New Article 3 para. 1(l) definition of '*Special Tax Regime,*' Select Draft Provisions of the US Model Income Tax Convention of 20 May 2015, p. 3.
519. The fact that the interest payments are beneficially owned by a resident of State Y in this case does not mean that State Y must subject to tax those interest payments.
520. OECD (2015), *supra* n. 226, p. 98.
521. *Ibid.*
522. *Ibid.*
523. OECD (2015), *supra* n. 226.
524. *Supra* s. 4.2.1.

limitation of tax treaties to assign taxing rights and not to enforce them, the literal wording of the STR rule only suggests an obvious conclusion, which is that tax treaties 'may', but not 'must', prevent DNT.

5.3.2 *The STR Rule and EU Law*

The practical application of a rule such as the one proposed under BEPS Action 6 (STR) can have some inconvenient consequences at the level of primary and secondary EU Law. With respect to EU primary law, the CJEU stated clearly in the *SIAT case* (2012) that domestic tax rules cannot determine the tax treatment of a payment made in one MS by reference to the characteristic of the tax system of another MS.[525] In brief, the case referred to the application of a domestic Belgian law that limited the deductibility of the payments for some services received by a Belgian resident company (SIAT). The justification of the Belgian Government to deny the deduction was the application of Article 54 of the 1992 Belgian Income Tax Code that provides that the payments for supply or services, among other kinds of payments, e.g., interest, shall not be regarded as business expenses where they are made to a non-resident taxpayer[526] if that payment is not subject thereto a tax or is subject to a '*tax regime which is appreciably more advantageous than the applicable tax regime in Belgium*' (emphasis added).[527] The taxpayer alleged that this domestic rule would infringe on his freedom to provide services.[528] The CJEU finally ruled in favour of the taxpayer, arguing that it was not clear what a 'tax regime which is appreciably more advantageous than the applicable tax regime in Belgium' means for purposes of the application of the rule, creating a level of uncertainty which can only be solved in a case-by-case basis.[529] Accordingly, it argued that the special rule of Article 54 was liable both to dissuade Belgian taxpayers from exercising their right to the freedom to provide services and from others to offer their services to recipients in Belgium.[530] It follows thus that such a special requirement constitutes a restriction on the freedom to provide services.[531]

In an analogy between the Belgian rule (Article 54) and the STR rule proposed under BEPS Action 6, especially considering the uncertainty of the term STR, which in a certain manner coincides with the undefined term 'tax regime appreciable more advantageous' under Belgian domestic law, it may be recommendable, at least from a policy perspective, to consider the position of the CJEU in cases like the one described

525. EU: Judgment in *Société d'investissement pour l'agriculture tropicale S.A. (SIAT) v. Belgian State*, C-318/10, EU:C:2012:415.
526. BE: Under Article 227(2) of the 1992 Belgian Income Tax Code, foreign companies that do not have their seat, principal place of business or centre of management or administration in Belgium are among the entities that are subject to tax on non-residents.
527. BE: Article 54 of the 1992 Belgian Income Tax Code.
528. The CJEU has consistently sustained that Article 49 EC precludes the application of any domestic rules, which have the effect of making the provision of services between MS more difficult. *See, e.g.*, EU: Joined Judgments *X and Passenheim-van Schoot*, C-155/08 and C-157/08 [2009], ECLI:EU:C:2009:368.
529. C-318/10, EU:C:2012:415, *supra* n. 525, paras 26 and 27.
530. *Ibid.*, para. 28.
531. *Ibid.*, para. 29.

above. Likewise, and although just a few services could be included under Article 21 OECD Model, there could be other fundamental freedoms jeopardised by the application of the STR rule, e.g., the freedom of capital derived by the limitation of deductibility of interest in case those interests are not subject to tax in the other Contracting State. Nothing would prevent the CJEU from applying a similar reasoning in such cases. Some could also argue, in contrast, that a restriction of fundamental freedoms could be justified under the aim of combating tax evasion or tax avoidance. However, it is worth recalling in this regard that, as sustained by the CJEU in the past, a restriction on fundamental freedoms could be justified in the need to combat tax evasion or tax avoidance only if the specific objective of such a restriction is to prevent a conduct consisting in the creation of 'wholly artificial arrangements' which do not reflect economic reality and with the view of escaping the taxes normally due on the profits or activities.[532]

Regarding EU secondary law, one should bear in mind that Article 1(1) of the EU Interest and Royalty Directive provides a general mandate that interest or royalty payments arising in an MS shall be exempted from taxes imposed on that MS (source State), provided that the beneficial owner of the interest or royalties is a company of an MS, or a PE of an MS's company also situated in an MS.[533] Contrary to this general prohibition, however, the application of the STR rule would imply that a source MS, which paid interest or royalties to the beneficial owner of the other MS (resident) where those items of income were subject to an STR, 'may tax' them. Thus, a potential violation of the Interest and Royalty Directive could arise if the source MS finally decides to exercise its right.[534]

The prohibition of Article 1(1) of the Interest and Royalty Directive can be, however, released in case it precludes domestic or agreement-based provisions required for the prevention of fraud or abuse.[535] Similarly, an MS may refrain from applying the directive or withdraw its benefits in cases where the principal motive or one of the principal motives of the transactions is tax evasion, tax avoidance or abuse.[536] Therefore, if by application of Article 5(1) or (2) of the EU Interest and Royalty Directive, the general prohibition is released, the STR might be applicable. Nevertheless, this should not prevent us from recognising that the limited wording of the rule - which opts for using the expression 'may tax', giving the source State the final decision to tax - still leaves a high degree of uncertainty with respect to its

532. EU: *Cadbury Schweppes* case and *Halifax* case, *supra* n. 123.
533. Article 1(1) of the Council Directive 2003/49/EC of 3 June 2003 on a common system of taxation applicable to interest and royalty payments made between associated companies of different Member States, OJ L 157/49 (2003), hereinafter 'Council Directive 2003/49/EC of 3 June 2003'.
534. As already stressed in this work, the STR rule uses the wording 'may tax,' instead of, e.g., 'must tax' or 'shall be taxed'. Therefore, it leaves up to the source state to finally exercise the assigned taxing right.
535. Article 5(1) of the Council Directive 2003/49/EC of 3 June 2003.
536. Article 5(2) of the Council Directive 2003/49/EC of 3 June 2003. This provision is similar to Article 15(1a) of the Council Directive 2009/133/EC of 19 October 2009 on the common system of taxation applicable to mergers, divisions, transfer of assets and exchanges of shares concerning companies of different Member States and to the transfer of the registered office of an SE or SCE between Member States.

practical application in these cases where the general prohibition of the directive does not apply.

6 FINAL REMARKS

When answering the core question of this chapter, which is whether tax treaties aim or not to prevent DNT as a broad tax policy goal, our answer should be clear and sound: No. As demonstrated during this chapter, tax treaties may certainly aim to counteract tax evasion and even sometimes tax avoidance. This is reflected in the wording of Article 26 (new Article 27) on the exchange of information. However, and recalling what was explained already in Chapter 1, neither tax evasion nor tax avoidance are equivalent concepts to DNT.[537] This does not mean that tax treaties might, under certain circumstances, be interpreted as aiming to prevent DNT. Indeed, this aim is especially evident when countries decide to include *subject-to-tax* or *switch-over clauses*, mostly to limit the application of the exemption method to relieve double taxation, demonstrating that a clear attempt to avoid a specific item of income in a cross-border transaction remains untaxed. This aim is, nevertheless, as exceptional as when tax treaties directly pursue the opposite outcome, namely, to achieve DNT, as it happens in the case of using *tax-sparing* or *matching-credit clauses* in tax treaties.

The above puts on evidence some important conclusions. First, DNT in a tax treaty context should also be regarded as a simple outcome whose occurrence can be or may not be desirable depending upon the specific circumstances surrounding a specific tax treaty. However, it is impossible to extract a general policy behind bilateral tax treaties that allows us to confirm that they, generally, aim to prevent the concurrence of DNT. This conclusion remains valid even after the implementation of the new OECD interpretation of Article 23A and 23B OECD Model in the OECD Commentaries, as well as the inclusion of Article 23A(4) OECD Model. None of these articles are effective enough to solve all the situations of DNT derived from either conflicts of qualification or conflicts of interpretation. Second, even when the prevention of DNT is expressly intended by some tax treaties, that is, either through a *subject-to-tax* or a *switch-over clause*, the scope of these clauses is very limited, not being able to apply to the generality of situations of DNT. This conclusion should not vary with the inclusion of a *'general subject-to-tax clause'* resembling, for example, the one included under Article 26(2) of the Nordic Tax Agreement. That is, neither the wording of the OECD Model nor the current tax treaty practice is enough to conclude that a general policy aim of avoiding DNT exists.

Special attention should, however, be paid to the proposals included in the BEPS Action 6 and their impact on the interpretation of double tax treaties with respect to the aim of avoiding DNT. Such proposals might suggest an interpretation of tax treaties not only as avoiding double taxation but also as preventing DNT. Nevertheless, this suggestion, in my view, should rapidly be discarded due to various reasons. First, the unhappy wording of the modified OECD Model preamble may only suggest that the aim

537. *Supra* Chapter 1, s. 4.

of preventing DNT occurs exclusively in cases where the DNT outcome is the result of tax evasion or tax avoidance. Second, the STR rule in case of Articles 11, 12 and 21 OECD Model would not suggest any obligation to the source State to tax the item of income. On the contrary, it is still facultative to this State to exercise or not its taxing right assigned, as demonstrated in the use of the word 'may be' instead of 'is' or 'must be', which could suggest otherwise. Therefore, to interpret the rule as generally preventing interest, royalties, or other income from remaining untaxed because of being subject to an STR would be at least imprecise. Finally, the application of such a rule could face some problems under EU law, especially derived from the current scope of the Interest and Royalty Directive. The implicit obligation to tax assigned to the source state within the STR rule could be impracticable with respect to transactions between MS within the EU. To do otherwise would amount to a violation of EU law.

Part II Hybrid Entities: A Domestic Decision with International Consequences

CHAPTER 3

The Hybrid Entities' Conundrum: A (Simple) Tax Characterisation Issue

1 INTRODUCTION

Chapters 1 and 2 have been so far devoted to establishing the boundaries of what DNT is, including its implications in the tax treaty context. This chapter turns now to analyse the second main element of this study, namely *hybrid entities*. For this purpose, the Chapter attempts to answer two simple questions: why hybrid entities (and reverse hybrid entities) exist and why one should care about them. The answer to these simple queries is, however, crucial for the further development of this study, especially when the interaction between hybrid entities and DNT is analysed in further chapters.[538]

Section 2 refers to some key concepts that are necessary to circumscribe the subsequent analysis on hybrids and reverse hybrid entities. This includes the distinction between legal and business entities, the difference between domestic and foreign entities, and the taxable and non-taxable status of entities from a domestic perspective. Section 3 turns the analysis into the concepts of *hybrid* and *reverse hybrid entities*, delimiting their terminology and subsequently analysing in a systematic manner the different existing manners to characterise foreign entities for tax purposes. This analysis includes the positive and negative characteristics of the different approaches to characterise entities, including the comparative approach, legal personality approach, overall approach, and fixed approach. The purpose of which is twofold. First, it aims to demonstrate that no system of characterisation truly prevails over the other. Second, there is no completely inviolable system of characterisation of foreign entities for tax purposes. Therefore, they appear as the result of specific domestic and sovereign tax policy decisions. Section 4 provides a detailed analysis of the US CTB system, probably the most famous 'elective system' to characterise entities for tax purposes in the world since it reserves the taxpayers the exclusive right to determine

538. *Infra* Chapters 5, 6 and 7.

when a foreign entity will be taxable or not for domestic tax purposes. It also provides a reference to the previous characterisation system used in the United States (i.e., *Kintner test*) as well as it analyses the cases of tax planning opportunities derived from the CTB election, specifically with reference to the avoidance of Subpart F income (CFC rules) and the inappropriate use of foreign tax credit (FTC). This Section also demonstrates that the electivity of the CTB system is more apparent than real, and when compared, e.g., with a resemblance or comparable system of characterisation, there is practically no difference in terms of the possibilities to predict a desired characterisation. Section 5 provides three concrete examples of different degrees of coordination in the characterisation of foreign entities: Spain, Denmark and the attempted coordination within the Proposal for an EU ATAD and the inclusion of Article 9a, dealing with cases of payments made to reverse hybrid entities. These examples attempt to demonstrate that coordination in the characterisation of entities is not only a utopian academic idea, but it can also be a concrete manner to deal with hybrids and reverse hybrid entities. Section 6 provides some final remarks.

2 KEY CONCEPTS

There are basically three previous and necessary distinctions to make before going into the conceptual study of hybrid entities, namely the distinction between legal and business entities, the difference between domestic and foreign entities, and the issue regarding taxable and non-taxable entities. I will briefly refer to them during the subsequent subsections.

2.1 Legal Entities and Business Entities

As expected, there is no straightforward and uniform definition of legal entities. Indeed, the concept necessarily varies from country to country according to the different civil and company law traditions. Nevertheless, a *legal entity* can generally be understood as 'a body having legal existence separate from its owners or participants [...], such that is capable of having its own rights and incurring its own liabilities'.[539] This separate existence is normally recognised in civil law countries as a separate legal personality and sometimes supposes also an important factor in determining the taxable status of entities.[540] In common law countries, however, where the concept of

539. IBFD Glossary, available online at the IBFD Tax Research Platform, accessed on 1 August 2023.
540. In Belgium, e.g., all entities that are residents for tax purposes, have legal personality, and are engaged in profit-making activities, are generally considered subject to corporate income tax. On the contrary, legal entities with no legal personality, such as partnerships, are considered as tax transparent. P. Vanhaute, *Belgium in International Tax Planning*, 2nd revised ed., IBFD, Amsterdam, 2008, Chapter 7.10, Online Books IBFD. In contrast, there are countries like Italy where, even though recognising the concept of legal personality, this is indeed completely irrelevant for purposes of applying the Corporate Income Tax. M. Grandinetti, *Italy* in: D. Gutmann (ed.) *Corporate Income Tax Subjects*, EATLP International Tax Series, Vol. 12, IBFD, Amsterdam (2015), p. 342.

legal personality is not always recognised, other elements can be considered.[541] For example, in the United States, whether an organisation is an entity separate from its owners for federal tax purposes is a matter of federal tax law, and it does not depend on whether the organisation is recognised as an entity under state law.[542] For example, a joint venture or other contractual arrangements may create a separate entity if the participant carries on a trade, business financial operation, or venture and divides the profits therefrom. On the contrary, a joint undertaking merely to share expenses does not create a separate entity for federal tax purposes. Similarly, mere co-ownership of property that is maintained, kept in repair, and rented or leased does not constitute a separate entity for federal tax purposes.[543]

Nonetheless, legal entities will not necessarily be considered business entities. Business entities will generally include a type of legal entity whose purpose is to carry on businesses. In civil law countries, the distinction is normally made between civil law and company law companies, distinguishing among them with respect to the existence of commercial reasons that justify their existence.[544] In common law countries, however, the distinction tends to be more straightforward and provided directly by statute. For example, in the United States, the Internal Revenue Code (IRC) states that a business entity is basically any entity recognised for federal tax purposes, including a disregarded entity with a single owner that is not properly classified as a Trust or otherwise subject to special treatment under the IRC.[545] This is why, in the United States and many other countries, the concept of business entities is necessarily reduced to corporations and partnerships.

Although the determination of legal and business entities seems to be *a priori* a matter of domestic law, it is interesting to note that it is also possible to find legal entities organised at a supranational level. Examples of the above are the European Company (SE),[546] the European Cooperative Society (SCE)[547] and the European Economic Interest Grouping (EEIG),[548] which are legal forms to a large extent governed by uniform EU law but which are still partly regulated by the national provisions of the MS of incorporation.[549]

---

541. This is arguable, however, in the case of the UK where the jurisprudence has clearly recognised that Limited Partnerships have no separate legal personality, whilst, e.g., LLPs and Scottish Partnerships do have. *See, e.g.*, UK: CA, 9 June 1998, *Memec Plc. v. Commissionaire of Inland Revenue*, Tax Treaty Case Law IBFD. For an analysis of *Memec Plc. v. Commissionaire of Inland Revenue, see* M. McGowan, *Classifying Entities and the Meaning of 'Tax Transparency': The UK Perspective*, Wolters Kluwer, 2023.
542. US: Treas. Reg. s. 301.7701-1(a)(1).
543. US: Treas. Reg. s. 301.7701-1(a)(2).
544. In Spain, e.g., as per the administrative practice of the DGT, a civil law entity might have a commercial object when it exercises an economic activity of production, exchange or services within the market. ES: DGT, Consulta Vinculante V2378-15 of 28 July 2015.
545. US: Treas. Reg. s. 301.7701-2(a) for the concept of business entities. *See also*, US: Treas. Reg. s. 301.7701-4 for Trusts.
546. EU: EC Regulation 2157/2001, Official Journal L 204/01.
547. EU: EC Regulation 1435/2003, Official Journal L 207/03.
548. EU: EEC Regulation 2137/1985.
549. L. Cerioni, *Cross-Border Mobility of Companies in the European Union: Tax Competition and Increased Scope for the CCCTB following Cartesio*, 64 Bull. Intl. Taxn. 12 (2010), Journals IBFD, p. 636. In 2012, the European Commission also presented the final proposal for a Council

Despite the above, this work will use the term *entity* as including any other arrangement, regardless of the legal position taken by a country on who derives the income from that entity or arrangement, and on whether this has or not a legal personality in a specific jurisdiction.

2.2 Domestic Entities and Foreign Entities

As a rule, countries have a clear understanding of what is a domestic entity, whilst such an understanding is not that clear when we talk about foreign entities. The reason seems to be obvious: each country decides sovereignly about their own legal forms. That is why countries generally opt to see foreign entities as the opposite of domestic ones, relying on the interpretation of the available legislation instead of providing a clear definition of them or simply using single criteria to determine the distinction between domestic and foreign entities.[550] An example of the above is the worldwide extended use of the concept of *place of incorporation* and *place of central management and control*, which also normally coincide with the criterion used to distinguish whether a company is a tax resident or not in a specific jurisdiction. In the United States, e.g., the Treasury Regulations consider an entity to be domestic if it is incorporated or organised in the United States, or under the law of the United States, or under the law of any state or the District of Columbia.[551] If an entity is organised in both a foreign country and in the United States, then it is also considered to be a domestic entity. All of the other entities are considered as foreign entities.[552] Similarly, in the Netherlands, an entity organised under Dutch law is considered a resident taxpayer or domestic entity.[553] Conversely, e.g., Ireland traditionally used the place of central management and control as the main criterion to determine whether an entity is domestic or foreign.[554] Other countries opt for using multiple choices to distinguish between domestic and foreign entities, recognising both the place of incorporation and the place of management and control as determining factors. In the United Kingdom, e.g., it is considered that if a company is incorporated in the country, it is a resident for

---

Regulation on the Statute for a European Foundation (FE). *See* EU: Proposal for a Council Regulation on the Statute for a European Foundation (FE), COM(2012) 35 final, 2012/0022 (AP), 8 February 2012, EU law IBFD. For further analysis on this proposal, *see, e.g.*, J.J.A.M. Korving and L.W.D. Wijtvliet, *A Consideration of the European Foundation: Alle Menschen werden Spender,* 67 Bull. Intl. Taxn. 9 (2013), Journals IBFD.

550. This makes the concept of foreign entities a residual (or default) one. *See* M. Lang and C. Staringer, *General Report* in: Cahiers de droit fiscal international Vol. 99B, *Qualification of Taxable Entities and Tax Treaty Protection* (IFA 2014), p. 34.
551. US: I.R.C s. 7701(a)(4) and s. 7701(a)(5).
552. *See* the exception for domestic corporations with a wholly owned Mexican or Canadian subsidiary, which may elect to be treated as a domestic corporation under certain circumstances. US: s. 1504(d).
553. NL: Article 2(4) of the Corporate Income Tax Act 1969.
554. A. Moore, *Ireland-Corporate Taxation* s. 1, Country Analyses, IBFD (accessed 1 August 2023). However, it is important to remember that since 1999 Ireland also had in place the place of incorporation as an alternative to be applicable in a very specific case, namely the case of a company operated in Ireland through a branch that it was ultimately controlled by a person in a country with a tax treaty in place with Ireland. *See* Mason and Daly, *supra* n. 36.

tax purposes. However, if an entity is incorporated abroad but centrally managed and controlled in the United Kingdom, it is also regarded as a domestic resident company.[555]

It is difficult to argue which one of the criteria, i.e., the place of incorporation or the place of central management and control, is the less easy to manipulate.[556] Indeed, e.g., if Ireland would use the place of central management and control as a single criterion with respect to other countries using the place of incorporation as a single criterion, some unsound outcomes might arise. For example, a company incorporated in Ireland before October 2013 and centrally managed and controlled somewhere else, e.g., the United States could have been considered tax resident nowhere because, whilst Ireland understood that the company was centrally managed in the United States, this latter country considered it incorporated there; therefore, it was not regarded as a domestic corporation.[557] After October 2013, however, these kinds of outcomes are no longer possible, and an Irish-incorporated company cannot be regarded as a tax resident anywhere for tax purposes.[558]

2.3 Taxable and Non-taxable Legal Entities

As well as the distinction between domestic and foreign entities, the distinction between taxable and non-taxable entities at a domestic level is not homogenous around the globe because it responds to specific and sovereign domestic tax policy decisions. Some countries determine whether an entity is taxable or not with reference to its corporate or private law status, e.g., using the legal personality of the entity as a factor to determine its tax status. Nonetheless, not always the legal personality is decisive in determining the tax status of an entity at a domestic level. In the case of *partnerships*,

555. The only caveat is the case of an entity treated as resident in a territory outside the UK and not resident in the UK for tax treaty purposes. In such a case, the entity will be regarded as non-UK resident. *See* M. Baldwin and T. Kiranoglu, *United Kingdom* in: Cahiers de droit fiscal international Vol. 99B, *Qualification of Taxable Entities and Tax Treaty Protection* (IFA 2014), p. 838. *See also, e.g.*, S. Oliver, *The Parent-Subsidiary of 23 July 1990: A United Kingdom Perspective*, 10 EC Tax Rev. 211 (2001).
556. In reference to the place of incorporation test used in the United States, Bittker and Lokken state that: '[A] place of management test is less arbitrary than the present U.S. rule [place of incorporation] only if that place is identified by factors that are not easily manipulated. For example, if the place of management is considered to be where the board of directors meets, a place-of-management test is even more pliable than the present U.S. rule.' B. Bittker and L. Lokken, *Fundamentals of International Taxation, US Taxation of Foreign Income and Foreign Taxpayers*, Thomson Reuters, Valhala NY, 2011, pp. 65-43.
557. This was the situation with AOI, AOE and ASI, the three Irish subsidiaries of Apple Inc. that originated a sound and public debate, because these three entities, due to the combination of the domestic rules in the United States and in Ireland, were regarded as tax residents nowhere. *See* Ting, *supra* n. 29, pp. 4-45.
558. Indeed, since 24 October 2013, where an Irish incorporated company is managed and controlled in a tax treaty country but is not resident there under that country's law, and it is not normally regarded as resident in Ireland because it is not managed and controlled in Ireland, it will be nevertheless regarded as resident in Ireland for tax purposes. This change is effective from 1 January 2015 as regards companies incorporated before 24 October 2013. *See* Moore, *supra* n. 554. *See also*, D. Stewart, *Ireland Targets 'Stateless' Companies in 2014 Budget*, 72 Tax Notes Int'l 3 (2013).

e.g., many countries recognise them as legal entities, subject to rights and obligations and able to appear in Court (i.e., having a separate legal personality), but they treat them for tax purposes as transparent entities, not able to assume tax obligations, such as the payment of taxes.[559] The advantage of relying on the corporate or private law status of an entity is, however, clear: there is no need to look at the structural substance of the entities.[560] That is why many countries follow this criterion.[561] In contrast, there are countries that simply separate between the corporate and the tax law status. In the United States, e.g., there is no immediate recognition of some legal forms as taxable entities at a federal level.[562] A US LLC, e.g., is treated as a corporation at the corporate state level, whilst it is treated as a disregarded entity for federal tax purposes.[563]

Although the domestic taxable status seems to be applicable without middle points, i.e., the entity is regarded as a separate taxable entity or not, there are some exceptions in which it is possible to distinguish semi-transparent entities or entities subject to a partial tax transparency regime. An interesting example of the above is the case of the French Limited Partnership (*societies en commandite simple*), which is regarded as a taxable entity, subject to corporate income tax with respect to the share of the profits of the limited partners, whilst it is regarded as a transparent entity with respect to the share of the profit of the general partners unless elected otherwise.[564] Similarly, the general partners of a Limited Partnership in Czech Republic are taxed at the level of the partners, whilst the limited partners are taxed at the level of the entity.[565] Likewise, as per the treatment of Trusts in Italy, certain beneficiaries are known, whilst others remain unknown.[566] A Trust will be transparent only in the part of the income attributed to the known beneficiaries, whilst it will remain opaque for the rest.[567] This partial or semi-taxable status, however, should not be confused with the situation in which an entity is granted a tax exemption that allows this entity not to be

559. In the United States, e.g., a partnership must file an income tax return even though it does not have to pay taxes. US: IRC s. 701 and s. 6031.
560. Lang and Staringer, *supra* n. 550, p. 27.
561. *Ibid.*
562. *Infra* s. 4.1.
563. However, LLCs with publicly traded interests are treated as corporations for federal tax purposes. *See* I.R.C. s. 7704. *See also*, P. McDaniel, M. McMahon, Jr. and D. Simmons, *Federal Income Taxation of Partnerships and S Corporations*, 4th ed., Foundation Press, New York, 2006, p. 2.
564. A. Coustel, *France* in: Cahiers de droit fiscal international Vol. 99B, *Qualification of Taxable Entities and Tax Treaty Protection* (IFA 2014), pp. 340-341. Indeed, the only entity treated as fully transparent under French domestic law is the real property co-ownership partnership, as defined by Article 1655 ter of the General Tax Code. *See* J. Benamran, *France-Corporate Taxation* s. 11, Country Analyses (accessed 1 August 2023).
565. T. Balco and H. Skalicka, *Czech Republic* in: Cahiers de droit fiscal international Vol. 99B, *Qualification of Taxable Entities and Tax Treaty Protection* (IFA 2014), p. 260.
566. A. Bavila, *Taxation of Trusts in Italy: Capital Gains on Trust Assets and Transparent Trusts*, 64 Bull. Intl. Taxn. 8/9 (2010), Journals IBFD, p. 482.
567. A. Crazzolara, *Italy* in: Cahiers de droit fiscal international Vol. 99B, *Qualification of Taxable Entities and Tax Treaty Protection* (IFA 2014), p. 445. It is interesting to note that 'trusts' were recognised only after Italy ratified the Hague Convention of 1 July 1985, which entered into force on 1 January 1992. The above created a lot of issues for practitioners, public officers and judges to understand a concept that comes from common law countries, e.g., the United Kingdom or Bermuda. For further analysis, *see* L. Corsini, *The Taxation of Trusts in Italy*, 53

taxed on certain items of income or when certain activities are exempt from taxation, e.g., in the case of a non-profit organisation. In general terms, a specific tax exemption or a full tax exemption will not change the taxable status of an entity, which will continue to be treated as a taxable entity even though it is exempted from Corporate Income Tax in a specific jurisdiction. Indeed, in the majority of the cases, the entity will continue to comply with some obligations inherent to taxable entities, such as filing tax returns or other tax formalities.[568] In other cases, the taxable status of an entity might certainly guarantee its entitlement to get a tax exemption. In Germany, e.g., only taxable entities are entitled to tax exemptions.[569]

Finally, it should be highlighted that the tax status of an entity should not vary just because it becomes part of a tax group regime. Indeed, and although this will depend exclusively upon the tax regime under analysis, it seems to be generally accepted that the tax status granted to a single entity is respected once it is part of a tax group.[570]

3 HYBRID ENTITIES AND REVERSE HYBRIDS

Having already stressed some key concepts regarding legal entities in general, this section turns now to properly study the origin and existence of *hybrids* and *reserve hybrids entities*. This includes specifically the study of the different systems to

---

Bull. Intl. Taxn. 3 (1999), Journals IBFD, p. 21. Specific provisions on trusts were not issued until the Law 296 of 27 December 2006, which entered in force on 1 January 2007. Bavila, *supra* n. 566.

568. Spain is an exemption, because totally tax exempt entities do not have to file tax returns and they are also excluded from all other tax formalities. *See* M. Villar, *Spain* in: Cahiers de droit fiscal international Vol. 99B, *Qualification of Taxable Entities and Tax Treaty Protection* (IFA 2014), p. 743.
569. DE: s. 5 of the German Corporate Income Tax.
570. In Germany, e.g., the effects of the tax group regime only extends to the transfer of the income from the subsidiary to the parent of the group, but it does not affect the taxability of the entities among the group. P. Dorfmüller, *Germany* in: Cahiers de droit fiscal international Vol. 99B, *Qualification of Taxable Entities and Tax Treaty Protection* (IFA 2014), p. 359. *See also*, DE: BFH of 29 October 1974, I R 240/72, BStBl. 1975 II, 126 and BFH of 7 December 1994, I K 1/93, BStBl. 1995 II, 175. Similarly, in Spain although the tax group is regarded as a taxpayer, the members of the group remain subject to the entire obligations in their individual capacity, except with respect to the payment of the corporate income tax of the group. *See* ES: Article 56(2) and (3) of the of the Corporate Income Tax Law [*Ley del Impuesto sobre las Sociedades*], Law 27/2014 (consolidated text) of 27 November 2014, BOE No. 288 of 28 November 2014. An exception to this, however, could be the case of the Polish tax group regime. A tax corporation group may be formed under Polish tax law by an agreement between two or more *Spzoos* or SAs that have their registered office in Poland, and it must exist for at least three tax years. Once the tax corporation group is formed, the income and losses of all the companies of the group is aggregated, also having the advantage that no transfer pricing rules are applied to the intra-group transactions, and the group members cannot linger file separate tax returns. In simple words, the tax group is technically a single taxpayer, and the members cease to be regarded as separate entities. Nonetheless, this interpretation is not entirely clear as exposed by the Directors of the Tax Chambers in Warsaw in different tax rulings, tax scholars and tax authorities. *See* P. Gozdziowska, B. Kuzniacki and T. Wickel, *Poland* in: Cahiers de droit fiscal international Vol. 99B, *Qualification of Taxable Entities and Tax Treaty Protection* (IFA 2014), pp. 638-639.

characterise entities for tax purposes, which is indeed the core issue regarding hybrid and reverse hybrid entities.

3.1 Terminology

Generally speaking, a *hybrid entity* is an entity considered as a taxable or opaque entity in the country of its establishment,[571] i.e., an entity different from its owners and subject to corporate income taxation in its country of organisation, whilst, in the other country, the same entity will be regarded as tax transparent;[572] namely, there will be no taxation at the level of the entity, but rather at the level of the partners.[573] Let us assume the following simple example. XCo is a corporation incorporated in country X, which has a wholly owned subsidiary in country Y (YSub). For country Y tax purposes, YSub is recognised as a taxable entity; namely, it is considered a separate legal entity subject to corporate income tax. Accordingly, the sole owner of YSub, i.e., XCo, will pay taxes only on the distribution received as a dividend from YSub. On the contrary, for Country X tax purposes, the same YSub entity is considered tax transparent. In simple terms, YSub is deemed not to exist for Country X tax purposes. Therefore, all the income, credit and expenses will flow through YSub to its sole owner, XCo. YSub is, therefore, a hybrid entity.

571. The terms 'taxable entity' and 'opaque entity' are used in an interchangeable manner during this work. Likewise, the term 'tax transparent' and 'fiscally transparent' entities are used in the same interchangeable manner.
572. The OECD Glossary of Tax Terms states that a *hybrid entity* is 'an entity that is characterised differently in two or more jurisdictions, for example, an entity that is treated as a partnership in one jurisdiction and as a corporation in another.' OECD, Glossary of Tax Terms, available at www.oecd.org, accessed on 1 August 2023. Likewise, the IBFD Tax Glossary states that a *hybrid entity* is generally, an entity that is characterised as transparent for tax purposes (e.g., as a partnership) in one jurisdiction and non-transparent (e.g., as a corporation) in another jurisdiction. An entity that is treated, from the point of view of a particular jurisdiction, as transparent in that jurisdiction and as non-transparent in the other jurisdiction is sometimes referred to as 'regular hybrid.' IBFD Glossary, available online at the IBFD Tax Research Platform, accessed on 1 August 2023.
573. Although this explanation coincides with the traditional tax treatment of 'Partnerships' as conduit entities where the various items of income and losses flow to the individual partners, its use is not limited exclusively to those entities in this work, and it may also include, e.g., single ownership entities not taxed at the level of the entity, but rather at the level of the single owner, such as the case of a Limited Liability Company (LLC) in the United States. *See, e.g.*, L. Cunningham and N. Cunningham, *The Logic of Subchapter K, A Conceptual Guide to the Taxation of Partnerships*, 4th ed., West, United States, 2011, p. 1, with respect to the tax treatment of US partnerships. *See also*, McDaniel, McMahon, Jr. and Simmons, *supra* n. 563, p. 1. Likewise, Australia, Germany and Sweden are also examples of countries that follow a tax transparency treatment for partnerships, like the one applied in the United States. However, there are some countries in which partnerships are, nevertheless, subject to tax at the entity level. For example, Belgium and Hungary. *See* J. Barenfeld, *Taxation of Cross-Border Partnerships, Double Tax Relief in Hybrid and Reserve Hybrid Situations*, Vol. 9 IBFD Doctoral Series, Amsterdam, 2005, s. 2.3.2.2, Online Books IBFD.

Figure 1 Hybrid Entity

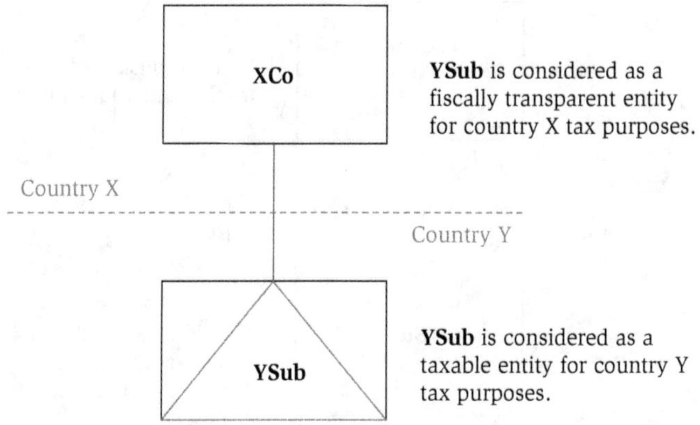

Accordingly, the same phenomenon of 'hybridity' can also be found in the opposite direction. This is to say an entity treated as tax transparent in the country of its establishment but considered as a taxable entity in the other country. These entities are known in doctrine as 'reserve hybrids'.[574] Taking the same example as above, YSub is regarded as a tax-transparent entity in its country of organisation, i.e., country Y, whilst as a taxable entity in the country of its sole owner (XCo), i.e., country X. Thus, country Y will not subject YCo to taxation at the level of the entity and will assume that all income, credits and expenses flow through YCo until its owner (XCo). Accordingly, country X will subject XCo to taxation only to the extent of the distributions made from YSub. In other words, YSub is considered under the eyes of country X as a taxable or tax-opaque entity.

574. With respect to the concept of *'reserve hybrid,'* the Glossary of the IBFD states that: '[A]n entity is a reverse hybrid when it is treated from the point of view of a particular jurisdiction as non-transparent and as transparent in the other. A hybrid entity is, therefore, also always a reverse hybrid, the difference depending on whether the classification is being made from the point of view of the jurisdiction treating the entity as transparent (hybrid) or non-transparent (reverse hybrid).' *See* IBFD Glossary, *supra* n. 572.

Figure 2 Reverse Hybrid

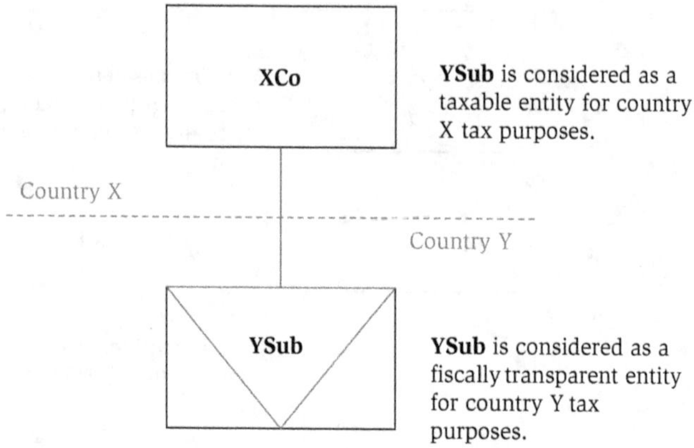

The core issue regarding the existence of hybrid and reverse hybrid entities remains thus in the different characterisation of an entity made by two or more jurisdictions, which can have an impact both with respect to the amount of taxes paid as well as to which country taxes should be paid. For this reason, the next sections of this chapter will deal in detail with this issue.

3.2 The Characterisation of Foreign Entities for Tax Purposes

As already stressed, the whole issue with respect to hybrids and reverse hybrid entities refers to the rules used to determine the tax status that a foreign entity will have in a specific jurisdiction, i.e., taxation at the level of the entity or at the level of the owners. Although the characterisation of foreign entities is made as per the specific domestic rules adopted in each country, which also depends exclusively on the specific domestic and sovereign tax policies, they can be divided as follows: (1) comparative approach; (2) legal personality approach; (3) overall approach; (4) fixed approach and (5) elective approach. All of them will be further explained.

3.2.1 Comparative Approach

Many countries around the world opt for a comparative approach or 'resemblance test' to characterise foreign entities for tax purposes. For this purpose, a foreign entity is recognised as a taxable entity or not considering a certain degree of comparability or equivalence to domestic taxable entities, and, in some cases, also considering the characteristics of the entity under foreign law. Germany, e.g., applies a resemblance test *(Rechtstypen-vergleich)* in a two-level manner. First, the foreign entity is evaluated in abstract according to the applicable foreign corporate law.[575] The reason for that is to distinguish the legal characteristics of the foreign entity from those domestic entity types in order to rule out non-applicable comparisons.[576] In other words, the test seeks to determine whether the foreign entity matches a German domestic one based on its functions and economic activity. For example, a French SICAV is, from a German perspective, considered equivalent to a German investment company by virtue of its economic activity and functions.[577] Second, and once this abstract evaluation is made, a specific legal comparison between the foreign and domestic corporate characteristics is made.[578] If there is no German entity to compare, the classification is made by way of an abstract structural comparison.[579] Therefore, whilst the general-abstract approach applied in the first level evaluates the applicable foreign corporate law without considering, for example, any potential design flexibility in the corporate governance documents, the second level or individual-concrete approach includes an evaluation of the specific characteristic of the entity.[580]

In 2004, however, it was issued the 'LLC letter',[581] which referred specifically to the characterisation of a US LLC and enumerated some criteria that should be considered when applying the comparison. These factors considered were as follows: (a) centralised management and representation; (b) limited liability; (c) free transferability of interests; (d) allocation of profits; (e) provision of capital; (f) perpetual duration of the entity; (g) profit distribution; (h) formal requirements for organisation;[582] and (i) other factors.[583] Nevertheless, it is still unclear whether the application of these criteria might be extended beyond the characterisation of a US LLC.[584]

Similarly, the Netherlands uses a resemblance test[585] that relies on the company law features of an entity determined according to its foreign incorporation statutes or

575. The Foreign law is determinative and particular attention is given to the conditions under civil law. C. Kahlenberg, *Classification of Foreign Entities for German Tax Purposes*, 54 Eur. Taxn. 4 (2014), Journals IBFD, p. 152. *See also*, U. Henkel, *Subjektfähigkeit grenzüberschreitender Kapitalgesellschaften*, RIW 7 (1991), p. 567.
576. Kahlenberg, *supra* n. 575, p. 153.
577. *Ibid.*, *see also*, J. Staigner and V. Köth, *Abkommensberechtigung einer französischen SICAV sowie des deutschen REIT*, BB 47 (2012), p. 2916.
578. Kahlenberg, *supra* n. 575, p. 153.
579. *Ibid.*
580. *Ibid.*
581. DE: Federal Ministry of Finance [*Bundesfinanzministerium*], 19 March 2004, IV B4-S1301 USA-22/04, *Schreiben betr. steuerliche Einordnung der nach dem Recht der Bundesstaaten der USA gegründeten Limited Liability Company*, BStBl I 2004, pp. 411-412.
582. Whilst the entry into the local German commercial register is a mandatory condition for the existence of stock corporations, partnerships limited by shares and limited liability companies (LLCs), it is not mandatory for the existence of commercial partnerships. In such a case, the registration in the local German commercial register will be only relevant with respect to third parties. DE: BFH of 13 June 1992, IX R 182/87, BStBl. 1992 II, 972.
583. For example, whether the foreign entity has legal personality can be also considered, although it does not play a decisive role for classification purposes. Accordingly, the number of investors is not a suitable criterion for distinguishing between corporation and partnerships. Dorfmüller, *supra* n. 570, p. 367.
584. Kahlenberg, *supra* n. 575.
585. The test is currently reflected in a degree published by the Dutch Minister of Finance dated on 11 December 2009. *See* NL: Decree of the State Secretary of Finance, CPP2009/519M of 11 December 2009. The decree has no legal binding power; however, as it is the interpretation

contracts.[586] The test is based on the following four questions: (a) is it possible for an entity to legally own the assets with which it performs its activities? (b) Are all the participants in the entity legally liable only to a limited extent, i.e., liable only for the amount of their capital contributions? (c) Does the entity have capital divided into shares for company law purposes, or can the capital be regarded as having been into shares? and (d) Is the entry of new, or the replacement of existing, participants possible without the consent of all participants, except in cases of inheritance or legacy? If the answer to three of the four questions is positive, then the foreign entity is considered a taxable entity.[587] The Dutch resemblance test is, however, not the only test used in the Netherlands to characterise foreign entities for tax purposes. Indeed, the Dutch Supreme Court applies a slightly different test. The Supreme Court raises the question

made by the State Secretary of Finance, taxpayers can rely on it based on the principle of legitimate expectations [*vertrouwensbeginsel*]. *See* M. De Graaf and J. Gooijer, *Netherlands* in: Cahiers de droit fiscal international Vol. 99B, *Qualification of Taxable Entities and Tax Treaty Protection* (IFA 2014), p. 563.

586. *Ibid*. Originally, however, the test was issued in the end of 2004, when the Ministry of Finance issued two decrees addressing the classification of foreign entities. The first of these decrees dealt with the classification of foreign entities in the context of the amended EC-Parent Subsidiary Directive. The second one attempted to clarify the Dutch approach to the classification of foreign entities for purposes of the Dutch participation exemption. *See* NL: Decrees of 18 December 2004, Nos CPP 2004/2730M and CPP 2004/1304M. *See* S. Laghmouchi, *Netherlands: Issues Arising under the Decrees on the Tax Treatment of Foreign (Hybrid) Entities*, 60 Bull. Intl. Taxn. 2 (2006), Journals IBFD, pp. 81-82. The test in 2004 was based on similar questions: '1) Can the entity hold legal title to the assets and liabilities used to carry out its activities?; 2) Is there at least one participant that has unlimited liability for debts and other obligations of the entity?; 3) Does the entity have a capital divided into shares?; 4) Is the admission or replacement of participants, other than by reason of inheritance or legacy, possible without the consent of all other participants? [...]. If test 1 was answered affirmative and test 2 negative, the foreign entity was classified as non-transparent. If test 1 was answered affirmative or negative and test 2 was answered affirmative, test 3 and 4 had to be taken into account. If test 3 and 4 were answered affirmative, the foreign entity was non-transparent. If test 3 or 4 was answered negative, the foreign entity was transparent. If the foreign entity was comparable to a Dutch limited partnership ('*commanditaire vennootschap*'), only the fourth test had to be applied. If the foreign entity was comparable to a Dutch limited partnership and the fourth test was answered affirmative, the entity was non-transparent according to the 2004 Decree.' *See* A.W.G. Lamers, *Classification of Foreign Entities in the Netherlands: Recent Developments*, 38 Intertax 12, 682 (2010) DOI: 10.54648/taxi2010072.

587. Prior to this four-question test, the characterisation system consisted in a six-criteria test contained in the Decree of 18 September 1997, No. DGO 97-00417, which stated the following questions: (1) Is a (formal) decision required to distribute the entity's profits to its participants? (2) Do the participants in the entity have limited liability? (3) Does the entity have legal title to the assets used in carrying on its activities? (4) Can the participants be replaced or admitted without the consent of all the other participants (i.e., is there free transferability of interests)? (5) Is the entity's capital divided into shares? (6) Is the entity subject to tax on its profits? An affirmative answer to all six precedent questions resulted in a foreign entity characterised as an opaque entity and eligible for the Dutch participation exemption. On the contrary, if one of the questions was answered in the negative, the foreign entity was regarded as a transparent entity for Dutch tax purposes. This 1997 Decree was a reaction to a decision of the Amsterdam Tax Court of Appeal dealing with the classification of a French *société en nom collectif* (SNC). An SNC has legal personality in France, its participants are liable for the SNC's debts, and the entity does not have capital divided into shares. The Amsterdam Tax Court of Appeal held therefore that, under Dutch civil law, an SNC should be considered to be similar to a Dutch '*vennootschap onder firma*', namely a transparent entity. *Ibid*., *see also*, NL: Decision of Amsterdam Tax Court of Appeal of 4 January 1995, No. 93/1467, Infobulletin, 95/315.

of who owns the rights and obligations from the conduct of the business and is, therefore, entitled to the profits. For this purpose, it considers the following factors: (1) the liability of the participants is limited to their contribution in the entity; (2) if the business is legally owned by the entity; and (3) if it is not actually being conducted on the account and at the risk of the participants in any other way.[588] If, based on these factors, it can be concluded that the rights and obligations from the conduct of a business are owned by the entity, this will be classified as a body corporate for Dutch tax purposes.[589] Thus, a body corporate will be considered non-taxable if the capital is wholly or partially divided by shares.[590] Nevertheless, if the partners are directly entitled to the profits of the entity, a second test is applied through which it is assessed whether the internal regulations imposed on the relationship between the entity and the partners resemble those of an open Dutch limited partnership or a partnership divided by shares.[591] In addition, although not officially recognised, there is also the possibility of obtaining an advance ruling with respect to the tax status of a foreign entity.[592]

In abstract, therefore, a resemblance or comparative test seems to be the simplest manner to characterise foreign entities for tax purposes. After all, the determination of whether a foreign entity is taxable or not for tax purposes is left exclusively to the domestic characteristics of the taxable entities compared to the foreign entity under analysis. Nevertheless, these types of tests or comparative approaches normally fail in different manners. First, they are unable to deal with the problem that other country's entities may be inherently different to their own.[593] Second, they require a high level of technical preparation within domestic tax authorities as well as important costs, mostly related to hiring foreign tax lawyers who can confirm the analysis of the corporate characteristics of the entity under scrutiny.[594] Third, and even in those cases in which all these costs are assumed, there is no 100% certainty that the system will not be subject to manipulation.[595] Indeed, it is a question of time that taxpayers get used to understanding how to manipulate the factors or questions that the resemblance test

588. De Graaf and Gooijer, *supra* n. 585, p. 564.
589. *Ibid.*
590. *Ibid., see also,* NL: Supreme Court 16 March 1994, no. 27.764, BNB 1994/191.
591. The distinctive criterion is whether the participations in the entity are freely transferable. *Ibid.*
592. As provided by De Graaf and Gooijer: 'What most commonly happens in Dutch practice is that, in bona fide situations, the tax inspector will be willing to give advance certainty depending on whether a specific foreign entity is considered to be transparent or non-transparent for domestic tax purposes. In fact, there is an experienced coordinating team within the Dutch tax administration that functions as a back office handling questions such as these that are submitted to individual tax inspectors all over the country.' *Ibid.*
593. Avery Jones stresses the example of the Lichtenstein '*Anstalt*', which is not clear whether it is a foundation or a trust. However, he also agrees that similar problems exist with respect to the different treatment of partnerships in civil and common law countries. *See* J. Avery Jones et al., *Characterisation of Other Sates' Partnerships for Income Tax*, 56 Bull. Intl. Fisc. Doc. 7 (2001), Journals IBFD, p. 289. For a reference to the '*Anstalt*', *see* M. Selig, *Half Trust, Half Company, All Anstalt: The History and Possible Tax Consequences of the Liechtenstein Anstalt Down Under,* 53 Intl. Fisc. Docn. 8/9 (1999), Journals IBFD.
594. *See, e.g.*, the Dutch tax administration and test already explained in this section.
595. *See, e.g.*, the '*Kintner test*' in the United States before the implementation of the CTB Regulations. *Infra* s. 4.2.

involves in order to obtain the desired characterisation, transforming the comparative system into a de facto elective system.[596] The above is not only a negative consequence for the tax administration making the comparative analysis, but it is also a tremendously unfair result for the taxpayers who cannot access sophisticated tax advisors in order to obtain a determined characterisation of an entity. Finally, one should also consider that an autonomous characterisation of entities might necessarily generate inconsistent results. In other words, there is no guarantee that a similar foreign entity will be characterised in different manners depending on who and how the comparative test is ultimately applied. This certainly increases the probabilities of generating hybrid and reverse hybrid entities.[597]

3.2.2 Legal Personality Approach

Conversely to the comparative approach, there are countries that prefer to look at the legal personality of the foreign entity and essentially grant the taxable status to those entities that are considered legal entities, namely entities separated from their owners.[598] In Belgium, e.g., the concept of legal personality serves as the main nexus to classify a foreign entity as taxable or not, and it is governed under Belgian international private law.[599] As a starting point, the place of principal establishment of the entity, i.e., where the company is effectively managed or the 'real seat', will be the primary conflict of law rule under Belgian international private law to be considered.[600] If the foreign entity has a legal personality and is treated as a taxable entity under the private law rules of the foreign jurisdiction, then Belgian law will recognize *de plano* that this foreign entity is a separate taxable entity.[601] If the foreign entity lacks legal personality under the laws of the foreign jurisdiction, it will be regarded as a transparent entity in Belgium, regardless of how the foreign jurisdiction treats that entity.[602] Similarly, in Switzerland, the determination of the foreign entity's legal personality in its country of organisation is considered.[603]

Nevertheless, the legal personality is rarely applied as an isolated factor to determine the characterisation of foreign entities. Indeed, this factor is normally used

596. *Ibid.*
597. *Supra* s. 3.1.
598. *Supra* s. 2.1.
599. De Broe, *supra* n. 255, p. 67.
600. *Ibid.*
601. Indeed, the fact that a taxpayer incorporates a foreign company to avoid or reduce tax liability is not enough to disregard the foreign entity for tax purposes. *Ibid.*
602. This may result in double taxation, e.g., if the foreign entity is treated as fiscally transparent and this country considers that the non-resident owners have a permanent establishment. The same situation could occur if the entity is regarded, even in absence of legal personality, as a taxable entity. P. Faes, *Belgium* in: Cahiers de droit fiscal international Vol. 99B, *Qualification of Taxable Entities and Tax Treaty Protection* (IFA 2014), pp. 151-152.
603. CH: Article 49(3) of the Federal Direct Tax Act [Bundesgesetz vom 18. Dezember 1987 über das international Privatrecht, SR 291], original text: '*Ausländische juristische Personen sowie nach Artikel 11 steuerpflichtige, ausländische Handelsgesellschaft und andere ausländische Personengesamtheiten ohne juristische Persönlichkeit werden den inländische juristischen Personen gleichgestellt, denen sie rechtlich oder tatsächlich am ähnlichen sind.*'

as a first-level test, and it is later combined with a resemblance or comparable test at a second level. In Belgium, e.g., if a foreign jurisdiction from which the foreign entity derives income does not recognize the concept of legal personality (e.g., the United States), the characteristics of this entity are compared against the characteristics of the legal entities under Belgium law in order to determine whether or not that entity is ultimately taxable in Belgium.[604] In other words, a resemblance test is applied as a second-level test after the legal personality test.[605]

Most of the difficulties in conceiving the legal personality as a unique proxy to determine the characterisation of a foreign entity derive exclusively from the nature of this concept. As noted by Avery Jones et al.: 'Legal person [...] is a concept that each country understands within its own legal system, and one tends to assume, wrongly, that it means much the same everywhere.'[606] An example of the above is the case of the EEIG in Europe, which is considered to have legal personality in most of the European countries, except in Germany and Italy, where it does not fit the concept of legal persons.[607] In Germany, this is due to the specific German legal tradition, whilst in Italy, this is because, under Italian law, there is a strict separation between the entity and its owners, which results in the fact that the owners cannot be personally liable for the entity's liabilities.[608] On the contrary, the members of an EEIG are so liable.[609]

---

604. In 1998, the Court of Appeal of Brussels classified a US general partnership as fiscally transparent entity, even though the concept of legal personality does not exist under US law. For this purpose, the Court took the features of the US general partnership and tested against those that would be attributed to a Belgian legal entity, arriving to the conclusion that the US partnership had no legal personality because all profits and losses were directly allocated to the partners; the partners were personally liable for the debts of the partnership; the partnership entered into dissolution in case of death, serious illness, bankruptcy or incapacity of one of the partners, and a partner could not withdraw from the partnership prior to its dissolution. *See* BE: Court of Appeals of Brussels, 30 April 1998, AFT, 1999, 119-125, cited in: Faes, *supra* n. 602, p. 157.
605. Similarly, in Switzerland, the legal or factual features of the foreign entity, e.g., bylaws and internal decisions that evidence how the entity is effectively organised, are compared to the Swiss entity to which it comes closest. However, there is not a uniform list of criteria provided by statute for this purposes. For further analysis, *see* S. Oesterhelt and S. Schreiber in: Zweifel/Beusch (eds) *Art. 49 of the Swiss Federal Law on Direct Taxation* [Bundesgesetz über die direkte Bundessteuer], 3rd ed., Helbling Lichtenhahn, Basel (2017), nos 42 et seq. However, e.g., the Swiss Tax Conference, an association of the Swiss federal and cantonal administrations, published in 2011 some guidelines or recommendations with respect to the treatment of a US LLC. In this regard, it was possible to circumscribe some factors normally considered to grant taxable status, which included: (a) whether or not the foreign entity has legal personality, and (b) whether or not the partners' liabilities are restricted. *See* J. Salom and H. Salomé, *Switzerland* in: Cahiers de droit fiscal international Vol. 99B, *Qualification of Taxable Entities and Tax Treaty Protection* (IFA 2014), p. 801. In the past, it was uncertain whether the participation in a US LLC was regarded as a participation in a Partnership or a Corporation for Swiss tax purposes. Nevertheless, these guidelines clarified that a US LLC was equal to a Swiss GmbH/Sàrl (*Gesellschaft mit beschränkter Haftung/société à responsabilité limitée*), namely a Swiss Corporation. *See* P. Hongler, *Swiss Tax Authorities Clarify Treatment of a Shareholding in a U.S. LLC*, 65 Tax Notes Int'l 8, 595-596 (2012).
606. Avery Jones et al., *supra* n. 593, p. 297.
607. *Ibid.*
608. *Ibid.*
609. *Ibid.*

3.2.3 *Overall Approach*

Other countries, instead of applying isolated criteria to qualify foreign entities for tax purposes, prefer to apply an overall approach in order to classify foreign entities for tax purposes.[610] The UK is a good example of the above because the UK does not apply fixed labels on foreign entities, i.e., opaque or transparent, but rather, it applies its tax legislation to determine the tax status of a particular entity for a particular tax situation.[611] The above also implies, e.g., that a partnership is considered a fiscally transparent entity but not for all tax purposes.[612]

The overall approach is, therefore, very uncertain for taxpayers since it depends specifically on the particular entity and tax situation analysed. This level of uncertainty, created mostly by inconsistent rules based on case law, can be illustrated in a couple of paradigmatic Court decisions.

The first of these cases is the *Memec Plc v. IRC* (1998) case law.[613] The case concerns a parent company (Memec), which entered into a silent partnership agreement under German law [*stille Gesellschaft*]. The other partner was a German GmbH, which was wholly owned by Memec. Accordingly, the partnership had no separate legal personality, but there was a contractual arrangement under which Memec had the right to receive a share of the profits of the business carried on by the other partner in return for a capital payment.[614] The German GmbH also had other subsidiaries from which it received dividends, which were also the main source of income of the German silent partnership and, thus, shared between the partners as per the arrangement. Memec argued the profits received by the German GmbH were indeed received by Memec, which was able to claim tax treaty relief for the double taxation generated.[615] Most notably, Memec stated that the German silent partnership did not create a new source of income under the arrangement because the arrangement was indeed transparent for tax purposes in the UK.[616] These arguments were originally rejected by the High Court, which considered that the question was not on the transparency or not of the German silent partnership but rather on the arrangement.[617] Indeed, the court considered that Memec has no rights in the shares of the subsidiaries and the

610. Lang and Staringer, *supra* n. 550, p. 35. The report refers to 'overall' or 'more comprehensive' approach in comparison to the reliance on single criteria. For a complete and updated analysis of the UK rules to classify entities for tax purposes, *see* McGowan, *supra* n. 541.
611. Baldwin and Kiranoglu, *supra* n. 555, pp. 835-836.
612. For this purpose, Baldwin and Kiranoglu provide the example of foreign private foundations and state: 'These are vehicles which are essentially corporate in nature, but which have some of the characteristics of settlement or trust. Because of the different definitions used in particular pieces of legislation, the same foundation may be both a close company for certain inheritance tax (IHT) purposes and also a 'settlement' for other IHT purposes. Give the broad range of terms and conditions on which foundations are established, the constitution of the particular foundation in question and the effect of its local governing law need to be considered in order to determine how the foundation affects the UK tax analysis.' *Ibid.*
613. UK: *Memec Plc. v. Commissionaire of Inland Revenue* (1998), *supra* n. 541.
614. Baldwin and Kiranoglu, *supra* n. 555, p. 848.
615. *Ibid.*
616. *Ibid.*
617. McGowan, *supra* n. 541, p. 34.

distribution made to them. However, it did not refer to the main issue, which was whether the German silent partnership could be regarded as fiscally transparent under English law.[618] However, when the case was appealed, the Court of Appeal referred specifically to the nature of the German silent partnership and to which extent the characteristics of the German silent partnership were shared by an English or Scottish partnership.[619] This decision was the basis for the guidelines of the HMRC International Manual INTM 180010, which listed six factors to consider whether an entity was treated as transparent or opaque for UK tax law purposes, including, e.g., references to the separate legal existence of the foreign entity and the level of responsibility on entity's liabilities, i.e., if the liabilities are assumed by the entity or personally by the owners of the entity.[620]

The factors published in the INTM 180010 governed the characterisation of entities at least until 1 July 2015, when the decision on *Anson v. Commissioner for HMRC*[621] came into play.[622] In brief, the *Anson* case referred to Mr Anson, a resident individual for UK tax law purposes who owned a US LLC in Delaware.[623] This entity was dedicated to managing various profitable venture capital funds.[624] A US LLC is, for US tax purposes, treated as a disregarded entity (fiscally transparent), whilst, in the UK, it was historically treated as a taxable entity.[625] The issues in question were to determine whether the profit remitted from the US to the UK was the same as Mr Anson was taxed in the US or not and whether he was finally entitled to a tax treaty relief.[626]

618. *Ibid.*
619. *Ibid.*, pp. 34-36.
620. UK: HMRC, INTM 180010. All the factors included are: (a) whether the foreign entity has a legal existence separate from that of the persons who have an interest in it; (b) whether the entity issues share capital or something else which serves the same function as share capital; (c) whether the business is carried on by the entity itself or jointly by the persons who have an interest in it that is separate and distinct from the entity; (d) whether the persons who have an interest in the entity are entitled to share in its profits as they arise, or whether the amount of profits to which they are entitled depends on a decision of the entity or its members, after the period in which the profits have arisen, to make a distribution of its profits; (e) who is responsible for debts incurred as a result of the carrying on of the business: the entity or the persons who have an interest in it; and (f) whether the assets used for carrying on the business belong beneficially to the entity or to the persons who have an interest in it. *See* M. Lemos, *'Non-Transparent': The Court of Appeal's Decision on the Delaware LLC in HMRC v. Anson*, XII GITC Rev. 2, 46 (2014).
621. UK: *Anson (Appellant) v. Commissioners for Her Majesty's Revenue and Customs (Respondent)* [2015] UKSC 44 on appeal from [2013] EWCA Civ 63, 1 July 2015.
622. Even up to that date the interpretation of the factors was debatable. *See, e.g.*, O. Popa, *UK Investors in US LLCs Exposed to Double Taxation–Is This the End of the Story?*, 53 Eur. Taxn. 6 (2013), Journals IBFD, p. 299. More recently, *see* McGowan, *supra* n. 541, pp. 42-52 (analysing the case in its different judicial stages).
623. Lemos, *supra* n. 621, p. 48. I will refer broadly to 'US LLC,' although the term is not precise because indeed every single State of the United States establishes different rules as regards to the organisation of LLCs. Nevertheless, the tax status is matter of federal tax law. *Infra* s. 4.
624. *Ibid.*
625. In fact, it is included as such in the list of classifications of foreign entities for UK tax purposes published by the HMRC. *See* UK: HMRC, INTM 180030 – *Foreign entity classification for UK tax purposes: List of Classifications of Foreign Entities for UK tax purposes.*
626. Mr Anson paid taxes in the US on his share on the LLC's profits at a rate of 45%. Accordingly, he also paid taxes in the UK on his after-tax amount remitted to the UK at a rate of 22%. He was thus subject to double taxation. Popa, *supra* n. 622.

The HMRC argued that the profits derived from the LLC and taxed in the US were not the same income subject to tax in the UK.[627] In other words, the HMRC considered the US LLC as a taxable entity, and therefore, Mr Anson could not credit the taxes already paid in the US on the share of profits in the LLC.[628]

The First-tier Tribunal ruled in 2010[629] in favour of the taxpayer, allowing double taxation relief under the treaty.[630] The tribunal emphasised that the partners were entitled to profits as they arose, and thus, Mr Anson was taxed on the same income in both countries, being entitled to tax treaty relief.[631] The Upper Tribunal, however, did not agree with this decision, considering that the First-tier Tribunal had erred in law in holding that the members of the US LLC had not merely a contractual but a proprietary entitlement to profits, although no evidence supported that conclusion.[632] In other words, it considered the US LLC as a taxable entity, and thus, Mr Anson was taxed in the UK on distribution and not on the same profits taxed in the US, not granting the tax treaty relief.[633]

Similarly, the Court of Appeal considered the US LLC as a taxable entity and did not grant the FTC to Mr. Anson.[634] In the decision of 1 July 2015, however, the UK Supreme Court interpreted that a UK-resident individual, a member of a US Delaware LLC, treated as fiscally transparent for US tax purposes, was entitled to an FTC under the treaty with the US for the amount of foreign taxes paid and calculated on the profits of the LLC.[635] In other words, it considered the US LLC in *Anson*'s case law as fiscally transparent. The UK Supreme Court, therefore, declined to apply the traditional position of considering a US LLC as a taxable entity and focused instead on the language of Article 23(2)(a) of the 1975 US/UK DTC (currently 24(4)(a) of the 2001 UK/US DTC) in terms of determining whether the UK tax was computed by reference to the same profits or income by reference to which the US tax is computed, finally granting the FTC. As provided by the Court: 'When UK tax is payable on a dividend received from a US Corporation, and US tax has been paid by the corporation on the

627. *Ibid.*, p. 300.
628. *Ibid.*
629. The case was anonymised as *Swift v. Commissioners for HM Revenue and Customs*. *See* UK: First-tier Tribunal, 22 February 2010, Case TC00399, Appeal No. SC/3106/08, *Swift v. Commissioners for HM Revenue and Customs,* Tax Treaty Case Law IBFD.
630. Popa, *supra* n. 622.
631. The Tribunal used the *Memec Plc*'s approach to determine whether the LLC was transparent or not for UK tax purposes. *Ibid.* This also coincides with the majority opinion of practitioners in the UK, who have stated that what makes an entity transparent for UK tax purposes is the ability of the members to remove profits from the organisation, without there being any person who can restrict that ability. Lemos, *supra* n. 620, p. 51.
632. *Ibid.*, p. 52. *Also,* UK: Upper Tribunal, 3 August 2011, FTC/39/2010, [2011] UKUT 318 (TCC), Tax Treaty Case Law IBFD; B. Arnold, *Tax Treaty Case Law News,* 66 Bull. Intl. Taxn. 1 (2012), Journals IBFD. *See also,* McGowan, *supra* n. 541, p. 46 (citing Mann J's comments in the case).
633. Popa, *supra* n. 622.
634. The arguments of the Court of Appeal, however, were slightly different and focused more on the source of the income. In fact, the Court held that the relevant test for determining whether a person is taxed on the same profits attends to whether the source of the income is the same. Lemos, *supra* n. 620, p. 52. Using *Memec Plc's* approach, the Court determined that the profit of the LLC did not belong to its members as they arose. Therefore, the sources of Mr Anson's income were different. Popa, *supra* n. 622.
635. UK: *Anson v. Commissioners for Her Majesty's Revenue and Customs* (2015), *supra* n. 621.

profits out of which the dividend was paid, there can be no question of the UK tax being "computed by reference to the same profits or income" as the profits of the corporation, if the source of the income is identified on the basis of UK (or, indeed, US) tax law.'[636] The above confirms the finding of the First-tier Tribunal, which stated that: '[I]n light of the terms of the LLC operating agreement and the views of experts is that the members of [the LLC] have an interest in the profits of [the LLC] as they arise.'[637] Therefore, in the same order of ideas, the Supreme Court states: 'If, then, Mr. Anson was entitled to the share of the profits allocated to him, rather than receiving a transfer of profits previously vested (in some sense) in the LLC, it follows that his "income arising" in the US was his share of the profits. That is therefore the income liable to tax under UK law, to the extent that it is remitted to the UK. There is no dispute as to the income which was taxed in the US: that was Mr. Anson's share of the profits of the LLC. Mr. Anson's liability to UK tax is therefore computed by reference to the same income as was taxed in the US. He accordingly qualifies for relief [...].'[638]

At least two important conclusions arise from the *Anson* case with respect to the characterisation of foreign entities.[639] First, it is the level of uncertainty in the UK rules of characterisation of foreign entities. As noted already, the HMRC recently stated in a list that a US LLC is treated as taxable entity. This certainly contradicts the UK Supreme Court's decision in *Anson*, providing again a broader level of uncertainty for all other forthcoming cases.[640] This issue is, in part, solved since the HMRC made public in September 2015 that it will continue to apply the practice of treating US LLCs as taxable entities, regardless of the outcome in *Anson*.[641] This is not an auspicious result for taxpayers because it implies that future potential cases of double taxation may occur. Second, *Anson* has already set up the discussion with respect to the UK system to characterise foreign entities, including those who, based on simplicity, claim for a system similar to that existing in the United States, i.e., CTB election.[642] As we will see further on in this work, one of the reasons the United States moved from a resemblance test (*Kintner* test) to an elective system (CTB election) was indeed the level of complexity in the old rules determining the tax status of entities, mostly from the tax

636. *Ibid.*, para. 92.
637. *Ibid.*, para. 119.
638. *Ibid.*, para. 121.
639. Other important conclusions that arise from *Anson* are related to the use of transparent entities and the access to tax treaty benefits, mostly considering Article 1(2) OECD Model. However, this issue will be further analysed in *infra* Chapter 4.
640. *See, e.g.*, S. Rogers, D. Cassidy and J. Mace, *U.K. Tax Treatment of U.S. LLCs Post-Anson*, 82 Tax Notes Int'l 4 (2016).
641. The document issued by the HMRC confirmed the following: '(i) when U.S. LLCs have already been treated as companies or corporations, HMRC will not challenge this view; (ii) the *Anson* ruling was specific to the facts and circumstances of that case, particularly Delaware law, and did not herald a wholesale shift in interpretation in this area; (iii) individual claims for double tax relief in reliance on Anson will be considered on a case-by-case basis; and (iv) HMRC proposes to continue in its existing approach to determine whether a foreign entity has 'ordinary share capital' for the purpose of various important corporate tax reliefs (including the substantial shareholding exemption).' *Ibid.*, pp. 367-368.
642. Lemos, *supra* n. 620, p. 57. *See also*, more recently, with a similar claim, McGowan, *supra* n. 541, p. 262.

authorities' point of view.[643] Under this assumption, it would not be a complete surprise that this discussion in the UK turns into a more serious debate in the near future.[644]

3.2.4 Fixed Approach

Tax scholars refer to 'fixed approach' to those cases in which all foreign entities are characterised in the same way, i.e., either fiscally transparent or opaque.[645] This labelled characterisation can be done in many ways. Italy, e.g., openly considers all foreign entities as taxable entities.[646] Other countries prefer to provide lists of taxable and non-taxable entities, such as the case of Luxembourg.[647] In other cases, e.g., in Greece, the taxable status of foreign entities is given based on arguments of neutrality or non-discrimination.[648] In other words, as all domestic entities are regarded as taxable entities, similarly, all foreign entities should also be treated like that.[649] There are also situations in which the absence of specific rules permits to interpret that all foreign entities are regarded as taxable entities.[650]

At first glance, the fixed approach is less costly for the tax administrations, which do not have to determine the tax status of foreign entities. Likewise, it contributes to predictability for taxpayers who know in advance how some foreign entities will be treated for domestic tax purposes. Similarly, one could say that it is less subject to abusive practices since taxpayers must rely completely on the knowledge of foreign law to plan a tax structure to reduce taxation. Nevertheless, as well as the other approaches already mentioned, it does not entirely avoid either the generation of hybrid and reverse hybrid entities or their potential misuse. For example, if Italy considers all the foreign entities as taxable entities,[651] the probability of generating cases of reverse hybrids is indeed very high because of the popularity of fiscally transparent structures among businesses around the world, particularly partnerships.

---

643. *Infra* ss 4.2. and 4.3.
644. McGowan, *supra* n. 541, pp. 249-272 (arguing for a partly elective system in the UK, which resembles the US CTB rules).
645. *See, e.g.*, Avery Jones et al., *supra* n. 593. *See also*, V. Kumar, *Conflicts of Qualification and Conflicts of Allocation of Income* in: E. Burgstaller and K. Haslinger (eds) *Conflicts of Qualification in Tax Treaty Law*, Linde, Vienna (2007), p. 39. Countries like Greece, Italy and Portugal follows this approach. *See* Lang and Staringer, *supra* n. 550, p. 35.
646. Crazzolara, *supra* n. 567, p. 447.
647. 'The opaque entities are listed in article 159 LIR, while the tax transparent entities are listed in article 175(1) LIR and §11 bis StAnpG.' *See* P. Berna, P. Mischo and F. van Kuij, *Luxembourg* in: Cahiers de droit fiscal international Vol. 99B, *Qualification of Taxable Entities and Tax Treaty Protection* (IFA 2014), p. 516.
648. A. Kardachaki and S. Psaroulis, *Greece* in: Cahiers de droit fiscal international Vol. 99B, *Qualification of Taxable Entities and Tax Treaty Protection* (IFA 2014), p. 392.
649. *Ibid.*
650. *See, e.g.*, M. Texeira De Abreu, Portugal in: Cahiers de droit fiscal international Vol. 99B, *Qualification of Taxable Entities and Tax Treaty Protection* (IFA 2014), p. 651; F. Yañez, Chile in: Cahiers de droit fiscal international Vol. 99B, *Qualification of Taxable Entities and Tax Treaty Protection* (IFA 2014), p. 197.
651. Crazzolara, *supra* n. 567, p. 447.

3.2.5 *Elective Approach*

Finally, there is an approach under which the taxpayer can elect the tax status of a determined foreign entity. Most countries, with some exceptions, do not follow this approach,[652] and, at this moment, the only example is given by the 'CTB regulations' in the United States, which, due to its special characteristics and complexities, will be separately analysed.

4 THE US ELECTIVE SYSTEM: THE 'STONE GUEST' IN A WORLDWIDE WALTZ

The United States represents the largest and most famous 'elective system' to characterise entities for tax purposes, reserving the taxpayers the exclusive rights to determine when a foreign entity will be taxable for US tax purposes. However, when comparing the previous experience based on a resemblance test, i.e., the *Kintner* test, it is possible to realize that the current system is indeed not less elective than the previous one, at least in practice. The above, however, does not mean to recognize that the CTB system represents an important source of disparities with respect to the characterisation of entities and, therefore, opportunities for tax planning, which can be mostly seen in the circumvention of Subpart F income (CFC rules in the United States) and FTC rules. Nonetheless, and as it will be demonstrated further on in this section, not always the circumvention of those rules attends to the CTB election, but rather to the poor design of those rules, being, therefore, the entity election completely irrelevant.

4.1 Introductory Issues: Domestic/Foreign and Taxable/Non-taxable Entities

When analysing the characterisation of entities for US tax purposes, it is important to clarify two previous issues: the distinction between domestic and foreign entities and the determination of whether an entity is taxable or not for US tax purposes.

652. In 2013, the Special Tax Treatment Control Act in South Korea allowed certain qualified foreign entities to opt to be treated as fiscally transparent in the same manner as domestic companies. Under the new rule, a foreign entity is qualified to make the election if it meets all the following criteria: (i) the foreign entity has certain similarities to the domestic entities which are allowed to make the election; (ii) the foreign entity has a PE in Korea; (iii) the foreign entity is treated as fiscally transparent in its country of organisation. S. Kim and J. Yoon, *Republic of Korea* in: Cahiers de droit fiscal international Vol. 99B, *Qualification of Taxable Entities and Tax Treaty Protection* (IFA 2014), p. 485. In contrast to the US CTB election, the South Korean rule seems to have the purpose of avoiding characterisation conflicts, mostly when there is a potential PE with potentially significant income. *See* Lang and Staringer, *supra* n. 550, p. 38. Other countries have recently introduced electivity exclusively within the domestic context, i.e., not applicable to foreign entities. This is the case of Italy, where since 1 January 2017 there is the possibility to elect the tax treatment of corporation and other entities (e.g., partnerships) either as tax transparent or taxable entities, as the taxpayers decide. The election can take five taxable periods and it is renewable. *See* IT: Article 55 bis Corporate Income Tax Act [*Imposta sul reddito d'impresa*], Official Journal [*Gazzetta Ufficiale*] No. 301 of 31 December 1986.

Generally speaking, the distinction between domestic and foreign entities in the United States is very straightforward: entities organised under US Law are domestic entities, whilst others are foreign.[653] Accordingly, the determination on whether a domestic entity is taxable or not for US tax purposes is made as follows: first, it is determined whether an organisation is recognised as a separate entity or not, i.e., an entity separate from its owners;[654] second, it is determined whether the entity is a 'business entity', which is basically any entity recognised for US federal tax purposes, including a disregarded entity with a single owner that is not properly classified as a Trust or otherwise subject to special treatment under the Internal Revenue Code.[655] A business entity with two or more owners is thus classified either as a Corporation,[656] subject to Corporate Income Tax at the level of the entity or as a Partnership,[657] not subject to taxation at the level of the entity but rather at the level of the partners.[658] Accordingly, a business entity with a single owner is classified either as a Corporation or a disregarded entity.[659] This distinction is crucial because all business entities not

653. US: IRS s. 7701(a)(4)-(5); US: Treas. Reg. s. 301.7701-5. There is one exception, however, which is the case of a domestic corporation that may elect to have a Canadian or Mexican subsidiary treated as a domestic corporation for US tax purposes if the subsidiary is organised and 'maintained solely for the purpose of complying with the laws [Canada or Mexico] as to the title and operation of property.' US: IRC s. 1504(d). *See also*, US: IRS Notice 2000-7, 2000-4 IRB 49 regarding the effect of repealing certain Canadian Banking Legislation on s. 1504(d) elections. The US jurisprudence has also been clear that a when the sole purpose was not to comply with Canadian Law, the election is not allowed. *See, e.g.*, US: *Kholer Co. v. US*, 124 F3d 1451 (Fed. Cir. 1997).

654. A 'cost sharing arrangement', e.g., is not recognised as a separate entity for federal tax purposes. *See* US: Treas. Reg. s. 301.7701-1(c). *See also*, US: Treas. Reg. s. 301.7701-1(a)(1) and Treas. Reg. s. 301.7701-1(a)(2), and the references to legal separate entities in the United States in *supra* s. 2.1.

655. US: Treas. Reg. s. 301.7701-2(a) for the concept of 'business entities', and US: Treas. Reg. s. 301.7701-4 for the concept of 'trusts'.

656. The term 'Corporation' is defined by statute to include: 'associations, joint stock companies, and insurance companies'. US: IRC s. 7701(a)(3). There are domestic entities that must be considered as such for US tax purposes, e.g., Banks, insurance companies. *See* US: Treas. Reg. s. 301.7701(2)(b). Accordingly, there are foreign entities that are listed as per se Corporations. US: Treas. Reg. s. 301.7701(2)(b)(8).

657. Partnerships include: 'a syndicate group, pool, joint venture, or other unincorporated organisation, through or by means of which any business, financial operation, or venture is carried on, and which is not, within the meaning of this title, a trust or state or a corporation [...]'. US: IRC s. 7701(a)(2). Likewise, a 'partner' is defined as: 'a member in such a syndicate group, pool, joint venture, or organisation'. US: IRC s. 7701(a)(2).

658. The pattern of taxation of partnerships (or pass-through entities), specially referred to the avoidance of economic double taxation has certainly encouraged its use in the United States. McDaniel et al. explains it as follows: 'Since the partnership is treated as a conduit for tax purposes, profits are taxed only once, in contrast to the taxation of corporate profits, first when earned by the corporation, and again, when distributed to shareholders.' McDaniel, McMahon and Simmons, *supra* n. 563, p. 1. Likewise, the use of losses makes a difference when electing between forming a corporation or a partnership. As McDaniel et al. state: 'In addition, when the enterprise realizes losses, the partners may deduct the losses currently on their own tax returns, while losses at the corporate level may not be deducted by shareholders.' *Ibid.* In addition to Partnerships, Limited Liability Companies (LLCs) are taxed either as Corporations or Partnerships. There is no single systematic treatment of LLCs for US federal tax purposes. However, most of LLCs are treated as Partnerships. *Ibid.*, pp. 1-2.

659. A disregarded entity is an organisation with a single owner, which can be recognised as an entity separate from its owner. US: Treas. Reg. s. 301.7701-3.

recognised as per se Corporations are regarded as 'eligible entities'[660], which means that they can elect to be classified either as a Corporation (taxable entity), a Partnership (non-taxable) or a disregarded entity. This is known as the 'Check-the-box' (CTB) election system or CTB regulations.

As noted, therefore, the CTB regulations apply primarily with respect to the characterisation of domestic entities, not being exclusively designed to characterise foreign entities for US tax purposes. The above relates to the fact that, in the United States, entities are formed according to state laws (and not according to federal law), which indeed creates a lot of problems with respect to the legal characteristics of entities.[661] For that reason, and since its very beginning, federal income tax developed its own system of characterisation for corporations, partnerships, trusts and states.[662] Regardless of this distinction, this work will subsequently refer to the rules of characterisation of foreign entities for US tax purposes as the federal tax rules only.

4.2 The 1954 *Kintner* Test

Before the implementation of the CTB regulations in 1996, the United States characterised foreign entities for tax purposes based on the concurrence of four corporate features, which included limited liability, continuity of life, centralized management, and free transferability of interests.[663] Hence, an entity with more than one owner was classified as an association and taxable as a corporation if it possessed at least three of these characteristics.[664] If it possessed fewer than three, then it was classified as a

660. *'Eligible entities'* are business entities not classified as a Corporation under Treas. Regs. s. 301.7701-1(b)(1), (3),(4),(5),(6),(7), or (8). US: Treas. Reg. s. 301.7701-3(a).
661. *See, e.g.*, P. Hobbs, *Entity Classification: The One Hundred-Year Debate*, 44 Cath. U.L. Rev. 437 (1995).
662. US: s. II.D. of the Revenue Act of 1913, Ch. 16, 38 Stat. 114, cited in: Dell'Anese, *supra* n. 4, p. 217.
663. US: *United States v. Kintner*, 216 F2d 418 (9th Cir. 1954). Subsequent Treasury regulations were issued because of this case law. *See* US: Treas. Reg. s. 301.7701-1 to 11, T.D. 6503, 1960-2 C.B. 409. Nevertheless, in 1935 the US Supreme Court already stated a sort of previous resemblance test. *See* US: *Morrissey v. Commissioner*, 296 US 344 (1935). This decision upholds both the Treasury's regulatory authority in the area of entity classification and the government's position concerning business trust. The decision described the corporate features that a trust should meet to be considered analogous to a Corporation, including ability to hold title to property, centralized management, continuity of life upon death of an owner, a structure that facilitates the transferability of beneficial interest and limited liability. *See* Dell'Anese, *supra* n. 4, p. 218. The above responded to a reaction during the early 1930s, where many professionals, especially doctors, began abandoning their solo practice in favour of large unincorporated groups in the form of trust or partnership agreements. *See* Hobbs, *supra* n. 661, p. 481. This issue was even more important after *Pelton v. Commissioner* (1937), where these types of organisations received the treatment of associations, taxed as Corporation, which allowed them, e.g., to adopt tax-favoured pension plans in comparison to those applicable to individuals. Sooner taxpayers started exploiting the corporate status. *Ibid.*, p. 482. *See also*, US: *Pelton v. Commissioner*, 82 F. 2d 473 (7th Cir. 1937).
664. Bittker and Lokken, *supra* n. 556, pp. 65-66. *See also*, M. Gianni, *International Tax Planning After Check-the-Box*, 2 J. Passthrough Entities 39, 9-10 (1999).

partnership for US tax purposes.[665] The treatment of entities with a sole proprietorship was not included under the *Kintner* resemblance test.[666]

The *Kintner* test, however, was not always easy to apply and let open a lot of possible outcomes, even when similar facts and foreign laws were under analysis. An example of this can be found in Rev. Rule 77-214 (1977)[667] and Rev. Rule 93-4 (1993);[668] both referred to the application of the *Kintner* test to a German GmbH [*Gesellschaft mit beschrankter Haftung*], owned by two subsidiaries, which were subsequently owned by a US Parent Corporation. In the case of Rev. Rule 77-214, the IRS stated that a German GmbH always possesses the corporate characteristics of limited liability[669] and centralized management.[670] On the other side, the presence of continuity of life[671] and free transferability of interest[672] would also exist unless separate interests exist to compel dissolution or to enforce transfer restrictions.[673] The GmbH's memorandum of association contained that the GmbH would be dissolved in case of death, insanity or bankruptcy of one of the shareholders [*Gesellschafter*], and any transfer of the GmbH's shares [*Geschäftsanteile*] would require the prior written approval of all the other shareholders. Because the GmbH was owned by two subsidiaries wholly owned by a US parent, the IRS ignored the provisions of the GmbH's memorandum of association and considered that the GmbH possessed both free transferability of interest and continuity of life, being recognised as a Corporation for US tax purposes.[674] In Rev. Rule 93-4, the IRS examined the same facts and foreign laws, arriving at the same conclusion, i.e., a GmbH is a Corporation for US tax purposes, although letting open some possibilities for achieving the opposite outcome, namely the tax treatment as a partnership.[675] Although the IRS concluded that a German GmbH always possesses the characteristics of limited liability and centralized management, coinciding with its previous Rev. Rule 77-214, it modified its previous position regarding continuity of life, stating that the presence or absence of separate interests is not relevant to the determination of whether an entity possesses continuity of life.[676] As the GmbH's memorandum of association requires dissolution upon bankruptcy of any shareholder, the GmbH lacks continuity of life, 'without further

665. *Ibid.*
666. *Ibid.*
667. US: IRS Rev. Rul. 77-214, 1977-1 C.B. 408.
668. US: IRS Rev. Rul. 93-4, 1993-1 C.B. 225.
669. DE: s. 13 GmbHG – Limited Liability Company Act – [limited liability].
670. DE: s. 35 GmbHG – Limited Liability Company Act – [management].
671. DE: s. 60 GmbHG – Limited Liability Company Act – [dissolution of a GmbH].
672. DE: s. 15 GmbHG – Limited Liability Company Act – [transferability of interest in the GmbH].
673. B. Spudis and M. Wilczynski, *Entity Classification Update: Rev. Rul. 93-4*, 71 Taxes 164, 165 (1993).
674. This is known as the 'single interest theory' applied by the IRS to justify the existence of free transferability of interest and continuity of life. *Ibid.*
675. *Ibid.*, p. 169.
676. As provided by Spudis and Wilczynski: '[...] the Service appears to be announcing that the single interest theory, as described in Rev. Rul. 77-214, is inapplicable to the corporate characteristic of continuity of life. In so ruling, the Service corrects its prior statement that dissolution must be compelled'. *Ibid.*, p. 166.

action', Rev. Rule 93-4 removes thus the need for any shareholder to compel dissolution.[677] With respect to the characteristic of free transferability, however, Rev. Rule 93-4 stated that because the two shareholders of the GmbH were subsidiaries of the same parent company, all decisions were subject to the influence of the parent company, applying the single interest theory.[678] This conclusion is nonetheless arguable because it is not clear that the single interest theory also applies to domestic entities.[679] Accordingly, no reference was made within the Rev. Rule 93-4 to the specific characteristic of the subsidiaries involved, when, in fact, according to that, some limitations to transfer interest may still exist depending on the entity involved.[680]

The *Kintner* test, although being the official manner to characterise foreign entities for tax purposes, was not always strictly followed. This is demonstrated, e.g., in the General Counsel Memorandum 34.376 (1970), where the IRS determined that an entity incorporated under the law of Nigeria also had to be treated as a Corporation for US federal tax purposes, considering that the concept of incorporation was similar to the US concept, regardless of the application of the *Kintner* test.[681] Similarly, in the General Counsel Memorandum 35.294 (1973), the IRS concluded that a Colombian company had to be recognised as a Corporation for US tax purposes because it was a separate juridical person under Colombian Law, regardless of the analysis of the factors under the *Kintner* test.[682] Later, the IRS would issue the General Counsel Memorandum 36.910 (1976), revoking the General Counsel Memorandum 35.294, which stated that all foreign entities should be characterised according to the *Kintner* test unless incorporated under common law principles.[683] This issue should be finally settled in the IRS Rev. Rule 88-8 (1976), where the IRS opted for considering all foreign entities as unincorporated and, thus, subject to the *Kintner* test in order to determine their characterisation for US tax purposes.[684]

The use of the *Kintner* test, therefore, puts on evidence some important consequences. First, the complexity and the level of legal uncertainty a resemblance test may

677. *Ibid.*
678. *Ibid.*
679. Spudis and Wilczynski state that Rev. Rul. 93-4 and Rev. Rul. 88-8 suggest that the single interest theory should be applied to both domestic and foreign entities. *Ibid.*, p. 168.
680. Certainly, less influence from the US Parent Company could exist if both subsidiaries owning the GmbH were German stock corporations [*Aktiengesellschaft*] rather than GmbHs. *See* s. 76, subsec. 1 and s. 117 AktG. This latter provides a responsibility of the directors of the company in case decisions where influenced, e.g., by shareholders. Nevertheless, s. 291 AktG [controlling company] can restrict the effects of s. 76, subsec. 1 AktG. Compare with: s. 35; s. 45 and s. 47 GmbHG.
681. US: IRS General Counsel Memorandum 34.376 of 13 November 1970, cited in: A. Gomez, *Rationalizing the Taxation of Business Entities*, 49 Tax Lawyer 2, 301 (1995). *See also*, Dell'Anese, *supra* n. 4, p. 220.
682. This position was subsequently limited by Rev. Rul. 73-254, by which the IRS clarified that the characterisation of a foreign unincorporated entity should be carry on through the *Kintner* test, regardless that this entity was recognised as a separate juridical person in its country of formation. *See* US: Rev. Rul. 73-254, 1973-1 C.B. 613. *Ibid., see also,* US: IRS General Counsel Memorandum 35.294 of 6 April 1973.
683. US: IRS General Counsel Memorandum 39.610 of 4 November 1976, cited in: Gomez, *supra* n. 681.
684. *Ibid.*

represent for taxpayers. Indeed, under a resemblance test, tax authorities really need to get involved in foreign laws to understand the proper characteristics of an entity. The above does not necessarily guarantee the same outcome, not even when the same entities and the same laws are under analysis, increasing thus the levels of uncertainty for taxpayers. Second, and even when such analysis is accurate – although most of the time costly – the opportunities for tax planning will nevertheless remain since taxpayers can always access careful consulting with local tax advisors to obtain the characterisation desired.[685] In other words, nothing prevents taxpayers from using drafting techniques and advice made by specialized tax attorneys or tax advisors to predetermine the classification type desired. This is exactly why the *Kintner* test remained in practice as a residual test applied mostly to unsophisticated taxpayers who were unable to pay the professional fees required to circumvent the rules,[686] being not less elective than its successor, namely the CTB regulations.[687] This, however, does not mean to categorise the *Kintner* test as better or worse than the subsequent elective system, but simply to emphasise that it proved at that time to be inadequate to serve its purpose, mostly after the appearance of small form of business with characteristics of both corporations and partnerships.[688]

4.3 The 1996 CTB Regulations

In 1996, the IRS issued the final regulations that simplified the old system of characterisation of foreign entities in the United States.[689] Generally speaking, the system allowed certain foreign business entities to be classified in a manner different from that provided in their countries of incorporation so long as they were not regarded as per se corporations for US tax purposes.[690] These foreign entities able to elect their tax treatment for US tax purposes are recognised as 'eligible entities'.[691]

685. Gianni, *supra* n. 664, p. 10. *See also*, S. Dean, *Attractive Complexity: Tax Deregulation, the Check-the-Box Election, and the Future of Tax Simplification*, 35 Hofstra L. Rev. 405, 430-431 (2005), who observed that well-advised taxpayers under the *Kintner* test could certainly avoid the application of corporate income tax.
686. Dell'Anese, *supra* n. 4, p. 222.
687. In the same opinion, Sicular states: 'Over time, of course, practitioners became increasingly adept at manipulating the four factors [*Kintner* test] to change the tax result, even for entities that were clearly corporations [...]. Getting there, of course took some amount of costly [...], but the U.S. tax saving frequently justified the cost. Entity classification thus was often effectively elective [...].' D. Sicular, *The New Look-Through Rule: W(h)ither Subpart F?*, 46 Tax Notes In'l 6, 601 (2007).
688. This is clearly explained by Hobbs, who states before the implementation of the CTB system: '[...] the resemblance test remains the methodology for entity classification today. However, it has not become cemented into the foundation of accepted tax doctrine. Indeed, given its history of inadequacy, it is remarkable that the resemblance test has survived'. Hobbs, *supra* n. 661, p. 519. And he continues: 'The resemblance test has proven inadequate because its underlying assumption is that all corporations resemble each other and that other organisations resemble corporations.' *Ibid.*
689. US: T.D. 8697, 61 Fed. Reg. 66584 of 18 December 1996.
690. US: Treas. Reg. s. 301.7701-2(b)(8) states the list of per se Corporations.
691. US: Treas. Reg. s. 301.7701-3(a).

Under the CTB system, an eligible foreign entity can elect to be classified either as an association, which is taxable as a corporation in the United States or as a partnership, which is taxable only at the level of the partners.[692] Accordingly, if an eligible foreign entity has only one member, it can choose to be classified either as an association or as a disregarded entity.[693] The election can be made at any time, and it must be accomplished with the formal requirements established by law.[694] Accordingly, the effective day of the election will normally be the one specified in the respective election form, although it is also possible to provide a specific date different from the one on which the election is filed, having even the chance of giving the election a retroactive effect.[695] Once the election has been made, it cannot be changed for a period of sixty months succeeding the date of the election.[696]

In the absence of an election, the tax status of a foreign business is settled by default rules, attending to the limited liability and the number of owners of the foreign entity.[697] According to these rules, a foreign-eligible entity will be considered a partnership if it has two or more members and at least one of them does not have limited liability.[698] On the contrary, it will be classified as an association taxable as a corporation if all members have limited liability[699] and as a disregarded entity if an eligible entity has a single owner who does not have limited liability.[700] Likewise, a foreign eligible entity is considered to have limited liability if the member has no personal liability for the debts of or claims against the entity by reason of being a member, based solely on the statute or law pursuant to which the entity is organised.[701] Conversely, a member has personal liability if the creditors of the entity may seek satisfaction of all or any portion of the debts or claims against the entity from the

692. *Ibid.*
693. *Ibid.*
694. An eligible entity is required to attach a Form 8832 ('Entity Classification Election') jointly with its Federal tax or information return of the taxable year in which the election is made. If the entity is not required to file a return for that year, a copy of the Form 8832 must be attached to the federal tax or information return of any direct or indirect owner of the entity for the taxable year in which the election is made. US: Treas. Reg. s 301.7701-3(c)(1)(ii).
695. The effective date cannot be more than seventy-five days prior to the date in which the election is filed and cannot be more than twelve months after the date in which the election is filed. If an election specifies an effective date of more than seventy-five days prior to the date the election if filed, it will be effective only seventy-five days prior to the date it was filed. Likewise, if the effective date exceeded twelve months after the date on which the election is filed, it will be effective twelve months after the date is filed. US: Treas. Reg. s. 301.7701-3(c)(1)(iii). Accordingly, US: IRS Rev. Proc. 2009-41 extended the time for filing the election to three years and seventy-five days prior to the date in which the election is filed. Entities that satisfy the requirements set out in Rev. Proc. 2009-41 must follow the prescribed procedures for obtaining relief for a late election. *See* US: IRS Rev. Proc. 2009-41 of 28 September 2009.
696. US: Treas. Reg. s. 301.7701-3(c)(1)(iv).
697. US: Treas. Reg. s. 301.7701-3(b)(2) that refers to the classification of foreign eligible entities that do not file an election. The default rules, however, do not apply with respect to the classification of entities made before 31 December 1996. These entities maintain their characterisation according to the *Kintner* test. US: Treas. Reg. s. 301.7701-3(b)(3)(ii).
698. US: Treas. Reg. s. 301.7701-3(b)(2)(1)(A).
699. US: Treas. Reg. s. 301.7701-3(b)(2)(1)(B).
700. US: Treas. Reg. s. 301.7701-3(b)(2)(1)(C).
701. US: Treas. Reg. s. 301.7701-3(b)(2)(ii).

member as such.[702] The determination is, therefore, left to the law in the foreign country where the entity is organised, except when a country allows the entity to specify in its organisational documents whether its members will have limited liability.[703] In such a case, these organisational documents turn also to be relevant.

As per all the rules described above, it is possible to extract some preliminary conclusions. First, although the CTB system is known for being elective, this election is subject to important limitations, which allow arguing that, indeed, it is just partially elective. This can be seen, e.g., in the fact that the election is relegated only to certain entities recognised as eligible entities and also based on limitations of time once the election is made. This issue was also recognised within the Joint Committee on Taxation (1997) reviewing the US elective system adopted, which stated: '[I]t could be said that the regime established under the check-the-box regulations is not completely elective, because entities eligible to elect either corporate or partnership under the regulations generally are unincorporated domestic entities.'[704] Accordingly, the default characterisation rules reduce the practical application of the election only to those situations in which an entity wishes to have a characterisation other than that provided by statute or, in cases, it decides to change a previous election. In all the other cases, therefore, the foreign entities will have a characterisation for US tax purposes regardless of any election made by the taxpayer. On the other hand, and in comparison with the previous *Kintner* test, the CTB system represents an important contribution to simplicity and legal certainty in the characterisation of foreign and domestic entities for tax purposes.[705] First, it eliminates the factual and legal comparisons established under the *Kintner* test, also reducing the costs for the tax administration.[706] Second, it represents a proof of 'fairness' or equal treatment of taxpayers, since after the CTB regulations, the election in the classification of entities is available to all types of taxpayers and not only those well-advised ones.[707] Indeed, as recognised within the US Joint Committee of Taxation (2010): 'The Check-the-box regulations were intended to relieve both taxpayers and the IRS from the need to expend considerable resources in determining the proper classification of unincorporated entities, when classification

702. *Ibid.*
703. *Ibid.*
704. US: Staff of the Joint Committee on Taxation, *Review of Selected Entity Classification and Partnership Tax Issues*, US Government Printing Office, Washington D.C. (1997), p. 16.
705. Indeed, it also allowed taxpayers to avoid domestic corporate status, and therefore, economic double taxation of income. In words of the Joint Committee on Taxation (1997): 'The principal impact is that taxpayers may now choose with greater simplicity and lower compliance costs whether they will pay two levels of tax on business income under the corporate tax rules, or whether they will pay only one level of tax under the partnership tax rules (or as a disregarded single-member entity).' *Ibid.*, p. 17. In the same opinion regarding simplicity and legal certainty for taxpayers, Mullis states: 'The criteria required to qualify to make a CTB election are simple and explicit. Once a classification election is made, it continues until an entity elects for a different classification.' K. Mullis, *Check-the-Box and Hybrids: A Second Look at Elective U.S. Tax Classification for Foreign Entities*, 64 Tax Notes Int'l 5, 373 (2011).This is in fact represented in the succeeding sixty months' limitation in which the election cannot be changed. US: Treas. Reg. s. 301.7701-3 c)(1)(iv).
706. Mullis, *supra* n. 705. *See also*, Dell'Anese, *supra* n. 4, p. 223; Gianni, *supra* n. 664.
707. *Ibid.*

was effectively elected for well-advised taxpayers.'[708] As such, it is possible to argue that the CTB regulations were not the result of isolated or random tax policy issues, disconnected from the reality of business in the United States, but rather a positive (written) legal response to classification rules that were becoming elective, and which could also involve other similar rules within the tax system.[709]

4.4 The CTB and Tax Planning Opportunities

The CTB regulations have not only improved in simplicity and fairness for taxpayers but have also created important new opportunities for tax planning through the use of hybrid entities, which were not originally intended under US tax law.[710] This is especially evident with respect to the avoidance of anti-deferral rules (CFC rules) and the use of foreign tax credits.[711] This, however, does not mean to recognize either that the existence of hybrid entities and reverse hybrids is a problem per se or that coordinated international measures should necessarily be adopted. Indeed, most of these issues still remain as domestic concerns that could be (and in some cases are) solved on a unilateral level.[712] Yet, and as I will argue later in this work, the coordination in the characterisation of entities seems to be a better manner to deal with the core of the issue, at least better than simply matching tax outcomes as proposed by the OECD.[713]

4.4.1 Avoidance of Subpart F Income

Under US tax law, a 'CFC' is a foreign corporation in which more than 50% of the total combined voting power of all classes of stock[714] or the total value of all stock, whichever is higher,[715] is owned by 'US shareholders', i.e., US persons owning directly,

708. US: US Joint Committee on Taxation, *Present Law and Background Related to Possible Income Shifting and Transfer Pricing* (JCX-37-10), 20 July 2010, p. 48.
709. As stated by the Joint Committee (1997): 'The check-the-box regulations could have the long-term effect of drawing attention to rules that may have become elective (whether under new regulations or under prior law) and of sparking a re-thinking of the rationale for such rules in some cases.' US: Joint Committee of Taxation (1997), *supra* n. 704, p. 18.
710. However, as I have argued somewhere else in this work, tax planning is not an *a priori* illegitimate activity. On the contrary, it becomes so depending on the level of tolerance in a determined country, which is given by its anti-avoidance measures. *Supra* Chapter 1, s. 4.2.1.
711. US: Staff of Joint Committee of Taxation (1997), *supra* n. 704, pp. 19-21.
712. *See, e.g.*, Denmark and the domestic anti-hybrid and anti-reverse hybrid rules discussed in *infra* s. 5.2.
713. *Infra* s. 5. OECD (2013), *supra* n. 2.
714. US: Treas. Reg. s. 1.951-1(g)(2) refers to the meaning of 'voting power'.
715. For example, if a domestic corporation owns exactly 50% of a foreign corporation's voting common stock (class A) and nonvoting preferred stock (class B). A foreign person owns the remaining stock, class A and B, in the same percentage. If at the beginning of the next year, the domestic corporation buys one share class B from the foreign person, the foreign corporation will be a CFC. US: Treas. Reg. s. 1.957-1(c), Example 8. Prior to 1987, the control was measured only by voting power. The alternative of total value was added to avoid manipulation. *See* Staff of Joint Committee on Taxation, 99th Cong., 2nd Sess., General Explanation of the Tax Reform Act of 1989, p. 988, cited in: Bittker and Lokken, *supra* n. 556, pp. 69-8.

indirectly,[716] or constructively,[717] 10% or more of the total voting stock of that foreign corporation.[718] In such a case, all those US shareholders owning 10% or more of the voting stock must include each year their pro rata share of certain CFC income, known as 'Subpart F' income in the US, which is generally passive income, regardless whether or not earnings are distributed from the subsidiary to the shareholders.[719] Therefore, CFC rules have the purpose of avoiding tax deferral through the incorporation of subsidiaries abroad, accelerating the taxation of certain income.

Therefore, under the US CFC rules, what makes a foreign entity to be considered a CFC is the fact of being characterised as a corporation for US tax purposes, i.e., as a taxable entity. Hence, partnerships for US tax purposes (i.e., tax transparent entities) will, in principle, not be subject to anti-deferral rules. However, since the CTB system is, in essence, elective, giving the taxpayer the possibility of changing the tax characterisation of an entity,[720] the possibilities to circumvent the US CFC rules increase. A classic example of the use of hybrid entities to circumvent Subpart F Income is earnings stripping through a disregarded loan.[721] Let us assume that a domestic corporation is the whole owner of a foreign entity (F1), organised as a corporation in country A and listed as a per se Corporation for US tax purposes. F1 subsequently owns 100% of another foreign entity (F2), organised in country B, a low-tax jurisdiction, where the entity is also a taxable entity for country B tax purposes. Let us also assume that F2 grants a loan to F1, and therefore, F1 pays back the interest associated with that loan (*see* Figure 3).

716. 'Indirect ownership' consists of stock beneficially owned by a US person through a foreign corporation, partnership, trust or state. In other words, the stock held by foreign entities is considered as indirectly owned proportionally by its shareholders or partners. US: IRC s. 958(a)(2). For example, if P (domestic corporation) owns 80% of F1 (foreign corporation), and F1 owns 80% of F2 (foreign corporation), and F2 owns 90% of F3 (foreign corporation), P is indirectly owner of 64% (0.80*0.80) of F2 and 57.6% (0.80*0.80*0.90) of F3. *See* example in Bitter and Lokken, *supra* n. 556, pp. 69-10. However, if P was a wholly owned subsidiary of another domestic corporation (e.g., U Corp.), there is no attribution of stock to it. *Ibid.*
717. Under US tax law, the concept used is '*constructive ownership*' and refers, in general terms, to the attribution rules of IRC s. 318, with some modifications. For example, under s. 318 a person is regarded to be the owner of stock owned by certain relatives (e.g., spouse), by his 50% controlled corporation, or by a partnership or trust in which he participates. For purposes of Subpart F rules, however, the percentage of stock ownership deemed to be controlling is reduced from 50% to 10%.
718. US: IRC s. 951(a). *See also*, P. McDaniel, H. Ault and J. Repetti, *Introduction to United States International Taxation*, 5th ed., Wolters and Kluwer, New York, 2005, p. 115.
719. '*Subpart F income*' as defined in IRC s. 952 consists of two principal categories of income: (1) insurance income, and (2) foreign base company income. This latter, as per the definition in IRC s. 954, includes: (a) foreign personal holding company income, (b) foreign base company sales income, (c) foreign base company service income, and (d) foreign base company oil related income. *See*, McDaniel, Ault and Repetti, *supra* n. 718, pp. 116-119. Generally, Subpart F income is income that the Congress found subject to tax haven manipulation. *See* Bittker and Lokken, *supra* n. 556, pp. 69-4.
720. Subject to the limitations stated in *supra* s. 4.3.
721. Mullis, *supra* n. 705, pp. 375-376.

Figure 3 Hybrid Entities and Subpart F Income

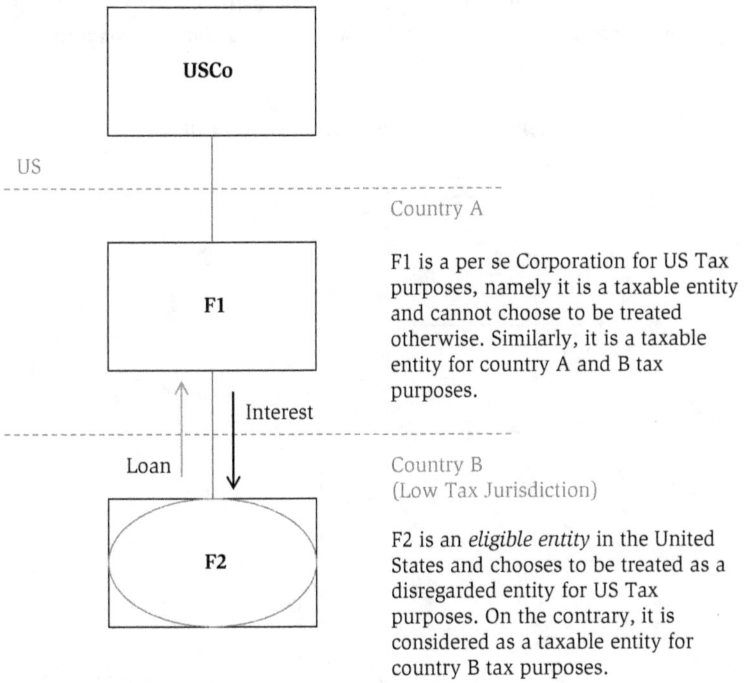

F2 is an eligible entity for US tax purposes, and it can elect to be treated either as a corporation or as a disregarded entity. If F2 elects to be disregarded for US tax purposes, the loan and the interest are also disregarded for US tax purposes. In other words, no interest income is recognised in the United States as Subpart F income. Accordingly, as F2 is a taxable entity in country B and F1 is also a taxable entity in country A, the interest amount paid from F1 to F2 is deductible at the level of F1, and most probably, not taxed in country B either (low/zero tax country). This latter outcome, i.e., non-taxation in country B, is, however, irrelevant for US tax purposes because the fact that the income was taxed or not in country B would not change the erosion of the domestic tax base due to the circumvention of CFC rules in the United States. This is at least the original concern expressed by the Staff of the Joint Committee on Taxation (1997) as follows: 'Under subpart F rules, the U.S. 10-percent shareholders of a controlled foreign corporation are required to include in income currently their shares of certain earnings of the controlled foreign corporation, whether or not the earnings are distributed to the shareholders [...] were the subsidiary to qualify as a partnership or a "nothing", its earning may not be included income currently by the

U.S. owner, making current inclusion, or not, a matter of choice.'[722] No reference is made with respect to the taxation or not in the other country.

Another way to circumvent Subpart F income using hybrid entities is given by a specific provision within the CFC rules, known as '*same-country exception*' (*see* Figure 4).[723]

Figure 4 'Same-Country' Exception

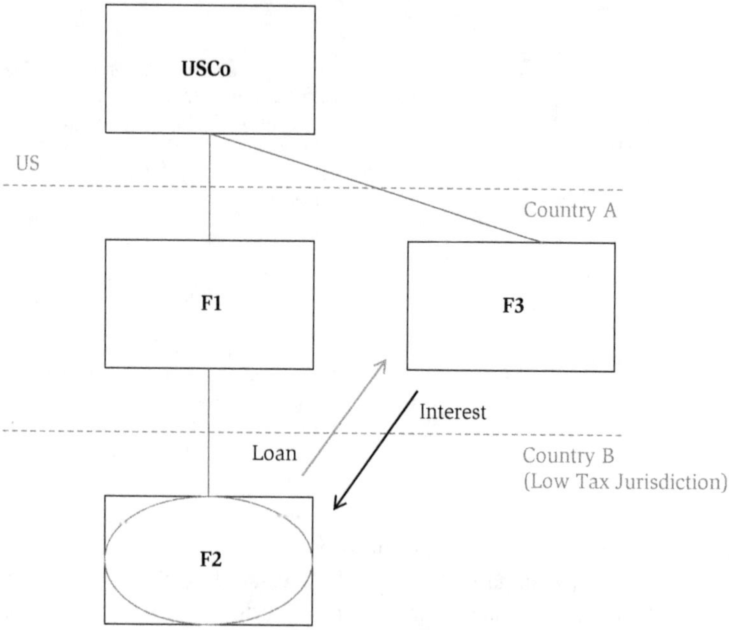

This exception states that Subpart F income will not include dividends, interest, rents and royalties received by a related corporation organised under the same laws of the CFC and which has a substantial part of its assets used in its trade or business located in that country.[724] As noted (Figure 4), we are assuming the same structure as in Figure 3, with the difference that a second foreign corporation (F3), wholly owned by the same domestic corporation that owns F1, is organised in country A. Likewise, let us assume that F2 grants a loan to F3 and receives interest payments back. Therefore,

722. US: Joint Committee of Taxation (1997), *supra* n. 704, p. 19. Similarly, it was addressed by the Staff of the Joint Committee on Taxation (2010), which stated: '[...] Treasury and the IRS recognised that such increased flexibility in entity classification in the foreign context could provide greater opportunities than under existing regulations for inconsistent, or hybrid, entity classification in which an entity is treated as a taxable entity in one country but as a flow-through entity in another country.' US: Joint Committee on Taxation (2010), *supra* n. 708, p. 48.
723. US: IRC s. 954(c)(3).
724. *Ibid.*

considering that F2 chose to be treated as a disregarded entity, the loan and interest between F3 and F2 are disregarded for US tax purposes. Accordingly, the fact that F2 is a disregarded entity implies that F3 is paying the interest 'directly' to F1, which is indeed organised in the same country. Thus, the same-country exception applies, and the interest amount paid to F2 is not included as Subpart F income of F1, which is clearly a CFC.

Unlike the example in Figure 3, where it is clear that the circumvention of CFC rules came up due to the tax characterisation of F2, in this second example (Figure 4) is not entirely clear that the characterisation of the foreign entity (F2) is properly the cause of the circumvention of the CFC rules. Indeed, as seen in Figure 5, the avoidance of Subpart F income might be perfectly achieved if F1 granted the loan directly to F3, being thus the characterisation of F2 completely anecdotic. Therefore, the issue in this case attends more to a deficient design of CFC rules rather than the use of the CTB election.

Figure 5 Same-Country Exception and the Irrelevancy of the CTB Election

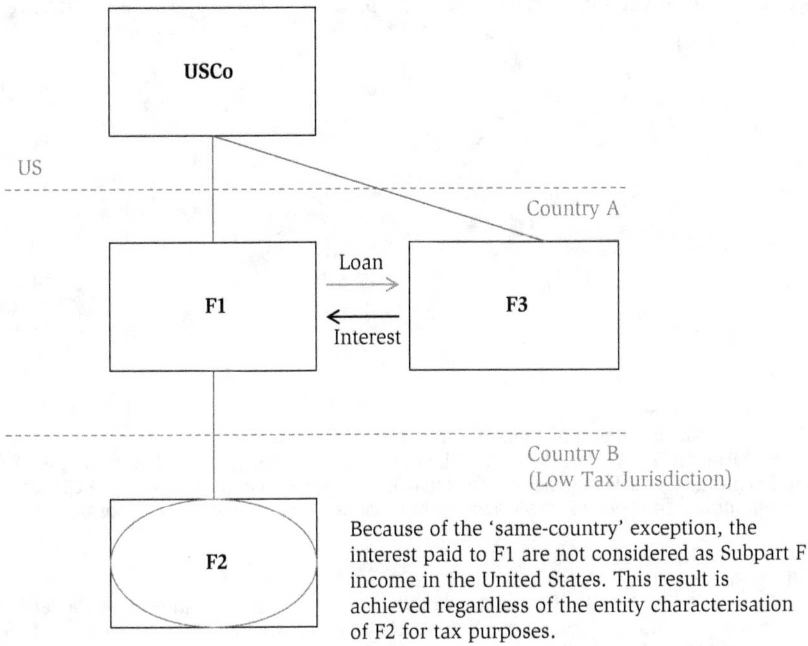

A similar situation occurs, e.g., with the *'manufacturing exception'* with respect to the generation of foreign base company sales income (FBC sales income).[725] As a general rule, FBC sales income is income from transactions in personal property (goods) where a related person is either the buyer or the seller.[726] However, if a CFC's income is derived in connection with the sale of personal property manufactured, produced or constructed by a CFC, that income is not considered FBC sales income.[727] In other words, income from manufacturing activities is not Subpart F income, and it should not be taxed as such in the United States. Although the exception makes sense since a CFC regime should not discourage the expansion of manufacturing operations carried on by MNEs in foreign countries, the relaxation of the text in 2008 certainly helped to extend the scope of the exception.[728] Indeed, after the modification of the statute in 2008, any CFC that makes a 'substantial contribution' through the activities of its employees, even though the foreign company itself is not a manufacturer, is considered as being included within the manufacturing exception.[729] This issue was also discussed during the hearing before the Permanent Subcommittee on Investigations of the Committee of Homeland Security and Governmental Affairs of the United States Senate, which referred to Apple Inc.'s offshore profit shifting.[730] Recalling what was referred to in Chapter 1 regarding the *Apple Inc.* case, Apple's tax structure is as follows (*see* Figure 6).

725. FBC sales income is part of subpart F income, *see supra* n. 719.
726. US: s. 954(d)(1). *See also*, Bittker and Lokken, *supra* n. 556, pp. 69-51. For example, A CFC's gross profits on a sale of goods are thus usually FBC sales income. Likewise, if a CFC acts as an agent for a related person in a transaction in goods, its commission fee is normally FBC sales income.
727. US: Treas. Reg. s. 1.954-3(a)(4)(i).
728. Ting, *supra* n. 29, p. 50.
729. US: Treas. Reg. s. 1.954-3(a)(4)(iv)(a). For this purpose, the participation of the CFC employees is crucial. Accordingly, even though the determination of whether the employees of the CFC made a substantial contribution depends on all relevant facts and circumstances, the regulations provides a nonexclusive list of activities of CFC employees, including, among others, the oversight and direction of the activities or process by which the good are produced; material selection, vendor selection or control of the raw materials, work-in-process or finished goods; management of manufacturing costs or capacities; quality control, etc. US: Treas. Reg. s. 1.954-3(a)(4)(iv)(b), from (1) to (7). *See also*, Bittker and Lokken, *supra* n. 556, pp. 69-59.
730. US: Permanent Subcommittee on Investigations of the Committee of Homeland Security and Governmental Affairs of the United States Senate, *Offshore Profit Shifting and the U.S. Tax Code – Part 2 (Apple Inc.)*, S. Hrg.113-90, US Government Printing Office, Washington (2013), hereinafter also 'U.S.: Apple's Hearing Report (2013).'

Figure 6 Apple's Tax Structure

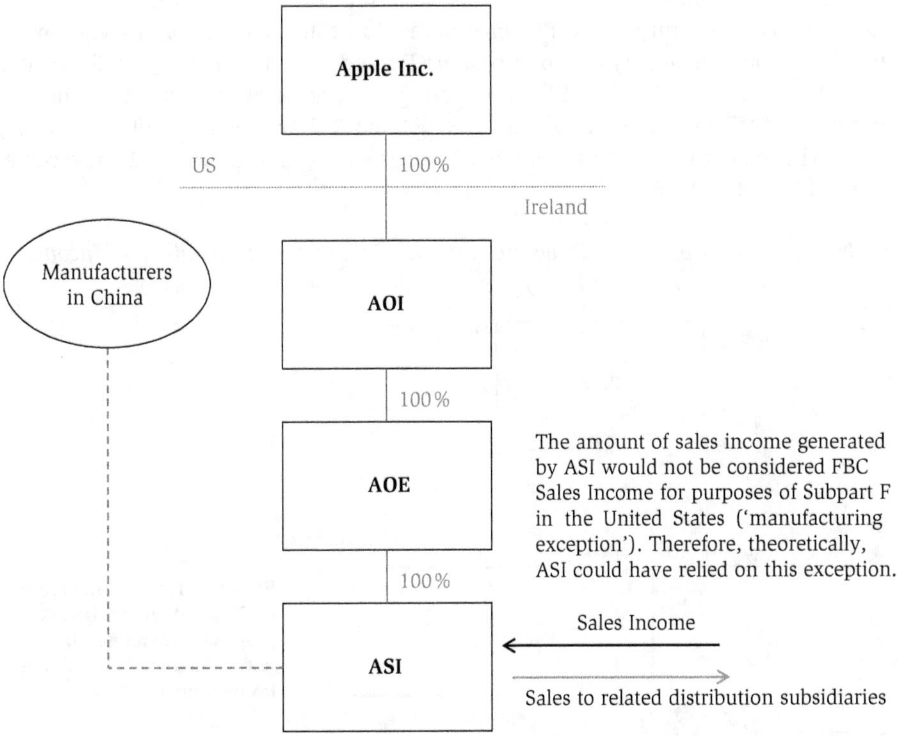

Apple Inc., a US Corporation, owns 100% of the stock in Apple Operations International (AOI), which subsequently owns 100% of the stock in Apple Operations Europe (AOE) and which subsequently owns 100% of the stock in Apple Sales International (ASI). This latter ASI engaged in unrelated contract manufacturers in China to assemble the products and subsequently sell them to distribution subsidiaries in Asia and Europe.[731] Therefore, theoretically, ASI could have relied on this exception, although that was not necessary because of the CTB election. ASI indeed avoided being regarded as a CFC through the CTB election. However, what it is interesting to stress here is that, even in the absence of the CTB election, ASI could have made use only of the manufacturing exception to obtain a similar result (i.e., the avoidance of potential FBC sales income), which demonstrates again that the electivity in the treatment of foreign entities for tax purposes is just a piece of the whole puzzle.[732]

731. Ting, *supra* n. 29, p. 44.
732. In this regard, Ting states that this is a demonstration that 'the U.S. tax law provides multiple shields to protect ASI's income from U.S. taxation'. *Ibid.*, p. 51.

There are cases, however, in which the CTB election is completely irrelevant to circumvent Subpart F income. This is the case, e.g., of multiple chain structures.[733] Let us assume the following hypothetical. A domestic corporation owns two CFCs: F1 incorporated in country A and FF1 incorporated in country C. Accordingly, F1 has a wholly owned subsidiary in country B (F2), and FF1 also has a wholly owned subsidiary in country D (FF2). F1 and FF1 are, per se, corporations. Therefore, they are not entitled to the CTB election. However, F2 and FF2 are eligible entities, and they elect to be treated as disregarded entities. Likewise, FF2 grants a loan to F2 and receives interest back (*see* Figure 7).

Figure 7 Multiple Chain Structures and the Circumvention of Subpart F Income

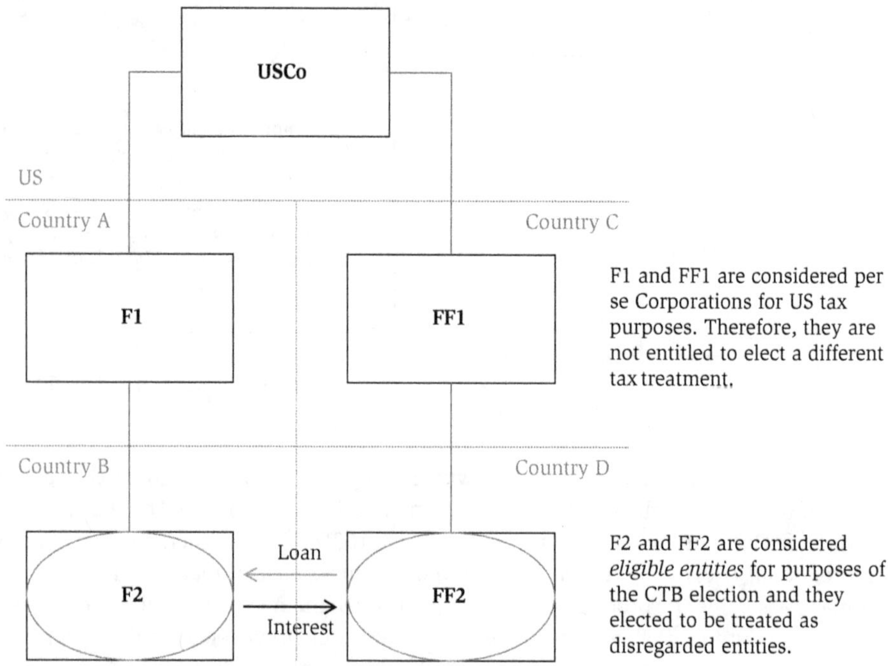

As per the example (Figure 7), the interest payments will be recognised as payments between FF1 and F1, and thus, Subpart F income. The 'same-country exception' does not apply in this case. Likewise, there will be Subpart F income, regardless of the election via CTB.

733. 'Check-the-box planning also cannot work if, for whatever reason, a corporation's foreign subsidiaries are in multiple chains, rather than being consolidated under a single foreign holding company.' Sicular, *supra* n. 687, p. 606.

In addition, a more extreme interpretation could even lead to the conclusion that, in some cases, the CTB election might create Subpart F income that would not otherwise exist in the absence of the election (*see* Figure 8).[734]

Figure 8 CTB Election and the Creation of Subpart F Income

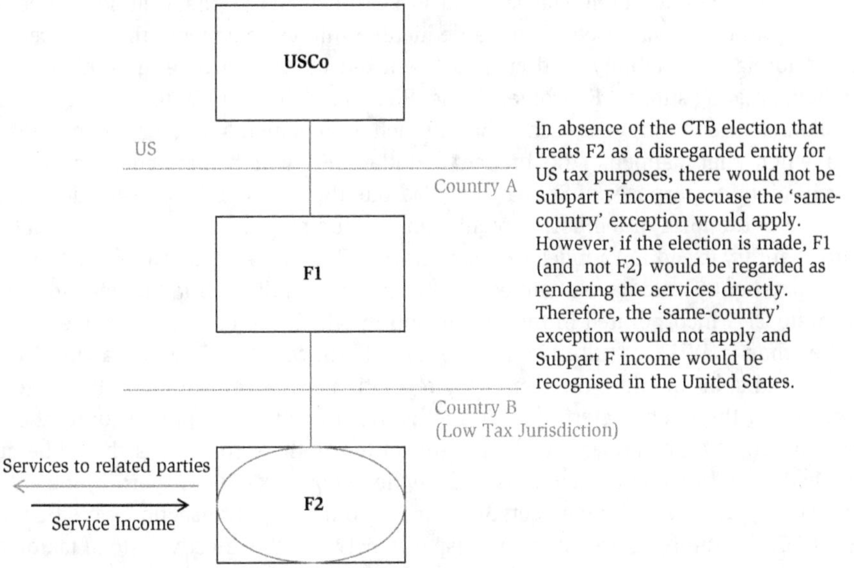

Taking the original example in Figure 3, where a domestic corporation owing F1, organised as a corporation in country A and listed as a per se corporation for US tax purposes, which subsequently wholly owns another foreign entity (F2), organised in country B, with the sole difference that F2 performs services for a related party in country B, i.e., same country of incorporation, and receives income accordingly. In the absence of the CTB election, the services performed by F2 are not considered foreign base company sales and services income because they are rendered in the same country of incorporation, namely country B. Nevertheless, if F2 elects to be treated as a transparent entity to circumvent other items of Subpart F income, it could risk the creation of a different type, i.e., service income. Indeed, in this case, the services would be rendered by F1, incorporated in country A, but rendered in a different country, namely country B. The same country exception would thus not be applicable, and the income should be recognised in the United States as CFC income. This result would not exist at all in the absence of the CTB election.

734. *Ibid.*

4.4.2 *Reaction from US Tax Law*

The formal reaction of the United States to the circumvention of Subpart F rules through the use of hybrid entities came first with Notice 98-11, right after the implementation of the CTB regulations.[735] The Notice attempted to tackle the situations in which a 'hybrid branch', namely, an entity with a single owner, is treated as a separate entity under foreign tax law and as a branch of a CFC that is its sole owner for US tax purposes, was used to make deductible interest payments that reduced the CFC's foreign tax liability, and created low-taxed interest income in another entity, without creating subpart F income.[736] The IRS and the Treasury stated that regulations would be issued to prevent such hybrid branch arrangements from being undertaken, and when that happens, the branch and the CFC will be treated as a separate corporation for purposes of Subpart F.[737] Despite the fact that those regulations came in force in the form of temporary regulations, including, e.g., rules providing that the same-country exception applied to payments by a CFC to a branch of a related CFC only if the payment would have qualified for the exception if the hybrid branch had been a separate CFC incorporated in the jurisdiction in which the payment is subject to tax (other than a WHT),[738] the IRS rapidly issued Notice 98-35[739] withdrawing Notice 98-11, and subsequently, the temporary regulations in force. Notice 98-35, however, maintained the re-characterisation of the hybrid branch as a separate corporation in case of hybrid branch payments.[740] For this purpose, three conditions should be met: (a) the hybrid branch payment must reduce the foreign tax of the payer; (b) the hybrid branch payment would have been Subpart F income if the transaction were between two CFCs;[741] and (c) there must be a disparity between the effective rate of tax on the payment in the hands of the payee and the hypothetical rate of tax that would have applied if the income had been taxed in the hands of the payer. For all other purposes, the hybrid branch is not treated as a separate entity.[742] None of these initiatives, however, finally achieved a permanent status.

Contrary to the above tendency, in 2006, although inspired by the arguments of Notice 98-11, Section 954(c)(6) was introduced within the Internal Revenue Code. This

735. US: Notice 98-11, 1998-6 I.R.B. 18.
736. US: Joint Committee on Taxation (2010), *supra* n. 708, p. 48.
737. US: Notice 98-11, 1998-6 I.R.B. 18. *See also*, US: T.D. 8767, 63 Fed. Reg. 14613, 26 March 1998.
738. US: Joint Committee on Taxation (2010), *supra* n. 708, p. 49. This rule interestingly focuses upon the taxation (or not) of the income in the foreign country, an issue that should be irrelevant if this income is finally included as Subpart F income in the United States. Similarly, Notice 98-11 stated: 'Treasury and the Service believe that it is appropriate to prevent taxpayers from using these types of hybrid branch arrangements to reduce foreign tax while avoiding the corresponding creation of Subpart F income.' US: Notice 98-11, 1998-6 I.R.B. 34.
739. US: Notice 98-35, 1998-27 I.R.B.
740. *Ibid.*
741. Specifically, the Notice refers to '*foreign personal holding company income*', which includes: (a) dividends, interest, rents and royalties; (b) net gains from the sale or exchange of property which gives rise to the income described in (a); (c) gain from certain commodities transactions; (d) gains from certain foreign currency transactions; and (e) income which is the equivalent of interest. *See* McDaniel, Ault and Repetti, *supra* n. 718, pp. 117-118.
742. US: Notice 98-35, 1998-27 I.R.B.

section states a 'look-through' rule by which dividends, interest, rents, and royalties received or accrued by a CFC, which is also a related person, shall not be treated as Subpart F income to the extent attributable to income of the related person that it is neither Subpart F income nor income effectively connected with the conduct of a trade or business in the United States.[743] In other words, if, for instance, CFC1, organised in country A, and CFC2, organised in country B, are both wholly owned by a US corporation, and CFC1 grants a loan to CFC2, and therefore, CFC2 pays interest back, those interests will not be included as Subpart F income of CFC1 to the extent they were not attributable to Subpart F income.

Figure 9 'Look-Through Rule' – IRC Section 954(c)(6)

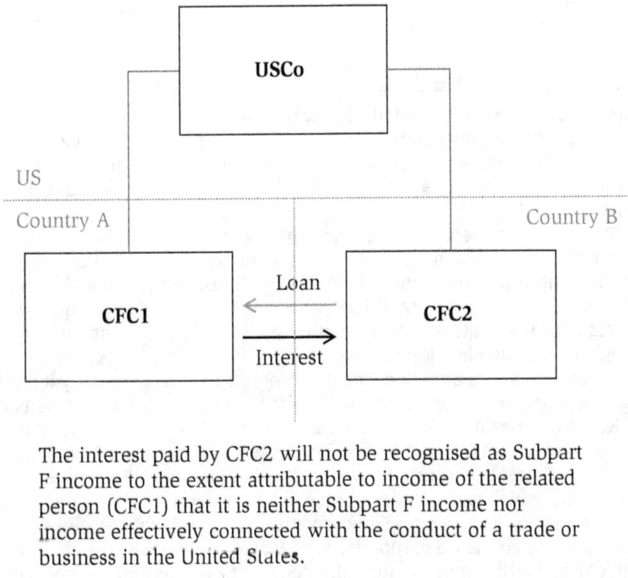

This provision is particularly interesting because it relaxes the position previously adopted with respect to hybrid branch arrangement and Subpart F income, and it represents, to a certain extent, an extension of the 'same-country exception'.[744] The above does not only highlight the contradictory nature of the CFC rules in the United States since they were issued[745] but also ratifies by statute a 'look-through' practice achieved already through the CTB election.[746]

743. US: IRC s. 954(c)(6)(A).
744. Ironically, also, the provision was very important in the case of Apple to avoid Subpart F income. As stated in the Apple's case hearing: 'Apple avoided them [Subpart F income] mostly through check-the-box regulations and the controlled foreign corporation (CFC) look-through rule.' US: Apple's Hearing Report (2013), *supra* n. 730, p. 15.
745. As stated by Sicular: 'The legislature's original intent in enacting Subpart F was to impose some constrains on the offshore movement of American capital, both to limit undue advantages enjoyed by investing abroad and to prevent tax avoidance through the use of offshore heavens

4.4.3 *Use of Foreign Tax Credit*

The US FTC is the method used to relieve juridical double taxation at a domestic level.[747] As such, the FTC allows US taxpayers to credit the payment of foreign taxes against their domestic tax liabilities, having as fundamental characteristic that the entity that bears the legal liability, and not necessarily the one that remits the payment of foreign taxes, is entitled to claim the credit.[748] The above can be seen, e.g., in the case that a foreign entity is required by law to withhold and remit the tax to the IRS in the case of interest paid to a non-resident. In this situation, the legal liability remains in the recipient of the interest paid and not in the entity in charge of the withholding of the tax, which is indeed a mere intermediary or 'withholding agent'.[749] The determination of the taxpayer on whom legal liability is placed is made according to foreign law.[750]

---

and shelters. As originally enacted, Subpart F reflected a compromise between the two conflicting goals of capital export neutrality [...] and 'competitiveness' or capital import neutrality [...] The last 45 years have not resolved the conflict, and that long-running tug-of-war is one of the reasons why Subpart F has always been unpredictable and confusing.' Sicular, *supra* n. 687, p. 590.

746. '[S]ince 1997 there has been a de facto look-through treatment in many cases through the use of the check-the-box rules to achieve. The use of the check-the-box rule to achieve look-through treatment in the international context was initially controversial and, while Treasury backed down from its initial attack on the technique, it was never quite given up. Section 954(c)(6) resolves the controversy, at least for a while; by providing an explicit, and broader, look-through rule, which is a logical next step.' *Ibid.*
747. US citizens, resident aliens and domestic corporations can elect annually if they want to deduct the foreign taxes paid or to use a credit against its US income tax liability instead. *See* McDaniel, Ault and Repetti, *supra* n. 718, p. 87. *See also*, US: IRC ss 901-908 and 960. This foreign tax credit is known as 'direct tax credit' as refers to the credit against foreign taxes paid directly by a US taxpayer to a foreign country. However, under US tax law, there is also a so-called indirect foreign tax credit, which is the credit granted to US corporations that directly own at least 10% or more of the voting stock in a foreign corporation from which it receives dividends. It is thus a legal fiction by which the US corporation is deemed to pay the taxes paid by the subsidiary in the foreign country attributable to those dividends. The indirect credit is also extended until the sixth-tier subsidiary to the extent that each parent owns directly at least the 10% voting requirement. After the third tier, it is necessary that the US parent has at least a 5% indirect ownership. *See* McDaniel, Ault and Repetti, *supra* n. 718, pp. 93-96. For a detailed explanation with respect to the different rules and calculation of the indirect foreign tax credit, *see* Bittker and Lokken, *supra* n. 556, pp. 72-189 to 72-243. For the rules about indirect foreign tax credit, *see* US: IRC s. 902 and correspondent Treasury Regulations. For the reference to indirect ownership, *supra* n. 716. For a brief historical reference of the US foreign tax credit, *see supra* Chapter 1, s. 3.2.1. For purposes of this section and the subsequent of this chapter, we will refer to FTC as 'direct foreign tax credit', unless otherwise provided.
748. US: Treas. Reg. s. 1.901-2(f)(1) and 1.901-2(g)(1).
749. US: Treas. Reg. s. 1.901-2(f)(2)(ii), Ex. 1.
750. Whether a particular foreign income tax is paid or accrued is sometimes an extremely difficult task. For example, a US parent Corporation may be liable for the taxes paid by a tax group in Luxembourg, even though most of the income of the group is not subject to tax in the United States. This is because, under Luxembourg law, the parent of the group was exclusively liable for the group's Luxembourg income tax. This was precisely the result in *Guardian Industries Corp v. Unites States* (2005), which is discussed later in this section. *See* Bittker and Lokken, *supra* n. 556, pp. 72-10 and 72-11. *See also*, US: *Guardian Industries Corp v. Unites States*, 477 f. 3d 1368, 1371 (Fed. Cir. 2007).

Hybrid entities can be used in this case to modify the person entitled to the FTC according to US tax law in a manner in which the FTC is claimed, although there is no corresponding income inclusion by the entity claiming the credit on foreign taxes.[751] This is known in doctrine as 'tax credit splitting'. Let us assume the following example: A domestic corporation is the whole owner of F1, a foreign corporation organised in country A, treated for US tax purposes as a disregarded entity, whilst as a corporation for country A tax purposes. Likewise, F1 is the whole owner of F2, also organised in country A and treated as a transparent entity for country A tax purposes, although elected to be treated as a corporation for US tax purposes.

Figure 10 Foreign Tax Credit Splitting

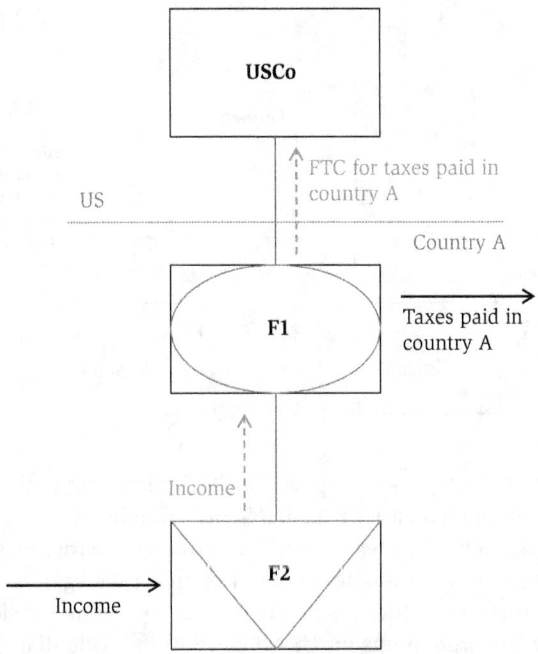

If income is earned by F2, the United States will consider that this income is attributable to F2 because this is regarded as a corporation for US tax purposes. However, on the other hand, country A will consider that income is attributable to F1, who is also legally liable for the payment of taxes in country A. Nevertheless, as the United States disregards F1 as an entity, it considers that the legal liability upon the foreign taxes paid is attributable to the US domestic corporation, which is finally

751. Mullis, *supra* n. 705, p. 377.

entitled to claim the FTC, regardless that no income was included at the level of the domestic parent company.[752]

Although with some minimal differences in the facts, this was the main issue discussed in *Guardian Industries Corp v. Unites States* in 2005.[753]

Figure 11 Tax Structure in Guardian Industries Corp. v. United States (2005)

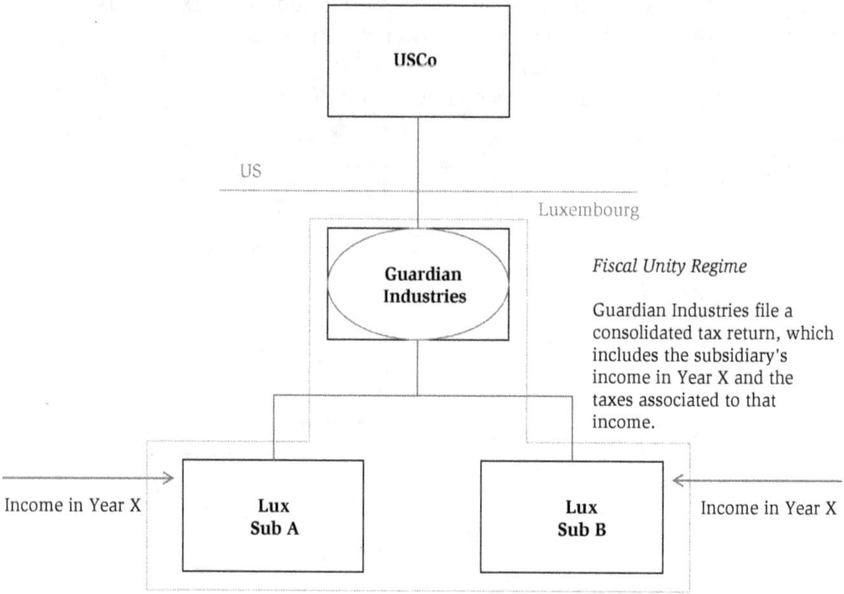

In *Guardian Industries*, the taxpayer, a US Corporation, indirectly owned 100% of the stock in Guardian Industries S.a.r.l. ('Guardian Industries'), which was an entity organised under the laws of Luxembourg.[754] Guardian Industries was a corporation for purposes of Luxembourg corporate income tax and a disregarded entity for US tax purposes.[755] Guardian Industries also owned stock in several subsidiaries in Luxembourg, all treated as corporations for US tax purposes.[756] Guardian Industries and the subsidiaries were also part of the same fiscal unity regime under the laws of Luxembourg.[757] Therefore, Guardian Industries reported income and paid taxes on the

752. Income was not included at the level of the domestic parent company, because the United States considers that income never flew from F2 to F1, because F2 is regarded as a Corporation for US tax purposes. However, income flew from F2 to F1 because as per the rules of country A, F2 is a transparent entity.
753. US: *Guardian Industries Corp v. Unites States* at *supra* n. 750.
754. J. Riedy, *IRS Uses Voluntary Payment Rule to Challenge Foreign Tax Credits Separated from the Income Base*, 34 Int'l. Tax J. 3, 11-12 (2008).
755. *Ibid.*
756. In the example in Fig. 11, they are represented by Lux SubA and Lux SubB, as a simplification.
757. Riedy, *supra* n. 754.

combined amount, i.e., including the subsidiaries' income.[758] Likewise, the taxpayer in the United States claimed an FTC for the foreign taxes paid by Guardian Industries, even though no income was reported in the United States.[759] The IRS argued that Guardian Industries and the subsidiaries were joint and severally liable for the Luxembourg corporate income tax. Therefore, the tax paid should be allocated among the subsidiaries.[760] The trial court, however, concluded that Guardian Industries was not joint and severally liable for the taxes paid in Luxembourg. The Federal Circuit confirmed that finding and affirmed that, under the Luxembourg consolidated return, Guardian Industries bore the legal liability for the consolidated group's taxes, which added to the fact that Guardian Industries was treated as a disregarded entity for US tax purposes, allowed the domestic parent company in the United States to claim the 100% of the FTC, regardless that no income was associated to those foreign taxes paid.[761] This decision would pave the origin of the US rules regulating tax credit splitting events discussed below.

4.4.4 *Reaction from US Tax Law*

Perhaps the first attempt to regulate in positive law the results achieved in *Guardian Industries* and the issues with respect to foreign tax credit splitting was through the proposed regulations under US Treasury Regulation Section 1.901-2(f).[762] The proposed regulations essentially attempted to provide rules that matched the results when an FTC was separated from the income on which the tax was provided using disregarded entities. In this regard, the proposed regulations stated, on the one hand, that if an entity is a reverse hybrid, i.e., considered as a corporation in the US and a fiscally transparent entity in its country of incorporation, the tax imposed on the owner's share of income from each reverse hybrid and the tax imposed by the foreign country on other income of the owner, is considered to be imposed on the combined income of each reverse hybrid and the owner, being thus allocated between the owner

758. *Ibid.*
759. *Ibid.*
760. US: Treas. Reg. s. 1.901-2(f)(3). This regulation states that if foreign income tax is imposed on the combined income of two or more related persons and they are jointly and severally liable for the income tax under foreign law, then the foreign law is considered to impose a legal liability on each person as per the amount of the foreign income tax attributable to its portion of the base for the tax. For example, following the hypothetical of Bittker and Lokken: '[I]f a domestic corporation's subsidiaries in country X file a consolidated tax return and the members of the country X are jointly and severally liable for the tax on the group's income, each subsidiary is the taxpayer with respect to the country X tax on its portion of the consolidated income. In contrast, if the country X parent is exclusively liable for the country X tax on all income of the country X group, the parent is deemed to have paid all of the group's country X tax, and other members of the group are deemed to have paid none of the tax.' *See* Bittker and Lokken, *supra* n. 556, p. 72-11.
761. Riedy, *supra* n. 754.
762. *Ibid.* Also, as provided by Rosenberg: 'The general theory behind matching (as a big picture concept) is that the FTC is intended to reduce double taxation on foreign-source income, which is only achieved if the credit is given to the same person who recognizes the foreign-source income for U.S. tax purposes.' R. Rosenberg, *New Foreign Tax Credit Anti-Splitting Rule*, 129 Tax Notes 6, 701 (2007).

and the reverse hybrid in a pro rata basis.[763] Let us assume the following simplified example. A and B are domestic corporations, owners of 95% and 5% of C, a partnership organised under the laws of country X. This partnership, however, is elected to be treated as a corporation for US tax purposes. In year X, C has an income of 500i and was subject to a CIT of 30% in country X. Partners A and B must pay taxes in country X for the amount of 142.5i and 7.5i, respectively.[764] Under the matching rule, however, if an owner's share in a reverse hybrid's income has no other income taxable by the foreign country where the reverse hybrid is organised, all of the foreign tax is allocated to and considered paid by the reverse hybrid.[765] In our case, therefore, C is liable for the whole amount of taxes that A and B paid because A and B did not have other income in country X. The payments are indeed treated as capital contributions to C.[766] (*See infra*).

Figure 12 Proposed Treasury Regulation Section 1.901-2(f) and Reverse Hybrids

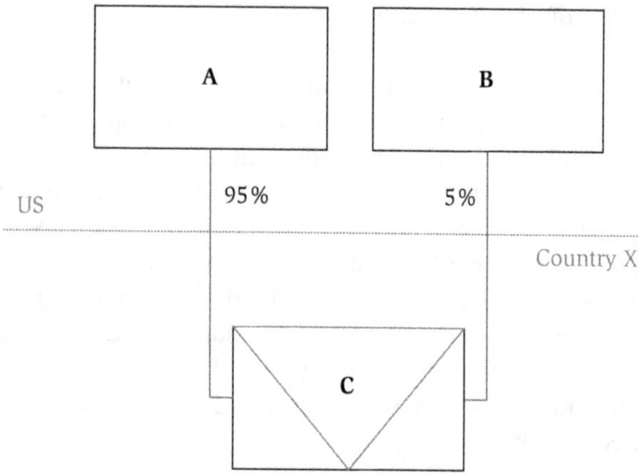

Year X' s Income of C = 500i
CIT in country X = 30% (150i)

The full amount of taxes is deemed to be paid by C for US tax purposes. A and B do not have FTC for the amounts paid because they did not receive other income from country X.

763. US: Proposed Treas. Reg. s. 1.901-2(f)(2)(iii).
764. US: Proposed Treas. Reg. s. 1.901-2(f)(6) Ex. 7.
765. US: Proposed Treas. Reg. s. 1.901-2(f)(2)(iii).
766. US: Proposed Treas. Reg. s. 1.901-2(f)(2)(v).

Accordingly, if foreign taxes are imposed on a hybrid entity, i.e., a taxable foreign entity regarded as fiscally transparent for US tax purposes, the hybrid entity is considered to be legally liable for such tax under foreign tax law and, therefore, deemed, for US tax purposes, to pay the foreign taxes.[767] In other words, the foreign taxes are allocated among the partners.[768] Assuming the same facts of the hypothetical above, with the only difference that C is an entity regarded as opaque for country X tax purposes whilst as fiscally transparent for US tax purposes, the outcome is that A is entitled to an FTC of 142.5i and B on the amount of 7.5i, which is calculated in proportion to the income attributable to them; namely, 475i are allocable to A, whilst 25i are allocable to B.[769]

Figure 13 Proposed Treasury Regulation Section 1.901-2(f) and Hybrid Entities

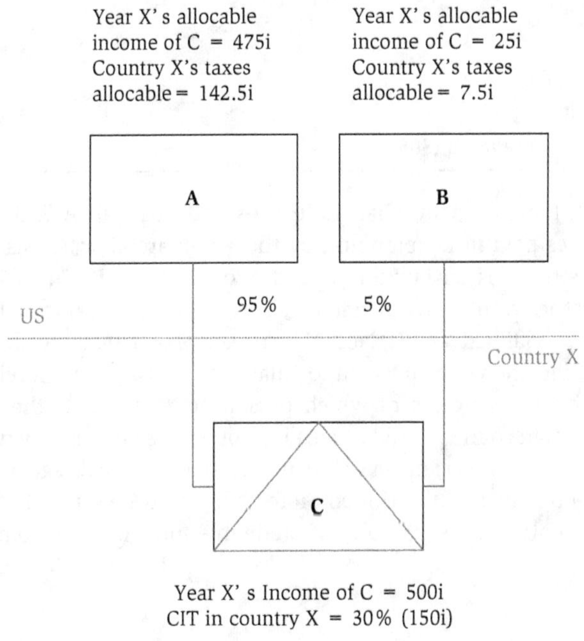

767. US: Proposed Treas. Reg. s. 1.901-2(f)(3).
768. Bittker and Lokken, *supra* n. 556, p. 72-19.
769. For some authors, however, this does not appear to change the results under the existing rules. *See, e.g.*, J. Riedy, *Proposed Code Sec. 901 Regulations Revise the Technical Taxpayer Rule*, 6 J. Tax'n Global Transactions 19, 22 (2006). Indeed, the proposed regulations did not change the rule by which income tax is considered paid, for US income tax purposes, by the foreign person on whom foreign law imposes legal liability for such tax and presented the regulations as a clarification of that general rule. For a critical analysis in this regard, *see, e.g.*, H. Levine and M. Miller, *Proposed Regulations 'Clarifying' the Technical Taxpayer Rule Don't Pass the Giggle Test*, 33 Int'l Tax J. 5 (2007).

On the other hand, the proposed regulations modified the results achieved in *Guardian Industries* since foreign income tax must be allocated to all members of the group in proportion to the income of each member.[770] Indeed, as per the proposed regulations, if foreign law imposes tax on the combined income of two or more persons, it is deemed that the legal liability is imposed on each of these persons for the amount of the foreign tax that it is attributable to such person's portion of the tax base.[771] Taking the example of Figure 11, let us assume that the gross income of the tax group in year X is 200i, which is subject to a 30% CIT in Luxembourg. We will also assume that under the laws in Luxembourg, the loss of Lux Sub B is allocated to Guardian Industries and Lux Sub A according to their income.

Figure 14 Income of the Group – Proposed Treasury Regulation Section 1.901-2(f)

Guardian Industries	100i[772]
Lux Sub A	100i
Lux Sub B	(60)i
Net Group Income	140i
Assumed Luxembourg taxes (30%)	42i

As noted, therefore, Guardian Industries and Lux Sub A had both 70i of net income; the taxes paid in Luxembourg by the group are allocated as follows: 21i on Guardian Industries, 21i on Lux Sub A and 0i on Lux Sub B. The above means that Guardian Industries would have declared its correspondent income in the United States and would have claimed an FTC of 21i instead of 42i paid by the whole group. Similarly, if no income were allocated to Guardian Industries, no foreign taxes would be allocated either, regardless of which person actually remits the taxes or which person of the foreign country could proceed to collect the taxes if they were not paid.[773] These regulations, however, never achieved the status of final regulations.[774]

In 2010, nonetheless, the United States adopted a new matching rule with the purpose of preventing the separation of creditable foreign taxes from the associated

770. US: Treas. Reg. s. 1.901-2(f)(2)(i).
771. Bittker and Lokken, *supra* n. 556, p. 72-15.
772. 'i' represents a foreign currency.
773. The term 'person' includes a disregarded entity. Bittker and Lokken, *supra* n. 556, p. 72-15. *See also*, Riedy, *supra* n. 754.
774. *See, e.g.*, D. Forst, *Recently Enacted Code Sec. 909 Targets 'Splitter' Transactions (Part 1)*, 14 J. Passthrough Entities 1 (2011). The proposed regulations also addressed an amendment to the voluntary payment rule in Proposed Treas. Reg. s. 1.901-2(e)(5). Under the proposed regulation, all foreign entities in which the same US person has a direct or indirect interest of 80% or more would be treated as a single taxpayer. For a further analysis, *see* Riedy, *supra* n. 754, pp. 11-12 and 69-71.

foreign income that originated them.[775] Under this new rule, if a foreign tax credit splitting event occurs with respect to a foreign income tax, this tax will not be taken into account for US tax purposes before the taxable year in which the 'related income' is also taken into account by the taxpayer.[776] The term 'related income' is referred to in the statute as any income, or earnings and profits, to which such portion of foreign income taxes relates.[777] Accordingly, it is understood that there is a 'foreign tax credit splitting event'[778] with respect to foreign income taxes if the related income is or will be taken into account by a 'covered person', which is, with respect to any person who pays or accrues the foreign income taxes: (a) any entity in which the payer holds, directly or indirectly, at least 10% ownership by vote or value;[779] (b) any person who holds, directly or indirectly, at least 10% ownership by vote or value in the payer;[780] and (c) any person who bears a relationship with the payer according to IRC Section 267(b) or 707(b).[781] Therefore, a splitting event will take place when foreign taxes and related income are allocated to different but related persons for US tax purposes, being a related person technically called a 'covered person' for this purpose.[782] In addition, and contrary to the proposed regulations under Treasury Regulation Section 1.901-2(f), the rules on foreign tax credit splitting event (Section 909) do not disallow the use of the FTC, but rather they suspend its use until the entity claiming the credit takes into account the related income.

The application of the new IRC Section 909 can be illustrated as follows. Let us assume a simplified structure based on *Guardian Industries* by which a domestic Corporation, USCo, wholly owns LuxCo, a Luxembourgish corporation acting as holding, which subsequently wholly owns OpCo, an operational subsidiary of LuxCo.[783] Both entities situated in Luxembourg are part of a single tax group. LuxCo is solely liable to file the tax returns of the group and to pay the CIT tax at a rate of 30% on the amount of 100i of income that OpCo generated in Year X. Accordingly, whilst OpCo remains treated as a corporation for US tax purposes, LuxCo elects to be treated as a disregarded entity. No dividends are distributed from OpCo to LuxCo in year X.

775. US: Staff of the Joint Committee on Taxation, *Technical Explanations of the Revenue Provisions of the Senate Amendment to the House Amendment to the Senate Amendment to the H.R. 1586, Scheduled for Consideration by the House of Representatives on August 10, 2010* (JCX-46-10), 10 August 2010, p. 4.
776. US: IRC s. 909(a). Nevertheless, the key is on the person. For example, if the same person has both the foreign taxes and the related income, and no covered person takes the income into account, the failure in recognising the income in the same year does not delay the use of the FTC. *See* Rosenberg, *supra* n. 762, p. 702. *See also*, Forst, *supra* n. 774, p. 12.
777. US: IRC s. 909(d)(3).
778. US: IRC s. 909(d)(4).
779. US: IRC s. 909(d)(4)(A).
780. US: IRC s. 909(d)(4)(B).
781. US: IRC s. 909(d)(4)(C). Letter (D) of s. 909(d)(4) also includes: 'any other person specified by the Secretary,' which may certainly expand the list of covered persons.
782. Rosenberg, *supra* n. 762.
783. This example is taken from Bittker and Lokken, s. 72.5A: 'Deferral of foreign income tax on Income not currently recognized,' with some modifications. *See* Bittker and Lokken, *supra* n. 556, pp. 72-87.

Figure 15 Application of IRC Section 909 'FTC Splitting Event'

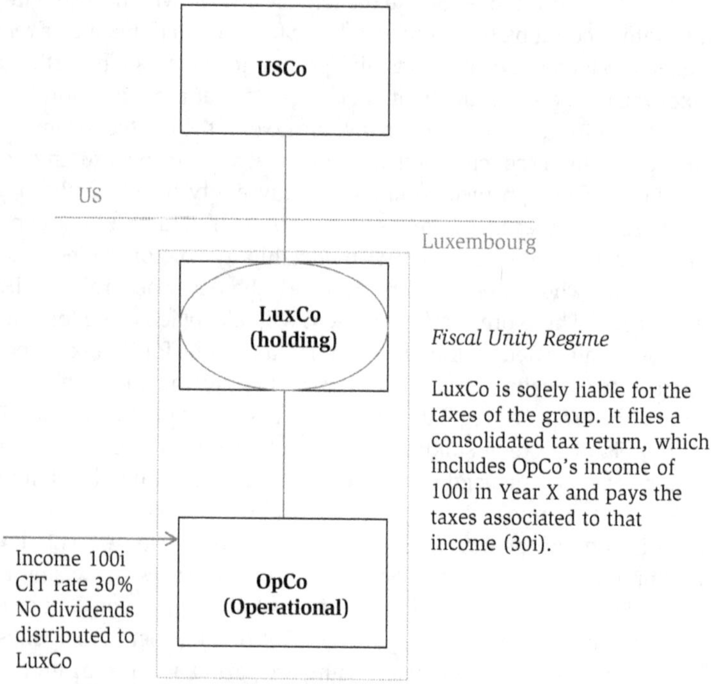

In the absence of IRC Section 909, LuxCo would be regarded, for US tax purposes, as solely liable for the taxes of the group. Accordingly, as LuxCo is a disregarded entity for US tax purposes, USCo could claim an FTC in the amount of 30i, regardless that this latter in the United States recognizes no income because indeed OpCo did not distribute dividends to LuxCo in Year X. Nevertheless, under IRC Section 909, OpCo would be regarded as a 'covered person' with respect to USCo, because this latter through LuxCo (disregarded as an entity in the US) owns at least 10% of OpCo. In addition, the amount of 100i, from which LuxCo paid 30i of taxes in Luxembourg, would be considered as 'related income', and there would be an FTC splitting event with respect to the taxes paid by LuxCo because, for US tax purposes, the related income of 100i is included only in the E&P of a covered person (OpCo).[784]

Despite the importance of IRC Section 909 to counteract situations in which, due to hybrid entities, an FTC is improperly granted, they are not exempt from criticism. First, it is argued that the definition of 'related income' is not as precise as it should be to determine when an FTC splitting event occurs. Indeed, it is undeniable that the definition of 'related income' is circular, i.e., it refers to income to which foreign taxes

784. *Ibid.*

relate.[785] One should argue, on the contrary, that similar matching rules exist with respect to the allocation of foreign taxes to income divided into two baskets (general active income and passive income) for determining the FTC for US tax purposes.[786] Nevertheless, such regulations attempt to match foreign taxes with income according to the foreign law's perception of the tax base, whilst the FTC splitting rules attempt to do the same, but according to US tax law.[787] For example, under these latter rules, no consideration is made with respect to the share of losses or whether a payment is debt or equity for foreign tax purposes.[788] The above makes the task of matching foreign taxes with related income an extremely difficult one.[789] Second, the focus on the person who takes the income into account for US tax purposes seems to deviate from the historic approach adopted by the IRS.[790] As noted, IRC Section 909 attempts to grant the FTC to the person who takes into account the related income for US tax purposes rather than for foreign tax purposes. This approach seems to deviate from the previous regulations that intended to match the FTC with the related income for foreign tax purposes.[791] Finally, although the concept of 'covered persons' includes only related persons, limiting thus the application of Section 909 to the cases in which FTC and related income are split, the statute gives the IRS the possibility of extending the concept of covered persons to 'any person that the Treasury specifies'.[792] In other words, cases in which the splitting of FTC and related income is made between unrelated persons are also hypothetically possible.

5 COORDINATION IN AN UNCOORDINATED WORLD

As noted so far, the whole issue regarding hybrid and reverse hybrid entities responds to the domestic characterisation of foreign entities for tax purposes. Thus, it seems to be legitimate to ask at this point whether coordination might be indeed a more accurate approach to avoid the misuse of these hybrid structures.[793]

785. US: IRC s. 909(d)(3).
786. According to US tax law, the credit for the amount of foreign taxes may not exceed the US tax, before the credit, on income from foreign sources. This is known as FTC limitation. US: IRC s. 904(a). The FTC limitation must be determined separately for foreign taxes on each of the two baskets: passive category and general category. US: IRC s. 904(d). *See also*, Bittker and Lokken, *supra* n. 556, pp. 72-93 and 72-123.
787. Rosenberg, *supra* n. 762, p. 703.
788. *Ibid.*
789. *Ibid., see also*, J. Bates, *Nature Abhors a Splitter: The FTC Splitter and Indirect FTC Rules*, 61 Tax Notes Int'l 7, 517 (2011).
790. Rosenberg, *supra* n. 762.
791. As provided in Treas. Reg. s. 1.901-2(f)(1): 'The person by whom tax is considered paid for purposes of section 901 and 903 is the person on whom foreign law imposes legal liability for such tax, even if another person (e.g., a withholding agent) remits such tax.' US: Treas. Reg. s. 1.901-2(f)(1).
792. US: IRC s. 909(d)(4)(D).
793. Coordination, however, must not be understood as synonymous of harmonisation. As it will be detailed at *infra* Chapter 6, I propose a rule ('*reactive coordination rule*'), which, on one hand, helps eliminating the hybrid mismatch itself, and, on the other hand, is applied in a simpler and more coherent manner.

This section provides three examples of different degrees of coordination in the characterisation of foreign entities: Spain, Denmark, the attempted coordination rule within the Proposal for an EU ATAD, and the recent Article 9a of the EU ATAD. These examples demonstrate that coordination in the characterisation of entities is beyond being a utopian academic idea, and it might be a very effective manner to deal with hybrids and reverse hybrid entities.

5.1 The Spanish Experience: An Example of Coordination in the Home Country?

The Spanish characterisation system of foreign entities for tax purposes is an interesting case of analysis. Originally designed as a resemblance test by statute, its practical application by the Spanish Tax Administration (DGT) considers specially the tax treatment given to the entity in its own jurisdiction, i.e., where the entity is established, reducing thus the possibilities of disparities in the characterisation of foreign entities practically to zero, at least in all cases in which Spain is the country classifying a foreign entity in a different manner. Disparities in the characterisation of Spanish entities will, however, still exist with respect to Spanish domestic entities characterised differently by a foreign country. In such a case, Spain does not change the domestic characterisation of its own entities to coordinate them with those in the foreign country.[794]

5.1.1 Spanish Legal Entities in Brief

Article 1665 of the Spanish Civil Code defines a 'legal entity' [Spanish: *sociedad*] as 'a contract by which two or more persons agree to put in common money, goods or industry, with the aim of distributing the benefits among them'.[795] A similar definition is held in Article 166 of the Spanish Commercial Code, which provides that an entity is: '[A] contract by which two or more persons agree to put in common money, goods, industry or any of these in a common fund, to obtain profits, will have commercial nature, whatever the type, as far as it has been incorporated according to this Code.'[796] Therefore, 'legal entities' [or *sociedades*] can be regarded as civil or commercial [or business] law entities under Spanish Law.[797]

The distinction between civil and business entities is crucial under Spanish law since, as a general rule, only business entities are subject to the Corporate Income Tax

794. This latter situation occurs, nevertheless, in the case of specific Danish provision dealing with the US CTB Regulations. *Infra* s. 5.2.
795. ES: Article 1165 of the Royal Decree of 24 July 1889 that publishes the Civil Code (hereinafter, 'Spanish Civil Code') [translation by the author].
796. ES: Article 166 of the Royal Decree of 22 August 1885 that publishes the Commercial Code (hereinafter, 'Spanish Commercial Code'). Articles 166-168 of the Spanish Commercial Code are currently repealed by the Law No. 19/1989 of 25 July 1989 on partial reform and adaptation of the commercial law to the Directives of the European Community with respect to legal entities [B.O.E. 27 July 1989] (translation by the author).
797. Other distinctions can be made, e.g., between public and private entities. *See* ES: Article 35 of the Spanish Civil Code.

Law.[798] All civil law entities, on the contrary, are subject to a special regime called 'Income Attribution Regime' or *[Regimén de Atribución de Rentas]*, which, in simple words, means that these legal entities will not be taxable. Instead, their income and the respective taxes will be attributed to their partners, who will suffer the final tax burden.[799] The above, however, does not mean Spain makes a systematic distinction between corporations and partnerships or between opaque and transparent entities in its internal legislation, at least not as it can be seen in common law countries such as the US or the UK, but it provides a very close distinction when separates between civil and business entities for purposes of the application of the Corporate Income Tax.[800]

5.1.2 The **'Income Attribution Regime'** *of the Spanish NRITL*

The special 'Income Attribution Regime' can also be applicable to foreign entities whose juridical nature is similar or identical to the Spanish entities. Indeed, according to Article 37 of the Spanish Non-Resident Income Tax Law (NRITL): 'Those entities incorporated abroad and whose juridical nature is identical or analogous to those of the entities subject to the income attribution regime, which are incorporated according to the Spanish Law, shall also be considered as entities subject to attribution of income regime.'[801] Thus, in simple words, non-resident or foreign entities having an identical or analogous legal nature to 'Spanish transparent entities', i.e., entities subject to the Spanish income attribution regime, will also be considered transparent. This analysis of equivalence or resemblance test includes several factors, such as the legal form of the foreign entity, legal personality, capital divided by shares, etc.

798. Since 2014, however, civil law entities with a commercial object will be subject to Corporate Income Tax. *See* ES: Article 7(a) of the Corporate Income Tax Law [*Ley del Impuesto sobre las Sociedades*], Law 27/2014 (consolidated text) of 27 November 2014, BOE No. 288 of 28 November 2014.

799. ES: Article 8.3 of the Personal Income Tax Law, Law 35/2006 of 28 November 2006 [*Ley de Impuesto a la Renta sobre las Personas Físicas (LIRPF)*]. Original Spanish text: '*No tendrán la consideración de contribuyentes las sociedades civiles no sujetas al Impuesto de Sociedades, herencias yacentes, comunidades de bienes y demás entidades a que se refiere el artículo 35.4 de la Ley 58/2003, de 17 de diciembre, General Tributaria. Las rentas correspondientes a las mismas se atribuirán a los socios, herederos, comuneros o partícipes, respectivamente, de acuerdo a lo establecido en la Sección 2ª del Titulo X de esta Ley.*' Articles 86 and 90 of the LIRPF regulate the 'Income Attribution Regime.'

800. Considering the transposition of EU law into Spanish law, several legal entities subject to tax transparency treatment have arisen. This is the case, e.g., of the Spanish Economic Interest Groups, the European Economic Interest Group and the Temporary Business Association [*Union Temporal de Empresas*]. *See* ES: Law No. 12/1991 of 29 April 1991 on Economics Interest Groups, and Law No. 18/1982 of 26 May 1982 on Temporary Business Associations. *See also*, EU: Council Regulation (EEC) No. 2137/85 of 25 July 1985 on the European Economic Interest Grouping – EEIG – (OJ L 199, 31 July 1985).

801. ES: Article 37 of the Spanish Non-Resident Income Tax Law–NRITL, Royal Legislative Decree No. 5/2004 of 5 March 2004 [translation by the author].

5.1.3 *The Spanish Characterisation Test in Practice*

Despite the textual wording of Article 37 Spanish NRITL, which can be read as a simple resemblance test,[802] Spanish tax scholars agree that when this test is applicable by the Spanish tax authority (DGT), the tax treatment given in the foreign country is the central element to determine the legal characterisation of the foreign entity in Spain.[803] In other words, the administrative practice of the DGT seems to settle a unique example of coordination in the characterisation of foreign entities that reduces practically to zero the possibilities of disparities in the characterisation of foreign entities, at least in all those cases in which Spain is the country classifying a foreign entity for domestic tax purposes.[804]

The above has been ratified in several binding rulings issued by the DGT up to this date. For example, a recent consultation in 2015[805] referred to the juridical nature of a 'German *Kommanditgesellschaft*' (German KG)[806] owned by some Spanish residents. As per the German tax law, a KG, independently of its legal personality, is subject to a tax regime in Germany by which the income of the entity is not subject to tax at the level of the entity but rather at the level of the partners. The DGT considered that the German KG had a similar or identical nature to the Spanish entities subject to the income attribution regime.[807] Thus, for purposes of Spanish Income Tax Law, such German KG will have the same tax treatment in Spain, which means that the Spanish partners should recognise the income of the KG according to their participation in the entity. Likewise, the DGT clarified that if dividends were distributed from the German KG to the Spanish partners, which were attributed to previous tax years in which the Spanish partners included their respective income attribution, they would not be subject to tax again in Spain.[808] This opinion with respect to the German KG resembles a previous binding ruling issued by the DGT in 2014.[809]

Similarly, the DGT stated in a general ruling of 2005, with respect to the consultation regarding a Scottish General Partnership, that this entity has a nature similar to or identical to the Spanish entities subject to the income attribution regime.[810] One of the elements considered in this consultation was the fact that the General Partnership, according to Scottish tax law, was regarded as transparent for Scottish tax purposes.[811] In 2007, in another general ruling, the DTG stated that a

802. *See, e.g.*, the cases of Germany and the Netherlands, *supra* s. 3.2.1.
803. *See, e.g.*, D. Jiménez-Valladolid de L'Hotellerie-Fallois and F. Vega Borrego, *Chapter 29: Spain* in *Corporate Income Tax Subjects* (ed. D. Gutmann), EATLP International Tax Series, Vol. 12 (2016), pp. 460-464. *See also* A. Mosquera Mouriño, *Régimen de atribución de rentas: especial referencia a las actividades económicas*, Carta Tributaria 4 (2012), pp. 3-16.
804. It is, however, always possible to get a ruling clarifying the tax status of an entity liable (or potentially liable) to tax in Spain. *See* ES: Articles 88 and 89 of the General Taxation Law [*Ley General Tributaria*], Law No. 58/2003 of 17 December 2003.
805. ES: DGT, Consulta Vinculante No. V3836-15 of 2 December 2015.
806. This could be equivalent to the concept of '*Limited Partnership*' used in common law countries.
807. ES: DGT, *supra* n. 805.
808. *Ibid.*
809. ES: DGT, Consulta Vinculante No. V1631-14 of 25 June 2014.
810. ES: DGT, Consulta General No. 0196-05 of 1 June 2005.
811. *Ibid.*

British partnership rendering legal services in Spain through an office should be regarded to have a nature similar or identical to the Spanish entities subject to the income attribution regime.[812] This conclusion was achieved bearing in mind specially the 'legal regime applicable to partnerships in the UK'.[813] On the contrary, when the tax transparency treatment of the entity is not clear at all, either because of the foreign legislation or for the lack of information when the taxpayer submitted the consultation, the DGT has considered the tax treatment of the entity as opaque. For example, in the binding ruling No. 0012-11 of 11 January 2011,[814] which referred to the legal nature of some international funds of capital risk using the form of limited partnerships, the DGT analysed the concurrence of several factors, including limited liability of the limited partners, the administration of the fund by a third party, and the existence of an agreement to distribute profits in which the limited partners have no influence. However, the taxpayer submitting the consultation in this case did not provide enough information regarding where exactly these funds were incorporated,[815] which, under the author's view, influenced the final decision of the DGT to consider these funds as opaque entities. Someone could also argue that the limited liability of the partners, as well as the other factors analysed by the DGT, were enough to achieve the same conclusion. Nevertheless, the DGT has opted clearly in other rulings to treat an LP or LLP as transparent entities when such treatment is clearly stated in the country of incorporation.[816]

Although it is arguable to affirm that Spain completely deviates from the resemblance test established by statute, it is possible to conclude from the administrative practice of the DGT that the tax characterisation of foreign entities given in the foreign country is the decisive factor in determining the tax characterisation in Spain.[817] The above can be seen, e.g., in a very recent binding ruling No. 3319-16 of 14 July 2016,[818] referred to a Spanish entity owned 100% by a German KG, which is

812. ES: DGT, Consulta General No. 0024-07 of 1 July 2007.
813. *Ibid.*, *see also*, ES: DGT, Consulta General No. 2110-04 of 30 December 2004, with respect to tax treatment given to a British partnership in Spain.
814. ES: DGT, Consulta Vinculante No. V0012-11 of 11 January 2011.
815. In this case the taxpayer is limited to inform that such funds were incorporated in the form of limited partnerships (LP), like the ones of Anglo-Saxons countries. *Ibid.*
816. For example, ES: DGT, Consulta Vinculante No. V1398-16 of 5 April 2016, referred to the nature of an LLP incorporated in the UK. In a similar response regarding the treatment of a British LLP, *see* ES: DGT, Consulta Vinculante No. V036-14 of 10 February 2014.
817. For example, other factors considered in the DGT Consulta General No. 0196-05 of 1 June 2005 were that, according to the UK tax law: (1) the general partnership had legal personality, although its capital was not divided in shares; (2) the unlimited liability of the partners; (3) the management if the entity is made by each of the members who act as agents of the entity and the rest of the members; (4) the partnership is not obligated to deposit annual accounts in the UK; (5) the partners are entitled to the profits without need of a decision or agreement at the entity level. None of these factors, however, were as relevant as the fact that the entity was not subject to tax in the UK at the level of the entity, but rather at the level of the partners. *See* ES: DGT, Consulta General No. 0196-05 of 1 June 2005.
818. ES: DGT, Consulta Vinculante No. V3319-16 of 17 July 2016.

subsequently owned by two partners: a general partner in Germany and a limited partner in the UK. The question referred exclusively to the potential application of the tax treaty between Spain and the UK. with respect to the limited partner of the German KG in the UK. Even though the DGT pronounced already with respect to the legal nature of the German KG for Spanish tax purposes, considering it as fiscally transparent, the DGT repeated in several passages of this recent ruling that the fact that the KG is regarded as transparent in Germany, and in this case also in the UK, permits to treat it also as tax transparent in Spain (i.e., subject to the 'Income Attribution Regime'), also making applicable the Spain-UK tax treaty.

On the other side, in my opinion, the level of coordination achieved with respect to the characterisation of foreign entities for tax purposes has to be with the similitude between the Spanish 'Income Attribution Regime' and the concept of 'transparent entities' mostly used, but not exclusively, in common law countries. Indeed, whilst a transparent entity will be an entity not subject to tax at the level of the entity but at the level of the partners, e.g., a partnership, an entity subject to the 'Income Attribution Regime' will be an entity whose income is attributed directly to the partners. In other words, a fiscally transparent entity. In the same order of ideas, if a foreign entity is taxable at the level of the entity (i.e., it is an opaque entity), it will also be considered as such for Spanish tax purposes. This coordinated outcome thus nullifies all the possibilities of disparities in the characterisation of foreign entities for Spanish tax purposes, i.e., when Spain classifies foreign entities, also reducing the complexity of the Spanish resemblance test and increasing the levels of legal certainty for taxpayers involved in legitimate tax planning structures through foreign entities.[819]

Finally, it is interesting to highlight that the Spanish solution provides, to a certain extent, a degree of coordination in the characterisation of the entity at source. Indeed, and contrary to other solutions that will be analysed further on in this work,[820] it is not the country receiving a hybrid payment which states the characterisation to be followed, but rather the country where this payment is sourced. This solution seems to

819. On the contrary, Villar argues that the question of characterising foreign entities in Spain is highly an individual task, which is very time consuming and leads to legal uncertainty. *See* Villar, *supra* n. 568. I do not disagree that the factors to be considered in the characterisation of a foreign entity are several, and as any other resemblance test, is costly. However, I estimate that the Spanish IFA report does not properly evaluate the extensive Spanish tax administrative practice, which clearly shows a tendency to recognise the tax treatment of the foreign entity in its country of organisation, which certainly reduces the time-consuming cost, at least partially. Indeed, for instance, if a taxpayer asking the DGT regarding the tax treatment of an entity, e.g., a US LLC, whose tax treatment in the United States is clear will, he will experience – most likely – a higher degree of certainty.

820. Especially the one proposed within the OECD Partnership Report, which attempts coordination in the characterisation of entities in the residence country. *Infra* Chapter 4 s. 3.

be, in principle, fairer with developing countries, and interestingly, it was also proposed in the original text of the EU ATAD Directive in 2016.[821]

5.2 The Danish Experience: Re-characterisation of Its Own Entities

Unlike the Spanish example above, Denmark has some specific rules providing for a certain degree of coordination in the characterisation of its own domestic entities with the one provided by a foreign country under certain circumstances.[822] In other words, if certain requirements are met, a domestic Danish taxable entity, considered tax transparent by a foreign country, can also be re-characterised as a transparent entity in Denmark. Likewise, a Danish transparent entity can be re-characterised as a taxable entity if the foreign country considers it as a taxable entity. Both rules are indeed a targeted reaction to the characterisation of entities derived specifically from a potential electivity in the characterisation of Danish entities by a foreign country (i.e., the US Check-the-box rules) rather than a general rule attempting to coordinate the characterisation of foreign entities for Danish tax purposes at any level.[823] The above, however, does not rest merits to this interesting example of coordination in the characterisation rules to deal with both hybrid entities and reverse hybrids.

5.2.1 Danish Reaction to Hybrid Entities

In 2004, Denmark adopted a rule by which a Danish taxable entity may be re-characterised as tax transparent if certain requirements are met:[824] (i) the taxable entity is a Danish resident entity or a PE of a foreign resident company; (ii) the Danish taxable entity is disregarded for foreign tax purposes; (iii) the income of the Danish company is included in the taxable income of the 'controlled foreign legal entity', i.e., an entity that owns more than 50% of the Danish company or holds more than 50% of the voting rights; and (iv) the foreign country is a member of the EEA or a tax treaty partner with

821. *Infra* s. 5.3. There is no doubt, however, that the deviation from the textual wording of the law made by the Spanish Tax Administration as to interpret the Income Attribution Regime affects the principle of legality and it might thus be considered undesirable. However, it is undeniable that from a pragmatic point of view, the interpretation of the Spanish Tax Administration provides an interesting solution of coordination regarding the issue of hybrid entities.
822. This can also be referred as 'coordination at residence', considering that Danish entities are re-characterised following the tax treatment given in the place where the parent company or investors are residents.
823. In this opinion, e.g., Dell'Anese, *supra* n. 4, p. 254. *See also*, A. Møllin Ottosen and M. Nørremark, *New Anti-Avoidance Rules in Denmark Targets Reverse Hybrids and Convertible Bonds*, 68 Bull. Intl. Taxn. 11 (2008), Journals IFBD, p. 513; J. Bundgaard, *Coordination Rules as a Weapon in the War Against Cross-Border Tax Arbitrage–The Case of Hybrid Entities and Hybrid Financial Instruments*, 67 Bull. Intl. Taxn. 4/5 (2013), Journals IBFD, pp. 200-201. All these authors coincide that the target of the 2004 and 2008 rules were exclusively the negative impact of the US CTB regulations.
824. DK: s. 2A of the Corporate Income Tax Law [SEL–*Selskabsskatteloven*]. This rule was adopted by the Bill 119 of 17 December 2003. *See*, J. Wittendorff, *Denmark's Hovmand Clarifies Pending Transparent Entities Legislation*, 33 Tax Notes Int'l 9, 758 (2004). *See also*, Dell'Anese, *supra* n. 4, p. 254.

Denmark.[825] If all the requirements are met, the Danish entity will be treated as a branch of the controlled foreign legal entity.[826]

As repeatedly argued by some authors, the reasons for these rules seem to be settled specifically to counteract some commonly used transactions in the past, which involved a Danish SPV financed with debt and owned by US persons, who always have the chance to elect how to treat the Danish company for tax purposes.[827] Therefore, since an SPV is a taxable entity for Danish tax purposes, the Danish company was able to deduct interest payments made to its US parent, although the interest income was never included in the United States due to the CTB election, treating the SPV as tax transparent for US tax purposes.[828] Interestingly, however, this domestic rule does not provide for a denial in the deduction made at the level of the SPV, but rather, it targets the real issue here, which is the different characterisation of the same entity by Denmark and the United States.[829] Since the SPV will, after the application of the rule, be considered also as tax transparent, the payment of interest will not be deductible any longer, although without the need to introduce a new domestic rule that denies the deduction.[830]

The application of the Danish anti-hybrid rule seems to be very straightforward. However, there are still some doubts about its real effectiveness. For example, the rule

825. Wittendorff, *supra* n. 824. J. Wittendorff, *Danish Parliament Enacts Transparent Entity Legislation*, 34 Tax Notes Int'l 1 (2004).
826. The fact that a Danish company is regarded as a branch does not entitle the company to take a deduction for payments made to the foreign parent company or to the group related entities, which are also treated as fiscally transparent under laws of the residence State of the foreign company. The payments are indeed considered to be made within the same legal entity. Accordingly, dividends paid from the Danish entity to the foreign controlled legal entity are not subject to WHT. *See* A. Riis and P.E. Lytken, *Denmark-Corporate Taxation* s. 10, Country Analyses IBFD (accessed on 1 August 2023). Nevertheless, 'if there is a direct link between external borrowings by the foreign parent company and the loan granted to the transparent entity, the interest paid by the foreign parent should be allocable to the transparent entity in accordance with ordinary principles of PE taxation'. Wittendorff, *supra* n. 824. *See also*, Dell'Anese, *supra* n. 4, pp. 254-255.
827. *See, e.g.*, N. Bjørnholm and A. Obery Hansen, *Denmark in International Tax Planning*, Online Books IBFD, 2005, p. 41–s. 4.16.2. Also, as provided by Bundgaard: 'Despite the general wording of the provision [Section 2A SEL], the practical scope appear to be Danish entities that are eligible for the U.S. check-the-box election. As a practical issue, this [application of the rule] includes primarily Danish companies organised in the form of a private limited company (*Anpartsselskab*–ApS). If an election is made according to US law to treat a Danish ApS as a transparent entity for US tax purposes, this may invoke this provision.' Bundgaard, *supra* n. 823, p. 201. Accordingly, Møllin Ottosen and Nørremark state: 'Different classifications of entities have been considered a problem mainly in relation to Danish limited partnerships whose direct owners are tax resident in the United States.' Møllin Ottosen and Nørremark, *supra* n. 823.
828. We are assuming, of course, that the Danish SPV is an eligible entity for purposes of the CTB election. *Supra* s. 4.3.
829. Indirectly, however, the deduction is denied since it is disregarded for Danish tax purposes after the re-characterisation. *Infra* Chapter 5 refers specifically to this solution, proposed by the OECD within the BEPS Action Plan 2, and known as 'primary response'.
830. A Danish company, which has been re-characterised as fiscally transparent, is also not considered as a Danish tax resident and thus is not subject to the benefits of the EU Directives and tax treaties signed by Denmark. Riis and Lytken, *supra* n. 826. Accordingly, the Danish company will no longer be subject to full-Danish corporate taxation. Wittendorff, *supra* n. 824.

requires re-characterising a domestic taxable entity as tax transparent so that the income of the Danish SPV is included in the taxable income of the US parent, which is assumed to be a controlled foreign entity. The above represents, first, an important practical limitation of the rule since no re-characterisation will occur in all those cases in which the Danish company has indeed no operating income in a specific taxable year. Second, the fact that Denmark treats a domestic taxable entity as tax transparent does not change the fact that the United States disregards the payments of the interests and any other transactions between the Danish company and the US parent. Therefore, the interests will not be subject to tax anywhere and no matter what because they will be disregarded for all tax purposes. Likewise, the rules are not entirely clear whether they apply in cases of a US taxpayer treating a Danish entity as transparent, without making use of the CTB election, but rather due to the default rules of classification in the United States.[831] Is, in this case, the Danish anti-hybrid rule applicable? If not, there would certainly be a range of situations that would not be covered under the rule, allowing a circumvention of it.[832] If yes, it would make more sense because, in such a case, the rule would counteract both the effect of the election and the default rules, coordinating completely the characterisation of entities. Indeed, as stressed already in this chapter, the CTB system is indeed just partially elective, and this is an issue that should not be underestimated.[833]

Another example of the limited application of the rules is the case of group-related entities.[834] Let us assume the example of a US corporation that directly owns a holding company (Holding 1) incorporated in country X, and this latter owns another holding company (Holding 2) incorporated in country Y, which finally owns a Danish company (DCo). Let us also assume that Holding 2 grants a loan to DCo and that this latter pays back interests associated with that loan (*see* Figure 16).

831. US: Treas. Reg. s. 301.7701-3(b)(3)(ii), with respect to the US default rule of characterisation of entities. *See also*, *supra* s. 4.3. for a further analysis.
832. This will certainly depend on the Danish law. If Danish law, e.g., allows to modify the responsibility of a Danish entity with two or more members (e.g., SPV, ApS, etc.), and one of these members becomes unlimited liable for the responsibilities of the entity, the Danish entity will be considered by default as a tax transparent entity for US tax purposes. US: Treas. Reg. s. 301.7701-3(b)(2)(1)(A).
833. *Supra* s. 4.3.
834. 'Unless the Danish subsidiary is held by the US parent company through one of more intermediate holding companies, which are not treated as fiscally transparent for US tax purposes, the Danish subsidiary is reclassified as a branch under section 2A.' *See* Riis and Lytken, *supra* n. 826.

Figure 16 Danish Anti-hybrid Rule and Group-Related Entities

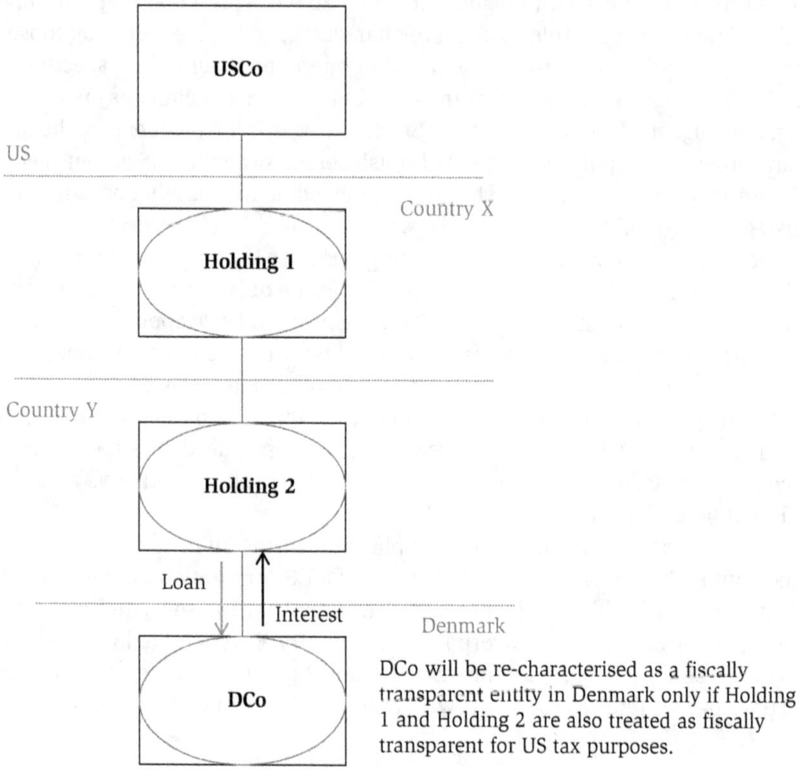

In this case, the Danish rule applies only to the extent that DCo and all the holding companies are treated as fiscally transparent under the tax rules of the foreign parent company, i.e., under the tax rules in the United States.[835] If the above does not happen, the interest will still be tax-deductible, although subject to the Danish thin capitalization rules.[836]

835. *Ibid.*
836. Wittendorff, *supra* n. 824, p. 759.

Figure 17 Danish Anti-hybrid Rule and Group-Related Entities (Second Assumption)

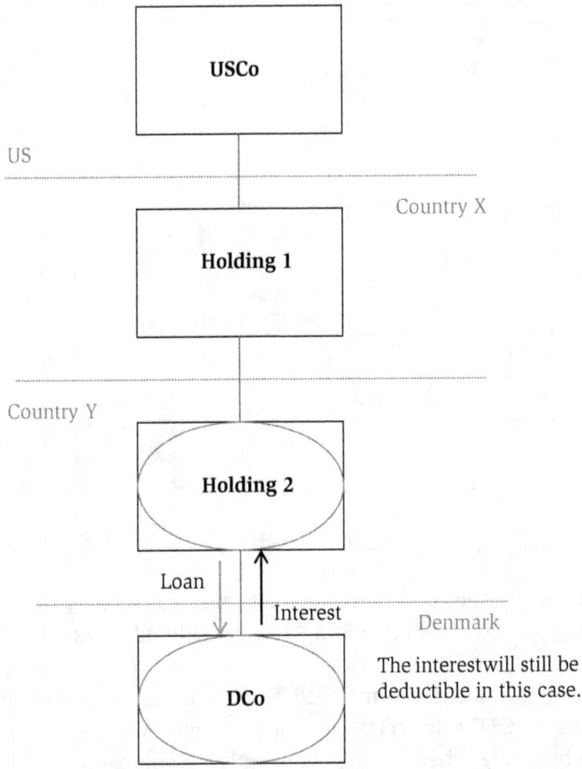

In the example above (*see* Figure 17), if Holding 1 is considered opaque for US tax purposes, whilst Holding 2 and DCo are regarded as tax transparent, the interests paid by DCo will still be deductible but subject to the Danish thin capitalization rules, assuming also that the income of the foreign creditor company is not included in the taxable income of the parent company in the United States.[837]

Let us now assume that Holding 2 does not exist anymore and that the structure only contemplates the US parent, Holding 1 and the Danish subsidiary, DCo.

837. *Ibid.* Ex. 3, Chart 2.

Figure 18 Danish Anti-hybrid Rule and Group Related Entities (Third Assumption)

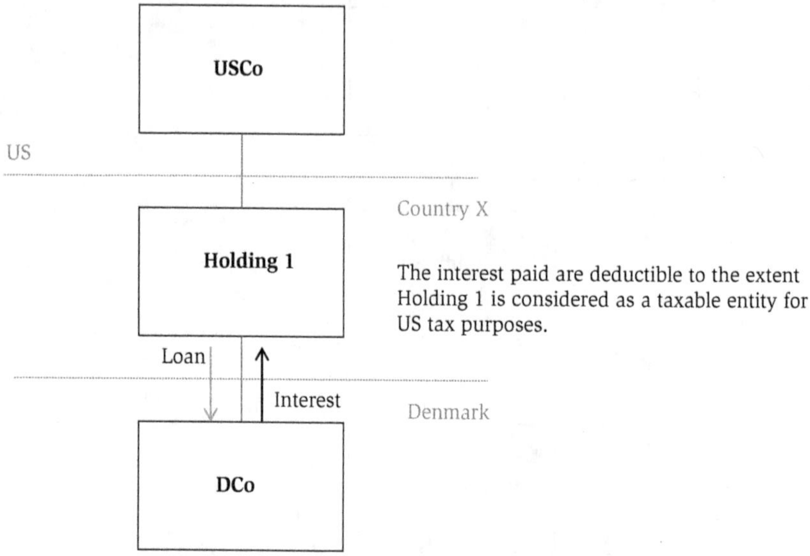

In such a case (*see* Figure 18), the interests paid from DCo to Holding 1 would also be deductible to the extent that Holding 1 is considered a taxable entity for US tax purposes.[838]

Although it is undeniable from all the assumptions above that the elective characteristic of the CTB rules certainly helps in circumventing the application of the Danish anti-hybrid rule when intermediary holding companies are involved,[839] one should also consider that in all those cases where the US parent decides to treat Holdings 1 and 2 as taxable entities in order to avoid the Danish anti-hybrids rule, they would most probably remain subject to CFC rules in the United States to the extent that Subpart F income is generated.[840] The above could perhaps not completely eliminate the abusive use of the CTB election, but at least increase the alternative costs for taxpayers when deciding about tax planning strategies involving holding companies in Denmark.[841]

838. *Ibid.* Ex. 1, Chart 2.
839. *Supra* s. 4.3.
840. Nonetheless, one should also consider that Subpart F income can be easily avoided in the United States without necessarily making use of the CTB election, e.g., through the 'same country exception.' *Supra* s. 4.4.1.
841. Although recognising that this is a very difficult issue to measure, Bundgaard states, from a practical experience, the following: '[T]he provision has had a significant effect on the structuring of the investments of US multinationals enterprises (MNEs) in Denmark.' *See* Bundgaard, *supra* n. 823, p. 201.

Finally, it is interesting to note the rationale behind the Danish anti-hybrid rule, especially with respect to the collection of taxes and the intention that income is taxed somewhere but not in Denmark. First, if a country wanted, as a general rule, to keep its taxing rights, thus collecting revenues, the Danish rule produced exactly the opposite effect, encouraging the collection of taxes in the other country. Indeed, the moment that all requirements are met, a Danish company will be re-characterised as tax transparent, therefore, not being subject to tax in Denmark anymore to the extent the income of the Danish company is recognised in the other country. This situation can be compared with the Spanish coordination in the characterisation of a foreign entity, which is made under a completely opposite idea, namely to follow the domestic treatment of a foreign entity in its country of organisation.[842] In this latter case, however, the possibility of revenue losses is lower.[843] Second, and regarding the aim of taxing the income somewhere, i.e., requesting that income of the Danish company be recognised in the other country, one should consider that this aim could be easily avoided in case the parent company is not necessarily located in the United States and rather in a low-tax jurisdiction. This issue could occur in theory since the Danish rule is written to be generally applied to all situations in which a Danish company is treated as tax transparent, so long all the other requirements are met, and not only in those cases in which the parent company is organised in the United States.[844] Likewise, the re-characterisation of a Danish entity as a tax-transparent entity does not change the characterisation made in the United States. This means a payment of interest from the Danish company to its parent will be completely disregarded in both countries. This solves the hybrid disparity, although strictly speaking keeps the interest income untaxed, i.e., disregarded as income.[845]

842. *Supra* s. 5.1.3.

843. For example, in a simple structure in which a Spanish company wholly owns a subsidiary in country X, and this country treats the entity as opaque, Spain will also follow this characterisation. Therefore, income will be taxed in country X. However, Spain could also tax the income by application of the CFC rules, decreasing the risk of tax deferral in Spain. Likewise, if the tax treatment of the subsidiary in its country of organisation was as fiscally transparent, Spain would follow that treatment and would again collect the taxes in the hands of the Spanish company (income is considered flowing through directly to the shareholders). In both cases, therefore, the revenue loss risk would be minimal.

844. Bundgaard, *supra* n. 823. Nevertheless, this rule would have any impact when applied to Spain. In such a case, as Spain will follow the Danish characterisation of the entity, there will be no space for the application of the Danish anti-hybrid rule. *Supra* s. 5.1.

845. This proves again the inconsistent logic behind the single taxation ideal. In contrast, however, Dell'Anese argues: '[T]he tax policy significance of the Danish initiative is clear: developed countries are beginning to take notice of U.S. entity classification rules [...]. They are also beginning to react, applying the single tax principle logic, to the US inaction in the outbound area, reaping this way all the tax advantage, as typical for first-movers in arbitrage situations.' Dell'Anese, *supra* n. 4, p. 256. *See also* the discussion about the single tax principle and the DNT outcome at *supra* Chapter 1, s. 3.

5.2.2 *Danish Reaction to Reverse Hybrids*

As per the case of hybrid entities, in 2008, the Danish Parliament adopted Bill No. L181, which contained measures to counteract the effects of cross-border structures involving *reverse hybrids*,[846] namely Danish entities considered as tax transparent in Denmark, whilst as taxable entities in the other country that is part of the transaction.[847] For this purpose, the rule provides that certain entities normally treated as fiscally transparent in Denmark, e.g., limited partnerships [*kommanditselskaber*], partnerships limited by shares [*partnerselskaber*] and branches of non-Danish entities, must be re-characterised as taxable entities if: (i) the direct owners/partners holding more than 50% of the capital or voting rights are tax residents in one or more foreign jurisdictions, the Faroe Islands, or Greenland;[848] and (ii) the jurisdiction where the owners are tax resident either considers the Danish entity to be a separate taxable entity, or it does not exchange information with the Danish tax authorities.[849] Accordingly, if the re-characterisation applies, it affects not only those who belong to the countries treating the Danish entity as a taxable entity or who do not exchange information with Denmark but also the other owners resident in countries treating the entity as tax transparent or those who indeed exchange information with Denmark.[850] Let us assume the following example where a US parent company has 51% of the voting rights in a Danish limited partnership [*kommanditselskaber*] – DLP – which is regarded as a fiscally transparent entity in Denmark. The remaining 49% belongs to owners who are residents in country X. Whilst the US owners elect to treat the DLP as a taxable entity, the owners in country X treat the DLP as fiscally transparent. Let us also assume that the DLP enters into a manufacturing agreement according to which a third party manufactures a product on behalf of the limited partner. According to this agreement, the DLP maintains the ownership of the IP, raw materials and final products. These latter are sold by DLP to unrelated parties outside Denmark.

---

846. It also contains measures to counteract convertible bonds. However, this topic will not be analysed here. For a reference, *see* Møllin Ottosen and Nørremark, *supra* n. 823. The rule is contained in DK: s. 2C of the Corporate Income Tax Law [SEL–*Selskabsskatteloven*].
847. *Supra* s. 3.1.
848. The 'direct owners/partners' do not need to be affiliated parties. Indeed, they can be separated companies or individuals that reside in foreign countries and that together hold more than 50% of the capital or voting powers. *See* Møllin Ottosen and Nørremark, *supra* n. 823, p. 514. Accordingly, non-Danish entities and branches, which are deemed to be fiscally transparent in their country of organisation, are disregarded for purposes of determining who are the direct owners/partners. The above is relevant, e.g., in the case a taxpayer decides to use an intermediary company (e.g., organised in country Y) between the US owners and the Danish transparent entity, which is deemed to be transparent in country Y, but as a taxable entity in the United States. In such a case, the entity in country Y is disregarded for purposes of determining who is the direct owner of the Danish entity. *Ibid.*
849. An exception to this anti-reverse hybrid rule applies for venture funds investing in medium- and small-sized companies if certain conditions are met. The reason for exempting venture funds is the desire to continue to encourage the start-up and growth of these types of businesses. Bundgaard, *supra* n. 823, p. 202.
850. Møllin Ottosen and Nørremark, *supra* n. 823, p. 514.

Figure 19 Danish Anti-reverse Hybrid Rule

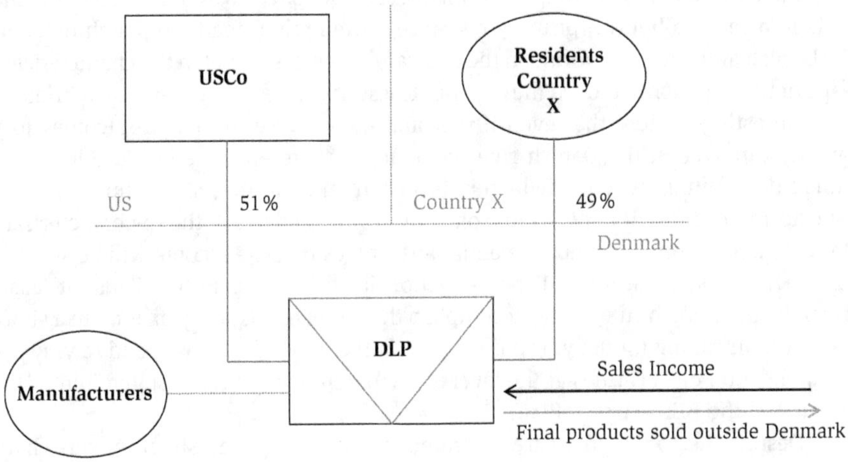

DLP is a fiscally transparent entity in Denmark. Likewise, country X also treats it as fiscally transparent. However, the US owners elected to treat it as a taxable entity.

In the absence of the Danish anti-reverse hybrid rule, the DLP is regarded as fiscally transparent in Denmark, and if there is no Danish PE either, the income derived from the sales is disregarded for tax purposes in Denmark (*see* Figure 19). This is to say, it flows through the owners in the United States and country X. Likewise, and because the US owners elected to treat the Danish entity as a taxable entity, the income is not taxed in the United States either, at least until dividends are distributed to the United States. Moreover, as income from manufacturing activities is not considered as Subpart F income ('manufacturing exception') in the United States, the application of the US CFC rules is also nullified.[851] Accordingly, as in this case, USCo owns more than 50% of the voting rights in DLP, and they elected to treat it as a taxable entity for US tax purposes; the DLP is re-characterised as a taxable entity in Denmark, also affecting those owners/partners who are not US residents.[852] In other words, the characterisation of the Danish entity is coordinated with the characterisation of the other country where the parent company is resident, i.e., the United States in this case. Thus, the DLP will be taxed in Denmark at a normal corporate tax rate of 25% on the income generated.[853]

851. US: Treas. Reg. s. 1.954-3(a)(4)(i). *See also*, *supra* s. 4.4.1.
852. Møllin Ottosen and Nørremark, *supra* n. 823, p. 514.
853. Other effects following the re-characterisation will include: (1) contrary to the normal rule that the owner of a fiscally transparent entity is deemed to own a proportionate part of the entity's assets and liabilities, this will be deemed to have an ownership in a separate entity. The above mans that any disposal of interest in the Danish entity will be regarded as a sale of shares, whose capital gains are not taxed in the hands of non-Danish residents; (2) a 'rollover principle' at the level of the owners of the entity, which ensures that they are generally not taxed on any

Interestingly, the Danish anti-reverse hybrid rule deviates from the recent OECD Action 2 of the BEPS Action Plan.[854] In brief, Action 2 provides for introducing a domestic rule denying a deduction at the level of the payer with respect to a payment made to a reverse hybrid (primary response), attempting finally to match outcomes. The Danish anti-reverse hybrid, on the contrary, attempts to match the characterisation of the entities, which is indeed the core of the issue with respect to reverse hybrids. Yet, it is interesting to note that even if the final target were to match outcomes to tax income somewhere, the Danish rule seems to be more effective because it does not require determining when a deduction has been taken in the third country payer, an issue normally difficult to determine on a big scale. In contrast, the re-characterisation of the domestic entity as a taxable entity guarantees that the income will be subject to tax in Denmark, regardless of the deduction in the third country. Thus, at least in principle, the Danish rule would accomplish the target of ensuring taxation in a simpler manner than calling for denying a deduction at the level of the payer and relying upon the application of CFC rules at the level of the parent company, as stated in the OECD Action 2 of the BEPS Action Plan.[855]

Despite the above, there are still some features of the Danish anti-reverse hybrid rule that are not completely convincing to apply as a solution at an international level. First, it is the one referred to the effect of the re-characterisation. It seems, at least *a priori*, unfair that the re-characterisation of a fiscally transparent entity as a taxable entity is applied to all partners, leaving the interest of minority shareholders subject to the tax treatment of the entity in the countries where the majority shareholders reside. Such a rule seems to be not only disproportionate and very disadvantageous for minority shareholders, but it could also give rise to important internal conflicts and negative consequences for the normal functioning of a business. Indeed, in the worst scenario, it could influence the decisions of domestic investors to carry out businesses based on the residents of the foreign investors and the tax treatment given to the entity in their country. This result is not only absurd, but it could generate important limitations to economic development. Second, and in my view, the Danish anti-reverse hybrid rule relies too much upon foreign laws with respect to the tax treatment of a domestic entity. This could ultimately increase the level of uncertainty for taxpayers, even violating basic domestic legal principles, such as the principle of legal certainty.

---

gains on the assets held by the entity as a consequence of the re-characterisation. On the contrary, the owners or participants of the re-characterised Danish entity are deemed to have acquired their ownership interest in the entity at a price equal to the tax value of the assets and liabilities held by the entity at the time of the re-characterisation; (3) assets and liabilities held by an entity that is re-characterised will be deemed to be acquired at the same time as the participant acquired them and at a similar price ('rollover principle' at the entity level); (4) dividends distributions from the re-characterised entity might be subject to WHT in Denmark. *Ibid.*, pp. 514-515.

854. OECD (2015), *supra* n. 6. A further analysis will be conducted at *infra* Chapter 5.

855. Indeed, if the OECD *primary response* is applied in case where a deductible payment is made to a reverse hybrid, the denial of the payment does not change the fact that the country of organisation considers the entity as fiscally transparent whilst the country where the parent company is located considers it as a taxable entity. In other words, the reverse hybrid issue will remain, and the income will be recognised neither in the country of organisation of the entity nor in the country of the parent company.

5.3 The EU ATAD: A Frustrated Example of Supranational Coordination

In January 2016, the European Commission issued a proposal for a Council Directive laying down rules against tax avoidance practices that might affect the functioning of the internal market.[856] The proposal for a directive contained a very interesting rule attempting to coordinate the characterisation of entities according to the characterisation given in the source MS. This rule, unfortunately, did not see the light, most probably attending to the global influence and why not to say it as well, the political pressure of the OECD and their *linking rules*.[857] Indeed, on 12 July 2016, a final text of the directive ('EU ATAD I')[858] came up with rules resembling the OECD *linking rules*, which have also been extended to deal with hybrid entity mismatches involving third countries outside the EU ('EU ATAD II').[859]

Nevertheless, and despite the frustrated process of coordination in the characterisation of entities within the EU, the EU ATAD II seems to retake the original approach proposed by the European Commission, at least with respect to issues involving reverse hybrid entities, establishing a rule that has nothing to do with the OECD BEPS approach, and which attempts to solve the issue of reverse hybrids through a re-characterisation rule triggered in the country where the reverse hybrid is established.[860]

856. EU: Proposal for a Council Directive laying down rules against tax avoidance practices that directly affect the functioning of the internal market, COM (2016) 26 final, hereinafter 'Proposal for EU ATAD'. The proposal for directive was part of a full Commission's Anti-Tax Avoidance Package that also included other initiatives at a regional level. Other initiatives included in the package were, e.g., a recommendation on tax treaties; a revision of the Administrative Cooperation Directive; a Communication on an external Strategy for Effective Taxation and a Chapeau Communication and Staff Working Document, explaining the political and economic rationale behind the individual measures that intends to address a number of issues in response to the 2013 BEPS project and which is also in line with some previous work in the area at the European level. *See* EU: Report of the Code of Conduct Group (Business Taxation), 16553/114 Rev. 1, FISC 225, ECOFIN 1166, Brussels (11 December 2014). *See also*, EU: Commission Communication, A Fair and Efficient Corporate Tax System in the European Union: 5 Key Areas for Action, COM (2015) 302 final, 17/6/2015. For an analysis of this Action Plan *see, e.g.*, S. Krauß, *EU-BEPS? Aktionsplan für eine faire und effiziente Unternehmensbesteuerung in der EU*, Internationales Steuerrecht 2 (2016), pp. 45 et seq. For a complete analysis of the different parts of the EU ATAD, *see* W. Haslehner, K. Pantazatou, G. Kofler, and A. Rust (eds), *A Guide to the Anti-Tax Avoidance Directive*, Edward Elgar Publishing, 2020. For a specific analysis on the anti-hybrid rules in the EU ATAD, *see* K. Spies, 'Hybrid Entities and Anti-Hybrid Rules in the EU ATAD (Article 9 and 9A ATAD)' in W. Haslehner, K. Pantazatou, G. Kofler, and A. Rust (eds), *A Guide to the Anti-Tax Avoidance Directive*, Edward Elgar Publishing, 2020.
857. *Infra* Chapter 5, s. 3. The political pressure of the OECD in the international context has been also highlighted considering the recent tax reforms on Pillar 1 and 2. *See*, for example, Agyemang and Fildes, *supra* n. 215, and Mansour, *supra* n. 215.
858. EU: Council Directive (EU) 2016/1164 of 12 July 2016 laying down rules against tax avoidance practices that directly affect the functioning of the internal market, OJ L193, (2016), hereinafter also 'ATAD I'.
859. EU: Council Directive (EU) 2017/952 of 29 May 2017 amending Directive (EU) 2016/1164 as regards hybrid mismatches with third countries, OJ L144/1 (2017), hereinafter also 'ATAD II'. I will refer to the amendment of ATAD as ATAD II, even though this is just an amendment of the text of July 2016 and not a different directive.
860. EU: Article 9a of the Council Directive (EU) 2017/952 of 29 May 2017 (ATAD II).

The abovementioned process of coordination, or attempted coordination, from the original proposal of ATAD until its final text (EU ATAD I) and its subsequent amendments dealing with mismatches with third countries, i.e., the EU ATAD II, will be subsequently analysed.

5.3.1 *The EU ATAD I (Original Text): A Coordination at Source*

The original proposal for an EU ATAD contained a specific provision dealing with hybrid entities, namely Article 10 of the original text of the proposal for directive. This article stated as follows:

> Where two Member States give a different legal characterisation to the same taxpayer (hybrid entity), including its permanent establishments in one or more Member States, and this leads to either a situation where a deduction of the same payment, expenses or losses occurs both in the Member State in which the payment has its source, the expenses are incurred or the losses are suffered and in another Member State or a situation where there is a deduction of a payment in the Member State in which the payment has its source without a corresponding inclusion of the same payment in the other Member State, the legal characterisation given to the hybrid entity by the Member State in which the payment has its source, the expenses are incurred or the losses are suffered shall be followed by the other Member State.[861]

Leaving aside for a moment the analysis of the connection between hybrid entities and the outcome of D/NI (DNT), which will be assumed in detail further on in this work,[862] the Proposal for EU ATAD provided a very interesting solution to deal with cases in which a different characterisation of the same entity is given in two MS. The solution, unlike other proposals launched at that time, especially the OECD *linking rules*, attempted to coordinate the characterisation of the entity as per the one given in the source country, countering thus the true reason of hybrid and reverse hybrid entities, rather than only alleviating the symptoms derived from the main issue.[863]

---

861. EU: Article 10(1) of the Proposal for EU ATAD.
862. The article refers to DD and D/NI. Whilst the former is excluded from the analysis of this work, the latter will be further analysed at *infra* Chapter 5.
863. Navarro, Parada and Schwarz, *supra* n. 481, p. 129. The solution proposed is partially in line with the recommendation of the European Parliament of December 2015, where the Parliament calls the European Commission for a proposal 'to either harmonize national definitions of debt, equity, opaque and transparent entities [...]; or prevent double non-taxation, in the event of a mismatch'. *See* EU: Recommendation C6 'Hybrid Mismatches' of the Resolution of the European Parliament with recommendations to the Commission on bringing transparency, coordination and convergence to corporate tax policies in the Union, 16 December, (2015/2010 (INL)), cited in: G. Fibbe and A.J.A. Stevens, *Hybrid Mismatches under the ATAD I and ATAD II*, 26 EC Tax Rev. 3, 155 (2017), note 19. A harmonized solution, i.e., harmonization in the rules characterising entities for tax purposes within the EU has also been proposed somewhere else. Most notably, Fibbe proposed in the past a uniform classification method within the EU by mutually recognising the tax classification in the host country. This mutual classification method would be based on the principle of mutual recognition of entities, and it would be materialised in an EU Directive. For further details on Fibbe's proposal, *see* G. Fibbe, *EC Law Aspects of Hybrid Entities*, Vol. 15, Doctoral Series IBFD, Amsterdam (2009), pp. 293-384. *See*

Let us assume the following simple example: X, an entity organised in MS1, has a subsidiary, Y, in MS2. For purposes of MS1, Y is not recognised for tax purposes (tax transparent), whilst for MS2's tax purposes, this is indeed a taxable entity subject to corporate income tax. Likewise, X grants a loan to Y, and it receives interest back accordingly (*see* Figure 20).

Figure 20 Article 10 EU ATA Directive (Original Text)

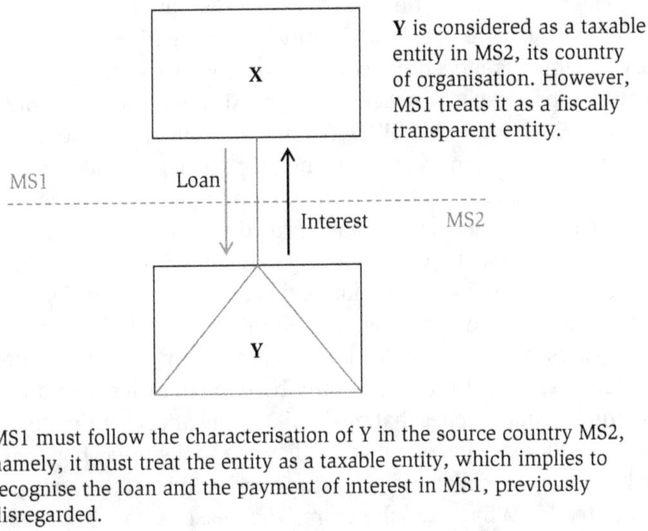

Therefore, any transaction between X and Y would be disregarded for MS1's purposes, whilst the same transactions would be recognised in MS2. In other words, the interest payments will be deductible in MS2 whilst not recognised as income in MS1, giving rise to a D/NI outcome.

The original Article 10 ATAD, however, instead of opting for a rule matching the outcomes of the transaction involving hybrids, i.e., denying a deduction in the country

also, EU: Judgment in *Columbus Container Services BVBA & Co. v. Finanzamt Bielefeld-Innenstadt*, C-298/05, ECLI:EU:C:2007:754, where the CJEU argued that a disparity derived from the autonomous classification of entities within EU MS was an issue beyond the fundamental rights and freedoms. Fibbe, based upon the outcome in *Columbus Container Services*, reinforces the idea of introducing a Directive on Mutual Recognition of Entities within the EU. As stated by Fibbe: 'If the ECJ did not consider in the *Columbus* case that the consequence of a classification conflict is a forbidden restriction [...]. Therefore, the new directive introduces a better system than the current tax classification methods that are applied autonomously [...]' Fibbe, *ibid.*, p. 378. Although I agree that the EU is a better place for achieving harmonised or coordinated results, harmonisation in the characterisation of entities would still be a utopic idea to implement in a global scale, beyond the EU. Similarly, if only implemented within the EU, it would still leave open issues of disparate characterisation of entities between MS and non-MS. For that reason, I am more inclined to propose a *reactive coordination rule*, which argues for coordination in the rules characterising entities rather than full harmonisation. For the details of this proposal, *see infra* Chapter 6.

of the payer to the extent that income is not included as such in the country of the payee, or letting this latter country to defensively react recognising the transaction between X and Y, it follows a different path.[864] Indeed, it provides that as MS1 and MS2 do not agree on the characterisation of entity Y, legally established in MS2, and this disagreement results in a D/NI outcome, MS1 should follow the characterisation of entity Y in MS2, i.e., the source country of the payment of interests. In other words, MS1 should align its characterisation of entity Y with the one provided in MS2, which is not only the country where the entity is legally established but also the source of the interest payments. This does not only avoid the D/NI outcome, which is arguably the true reason for the mismatch but also directly solves the disparity in the characterisation of entity Y, which is indeed the core of the issue at stake.

The solution proposed by Article 10 EU ATAD does not only differ from the one proposed by the OECD within the BEPS Action Plan 2 but also makes much more sense in a regional-coordinated context such as the EU,[865] where similar domestic measures have been adopted or operate in a very similar manner, at least in practice.[866] Similarly, coordinating the characterisation at source provides major advantages. First, it avoids implementing more invasive measures, obligating an MS to deny a deduction when a correspondent inclusion of income is not made in the other MS or forcing an MS to tax a payment received by an entity, even though this MS decided sovereignly to exempt it. Second, it attends specifically to the core issue regarding hybrid entities, namely the different characterisation of the same entity by two countries, avoiding complexities and consequentialist approaches that might ultimately affect legitimate transactions.[867]

Regardless of the above, one could still argue that similar regional coordination could also be achieved following the characterisation of the entity given in the residence country.[868] What are, therefore, the reasons to give preference to the characterisation of the entity in the country where the payment is sourced rather than the country where the investors are residents? Both tax policy and practical reasons might justify the preference for the source country.[869] First, as the country producing the hybrid entity mismatch is precisely the country of the investors, there are strong tax

864. For a further analysis on the OECD *linking rules*, *see infra* Chapter 5, s. 3.
865. I have already argued in this sense before. *See, e.g.*, Navarro, Parada and Schwarz, *supra* n. 481, p. 129.
866. For example, Spain. *Supra* s. 5.1.
867. *Infra* Chapter 5, s. 5.
868. This is indeed the solution proposed within the 1999 OECD Partnership Report with respect to transparent entities and the access to tax treaty benefits. *Infra* Chapter 4, s. 3.1.
869. The Proposal for EU ATAD refers to 'source country'. However, as it will be explained later in this work, I am more inclined for using the term 'home country' (i.e., where the entity is legally established or incorporated) to create a coordinated solution in the characterisation of entities. This is because the use of the concept 'source country' might not always coincide with the 'home country' of the entity, e.g., in case of payments made to a hybrid entity in a triangular situation). Moreover, I believe that when the original text of Article 10 of the Proposal for EU ATAD refers to 'source country' is indeed referring to 'home country'. The reason for using finally the terminology of 'source country' is related to the fact that the Proposal for EU ATAD is covering payments made by a hybrid entity that derive in a D/NI outcome. Therefore, in such cases, the source and home country will always coincide. For the proposal for a 'reactive coordination rule', which explains the use of the term 'home country' rather than 'source country', *see infra* Chapter 6, s. 2.1.

policy reasons to argue that a coordination in the characterisation of entities should be settled following the characterisation of the entity as per the rules of the country where this is legally established, and not in the other way around. In other words, the country that is primarily called to react in the case of a mismatch is the country producing such mismatch, i.e., the country of residence of the investors.[870] Second, there are also practical reasons, e.g., following the characterisation at source might be an easier way to deal with reverse hybrid entity mismatches in cases where the reverse hybrid entity receives payments. Indeed, up to now, reverse hybrid entity mismatches are mostly counteracted, either denying a deduction in the country where the payment is made or relying on the use of CFC rules in the country of the investors.[871] Nevertheless, this situation could be simply solved, making the country of the investors follow the classification of the entity in its country of establishment. This is to say, also considering the entity as tax transparent. Let me illustrate the above as follows: X, a corporation incorporated in MS1, has a subsidiary, Y, in MS2. This latter considers the entity as transparent, whilst the former as a taxable entity. Y receives interest income from a third country. If Y, therefore, receives interest from a third country, MS2 will not tax that item of income because it considers that Y is a non-taxable entity. MS1, on the other hand, considers that the entity exists and thus will not consider that the income flows through Y, being finally allocated to X.

Figure 21   Article 10 EU ATA Directive (Original Text) and Reverse Hybrids

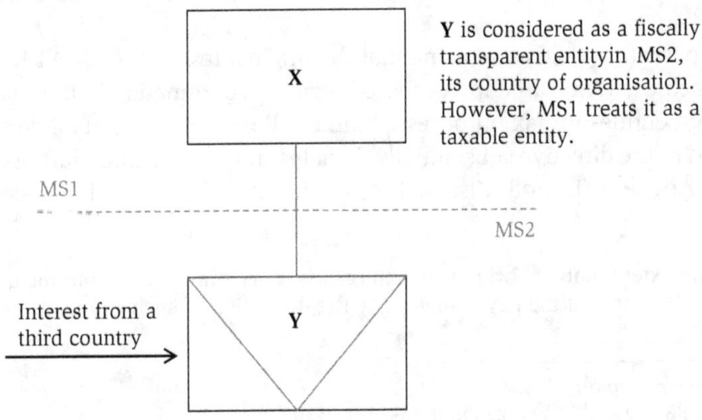

For MS2 tax purposes, the interest should flow through and be allocated to X. Therefore, they are not taxed at the level of Y. In contrast, MS1 considers that the interest are allocated in Y and no income arises until dividends are distributed.

870. J. Lüdicke, *'Tax Arbitrage' with Hybrid Entities: Challenges and Responses*, 68 Bull. Intl. Taxn. 6/7 (2014), Journals IBFD, p. 317.
871. However, the OECD also proposes limiting the tax transparency in the country where the reverse hybrid entity is organised. *See* OECD (2015), *supra* n. 6, p. 64, Recommendation 5.2.

In the absence of Article 10 of the EU ATAD (original text), the solution to this reverse hybrid case would be left exclusively to the capacity of MS1 to use its CFC rules in order to recognise the interest income in MS1 (*see* Figure 21).[872] Nevertheless, if Article 10 were applied, MS1 should also consider Y as a transparent entity, and therefore, it would tax the interest in the hands of X without having to rely exclusively on its CFC legislation. Thus, in principle, the solution proposed by the original text of the EU ATAD seems to bring us to a simpler solution, also targeting the problem in its core, that is, eliminating the disparate tax treatment of the entity in MS2.

Regardless of the above, the application of the proposed Article 10 also had important limitations, mostly derived from its restricted regional scope.[873] Indeed, the rule was created to apply only to hybrid and reverse hybrid entity mismatches generated within the EU. In other words, assuming any of the examples mentioned above, with the only difference that the residence country's entity (MS1) is the United States, the results would evidently change to the extent that Y in both examples is an eligible entity for purposes of the CTB election.[874] This could raise serious issues regarding competition between EU and US investors willing to invest within Europe, resulting in the latter group having a competitive advantage in comparison with the former one.[875] This issue is, however, (partially) solved with the extension of the rule to cases involving hybrid entity mismatches outside the EU according to the amendments introduced to the EU ATAD or referred to in this work as ATAD II.[876]

5.3.2 *The EU ATAD I (Final Text): When Political Pressure Comes First*

Despite the potential positive outcome that the original text of the EU ATAD proposal could have achieved, i.e., an unprecedented regional coordination in the characterisation of foreign entities for tax purposes within the European internal market, the final text included in the directive substantially deviates from its original draft. As provided in the final Article 9 (Hybrid Mismatches) of the EU ATAD I, with respect to D/NI outcomes:

> 2. To the extent that a hybrid mismatch results in a deduction without inclusion, the Member State of the payer shall deny the deduction of such payment.[877]

872. *See*, however, *supra* n. 871.
873. Navarro, Parada and Schwarz, *supra* n. 481, p. 130.
874. *Supra* s. 4.3.
875. I have also proposed somewhere else that, considering the unlikeliness that the United States decides to amend its characterisation system when applied to EU entities, this issue should simply be assumed as a stranded cost in the implementation of the proposal. *See* Navarro, Parada and Schwarz, *supra* n. 481, p. 130.
876. However, there are still doubts with respect to certain transactions included within the scope of the EU ATAD II. For example, payments made to a reverse hybrid entity in case the reverse hybrid entity is not organised within the EU. The wording of Article 9a suggests that those cases would not be within the scope of the directive. However, some authors disagree on this statement. *See, e.g.*, Fibbe and Stevens, *supra* n. 863, p. 165. *See also* a further analysis of the EU ATAD II in *infra* s. 5.3.3. The other limitation, in my view, is the link to specific outcomes (DD and D/NI). This issue will be, however, analysed at *infra* Chapter 5.
877. Article 9 of the Council Directive (EU) 2016/1164 of 12 July 2016 (ATAD I).

Interestingly, the core issue regarding hybrid and reverse hybrid entities, i.e., the characterisation of entities, is relegated to the backyard in the final text of the EU ATAD I, again giving priority to the artificial matching of tax outcomes.[878] This result can only be explained due to political reasons. Indeed, since the modification of the PSD in 2014,[879] which included a rule by which a parent company is refrained from taxing profits distributed by qualifying subsidiaries of another Member State only to the extent that the distributions are not tax deductible in the Member State of the subsidiary,[880] there was no equivalent rule at the EU law level denying a deduction if a correspondent inclusion of income did not take place.[881] Whilst the former rule included within the PSD is equivalent to the so-called defensive rule, the latter one included in the EU ATAD I is equivalent to what is known as 'primary response'; both measures are designed within the scope of the OECD BEPS Action Plan 2 in order to counteract 'hybrid mismatches'.[882] In other words, if the text had been approved in its original wording, we would have two incompatible rules solving the same issue at an EU level. First, the PSD provided for a compulsory taxation when income was deducted in the MS of the payer, i.e., the OECD 'defensive rule'. Second, a rule attempting to solve the problem through the coordination in the characterisation of entities at source, i.e., a completely different solution to the one proposed by the OECD. As this latter rule is contained in a wider and *ex post* directive, it might have implied a tacit derogation of the former, or which is the same, it could have repealed the legal basis created to implement the OECD solutions on hybrid mismatches unless, of course, a modification in the PSD would have also taken place.[883] Therefore, in my view, it is evident that the switch from a rule coordinating the characterisation of entities among MS to one denying a deduction when income is not correspondently included in the other MS, or allowing a deduction only in the MS where the payment has its source, represents a surrender to the political pressure at the OECD level to align the OECD rules with the EU rules. This ultimately represents a missed opportunity to provide a more coherent rule, which could have been in line with the idea of a European internal market and

878. The arguments on why I argue that matching outcomes, i.e., DD and D/NI, is an artificial construction will be further analysed in connection with the concept of hybrid mismatch arrangements at *infra* Chapter 5. However, this analysis excludes the cases of DD.
879. EU: Council Directive 2014/86/EU of 8 July 2014 amending Directive 2011/96/EU on the common system of taxation applicable in the case of parent companies and subsidiaries of different Member States, OJ 219/40 (2014), hereinafter 'Council Directive 2014/86/EU of 8 July 2014 amending Directive 2011/96/EU'.
880. If the profit distributions are tax deductible in the Member State of the subsidiary, then the parent company's Member State will be obliged to tax them. *Ibid.*
881. C. Marchgraber, *Tackling Deduction and Non-Inclusion Schemes–The Proposal of the European Commission*, 54 Eur. Taxn. 4 (2014), Journals IBFD, p. 142. *See also*, Navarro, Parada and Schwarz, *supra* n. 481, p. 128.
882. A further analysis on *linking rules* will be made at *infra* Chapter 5.
883. As this author has argued somewhere else with respect to the Proposal for EU ATAD: '[...] a positive immediate result can be concluded: there will be no need to force a sovereign Member State to deny a deduction or to tax an in tem of income to counteract a hybrid mismatch. The above however will require a modification in the current Parent-Subsidiary Directive'. Navarro, Parada and Schwarz, *supra* n. 481, p. 129.

which would have targeted better the core of the issue regarding hybrid entity mismatches.[884]

5.3.3 *The EU ATAD II: Confirming (but Not Exclusively) the OECD Standards*

As stressed already, on 29 May 2017, it was published the final text of the ATAD which extended the scope of application of the rules to mismatches to third countries outside the EU.[885] This amendment to the text of the ATAD, which I will refer to as ATAD II, follows the OECD recommendations established in the OECD BEPS Action 2, also introducing a very interesting rule to deal with payments made to reverse hybrid entities, which is perhaps more in line with the original intent of the EU ATAD.[886]

5.3.3.1 *Article 9(2) EU ATAD: The OECD Approach*

With respect to Article 9 EU ATAD, referred to D/NI outcome, it reads now as follows:

> To the extent that a hybrid mismatch results in a deduction without inclusion: (a) the deduction shall be denied in the Member State that is the payer jurisdiction; and (b) where the deduction is not denied in the payer jurisdiction, the amount of the payment that would otherwise give rise to a mismatch outcome shall be included in income in the Member State that is the payee jurisdiction.[887]

884. As Fibbe and Stevens also argue as regards to the EU ATAD I and II: '[...] the approach chosen by the Council does seem to close many of the existing loopholes where hybrid mismatches are used. Main remaining question is whether all twenty-seven Member States will be able to consistently implement the complex anti-mismatch rules. *The authors see it as a missed chance that in the ATAD it has not been decided to address the very cause of hybrid mismatches*' (emphasis added). Fibbe and Stevens, *supra* n. 863, p. 153.
885. The first proposal came up, however, on 25 October 2016, which subsequently derived in a second draft published on 2 December 2016. *See* EU: Proposal for a Council Directive amending Directive (EU) 2016/1164 as regards hybrid mismatches with third countries, COM (2016) 687 final, 25 October 2016, hereinafter 'Proposal ATAD II (25 October 2017).' Later, a text was made public on 17 February 2017, which was accepted by the European Council during the ECOFIN meeting of 21 February 2017. *See* EU: Proposal for a Council Directive amending Directive (EU) 2016/1164 as regards hybrid mismatches with third countries, 6333/17 FISC 46 ECOFIN 95, 17 February 2017, Article 9(2), hereinafter, 'Proposal ATAD II (17 Feb. 2017).' The final text approved and released on 29 May 2017 has nevertheless no variations in comparison with the latest one of February 2017. EU: Council Directive (EU) 2017/952 of 29 May 2017 (ATAD II).
886. The amendments to ATAD (ATAD II) also include measures related to dual inclusion of income and hybrid transfers, which will not be treated in this work. The rules related to imported mismatches will be mentioned further on in this work at *infra* Chapter 5, s. 2.4.3.
887. Article 9(2) of the Council Directive (EU) 2017/952 of 29 May 2017 (ATAD II). A mirror article can be found in the launched proposal of 17 February 2017. *See* EU: Proposal ATAD II (17 February 2017). The wording of the article was slightly different in the draft of 25 October 2016. However, the idea remained the same, namely the inclusion of a *primary response* and a *defensive rule* to counteract hybrid mismatches. As provided in Article 9(2) of this draft: 'To the extent that a hybrid mismatch involving a third country results in a deduction without inclusion: (i) if the payment has its source in a Member State, that Member State shall deny the deduction, or (ii) if the payment has its source in a third country, the Member State concerned shall require the taxpayer to include such payment in the taxable base, unless the third country

The wording is not a surprise because it simply aligns, or attempts to align, the EU legislation on hybrid mismatches with the OECD proposal.[888] This intention is indeed evident from the wording used in the preamble of the Directive, which provides as follows: 'In response to the need for fairer taxation and, in particular, to follow up on the OECD BEPS conclusions, the Commission presented its Anti-Tax Avoidance Package [...].'[889] Likewise, it states: 'Directive (EU) 2016/1164 includes rules on hybrid mismatches between Member States and should thus also include rules on hybrid mismatches with third countries [...].'[890] The aligning intention can also be seen in the modification of certain specific requirements related to the scope of the rules in order to make them closer to the OECD proposal.[891] For example, the EU ATAD I contained a more restricted definition of 'associated enterprises'[892] when compared to the definition introduced in the EU ATAD II.[893] Indeed, this latter measure includes within the concept of 'associated enterprises' also the cases of persons being part of the same consolidated group, a person 'acting together' with another person with respect to the voting rights or capital ownership of an entity, or an enterprise in which the taxpayer has a significant influence in the management, or the other way around, when an enterprise has a significant influence in the management of the taxpayer, which are concepts expressly included within the OECD BEPS Action 2.[894] Once again, however, it would have been more interesting to see an approach more in line with the idea of a European (coordinated) internal market, although still in line with the OECD BEPS

---

has already denied the deduction or has required that payment to be included.' *See* Article 9(2) of the Proposal ATAD II (25 October 2017). MS had until 31 December 2019 to publish the adopt the measures into domestic laws, which should also come into force from 1 January 2020, with the exception of the new Article 9a ('tax residency mismatches'), whose text can be communicated to the Commission until 31 December 202, and it comes into force from 1 January 2022. *See* Article 2 of the Council Directive (EU) 2017/952 of 29 May 2017 (ATAD II). *See also*, EU: European Commission Press release, *Fair Taxation: Commission Welcomes New Rules to Prevent Tax Avoidance Through Non-EU Countries*, 21 February 2017.

888. Also in this opinion, *see* Fibbe and Stevens, *supra* n. 863, p. 156.
889. EU: Council Directive (EU) 2017/952 of 29 May 2017 (ATAD II), rec. 3.
890. *Ibid.*, rec. 8.
891. The OECD BEPS Action Plan 2 limits the application of the proposed *linking rules* to '*control groups*' (and structured arrangements). *Infra* Chapter 5, ss 3.3.1 and 3.3.2. The EU ATAD refers instead to '*associated enterprise*', although in practice both concepts, after the modifications introduced by the EU ATAD II, include the same assumptions.
892. Article 2(4) of the Council Directive (EU) 2016/1164 of 12 July 2016 (ATAD I) provides that: '"associated enterprises" means: (a) an entity in which the taxpayer holds directly or indirectly a participation in terms of voting rights or capital ownership of 25 percent or more or is entitled to receive 25 percent or more of the profits of that entity; (b) an individual or entity which holds directly or indirectly a participation in terms of voting rights or capital ownership of 25 percent or more or is entitled to receive 25 percent or more of the profits of the taxpayer [...] For the purposes of Article 9 [hybrid mismatches] and where the mismatch involves a hybrid entity, this definition is modified so that the 25 percent requirement is replaced by a 50 percent requirement'.
893. EU: Council Directive (EU) 2017/952 of 29 May 2017 (ATAD II), recs 13 and 14.
894. To compare, *see* the concepts of '*control group*' and '*acting together*' under the OECD BEPS Action Plan 2 at *infra* Chapter 5, s. 3.3.1.

Action 2, but directly addressing the core of the hybrid entity mismatches. The EU is indeed the best scenario to achieve this aim.[895]

5.3.3.2 *Article 9a EU ATAD: The Characterisation of Entities Is Back on the Scene*

Regardless of the tendency to align the EU legislation on hybrid entity mismatches with the one proposed by the OECD, it is interesting to highlight a small deviation of this tendency, which can be found in Article 9a EU ATAD dealing with payment received by reverse hybrid entities established in an MS.

Article 9a EU ATAD reads as follows: 'Where one or more associated non-resident entities holding in aggregate a direct or indirect interest in 50% or more of the voting rights, capital interests or rights to a share of profit in a hybrid entity that is incorporated or established in a Member State, are located in a jurisdiction or jurisdictions that regard the hybrid entity as a taxable person, the hybrid entity shall be regarded as a resident of that Member State and taxed on its income to the extent that this income is not otherwise taxed under the laws of the Member State or any other jurisdiction.'[896] As per the wording of the article, it is possible to affirm that it attempts (to a certain extent) to coordinate the characterisation of entities as a solution to the reverse hybrid mismatch rather than constructing a rule focused exclusively on the tax outcomes in a transaction.[897] The above can be seen in the wording of the article when it says: '[...] the hybrid entity shall be regarded as a resident of that Member State and taxed on its income to the extent that this income is not otherwise taxed under the laws of the Member State or any other jurisdiction'.[898] Thus, in other words, the article is providing for a re-characterisation of the entity at the level of the MS where this is organised, which at least gets closer to the true issue regarding reverse hybrid entities: the disparate characterisation for tax purposes.[899]

895. Fibbe and Stevens share this criticism and argue for a more 'principled based EU approach' in terms of 'introducing either a consistent system of anti-abuse rules whereby always the same country (source country or investor country; from an EU policy perspective the source country seems preferable) should make the adjustments or by implementing a uniform classification method [of entities] between Member States.' Fibbe and Stevens, *supra* n. 863, p. 156, n. 22.
896. Article 9a(1) of the Council Directive (EU) 2017/952 of 29 May 2017 (ATAD II).
897. In this opinion, *see also* Fibbe and Stevens, *supra* n. 863, p. 164.
898. *Ibid.* Despite the confusion that the reference to a '*hybrid entity*', it is clear that the article refers to the case of a '*reverse hybrid*', i.e., an entity considered as tax transparent in its country of organisation, whilst as non-tax transparent in the country of the investors.
899. The reverse entity mismatch rule resembles what we have already studied with respect to the Danish anti-reverse hybrid provisions. Briefly recalling, the Danish rule provides that some entities, normally treated as fiscally transparent in Denmark, must be re-characterised as taxable entities if the direct owners/partners holding more than 50% of the capital or voting rights are tax residents in one or more foreign jurisdictions, and these jurisdictions considers the Danish entity to be a separate taxable entity. *Supra* s. 5.2.2.

The rule on Article 9a EU ATAD also seems to apply with priority over the rule contained in Article 9(2) (*linking rules*). The above seems to be confirmed in recital 29 of the preamble of the Directive, which says: 'The hybrid mismatch rules in Article 9(1) and (2) only apply to the extent that the situation involving a taxpayer gives rise to a mismatch outcome. No mismatch outcome should arise when an arrangement is subject to adjustments under Article 9(5) or 9a, and, accordingly, arrangements that are subject to adjustment under those parts of this Directive should not be subject to any further adjustment under the hybrid mismatch rules.'[900] In simple words, to the extent that Article 9a has solved the reverse hybrid entity mismatch, there is no need to apply the rules of Article 9(2) EU ATAD. The above also seems to be the case when CFC rules contained in the EU ATAD may solve the reverse hybrid entity mismatch first. According to the recital 30 EU ATAD: 'Where the provisions of another directive, such as those in Council Directive 2011/96/EU [EU ATAD I], lead to the neutralization of the mismatch in tax outcomes, there should be no scope for the application of the hybrid mismatch rules provided for in this Directive.'[901] A similar priority (regarding CFC rules) is confirmed under the OECD BEPS Action Plan 2.[902]

The rule in Article 9a EU ATAD is, however, still ineffective in targeting payments made to a reverse hybrid entity in all those cases when the reverse hybrid is incorporated in a third country outside the EU. Let us assume the following hypothetical: MS1 is a corporation incorporated in an MS of the EU, which has a subsidiary in a third country outside the EU. This latter (Sub) has subsequently a subsidiary in another MS (MS2). Sub and MS2 engaged in a loan agreement through which MS2 pays interest to Sub. Sub is tax transparent entity in its country of establishment (outside the EU), although both MS consider it as an opaque entity (*see* Figures 22 and 23).

900. EU: Council Directive (EU) 2017/952 of 29 May 2017 (ATAD II), rec. 29.
901. EU: Council Directive (EU) 2017/952 of 29 May 2017 (ATAD II), rec. 30.
902. OECD (2015), *supra* n. 6, p. 64. *See also, infra* Chapter 5, s. 4.2 referred to the interaction between CFC rules and *linking rules*. In addition, it is interesting to remark that the rule in Article 9a EU ATAD seems to be, in principle, in contradiction to Article 62 of the CCTB proposal, which provides that where an entity is treated as transparent in an MS where it is established, a taxpayer holding an interest in the entity shall include in his tax base his share in the income of the entity. *See* EU: Proposal for a Council Directive (EU) 2016/0337 of 25 October 2016 on a Common Corporate Tax Base, COM (2016) 685 final, Article 62(1) on allocation of the income of transparent entities to taxpayers holding an interest. *See also,* Fibbe and Stevens, *supra* n. 863, p. 164.

Figure 22 Article 9a EU ATAD

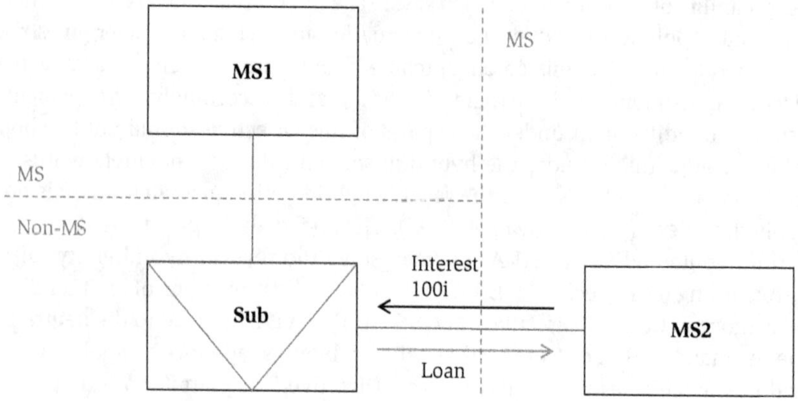

In such a case, Article 9a EU ATAD is inapplicable. However, Article 9(2) may still apply, obligating MS2 to deny the deduction of the interest payments in that MS. Yet, if MS2 is also located in a non-EU MS, both Article 9(2) and 9a EU ATAD II are inapplicable, i.e., those mismatches would be out of the scope of the EU ATAD.

Figure 23 Article 9a EU ATAD

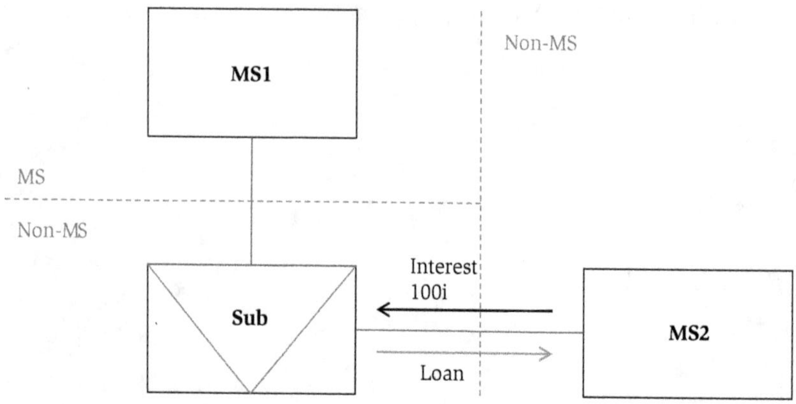

In this scenario, therefore, the only option to solve the reverse hybrid entity mismatch would be to attend to the possibility that the third countries, i.e., where Sub and MS2 are organised, have introduced the OECD recommendations (i.e., *linking rules* or the rule by which the non-MS country where the reverse hybrid is organised denies the tax transparency treatment), or that the CFC rules in MS1 are effective enough to counteract the mismatch.

Yet, this author still argues that these types of rules, i.e., rules attempting to coordinate the characterisation of the entities, make more sense than those based exclusively on the matching of tax outcomes. First, and as repeatedly stressed in this work, coordination rules focus on the core of the issue regarding hybrid and reverse hybrid entities, namely the different characterisation of entities. Second, they are simple to administer both for taxpayers and tax administrations. After all, matching the characterisation of the entities is easier than determining whether a deduction was or not taken in the other State or whether income was or not included. Nevertheless, I consider that some questions remain still unsolved.

First, there is still not enough justification for providing rules matching the characterisation of the entity as per the one provided in the residence country of the majority controlling partner rather than the characterisation given in the MS where the entity is organised.[903] Of course, the immediate consequence of this rule is that the tax revenues are maintained within the EU, which could be enough policy justification for many.[904] However, re-characterising an entity in the MS where the entity is organised may also create uncertainty for those taxpayers who originally decided to carry on business using these types of organisations rather than tax-opaque ones.[905] Second, there are still some doubts regarding the effect that the re-characterisation might have on those minority shareholders or partners who reside in countries where the entity is considered fiscally transparent. Will the re-characterisation proposed also affect those shareholders? The intuitive answer should be no. However, the experience of other countries, like Denmark, which offer similar solutions as the one proposed in the EU ATAD, demonstrates that they will finally affect those shareholders who originally did not have any mismatch.[906] Third, one should also consider the potential double taxation if the entity in the MS is re-characterised as a taxable entity. In such a case, the income received by the entity will be subject to tax in the MS where the entity is organised and might also be subject to taxation in the country of the majority of owners/partners treating the entity as a taxable entity because of the application of CFC rules. The priority of CFC rules, which is granted in the EU ATAD, seems to be dealing correctly with this issue, though, because it switches off the application of Article 9a in case the mismatch was already solved through the CFC legislation in MS1.[907]

All in all, this author is still of the idea that a *reactive coordination rule*, which respects the characterisation of the entity given in the country of establishment (i.e.,

903. *Supra Fig. 19: Danish anti-reverse hybrid rule.*
904. Revenues will be maintained within the EU, because the entity will be treated as a taxable entity, being thus subject to corporate income tax in the MS where it is organised (EU MS).
905. As noted already, in some cases the decision to opt for a traditional transparent entity, such as a partnership rather than a corporation, attends to the simple fact of avoiding economic double taxation. This pattern is evident, e.g., in the case of the United States, where the use of partnerships was basically because of the avoidance of double taxation. *See* the explanation of McDaniel, McMahon and Simmons at *supra* n. 563. *See also*, in the context of the OECD proposal for a global minimum tax (OECD Pillar 2), L. Parada, 'Tax Neutrality Regimes and GloBE' in W. Haslehner, K. Pantazatou, G. Kofler and A. Rust (eds) *The Pillar 2 Global Minimum Tax*, Edward Elgar Publishing, 2022-23.
906. Møllin Ottosen and Nørremark, *supra* n. 823, p. 514.
907. This outcome could be avoided granting an indirect FTC, although this is not something that can be guaranteed in all cases.

home country), might still bring better outcomes. This idea will be elaborated in further detail in Chapter 6.[908]

6 FINAL REMARKS

When answering the questions of why hybrid entities (and reverse hybrids) exist and why one should be concerned about them, this chapter has left us with important conclusions. First, hybrid entities and reverse hybrids are the results of domestic and sovereign tax policy decisions that determine the tax treatment that a foreign entity will have for domestic tax purposes. This result should not be surprising at all, considering that tax systems around the world are neither uniform nor consistent in their tax policies, and they normally differ from each other in many aspects. Second, one should also note that there are no rules to characterise entities that fit all the requirements to be considered completely inviolable. Indeed, and contrary to the doctrine that tends to blame elective systems as a major source of hybrid and reverse hybrids, this chapter has demonstrated that this result is not less likely to occur with other characterisation rules, e.g., resemblance tests. Indeed, resemblance or comparative tests normally fail to create a consistent characterisation of foreign entities due, most of the time, to the incompatible characteristics between foreign and domestic entities. Similarly, these tests tend to be generally not less elective than a formally elective system that relies completely on a taxpayer's election. A good example of the above is the *Kintner* test in the United States, which was in force before the issuance of the CTB regulations. Under this system, a sophisticated taxpayer could, after proper legal advice, set up the structures that most accurately fit his pretensions, predicting thus in advance the desired tax treatment of those entities. However, this does not mean to recognise the influence of the CTB system to circumvent Subpart F Income and to inappropriately claim an FTC. However, and as demonstrated already, some of these circumventions did not attend exclusively to the CTB election but rather to the poor design of domestic anti-deferral and FTC rules. The above, therefore, reinforces the idea that determining whether a characterisation system is elective or not is certainly not the true path to solving the issues of hybrids and reverse hybrid entities. In other words, the analysis of the existing systems to characterise foreign entities for tax purposes cannot be made in isolation, disregarding, e.g., the design of other rules within the tax system, including, for example, anti-deferral rules, as well as their interaction with the characterisation rules in the global world.

In the same order of ideas, this chapter has attempted to demonstrate how the coordination in the characterisation of foreign entities, i.e., the real issue regarding hybrids and reverse hybrid entities, is far from being just a utopian academic idea and could become indeed relevant to properly deal with issues involving hybrids. This tendency can indeed be seen in different countries and to different extents of development, including both domestic and supranational law. For example, in Spain, unlike being a casual practice rather than an intended law rule, it results in an effective

908. *Infra* Chapter 6.

coordination in the characterisation of entities, nullifying the appearance of hybrid entities and reverse hybrid entities in all those cases in which Spain is the country characterising a foreign entity located in a country from where Spanish residents receive income. This idea was also recently included within the original proposal for an EU ATAD (2016), which provided that in all those cases in which different characterisation of entities by two MS existed, deriving in certain outcomes, the resident MS should follow the characterisation of the source MS in order to solve the disparity. Unfortunately, this rule was not ultimately included in the final text of the EU ATAD (2016), which opted to follow the OECD recommendations on these matters. However, the amendments to the EU ATAD in 2017 (ATAD II) included a rule dealing with reverse hybrid entities and third countries, which provides for a re-characterisation of a fiscally transparent entity when the entity is regarded by the majority of the shareholders, residents in a third country, as a taxable entity. This rule resembles the approach already adopted by Denmark with respect to hybrid and reverse hybrid entities, which attempts to coordinate the characterisation of entities through a re-characterisation of its own domestic entities, producing interesting results. This approach, however, still has the disadvantage of relying excessively on foreign laws, also increasing the levels of uncertainty for taxpayers. Yet, in my opinion, rules aimed at matching the characterisation of entities are indeed a more effective manner to deal with hybrids and reverse hybrids entities than those attempting to create an artificial match of tax outcomes. After all, hybrids and reverse hybrid entities exist exclusively because of the different characterisation of the same entity by two jurisdictions. This idea will be reinforced further on in this work.[909]

909. *Infra* Chapter 6.

CHAPTER 4

Hybrid Entities and the Entitlement to Tax Treaty Benefits

1 INTRODUCTION

Tax treaties have the purpose of allocating taxing rights between the source and residence jurisdiction in order to avoid double taxation.[910] This division of taxing rights implies that either of these countries will give up part of their sovereignty to tax an item of income when two persons, considered residents for purposes of the treaty, are subject to taxation in both countries on the same income.[911]

Although the determination of persons and residents for tax treaty purposes is rather clear in the case of individuals, it can be quite problematic when referring to

910. On the other hand, as stressed in Chapter 2, the aim of avoiding DNT as a general tax policy goal of tax treaties is debatable. This conclusion remains valid even after the implementation of the new OECD interpretation of Articles 23A and 23B OECD Model within the OECD Commentaries and the inclusion of a new Article 23A(4) OECD Model, because none of these articles are effective enough to solve all the situations of DNT derived from either conflicts of qualification or interpretation. *Supra* Chapter 2, s. 3.4. The above can also be concluded after the recent proposal to modify the title and preamble of the OECD Model in order to include a reference to the avoidance of DNT and the inclusion of an *STR rule* under Action 6 of the BEPS project. *Supra* Chapter 2, ss 5.3 and 6. On the one hand, the unsatisfactory wording of the modified OECD Model preamble appears to only suggest that the prevention of DNT is exclusively relegated to the cases where this outcome is the result of tax evasion or tax avoidance. *Supra* Chapter 2, ss 5.1 and 5.2. Likewise, the *STR rule* does not suggest any obligation to the source State to exercise its taxing rights as demonstrated in the use of the word 'may be' instead of 'is' or 'must be'. *Supra* Chapter 2, s. 5.3. Despite the above, nothing prevents that some specific tax treaties might include provisions aiming to prevent DNT, e.g., *subject-to-tax* or *switch-over clauses. Supra* Chapter 2, ss 4.2.1 and 4.2.2.

911. However, as already stressed in Chapter 2, the relief of double taxation is also limited to the cases of juridical double taxation. Economic double taxation, on the other hand, i.e., when a same element of income or the same economic transaction is subject to the same type of tax in the hands of two or more different taxpayers, seems not to be included in the treaty relief. *See* references to this discussion in *supra* Chapter 2, *supra* n. 196. In contrast, *see* analysis of s. 5.3.2.4 of this chapter and the proposal for a reverse saving clause.

entities, mostly when those entities are treated differently for tax purposes by the Contracting States. Accordingly, this disparity in the characterisation of entities may give rise to conflicts *of allocation of income*, i.e., where the same income is attributed to different taxpayers in the source and residence states within the tax treaty context.[912]

The concern regarding conflicts of allocation of income was originally assumed in 1999 when the OECD issued a report referring specifically to the case of partnerships. In this report, the OECD suggested that a residence-source conflict of allocation of income (or attribution conflict) might be solved if the source state relies on the attribution principles of the residence state. This idea was later recognized as positive law in Article 1(6) US Model, which also included cases of tax-transparent entities that were not necessarily partnerships, and it is also part of the current Article 1(2) OECD Model, whose text mirrors the US Model provision, and which is also replicated in Article 3(1) of the MLI.[913] This chapter analyses these provisions and raises some concerns with respect to their application.

Section 2 briefly refers to the general rules regarding the entitlement to tax treaty benefits with respect to entities. Section 3 analyses the principles established within the OECD Partnership Report with regard to conflicts of allocation of income. For this purpose, it analyses the general principles settled in the report, its exceptions and the formal and substantial critics raised with respect to the position adopted. Section 4 analyses Article 1(6) US Model, which is the first positive recognition of the principles settled in the OECD Partnership Report and the immediate precedent of Article 1(2)

912. The disparities in the characterisation of entities might also give rise to what is known in doctrine as '*conflicts of qualification*'. Nevertheless, as these conflicts depend on the nature of an item of income, rather than exclusively on the discrepancies as regards the characterisation of an entity either as fiscally transparent or tax opaque, they will not be included in the analysis of this work. In this opinion *also*, e.g., Fibbe, *supra* n. 863, p. 216 and p. 219. However, a good example illustrating a conflict of qualification derived from the different characterisation of entities can be found in the OECD Commentary on Article 23A OECD Model. The example consists of a partnership organized in State A, which has a PE in State E. Accordingly, its owner, who is a resident of State R alienates its interest in the partnership. Whilst State E considers the partnership as tax transparent, State R, the State of the partner, considers it as a taxable entity. Derived from the different characterisation of the partnership thus State R and State E apply a different provision of the treaty. In other words, they apply a disparate characterisation of the *income* influenced by the different tax treatment of the entity. State R, on one hand, considers that the alienation of the interest corresponds to the alienation of the shares in a company, and thus, it is regulated under Article 13(5) OECD Model (which exempts the owner from taxation). State E, on the other hand, considers the owner to be alienating the underlying assets of the business in State E (PE), and thus, it might tax the income according to Article 13(1) or (2) OECD Model. The solution provided by the OECD in this case, and which derives from the 1999 OECD Partnership Report is that the State of residence (State R) should apply either the exemption or credit method to relief double taxation, following thus the characterisation of the income in the State of source. This line of reasoning is founded in the wording of Article 23A and 23B OECD Model, which require the State of residence to check whether the income may be taxed in the State of source 'in accordance with the provisions of the Convention'. R. Danon, *Qualification of Taxable Entities and Treaty Protection*, 68 Bull. Intl. Taxn. 4/5 (2014), IBFD Journals, p. 200. A further discussion on the interpretation of the phrase '*in accordance with the provisions of this Convention, may be taxed*', referred to conflicts of qualification and DNT can be found at *supra* Chapter 2, s. 3.3.
913. The proposal of including Article 1(2) OECD Model is already ratified in the text of the recently released draft contents of the 2017 update to the OECD Model. *See* OECD (2017) and OECD (2017a), *supra* n. 488.

OECD Model. This Section first provides a general interpretation of the wording of this provision. Second, it illustrates the application of Article 1(6) US Model through seven examples, which are divided into two groups: (i) strict bilateral cases and (ii) triangular cases. Finally, this section provides some examples where the interplay between Article 1(6) US Model and other tax treaty and domestic provisions are either not entirely clear or they simply conflict with each other. The above includes the interplay with the concept of *beneficial owner* in Articles 10, 11 and 12 US Model; the *saving clause* of Article 1(4) US Model; the US CTB regulations and I.R.C. Section 894(c). Section 5 follows a similar path. It first provides a general interpretation of the wording of Article 1(2) OECD Model. Later, it analyses seven illustrations explaining the application of Article 1(2) OECD Model, which are also divided into two groups: (i) strict bilateral cases and (ii) triangular cases. Finally, it addresses some specific issues regarding its application, which includes the interplay with the concept of *beneficial owner*, the *saving clause* and double taxation relief, and the negative impact that Article 1(2) OECD Model has with respect to developing countries. Section 6 briefly addresses Article 3(1) MLI, whose text mirrors Article 1(2) OECD Model. Accordingly, this section analyses Article 11 and Article 3(3) MLI as two different options for a *saving clause* included within the text of the MLI, as well as Article 3(2) and Article 5 – Option C regarding the interplay between the *saving clause* and the obligation to relieve double taxation. Section 7 provides some final remarks.

2 THE GENERAL APPLICATION OF TAX TREATIES TO ENTITIES

Generally, a double tax treaty applies only to persons who are residents of one or both Contracting States. Therefore, in order to determine the application of a tax treaty to any entity, i.e., corporate or non-corporate entity, one should primarily consider two basic questions: (i) is the entity a person as per the definition of the OECD Model? and subsequently, (ii) is this person a resident of a Contracting State as defined in the OECD Model?[914]

With regard to the first question, Article 3(1)(a) OECD Model defines a *person*, for purposes of the Convention, as any 'individual, company and any other body of persons'.[915] In principle, the reference to 'any body of persons' generated some questions as to whether partnerships and other non-corporate entities were considered persons for tax treaty purposes. This conflict, however, was solved in the 1999 OECD

914. P. Baker, *The Application of the Convention to Partnerships, Trusts and Other, Non-Corporate Entities*, 2 GITC Rev. 1, 1-2 (2002). Nevertheless, the introduction of an LOB clause within tax treaties may also imply that a third important question is raised, which is 'Is that resident a qualified resident under the treaty?', which is indeed the essence of a Limitation of Benefits provision in tax treaties. An exhaustive analysis of LOB clauses in tax treaties exceeds the purpose of this chapter. However, for more information, *see*, for example, F. Vega Borrego, *Limitation of Benefits Clauses in Double Tax Conventions*, Kluwer Law International, 2006. More recently, *see* J. Bates et al., *Limitation on Benefits Articles in Income Tax Treaties: The current State of Play*, 41 Intertax 7 (2013) DOI: 10.54648/taxi2013036. In the EU law context, *see also* P. Baker, *The BEPS Action Plan in the Light of EU Law: Treaty Abuse*, British Tax Review 3 (2015).
915. Article 3(1) OECD Model Tax Convention.

Partnership Report, which stated: 'While the practices of Member countries are not entirely uniform in this respect, the Committee has determined that partnerships should be considered to be "persons" within the meaning of the definition found in Article 3.'[916] Subsequently, the last sentence of paragraph 2 on the Commentary on Article 3 was replaced by the following: 'Partnerships will also be considered to be "persons" either because they fall within the definition of "company" or, where this is not the case, because they constitute other bodies of persons.'[917] At present, therefore, there is no doubt that partnerships are regarded as persons for tax treaty purposes.

Article 4(1) OECD Model, on the other hand, states that a *resident* for purposes of the treaty is 'any person who, under the law of that state, is liable to tax therein by reason of his domicile, residence, place of management or any other criterion of a similar nature [...]'.[918] As discussed already in Chapter 2,[919] the view of the term '*liable to tax*' is that of a person who, by reason of various criteria, e.g., residence, domicile, etc., is subject to '*comprehensive taxation*'.[920] The OECD Commentaries do not define '*comprehensive taxation*' in a systematic manner. However, it is widely recognised and accepted in doctrine and in the tax treaty practice that a person is considered liable to comprehensive taxation even if a State does not impose a tax effectively.[921] For example, an entity enjoying a complete exemption from tax is still regarded as resident for purposes of the tax treaty to the extent that the residence state asserts jurisdiction to tax the entity on its worldwide income in accordance with one of the internationally accepted bases to full liability, i.e., place of incorporation or place of management of the entity.[922] Prima facie, therefore, both corporate and non-corporate entities would be regarded as residents for purposes of the treaty to the extent they are fully liable to tax. Nevertheless, the issue is precisely that most of the non-corporate entities, e.g., partnerships and disregarded entities with a sole owner, are granted full tax transparency, which is indeed inconsistent with the assertion of full tax liability based on

916. OECD (1999), *supra* n. 1, para. 30.
917. OECD Commentary on Article 3 concerning general definitions, para. 2.
918. Article 4(1) OECD Model.
919. *Supra* Chapter 2, s. 3.1.
920. OECD Commentary on Article 4 concerning the definition of resident, paras 8 and 8.6.
921. OECD Commentary on Article 4 concerning the definition of resident, para. 8.6. This is also the main reason why placing the terms 'liable to tax' and 'subject to tax' on an equal footing is incorrect. Whilst the former supposes full tax liability, which is provided even in the absence of an effective taxation, the latter necessarily assumes the effective payment of taxes. The requirement provided by Article 4(1) OECD Model certainly does not request effective taxation. *See* the full discussion at *supra* Chapter 2, s. 3.1. *See also* the reference to the case law UK: *Paul Weiser v. Commissioner for Her Majesty's Revenue and Customs* (2012), which finely illustrates the distinction between 'liable to tax' and 'subject to tax' at *supra* n. 345. For the view that 'liable to tax' does not correspond to 'subject to tax', *see, e.g.*, De Broe, *supra* n. 255. *See also*, Ismer and Riemer, *supra* n. 333, Article 4 at m.no. 26. *See also* the analysis at *supra* Chapter 2, s. 3.1 as regards the interpretation of the term 'liable to tax' and DNT.
922. Baker, *supra* n. 914. Similarly, para. 8 of the Commentary on Article 4 provides the example of pension funds, charities and other organizations that may be exempted from tax, but they are exempt only if they meet all the requirements for exemption specified in the tax laws [i.e., if they are fully liable to tax]. The Commentary recognises that 'most States would view such entities as residents for purposes of the Convention'. OECD Commentary on Article 4 concerning the definition of resident, para. 8.6.

worldwide taxation.[923] This is perhaps the reason why the 1999 OECD Partnership Report concluded that partnerships are not residents for purposes of Article 4(1) OECD Model.[924] In such a case, however, the partners are the ones who should be entitled to the benefits provided by a tax treaty to the extent that they are *liable to tax* on their share of the partnership income in those countries.[925]

Let us assume a basic illustration to explain the above. Assume that R is an entity organised in State R, which has two partners, A and B, who are residents of State R. Likewise, entity R receives interest payment from an independent debtor in State P. We will also assume that both State R and State P consider entity P as tax transparent and that the general WHT rate on interest paid abroad in State P is 30%.

Figure 24 Entitlement to Tax Treaty Benefits/Transparent Entities

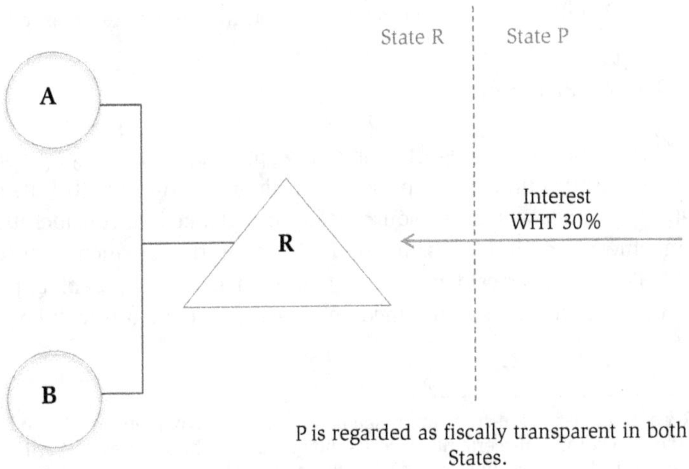

In such a case, and as per Article 11(2) of the treaty R-P, State P should apply a reduced WHT of 10% if the interest payments are paid to the beneficial owners of the other Contracting State, which, in this case, would most probably be A and B.[926] Likewise, according to Article 11(1) of the treaty R-P, State R should grant a relief from double taxation to partners A and B. In simple words, entity P is neither regarded as

923. As well explained by Baker: '[T]he problem with many non-corporate entities is that they are partially or fully transparent for tax purposes in their state of establishment or management. It would be entirely inconsistent for a state to accord full fiscal transparency to an entity and yet assert jurisdiction to tax that entity on its worldwide income.' Baker, *supra* n. 914, p. 3.

924. Paragraph 34 of the OECD Partnership Report states: 'If the State in which the partnership has been organized treats that partnership as fiscally transparent, then the partnership is not "liable to tax" in that State within the meaning of Article 4, and so cannot be a resident for purposes of the Convention [...].' OECD (1999), *supra* n. 1, para. 34, p. 14.

925. *Ibid.*, para. 47, p. 17. *See also*, OECD Commentary on Article 8 concerning the definition of resident, para. 8.8.

926. State P also considers entity P as tax transparent. Therefore, it will recognise that income is allocated to the partners, who should coincide with the beneficial owners.

receiving the interest payments nor granted thus any benefits of the treaty. The treaty R-P is thus applicable with regard to A and B, who are residents of State R receiving interest from State P.

3 THE 1999 OECD PARTNERSHIP REPORT

In 1999, the OECD issued the Partnership Report, which provided some important conclusions with respect to the application of the OECD Model to partnerships and other non-corporate entities.[927] Jointly with recognizing that partnerships can be regarded as persons for purposes of Article 3(1) OECD Model,[928] although not considered as residents for purposes of Article 4(1) OECD Model,[929] it provided important conclusions with respect to the cases of different characterisation of the same entity in the country of residence and the country of source, giving rise to issues with respect to the allocation of income and the entitlement to tax treaty benefits.[930]

3.1 General Principle

As a general rule, the OECD suggests that when applying a tax treaty, the source state should rely on the attribution principles of the residence state and attribute the income accordingly.[931] In other words, the source state should take into consideration the way in which income arising in its jurisdiction is treated in the jurisdiction of the resident taxpayer.[932] Thus, if the residence state follows a non-transparent approach with respect to the entity through which income is received, the entity will be regarded as

927. The Report adopted a case-study approach under different hypotheticals. The individual study of all those hypotheticals certainly exceeds the purpose of this chapter. Nevertheless, some of them are considered later in this work for purposes of stressing some fundamental ideas.
928. OECD (1999), *supra* n. 1, para. 30, p. 12.
929. *Ibid.*, para. 47, p. 17.
930. This section does not deal with qualification conflicts, i.e., where the residence and source State apply different articles of the tax treaty based on differences in their domestic laws. This issue was already analysed at *supra* Chapter 2, s. 3.3, referred specifically to cases of DNT and the new interpretation of Article 24A(1) OECD Model. *See also* on this topic: F. Engelen and P. Pötgens, *Report on 'The Application of the OECD Model Tax Convention to Partnerships' and the Interpretation of Tax Treaties*, 40 Eur. Taxn. 7 (2000), Journals IBFD; A Lamers and J. Stevens, *Classification Conflicts: The Cross-Border Tax Treatment of the Profit Share of Limited Partners*, 44 Eur. Taxn. 4 (2004), Journals IBFD.
931. H. Ault, *Issues Related to the Identification and Characteristics of the Taxpayer*, 56 Bull. Intl. Taxn. 6 (2002), Journals IBFD, p. 264. As provided in the OECD Commentaries on Article 1, modified after the OECD Partnership Report: '[...] the state of source should take into account, as part of the factual context in which the convention is to be applied, the way in which an item of income, arising in its jurisdiction, is treated in the jurisdiction of the person claiming the benefits of the convention as a resident'. OECD Commentary on Article 1 concerning the persons covered by the convention, para. 6.3. This approach, according to Wheeler, was anticipated by Hugh Ault during the IFA Meeting in London on the concept of beneficial owner. J. Wheeler, *The Attribution of Income to a Person for Tax Treaty Purposes*, 59 Bull. Intl. Fisc. Doc. 11 (2005), Journals IBFD, p. 488.
932. M. Steindl and M. Stiastny, *The Impact of the OECD Partnership Report (1999) on Tax Avoidance in Outbound Cases*, 68 Bull. Int'l. Taxn. 2 (2014), Journals IBFD, p. 112.

liable to tax and, therefore, entitled to the benefits of the treaty.[933] On the contrary, if the resident state considers the entity as tax transparent, income will be allocated to its partners to the extent they are also considered residents of that State.[934]

The application of the principles stated in the 1999 OECD Partnership Report can be illustrated through Example 4 of the Report, which provides the following hypothetical: P is a partnership established in State P. A and B are P's partners who reside in State P. State P treats P as a tax-transparent entity, whilst States S treats it as a taxable entity. P derives royalty income from State S that is not attributable to a PE in State S.[935]

Figure 25 OECD Partnership Report, Example 4

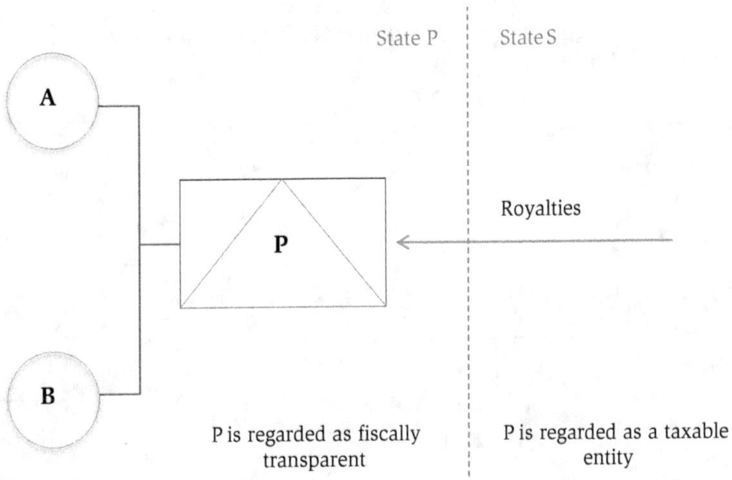

In this hypothetical, State S shall follow the characterisation of entity P given in the residence state to determine to whom the income is attributed. As A and B are residents of State P, the royalty income is considered to be paid to A and B, who are then entitled to the treaty benefits.[936] However, if we disregard the application of the OECD Partnership Report, one should consider that entity P is not a resident for purposes of Article 4(1) OECD Model. Therefore, the treaty S-P may not be applicable, at least from the perspective of State P.[937] In other words, the royalties might be subject

933. *Ibid.*
934. *Ibid.*
935. OECD (1999), *supra* n. 1, Ex. 4, p. 23.
936. The above means that, in principle, State S should reduce its WHT and State R would grant a relief in case of double taxation. However, it is arguable that State S considers A and B as the beneficial owners for purposes of Article 12 OECD Model, and finally apply a reduced WHT. This issue is further on analysed at *infra* s. 3.3.2.3.
937. For State S, on the contrary, the treaty P-S is applicable with or without the considerations on the principles of the OECD Partnership Report, because State S considers entity P as a taxable entity.

to double taxation since State S will not limit its taxing rights in favour of the resident country.

Similarly, in triangular cases, the source state is bound not only by the tax characterisation of the entity in the residence state of the partnership but also by the tax treatment in the residence state of the partners.[938] Once again, the characterisation of the entity given in the source state is completely irrelevant. Let me take Example 9 of the OECD Partnership Report to illustrate this. Let us assume that entity P is established in State P, and A and B are entity P's partners who reside in a different State, i.e., State R. Entity P owns shares in X, a company resident in State S. X pays dividends to P. States P and S treat the partnerships as a taxable entity whilst State R treats it as fiscally transparent.[939]

Figure 26 OECD Partnership Report, Example 9

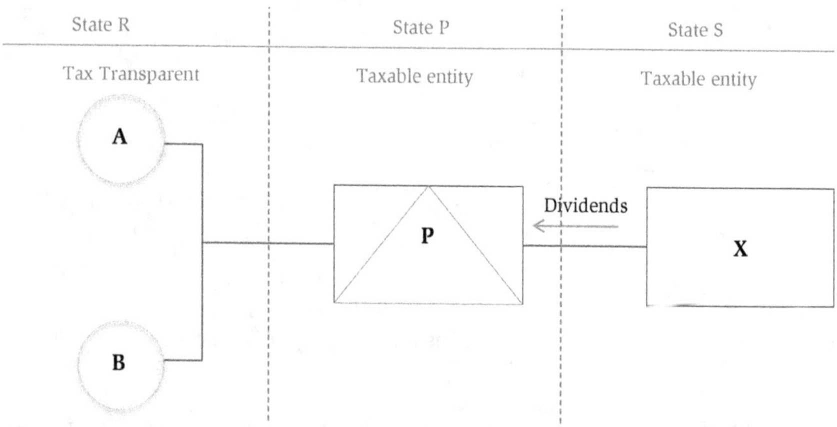

As noted, State S is bound not only by the characterisation of entity P in country P but also by the characterisation of State R, where the partners of P reside. The double entitlement to treaty benefits is solved in a pragmatic manner providing that State S should apply the lowest WHT resulting from the application of the treaties P-S and R-S.

The OECD Partnership Report states that in this case, the tax treatment given to entity P in State S is irrelevant for purposes of determining to whom the income shall be attributed.[940] State S, however, will consider the tax treatment given in both State P and State R. In this regard, the tax treaty between States P-S is applicable since P is considered a resident of State P by this State. A and B, on the other hand, are potentially

938. Steindl and Stiastny, *supra* n. 932.
939. OECD (1999), *supra* n. 1, Ex. 9, p. 29.
940. *Ibid.*

liable to tax as residents of State R. Therefore, State S should, in principle, limit its taxing rights with regard to the treaty R-S. In other words, State S should be limited in its taxing rights by the tax treatment in State R and State P, providing a double entitlement to tax treaty benefits, i.e., to the entity P and to its partners, although by application of two different treaties. The solution proposed by the OECD in the Partnership Report in this case is, however, that State S applies the lowest WHT resulting from those two applicable treaties.[941] For example, if the treaty P-S provides for 10% WHT and the treaty between R-S provides for 15% WHT, State S should tax the dividends at a rate of 10% WHT to satisfy both treaty obligations. The above, however, does not prevent the double taxation that might arise because of the non-application of the treaty R-P.[942]

3.2 Exception

The OECD contemplates an exception to the general recommendation: the general rule will not apply to restrict the source state's right to tax its own residents. As provided in the OECD Commentary on Article 1, updated as per the recommendations of the Report: 'Where a partnership is treated as a resident of a Contracting State, the provisions of the Convention that restrict the other Contracting State's right to tax the partnership on its income do not apply to restrict that other State's right to tax the partners who are its own residents on their share of the income of the partnership.'[943] In other words, if the residence state of the partnership treats it as a taxable entity and the source State considers it transparent, the source state would not be limited to tax its own residents, partners of the partnership, on the ground that the residence state does not allocate the income to the partners. Let us assume the following hypothetical to illustrate this. P is a Partnership established in country P and has two partners: A and B. Whilst B is resident in country P, A is resident in country S, the source state. P receives royalties from country S. P is considered a taxable entity in country P, whilst it is fiscally transparent in country S.[944]

941. *Ibid.*, Ex. 9, para. 74, pp. 29-30.
942. There is no relationship residence-source between R and P. Thus, there is no treaty applicable, assuming also that P is not regarded as a PE, because in such a case, the treaty R-P would be applicable, and State R should grant double taxation relief. *See* a further analysis in *infra* s. 3.3.2.1.
943. OECD Commentary on Article 1 concerning the persons covered by the convention, para. 6.1.
944. This example is inspired on Ex. 16 of the OECD Partnership Report. *See* OECD (1999), *supra* n. 1, p. 45.

Figure 27 Example Inspired in Example 16, OECD Partnership Report

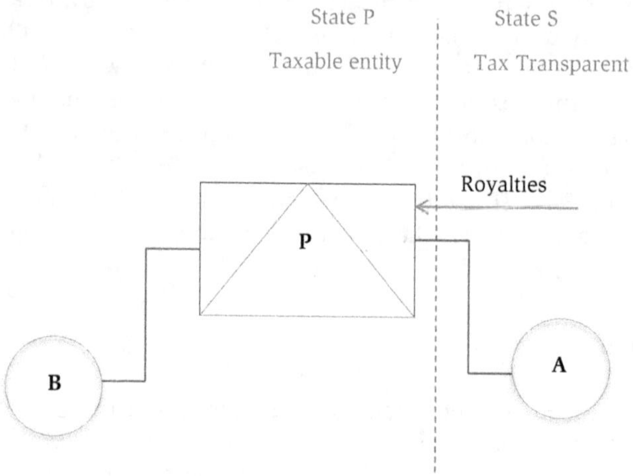

State S is not restricted to tax its own resident, i.e., partner A, regardless of the characterisation of entity P given in the residence state in this case.

As per Article 12 OECD Model, the royalties arising in a Contracting State and beneficially owned in the other Contracting State should be taxable only in this latter State, i.e., the residence state.[945] Therefore, since P is a taxable entity in State P, this State has the exclusive right to tax those royalties unless specifically prevented by a provision within the treaty or the application of CFC rules.[946] Nevertheless, the exception to the general recommendation of the Report provides that in this case, State S would not be limited by Article 12 OECD Model and could also tax partner A on its share of the royalties, i.e., partnership's income. Indeed, as provided in the Report: 'Article 12 of the Convention does not affect taxation that is based on residence but only taxation that is based on source.'[947] In other words, Article 12 would not apply in this case because the royalties would have not been paid from a Contracting State (State S) to the other Contracting State (State P). On the contrary, under State S's perspective, partner A and not entity P received the royalties, and partner A is a resident of State S.[948]

945. Article 12(1) OECD Model Tax Convention.
946. This was indeed the minority opinion sustained by the OECD delegates. As stated within the OECD Partnership Report: 'The delegates who adopted that interpretation therefore concluded that unless the case fell under the application of CFC rules or the Convention included a special provision allowing State R [State S in our example] to tax its residents in such circumstances (e.g., a specific provision applicable to partnerships or a so-called "saving clause" such as is found in Conventions concluded by the United States), the Convention would prevent State R [State S in our example] on taxing partner B [A in our example] on his share of the royalties.' OECD (1999), *supra* n. 1, Part III para. 126, p. 46.
947. OECD (1999), *supra* n. 1, Part III para. 127, p. 46.
948. *Ibid.*

This position, agreed by the majority of the OECD delegates, could certainly lead to double taxation unless State S consider that partner A has a PE in State P, and thus, State S is obligated to provide double tax relief under the tax treaty.[949] The above, however, seems not to be a reason enough to prevent State S from taxing partner A.[950] Yet, the double tax issue may become permanent in cases involving other types of transparent entities rather than partnerships. As explained by Danon, this could be perfectly possible in a similar situation involving a trust rather than a partnership.[951] Following the reasoning of Danon, let us assume the following hypothetical where State P is the country where a trust (T) is established. The settlor of the trust is a resident of this State, whilst the beneficiary is a resident of State S, from where the trust receives annual royalties. The trust is regarded as fiscally transparent in both States.

Figure 28 Example with Trust

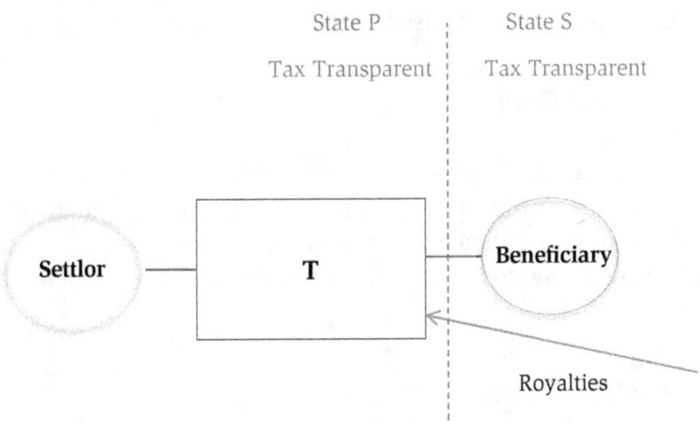

In this hypothetical, following the exception to the general recommendation of the Report, Article 12 OECD Model would not be applicable to limit the taxation rights of the source country S to tax the beneficiary, who is also a resident of this country. State P, on the contrary, would tax the same income in the hands of the settlor, who is a resident of State P. The difference is that the beneficiary, unlike partner A in the previous example, does not maintain a PE in State P. In this situation, therefore, the avoidance of double taxation becomes impossible.[952]

949. Although minimised, double taxation would still exist in the cases where there is no PE in State P.
950. As provided by the OECD Partnership Report: 'The fact that double taxation results because of the differing income allocations of State R and P [S and P in our example] is not a reason to limit its right to tax its residents.' OECD (1999), *supra* n. 1, Part III para. 127, p. 47.
951. Danon, *supra* n. 912, p. 197.
952. Danon argues that this solution is inconsistent. He sustains that 'the only reason why the OECD arrives at this result is precisely because, without any sound argument, it suddenly implicitly applies the internal attribution rules of the source state, thereby causing the income to be allocated to one of its residents [...]. More generally, what the OECD Partnership Report is

3.3 Critics

Critics upon the general recommendations of the OECD Partnership Report have been elaborated both in form and in substance.

3.3.1 Formal Critics

Formally speaking, the Report is criticised for its case-by-case approach rather than a more general and theoretical one. Indeed, it is undeniable that a case-by-case approach is more practical and illustrative. However, it also creates a lot of uncertainty because it is impossible to cover all the potential issues that may arise in every single situation using just a few hypotheticals.[953] Similarly, the Report is criticised for limiting its analysis to the case of partnerships without including the case of other non-corporate entities, such as trusts or LLCs.[954] However, there is no doubt that the same criteria used for partnership may also be used for other non-corporate entities.

3.3.2 Substantial Critics

Substantially speaking, the Report also left important gaps for criticism, which can be summarised in three main areas: (i) unresolved conflicts of attribution; (ii) a preference for a solution favouring residence States; and (iii) the interplay with other attribution rules, especially with the concept of *beneficial ownership* of Articles 10, 11 and 12 OECD Model.

3.3.2.1 Unresolved Conflicts of Attribution

With regard to the unresolved conflicts of attribution, these may arise either in the form of 'residence-residence' conflicts or 'source-source' conflicts.[955] The 'residence-residence' conflicts, on the one hand, can be illustrated using the following hypothetical: P is a partnership organised in State P, which has two partners, A and B, who are residents of State R. Accordingly, P receives interest and royalties from State S. Whilst State P and S treat the partnership as a taxable entity, State R, the residence state of the

---

doing is erroneously turning a source-residence into a residence-residence conflict of attribution'. Although he argues '[...] the real and unresolved residence-residence conflict of attribution comes into play where income sourced in a third state is allocated to residents of two different resident states'. *Ibid.*, p. 198. *See also infra* s. 3.3.2.1, referring to 'residence-residence' and 'source-source' conflicts. For more issues regarding the taxation of trusts in the international context, *see* M. Brabazon, *International Taxation of Trust Income: Principles, Planning, and Design*, Cambridge University Press, 2019.

953. One of the major criticisms to the 1999 OECD Partnership Report came from Prof. M. Lang. *See* M. Lang, *The Application of the OECD Model Tax Convention to Partnerships, A Critical Analysis of the Report Prepared by the OECD*, Wolters Kluwer, Alphen aan den Rijn (2000). *See also, e.g.*, Danon, *supra* n. 912, p. 199.
954. This is, however, clarified in the OECD proposal on Article 1(2) OECD Model. *See* the analysis in *infra* s. 5.
955. This terminology is indeed used by Danon. *See* Danon, *supra* n. 912, pp. 198-200.

partners A and B, considers it as fiscally transparent, although it does not constitute a PE for tax treaty purposes.

Figure 29 Triangular Case Illustrating a 'Residence-Residence' Conflict

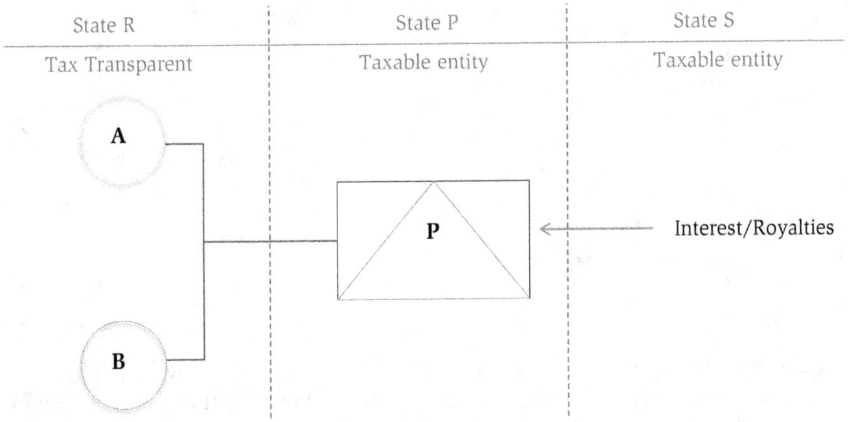

As per the recommendation of the OECD Partnership Report, if State S has a treaty with both P and R, then both treaties would be applicable, and State S would be obliged to impose the lowest rate upon interest and royalties.[956] Similarly, State R and State P will impose taxation as well.[957] However, State R will not be able to grant double taxation relief under a treaty with P because the relationship between both is not as residence-source countries but rather as residence-residence. In other words, the interest and royalties will be subject to double taxation.[958]

Similarly, 'source-source' conflicts of allocation may arise without a proper solution when a payment derived from an entity considered opaque in its country of organization whilst fiscally transparent in the country of residence of its partners and the country where the recipient of the income is located, giving rise therefore to an item of income sourced twice.[959] This can be illustrated in the following hypothetical. Let us assume that P is a partnership organised in State P, which has two partners, A and B, who are residents of State R. Partnership P pays interest to C, a company organised in State S. Whilst States R and S treat P as fiscally transparent, State P considers it as a taxable entity.

956. OECD Commentary on Article 1 concerning the persons covered by the convention, para. 6.5. *See also*, OECD (1999), *supra* n. 1, Part II.4, para. 74, Ex. 9., p. 30.
957. If the income is royalties, they [State R and State P] will indeed have the exclusive right to tax as per Article 12 OECD Model.
958. The double taxation issue would be minimized if P was considered a PE. In such a case, State R should grant a double taxation relief on the interest and royalties attributed to the PE. *See* Danon, *supra* n. 912, pp. 198-199.
959. *Ibid.*, p. 199.

Figure 30 Triangular Case Illustrating a 'Source-Source' Conflict

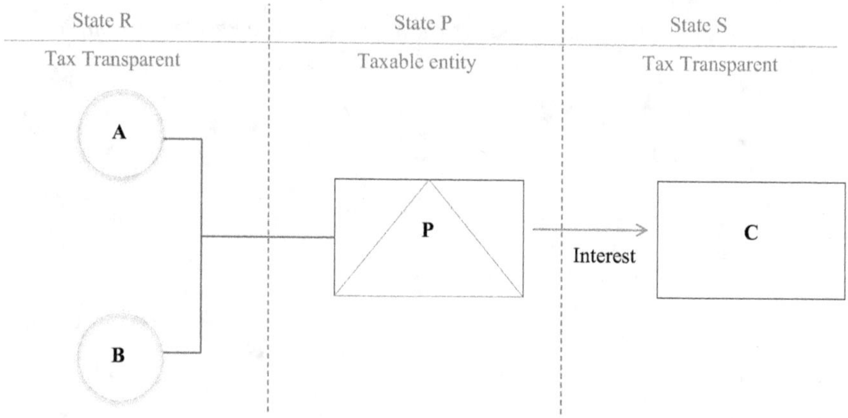

As per Article 11(5) OECD Model, the interests are deemed to be paid both from country R and country P. Therefore, State S should provide double taxation relief with respect to the treaty with R and P. Nevertheless, it is possible that no tax credit is allowed in State C with respect to the total WHT levied in State R and P, leading thus to an unsatisfactory result of double taxation.[960]

3.3.2.2 *Preference for the Residence State*

Another sound critic against the principles stated in the OECD Partnership Report is its remarked preference for the residence state rather than the source state.[961] Indeed, as already stressed, the OECD Partnership Report provides that it is the residence state that decides, in case of conflicts of allocation of income, whether the tax liability is imposed on the partnership or the partners, and the source state must then apply the tax treaty accordingly.[962]

This preference for the residence state, as explained by Wheeler, does not consider the cases in which the source state may consider that attribution unacceptable.[963] Indeed, the principle stated in the OECD Partnership Report is built on the

960. *Ibid.*
961. In 2005, and with respect to the OECD Partnership Report, Wheeler argued: 'A more serious problem with this approach is that it does not take sufficient account of the concerns of the source state about income conduits.' Wheeler, *supra* n. 931, p. 488.
962. J. Wheeler, The *Missing Keystone of Income Tax Treaties*, 3 World Tax J. (2011), Journals IBFD, p. 260. However, '[...] determining the direction taken by the income flow is a prior stage that should not be determined by one state alone. It is not satisfactory to give the initiative in this respect to the residence state, leaving the source state to combat an attribution that it finds unacceptable by using a concept as problematic as beneficial owner'. *Ibid.*, p. 261.
963. *Ibid.*, for example, if the State of source considers that a payment of interest is not paid to the *beneficial owner* of the interest payments, it might in theory deny the reduced WHT under Article 11. *See also* the further analysis at *infra* s. 3.3.2.3.

grounds that income is attributed to a person, either the partners or the partnership, who carries out the business or makes the investment. Nevertheless, States sometimes go beyond these paths and attribute income based on less direct connections with the income.[964] In a similar view, Lang argues: '[I]t makes sense to assume that it is not up to the residence State to decide who shall be entitled to the treaty benefits in the source State. It is the source State that decides on the taxpayer status.'[965] Wassermeyer also stresses that the domestic law of the state granting the tax benefits [source state] is crucial for purposes of tax liability and income allocation.[966] The approach argued by these two authors, i.e., favouring the position of the source state, has been indeed confirmed by a case law decision by the Austrian Supreme Court [*Verwaltungsgerichthof*] in 2006.[967] In a complementary approach, Wheeler also proposed in 2005 that the law of the State where the intermediary company is located, in case of conduits, should also be decisive. This option has been, however, criticised for encouraging taxpayers to shift income to jurisdictions with a tax treaty providing for zero source taxation.[968]

3.3.2.3 *The (Original Missed) Interplay with the Concept of Beneficial Owner*

The principle stated in the OECD Partnership Report appears not to be completely in line with the mechanics of tax treaties, especially when referring to the interplay between this principle and the concept of *beneficial owner* in Articles 10, 11, and 12 OECD Model.[969]

The above can be illustrated using the following example. Let us assume that entity P is established in State P. A and B are P's partners who reside in State R. P owns shares in X, which is a company resident in State S. X pays dividends to P. States P and S treat entity P as a taxable entity whilst State R treats as fiscally transparent. Likewise, whilst the treaty between P-S provides for a 10% WHT, the treaty between R-S provides for a 5% WHT.

964. *Ibid.*
965. Lang, *supra* n. 953, p. 38.
966. F. Wassermeyer, *Doppelbesteuerung (OECD-Musterabkommen* 2010 *Kommentar)* in: F. Wassermeyer, C. Kaeser, M. Lang and J. Schuch (eds), Linde, Vienna, 2015, Article 12, m.no. 33.
967. AT: VwGH, 18 October 2006, case 2003/13/0052, and an analysis of the case in: M. Lang, *Tendenzen in der Rechtsprechung des österreichischen Verwaltungsgerichtshofs zu den Doppelbesteuerungsabkomme,* IFF Forum für Steuerrecht 2012, pp. 27-29. *See also*, Steindl and Stiastny, *supra* n. 932, p. 114.
968. Steindl and Stiastny, *supra* n. 932, p. 114.
969. For the discussion regarding the meaning of *beneficial owner, see* the references at *supra* n. 352.

Figure 31 The OECD Partnership Report and the Beneficial Ownership Requirement

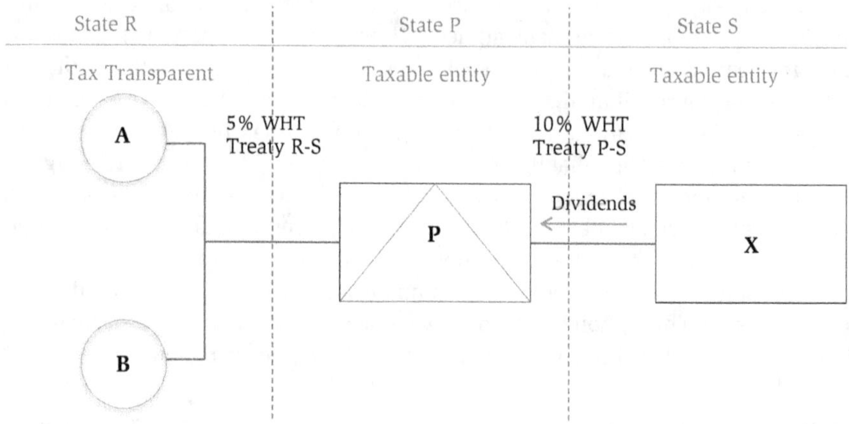

If we consider the solution stated in the OECD Partnership Report and reproduced in the OECD Commentaries, we should say that this situation is solved if State S taxes the dividend at the lowest WHT rate between the two applicable treaties, i.e., 5% WHT stated in the treaty R-S. However, the wording of Article 10(2) OECD Model provides for a reduced WHT to the extent the *beneficial owner* of the dividends is a resident of the other Contracting State. In this case, however, the solution provided in the OECD Partnership Report and reproduced in the OECD Commentaries seems to disregard the interplay between the benefits of the treaty and the special requirement of the *beneficial owner* of Article 10(2) OECD Model.

The OECD Partnership Report assumes that there is only one beneficial owner, i.e., partnership P. This is correct from the perspective of State S (source state), which sees P as a taxable entity. However, in the same logic, State S should not restrict its taxing rights with regard to A and B, who are not the *beneficial owners* of the same dividends. In simple words, solving the conflict by just providing that the source state should apply the lowest WHT rate when comparing the treaties with the partnership and the partners seems to be awkward. Unfortunately, the proposed OECD Commentaries on Article 1(2) OECD Model still leaves open the discussion with regard to the beneficial ownership requirement in Articles 10, 11, and 12 OECD Model. Indeed, the proposed OECD Commentaries on Article 1(2) OECD Model simply provide that nothing prevents the source state from determining, in this case, that a different person may be regarded as the beneficial owner.[970]

970. A further analysis at *infra* s. 5.3.1.

4 THE US MODEL: THE LEGAL PRECEDENT FOR THE OECD PROPOSAL

Although there are no doubts that the principles settled in the 1999 OECD Partnership Report are reproduced in Article 1(6) of the US Model, this provision can also be found in tax treaties concluded by the United States since 1996 and even older ones.[971] Accordingly, the formal inclusion within the US Model came only in its 2006 version,[972] applying indistinctly both to partnerships and other kinds of entities, including, e.g., trusts and LLCs.[973] This provision is analysed in the subsequent subsections.

4.1 General Interpretation of Article 1(6) US Model

Article 1(6) US Model (2016) states that: 'For purposes of this Convention, an item of income, profit or gain derived by or through an entity that is treated wholly or partly fiscally transparent under the taxation laws of either Contracting State shall be considered to be derived by a resident of a Contracting State, but only to the extent that the item is treated for purposes of the taxation laws of such Contracting State as the income, profit or gain of a resident.'[974] A slightly similar wording was used in the previous US Model (2006), which provides: 'An item of income, profit or gain derived through an entity that is fiscally transparent under the laws of either Contracting State shall be considered to be derived by a resident of a State to the extent that the item is treated for purposes of the taxation law of such Contracting State as income, profit or gain of a resident.'[975]

Regardless of the slightly different wording, the provisions state the same: if an item of income is received by a fiscally transparent entity, considered as such by any of the Contracting States, it shall be regarded as received by the residents of the State considering the entity as tax transparent so long as the item of income is subject to tax at the partners' level in that State. That is to say, the benefits derived from a tax treaty can be claimed only by the partners of the transparent entity to the extent these are also regarded as residents in the State, characterising the entity as fiscally transparent. In other words, Article 1(6) US Model obliges the State of source to grant treaty benefits by the sole fact that the State of residence attributes the income derived through a fiscally transparent entity to one of its residents.[976]

Nevertheless, Article 1(6) US Model is not designed as an '*anti-hybrid entity*' rule but rather as a rule that clarifies to whom income is being allocated, and thus, the

971. Biitker and Lokken, *supra* n. 556, p. 65-59.
972. R. Avi-Yonah and M. Tittle, *The United States Model Income Tax Convention*, Bull. Int'l Taxn., Vol. 61, p. 224 (2007), Journals IBFD.
973. US: United States Model Technical Explanation accompanying the United States Model Income Tax Convention of 15 November 2006, p. 7. The inclusion of trusts and LLCs is important, because it was in fact one of the concerns arose in the Partnership Report in 1999. *See* OECD (1999), *supra* n. 1.
974. US: 2016 United States Model Income Tax Convention of 17 February 2016, Article 1(6).
975. US: 2006 United States Model Income Tax Convention of 15 November 2006, Article 1(6).
976. R. Doernberg and K. van Raad, *Hybrid Entities and the U.S. Model Income Tax Treaty*, 19 Tax Notes Int'l 8, 746 (1999).

benefits of a treaty are being granted when income is received through transparent entities. For example, it applies even if both Contracting States treat the entity as fiscally transparent.[977] However, this does not mean to recognise its particular importance in cases where *hybrid* or *reverse hybrid entities* are involved.[978] Likewise, as per the technical explanations of the 2006 US Tax Treaty Model, Article 1(6) has basically two main purposes.[979] First, it aims to eliminate the technical problems that investors would have prevented using transparent entities to claim treaty benefits, even though such investors would be subject to tax on the income derived through such entities.[980] Second, it attempts to directly prevent the use of transparent entities to claim treaty benefits in circumstances where the person investing through such an entity is not subject to tax on the income in its State of residence.[981] Article 1(6) US Model involves thus a series of preconditions within its wording, which are analysed as follows.

4.1.1 *The Reference to* 'Income, Profit or Gain'

Article 1(6) US Model refers to '*income, profit or gain*' received by a fiscally transparent entity. Therefore, the provision includes several numbers of items of income, such as business profits, income from services, dividends, royalties, rental income and gains derived from the sale of property.[982] All of these items of income correspond to the substantive rules of Articles 6 through 21 US Model.[983] Likewise, there is no reference to 'capital' because there is no provision on the taxation of capital within the US Model.[984] Finally, it is also clear that the determinations of income should be made on an 'item by item' and not 'entity-by-entity' basis.[985]

977. The reference to '*either Contracting State*' in the wording suggests that at least one Contracting State should treat the entity as fiscally transparent, but it does not restrict its application if both States do that. This is stated clearly in the OECD proposal, which mirrors Article 1(6) US Model. *Infra* s. 5.
978. As stressed in Chapter 3, the US Check-the-box regulations are indeed an important source of hybrid and reverse hybrid entities. *See* the analysis of the US Check-the-box system at *supra* Chapter 3, s. 4.
979. *Ibid.*
980. *Ibid.* The reference to '*subject to tax*' made in the 2006 Technical Explanation of the US Tax Treaty Model may mislead readers to the wrong idea that Article 1(6) of the US Tax Treaty Model is aimed at avoiding the result of DNT. However, this interpretation is incorrect. If we analyse the use of the term 'subject to tax' in a treaty context, we immediately realise that it refers to the definition of residents or people liable to tax by reason of their domiciles, residence or citizenship. In simple words, and as we will see later in this chapter, the article is trying to ensure that the tax treaty benefits arrive to a resident of any of the treaty partners and not to a third person, who is not part of the bilateral treaty.
981. *Ibid.*
982. US: Technical Explanation of the 2006 United States Model Income Tax Convention, of 15 November 2006, p. 5.
983. *Ibid.*
984. J. Kollmann, A. Roncarati and C. Staringer, *Treaty Entitlement for Fiscally Transparent Entities: Article 1(2) of the OECD Model Convention* in: M. Lang, P. Pistone, S. Staringer (eds) *Base Erosion and Profit Shifting (BEPS). The Proposal to revise the OECD Model Convention*, Linde, Vienna (2016), p. 21.
985. A. Nikolakakis et al., *Some Reflections on the Proposed Revision to the OECD Model and Commentaries, and on the Multilateral Instrument, with respect to Fiscally Transparent Entities*, 3 BTR 311 (2017). *See also*, *infra* s. 5.1.1. as regards the OECD Model.

4.1.2 *Income, Profit and Gain Derived* 'by or Through'

The wording of the 2016 US Model also refers to income derived '*by or through*' an entity. This wording certainly differs from the wording of the 2006 US Model, which only referred to income '*derived through*'.[986]

When analysing the 2006 Technical Explanation of the US Model, it seems to be clear that the terms '*by*' and '*through*' are used in an interchangeable manner. For example, the Technical Explanations state: 'Under paragraph 6, an item of income, profit or gain *derived by* such a fiscal transparent entity will be considered to be derived by a resident of a Contracting State [...]' (emphasis added).[987] Likewise, they provide: 'In the case of a partnership, the persons who are, under U.S. tax laws, treated as partners of the entity would normally be the persons whom U.S. tax laws would treat as deriving the interest income *through* the partnership.'[988] Yet, what seems to be clear is that, depending on the perspective (i.e., residence or source state), income might be considered derived by or through an entity, although this does not affect the fact that the country treating the entity as fiscally transparent should assign the benefits of the treaty to the owners of that entity only to the extent that they are also residents in that State. However, this might be interpreted from Article 1(6) US Model without the need to modify its wording.

Although the real practical reasons for a change in the wording of the provision are still doubtful, mostly in the absence of technical explanations for the new 2016 US Model, some hints might be found within the OECD Article 1(2) OECD Model, which uses a similar wording.[989] In this case, the wording '*derived by or through*' seems to be interpreted as ensuring the application of the provision to two types of cases. First, where the source state treats the entity X as transparent, and thus, the income is *derived through* the fiscally transparent entity. Second, where the source state treats entity X as tax opaque (being regarded as tax transparent by the residence state), and thus, the income is *derived by* such entity.[990] Therefore, the reference to income derived '*by or through*' seems to have a broad meaning and is applied 'regardless of the view taken by each Contracting State as to who derives that income for domestic purposes and regardless of whether or not that entity or arrangement has legal personality or constitutes a person as defined in subparagraph 1(a) of Article 3'.[991] In simple terms,

986. Compare the wordings in *supra* s. 4.1.
987. US: Technical Explanation of the 2006 United States Model Income Tax Convention of 15 November 2006, p. 6.
988. *Ibid.*
989. *Infra* s. 5.1.2.
990. *Ibid.*
991. OECD (2015), *supra* n. 6, p. 141, Proposed Commentary on Article 1, para. 26.8.

this wording would reinforce the two functions of the provision, i.e., to grant and deny treaty benefits from the perspective of the source state.[992]

4.1.3 The Reference to 'Entities' *(and Not* Arrangements*)*

The exclusive reference to '*entities*' within the wording of Article 1(6) US Model seems to be very clear and straightforward: the provision only applies to legal entities that qualify as a person as per the definition of Article 3(1) US Model, which is treated as fiscally transparent at least by one of the Contracting States.[993] Unlike the OECD Model, the US Model definition of person includes specifically partnerships, trusts, estates, companies, and any other body of persons.[994] Therefore, the status as a person of partnerships and other transparent entities was never considered an issue. In contrast, the definition of persons within the OECD Model generated some questions before 1999 as to whether the wording 'any body of persons' would also include partnerships and other non-corporate entities as well.[995] This discussion was, however, settled after the issuance of the OECD Partnership Report and the modification of the OECD Commentaries, which recognised that: 'Partnerships will also be considered to be 'persons' either because they fall within the definition of "company" or, where this is not the case, because they constitute other bodies of persons.'[996] All in all, therefore, the scope of application of Article 1(6) US Model seems to be rather clear, including within the notion of '*entities*', both corporate and non-corporate ones.

4.1.4 'Wholly or Partial' *Fiscal Transparency*

Finally, the wording of the 2016 US Model refers to entities that are '*wholly or partially transparent*'. This wording, however, does not make much sense because it was clear since the 2006 US Model that Article 1(6) was applicable not only to partnerships but also to other transparent entities in general, including common investment trusts under

992. This is, however, evident from the wording within the 2006 US Model, which refers to the source State attribution 'to the extent' of residence State attribution. *See* Nikolakakis et al., *supra* n. 985, p. 311.
993. The 2006 Technical Explanation of the US Model states: 'Entities falling under this description in the United States include partnerships, common investment trusts under section 584 and grantor trusts. This paragraph also applies to U.S. limited liability companies ("LLCs") that are treated as partnerships or disregarded entities for U.S. tax purposes.' US: Technical Explanation of the 2006 United States Model Income Tax Convention, of 15 November 2006, p. 6.
994. US: 2006 United States Model Income Tax Convention of 15 November 2006, Article 3(1).
995. OECD Model Convention, Article 3; OECD Commentary on Article 3 concerning general definitions, para. 2. *See also* the discussion at *supra* s. 2.
996. *Ibid.*

I.R.C. Section 584 and grantor trust and LLCs.[997] Thus, the change in the wording seems to have a more practical reason, which is to align the wording with Article 1(2) OECD Model, facilitating, therefore, the negotiations of treaties.[998]

4.2 Illustrations Regarding the Application of Article 1(6) US Model

The application of Article 1(6) US Model is illustrated below through a series of examples. All these examples involve the United States as either the resident or source State and are divided into two groups: (i) strict bilateral cases and (ii) triangular cases. Likewise, all the examples assume that no PE is constituted in the source state, and all treaties include Article 1(6) US Model. Finally, all the examples also assume that all anti-abuse restrictions within domestic laws and tax treaties have been passed before the application of Article 1(6) US Model.[999]

4.2.1 Application of Article 1(6) US Model in Strict Bilateral Cases

This Section contains four illustrations of strict bilateral situations analysing the implications of Article 1(6) US Model. Whilst Examples 1 and 2 refer to income received by or through a hybrid entity, Examples 3 and 4 refer to income received through a reverse hybrid entity.

4.2.1.1 Example 1: Foreign Entity with US Owners

Let us assume a foreign entity, P, which is organized and resident in State P and has two owners, A and B, who are US citizens. Accordingly, entity P receives interest payments from a debtor in the foreign State P. Whilst State P considers the entity as a taxable entity, the partners A and B in the United States have elected to treat the entity as tax transparent for US tax purposes.[1000] Thus, from a US perspective, the income is allocated to partners A and B instead. State P also applies a 30% WHT on interest paid abroad of 30%, which is calculated on the gross amount of these payments.

997. US: Technical Explanation of the 2006 United States Model Income Tax Convention of 15 November 2006, p. 6.
998. *Infra* s. 5.1.4.
999. This includes, e.g., substance over form doctrine or LOB provisions within US tax treaties. For a brief reference about the LOB provision in the new 2016 US Model and its interpretation with regard to pursuing single taxation, *see supra* Chapter 1, s. 3.2.3.2.
1000. For a detailed analysis with respect to the election under the CTB regulations, *see supra* Chapter 3, s. 4.3.

Figure 32 Example 1: Foreign Entity with US Owners

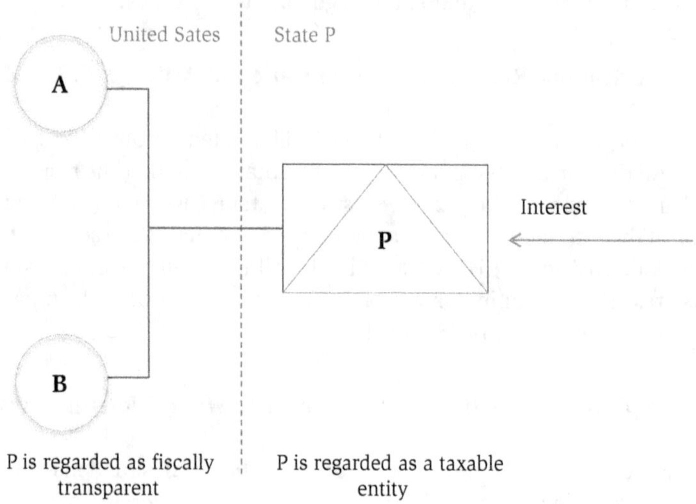

As foreign entity P is an eligible entity, partners A and B decided to file the election to treat foreign entity P as tax transparent for US tax purposes.

Whilst, on the one hand, for State P, this is strictly a domestic situation, partners A and B, on the other hand, would like to claim the benefits of the treaty between the United States and State P because, from a US perspective, income is allocated and taxed at the level of A and B. The conflict is thus given by the different tax characterisation of entity P.

If we look at the application of Article 1(6) US Model, all the preconditions are met. That is, there is indeed interest income being derived through an entity that one of the Contracting States (the United States in this case) considers as tax transparent, and the income is allocated to A and B, who are also US citizens, i.e., residents for purposes of the treaty. This implies that State P will limit its taxing rights and will apply a reduced WHT of 15% according to Article 11 of the United States/State P tax treaty. Likewise, owners A and B may claim a tax credit as per Article 23 of the United States/State P tax treaty.

The solution of Article 1(6) US Model in this case works certainly in favour of the United States, i.e., the residence state in this bilateral case. Indeed, the source state (State P) shall limit its taxing rights just because the partners of the entity are US citizens and decided to file the election to treat the foreign entity P as tax transparent. In other words, the CTB rules seem to be the real reason for the application of Article

1(6) US model to a situation that, in principle, might be perfectly treated as a domestic one.[1001]

Likewise, the solution given by Article 1(6) US Model presents problems from the perspectives of both the source and residence states. From the source state's perspective, it does not consider the proper interplay with the concept of *beneficial owner* under Article 11 of the United States/State P tax treaty. Indeed, for State P, partners A and B will be rarely considered as the beneficial owners of the interest under the rules of this State.[1002] On the other hand, from the residence state's perspective, it is arguable that Article 23 of the United States/State P tax treaty can be interpreted so extensively as to provide relief to A and B when technically there is no direct payment of taxes. In other words, entity P will be subject to tax in State P because it is a resident of that State. However, unless Article 23 is interpreted as providing an indirect tax credit, A and B should not be relieved from double taxation.[1003]

4.2.1.2 Example 2: US Corporation with US Owners

Let us assume now that a US Corporation (USCo) [per se Corporation][1004] has two owners, A and B, who are US citizens and who receive interest payments from State P. Whilst for US tax purposes, a US Corporation is indeed a taxable entity, for State P tax purposes, this is a tax-transparent entity. State P generally applies a 30% WHT on interest paid abroad, which is calculated on the gross payments.

1001. Nonetheless, it is important to remember that even if this situation was treated as a domestic one, the United State could tax A and B (US citizens) by reason of Article 1(4) US Model, i.e., the 'saving clause'.
1002. *See* a further analysis in *infra* s. 4.3.1.
1003. The interpretation of Article 23 US Model as to provide an indirect tax credit is, nevertheless, arguable. For a comparison with the solution proposed within the OECD Model, *see infra* s. 5.3.2. The solution to the interpretation of Article 23 in a similar case provides that, unless the relief refers to taxes applied according to the treaty, no relief should be given to A and B. In other words, if the taxation imposed to entity P is derived exclusively by the fact of being a resident of State P, there is no obligation to relief of double taxation in the other State. *See* OECD (2015), *supra* n. 226, para. 64 (replacement of Article 23B OECD Model), p. 88.
1004. For the implications regarding being considered a per se Corporation and the application of the CTB election, *see supra* Chapter 3, s. 4.3.

Figure 33 Example 2: US Corporation with US Owners

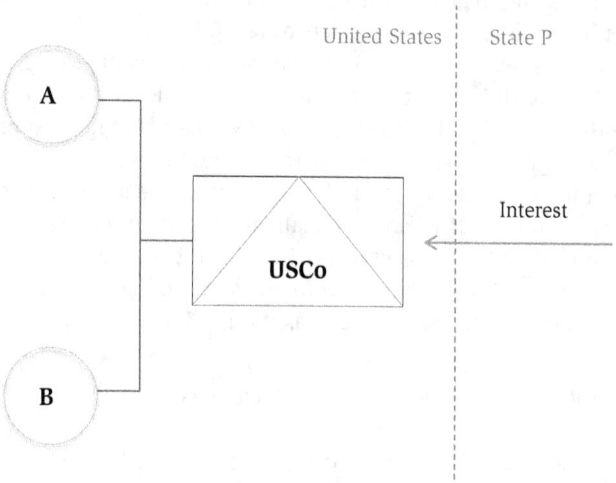

USCo is a per se Corporation. Therefore, USCo is a taxable entity in the United States. Accordingly, this characterisation cannot be changed using the CTB election at a domestic level. State P, on the other hand, considers USCo as a fiscally transparent entity.

The conflict in this case is because of the different perspectives between the United States and State P regarding the tax characterisation of USCo and, consequently, the application of the United States/State P tax treaty. On the one hand, the United States considers USCo as a taxable entity, whilst State P considers USCo as a tax-transparent entity. Therefore, from the US perspective, USCo is the tax resident for treaty purposes who receives the interest payments from State P and, thus, who is entitled to claim the benefits of the treaty between the United States and State P. On the other hand, according to State P, partners A and B are the ones receiving the interest payments and the beneficial owners of them. In other words, A and B are the ones entitled to claim the benefits of the treaty between the two countries and not USCo.

The preconditions of Article 1(6) US Model to grant the benefits of the treaty to A and B are, nevertheless, not met because A and B are not considered residents of State P. Therefore, Article 1(6) US Model acts in this case to deny the benefits of the treaty to A and B and to ensure that they are granted to USCo. In other words, Article 1(6) US Model ensures that the characterisation of USCo in the United States prevails.

Yet, it is interesting to note that for the source state (State P), it would be irrelevant whether the income is allocated to A and B or to USCo because, in both cases, it would apply the treaty between the United States and State P, reducing its WHT to 15% according to Article 11 of the United States/State P tax treaty. In other words, Article 1(6) US Model is relevant in this case only to determine who in the residence state may claim the relief of double taxation as per Article 23 of the United States/State P tax treaty. Likewise, as noted below, if A and B were residents of State P, the application of Article 1(6) US Model would be redundant because the preconditions of Article 11 US Model would not be met anyway, i.e., there would be no interest payments arising in a Contracting State and beneficially owned in the other Contracting State. The interest payments, in this case, would arise in the same State where the beneficial owners of the payments are residents. Therefore, it would not go beyond being a domestic issue. However, nothing would prevent the United States from taxing USCo (a taxable entity) as a resident anyway, generating a situation of double taxation.[1005]

Figure 34 Example 2 (Variation): US Corporation with Resident's Owners in the State of Source

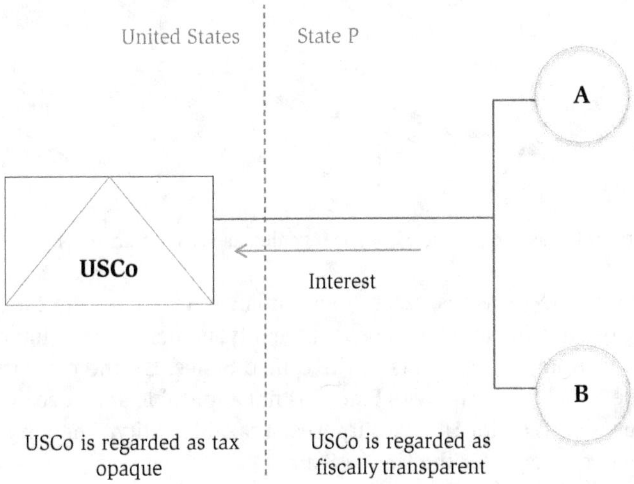

Article 1(6) US Model is irrelevant in this case, because the preconditions for application of Article 11 US Model are not met. Likewise, interest will be taxed both in the United States, at the level of USCo, and in State P, as the share of income in the 'foreign partnership'.

4.2.1.3 *Example 3: Foreign Partnership with US Owners*

Let us now assume that a foreign partnership P is organised and it is resident in State P. It has two owners, partners A and B, who are both US citizens. Accordingly, foreign partnership P receives interest payments from a debtor in State P. The US partners of partnership P, A and B elected to treat the foreign partnership P as a taxable entity in the United States, whilst this is indeed a tax-transparent entity under the domestic laws

1005. *See* the interplay between Article 1(6) US Model and Article 1(4) US Model ('saving clause') at *infra* s. 4.3.2.

of State P. Likewise, State P applies a general 30% WHT on interest paid abroad, which is calculated on the gross amount of payments.

Figure 35 Example 3: Foreign Partnership with US Owners

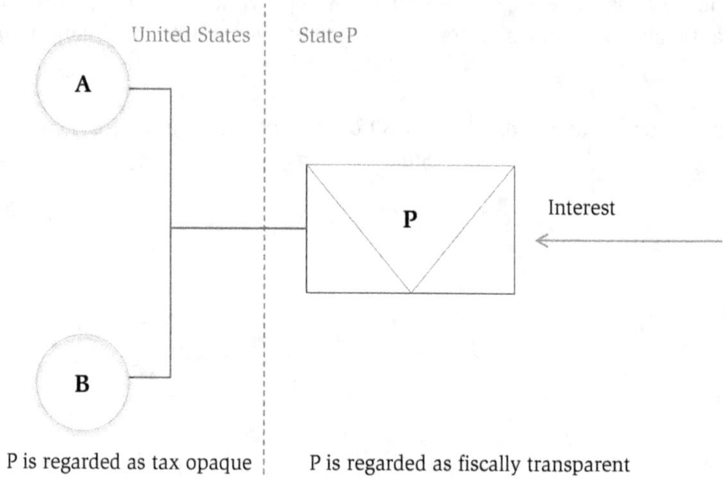

As well as the previous cases, the conflict is given by the fact that State P considers the partnership as a tax transparent entity, namely that the interest payments are allocated to A and B, residents of the United States. On the contrary, the United States considers that the treaty with State P is not applicable at all because, in fact, the foreign partnership P is, for US tax purposes, a taxable entity. The whole transaction raises no treaty concerns for the United States.

As regards the application of Article 1(6) US Model, the income is received through partnership P, considered fiscally transparent in State P. However, it is not allocated to residents of this State. On the contrary, A and B are US citizens and residents in the United States. Therefore, Article 1(6) US Model applies in this case to deny the benefits of the treaty to partners A and B and to confirm that the payments of interest in this case are a mere domestic situation.[1006] Yet, nothing prevents the United States from taxing the interest through the application of CFC rules, which may

1006. The denial of the benefits of the treaty also includes the possibility that A and B claim the reduced WHT at source. In other words, it could not be argued that the source State should still reduce its WHT as per Article 11 US Model and that the benefits of the treaty to A and B are limited only to the double taxation relief of Article 23 US Model.

ultimately trigger double taxation. Double taxation, however, might be avoided in this case through the application of the domestic US tax credit system.[1007]

4.2.1.4 *Example 4: Domestic Partnership with US Owners*

Let us assume now that a US partnership (USP) has two owners, A and B, who are both US citizens. Accordingly, some interest payments are paid from State P. Whilst USP is indeed tax transparent for US tax purposes, State P considers it as a taxable entity. State P applies a general WHT on interest paid abroad of 30%, calculated on the gross payments.

Figure 36 Example 4: Domestic Partnership with US Owners

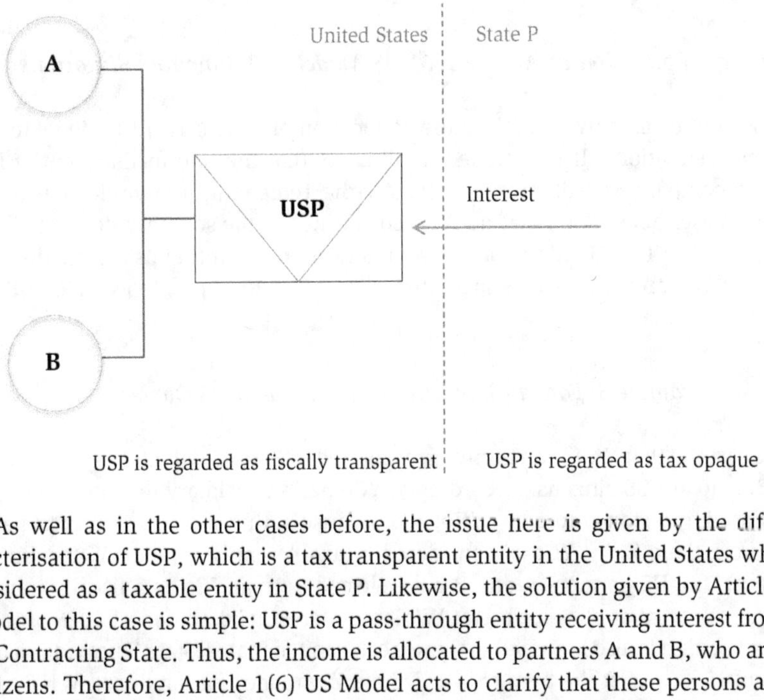

As well as in the other cases before, the issue here is given by the different characterisation of USP, which is a tax transparent entity in the United States whilst it is considered as a taxable entity in State P. Likewise, the solution given by Article 1(6) US Model to this case is simple: USP is a pass-through entity receiving interest from the other Contracting State. Thus, the income is allocated to partners A and B, who are also US citizens. Therefore, Article 1(6) US Model acts to clarify that these persons are the ones who should claim the relief from double taxation under Article 23 of the

1007. US: I.R.C. s. 960 provides for an FTC with respect to the taxes paid at the level of the foreign subsidiaries. If a corporation claims the credit (not as in the example above), the applicable provision is I.R.C. s. 902. Likewise, the deemed FTC under s. 960 is available for taxes paid by subsidiaries until the sixth tier. *See* McDaniel, Ault and Repetti, *supra* n. 718, p. 121.

United States/State P tax treaty and who may also enjoy the reduced WHT at source. The solution seems to be satisfactory from the point of view of the residence state, i.e., the United States.

However, from the point of view of the source state, the application of Article 1(6) US Model may not solve all the conflicts regarding the application of the treaty. Indeed, the fact that Article 1(6) US Model clarifies that A and B should be granted the benefit of the treaty does not change the fact that State P still considers USP, and not partners A and B, as the *beneficial owner* of the interest income.[1008] In other words, the reduced WHT at source as per Article 11 of the United States/State P tax treaty could still not be granted if State P considers that A and B are not the beneficial owners of the interest. The above might also generate conflicts regarding the application of Article 23 of the United States/State P tax treaty because the double taxation relief may, in that case, cover only the amount of reduced WHT and not the full amount of WHT if State P decides not to apply the reduced WHT at source.

4.2.2 *Application of Article 1(6) US Model in Triangular Situations*

This section turns now to analyse the application of Article 1(6) US Model to specific triangular situations. It is assumed in all cases that the intermediary entity is not a conduit company, agent or nominee. All the remaining assumptions used in the bilateral cases above, i.e., that no PE is constituted in the source state, that all treaties include Article 1(6) US Model and that in all cases, the anti-abuse restrictions within domestic law and tax treaties are satisfied in order to apply Article 1(6) US Model, remain the same.

4.2.2.1 *Example 5: Foreign Intermediary Entity with US Owners*

Let us assume that YCo is an entity incorporated in State Y, which has two partners, A and B, who are US citizens. Accordingly, YCo has a subsidiary in State Z, ZCo, which is financed by a loan granted by YCo, and because of this, it receives interest payments back from State Z.[1009] YCo is considered a taxable entity in State Y and in State Z. However, the US partners A and B have elected to treat YCo as a fiscally transparent entity. Country Z applies a general WHT on interest paid abroad of 30% of the gross amount paid. It is also assumed that the treaty United States/State Z provides a reduced WHT of 15%, whilst the treaty State Y/State Z provides for a reduced WHT of 10%.

1008. *See also, infra* s. 4.3.1.
1009. The example assumes that the loan and interest are at arm's length.

Figure 37 Example 5: Foreign Intermediary Entity with US Owners

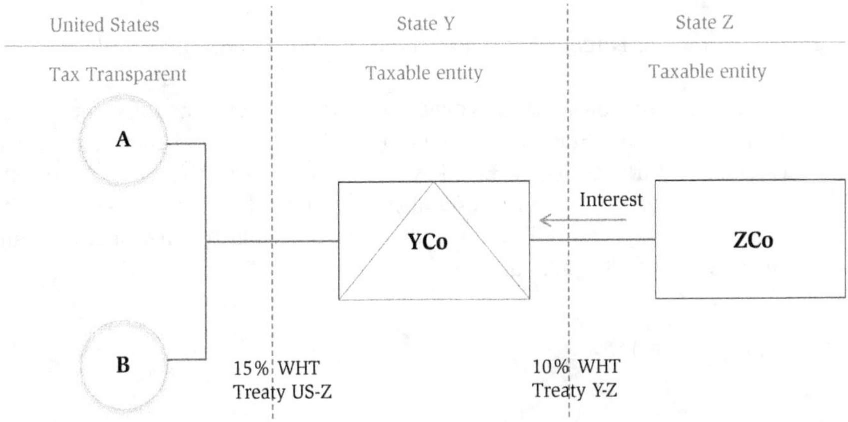

Whilst for US tax purposes YCo is tax transparent, State Y and Z consider it as tax opaque. Likewise, State Z applies a general a 30% WHT on the gross payments of interest abroad. The tax treaty between United States/State Z provides for a reduced WHT of 15% whilst the tax treaty between State Y/State Z provides for a reduced WHT of 10%.

According to the treaty between State Y and State Z, which is assumed to follow the OECD Model, State Z should reduce its WHT to 10% as per Article 11 of the State Y/State Z tax treaty. Likewise, State Y should grant a relief of double taxation as per Article 23 of the State Y/State Z tax treaty. This result is achieved by the sole fact that both States coincide in characterising YCo as a taxable entity. Therefore, the income and the benefits of the treaty are undoubtedly allocated to YCo.[1010]

Regarding the treaty between the United States and State Z, especially with respect to Article 1(6) of the United States/State Z tax treaty, income is received through an entity considered as tax transparent by one of the Contracting States (United States), and it is allocated to the partners A and B, who are US citizens. Therefore, in principle, State Z (source state) should comply with both treaties, which under the principles of the OECD Partnership Report would mean that State Z must apply the lower WHT rate (10%) between the two applicable treaties. This solution,

1010. Even in the case State Y/State Z tax treaty would include a provision like Article 1(6) US Model (e.g., Article 1(2) OECD Model), it would not apply because none of the Contracting States treat YCo as a fiscally transparent entity.

however, is not only misaligned with the concept of *beneficial owner*[1011] but also leaves open a potential double taxation issue.[1012]

4.2.2.2 Example 6: Foreign Entity Receiving US-Sourced Income

Let us assume the same basic facts as given in Example 5, with the difference that the United States is now the State where the interest is sourced and that State X is the residence state of partners A and B. Likewise, let us assume that YCo is treated as fiscally transparent for US tax purposes whilst it is regarded as a taxable entity in State Y and State X. Finally, we will assume that all applicable treaties provide similar reductions of WHT of 15% at source.

1011. The application of Article 1(6) US Model in this case would not change the fact that the source State still considers YCo as a taxable entity, and thus, as the *beneficial owner* of the interest payments. Thus, for purposes of applying Article 11 United States/State Z tax treaty, State Z could still argue that the interest payments are not beneficially owned by A and B in the United States.

1012. If the United States does not have a treaty with State Y, or if having a treaty, YCo is not regarded as a PE, there will be no double taxation relief for the taxes imposed at the level of YCo in State Y. A similar example was discussed at *supra* s. 3.3.2.1 in relation to the unresolved conflicts of allocations under the principles of the OECD Partnership Report. Likewise, as well explained by Danon, if the same situation is analysed regarding a trust, being the trust and the settlor residents in State Y (using our example) and the beneficiary being resident in the United States and having both the United States and State Y treating the trust as transparent, the relief of double taxation becomes impossible. *See* Danon, *supra* n. 912, pp. 198-199, Figure 7. Yet, it is interesting to note, e.g., that the exchange of notes of 24 July 2011 with regard to the treaty between the United States and the United Kingdom expressly provides double tax relief in such a situation. As stated in the exchange of notes: 'In the case the same item of income, profit or gain derived through a trust is treated by each Contracting State as derived by different persons resident in either State, and a) the person taxed by one State is the settlor or grantor of a trust; and b) the person taxed by the other State is a beneficiary of that trust, the tax paid or accrued by the beneficiary shall be treated as if it were paid or accrued by the settlor or grantor for the purposes of determining the relief from double taxation to be allowed by the State of which that settlor or grantor is a resident (or, in the case of the United States, a citizen) [...].' US: United States response to United Kingdom note setting forth additional agreements regarding the US-UK Double Taxation Convention, signed on 24 July 2001, London.

Figure 38 Example 6: Foreign Entity Receiving US-Sourced Income

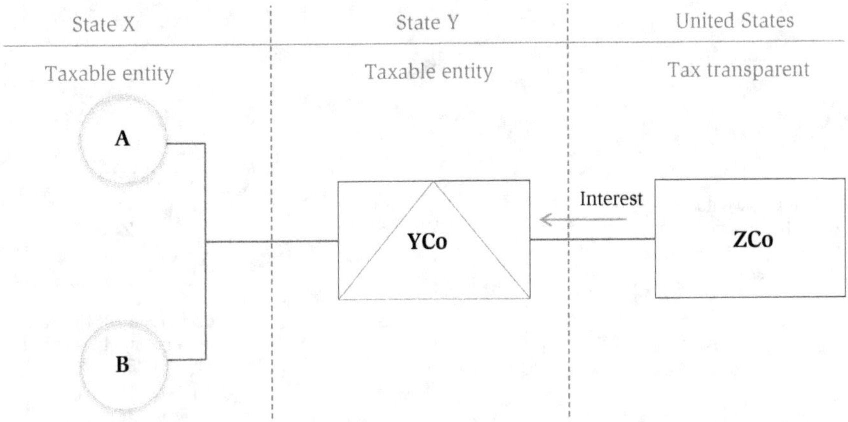

If we first analyse the treaty between the United States and State Y, it is easy to figure out that Article 1(6) of the State Y/United States tax treaty applies to deny A and B the benefits of the treaty. In other words, as there is an item of income received through an entity considered, in this case, tax transparent in the United States (source state), but the income is not allocated to US residents, Article 1(6) of the State Y/United States ensures that the benefits are not allocated to A and B, but rather to YCo. In other words, it is YCo which may claim the reduced WHT under Article 11 of the State Y/United States and the relief from double taxation under Article 23. However, there is still an issue because the application of Article 1(6) US Model, in this case, does not prevent the fact that, from a US perspective, the *beneficial owner* of the interest may be A and B and not YCo, which is still a tax transparent entity from a US perspective. In simple words, it could still be arguable that the United States decides to limit its taxing rights, reducing its WHT to 15%, because, for the United States, the preconditions of Article 11 of the State Y/United States are simply not met.[1013]

State X, on the other hand, i.e., the State where the partners of YCo are residents, also has a treaty with the United States. In this case, Article 1(6) of the treaty State X/United States also applies to deny the benefits of that treaty to A and B because these two are not residents of the State, treating the entity a tax transparent, i.e., the United States. The application of Article 1(6) of the State X/United States, however, does not solve the question regarding who the *beneficial owner* of the interest is. In this case, it seems to be clear that the United States will still consider A and B as the beneficial owners of the interest and not YCo. Thus, the United States might still decide to apply Article 11 of the State X/United States regarding A and B, even though by application of Article 1(6) of the State X/United States, these two are not entitled to the benefits of the treaty.[1014]

1013. *See also infra* s. 4.3.1.
1014. *Ibid.*

Figure 39 Example 6: Article 1(6) v. Beneficial Owner (Article 11)

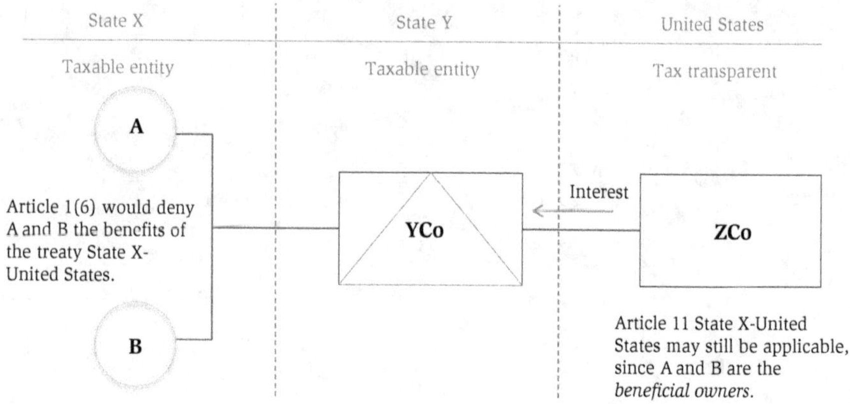

Accordingly, even in the hypothetical that A and B were US residents, the preconditions of Article 11 of the State X/United States would not be met, i.e., there would not be a payment of interest arising in a Contracting State and being beneficially owned in the other Contracting State.[1015] On the contrary, in this case, interest would arise and would be paid to residents of the same State. This situation would, therefore, amount to a mere domestic issue.

Figure 40 Example 6: Variation: A and B Are US Owners

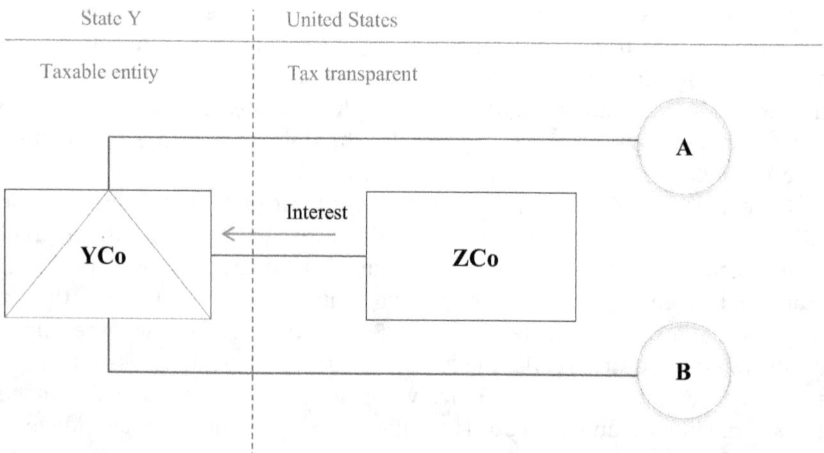

1015. Article 11(1) of the US Model states: 'Interest arising in a Contracting State and *beneficially owned* by a resident of the other Contracting State may be taxed only in that other State' (emphasis added). US: 2006 United States Model Income Tax Convention of 15 November 2006, Article 11(1).

4.2.2.3 *Example 7: US Intermediary Partnership*

Let us assume now that a US partnership P has two foreign owners, A and B, who are residents of State X. Accordingly, it receives interest payments from ZCo, an entity legally organised in State Z. Whilst the US partnership P is fiscally transparent in the United States, it is considered as a taxable entity in both State X and State Z. Country Z applies a general 30% WHT on gross interest paid abroad. It is also assumed that both the treaty United States/State Z and the treaty X-Z provide for a similar reduced WHT of 10%.

Figure 41 Example 7: US Intermediary Partnership

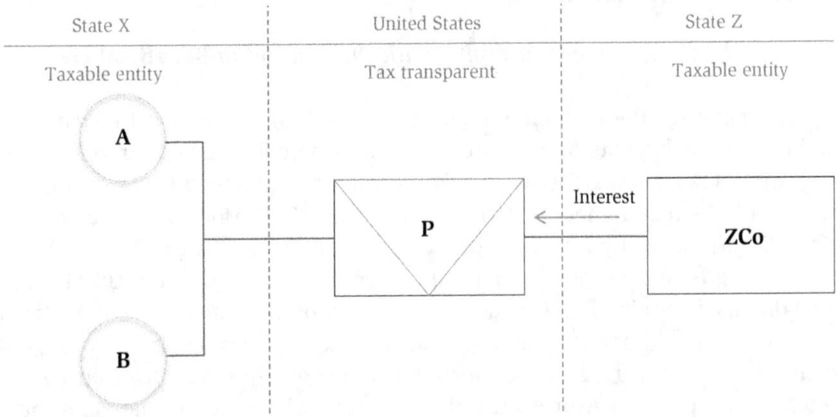

Article 1(6) US Model works, in this case, to deny A and B access to the benefits of the treaty the United States/State Z. Indeed, only to the extent A and B are US residents or citizens can they access the benefits of such treaty as per Article 1(6) of the United States/State Z tax treaty. Nevertheless, as the tax characterisation of US partnership P in the United States has not changed, the treaty is not applicable from a US perspective anyway because P is not a resident for purposes of the treaty.[1016] From State Z's perspective, however, the treaty might still be perfectly applicable because P is, for its tax purposes, a taxable entity. The tax characterisation of YCo has not changed by reason of Article 1(6) of the United States/State Z tax treaty. Therefore, it might be that State Z will still decide to limit its taxing rights and reduce its WHT to 10%. This would not be, however, an optimal result for State Z.

The treaty X-Z, on the other hand, is clearly not applicable in this case because both Contracting States consider P as a taxable entity. This is to say, neither of them considers that the interest payments are being paid to A and B. This conclusion does not change at all if a provision similar to Article 1(6) US Model is introduced within the treaty State X/State Z because in such a case, the precondition for the application of the

1016. Article 4 of the 2016 US Model.

provision (i.e., that income is received through an entity regarded as fiscally transparent by at least for one of the Contracting States) is simply not met.[1017]

4.3 The Interplay of Article 1(6) US Model with Other Tax Treaty and Domestic Provisions

As noted in the previous illustrations, Article 1(6) US Model provides a practical solution regarding the question of who should be granted the benefits of a treaty when income is received through a transparent entity. Nevertheless, this provision cannot be analysed in isolation.

This Section provides some examples where the interplay between Article 1(6) US Model and other tax treaty and domestic provisions are either not entirely clear, or they simply conflict with each other.[1018]

4.3.1 The (Still Missed) Interplay with the Concept of Beneficial Owner

As stressed already, the solution provided by Article 1(6) US Model with regard to who should enjoy the benefits of a tax treaty when income is received through an entity considered as tax transparent, at least for one of the Contracting States, is not always aligned with the requirement of Articles 10, 11, and 12 US Model, that income should be *beneficially owned* by a resident of the other Contracting State.[1019]

Although the concept of beneficial owner is not defined in the US Model, it is stated that its determination is made under the law of the State imposing the tax, i.e., the source state.[1020] For example, as provided in the Technical Explanations regarding Article 11 US Model used in the illustrations above: '[t]he *beneficial owner* of the interest for purposes of Article 11 is the person to which the income is attributable under the laws of the source State'.[1021] Therefore, if a person receiving the interest is acting as an agent or nominee, regardless of being resident, it will not be considered the beneficial owner of them.[1022] That is, the *beneficial ownership* requirement should still be relevant to determine the application of Article 11 US Model, regardless of the results achieved by Article 1(6) US Model.

The conflictive interplay between the results of Article 1(6) US Model and the *beneficial ownership* requirement was illustrated in some examples analysed in the

1017. Compare the analysis at *infra* s. 5.2.2.3 (Ex. 7) on Article 1(2) OECD Model.

1018. Although some of these issues have been already mentioned in the illustrations at *supra* ss 4.2.1 and 4.2.2 (e.g., the interplay with the concept of *beneficial owner*) they are systematically analysed in this section.

1019. Although I recognise that the concept of *beneficial owner* is indeed conflicting, it is not the intention of this work to provide an exhaustive analysis of it. That would certainly exceed the purpose of this work. For a further study of the concept, however, *see* the references at *supra* n. 352. Likewise, the analysis of the concept of *beneficial owner* with regard to its interpretation as avoiding DNT within the OECD Model can be found at *supra* Chapter 2, s. 3.2.

1020. US: Technical Explanation of the United States Model Income Tax Convention of 15 November 2006, p. 33 referred to para. 3, Article 10 US Model (Dividends) and p. 42 referred to para. 1, Article 12 (Royalties).

1021. *Ibid.*, p. 39 referred to para. 1, Article 11 (Interest).

1022. *Ibid.*

previous Section of this chapter.[1023] For instance, in Example 4 above, it is evident that the solution provided by Article 1(6) US Model to grant the benefit of the treaty United States/State P to A and B, the partners of USP (a US partnership), does not prevent the source state (State P) from considering USP (a taxable entity under the domestic laws of State P) as the beneficial owner of the interest.[1024] In other words, State P could perfectly deny the reduced WHT to A and B, who are residents but not beneficial owners as per the rule of the source state.[1025] Similarly, e.g., the strict application of Article 1(6) US Model in Example 5 reveals again the misalignment between the provision and the *beneficial owner* requirement of Article 11 US Model.[1026] In this case, the entity receiving the interest is considered a taxable entity both in the source state (State Z) and the State of the legal organisation of the entity (State Y).[1027] Thus, A and B, US partners, obtain the benefits of the treaty United States/State Z, even with a lower WHT of 10% because of the application of the OECD partnership solution when the two applicable treaties provide for different WHT rates, and regardless of the fact that the source state might still consider YCo as the *beneficial owner.*

The US Model does not provide any hints to solving this conflicting position between the solution of Article 1(6) US Model and the concept of *beneficial owner* in Articles 10, 11, and 12 US Model.

4.3.1.1 *Alternative Approaches Within the US Tax Treaty Practice*

Even though the US Model does not directly assume the interplay between Article 1(6) and the concept of *beneficial owner* in Articles 10, 11, and 12, some solutions to this conflicting position between the two provisions may be found within the US tax treaty practice. As follows, the author stresses two different solutions. The first one is found within the Poland/United States Tax Treaty (2013) and implies the non-application of Article 1(6) under some circumstances. Although this rule seems to be oriented for a different purpose, it indirectly helps solve the conflicting position between Article 1(6) and the *beneficial ownership* requirement. The second one is found within the Canada/United States Tax Treaty (1980 as amended in 2007) and attempts directly to solve the conflict through a rule that deems who should be the *beneficial owner.*

4.3.1.1.1 Poland/United States Tax Treaty

The treaty between the United States and Poland contains a provision, which provides that Article 1(6) US Model is not applicable if certain conditions are met. As stated in Article 1(6)(b) of the treaty United States-Poland: 'Subparagraph a) shall not apply to an item of income, profit or gain if the entity described in subparagraph a) is not fiscally transparent under the laws of the State in which the income, profit or gain arises, is organized in a third state, and is eligible for benefits under a convention for the

1023. *Supra* s. 4.2.
1024. *Supra* s. 4.2.1.4.
1025. *Ibid.*
1026. *Supra* s. 4.2.2.1.
1027. *Ibid.*

avoidance of double taxation between the third state and the State in which the income, profit or gain arises with respect to that item of income, profit or gain that are more favorable than the benefits provided by the provisions of this Convention with respect to that item.'[1028] Therefore, at least three preconditions should be met in order to disallow the application of the general rule contained in Article 1(6)(a) Poland/United States Tax Treaty: (i) that the entity is considered as tax opaque under the law of the State where the interest payments are sourced; (ii) that the entity receiving the interest payments is organized in a third State (i.e., neither the United States nor Poland), and (iii) that the entity in this third State is eligible for the benefits of a treaty with the State of source, and which are more favourable than the benefits provided by the Poland/United States Tax Treaty.

The application of this rule is illustrated using an example like Example 5 above, although with some modifications.[1029] Let us assume that a US Corporation (USCo), resident in the United States, is the sole owner of FCo, an entity organised in State F. Accordingly, FCo receives interest payments from Poland. Whilst for US tax purposes, FCo is regarded as a tax transparent entity, for Polish and State F tax purposes, it is considered as a tax opaque entity. Likewise, whilst the treaty State F/Poland provides for a reduced WHT of 0%, the treaty United States/Poland provides for a reduced WHT of 5%.

Figure 42 Article 1(6)(b) United States/Poland Double Tax Treaty

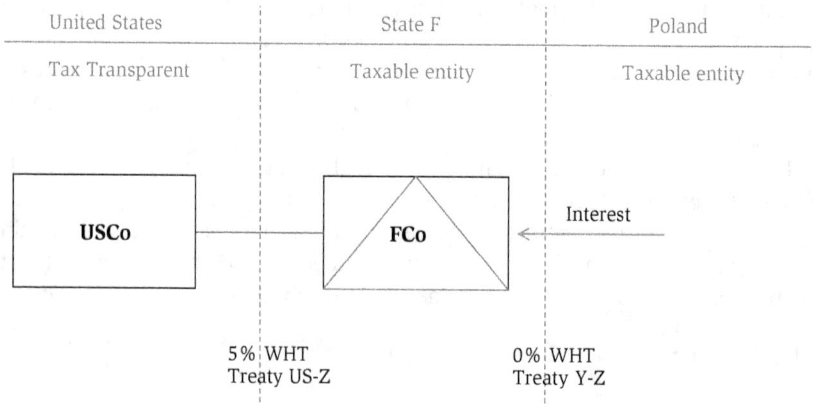

The preconditions of Article1(6)(b) US-Poland tax treaty are met. Thus, Article 1(6)(a) US-Poland tax treaty [Article1(6) US Model] does not apply in this case. In other words, USCo is not deemed as deriving the interest payments.

1028. US/PL: Article 1(6)((b) of the Convention between the United States of America and the Republic of Poland for the Avoidance of Double Taxation and the Prevention of Fiscal Evasion with respect to Taxes on Income of 13 February 2013.

1029. This example is inspired in the one used within the Technical Explanations of the treaty US/Poland. US/PL: Department of the Treasury Technical Explanation of the Convention Between the United States of America and the Republic of Poland for the Avoidance of Double Taxation and the Prevention of Fiscal Evasion with respect to Taxes on Income of 13 February 2013, pp. 6-7. For example 5, *supra* s. 4.2.2.1.

All the preconditions for the non-application of Article 1(6) US Model are thus met. First, FCo is considered by Poland as a taxable entity. Second, FCo is organised in State F (a third State). Third, FCo, as a taxable entity in State F, is eligible for the benefits of the treaty between State F and Poland, which also provides for a more beneficial reduction of WHT when compared with the treaty United States/Poland. In this case, therefore, USCo is not deemed as deriving the interest payments, and therefore, it is not entitled to the benefits of the treaty United States/Poland.

The solution provided in the United States/Poland tax treaty is unique since it is not included in other tax treaties signed by the United States, which also include Article 1(6) US Model in their texts.[1030] Likewise, the solution aligns in a better manner with the allocation of the benefits of the treaty and the concept of *beneficial owner* since it is evident for the source state (Poland) that the beneficial owner of the interest payments is FCo, which is regarded in this country as a taxable entity.[1031] Therefore, if the application of Article 1(6) of the United States/Poland tax treaty would imply that a reduced WHT is also granted to USCo, this would most probably conflict with the fact that Poland would not consider USCo as the beneficial owner of the interest. Accordingly, the solution seems to be more beneficial for the source state, which must not limit its taxing rights just because of a different characterisation of an entity given in the residence state of the partners of that entity when the entity is considered a taxable entity by the source state.[1032]

4.3.1.1.2 Canada/United States Tax Treaty

Another solution can be found within the Technical Explanations to the Protocol 2008, referred to in the 2007 amendment to the Canada/United States tax treaty (1980), which specifically clarifies the interaction between Article IV(6) and IV(7) of the Canada/United States tax treaty [Article 1(6) US Model] and the concept of *beneficial owner* in Articles 10, 11, and 12 of the same treaty.[1033] According to the Technical Explanations to the Protocol 2008: 'Special rules apply in the case of income, profits or gains derived through a fiscally transparent entity, as described in new paragraph 6 of

1030. Nevertheless, one should bear in mind that this provision seems to be the result of a bilateral negotiation and it is not included within the US Model.
1031. Although it is arguable to say that this solution was created for that exclusive purpose. In fact, it seems to be more connected with the idea of avoiding double benefits obtained from treaties in triangular cases.
1032. The characterisation of the entity in State F seems to be completely irrelevant, as it is also confirmed today within the US Technical Explanations of the 2006 US Model. US: Technical Explanation of the United States Model Income Tax Convention of 15 November 2006, p. 6.
1033. US/CA: Convention between Canada and the United States of America with respect to Taxes on Income and on Capital of 26 September 1980 (As amended through 2007), Article IV(6) and IV(7).

Article IV. Residence State principles determine who derives the income, profits or gains, to assure that the income, profits or gains for which the source State grants benefits of the Convention will be taken into account for tax purposes by a resident of the residence State. Source country principles of beneficial ownership apply to determine whether the person who derives the income, profits or gains, or another resident of the other Contracting State, is the beneficial owner of the income, profits or gains. The source State may conclude that the person who derives the income, profits or gains in the residence State is a mere nominee, agent, conduit, etc. for a third country resident and thus deny the person the benefits of the Convention. If the person who derives the income, profits or gains under paragraph 6 of Article IV would not be treated under the source State's principles for determining beneficial ownership as a nominee, agent, custodian, conduit, etc. that person will be treated as the beneficial owner of the income, profits or gains for purposes of the Convention.'[1034] In simple words, the source state should determine whether the partner(s) of a fiscally transparent entity, considered as such by the residence state, is an agent, nominee, custodian or conduit or not, i.e., whether this is the *beneficial owner*. If the source state considers that the partner deriving the income under Article IV(6) of the Canada/United States tax treaty is indeed an agent, nominee, custodian or conduit for a non-resident of the other Contracting State, then it may deny the benefits of Article 11 Canada/United States tax treaty. However, if the source state still considers that the partner deriving the income under Article 1(6) is indeed an agent, nominee, custodian or conduit, but for a resident of the other Contracting State, then it should grant the benefits of the treaty anyway.[1035] The solution thus seems to assimilate the concepts of *resident* and *beneficial owner*, at least for purposes of application of Article 1(6) US Model.

The above might be illustrated using the same example provided in the Technical Explanations.[1036] Let us assume a Canadian entity, CanLP, which is considered fiscally transparent in Canada but, as a taxable entity in the United States, receives interest payments sourced in the United States. Accordingly, CanCo, a company resident in Canada, wholly owns CanLP.

1034. US/CA: Technical Explanation of the Protocol done at Chelsea on 26 September 2007 amending the Convention between the United States of America and Canada with respect to Taxes on Income and on Capital done at Washington on 26 September 1980, as amended by the Protocols of 14 June 1983, 28 March 1994, 17 March 1995, and 29 July 1997, p. 9.
1035. *Ibid.*
1036. *Ibid.*

Figure 43 Example from the Technical Explanations to the Protocol 2008

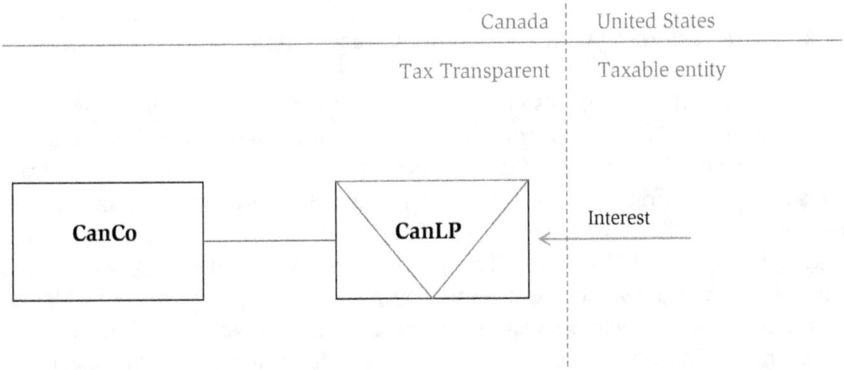

Even if the United States considers CanCo to be a nominee, agent, custodian or conduit, i.e., not a *beneficial owner*, the benefits of Article 11 of the Canada/United States tax treaty should be allocated to CanCo if this entity is a nominee, agent, custodian or conduit of a *Canadian resident*.

According to Article IV(6) of the Canada/United States tax treaty [Article 1(6) US Model], it is CanCo which derives the interest payments and should enjoy the reduced WHT of Article 11 of the Canada/United States tax treaty.[1037] Likewise, the United States, the source State in this case, should consider CanCo as the *beneficial owner* of the interest unless CanCo is found to be a nominee, agent, custodian or conduit for a person who is not a resident of Canada.[1038] However, even if the United States considers CanCo to be a nominee, agent, custodian or conduit, i.e., not a *beneficial owner*, it should allocate the benefits of Article 11 of the Canada/United States tax treaty if CanCo is a nominee, agent, custodian or conduit of a Canadian resident.[1039]

Even though I recognise that the solution given by the Canada/United States treaty is practical and solves the conflictive position between the two provisions under analysis, it might rarely be used within the US Model as a standard solution because, in fact, it represents an exception to the rule that the *beneficial owner* is determined exclusively under the domestic laws of the source state. Indeed, nothing within Article 1(6) US Model provides that the characterisation of the entity by the source state should be changed by application of this provision. Thus, it is still expected that the source state (in the absence of the explanation included within the Technical Explanations above) will keep considering a tax-opaque entity as the *beneficial owner* of the interest paid. The success of the solution provided is, therefore, tied to the commercial relations between the States negotiating the treaty, i.e., the United States and the other

1037. *Ibid.*
1038. *Ibid.*
1039. *Ibid.*

Contracting State. Thus, a solution such as the one found in the Canada/United States tax treaty certainly responds to that pattern of close economic connections.[1040]

4.3.2 *The Interplay with the* 'Saving Clause' *(Article 1(4) US Model)*

Article 1(6) US Model must also be analysed with regard to its interplay with Article 1(4) US Model. This provision contains the traditional '*saving clause*' found in all the tax treaties signed by the United States, which basically establishes that the Contracting States reserve their rights to tax their residents and citizens as provided in the internal laws, notwithstanding any tax treaty provision to the contrary.[1041] As provided within paragraph 4, Article 1 US Model: 'Except to the extent provided in paragraph 5, this Convention shall not affect the taxation by a Contracting State of its residents (as determined under Article 4 (Resident)) and its citizens. Notwithstanding the other provisions of this Convention, a former citizen or former long-term resident of a Contracting State may, for the period of ten years following the loss of such status, be taxed in accordance with the laws of that Contracting State.'[1042] A simple example of the saving clause's application would be a person resident in the other Contracting State, who is also a US citizen, and who renders services in the United States without constituting a PE. Under normal circumstances, in application of Article 7 of the US Model, the United States would be prevented from taxing this income because of the fact that there is no PE in the United States. However, as the resident of the Contracting States is also a US citizen, the United States reserves the right to tax this citizen on his worldwide income, overriding the application of the treaty.[1043]

1040. However, a similar rule has been proposed by a group of academics as a solution that may be applicable in the context of the OECD Model to deal with to the conflict between Article 1(2) OECD Model and the beneficial ownership's requirement of Articles 10, 11, and 12 OECD Model. This proposal is analysed at *infra* ss 5.3.1.1; 5.3.1.2 and 5.3.1.3.

1041. McDaniel, Ault and Repetti, *supra* n. 718, p. 181.

1042. Article 1(4) of the 2016 US Tax Treaty Model.

1043. Example taken from the US: Technical Explanation of the United States Model Income Tax Convention of 15 November 2006, p. 3. The application of the saving clause was also a key issue in: UK: CA, 23 March 2011, *Bayfine UK v. Commissioner for H M Revenue and Customs*, [2011] EWCA Civ 304, Tax Treaty Case Law IBFD. In this case, whilst the United Kingdom claimed exclusive rights to tax since no PE was constituted in the United States, the United States applied taxation according to Article 1(3) of the UK-US tax treaty [*saving clause*]. For a more detailed analysis, considering all the other factors involved within the case, *see* B. Arnold, *Tax Treaty News*, 64 Bull. Intl. Taxn. 10 (2010), Journals IBFD, pp. 495-496. *See also*, Cleave, *supra* n. 347.

Figure 44 Example of the Saving Clause's Application

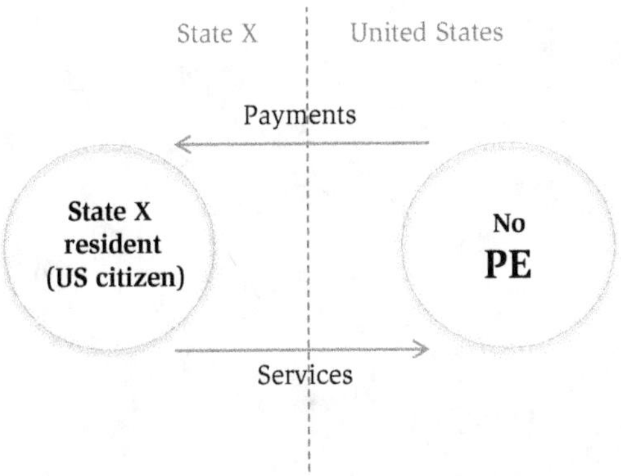

In principle, there are no profits attributable to a PE in the United States. Thus, the United States should refrain from taxing the payment from services. However, as the State X resident is also a US citizen, Article 1(4) US Model applies disregarding the treaty.

The specific interplay between Article 1(4) US Model [*saving clause*] and Article 1(6) US Model [*transparent entities*] can be illustrated as follows. Let us assume the case of a US LLC owned by a resident of State X and receiving royalties sourced in the United States. The sole owner of the LLC decides to treat the LLC as a US Corporation according to the CTB election, although this is still considered fiscally transparent in State X.[1044] In this scenario, the United States will tax the LLC on its worldwide income on a net basis, regardless of whether the other Contracting State (State X) views the LLC as fiscally transparent. In other words, under a strict application of Article 12 US Model, the royalties should be taxed exclusively in State X, at the level of resident X, who is the sole owner of the LLC receiving the income and being entitled to the benefits of the treaty United States/State X according to Article 1(6) US Model. Nonetheless, the United States reserves its right to tax the LLC on its worldwide income, which includes the royalties sourced in the United States.

1044. The example is inspired in the explanation of the interplay in the US: United States Model Technical Explanation accompanying the United States Model Income Tax Convention of 15 November 2006, p. 7. The example also mirrors example 17 of the OECD Partnership Report. *See* OECD (1999), *supra* n. 1, p. 47.

Figure 45 Saving Clause and Article 1(6) US Model

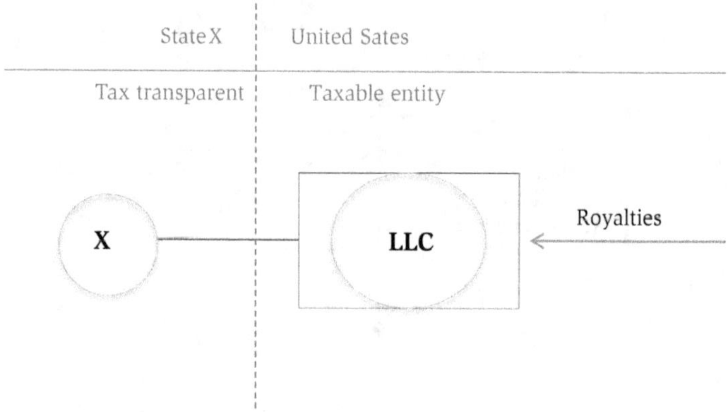

Regardless that Article 1(6) US Model grants the benefits of the treaty to Resident X, as the LLC is treated as a taxable entity in the United States, the United States reserves its right to tax the LLC on its worldwide income as per Article 1(4) US Model.

The application of the saving clause, therefore, raises concerns regarding the double taxation relief in State X (Article 23) because unless an indirect tax credit is provided, partner X will be taxed in State X on the same income already taxed in the United States, but with no double taxation relief under the treaty.[1045] Yet, the interpretation of Article 23 US Model as granting an indirect tax credit is still arguable.[1046]

4.3.3 *Article 1(6) US Model and the CTB Regulations*

As already analysed in Chapter 3, the CTB regulations allow certain foreign business entities to be classified in a manner different from that provided in their countries of incorporation so long as they are not regarded as per se Corporations for US tax purposes.[1047] These entities, called *eligible entities*, may elect their tax treatment for US

1045. In practice some countries grant an indirect tax credit. *See* J. Lüdicke, *Exemption and Tax Credit in German Tax Treaties: Policy and Reality*, 64 Bull. Intl. Taxn. 12 (2010), Journals IBFD, p. 615; W. Schön, *International Tax Coordination for a Second-Best World (Part II)*, 2 World Tax J. 1(2010), Journals IBFD, p. 67. *See also*, Kollmann, Roncarati and Staringer, *supra* n. 984, p. 24.

1046. In contrast, if, for example, a USCo is the sole owner of a foreign entity receiving royalties from the same State where this is a resident, and considered as tax transparent for US tax purposes, an indirect tax credit would be granted to the extent the USCo owns at least 10% of the foreign subsidiary and receives dividends from this latter. US: IRC s. 902. This indirect tax credit is, nonetheless, granted under domestic law and it does not imply to interpret Article 23 US Model as to granting an indirect tax credit. This interpretation of the Article 23 would be certainly very extensive.

1047. US: Treas. Reg. s. 301.7701-2(b)(8) states the list of per se Corporations.

tax purposes.[1048] Therefore, if a US LLC is generally considered a disregarded entity, the foreign owner may elect to treat it as a taxable entity for US tax purposes. Accordingly, if a foreign partnership is regarded in its country of organisation as fiscally transparent, the US partners might elect to treat it as a taxable entity for US tax purposes.[1049]

The possibility to re-characterise foreign entities for US tax purposes does not only increase the number of possible disparities in the tax characterisation of entities, giving rise to *hybrid* and *reverse hybrid entities* but may also condition, to a certain extent, the application of Article 1(6) US Model. For example, in Example 1 above, the CTB election seems to be the true reason to trigger the application of Article 1(6) US model.[1050] Indeed, in the absence of the election, the treaty between the United States and State P should not be applicable at all, and the interest payment received by entity P should not go beyond being a domestic concern.[1051] Thus, the domestic CTB election, in this case, is the cause of the application of the treaty and the allocation of the benefits to A and B, US owners of entity P.[1052] The same situation might occur the other way around. As noted in Example 3 above, it is the election to treat entity P, a foreign fiscally transparent entity, as tax opaque for US tax purposes, which conditions the application of Article 1(6) US Model, in this case, to deny the benefits of the treaty to A and B and to ensure the non-application of the treaty.[1053]

In some triangular situations, the benefits of treating a foreign entity as tax transparent might give rise to the application of a more beneficial tax treaty under Article 1(6) US Model. Let me recall Example 5 above, whereby the sole fact that A and B, US owners of a foreign entity organised in a third country and treated as fiscally transparent under the CTB election in the United States, might benefit from a reduced WHT under a tax treaty different from that between the United States and the source state of the income.[1054] This situation, however, is elegantly solved within the US treaty practice, making a 'switch-off' in the application of Article 1(6) US Model under certain circumstances.[1055]

All in all, the possibility of electing the tax treatment of a given entity organised within or outside the United States should be considered as an important tool to determine the application of Article 1(6) US Model, and therefore, the application or not of the benefits of a tax treaty to certain residents. In this case, unlike the tax planning opportunities analysed in Chapter 3 with respect to the application of CFC rules or the use of an FTC,[1056] which also depend on the design features of these domestic rules (i.e., CFC rules and FTC), the CTB election seems to play a more direct

1048. *Supra* Chapter 3, s. 4.3.
1049. *Ibid.*
1050. *Supra* s. 4.2.1.1.
1051. *Ibid.*
1052. *Ibid.*
1053. *Supra* s. 4.2.1.3.
1054. *Supra* s. 4.2.2.1.
1055. US/PL: Article 1(6)(b) of the Convention between the United States of America and the Republic of Poland for the Avoidance of Double Taxation and the Prevention of Fiscal Evasion with respect to Taxes on Income of 13 February 2013. *See also* the analysis at *supra* s. 4.3.1.1.1.
1056. *Supra* Chapter 3, s. 4.4.

role when analysing the application of Article 1(6) US Model and the access or not to the benefits of a tax treaty.

4.3.4 *Article 1(6) US Model and I.R.C. Section 894(c)*

As well as Article 1(6) US Model, domestic I.R.C. Section 894(c) addresses the issue of hybrid entities and, thus, should be considered when analysing the scope of application of Article 1(6) US Model. This domestic provision specifically states that a foreign person shall not be entitled to a reduced WHT granted by a treaty to the extent that income is not attributed to that foreign person in the foreign country. The treaty does not contain a provision addressing the cases of income received through a transparent entity, and the foreign country does not impose a tax on the distribution of that income from the entity to such person.[1057]

The US Treasury Regulations under Section 894(c) adopt different approaches depending on whether there is a '*domestic reverse hybrid*' involved or not.[1058] As per the definition in the Treasury Regulations, a *domestic reverse hybrid* entity is a domestic entity that is treated as not fiscally transparent for US tax purposes and as fiscally transparent under the laws of the person holding the interest in the entity in the other State.[1059] For example, a US LLC which was elected by its non-resident sole proprietorship is to be treated as a Corporation in the United States (i.e., a taxable entity), although it is considered fiscally transparent in his/her residence state.[1060] A '*non-reverse domestic hybrid*' entity is exactly the opposite, i.e., an entity considered fiscally transparent in the United States and/or any other jurisdiction. The rules under Section 894(c) apply differently in each case.[1061]

With regard to *domestic reverse hybrid entities*, a distinction must be made with respect to payments received by a domestic hybrid entity or payments made by a domestic hybrid entity.[1062] With respect to payments received by a domestic hybrid entity, a tax treaty cannot reduce the tax applied to such payments that are from US sources.[1063] Thus, even though another country might tax a foreign holder of interest in the entity with regard to the US-sourced income, the United States will not apply the tax treaty rates to such a person.[1064] In simple words, the foreign interest holders of a domestic reverse hybrid entity are not entitled to the benefits of a reduction of US income tax according to a tax treaty to which the United States is a party when items of income are received by such entity and sourced in the United States. This is illustrated with the example from section 4.3.2, which assumes the case of a US LLC

1057. US: I.R.C. s. 894(c).
1058. McDaniel, Ault and Repetti, *supra* n. 718, p. 85.
1059. US: Treas. Reg. s. 1.894-1(d)(2)(i). The reference to 'reverse hybrid entity' should not be thus confused with the traditional distinction between hybrids and reverse hybrid entities. *Supra* Chapter 3, s. 3.
1060. *See* example at *supra* s. 4.3.2.
1061. US: Treas. Reg. s. 1.894-1(d)(2)(i).
1062. US: Treas. Reg. s. 1.894-1(d)(2)(ii)(A) and Treas. Reg. s. 1.894-1(d)(2)(ii)(B).
1063. US: Treas. Reg. s. 1.894-1(d)(2)(i).
1064. McDaniel, Ault and Repetti, *supra* n. 718, p. 85.

owned by a resident of State X and which receives royalties sourced in the United States. The sole owner of the LLC decides to treat the LLC as a US Corporation according to the CTB election, although this is still considered fiscally transparent in State X. We will also assume that there is no Article 1(6) US Model included within the treaty United States/State X.

Figure 46 I.R.C. Section 894(c)s Illustration

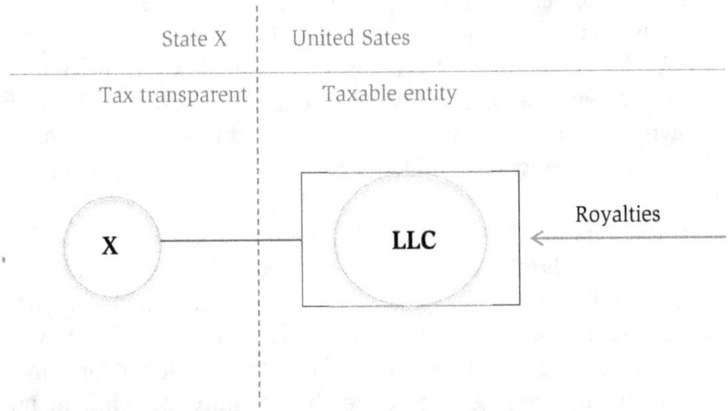

I.R.C. Section 894(c) provides that the interest holder X will not enjoy a reduced WHT, regardless that, according to State X, the royalties are received by him.

In this case, I.R.C. Section 894(c) provides that the interest holder X will not enjoy a reduced WHT, regardless that, according to State X, the royalties are received by him. This provision might thus be interpreted as a protection of the base erosion at source and acts indeed as a complementary rule when Article 1(6) US Model has not been included within a tax treaty signed by the United States.[1065] Nonetheless, from the point of view of treaty obligations, the provision is indeed arguable since it basically operates as a treaty override.[1066] For example, if we assume that State X does not include Article

1065. This is interpreted from the wording of I.R.C. s. 894(c), which requires that 'the treaty does not contain a provision addressing the cases of income received through a transparent entity [...]'. US: I.R.C. s. 894(c).

1066. The above practice should not be, however, a surprise since Article VI of the United States Constitution provides that international tax treaties and domestic legislation are in equal footing. Therefore, where tax treaties and legislative provisions conflict with each other, domestic legislation prevails. *See* McDaniel, Ault and Repetti, *supra* n. 718, p. 178. However, the courts in the United States have also been clear that when legislative provisions override tax treaty obligations, this must be expressly stated within the domestic provision. *See*, e.g., US: *Cook v. United States*, 288 US 102 (1933). *See also*, US: Restatement (Third) of Foreign Relations Law of the United States (1987), s. 114(1). The issue with regard to the relation between treaties and domestic legislation was expressly addressed in US: I.R.C. s. 7852(d)(1), which provides: 'For purposes of determining the relationship between a provision of a treaty and any law of the United States affecting revenue, neither the treaty nor the law shall have preferential status by reason of its being a treaty or law.' Likewise, US: I.R.C. s. 894(a) states:

1(6) US Model yet recognises strictly the principles of the OECD Partnership Report, introduced in the OECD Commentaries, the result should be the same as if the provision was introduced in the tax treaty with the United States. In such a case, however, this domestic provision will apply to deny the treaty benefits to a resident of the other Contracting State.[1067]

With regard to payments made *from* a domestic reverse hybrid entity, these payments will be characterized for tax treaty purposes as being paid by a non-transparent entity.[1068] Therefore, in the example above, if a payment is made from the US LLC to its sole proprietorship in State X, it will be considered as a payment made from a tax-opaque entity in order to apply the United States/State X tax treaty.[1069] Likewise, the Treasury Regulations provide special rules when the domestic reverse hybrid entity has received a tax-free dividend from a domestic subsidiary.[1070] In such a case, the payment from the domestic reverse hybrid to its interest holder abroad is considered as a non-deductible dividend, regardless that it is, in fact, an interest payment.[1071]

On the other hand, the Treasury Regulations provide that in the case of a '*non-reverse domestic hybrid*' entity, i.e., an entity considered as fiscally transparent in the United States and/or any other jurisdiction, an item of income shall be eligible for a reduced WHT under the treaty in which the United States is part of, only to the extent that an item of income is considered as derived by a resident for purposes of the treaty.[1072] Thus, the income might be derived by an entity receiving the income if the entity is considered to be tax opaque in its jurisdiction, or if the entity is considered fiscally transparent, it will be considered derived by the persons holding an interest in that entity to the extent the interest holder is not considered as fiscally transparent in its jurisdiction.[1073] Therefore, it is possible to conclude that the taxing jurisdiction exercised over the item of income controls the application of the treaty benefits with regard to '*non-reverse domestic hybrids*'.[1074]

Still, if all countries around the world implemented, bilaterally or multilaterally, Article 1(2) OECD Model, it seems to be, at least in principle, unnecessary to have a domestic provision such as I.R.C Section 894(c). Indeed, due to Article 1(2) OECD

'The provisions of this title shall be applied to any taxpayer with *due regard* to any treaty obligation of the United States which applies to such taxpayer' (emphasis added). Yet, as provided by McDaniel et al.: 'The extent to which these legislative changes will in fact affect the relation between treaties and statutes remains for the courts to decide in the context of particular situations of conflict that may arise in the future.' McDaniel, Ault and Repetti, *supra* n. 718, p. 179.

1067. Thus, the application of this domestic provision as to deny the benefits of a treaty for certain payment received through hybrid entities will be prevented only to the extent that the other Contracting State agrees in introducing Article 1(6) US Model within its treaty with the United States and accomplishes also with the other preconditions of US: I.R.C. s. 894(c).
1068. US: Treas. Reg. s. 1.894-1(d)(2)(ii)(A).
1069. *Ibid.*
1070. US: Treas. Reg. s. 1.894-1(d)(2)(ii)(B).
1071. *Ibid.*
1072. US: Treas. Reg. s. 1.894-1(d)(1).
1073. *Ibid.*
1074. McDaniel, Ault and Repetti, *supra* n. 718, p. 85.

Model, income would be attributed to a foreign person in the foreign country because of a specific treaty provision addressing the cases of income received through a transparent entity, and the foreign country would most probably impose a tax on the distribution of that income from the entity to such person. Nevertheless, the wording of I.R.C. Section 894(c) seems to require not only a provision similar to Article 1(6) US Model as granting a reduced WHT but also that the income received by a foreign person through a tax transparent entity is allocated to that person and taxed there.[1075] This latter requirement leaves open the possibility that in the absence of effective taxation, I.R.C. Section 894(c) might still be applicable. Paradoxically, however, if all countries around the world start introducing similar domestic provisions to protect their tax bases at source, Article 1(2) OECD Model (or similar provisions) might become completely irrelevant.

5 THE OECD MODEL'S PROPOSAL: A RESIDENCE STATE'S PERSPECTIVE

Chapter 14 of the OECD BEPS Action Plan 2 originally contained a detailed proposal calling for the inclusion of a positive norm within the OECD Model dealing with cases in which one or two of the Contracting States treat an entity or arrangement as fiscally transparent.[1076] This proposal was inspired in the 1999 OECD Partnership Report, and it is now ratified in the final text of Article 1(2) OECD Model, which is replicated in Article 1(3) MLI.[1077] However, unlike the OECD Partnership Report, Article 1(2) OECD Model addresses not only cases of partnerships but also other entities considered as fiscally transparent.[1078] Similarly, it aims to ensure not only that the benefits of tax treaties are granted in appropriate cases but also that these are not granted in cases where neither Contracting State treats the income received through a fiscally transparent entity as the income of one of its residents.[1079] The specificities of this provision are subsequently analysed.

1075. US: I.R.C. s. 894(c)(1)(C).

1076. OECD (2015), *supra* n. 6, pp. 139 et seq. *See also* the released draft contents of the 2017 update to the OECD Model and the public comments received with regard to the draft. *See* OECD (2017) and OECD (2017a), *supra* n. 488.

1077. OECD Model Tax Convention on Income and Capital: Condensed Version 2017. For the analysis of the MLI provision, *see infra* s. 6 of this chapter.

1078. As provided by the OECD: 'The Partnership Report (OECD, 1999), however, did not expressly address the application of tax treaties to entities other than partnerships. To address that issue, as well as the fact that some countries have found difficult to apply the conclusions of the Partnership Report, it was decided to include in the OECD Model Tax Convention (OECD, 2014), the following provision, which will ensure that income of transparent entities is treated, for the purposes of the Convention, in accordance with the principles of the Partnership report.' *Ibid.*, p. 139.

1079. *Ibid.*, this reference would also clarify that Article 1(2) OECD Model may also be aimed as denying treaty benefits. *See also* in this opinion: Kollmann, Roncarati and Staringer, *supra* n. 984, pp. 23-24; A. Schnitger and M. Oskamp, *Empfehlungen der OECD zur Neutralisierung von 'Hybrid Mismatches' auf Abkommensebene*, 23 IStR 11 (2014), p. 390.

5.1 General Interpretation of Article 1(2) OECD Model

Paragraph 2 of Article 1 of the OECD Model reads as follows: 'For the purposes of this Convention, income derived by or through an entity or arrangement that is treated as wholly or partly fiscally transparent under the taxation law of either Contracting State shall be considered to be income of a resident of a Contracting State but only to the extent that the income is treated, for purposes of the taxation by that State, as income of a resident of that State.'[1080] Unsurprisingly, the wording used in the OECD Model is very similar to that already utilised in the 2006 US Model, and it is almost identical to the 2016 US Model.[1081] The wording of the OECD provision, as well as the preconditions for its application, are now analysed.

5.1.1 *The Reference to* 'Income' *(Only)*

Paragraph 26.9 of the Commentary on Article 1 states: 'The word "income" must be given the wide meaning that it has for the purposes of the Convention and therefore applies to various items of income that are covered by Chapter III of the Convention (Taxation of Income), including, for example, profits of an enterprise and capital gains.'[1082] Therefore, it is clear that all the types of income between Articles 6 and 21 OECD Model are included within the meaning of '*income*', including profits, business profits, income from services, dividends, royalties, rental income, etc.[1083] Likewise, the Commentary on Article 1 allows us to conclude that 'capital' (Article 22 OECD Model) is not included within the scope of Article 1(2) OECD Model.[1084] In the same order of ideas, it is possible to sustain that the reference to '*income*' and not to '*income, profit or gain*' in Article 1(6) US Model does not represent a substantial difference because, in both cases, it is evident that the provision applies only as regards taxes on income.[1085]

Another important issue is that Article 1(2) OECD Model applies separately to each item of income. As provided in the OECD Commentaries: 'As with other provisions of the Convention, the provision applies separately to each item of income of the entity or arrangement.'[1086] This is connected with the partial transparency

1080. OECD (2017), *supra* n. 1077.
1081. *Supra* s. 4.1.
1082. OECD Commentary on Article 1, para. 8.
1083. *Ibid*. This argument is based on the idea that the term '*income*' within the OECD Model should have an autonomous interpretation. In this sense, the allocation rules of Articles 6-21 OECD Model should govern the taxation of income and should provide guidance with regard to the meaning of the term 'income'. *See* Ismer/A. Blank in: Reimer and Rust (eds) *Klaus Vogel on Double Taxation Conventions*, Article 2 at m.no. 36.
1084. Kollmann, Roncarati and Staringer, *supra* n. 984, p. 19. Also in this opinion: E. Schaffer, *Chapter 5: Implications of BEPS Action 2 and Its Relevance for the Application of Article 17 of the OECD Model* in: M. Lang (ed.) *Domestic Attribution of Income and Taxation of International Entertainers and Sportspersons: Theory and Practice of Art. 17 OECD Model Convention*, IBFD, Amsterdam (2017), Online Books IBFD.
1085. *Supra* s. 4.1.1. *See also*, Schaffer, *supra* n. 1084.
1086. OECD Commentary on Article 1, para. 11.

treatment that some entities receive at a domestic level,[1087] including the case of trusts.[1088]

5.1.2 *Income Derived* 'by or Through'

Article 1(2) OECD Model requires that income is derived '*by or through*' an entity or arrangement. However, there are no hints within the OECD Commentaries with regard to the distinction that the wording of the article attempts. Indeed, the OECD Commentaries on Article 1(2) OECD Model simply state: 'The reference to "income derived by or through an entity or arrangement" has a broad meaning and covers any income that is earned by or through an entity or arrangement, regardless of the view taken by each Contracting State as to who derives that income for domestic tax purposes and regardless of whether or not that entity or arrangement has legal personality or constitutes a person as defined in subparagraph a) of paragraph 1 of Article 3.'[1089] In principle, therefore, the wording seems to be redundant.[1090] However, as suggested by some commentators already, the reference to '*by or through*' would have the purpose of ensuring the application of Article 1(2) OECD Model to cases where the source state treats an entity X as transparent, and thus, considers that the income is '*derived through*' that entity. Similarly, it would cover cases where the source state treats entity X as tax opaque (being regarded as tax transparent by the residence state), and thus, that the income is '*derived by*' such entity.[1091] This interpretation has some logic if one considers that Article 1(2) OECD Model does not attempt to affect the determination of persons or events in the source state.[1092] Indeed, as argued somewhere else already, Article 1(2) OECD Model simply determines who is entitled to the benefits of a tax treaty. This means that it will always be necessary to look at the specific allocative rules within treaties to determine whether the benefits of it are ultimately granted.[1093]

Moreover, as stated in the tax literature already, one could argue that the wording '*derived by or through*' used in Article 1(2) OECD Model simply reinforces the alleged

1087. *Infra* s. 5.1.4.
1088. For example, the OECD Commentaries assumes the case of a trust where it is established that all dividends received by the trust will go directly to the beneficiaries during its lifetime, but they will be accumulated afterwards. If one of the Contracting States considers that the beneficiary is taxable on the distributed dividends that will be accumulated, Article 1(2) OECD will apply then to the dividends as different categories, independently whether they were received in the same month. *See* different authors at *supra* n. 1086.
1089. OECD Commentary on Article 1, para. 7.
1090. In the case of the wording of Article 1(6) US Model 2016, the reference to 'by or through' seems to be also irrelevant since the 2006 US Model only refers to 'income through' (not 'by') and the 2006 Technical Explanations uses the terms in an interchangeable manner. *Infra* s. 4.1.2.
1091. Nikolakakis et al., *supra* n. 985, p. 303. *See also*, Schaffer, *supra* n. 1084.
1092. Nikolakakis et al., *supra* n. 985, p. 303.
1093. L. Parada, *Hybrid Entities and Conflicts of Allocation of Income Within Tax Treaties: Is New Article 1(2) of the OECD Model (Article 3(1) of the MLI) the Best Solution Available?*, British Tax Rev. 3(2018), p. 343.

double function of this provision.[1094] That is, on the one hand, as to grant treaty benefits in case an item of income is received by a fiscally transparent entity whose partners are also residents of the state which considers the entity to be fiscally transparent, and, on the other hand, as to deny the benefits of a tax treaty in case the partners of the entity are not regarded as residents by the state which considers such an entity to be fiscally transparent.[1095]

5.1.3 *The Reference to* 'Entities or Arrangements'

The absence of a clear definition of the term '*arrangements*' has left a wide shadow of uncertainty with regard to what the proper interpretation of the OECD provision should be, and, therefore, to which extent the scope of Article 1(2) OECD Model is indeed wider than the correspondent provision in the US Model, which does not include any reference to 'arrangements'.

The reference to '*arrangements*' might be interpreted, on the one hand, as covering all those cases of transparent vehicles other than partnerships. As stressed already, one of the main limitations of the 1999 OECD Partnership Report was that it was not possible to extend the application of the conclusions achieved to entities other than partnerships.[1096] Therefore, the reference to '*arrangements*' would attempt to cover all those alternative businesses beyond the concept of partnerships, including, e.g., CIVs and trusts.[1097] Although this interpretation seems to be logical since the OECD recognises that the Partnership Report did not properly address the application of tax treaties to entities other than partnerships, it is evident that non-corporate entities, in general, and the only two examples of vehicles used within the proposed Commentaries on Article 1(2) OECD Model, may be perfectly fitted within the term '*entities*' without need of referring to '*arrangements*'.[1098]Therefore, the intention behind the wording of Article 1(2) OECD Model seems still to be different.

As argued by some commentators, the inclusion of the term '*arrangements*' reveals to a certain extent the intention to set up a flexible concept that anticipates the appearance of future vehicles treated as fiscally transparent and to which income is allocated but which is not regarded as entities.[1099] In other words, there is an intention to extend the personal scope of Article 1(2) OECD Model beyond Article 1(6) US Model. This exercise is, however, very risky. First, it affects the certainty required within a treaty provision that should be very clear with regard to whom a treaty benefit is being granted. Second, it leaves a wide shadow over the interpretation of a notion that lacks

1094. These two functions are separately stated within the United States/Canada Tax Treaty, Article IV(6) and IV(7). *See* United States-Canada Income and Capital Tax Treaty (as amended through 2007), Tax Treaties IBFD. This distinction is, nevertheless, unusual. Nikolakakis et al., *supra* n. 985, p. 304.
1095. Parada, *supra* n. 1093.
1096. *Supra* s. 3.
1097. OECD Commentary on Article 1, paras 22-48. *See also*, OECD (2015), *supra* n. 6, p. 140, Proposed Commentary on Article 1(2), paras 26.4 and 26.5.
1098. Schaffer, *supra* n. 1084.
1099. *Ibid.*

a clear explanation within the OECD Commentaries. In this regard, and to the extent no specific examples of 'arrangements' are provided or a definition of the term is included within the Commentaries, I agree with the conclusion that the interpretation of the personal scope of the provision remains exactly as it is with respect to Article 1(6) US Model.[1100]

5.1.4 'Wholly and Partial' *Fiscal Transparency*

Another precondition for the application of Article 1(2) OECD Model is that the entity or arrangement is considered '*wholly or partly*' as fiscally transparent. The above involves both the issues of determining what a 'fiscally transparent entity is', as well as what are the cases of '*partial fiscal transparency*' that the provision refers to.

As for '*fiscal transparency*', the OECD Commentaries offer the following definition: 'The concept of 'fiscally transparent' used in the paragraph to situations where, under the domestic law of a Contracting State, the income (or part thereof) of the entity or arrangement is not taxed at the level of the entity or arrangement but at the level of the persons who have an interest in that entity or arrangement.'[1101] The OECD provides an example within the Commentaries, which covers the situation in which the amount of taxes payable is determined separately at the level of the entity but with respect to the personal characteristics of the persons liable to tax. With regard to this example, it states: 'The fact that the income is computed at the level of the entity or arrangement before the share is allocated to the person will not affect that result.'[1102] In addition, the proposed Commentaries state that countries are, nevertheless, free to clarify this definition of '*fiscally transparent*' within their bilateral conventions. Although this latter solution is indeed valuable since bilateral tax treaties are the best place where countries might clarify the doubts with regard to specific, transparent forms existing in each of the Contracting States, it might also be risky to have so many different definitions of '*fiscal transparency*', which might result in ambiguous interpretations of the term, deteriorating the required legal certainty with regard to allocation conflicts, and thus, affecting both taxpayers and tax administrations.[1103]

Despite the fact that the concept of '*fiscal transparency*' clearly refers to cases in which an entity is not taxable at its level but rather at the level of the owners of that entity, some authors have suggested a broader interpretation of the concept and thus, a potential broader application of Article 1(2) OECD Model due to these other potential conflicts of transparency.[1104] These authors have illustrated the above through the following example involving CFC rules. Let us imagine a company (ACo) incorporated in State A which has 100% of the ownership of another company incorporated in State

1100. Also in this opinion: Nikolakakis et al., *supra* n. 985, p. 335. For these authors, the reference to '*arrangements*' should also be clarified.
1101. OECD Commentary on Article 1, para. 9.
1102. *Ibid.*
1103. M. Lang, *Dreifache Nichtbesteuerung als Ergebnis der Anwendung von Doppelbesteuerungsabkommen*, 25 SWI 5 (2015), pp. 198-208.
1104. *See* Kollmann, Roncarati and Staringer, *supra* n. 984, pp. 17-18.

B (BCo). This latter company receives royalties from State C. Likewise, all the States consider BCo as a taxable entity.[1105]

Figure 47 Illustration Using CFC Rules

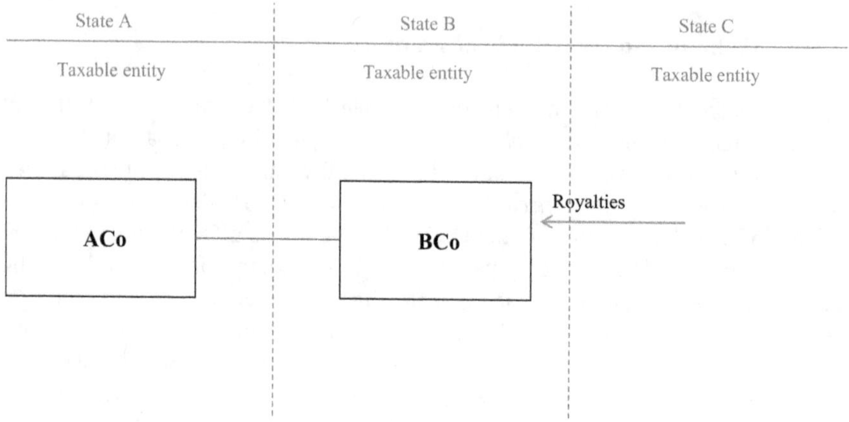

Due to the application of Article 12 of the treaty B-C, the royalties are taxed in State B exclusively. State A also taxes the royalties as 'deemed dividends' because of the application of CFC rules. However, the treaty A-C is not applicable, because the royalties are not attributed to ACo. Indeed, State A considers BCo as a taxable entity as well.

For these authors, this case might imply a 'conflict of transparency', even though all countries agree that BCo is a taxable entity.[1106] In other words, CFC rules would deem BCo to be transparent and, thus, attribute the undistributed profits to ACo. It is evident, however, that Article 1(2) OECD Model does not apply in this case because none of the countries involved considers BCo as 'tax transparent'.

I certainly disagree with this interpretation. First, this case does not represent a conflict of attribution of income for tax treaty purposes because the royalties, for purposes of the treaty B-C, are clearly attributed to BCo, who is most probably also the beneficial owner according to the application of Article 12 OECD Model. State B, therefore, has the exclusive right to tax those royalties. Second, treaty A-C is not applicable at all since State A considers BCo as tax opaque. Therefore, the second attribution, i.e., the 'deemed dividend' by which State A also taxes the undistributed profits of BCo, is due to a different legal fiction that has nothing to do with the legal characterisation of entity BCo. Indeed, this legal fiction operates by the sole fact that ACo controls BCo, and this latter receives passive income (royalties). In simple words, there is no 'deemed transparency' with regard to this second attribution, but rather a different legal fiction that allows exceptionally the taxation of a non-resident (BCo) on foreign source income to avoid tax deferral. Therefore, Article 1(2) OECD Model has

1105. *Ibid.*
1106. *Ibid.*

nothing to do with this potential case of double taxation, which could (and perhaps should) be solved strictly at a domestic level.[1107] Moreover, it would be completely unfair for the source state in this case (State C) to apply the treaty A-C by extending the interpretation of the concept of *fiscal transparency* under Article 1(2) OECD Model, which would also oblige this State to limit its taxing rights as regards State A.

It is also interesting to note that the precondition that the entity or arrangement is considered fiscally transparent applies not only with respect to cases of full transparency but also to cases of '*partial transparency*'. The concerns about '*partial transparency*' are nevertheless not novel. They were indeed originally raised within the 1999 OECD Partnership Report, which stated: 'The Committee first discussed cases where domestic tax laws create intermediary situations where a partnership is partly treated as a taxable unit and partly disregarded for tax purposes. While this may create practical difficulties with respect to a very limited number of partnerships, it is a more important problem in the case of other entities, such as trusts. For this reason, the Committee decided to deal with this issue in the context of follow-up work to this report'.[1108] Likewise, the OECD Commentaries on Article 1(2) OECD Model specifically addresses the issue, establishing that: 'In case of an entity or arrangement which is treated as partly fiscally transparent under the domestic laws of one of the Contracting States, only part of the income of the entity or arrangement might be taxed at the level of the persons who have an interest in that entity or arrangement as described in the preceding paragraph while the rest would remain taxable at the level of the entity or arrangement.'[1109] As noted in the Commentaries, this is particularly the case of LLPs and trusts. The above reinforces the idea that the personal scope of Article 1(2) OECD Model is indeed not different from Article 1(6) US Model, which, although its 2016 Model includes the wording '*partially transparent*', it was clear since 2006 that the provision was applicable not only to partnerships but also to other transparent entities in general, including common investment trusts under I.R.C. Section 584 and grantor trust and LLCs.[1110]

5.2 Illustrations Regarding the Application of Article 1(2) OECD Model

The application of Article 1(2) OECD Model is illustrated through a series of examples that are divided into two groups: (i) strict bilateral cases and (ii) triangular cases. All the examples follow almost the same facts used in the examples that analysed the application of Article 1(6) US Model to both bilateral and triangular situations. This allows us to compare the results and to analyse the differences and similarities between the two provisions. Likewise, and as well as in the examples regarding Article 1(6) US

1107. Another option would be modifying Article 23 OECD Model to exceptionally grant relief of double taxation at the level of State A under the treaty A-C. However, this could imply also that State C has also to limit its taxing rights due to the application of the treaty, and solely because of the CFC rules in State A.
1108. OECD (1999), *supra* n. 1, para. 37.
1109. OECD Commentary on Article 1, para. 10.
1110. US: Technical Explanation of the United States Model Income Tax Convention of 15 November 2006, p. 5.

Model, all the examples below assume that no PE is constituted in the source state, and all treaties include Article 1(2) OECD Model. Accordingly, all the examples also assume that all anti-abuse restrictions within both domestic law and tax treaties have been passed before the application of Article 1(2) OECD Model.

5.2.1 *Application of Article 1(2) OECD Model in Strict Bilateral Situations*

This section contains four illustrations of strict bilateral situations analysing the implication of Article 1(2) OECD Model. Whilst Examples 1 and 2 refer to income received by or through a hybrid entity, Examples 3 and 4 refer to income received through a reverse hybrid entity.

5.2.1.1 *Example 1*

Entity P is organised and resident in State P and has two owners, A and B, who are residents of State R. Accordingly, Entity P receives interest payments from a debtor in State P. Whilst State P considers the entity as a taxable entity, State R considers the same entity as tax transparent, and thus, the income is allocated to partners A and B. State P applies a general 30% WHT on gross interest paid abroad.

Figure 48 Article 1(2) OECD Model: Example 1

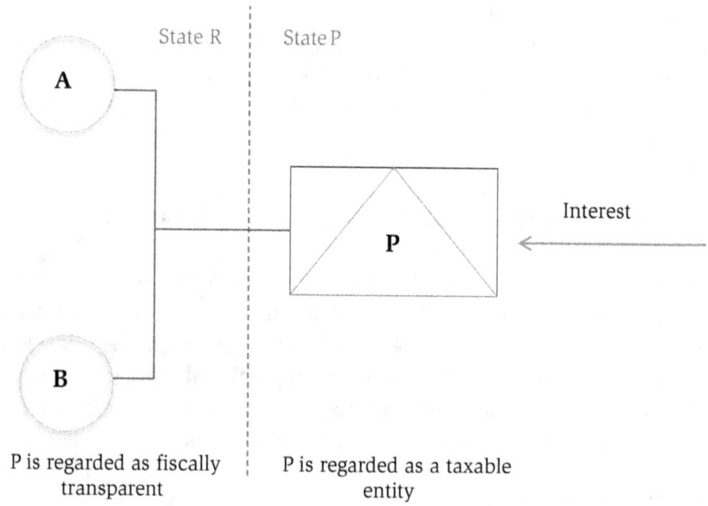

From the perspective of State P (source state), this is a purely domestic issue. However, Article 1(2) of the treaty R-P allows the application of the treaty between the two countries, granting to A and B the benefits of that treaty. In other words, the preconditions of Article 1(2) OECD Model are met since there is an entity considered fiscally transparent by one of the Contracting State, which is receiving income from the other Contracting State and that income is allocated to the partners, who are also residents of the State considering the entity as tax transparent.

Although the solution is practical, it might be contended from the point of view of the source state (State P). Indeed, Article 1(2) of the treaty R-P makes the treaty applicable by the sole fact that entity P is characterised as fiscally transparent in the residence state, obliging the source state to apply the treaty and, thus, to limit its taxing rights. Likewise, the solution does not consider the proper interplay with the concept of beneficial owner required in Article 11 of the treaty R-P to apply the reduction in the WHT at source. Indeed, it may be very difficult for the source state to consider A and B as the beneficial owners of the interest paid in this case.[1111]

From the perspective of the residence state, the solution also presents some problems. If entity P is subject to taxation in State P due to the rights that State P reserves to tax its own residents, it is arguable that State R may grant a relief from double taxation under Article 23B OECD Model when A and B have paid no taxes in State P. Indeed, granting a relief in this case may be interpreted as if Article 23 would provide an indirect tax credit, which, in the opinion of some commentators, is indeed a very broad interpretation of this provision. This issue is further analysed in this chapter.[1112]

5.2.1.2 *Example 2*

Let us assume now that entity R is organised in State R and has two owners, A and B, who are also residents of State R. Accordingly, some interest payments are paid from State P. Whilst State R considers entity R as tax opaque, State P considers it as tax transparent. State P also applies a general 30% WHT on gross interest paid abroad.

1111. This issue is further on analysed in this chapter at *infra* s. 5.3.1.
1112. *Infra* s. 5.3.2.

Figure 49 Article 1(2) OECD Model: Example 2

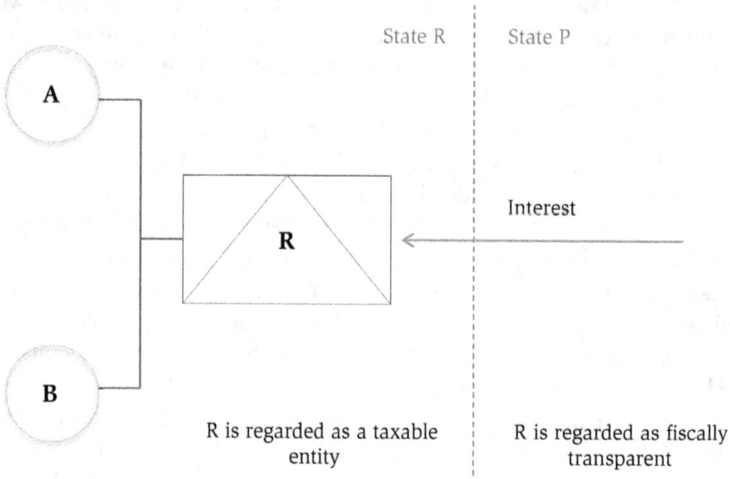

As per Article 1(2) OECD Model, there are interest payments received through an entity that one of the Contracting States considers as tax transparent. However, the income is not allocated to the partners of that entity who are also residents in the State, treating the entity as tax transparent. Therefore, Article 1(2) of the treaty R-P acts in this case as denying A and B the benefits of the treaty and ensuring that the benefits of this are allocated to entity R.

In the same order of ideas, Article 1(2) of the treaty R-P clarifies who is entitled to claim the double tax relief in the residence state under Article 23 of the same treaty. However, the solution of Article 1(2) of the treaty R-P possesses a bit more uncertainty with regard to the proper application of Article 11 because it is doubtful that State P will consider entity R as the beneficial owner of the interest payments and is therefore likely to opt for reducing its WHT at source anyway.

On the other hand, if A and B were residents of State P, the application of Article 1(2) of the treaty R-P would be redundant because the preconditions of Article 11 would not be met anyway, i.e., there would be no interest payments arising in a Contracting State and paid to residents in the other Contracting State. The interest payments, in this case, would arise in the same State where the recipients of the payments are residents. Therefore, it would not go beyond being a domestic concern. However, nothing would prevent State R from taxing entity R, which is, in its perspective, a taxable entity. Thus, double taxation may ultimately arise and be unavoidable in this case.[1113]

1113. Unless a double taxation relief is provided domestically, i.e., in State P, of course.

Figure 50 Article 1(2) OECD Model: Example 2 (Variation)

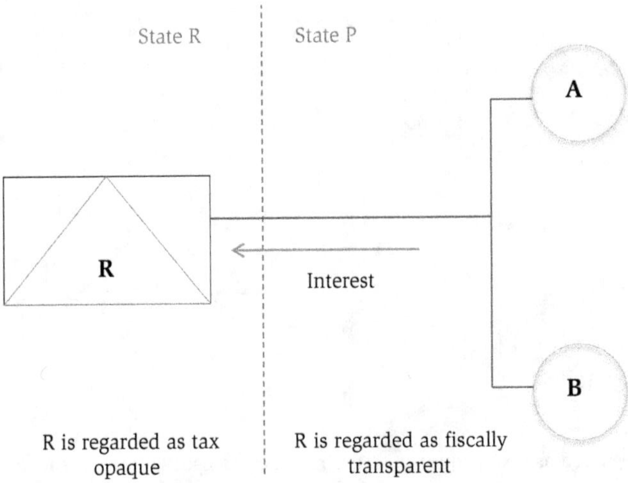

Article 1(2) OECD Model is irrelevant in this case because the preconditions for application of Article 11 OECD Model are not met. Likewise, interest will be taxed both in State R, at the level of entity R, and in State P, at the level of A and B as the share of income in the foreign partnership. Double taxation might thus arise.

5.2.1.3 *Example 3*

Let us assume now that entity P is organized and is resident in State P and has two owners, A and B, who are residents of State R. Accordingly, entity P receives interest payments from a debtor in State P. State R considers the entity as tax opaque, whilst State P considers the same entity as fiscally transparent. Entity P is thus a reverse hybrid entity. State P applies a general 30% WHT on gross interest paid abroad.

Figure 51 Article 1(2) OECD Model: Example 3

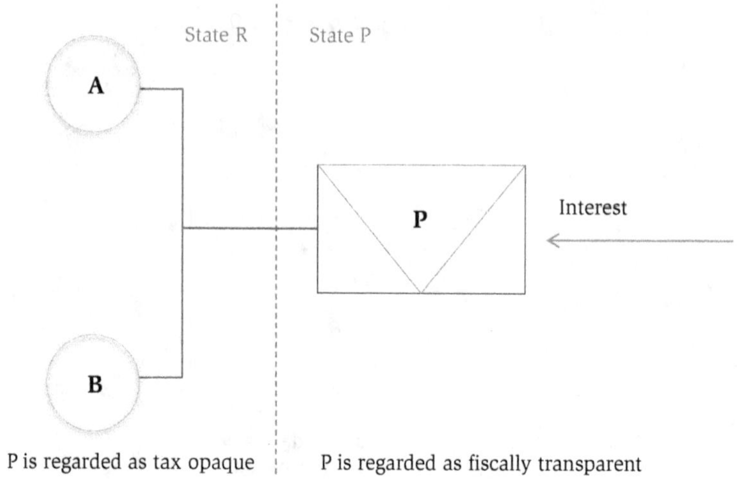

As regards the application of Article 1(2) of the treaty R-P, the interest income is received through an entity (P) considered fiscally transparent in State P, but it is not allocated to residents of this State. Therefore, Article 1(2) OECD Model applies in this case to deny the benefits of the treaty to A and B and to confirm that the payments of interest in this case is a mere domestic situation. Yet, nothing prevents State R from taxing the interest through the application of its domestic CFC rules. If that is the case, double taxation may be avoided in this case only to the extent a domestic relief is granted in State R.[1114] Likewise, the solution of Article 1(2) does not prevent State P from still considering A and B as the beneficial owners of the income.

5.2.1.4 Example 4

Let us assume now that entity R is organised and is resident in State R. Entity R has two owners, A and B, who are also residents of State R. Accordingly, interest payments are paid from State P. Whilst State R considers entity R as tax transparent, State P considers it a taxable entity. State P applies a general 30% WHT on gross interest paid abroad.

1114. This is the case, e.g., of the United States. US: I.R.C. ss 960 and 902. *See* the explanation in a similar example referred to the US Model provision at *supra* s. 4.2.1.3.

Figure 52 Article 1(2) OECD Model: Example 4

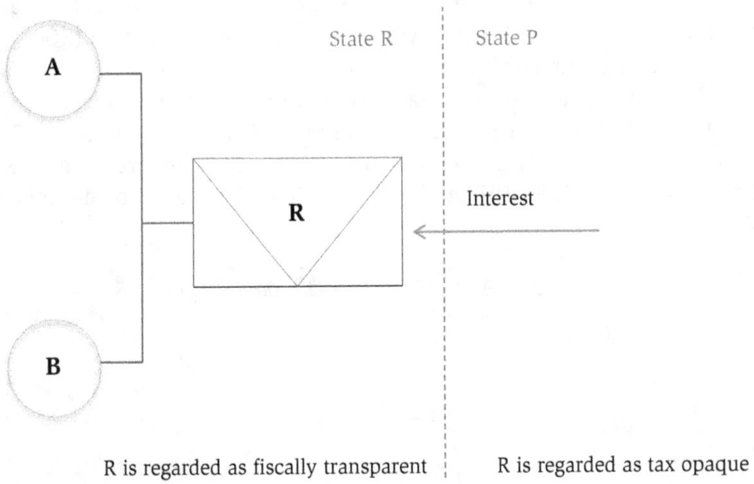

According to Article 1(2) of the treaty R-P, entity R is a fiscally transparent entity receiving interest from State P, which is allocated to partners A and B, who are also residents of State R. Therefore, Article 1(2) of the treaty R-P clarifies that partners A and B are the ones who should claim the benefits of the treaty between State R and State P. This solution seems to be satisfactory from the point of view of the residence state.

From the source state's perspective, however, the application of Article 1(2) of the treaty R-P might still leave open some uncertainty as regards the application of the treaty between State R and State P. Indeed, the fact that Article 1(2) clarifies that A and B should be granted the benefit of the treaty does not change the fact that State P still considers entity R, and not A and B, as the beneficial owner of the interest income. In other words, State P might still deny the reduced WHT at source because A and B are not the beneficial owners of the interest. This might also generate conflicts as regards the application of Article 23 because the double taxation relief might cover only the amount of reduced WHT under the treaty and not the full amount of WHT if the source state does not reduce its WHT under Article 11.

5.2.2 *Application of Article 1(2) OECD Model in Triangular Situations*

This Section turns now to analyse the application of Article 1(2) OECD Model to specific triangular situations. For this purpose, the previous assumptions that no PE is constituted in the source state and that all treaties include Article 1(2) OECD Model apply here unchanged. Likewise, in all cases, it is assumed that the intermediary entity is not a conduit company, agent or nominee.

5.2.2.1 *Example 5*

Let us assume that YCo is an entity incorporated in State Y, which has two partners, A and B, who are residents of State X. YCo has a subsidiary in State Z (ZCo), which is financed by a loan granted by YCo from which it receives interest payments back from State Z.[1115] YCo is considered as a taxable entity in State Y and in State Z. However, it is regarded as a fiscally transparent entity in State X. Likewise, although Country Z applies a general 30% WHT on gross interest paid abroad, the treaty State X/State Z provides for a reduced 10% WHT and the treaty State Y/State Z provides for a reduced 5% WHT.

Figure 53 Article 1(2) OECD Model: Example 5

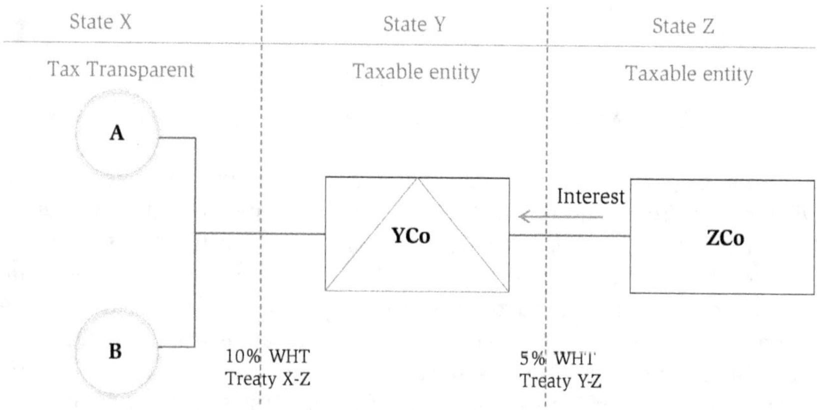

YCo is regarded as tax transparent in State X, whilst State Y and Z consider it as tax opaque. Likewise, State Z applies a 30% WHT on the gross payments of interest abroad, although the treaty State X/State Z provides for a reduced WHT of 10%, and the treaty State Y/State Z provides for a reduced WHT of 5%.

According to the treaty Y-Z, State Z should reduce its WHT to 5% according to Article 11, and State Y should grant a relief of double taxation as per Article 23. Both the income and the benefits of the treaty are allocated to YCo. Likewise, Article 1(2) treaty Y-Z does not apply because YCo is considered a taxable entity in both Contracting States.

The treaty X-Z is, nevertheless, also applicable. According to Article 1(2) treaty X-Z, income is being received by or through an entity or arrangement considered fiscally transparent by one of the Contracting States, and it is allocated to the partners A and B, who are also residents of the State treating the entity as tax transparent, i.e., State X. Therefore, in principle, State Z should apply both treaties, which under the principles of the OECD Partnership Report would mean that State Z must apply the

1115. The example assumes that the loan and interest are arm's length.

lower WHT rate (5%) as regards both treaties.[1116] This solution, however, is not only misaligned with the concept of beneficial owner[1117] but also leaves open a potential double taxation issue.[1118]

5.2.2.2 *Example 6*

Let us assume the same basic facts as in Example 5, with the sole difference that YCo is treated as fiscally transparent in State Z whilst it is regarded as a taxable entity in States X and Y. Likewise, this hypothetical also assumes that all applicable treaties provide similar reductions of WHT of 10% at source.

Figure 54 Article 1(2) OECD Model: Example 6

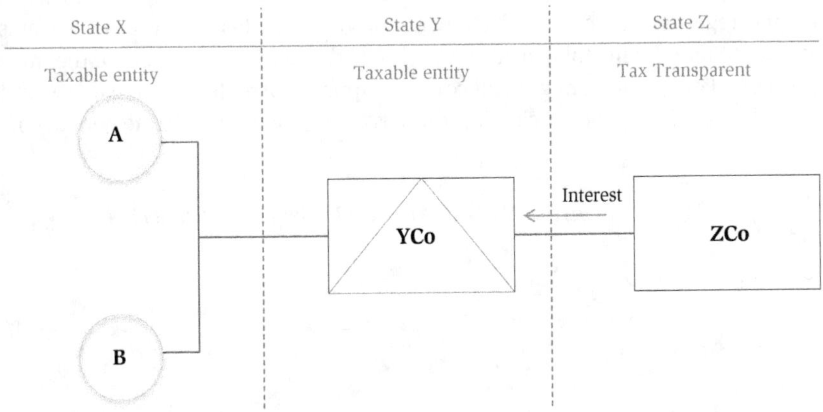

Both the tax treaties between State X/State Z and the tax treaty between State Y/State Z provide for a 10% reduced WHT.

If we first consider the treaty Y-Z, it is easy to figure out that Article 1(2) treaty Y-Z applies in this case to deny A and B the benefits of the treaty and to ensure that these

1116. OECD Commentary on Article 1 concerning the persons covered by the Convention, para. 6.5. The situation could be a bit worse for the source state if we consider that the treaty between State X/State Z provides for a reduced WHT of 5%, whilst the treaty between State Y/State Z provides for a reduced WHT of 10% (exactly the opposite as in the example). In such a case, it is evident that the application of the treaty between States X and Z is due exclusively to the different characterisation of the entity YCO in State X, limiting the taxing rights of the source state by application of a treaty that, in absence of that different tax characterisation, should simply not apply. *See* Parada, *supra* n. 1093, p. 347.
1117. *Infra* s. 5.3.1.
1118. If State X does not have a treaty with State Y, or if having a treaty, YCo is not regarded as a PE, there will be no double taxation relief for the taxes imposed at the level of YCo in State Y. For an alternative manner to solve this issue, *see* the explanation regarding the treaty between the United States and Poland, which provides for the non-application of Article 1(6) US Model if certain requirements are met. *Supra* s. 4.3.1.1.1.

benefits are allocated to YCo. In other words, as there is an item of income received through an entity considered, in this case, tax transparent in State Z, but the income is not allocated to residents of that State, Article 1(2) treaty Y-Z ensures that the benefits are not allocated to A and B, but rather to YCo. The application of Article 1(2) OECD Model, however, does not prevent the fact that State Z still considers A and B, and not YCo, as the beneficial owners of the interest. However, the reduced WHT of 10% at source could still be arguable under State Z's perspective because the preconditions of Article 11 treaty Y-Z would not be met.

As regards the treaty X-Z, Article 1(2) treaty X-Z also applies to deny the benefits of that treaty to A and B because these two are not residents of the State, treating the entity as tax transparent, i.e., State Z. Thus, A and B could get neither the reduced WHT at source under Article 11 nor the double taxation relief under Article 23 of the treaty X-Z.

The application of Article 1(2) of the treaty X-Z, however, does not solve the question as regards who the beneficial owner of the interest is. In this case, it seems to be clear that State Z will still consider A and B as the beneficial owners of the interest and not YCo. Thus, State Z might still consider applying Article 11 as regards A and B, although, by application of Article 1(2), these two are not entitled to the benefits of the treaty.

Figure 55 Article 1(2) v. Article 11 (Beneficial Owner)

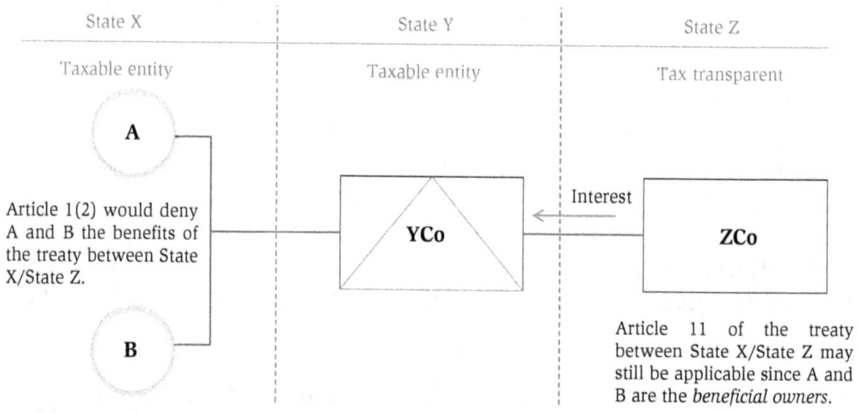

On the other hand, even in the hypothetical that A and B were residents of State Z, the preconditions of Article 11 of the treaty X-Z would not be met, i.e., there would not be a payment of interest arising in a Contracting State that is being paid to residents in the other Contracting State. In contrast, in this case, interest would arise and would be paid to residents of the same State. This situation would thus remain a domestic one.

Figure 56 Example 6 (Variation)

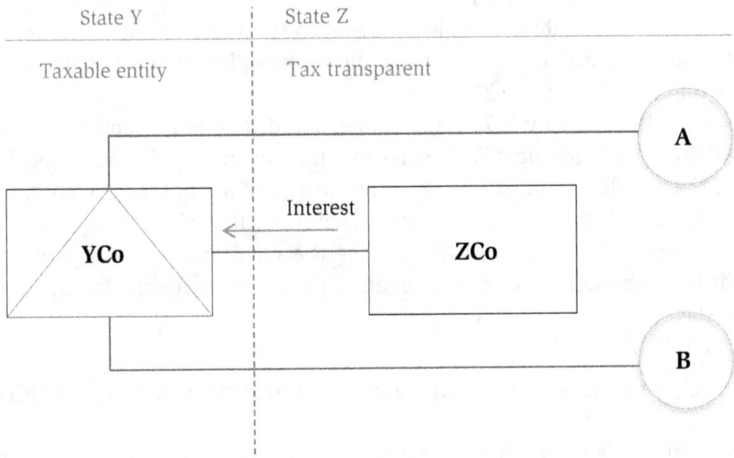

5.2.2.3 *Example 7*

Let us consider the same facts as Example 6 above, with the only difference that YCo is considered fiscally transparent in State Y whilst as a taxable entity in State X and State Z.

Figure 57 Article 1(2) OECD Model: Example 7

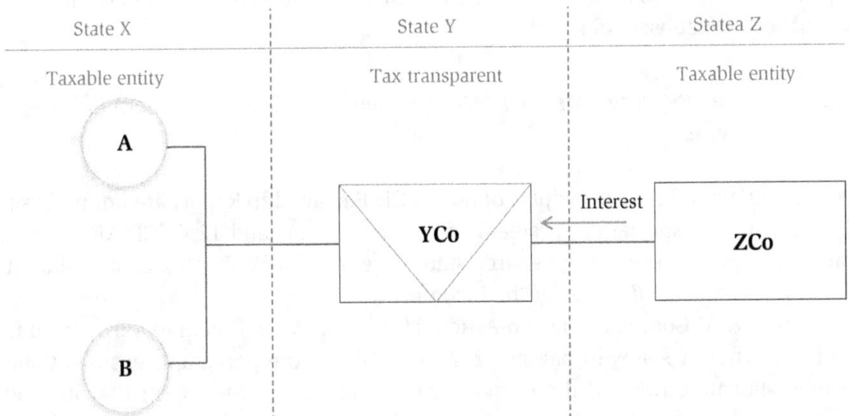

As regards the treaty Y-Z, Article 1(2) works to deny the benefits of the treaty to A and B, which are not considered residents of the State, which considers YCo as tax transparent, i.e., State Y. This solution, however, does not prevent that State Y still considers YCo as tax transparent. In other words, Article 1(2) of the treaty Y-Z does change the characterisation of the entity receiving the income neither at the source state nor at the residence state. Therefore, from the strict perspective of State Y, the treaty Y-Z is not applicable because YCo is not a resident for purposes of the treaty. Nonetheless, State Z might still apply a reduced WHT under Article 11 of the treaty Y-Z because State Z considers YCo as a taxable entity. This would not be, however, a desirable outcome from State Z's perspective.

As regards the treaty X-Z, on the other hand, this is evidently not applicable. Since neither State X nor State Z consider that the income is paid to and received by A and B, the preconditions of Article 11 of the treaty X-Z are not met. Accordingly, both States agree that YCo is a taxable entity. Therefore, the introduction of Article 1(2) within the treaty State X-Z does not change the result because the precondition of having at least one Contracting State treating the entity as fiscally transparent would not be met.

5.3 Other Issues with Regard to the Application Article 1(2) OECD Model

As noted in the illustrations above, Article 1(2) OECD Model may solve many issues with regard to whom income, for the purpose of a tax treaty, should be (or should not be) allocated, and thus, whether the benefits of the treaty should be ultimately granted. This is especially troubling in cases where Contracting States do not agree on how to treat an entity for tax purposes. Nevertheless, the solutions provided by Article 1(2) OECD Model are not always desirable. This is especially evident in cases where the application of Article 1(2) OECD Model puts the source state in an unfavourable position as regards the residence state or when the application of this provision conflicts with other attribution rules within tax treaties, in particular, with the concept of beneficial owner of Articles 10, 11 and 12 OECD Model. These issues are analysed in the subsequent subsections.

5.3.1 *The (Repeated Missed) Interplay with the Concept of* Beneficial Owner

As stressed already, the principles of the OECD Partnership Report are not necessarily aligned with the special requirement of Articles 10, 11, and 12 OECD Model, which states that for purposes of the source state to reduce its WHT, the income should be 'paid to' the *beneficial owner* of the income.[1119]

The OECD Commentaries on Article 1(2) OECD Model seem to partially address the issue when it states in paragraph 22.14: 'Whilst the paragraph ensures that the various allocative rules of the Convention are applied to the extent that income of fiscally transparent entities is treated, under domestic law, as income of a resident of a Contracting State, *the paragraph does not prejudge the issue of whether the recipient is*

1119. *Supra* s. 3.3.2.3. This was also discussed with regard to Article 1(6) US Model and that is why the author refers to it as the 'repeated missed' interplay with the concept of *beneficial owner*. *See supra* s. 3.2.3.1.

the beneficial owner of the relevant income.' (Emphasis added).[1120] Nevertheless, a closer look at the Commentary brings us a different insight.

Let us take Example 5 used in *supra* section 5.2.2.1 and assume that YCo is an entity incorporated in State Y, which has two partners, A and B, who are residents of State X. Accordingly, YCo has a subsidiary in State Z (ZCo), which is financed by a loan granted by YCo from which YCo receives interest payments back from State Z.[1121] YCo is considered as a taxable entity in State Y and in State Z. However, it is regarded as a fiscally transparent entity in State X. Likewise, although Country Z applies a general 30% WHT on gross interest paid abroad, the treaty State X/State Z provides for a reduced 10% WHT whilst the treaty State Y/State Z provides for a reduced 5% WHT.

Figure 58 The Interplay Between Article 1(2) OECD Model and the Beneficial Owner

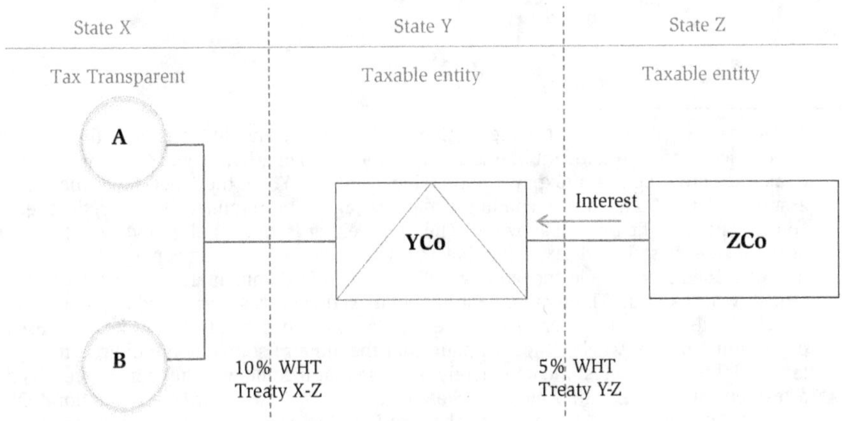

Whilst YCo is regarded as tax transparent in State X, State Y and Z consider it as tax opaque. Similarly, State Z applies a general 30% WHT on the gross payments of interest abroad. However, the treaty between State X/State Z provides for a reduced WHT of 10%, and the treaty between State Y/State Z provides for a reduced WHT of 5%.

Following the OECD Commentaries, Article 1(2) OECD Model should not prejudge the issue of whether or not YCo is the beneficial owner of the dividends paid.[1122] Although the term '*beneficial owner*' is indeed obscure and elusive,[1123] it is clear in this

1120. OECD Commentary on Article 1, para. 13.
1121. The example assumes that the loan and interest are arm's length.
1122. OECD Commentary on Article 1, para. 13.
1123. *See* the references at *supra* n. 352 regarding the discussion about the meaning of *beneficial owner*.

case that State Z will consider YCo, a taxable entity, as the beneficial owner of the dividends.[1124] In other words, State Z could still deny the application of the lowest WHT of 5% (treaty Y-Z) to A and B because, in fact, A and B are not the beneficial owners of the interest. Nevertheless, according to the principles of the OECD Partnership Report, recognised in the OECD Commentaries, State Z should indeed comply with both treaties (Y-Z and X-Z), applying the lower WHT rate (5%) to both treaties.[1125] This solution is certainly not aligned with the concept of beneficial owner[1126] and may also contradict the purpose of the treaty itself, leaving open a potential double taxation issue as well.[1127]

1124. The debate regarding which state, residence or source, should determine the beneficial owner, seems to be redundant in this case. On the one hand, both countries consider YCo as a taxable entity, i.e., as a taxpayer and resident in State Y. On the other hand, the example assumes that YCo is not a conduit company, agent or nominee, that might affect its consideration as the beneficial owner. Therefore, either from the point of view of the source or the residence state, it is expected that YCo will be regarded as the beneficial owner of the interest. The above would indeed align with the OECD Commentaries on Article 11 OECD Model, which states: 'The requirement of beneficial owner was introduced in paragraph 2 of Article 11 to clarify the meaning of the words "paid to a resident" as they are used in paragraph 1 of the Article. It makes plain that the State of source is not obliged to give up taxing rights over interest income merely because that income was immediately received by a resident of a State with which the State of source had concluded a Convention.' OECD Commentary on Article 11 concerning the taxation of interest, para. 9. Accordingly, it states: 'The term "beneficial owner" is not used in narrow technical sense, rather, it should be understood in its context and in light of the object and purpose of the Convention, including avoiding double taxation and the prevention of fiscal evasion and avoidance.' *Ibid.*, in a similar triangular example, Sanghavi arrives to the same conclusion. His example considers a company SCo, resident in State S, which pays dividends to HCo, resident of State H. HCo is wholly owned by RCo, a company established in State R. Whilst State S and H consider HCo as a taxable entity, State R considers it as a fiscally transparent entity, because of an option given in State R. As stated by Sanghavi: 'However, article 10(2) restricts the source state's taxing rights only if the beneficial owner of the dividends is a resident of the other contracting states [...] it is clear that the "beneficial owner" generally refers to a singular entity [HCo].' D. Sanghavi, *BEPS Hybrid Entities Proposal: A Slippery Slope, Especially for Developing Countries*, 85 Tax Notes Int'l 4, 360 (2017) DOI: 10.2139/ssrn.2915454, Figure 1.

1125. OECD Commentary on Article 1 concerning the persons covered by the Convention, para. 6.5. However, if YCo is regarded as tax transparent in State Y, it is obvious that State Z must not grant any benefit of the treaty to State Y. For an alternative solution, *see* the treaty United States/Poland, analysed in *supra* s. 4.3.1.1.1.

1126. The application of Article 1(2) OECD Model in this case would not solve the conflict that YCo might still be the beneficial owner of the interest payments. Thus, for purposes of applying Article 11 OECD Model, State Z could still argue that the interests are not beneficially owned by A and B in State X.

1127. For example, if State X does not have a treaty with State Y, or if having a treaty, YCo is not regarded as a PE, there will be no double taxation relief for the taxes imposed at the level of YCo in State Y. Moreover, if the same situation is analysed using a trust, the relief of double taxation becomes impossible. *See* Danon, *supra* n. 912, pp. 198-199.

Figure 59 Solution as Per the Commentaries on Article 1(2) OECD Model

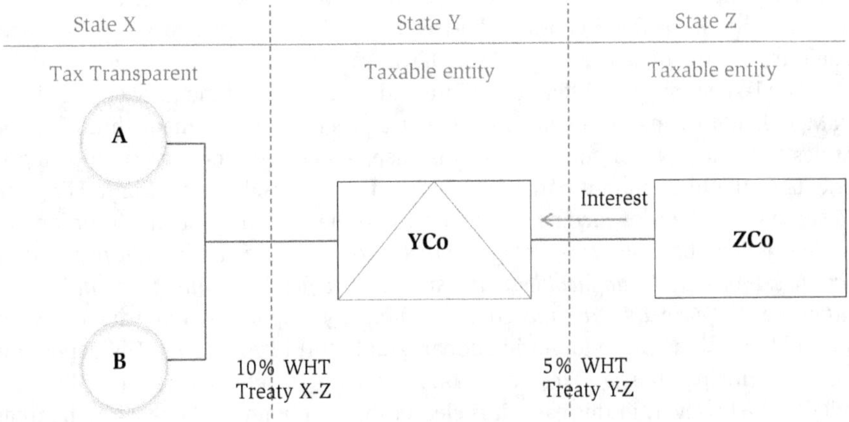

Whilst Article 1(2) OECD Model provides that partners A and B are the beneficiaries of the treaty X-Z, this solution does not coincide with the fact that for State Z considers YCo and not partners A and B as the *beneficial owner* of the interest payments. Therefore, there would be no reason for State Z to apply a reduced 5% WHT at source.

The second part of the Commentary does not help to clarify the interplay either. As provided in the second part of paragraph 24.16: 'Where, for example, a fiscally transparent partnership receives dividends as an agent or nominee for a person who is not a partner, the fact that the dividend may be considered as income of a resident of a Contracting State under the domestic law of that State *will not preclude the State of source from considering that neither the partnership nor the partners are the beneficial owners of the dividend*' (emphasis added).[1128] The example is straightforward and clear in terms that no nominee or agent, partnership or partner of it is indeed the beneficial owner of the dividends. However, it does not clarify which of the two, i.e., partners or partnerships, should be considered *beneficial owners*. Interestingly, however, is that the paragraph emphasises that the determination of who is the *beneficial owner* should be made in accordance with the domestic laws of the source state.[1129] Although some commentators might criticise this statement,[1130] I agree with the fact that, by logic, it is

1128. OECD Commentary on Article 1, para. 13.
1129. *Ibid.*
1130. For example, Sanghavi states with regard to this second part of para. 13 (proposed para. 26.14) of the Commentary on Article 1: 'It is also strange that the commentary suggests that the beneficial owner should be determined exclusively in accordance with the tax principles of the source state. A situation in which the source state considers a partnership to be the beneficial owner of dividends, but the other state treats that partnership as transparent would, absent unilateral relief, likely result in unrelieved double taxation because the partnership will not qualify as a treaty resident.' Sanghavi, *supra* n. 1124, p. 361. I disagree with Sanghavi's statement in the sense that, in practice, the partnership will not be subject to tax in the residence state, but rather its partners, but only to the extent they are also residents in that

the source state, i.e., the State whose taxing rights are limited by a tax treaty, who should determine to whom interest, dividends or royalties are '*paid to*', independently of the residence status as per the domestic laws of the residence state. Of course, this idea does not solve the dichotomy between beneficial owner and the persons who benefit from a treaty as per Article 1(2) OECD Model either.

The issue is slightly differently addressed in the UN Commentary on Article 1(2) UN Model, addressing the application of tax treaties to payments made through hybrid entities.[1131] The UN Commentary, in this case, states: 'As first step in applying the benefits of the Convention, paragraph 2 identifies the resident of a Contracting State that derives an item of income for which treaty benefits are sought. In order to be entitled to such benefits, *such resident must also satisfy any additional requirements that are set forth in the applicable treaty, such as beneficially owning the item if income under the tax principles of the source State*, any applicable requisite ownership thresholds (such as those found in subparagraph 2(a) of Article 10 (Dividends), and either a principal purpose test or a limitation on benefits provision.' (Emphasis added).[1132] However, in this case, it is clearer that to obtain the benefits of the treaty, it is not only necessary to be a resident for purposes of the treaty but also to comply with the beneficial ownership requirement of Articles 10, 11, and 12 UN Model, the solution again clashes with Article 1(2) UN Model. Using the same example as above, we would conclude that State Z would consider YCo as the beneficial owner. Indeed, in this case, there is no doubt that this determination is made exclusively '*under the tax principles of the source State*' (emphasis added), which considers YCo as a taxable entity. On the other hand, however, Article 1(2) UN Model will consider A and B as the person receiving the dividends and who benefit from the treaty X-Z, but who, nevertheless, are not the beneficial owners of the dividends according to State S. Once again, therefore, the solution of Article 1(2) UN Model clashes with the beneficial ownership requirement, providing an inconsistent outcome.

State. If they were residents of a third State, it should be analysed what is the tax treatment that this State gives to the partnership and whether this tax treatment coincides or not with the one given in the source state. Thus, if this third country, i.e., where the partners are residents, treats the partnership as a taxable entity, there will be no double taxation issue, because the partners will not be allocated the income derived through the partnership. However, if this State considers the partnership as fiscally transparent, the residence state of the partners will exercise its taxing rights. In this case, double taxation will arise, but only to the extent the residence state does not grant double taxation relief under Article 23 OECD Model at all, or it grants double taxation relief, but only up to the amount of taxes at source limited by the treaty. This, however, does not mean to proceed again with ad hoc solutions giving also the residence state the possibility to determine who is the beneficial owner of the income, or to establish an exception with regard to the determination of the beneficial owner by the source state. Instead, it is perhaps the design or the scope of Article 1(2) OECD Model, which should be questioned. This is indeed what I assume in the proposal developed at *infra* Chapter 6.

1131. UN: Committee of Experts on International Cooperation in Tax Matters, 11th session, Item 3 (a)(i) of the provisional agenda, Application of treaty rules to hybrid entities, New provision for the United Nations Model Double Taxation Convention between Developed and Developing Countries to address the application of tax treaties to payments made through hybrid entities, Geneva 11-14 October 2016, Annex I: United Nations Model Double Taxation Convention between Developed and Developing Countries: proposed changes to address the application of tax treaties to payments made through hybrid entities, pp. 4 et seq.

1132. UN: Commentary on Article 1(2) UN Model, para. 6.

Figure 60 Solution under the Commentaries on Article 1(2) UN Model

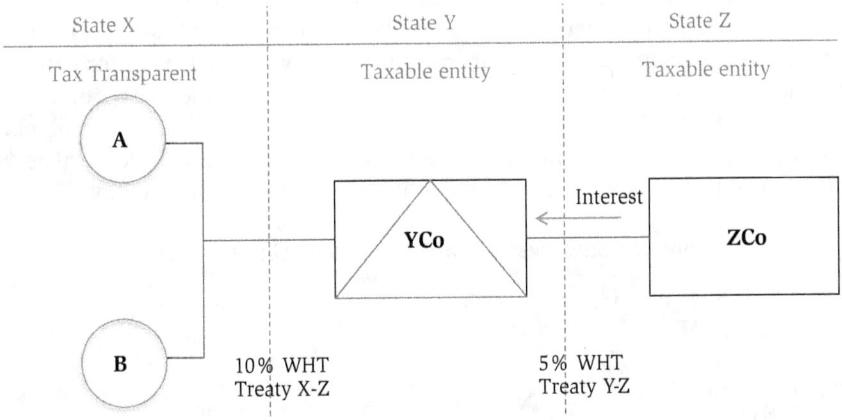

Whilst Article 1(2) UN Model provides that partners A and B are granted the benefits of the treaty X-Z, this solution does not coincide with the fact that for State Z, YCo is the *beneficial owner* of the interest payments, and not partners A and B. Once again, the solution of Article 1(2) UN Model clashes with the beneficial owner requirement of Articles 10, 11 and 12 UN Model.

5.3.1.1 *A 'Deemed' Beneficial Owner: An Alternative Solution*

It is evident from the examples above that the dichotomy between the solution provided by Article 1(2) OECD Model with regard to who should enjoy the benefits of a tax treaty when income is received by or through an entity (or arrangement, whatever that means) and the concept of *beneficial owner* in Articles 10, 11, and 12 OECD Model, is very difficult to solve.[1133] Indeed, if one gives priority to the *beneficial owner*'s determination by the source state, the Article 1(2) OECD Model remains ineffective in many cases. On the contrary, if one gives priority to the determination of who should get the benefits of a treaty when income is received by or through a fiscally transparent entity under Article 1(2) OECD Model, the *beneficial ownership* requirement clashes again and may deny those benefits. In simple terms, one remains within the effect created by the incompatibility of the two provisions.

Considering the above, a recognised group of academics have recently proposed an alternative to solve this dichotomy between Article 1(2) OECD Model and the *beneficial ownership* requirement. The proposal is based on the common agreement that the benefits of a treaty as per the application of Article 1(2) OECD Model should not fail to be granted where income being attributed to a resident of the other Contracting State, assuming no relevant party is acting as an agent or nominee or other

1133. Nikolakakis et al., *supra* n. 985, pp. 333-334. These academics include A. Nikolakakis, S. Austry, J. Avery Jones, P. Baker, P. Blessing, R. Danon, S. Goradia, J. Hattingh, K. Inoue, J. Lüdicke, G. Maisto, T. Miyatake, K. van Raad, R. Vann and B. Wiman.

intermediary for a third party from the source state's perspective.[1134] The proposal is divided into two steps.

The first step suggests that the source state should determine if the entity is an agent, nominee or other intermediary. If yes, the source state should skip the entity and go to the next person, i.e., the member(s) of the entity. If this person (or entity) for which the entity is a nominee, agent or other intermediary is considered tax opaque,[1135] then Article 1(2) OECD Model is not in play.[1136] If this person (or entity) is a nominee, agent or other intermediary for another fiscally transparent entity, then Article 1(2) OECD Model is in play with regard to that other fiscally transparent entity.[1137]

Figure 61 Step One: 'Deemed' Beneficial Owner's Proposal

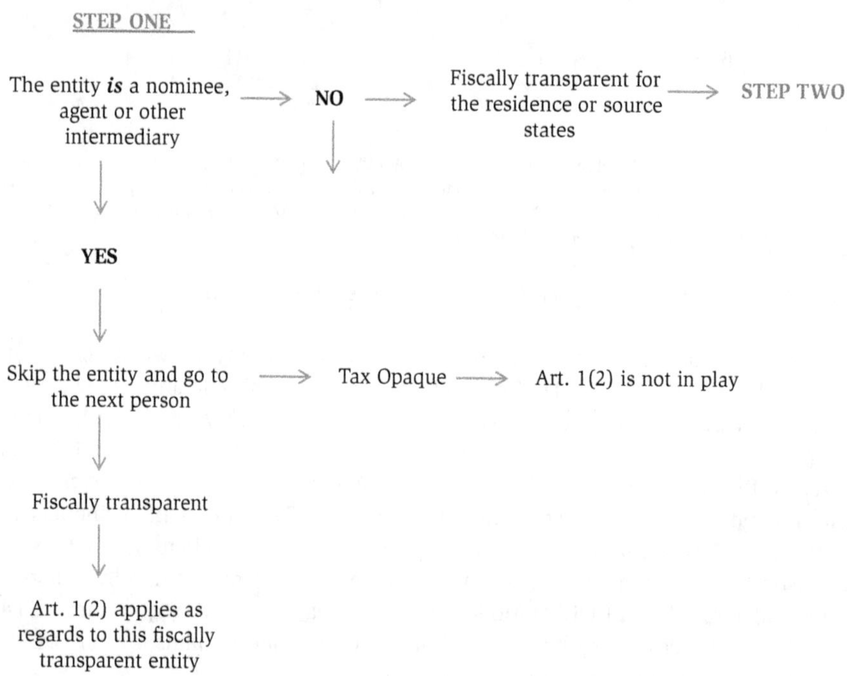

1134. *Ibid.*
1135. It is not specified in the proposal, but I assume that the consideration of tax opaque or fiscally transparent refers to the consideration of the residence state, even though the determination of nominee, agent or other intermediary is done from the perspective of the source state.
1136. Nikolakakis et al., *supra* n. 985, p. 336.
1137. *Ibid.*, the wording is confusing, but it seems to state that Step 2 of the proposal must be applied.

The second step applies only to the extent that the entity is considered as a fiscally transparent entity and it is not a nominee, agent or other intermediary, or where it is a nominee, agent or other intermediary for another fiscally transparent entity.[1138] For this purpose, we must distinguish if the entity is considered fiscally transparent from the perspective of the source state or from the perspective of the residence state. If the entity is regarded as fiscally transparent from the source state perspective but is considered opaque by the residence state, then the source state must consider the entity as the *beneficial owner*.[1139] On the other hand, if the residence state also considers the entity as fiscally transparent, then one should take a look at the members of the entity. If the members are residents of the residence state, then the source state must consider those residents as the *beneficial owners* unless the resident is considered a nominee, agent or other intermediary.[1140] If the resident is indeed a nominee, agent or other intermediary, then the step requires a scrutiny of the principal. If the principal is a resident of the residence state and also an opaque entity [it seems to be also from the State of residence's perspective], then the source state should consider that the *beneficial owner* requirement is met. On the contrary, if the principal is not a resident of the residence state and is considered tax opaque [from the State of residence's perspective], then the *beneficial owner* requirement will not be satisfied.[1141]

1138. *Ibid.*

1139. '[...] the source state should be required to apply the treaty as if the beneficial owner is the entity, regardless of the legal nature of the entity or the effect of that in the source state's normal application of the beneficial owner principles'. *Ibid.*, it is thus clear that a 'deemed' beneficial owner has been created in order to solve the discrepancies with Article 1(2) OECD Model Tax Convention.

1140. It is correct to affirm in this case that if the resident is not regarded as a nominee, agent or other intermediary, it will coincide with the source state's determination of the beneficial owner. However, this is the result of the tax characterisation of the entity by both States as fiscally transparent. If residence and source States treat the entity as fiscally transparent, it is almost impossible that they conflict with regard to who is the beneficial owner and the person being entitled to the benefits of the treaty.

1141. This is the same solution offered in the treaty Canada/ United States analysed in some sections above. *Supra* s. 4.3.1.1.2. In that treaty it is provided that if State of source considers that the partner deriving the income under Article IV(6) of the Canada/United States tax treaty [Article 1(6) US Model] is an agent, nominee, custodian or conduit for a *non-resident* of the other Contracting State, then the State of source may deny the benefits of Article 11 Canada/United States tax treaty. However, if the State of source still considers that the partner deriving the income is an agent, nominee, custodian or conduit, but for a *resident* of the other Contracting State, then it should be granted the benefits of the treaty anyway. The concepts of *residence* and *beneficial ownership* are merged to get a pragmatic solution.

Figure 62 Step Two: 'Deemed' Beneficial Owner's Proposal

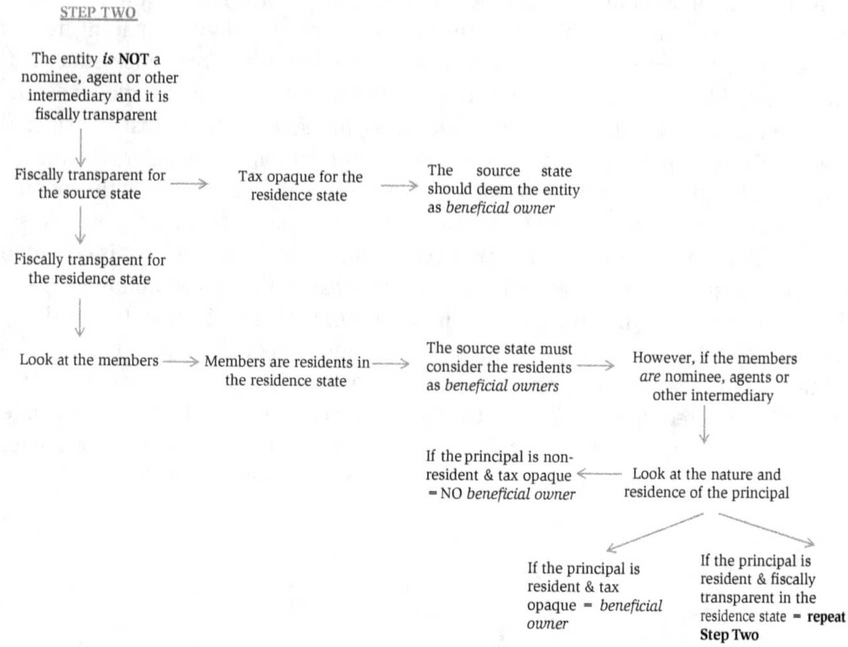

In the same order of ideas, if the entity was not considered as a nominee, agent or other intermediary and the source state considers the entity as tax opaque, step two would apply as follows.[1142] If the residence state also considers the entity as opaque, Article 1(2) OECD Model does not apply.[1143] On the contrary, if the residence state considers the entity as fiscally transparent, then the source state must apply the treaty as if the *beneficial owner* were the entity's member unless they are regarded as nominees, agents or other intermediaries by the source state.[1144] If the members are considered nominees, agents or other intermediaries, then one should look at the residence of the principal. If the principal is a resident of the residence state and a tax-opaque entity, then it should be considered as the *beneficial owner* for purposes of the treaty. On the contrary, if the principal is a resident in the residence state but fiscally transparent, then step two is repeated. If the principal is not a resident of the residence state, then it is not regarded as the *beneficial owner* for purposes of the treaty.[1145]

1142. Nikolakakis et al., *supra* n. 985, p. 337.
1143. *Ibid.*, it is clear that the precondition of having at least one of the Contracting States treating the entity as fiscally transparent would not be met in order to apply Article 1(2) OECD Model.
1144. *Ibid.*
1145. *Ibid.*

Figure 63 Step Two: 'Deemed' Beneficial Owner's Proposal

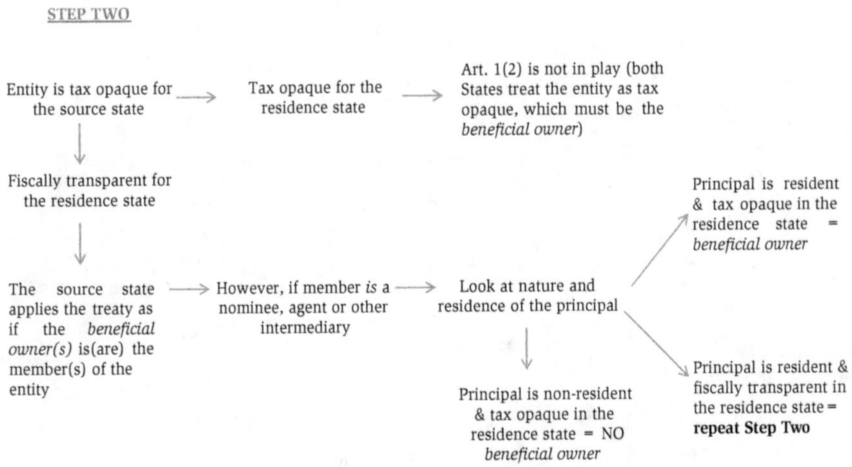

5.3.1.2 *Testing the Proposal for a 'Deemed' Beneficial Owner*

If we test the proposed solution with the illustrations given in *supra* Sections 5.2.1 and 5.2.2, the results would be as follows:[1146]

> *Example 1:*[1147]
>
> In this example, Article 1(2) of the treaty R-P makes the treaty between these two States applicable by the sole characterisation of entity P in State R, i.e., the residence state, generating a conflict with the concept of beneficial owner in Article 11 of the treaty R-P. Let us now apply the proposed solution.

1146. This is my interpretation of the proposed solution and might not necessarily coincide with the one sustained by the authors in their proposal.
1147. *Supra* s. 5.2.1.1.

Figure 64 Testing the Deemed B.O. Proposal (Example 1)

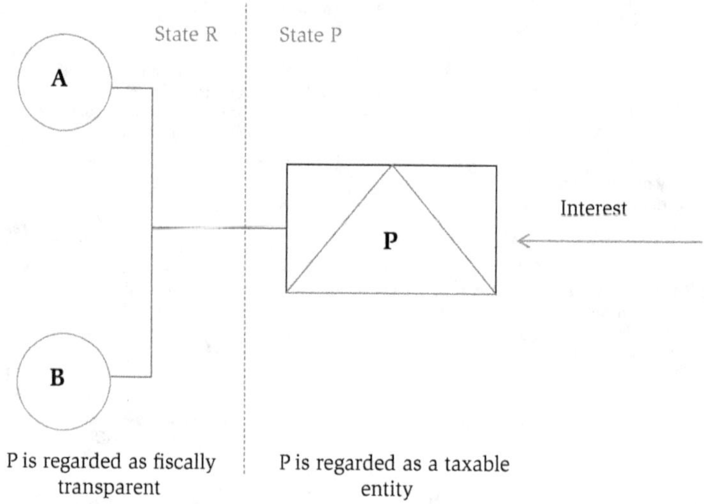

If entity P *is not* a nominee, agent or other intermediary under State P's perspective, but State R treats it as tax transparent, then A and B are deemed B.O. of the income. On the contrary, if entity P is a nominee, agent or other intermediary, State P should skip the entity and look at A and B (individuals) as the B.O. The tax characterisation of entity P in State P is irrelevant in this case.

As noted in Figure 64, if entity P *is not* a nominee, agent or other intermediary under State P's perspective, but State R considers the entity as fiscally transparent, the solution would be that State P should apply the treaty R-P, granting a reduced WHT under Article 11, deeming A and B as the beneficial owners. Although the proposed alternative solves the dichotomy between Article 1(2) and Article 11 (beneficial owner) in a pragmatic way, the question of why the source state (State P) should apply the treaty R-P by the sole characterisation of the entity in State R remains unanswered. On the contrary, if entity P *is* a nominee, agent or other intermediary (i.e., not the beneficial owner), State P should skip the entity and look at the members A and B. In such a case, Article 1(2) is not in play because partners A and B are not tax-transparent (they are individuals). In other words, A and B are now deemed to be the beneficial owner by State P, and they are also the persons receiving the benefits of the treaty under State R's perspective, which considers the entity as fiscally transparent. Although the solution completely disregards the tax characterisation of the entity in the source state, this seems to be irrelevant since the source state considers the entity as a nominee, agent or other intermediary, i.e., not as the beneficial owner.

Example 2:[1148]

In this example, Article 11 of the treaty R-P applies to reduce the WHT at source. However, Article 1(2) OECD Model denies the benefits of the treaty to A and B (beneficial owners under the State P's perspective) and provides that the benefits of the treaty should be allocated to entity R. Once again, State P might not agree in reducing its WHT with respect to entity R, but rather with respect to A and B, who are the beneficial owners. Let us now apply the proposed solution.

Figure 65 Testing the Deemed B.O. Proposal (Example 2)

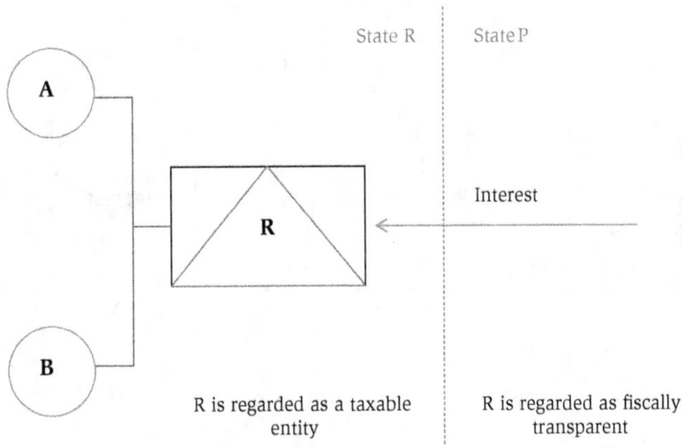

If entity R *is not* a nominee, agent or other intermediary under State P's perspective, and State R treats it as tax opaque, then entity R is deemed the B.O. of the income. On the contrary, if entity P is a nominee, agent or other intermediary, State P should skip the entity and look at A and B (individuals) as the deemed B.O. The tax characterisation of entity R in State R is irrelevant, and Article 1(2) is not in play.

As noted in Figure 65, if entity R *is not* a nominee, agent or other intermediary under State P's perspective, and this State treats the entity as fiscally transparent, being rather opaque for the residence state (State R), the proposed solution provides that State P should deem entity R as the beneficial owner. Again, the solution is pragmatic and solves the conflict, although it limits the exclusivity of the State of source to determine under its domestic law who is the beneficial owner. On the contrary, if entity R *is* a nominee, agent or other intermediary under State P's perspective, this State should look at the members of the entity, i.e., A and B. As both are individuals (not fiscally transparent), Article 1(2) OECD Model is not in play, and Article 11 should apply to reduce the WHT at source with respect to A and B, who are now considered the beneficial owners of the interest, regardless of the tax characterisation of entity R in State R.

1148. *Supra* s. 5.2.1.2.

Example 3:[1149]

In this example, Article 1(2) of the treaty R-P acts to deny the benefits of the treaty to A and B and to confirm that this is indeed a domestic situation. Nevertheless, the treaty might still be applicable from the perspective of State P, which considers entity P as fiscally transparent and A and B as the beneficial owners of the interest. Let us now apply the proposed solution.

Figure 66 Testing the Deemed B.O. Proposal (Example 3)

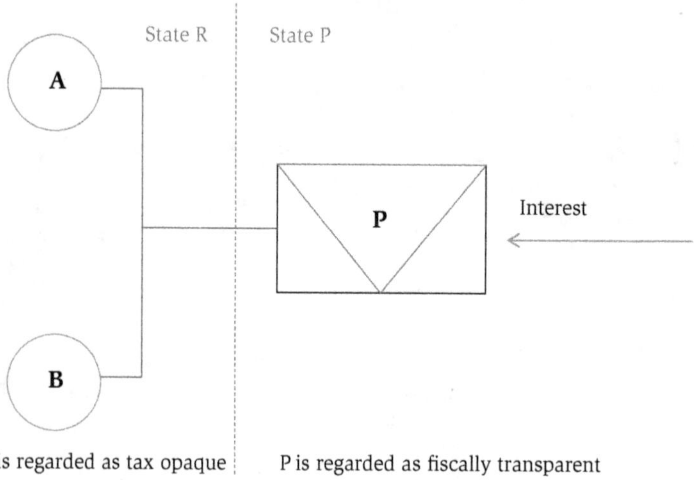

If entity P *is not* a nominee, agent or other intermediary under State P's perspective, and State R treats it as tax opaque whilst State P as tax transparent, then entity P is deemed the B.O. of the income. On the contrary, if entity P is a nominee, agent or other intermediary, State P should skip the entity and look at A and B (individuals) as the deemed B.O. This means, regardless of the outcome under Article 1(2), the source state will reduce its WHT and apply the treaty as regards A and B, who should get a relief from double taxation in the residence state

As noted in Figure 66, if entity P *is not* a nominee, agent or other intermediary under State P's perspective, and it is regarded as fiscally transparent by this State (source state) whilst as a taxable entity by State R (residence state), then State P should deem entity P as the beneficial owner, solving the conflict with Article 1(2). On the contrary, if entity P *is* considered as a nominee, agent or other intermediary from State P's perspective, then State P must look at members A and B. Both are individuals (non-transparent). Therefore, Article 1(2) is not in play, and State P will have to consider reducing its WHT under Article 11 with respect to A and B, who should be capable, in principle, of getting relief under Article 23 as well. This outcome disregards the tax characterisation of entity P in the

1149. *Supra* s. 5.2.1.3.

residence state (State R). In other words, Article 1(2) shall not apply to deny the benefits of the treaty to A and B.

Example 4:[1150]

In this example, Article 1(2) grants the benefits of the treaty R-P to A and B. However, State P considers that the beneficial owner is entity R and not A and B. Let us thus apply now the proposed solution.

Figure 67 Testing the Deemed B.O. Proposal (Example 4)

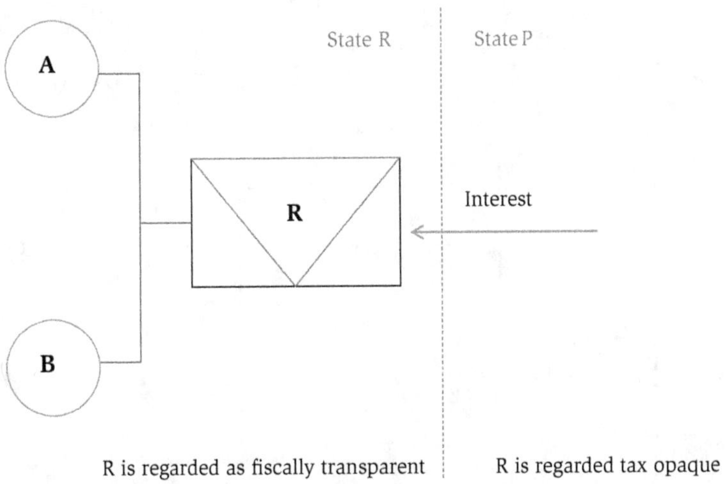

If entity R *is not* a nominee, agent or other intermediary under State P's perspective, and State R treats it as tax transparent, then A and B are deemed the B.O. of the income. On the contrary, if entity P is a nominee, agent or other intermediary, State P should skip the entity and look at A and B (individuals) as the deemed B.O. The tax characterisation of entity R in State P is irrelevant.

As noted in Figure 67, if entity R *is not* a nominee, agent or other intermediary under State P's perspective, but it is considered fiscally transparent by the residence state (State R), then State P should deem A and B as the beneficial owners. The proposed solution works to solve the conflictive position between Article 1(2) and the beneficial ownership requirement of Article 11 of the treaty R-P. On the contrary, if entity R *is* a nominee, agent or other intermediary under State P's perspective, then State P must look at the members A and B. Both are individual persons (non-transparent). Therefore, Article 1(2) is not in play.

1150. *Supra* s. 5.2.1.4.

Namely, A and B would be granted the benefits of the treaty and would also be considered the beneficial owners for purposes of Article 11 of the treaty R-P.[1151]

Example 5:[1152]

Let us now analyse the application of the proposed rule in a triangular case. In example 5, the relevant treaty is X-Z because in the treaty Y-Z, both States consider YCo as a taxable entity, and thus, Article 1(2) does not apply.

Figure 68 Testing the Deemed B.O. Proposal (Example 5)

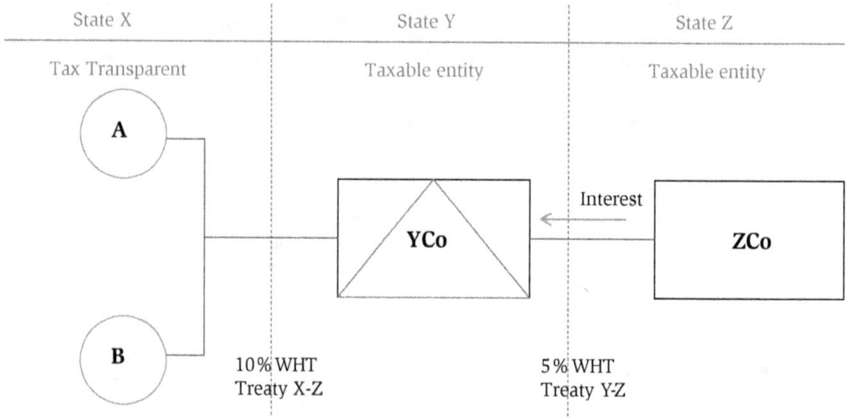

If YCo *is not* a nominee, agent or other intermediary under State Z's perspective, and State X treats YCo as tax transparent, then A and B are deemed the B.O. of the income. However, two B.O. exist in parallel now. YCo regarding the treaty between Y-Z, and A and B (deemed) regarding the treaty X-Z. On the contrary, if YCo is considered as a nominee, agent or other intermediary, State Z should skip the entity and look at A and B (individuals) as the deemed B.O. The expected outcome in this case is that Article 11 of the treaty Y-Z should not apply.

As noted in Figure 68, if YCo *is not* a nominee, agent or other intermediary under State Z's perspective, and State X (residence state) considers YCo as fiscally transparent whilst this is treated as tax opaque in State X (source state), then State Z must deem A and B as the beneficial owners of the interest. This pragmatic solution solves the dichotomy between Article 1(2) and the concept of beneficial owner and grants A and B the lowest WHT of 5% (from the treaty Y-Z). Accordingly, it creates two beneficial owners for the same income. One is YCo (the real one), as regards the treaty Y-Z, whilst the other ones are A and B (the 'deemed' ones), as regards the treaty X-Z. I do not really see a reason how this solution can be accepted without hesitation from the strict perspective of the source state. On the contrary, if YCo *is* considered as a nominee, agent or other intermediary under

1151. Indeed, the fact that entity is considered as a nominee, agent or other intermediary under State P's perspective, means that it cannot be the beneficial owner for the purposes of Article 11 of the treaty R-P.
1152. *Supra* s. 5.2.2.1.

State Z's perspective, this State should look at the members A and B. As both are individuals (non-transparent), Article 1(2) is not in play. Therefore, A and B are the beneficial owners of the interest under State Z's perspective, and they are also the residents who receive the income and are granted the benefits of the treaty in State X. However, one could still question whether the fact that YCo is considered a nominee, agent or other intermediary under State Z's perspective changes or not the consideration of who the beneficial owner under the treaty Y-Z is. In other words, if YCo is considered as a nominee, agent or other intermediary by State Z, the expected result is that Article 11 of the treaty Y-Z does not apply.

Example 6:[1153]

In example 6, both applicable treaties are relevant. In both treaties, Article 1(2) applies to deny the benefits of the treaty to A and B. However, in both cases, A and B are indeed seen as the beneficial owners of the interest. Let us now apply the proposed solution.

Figure 69 Testing the Deemed B.O. Proposal (Example 6)

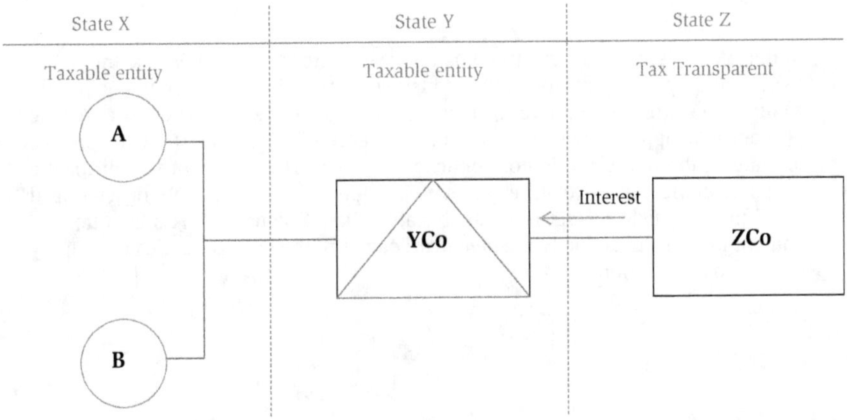

As for the treaty Y-Z and X-Z, if YCo *is not* a nominee, agent or other intermediary under State Z's perspective, and State Z treats YCo as tax transparent whilst State Y as tax opaque, then YCo is deemed the B.O. of the income. YCo regarding the treaty between Y-Z, and A and B (deemed) regarding the treaty X-Z. On the contrary, if YCo is considered as a nominee, agent or other intermediary, State Z should skip the entity and look at A and B (individuals) as the deemed B.O. State Z will provide a reduced WHT only as regards the treaty X-Z, and A and B should get a relief from double taxation. Article 1(2) is not in play.

1153. *Supra* s. 5.2.2.2.

As regards the treaty Y-Z above, if YCo *is not* a nominee, agent or other intermediary under State Z's perspective, and it is considered as fiscally transparent by this country (source state) whilst as tax opaque by State Y (residence state), the source State (Z) should deem YCo as the beneficial owner. Therefore, the treaty Y-Z is now fully applicable, and State Z should limit its taxing rights based on a 'deemed' *beneficial owner*.[1154] Considering the same situation as regards the treaty X-Z, i.e., YCo *is not* a nominee, agent or other intermediary under State Z's perspective, the solution is the same as above. That is, YCo is deemed to be the beneficial owner, and therefore, the treaty X-Z is no longer applicable.[1155]

As for the treaty Y-Z, if YCo *is* considered a nominee, agent or other intermediary under State Z's perspective, this State should look at the members of the entity. As A and B are both individuals (not fiscally transparent), Article 1(2) is not in play. Accordingly, since YCo is just a nominee, agent or intermediary, State Z might clearly deny a reduced WHT under Article 11 of the treaty Y-Z. On the other hand, State Z will consider reducing its WHT under Article 11 with respect to A and B (treaty X-Z), and it should, in principle, get relief under Article 23, regardless of the tax characterisation in its residence state (State R). In other words, Article 1(2) does not apply anymore to deny the benefits of the treaty to A and B.

Example 7:[1156]

In this example, the relevant treaty is between States Y and Z because the treaty X-Z is not only not applicable, but it considers that both the residence state (State X) and the source state (State Z) treat YCo as a taxable entity. Therefore, Article 1(2) does not apply. Let us thus focus on the treaty Y-Z. From the strict perspective of State Y, the treaty Y-Z is not applicable because YCo is not a resident for the purposes of the treaty. Nonetheless, State Z might still consider applying a reduced WHT under Article 11 OECD Model because State Z considers YCo as a taxable entity and, thus, most likely the *beneficial owner* of the interest. Let us now apply the proposed solution.

1154. However, State Z keeps considering YCo as a transparent entity.
1155. This is consistent with the solution of Article 1(2) OECD Model, which in this case denies the benefits of the treaty X-Z to A and B.
1156. *Supra* s. 5.2.2.3.

Figure 70 Testing the Deemed B.O. Proposal (Example 7)

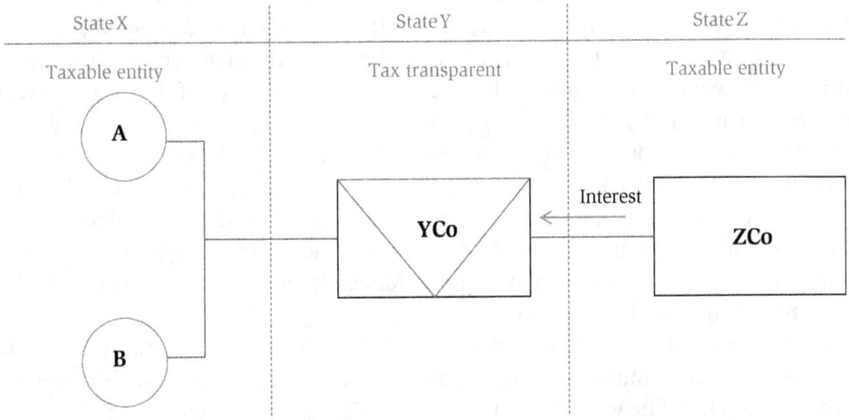

If YCo *is not* a nominee, agent or other intermediary under State Z's perspective, and State Y treats YCo as tax transparent whilst State Z as tax opaque, then A and B are deemed the B.O. of the income. On the contrary, if YCo is considered as a nominee, agent or other intermediary, State Z should skip the entity and look at A and B (individuals) as the deemed B.O. This simply confirms that no treaty is applicable in this case.

As noted in the Figure above, if YCo *is not* considered as a nominee, agent or other intermediary under State Z's perspective, and the residence state (State Y) considers YCo as fiscally transparent whilst the source state (State Z) considers it as a taxable entity, State Y (residence state) must apply the treaty as if the beneficial owners were the partners of YCo, i.e., A and B, residents of State X. In other words, the 'deemed' *beneficial owner*, in this case, allows State Z to confirm that the reduced WHT at source under Article 11 of the treaty Y-Z will not apply as regards YCo. In other words, it confirms that the treaty Y-Z is simply not applicable both for State Y and Z. On the contrary, if YCo *is* considered as a nominee, agent or other intermediary under State Z's perspective, State Z must skip the entity and look at members A and B. As both A and B are individual persons (not fiscally transparent in their residence state), Article 1(2) is not in play. This outcome simply confirms that neither the treaty X-Z (originally not applicable) nor the treaty Y-Z are now applicable.

5.3.1.3 *The Pragmatism of 'Deemed' Rules: Criticism*

The pragmatic solution for a deemed beneficial owner seems to rely on some basic ideas. First, whilst the tax characterisation of the entity in the residence state appears to be relevant to solving the dichotomy between Article 1(2) OECD Model and the *beneficial ownership* requirement of Articles 10, 11, and 12 OECD Model, the tax characterisation of the entity at source lacks it. In other words, it is assumed by the proponents that the tax characterisation of the entity at source plays no role in the determination of the beneficial owner. For example, if the entity is not a nominee, agent or other intermediary under the source state's perspective, and it is also considered a taxable entity by this country although as fiscally transparent by the residence state, the solution simply proposes to treat the members of that entity as 'deemed' beneficial owners to the extent that they are also not considered a nominee, agent or other intermediary. And even in the case the members are regarded as nominees, agents or other intermediaries, it is the tax residence of the principal which decides the conflict. Indeed, if the principal is a resident and tax opaque in the residence state, it is deemed as the beneficial owner. In simple terms, the concepts of *beneficial owner* and *resident* for purposes of the treaty are merged to solve the dichotomy. Similarly, if the entity is originally not considered as a nominee, agent or other intermediary by the source state, and it is treated as fiscally transparent by the same State although as tax opaque by the residence state, the source state should deem the entity as the beneficial owner.

The above brings us to the second characteristic of this proposal, which is that even though it relies initially on the source state's approach to determine the beneficial owner, which is in line with the proposed OECD Commentaries on Article 1(2),[1157] this idea is rapidly disregarded. Indeed, it is evident from the proposal that even though the source state considers an entity as tax opaque and not as a nominee, agent or other intermediary, it must make this decision contingent on the fact that the State of residence also considers that entity as tax opaque.[1158] Otherwise, the proposed solution provides that the members of the entity are the 'deemed' beneficial owners.[1159] In the same order of ideas, even though the source state considers an entity as tax transparent and not as a nominee, agent or other intermediary, the determination of the beneficial owner is still contingent on the fact that the residence state also considers the entity as tax transparent to finally confirm that the members of the entity are the beneficial owners. The prevalence of the residence state tax characterisation is such that if the residence state would consider an entity as opaque whilst the source state as tax transparent, then the source state must 'deem' the entity as the beneficial owner. Therefore, I dare to say that the whole proposal relies almost exclusively on the tax characterisation of the entity in the residence state, even though no justifications for this approach are provided.

As regards the outcomes derived from the test of the proposed solution in the section above, I recognize that the proposed solution is indeed pragmatically effective in solving the dichotomy between Article 1(2) OECD Model and the application of the beneficial ownership requirement of Articles 10, 11, and 12 OECD Model.[1160] However, there are still some very arguable outcomes. For instance, in Example 5 above (triangular case), the application of the proposed solution does not only create two beneficial owners, one real and one 'deemed', but it puts the source state in the

1157. Proposed Commentary on Article 1(2), para. 26.14, OECD (2015), *supra* n. 6, p. 142.

1158. Although in such a case, Article 1(2) OECD Model is not applicable at all.

1159. If they are also considered as nominee, agents or other intermediary, the solution is even more straightforward and calls for a scrutiny of the residence of the principal. *See* Nikolakakis et al., *supra* n. 985, p. 337.

1160. For example, the results in examples 2 and 3, where the State of source consider initially that the entity is a nominee, agent or other intermediary. *Supra* s. 5.3.1.2.

position of again applying the two treaties involved, i.e., the treaty Y-Z and the treaty X-Z.[1161] In this particular case, however, the two treaties provide for different reductions in their WHT, being the source state obliged to apply the lower reduction as regards both treaties and now also under the confirmation that both the entity and its owners must be considered as the beneficial owners of the interest.[1162] Considering that the proposed solution is inspired by the treaty practice between Canada and the United States, some exceptions might also be applied considering other similar US tax treaty practices, such as the case of the tax treaty between Poland and the United States.[1163] As analysed already in this work, in a very similar situation (as Example 5), Article 1(6) US Model (i.e., Article 1(2) OECD Model) becomes not applicable if some preconditions are met.[1164] These preconditions are: (i) that the entity is considered as tax opaque under the law of the source state; (ii) that the entity receiving the interest payments is organised in a third State (not the treaty partners' States); and (iii) that the entity in this third State is eligible for the benefits of a treaty with the source state (i.e., it is a taxable entity there), and which are more favorable than the benefits provided between the treaty partners (i.e., the residence state of the members of the entity and the source state).[1165]

In spite of the fact that a dichotomy between Articles 1(2) and 10, 11, and 12 OECD Model (as regards the *beneficial ownership* requirement) seems to be addressed only through the use of 'deeming rules', or exceptions to the general principles, I still believe that this conflict might be solved perhaps in a simpler manner, without attending perhaps to the implementation of deeming rules within tax treaties. In other words, a step towards simplicity is crucial at this point. This step should start from the basis that perhaps Article 1(2) OECD Model is not the ideal solution to the problem of hybrids and reverse hybrid entities, i.e., a domestic problem with tax treaty implications. This author thus still argues in favour of a simpler domestic rule, which might also have a positive impact on the application of tax treaties.[1166]

5.3.2 *The OECD* 'Saving Clause' *and Relief from Double Taxation*

As well as the conflict with the beneficial ownership requirement in some allocative rules of the OECD Model, the solution of Article 1(2) OECD Model regarding who is entitled to the benefits of a tax treaty when income is received by or through a fiscally transparent entity, may also be limited by the application of the new OECD saving

1161. *Supra* s. 5.3.1.2.
1162. *Ibid.*
1163. US/PL: Article 1(6)((b) of the Convention between the United States of America and the Republic of Poland for the Avoidance of Double Taxation and the Prevention of Fiscal Evasion with respect to Taxes on Income of 13 February 2013. *Supra* s. 4.3.1.1.1.
1164. *Ibid.*
1165. *Ibid.*
1166. *Supra* Chapter 6, referred to the proposal for a '*reactive coordination rule*'.

clause, generating conflicts regarding the entitlement to double taxation relief under Article 23 OECD Model. These issues are analysed below.

5.3.2.1 *The OECD Saving Clause in a Nutshell*

Paragraph 3 of Article 1 OECD Model reads as follows:

> This Convention shall not affect the taxation, by a Contracting State, of its residents except with respect to the benefits granted under paragraph 3 of Article 7, paragraph 2 of Article 9 and Articles 19, 20, 23 [A] [B], 24, 25 and 28.[1167]

This provision, known in doctrine as the 'saving clause',[1168] aims at ensuring the Contracting States' right to tax its own residents, regardless of the application of the treaty and to the extent no other exceptions to the application of this provision apply.[1169] In other words, the OECD saving clause allows a Contracting State to impose taxation on its residents just because of being residents, even if a tax treaty imposes on it an obligation to limit its taxing rights fully or partially.[1170]

Although the wording of the OECD saving clause resembles almost exactly the US saving clause in Article 1(4) US Model, the OECD saving clause is certainly less complex and perhaps more limited in scope than the similar version in the US

1167. OECD (2017), *supra* n. 488, Article 1(3) OECD Model. The OECD BEPS proposal on Action 2, as regards tax treaties, came originally with a phrase in brackets saying: '[In no case shall the provisions of this paragraph be construed so as to restrict in any way a Contracting State's right to tax the residents of that State].' OECD, *Neutralizing the Effects of Hybrid Mismatch Arrangements*, OECD Publishing, Paris, 2014, p. 86. Similarly, para. 26.16 of the proposed Commentary on Article 1 provided: 'The last sentence of the paragraph clarifies that the paragraph is not intended to restrict in any way a State's right to tax its own residents.' *Ibid.*, p. 91. Although the final draft of the OECD BEPS Action 2 deleted this phrase, it kept para. 26.16 of the Commentaries on Article 1, which now provides: 'As confirmed by paragraph 3, paragraph 2 does not restrict in any way a State's right to tax its own residents.' OECD (2015), *supra* n. 6, p. 143.
1168. *Supra* s. 4.3.2. This provision resembles Article 1(4) US Model (saving clause).
1169. This has also been even recognised as a sort of general principle. For example, as stated in the Judgment of 17 September 2004, Tokyo District Court, 254 Zeimu Sosho Siryo: Electronic Version (Document on Tax Litigation) [ZSS] 244: 'As aforementioned, tax conventions generally do not amend national tax legislations of one state applicable to its residents. Therefore, unless otherwise provided for in tax conventions, contracting states reserve their rights to tax their own residents in accordance with their national tax legislations. This principle is called "Saving", and in the light of the above-mentioned concept of tax conventions, that principle must be applied even if tax conventions do not include a specific provision', cited in: Y. Suzuki, *Principle or Clause of 'Saving' in Tax Conventions: Introduction and Analysis of One Japanese Case*, WU International Taxation Research Paper Series No. 2015-07, available at SSRN.
1170. For more on the OECD saving clause, *see* L. Parada, *The OECD 'Saving Clause': An American Tailored Provision Made to Measure the World*, Rivista di diritto finanziario e scienza delle finanze, LXXVIII, 1, I, 13-52 (2019).

Model.[1171] Additionally, and as well as in the case of the US saving clause, the OECD saving clause is surprisingly limited by a series of exceptions, although all those cases excluded from the application of the saving clause assume that the same income is attributed to the same taxpayer, which is precisely the opposite than in cases involving the use of hybrid entities, that is, when two Contracting States do not agree with who is the taxpayer.[1172]

5.3.2.2 *The OECD Saving Clause and Hybrid Entities*

As noted already in this work, Article 1(2) OECD Model provides a potential solution to the problem of who is entitled to the benefits of a tax treaty when income is received by or through a fiscally transparent entity. In simple words, if income is received by an entity or arrangement that is considered tax transparent for one of the Contracting States, the benefits of the treaty will be allocated to the owners of that entity to the extent that they are also residents of the State treating the entity as tax transparent. However, at the same time, the OECD saving clause reserves the right of Contracting States to tax their residents regardless of the application of the treaty. This could bring us to odd situations, such as the case in which a Contracting State acting as source state and as the state in which a hybrid entity is located may, by application of Article 1(2), grant the benefits of a tax treaty to the resident partners in the residence state, but still tax the entity at source outside the tax treaty context. That is, by the sole fact of being a resident in that state, generating a situation of double taxation.

Let me illustrate the above with the following example. Let us assume that entity P is organized and resident in State P and has two owners, A and B, who are residents of State R. Accordingly, entity P receives interest from the same State P. Whilst State P considers the entity P as a taxable entity, State R considers the same entity as fiscally transparent. State P applies a general 30% WHT on gross interest paid abroad of 30%.

1171. For example, the OECD saving clause does not have to deal with conflicting cases where a taxpayer is a citizen of one Contracting State and resident in the other Contracting State, or with cases of former resident taxpayers. *See* Parada, *supra* n. 1170, p. 27. However, one could also argue that the scope of the OECD saving clause seems to be broader than just simply ensuring residence-based taxation, opening the door for countries to apply their own domestic anti-abuse legislation in cases where the result is precisely that the same income is attributed to different taxpayers in the two Contracting States. *See* G. Kofler, *Some Reflections on the 'Saving Clause'*, 44 Intertax 8/9 (2016), p. 575 DOI: 10.54648/taxi2016048. For an analysis of the US saving clause, *see supra* s. 4.3.2 of this chapter.

1172. Kofler, *supra* n. 1171, p. 579.

Figure 71 Article 1(2) OECD Model and OECD Saving Clause (Example 1)

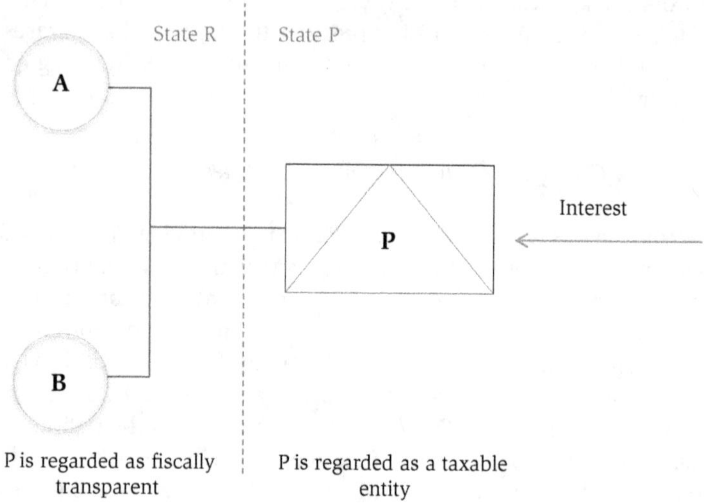

According to Article 1(2) OECD Model, partners A and B are entitled to the benefits of the treaty between R-P, i.e., a reduced withholding tax on interest in the source state, because indeed State R considers entity P as fiscally transparent and treats the interest as being received by two of its residents, that is, A and B. However, in the application of the saving clause, State P might also tax entity P – which is indeed a taxable entity in that country – regardless of the application of the treaty. In other words, State P, by application of its domestic law, has the right to tax entity P on its worldwide income. The question is, therefore, whether partners A and B might be able to claim a double taxation relief under Article 23 of the treaty R-P in State R based on the taxation of the interest in the hands of entity P by application of the saving clause. Unfortunately, the answer is not straightforward.[1173]

On the one hand, there will be those who argue for an extensive interpretation of Article 23 OECD Model, supporting a double taxation relief in State R. The reasoning behind this is simple and attends to the fact that double taxation should be avoided as per the traditional object and purpose of tax treaties. This reasoning might be well supported by treaty practice. For instance, the tax treaty between Germany-Australia (2015), although not specifically providing an indirect tax credit, recognises the double tax issue and allows the possibility of a MAP to solve it.[1174] Similarly, the United

1173. Indeed, the application of the saving clause and the relief from double taxation represents a situation of residence-residence tax treaty relation rather than one of residence-source.

1174. As stated in the Protocol: 'If, in accordance with paragraph 2 of Article 1, income is taxed in a Contracting State in the hands of an entity or arrangement that is treated as wholly or partially fiscally transparent under the laws of the other Contracting State and is also taxed in the hands of a resident of that other State as a participant in such entity or arrangement, *and this results in double taxation*, the competent authorities of the Contracting States shall consult each other pursuant to Article 25 to find the appropriate solution' (emphasis added).

Kingdom has the practice of providing for a tax credit where the same income is taxed by the other State, even when this is taxed in the hands of two different persons, and regardless of the existence of a fiscally transparent entity,[1175] although the UK case law may not be entirely consistent.[1176] However, even if a credit could be granted, one should not underestimate the challenges associated with the determination of the tax credit in practice. Indeed, in the example above, it will be very difficult to ensure that the income taxed in State P corresponds to the same income that is taxed in the hands of A and B later. This is important because if the conclusion is that the taxation of the interest in the hands of entity P relies exclusively upon its status as resident in State P and not in the application of Article 11 of the R-P treaty, there will be – in principle – no obligation for State R to provide relief from double taxation.[1177]

On the other hand, there will be those who argue that it is very difficult to grant relief from double taxation in practice when no taxes have been paid directly by A and B in State P.[1178] In other words, unless one interprets Article 23 OECD Model extensively to include a potential indirect tax credit, relief from double taxation in State R would result inappropriate, at least from a strict interpretation of the treaty.[1179]

Things may become even odder if we consider the application of a complete distributive rule, such as the case that no PE is constituted in the source state or that instead of interest income, entity P receives royalties. In both cases, the exclusive taxing rights will be allocated to the residence state. Therefore, the question is whether the source state may still tax such income on its resident entity, even though the specific distributive rule prevents it from doing so.[1180] Let me illustrate this by taking

---

See AUS/DE: Protocol to the Agreement between Australia and the Federal Republic of Germany for the elimination of Double Taxation with respect to Taxes on Income and on Capital and the prevention of Fiscal Evasion and Avoidance, of 12 November 2015, Article 2 of the Protocol with reference to paragraph 2, Article 1 of the Convention.

1175. Nikolakakis et al., *supra* n. 985, p. 347.

1176. *See, e.g.*, UK: CA, 23 March 2011, *Bayfine UK v. Commissioner for H M Revenue and Customs*, [2011] EWCA Civ 304, where the United Kingdom claimed exclusive rights to tax since no PE was constituted in the United States. In this case, the United States applied taxation according to Article 1(3) of the UK-US tax treaty [*saving clause*]. For a detailed analysis, *see* Arnold, *supra* n. 1043, pp. 495-496. *See also*, Cleave (2011), *supra* n. 347 (on the Bayfine case). Similarly, *see* UK: *Anson (Apellant) v. Commissioners for Her Majesty's Revenue and Customs (Respondent) [2015] UKSC 44 on appeal from [2013] EWCA Civ 63*, 1 July 2015, where relief was granted on the view that the income of the entity should be attributed to the members as such (as the 'same income'), even though the member did not have a direct or indirect proprietary interest in the any of the entity's property income. *See* more in, for example, Lemos, *supra* n. 620, p. 46. *See also*, Popa, *supra* n. 622. *See also*, Rogers, Cassidy and Mace, *supra* n. 640. More recently, *see* McGowan, *supra* n. 541, pp. 42-52 (analysing the case in its different judicial stages).

1177. Parada, *supra* n. 1170, p. 36.

1178. However, this may not be necessarily a problem if the residence state applies the exemption method rather than the credit method to relieve double taxation.

1179. In this sense, Lang argues: "I am not convinced about the legal basis for such an indirect tax credit, even though it eliminates double taxation. It might be difficult to interpret article 23 so extensively that an indirect credit has to be granted'. Opinion of M. Lang in the conference 'Practical Problems of Tax Treaty Interpretation and Application', held in Vienna on 21 October 2013, and summarized in: K. Dziurdz, D. Fuentes and E. Pinetz, *Case Studies on Partnerships and Other Hybrid Entities*, 68 Bull. Intl. Taxn. 3 (2014), p. 153.

1180. Parada, *supra* n. 1170, p. 37.

the example of Figure 71 with the only variation that instead of interest, entity P receives royalties.[1181]

Figure 72 Article 1(2) OECD Model and OECD Saving Clause (Example 2)

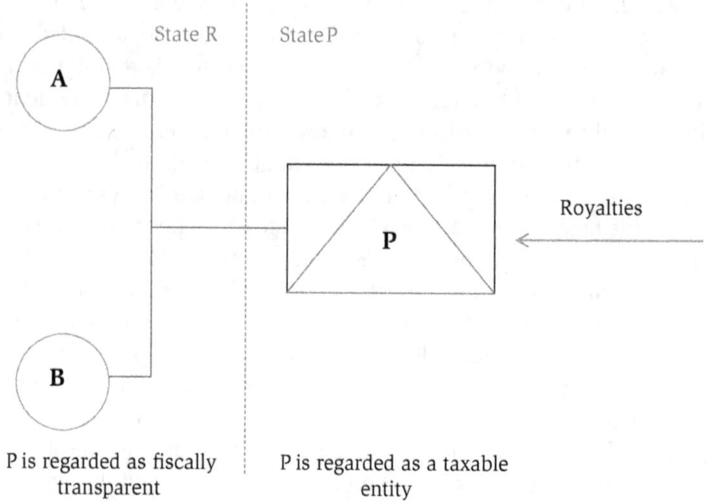

Following the OECD Partnership Report's majority opinion, State P (source state) would not limit its taxing rights by the treaty since this situation amounts to a purely domestic issue.[1182] In other words, State P would be simply exercising its sovereign right to tax a domestic resident entity on its domestic income, and the treaty would not impose a limit to this right at all. However, the OECD Partnership Report's minority opinion argued that State P, in our example, should provide relief from double taxation by allowing State R to exercise its exclusive taxing right upon the royalties in the hands of the partners of entity P, i.e., A and B.[1183] This would suggest that the residence state may be obliged to provide relief from double taxation even in the absence of a PE in the source state, which is nonetheless arguable, at least following a strict interpretation of the wording of Article 23 OECD Model.[1184] This leaves us again without a definitive answer.[1185]

1181. This example resembles Example 17 of the OECD Partnership Report. *See* OECD (1999), *supra* n. 1.
1182. *Ibid.*, para. 131.
1183. *Ibid.*, para. 132.
1184. *Ibid.*, para. 133 in connection to paras 100 and 104-105.
1185. Dziurdz, Fuentes and Pinetz, *supra* n. 1179.

5.3.2.3 *The New OECD Commentaries*

Conscious of the issues regarding the application of the saving clause and the tax treaty relief under Article 23 OECD Model, especially in cases where the same income is attributed to different taxpayers, such as the case of hybrid entities, the OECD proposed in paragraph 64 of the OECD BEPS Action 6 some modifications to the Commentaries on Articles 23A and 23B.[1186] This proposal has already been introduced in the 2017 OECD Model as a new paragraph 11.1 of the Commentaries on Articles 23A and 23B, which reads as follows:

> In some cases, the same income or capital may be taxed by each Contracting State as income or capital of one of its residents. This may happen where, for example, one of the Contracting States taxes the worldwide income of an entity that is a resident of that State, whereas the other State views that entity as fiscally transparent and taxes the members of that entity who are residents of that other State on their respective share of the income.[1187]

This situation described in the paragraph above resembles, to a certain extent, the conflictive interaction between the solution provided in Article 1(2) OECD Model and the application of the OECD saving clause.[1188] Paragraph 11.1 continues as follows:

> the phrase (*except to the extent that these provisions allow taxation by that other State solely because the income is also income derived by a resident of that State*) clarifies in such cases, both States are not reciprocally obliged to provide relief for each other's tax levied exclusively on the basis of the residence of the taxpayer and that each State is therefore only obliged to provide relief of double taxation to the extent that taxation by the other State is in accordance with provisions of the Convention that allow taxation of the relevant income as the State of source or as a State where there is a permanent establishment to which that income is attributable, thereby excluding taxation that would solely be the result of the residence of a person in that other State (emphasis added).[1189]

Based on the text above, one could conclude that Paragraph 11.1 leaves no doubts that the residence state has no obligation to provide double taxation relief under Article 23 OECD Model to the extent this taxation is based exclusively on the residence of the taxpayer in the source state and not the application of the treaty, which is precisely what the OECD the saving clause seems to allow.[1190]

1186. OECD (2015), *supra* n. 226, para. 64 (replacement of Article 23B OECD Model), p. 88.
1187. OECD Commentary on Articles 23A and 23B, para. 11.1
1188. *Supra* s. 4.3.2.2.
1189. Originally, the wording said: '... in accordance with paragraph 3 of Article 1'. For the specific proposal on Action 6, *see* OECD (2015), *supra* n. 226.
1190. Parada, *supra* n. 1170, p. 38.

It is arguable that this solution could not be achieved by the simple interpretation of Article 23 OECD Model.[1191] However, the inclusion of paragraph 11.1 to the OECD Commentaries on Article 23 provides some certainty, especially considering that the questions remained open since the 1999 OECD Partnership report.[1192] Yet, paragraph 11.1 of the Commentary on Article 23 still leaves some open questions.

First, the true intention behind the existence of a saving clause within the OECD Model is still unclear.[1193] Most notably, it challenges the existence of a saving clause in itself because if a new paragraph 11.1 clarifies that a Contracting State may tax one of its residents on worldwide income and due to its residence status exclusively, and at the same time clarifies that in such a case the other Contracting State has no obligation to relieve double taxation based on the tax treaty that both states signed, the existence of a saving clause to ensure such residence-based taxation becomes superfluous. As acknowledged in the OECD BEPS Action Plan 2 (Deliverable 2014): 'A proposal included in the Treaty Abuse Discussion Draft would make that paragraph [paragraph 3, Article 1] unnecessary'.[1194] This quotation refers precisely to the draft proposal of a new paragraph 11.1 within the commentaries on Article 23 OECD Model, which, although introduced in the 2017 OECD Model, kept the saving clause untouched. The foregoing serves to reinforce the idea already stressed in this work, which is that the purpose of the saving clause would be certainly beyond simply ensuring residence taxation.[1195]

Second, paragraph 11.1 clarifies that the taxpayer in the residence state will remain in a permanent double taxation status unless a domestic relief is provided. Let me illustrate this again using the facts from the example in Figure 72.

1191. OECD (1999), *supra* n. 1, para. 133 in connection to paras 100 and 104-105.
1192. *See* discussion at *supra* s. 5.3.2.2 of this chapter.
1193. On the discussion regarding the rationale behind the OECD saving clause, *see* Kofler, *supra* n. 1171 (arguing that the saving clause may open the door for the application of domestic anti-avoidance rules). *See also*, J. Sasseville, *A Tax Treaty Perspective: Special Issues*, in: G. Maisto (ed.), *Tax Treaties and Domestic Law*, EC and International Tax Law Series, Vol. 2, IBFD, Amsterdam (2006), p. 49 (arguing that 'the true purpose of the saving clause, as regards residence taxation, is to prevent the treaty from restricting residence taxation in an unintended way'). Therefore, the purpose of the OECD saving clause appears to be broader than simply ensuring residence taxation in the source state.
1194. OECD (2014), *supra* n. 48.
1195. *Ibid*.

Figure 73 Saving Clause and Unrelieved Double Taxation

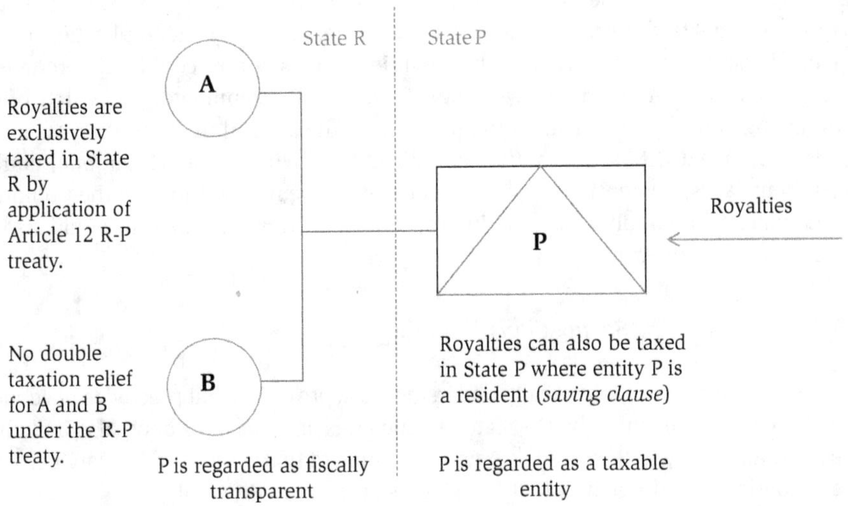

In this case, the partners of entity P will be taxed on the amount of interest received through entity P. This is due to the application of Article 1(2) of the treaty between States R-P, as well as by the application of the specific allocative rule in Article 12.[1196] However, this does not truly prevent entity P from being taxed on those royalties, although not by the application of Article 12 of the R-S treaty, but exclusively due to its status as a resident in State P (source state). Similarly, partners A and B have no right to claim relief from double taxation under the treaty between States R-P unless entity P is regarded as a PE in State P, and those royalties are indeed attributed to that PE, which is assumed not to happen in this case. As a result, therefore, A and B will remain in a permanent situation of unrelieved double taxation.[1197]

The double taxation outcome above seems to contradict the traditional object and purpose of tax treaties, which, beyond formalisms, is intended to avoid double taxation.[1198] Indeed, if we attend strictly to this aim, the double taxation resulting from the application of the saving clause in the cases of hybrid entities should be prevented.[1199] Therefore, the question seems to be how rather than why to prevent double taxation in these cases. As stressed already in this work, the textual interpretation of Article 23 OECD Model does not allow us to conclude that a double taxation obligation exists. Thus, some alternatives are needed.

1196. This example also assumes that A and B are indeed the beneficial owners of the income.
1197. Parada, *supra* n. 1170, p. 40, Example 6.
1198. For the discussion on the object and purpose of tax treaties, *see* Chapter 2 of this book.
1199. This interpretation also appears to recognise the practice of some countries as to grant double taxation relief in those situations. *See*, for example, the cases of the treaty Germany-Australia or the treaty practice in the UK at *supra* n. 1175 and 1177.

5.3.2.4 *A 'Reverse Saving Clause' as an Alternative Solution*

As I already argued in the tax literature, the introduction of a 'reverse saving clause' may help mitigate the cases of double taxation generated by the application of the saving clause in cases involving hybrid entities. This solution could be materialised through a modification in the wording of the OECD Commentaries, which offers Contracting States an opportunity to opt out from the general interpretation of Article 23A and 23 B OECD Model, granting an indirect tax credit to relief (economic) double taxation in cases they decide to.[1200] In other words, the new wording of the Commentaries will leave no doubts that if an indirect tax credit was granted, this would also be in accordance with Article 23.

5.3.2.4.1 A '*Reverse Saving Clause*' in Brief

A reverse saving clause is generally understood as a provision that precludes residence-based taxation of an entity by the State in which this entity is a resident, also including the distributions by that entity.[1201] A good example of this could be the treaty between the Netherlands and Belgium (2001), which states in the Protocol:

> Where a company is subject to tax as such in a Contracting State but the income or capital of this company is, in the other Contracting State, taxed as income or capital of the participants in this company, *the provisions of this Convention shall not be allowed to result in double taxation* or a total or partial exemption of such income or capital. In order to avoid such effect, the tax, the income and the capital of the company shall be considered as the tax, income and capital of the participants in this company in proportion to their entitlement to the company's capital. *To the extent necessary, the participants in the company should be allowed, each for their part, to credit the tax levied on the company in respect of this income or this capital (including any tax withheld at the source in third States) against the tax for which they are liable in respect of the same income or the same capital,* and that the State of residence of the company waives possible taxation of the participants in this company who are residents of the other Contracting State in respect of the profits distributed by this company to such participants (emphasis added).[1202]

Accordingly, the Protocol provides:

> Where a company is not subject to tax as such in a Contracting State and is subject to tax as such in the other Contracting State, the other Contracting State shall apply, at the request of the company, the provisions of Chapters III, IV and V of this convention insofar as these provisions would have had to be applied if the persons having rights in the company's capital had directly received or possessed, each proportionally to its share in that company, the income or capital of said company. The application of the preceding sentence shall in no way affect that the other

1200. Parada, *supra* n. 1170.
1201. Nikolakakis et al., *supra* n. 985, p. 354.
1202. Convention between the Kingdom of Belgium and the Kingdom of the Netherlands for the Avoidance of Double Taxation and the Prevention of Fiscal Evasion with respect to Taxes on Income and on Capital and its Protocol I of 15 June 2001, Article 2 of the Protocol with respect to Article 3(1)(c) of the Convention.

Contracting State shall determine, pursuant to its domestic laws, the taxable base of the company and shall reduce this base only insofar as such reduction results from the preceding sentence.[1203]

A reverse saving clause appears, therefore, as a practical and, to a certain extent, also a fairer solution to the double taxation generated by the application of the saving clause in cases involving hybrid entities, providing an indirect tax credit for the participants regarding the taxes paid at the level of the entity. Let me illustrate this using the following example.[1204] Let us assume that P is a partnership established in State P and owned by A and B (equally), who are residents in State R. State R considers entity P as a tax-transparent entity whilst State P considers entity P as a taxable entity. Entity P 100 of interest income from State P that is not attributable to a PE in there. In addition, State P imposes a corporate income tax of 30%, whilst A and B are subject to the highest progressive bracket of personal income tax (40%) in State R.

Figure 74 Reverse Saving Clause (Ex-Post Effect)

	Partners A/B (individually considered)	Entity P taxation
Interest Income	35	100
Gross-up	15	-
Taxable Income	50	100
Tax	20	30
Tax Credit	(15)	-
Total tax burden	5	30

As demonstrated in the table above, the individual position of owners A and B (regarding double taxation) is better off after the application of the reverse saving clause.[1205] Indeed, after the application of the reverse saving clause, each partner of entity P (A and B) will receive a credit of 15 for the taxes paid at the level of the entity in the source state P. Therefore, their overall tax burden is substantially reduced, alleviating the double tax effect derived from the taxation of entity P as a resident of state P (source state).

5.3.2.4.2 An Optional '*Reverse Saving Clause*'

As I have argued somewhere else already, the introduction of a reverse saving clause could be easily offered as an option for those countries who want to opt for it. This could be materialised as an alternative or exception to the general interpretation in paragraph 11.1 of the OECD Commentaries on Articles 23 OECD Model, which in

1203. *Ibid.*, Article 4(b) of the Protocol with respect to Article 4 of the Convention.
1204. This is based on the example in Parada, *supra* n. 1170, p. 43, Figure 7.
1205. *Ibid.*

practice implies two simple modifications to the current text of the OECD Commentaries.[1206] First, including the expression 'in principle' in the text of paragraph 11.1 of the Commentary on Article 23A and 23B, which would now read as follows:

> the phrase (*except to the extent that these provisions allow taxation by that other State solely because the income is also income derived by a resident of that State*) clarifies in such cases, both States are ***in principle*** not reciprocally obliged to provide relief for each other's tax levied exclusively on the basis of the residence of the taxpayer and that each State is therefore only obliged to provide relief of double taxation to the extent that taxation by the other State is in accordance with provisions of the Convention that allow taxation of the relevant income as the State of source or as a State where there is a permanent establishment to which that income is attributable, thereby excluding taxation that would solely be the result of the residence of a person in that other State [emphasis and bold added].

Second, introducing a new paragraph within the same paragraph 11.1 of the Commentaries on Articles 23 OECD Model which reinforces the idea of offering an indirect tax credit in case the Contracting States decide to do so. This new paragraph would read as follows:

> However, where a company is subject to tax as such in a Contracting State but the income or capital of this company is, in the other Contracting State, taxed as income or capital of the participants in this company because the income is also income derived by a resident of that State, the Contracting States may also agree that the income and the capital of the company shall be considered as the tax, income and capital of the participants in this company in proportion to their entitlement to the company's capital in order to avoid double taxation.[1207]

Therefore, considering these modifications, Article 23 should be, in principle, interpreted as not imposing any obligation on the residence state to provide double taxation relief to the extent this outcome is based exclusively upon the residence of the taxpayer in the source state. However, the modifications proposed would allow both Contracting States to decide otherwise, that is, to provide double tax relief. If that is the case, this decision will be supported by the interpretation of Article 23.[1208]

The proposed solution possesses some advantages, including its consistent approach with the main object and purpose of tax treaties, which is to avoid double taxation.[1209] It also does not alter the traditional understanding that 'in principle' Article 23 does not impose an obligation to relieve double taxation based exclusively on the residence status of the taxpayers,[1210] and it is easy to implement as well.[1211] However, it carries some evident disadvantages, too. For example, it is widely known

1206. Parada, *supra* n. 1170 (where an optional reverse saving clause was originally proposed).
1207. This text is inspired in the tax treaty practice analyses already at *supra* s. 4.3.2.4.1 of this chapter.
1208. *Ibid.*, pp. 44-45.
1209. However, this should be read with the caveat that tax treaties do not exist primarily to alleviate double taxation. For a full analysis on this matter, *see supra* Chapter 2 of this book.
1210. In this opinion, for example, Lang cited in: Dziurdz, Fuentes and Pinetz, *supra* n. 1179.
1211. Indeed, an optional reverse saving clause could be considered a formal recognition of a practice already in force in some countries around the world. *See* Parada, *supra* n. 1170. *See also*, *supra* s. 4.3.2.4.1 of this chapter.

that the interpretative role and the legal nature of the OECD Commentaries can be an obstacle to making this proposal widely spread, especially considering that the OECD Commentaries are neither an instrument made in connection with the conclusion of a treaty nor preparatory work used or produced in preparing an individual treaty.[1212] Therefore, they could arguably have an interpretative role. Similarly, the optional character of the proposed reverse saving clause may appear in principle as disadvantageous because it may bring some countries to sign treaties opting for a reverse saving clause whilst others do not, which may ultimately create opportunities for treaty shopping.[1213] Yet, and as argued somewhere already, this concern appears to be more apparent than real since all the provisions within the OECD Model, as well as its Commentaries, are subject to reservations and observations taken into account during the treaty negotiation process.[1214] Therefore, the concern that some countries may opt in some cases for the proposed reverse saving clause and in others not becomes completely irrelevant because the same concern can be applied to all other provisions and Commentaries within the OECD Model.[1215] Finally, some may rightfully argue that tax treaties should not be concerned about residence-residence double taxation, which is indeed the situation when a saving clause applies,[1216] and ultimately, they should not provide a double taxation relief in cases of economic double taxation.[1217] However, this approach is rather formalistic than policy-oriented and should, in any case, be regarded as an unbreakable tax treaty principle.[1218] Indeed, if tax treaties represent the goodwill of two countries to limit their sovereign taxing rights in order to avoid double taxation, they should also be flexible enough to recognise that, in some cases, that double tax burden may well derive from income being taxed twice in the hands of two different taxpayers and that no serious policy reasons justify leaving the solutions to these cases of double taxation exclusively to domestic provisions or isolated tax treaty practices of countries.[1219]

5.3.3 Article 1(2) OECD Model and Developing Countries: Brief Comments

All the illustrations regarding the application of Article 1(2) OECD Model allow us to see its preferential results for the residence state. It is interesting, thus, that developing countries, normally acting as source states in bilateral relations, may be willing to

1212. *See, e.g.*, Reimer, *supra* n. 268, p. 135. Conversely, in *Thiel v. Federal Commissioner of Taxation* in Australia, there is a clear reference to the OECD Commentaries as 'supplementary means of interpretation' for the purposes of Article 32 of the VCLT. *See* AU: *Thiel v. Federal Commissioner of Taxation* [1990] HCA 37; 171 CLR 338, cited in: Krever and Mellor, *supra* n. 243, p. 42.
1213. Parada, *supra* n. 1170, p. 49.
1214. *Ibid.*, pp. 50-51.
1215. *Ibid.*
1216. For an analysis on 'residence-residence' and 'source-source' conflicts of attribution of income within tax treaties, *see* R. Danon, *Qualification of Taxable Entities and Treaty Protection*, 68 Bull. Intl. Taxn. 4/5 (2014).
1217. Lang, *supra* n. 222.
1218. Parada, *supra* n. 1170, p. 48.
1219. *Ibid.*

include such a provision within their tax treaty network. Contrary to this logic, however, the UN Committee of Experts on International Cooperation in Tax Matters has agreed to include within the UN Model a provision like Article 1(2) OECD Model.[1220] This does not only contradict the historic position of the UN Committee of Experts as not recognising the principles of the OECD Partnership report[1221] but may also negatively impact the tax base of developing countries.

Let me illustrate the economic impact of a provision like Article 1(2) OECD Model introduced within the UN Model using the following example.[1222] Let us imagine a company R that is resident in State R, which is the sole proprietorship of an entity H, resident in State H, and which provides services to its client in a third country S, a developing country, constituting a PE in this country. Likewise, whilst State H and State S consider entity H as a taxable entity, State R considers it as a fiscally transparent entity. It is also assumed that the treaty between State R and State S follows the OECD Model and does not include a service PE provision.[1223]

Figure 75 Article 1(2) OECD Model and Developing Countries

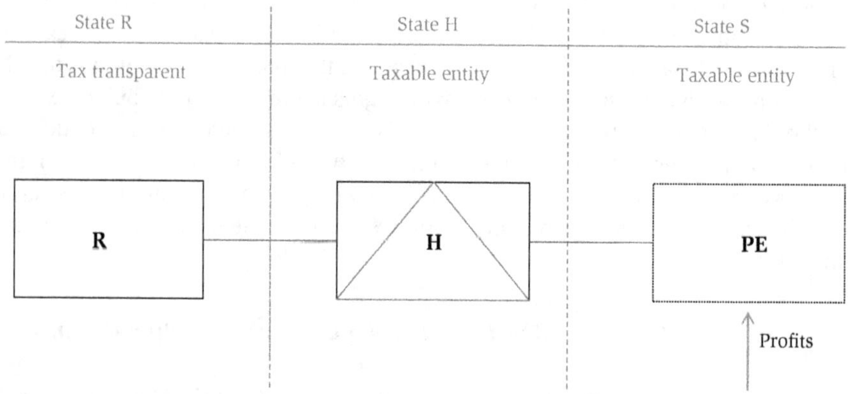

Under the treaty H-S, there is a service PE in State S. Thus, State S has the right to tax the profits attributable to that PE. However, by application of Article 1(2) R-S treaty, those profits are income of R. Under the treaty between R-S, there is no PE constituted in State S.

1220. UN (2016), *supra* n. 1131.

1221. The principles of the OECD Partnership Report were never acknowledged. This idea is not derived from the official minutes of meetings sustained by the Committee of Experts discussing the principles of the OECD Partnership Report, but by the reading of paras 5 and 6 of the Commentary on Article 1 UN Model. *See* UN: United Nations Model Tax Convention between Developed and Developing Countries, UN, New York, 2011, p. 42.

1222. Regardless that the analysis is focused on the impact in the tax base of developing countries, the legal concern raised here regarding to the interplay between Article 1(2) OECD Model and the concept of beneficial owner can be indeed reproduced in the case of a provision within the UN Model.

1223. This example is extracted from Sanghavi to explain what he calls the 'economic anomalies' of Article 1(2) OECD Model. *See* Sanghavi, *supra* n. 1124, pp. 361-362, Figure 2.

According to the treaty between State H and State S, the business profits generated by entity H are attributable to its PE in State S. Thus, State S has the right to tax those profits attributable to the PE according to Article 7 of the treaty H-S. Of course, State H will tax the same profits in the hands of entity H, providing relief from double taxation as per the treaty H-S. However, according to Article 1(2) R-S treaty, the profits must also be attributed to company R, which is also entitled to the benefits of the treaty R-S. This result is given by the sole fact that State R treats entity H as fiscally transparent, and the income is allocated to a resident of State R. Likewise, considering that the treaty R-S does not contain a service PE provision, i.e., there is no PE as per the understanding of the treaty R-S, Article 7 of the R-S treaty prevents State S from taxing any of the profits associated to the services rendered in State S. Moreover, double taxation may occur since State H will anyway tax the profits of entity H in State H, and these profits will be taxed again in State R, at the level of company R. Therefore, unless under the treaty R-H entity H is regarded as a PE in State H, there will be no relief from double taxation in State R. The same results if States R and State H do not have a treaty at all.

It is surprising that the outcome above explained by which the source state (State S) must give up its taxing rights just because the residence state of the partner (company R) considers entity H as fiscally transparent is indeed accepted by State S when indeed the erosion of its tax base and the negative economic impact is rather evident. This situation also resembles the example analysed at *supra* section 5.3.1, where the source state should give the benefits of a reduced WHT not only to the country where the intermediary entity was established, which is correct since both countries treated that intermediary entity as a taxable entity, but also to the State where the partners of this entity were residents. In this latter case, simply because the residence state of the partners treated the entity established in a third State as fiscally transparent.[1224] This certainly benefited the residence state of the partners since the reduction of the WHT was lower in the treaty between the residence of the partners and the source state in comparison to the treaty between the residence state of the entity and the source state. Once again, the sole fact that the residence state of the partners considers the intermediary entity as fiscally transparent granted the partners a more beneficial tax treaty, jeopardising the position of the source state. Therefore, from a policy perspective, it is arguable that a provision such as the one introduced in the OECD Model may have any benefits for developing countries once introduced in the UN Model, which is an instrument that by nature aims to protect the interest of developing countries in the negotiation of tax treaties.

1224. The 'deemed' *beneficial owner* proposal reaffirms this conclusion as well. *Supra* s. 5.3.1.1. However, the alternative stated within the United States/Poland tax treaty seems to be a suitable and fairer alternative from a source state's perspective. *Supra* s. 4.3.1.1.1.

6 TRANSPARENT ENTITIES AND THE MLI: SOME BRIEF REMARKS

This last Section has the purpose of briefly stressing some issues with regard to Article 3(1) MLI and some other related provisions within the MLI dealing with transparent entities.[1225] As most of the provisions resemble or directly refer to the interpretation of the OECD Model proposal in Article 1(2), this section will stress only the most important commonalities and differences, avoiding any unnecessary repetition.[1226]

6.1 Article 3(1) MLI: A Mirror of Article 1(2) OECD Model

Article 3(1) MLI states as follows:

> For the purposes of a Covered Tax Agreement, income derived by or through an entity or arrangement that is treated as wholly or partly fiscally transparent under the tax law of either Contracting Jurisdiction shall be considered to be income of a resident of a Contracting Jurisdiction but only to the extent that the income is treated, for purposes of taxation by that Contracting Jurisdiction, as the income of a resident of that Contracting Jurisdiction.[1227]

Therefore, as it can be easily noted, both the text of Article 1(2) OECD Model and the text of Article 3(1) MLI are exactly the same. Indeed, the MLI Explanatory Statements notes that Article 3(1) MLI replicates the text of Article 1(2) OECD Model 'with changes made solely to conform the terminology used in the model provision to the terminology used in this Convention'.[1228] Therefore, since the MLI Explanatory Statements do not elaborate further on the interpretation of Article 3(1) MLI, one might presume that the intention is to give relevance to the OECD Commentaries on Article 1(2) in this regard.[1229] Therefore, the analysis and conclusions achieved as regards the interpretation and application of Article 1(2) OECD Model can also be extended to

---

1225. OECD (2016), Text of the Multilateral Convention to Implement Tax treaty Related Measures to prevent Base Erosion and Profit Shifting, adopted on 24 November 2016, Part II-Hybrid Mismatches (hereinafter also, 'MLI text'); OECD, *Explanatory Statement to the Multilateral Convention to Implement Tax Treaty Related Measures to Prevent Base Erosion and Profit Shifting*, OECD Publishing, Paris, 2016 (hereinafter also, 'MLI Explanatory Statements'). For a critical analysis of the MLI, *see* J. Zornoza, *Acción 15. El instrumento multilateral y el plan de acción BEPS* in: J. Ramos (coord.), *Erosión de la Base Imponible y Traslado de Beneficios: Estudios sobre el plan BEPS de la OCDE*, Aranzadi, Navarra (2016), pp. 425-452. *See also*, N. Bravo, *A Multilateral Instrument for Updating the Tax Treaty Network* (IBFD Doctoral Series, 2020). *See also*, R. García Antón, *Multilateral Dynamics in Bilateral Settings: Back to Realpolitik* British Tax Review 4 (2019) (stressing the constant tensions between global standards and bilateral approaches in the path towards multilateralism).

1226. However, for a recent analysis on hybrid entity mismatches and the MLI, *see* L. Parada, *Hybrid Entity Mismatches and the MLI: A Tax Policy Assessment*, 49 Intertax 10 (2021) DOI: 10.54648/taxi2021085.

1227. OECD (2016), MLI Text, *supra* n. 1225, Article 3(1).

1228. OECD (2016), MLI Explanatory Statements, *supra* n. 1225, para. 40.

1229. For example, the MLI Explanatory Statements establish: 'The commentary that was developed during the course of the BEPS Project and reflected in the Final BEPS Package has particular relevance in this regard.' *Ibid.*, para. 12. In the same opinion: Nikolakakis et al., *supra* n. 985, pp. 298-299.

Article 3(1) MLI without the need for further analysis.[1230] Finally, it is perhaps important to note that Article 3(1) MLI is not required as a minimum standard. Therefore, a Party may opt completely out of this article.[1231]

6.2 '*Saving Clause*' and Relief from Double Taxation

As well as the OECD Model, the MLI includes expressly two provisions dealing with the rights of the Contracting States to tax their own residents. These provisions are optional, and they can be selected in a detailed version, i.e., Article 11 MLI, or in a simplified one, i.e., Article 3(3) MLI with regard to Article 3(1) MLI.[1232] In both cases, the ultimate purpose of the provision is to ensure that Contracting States within a tax treaty are not precluded from taxing their own residents.[1233] However, whilst the version of Article 11 MLI seems to retain the obligations to provide double taxation relief under provisions such as Article 7(3), Article 9, Article 19, Article 20, Article 23A and 23B, Article 24, Article 25 and Article 28 OECD Model, Article 3(3) MLI does not expressly preserve treaty obligations regarding those articles.[1234] Therefore, the inclusion of one provision or the other might not have the same effect.[1235]

There are also two other provisions in the MLI dealing with tax credits and exemption obligations that should be considered. The first one is Article 3(2), which provides:

> Provisions of a Covered Tax Agreement that require a Contracting Jurisdiction to exempt from income tax or provide a deduction or credit equal to the income tax paid with respect to income derived by a resident of that Contracting Jurisdiction which may be taxed in the other Contracting Jurisdiction according to the provisions of the Covered Tax Agreement shall not apply to the extent that such provisions allow taxation by that other Contracting Jurisdiction solely because the income is also income derived by a resident of that other Contracting Jurisdiction.[1236]

As noted, the wording mirrors the already analysed paragraph 11.1 of the OECD Commentaries on Articles 23A and 23B,[1237] stating that both States *are not* reciprocally obliged to provide relief for each other's tax levied exclusively on the basis of the residence of the taxpayer. In contrast, they are only obliged to provide relief of double

1230. *Supra* s. 5.
1231. OECD (2016), MLI Explanatory Statements, *supra* n. 1225, para. 46.
1232. Article 3(3) MLI states that, with respect to Covered Agreements for which one or more parties have made the reservation of Article 11(3) MLI, the following sentence must be added to Article 3(1): 'In no case shall the provisions of this paragraph be construed to affect a Contracting State Jurisdiction's right to tax the residents of that Contracting Jurisdiction.' OECD (2016), MLI Text, *supra* n. 1225, Article 3(3). For an analysis regarding the optionality of the saving clause within the MLI, *see*, e.g., V. Chand, *Should States Opt for the Saving Clause in the Multilateral Instrument?*, 86 Tax Notes Int'l. 8 (2017).
1233. Nikolakakis et al., *supra* n. 985, p. 345.
1234. OECD (2016), MLI Text, *supra* n. 1225, Article 11 and Article 3(3).
1235. Nikolakakis et al., *supra* n. 985, p. 345.
1236. OECD (2016), MLI Text, *supra* n. 1225, Article 3(2).
1237. *Supra* s. 5.3.2.

taxation to the extent that taxation by the other State is in accordance with provisions of the Convention that allow taxation of the relevant income as the State of source or as a State where there is a permanent establishment to which that income is attributable.[1238]

Similarly, Article 5 MLI – Option C, which applies only to credit-based relief along the lines of Article 23B OECD Model, would limit the obligation of the residence state to the extent that the treaty allows taxation by the other Contracting State solely because the income is also income of a resident of that other Contracting State.[1239] Indeed, as provided by the article: 'Where a resident of a Contracting Jurisdiction derives income or owns capital which may be taxed in the other Contracting Jurisdiction in accordance with the provisions of a Covered Tax Agreement (except to the extent that these provisions allow taxation by that other Contracting Jurisdiction solely because the income is also income derived by a resident of that other Contracting Jurisdiction), the first-mentioned Contracting Jurisdiction shall allow […].'[1240]

Therefore, as well as stressed with respect to paragraph 11.1 to the Commentaries on Article 23A and 23B OECD Model, the approach adopted within the MLI may create similar problems of double taxation relief, especially with the interaction between Article 3(1) MLI and the saving clause options offered. The analysis in previous sections is therefore perfectly applicable here as well.[1241]

7 FINAL REMARKS

The allocation of taxing rights between countries due to the application of a tax treaty is not an easy task because it assumes to renounce part of the sovereignty of a State to tax. This task becomes even more complex when countries do not agree on the tax treatment that a foreign entity should have for domestic tax purposes. Such a decision is also crucial for tax treaty purposes since tax treaties do not deal with the characterisation of entities, as this is strictly a domestic tax issue.

Since the OECD Partnership Report in 1999, the solutions provided have been, intentionally or not, designed in a way winners and losers seem to appear clearly established, giving residence states a more favourable position when compared to source states. The above can be noticed in the materialisation of those principles both in Article 1(6) US Model and Article 1(2) OECD Model. However, this does not rest merit to these provisions that mirror one another, although it must be recognised that this is perhaps the source of the problem as well.

Article 1(6) US Model is a provision created to protect the position of the United States both as a resident and source state. When the provision is analysed with the

1238. OECD (2015), *supra* n. 226, p. 89, text of para. 11.1 to the Commentary on Article 23A and 23B.
1239. Nikolakakis et al., *supra* n. 985, p. 347. These authors stress that, curiously, there is no such option as regards the exemption-based relief along the lines of Article 23A OECD Model, regardless that para. 64 of the OECD BEPS Action Plan 6 (current paragraph 11.1 of the Commentaries) provides such a proposal.
1240. OECD (2016), MLI Text, *supra* n. 1225, Article 5, Option C.
1241. For more on the MLI and hybrid entities, *see* Parada, *supra* n. 1226.

United States as the residence state, it fits perfectly with the policy that the benefits of a treaty signed by the United States are not allocated to persons other than US persons. Therefore, when an item of income is received through an entity that the United States considers fiscally transparent, the income and the benefits of the treaty are allocated to the US partners only. In contrast, where the United States is the source state, the application of the '*saving clause*' again protects the position of the United States, allowing the taxation of its own residents regardless of the application of a tax treaty. Article 1(2) OECD Model, on the other hand, follows the same patterns, regardless that the OECD Model is used by developed and developing countries and that these latter countries remarkably rely mostly on source taxation. In this regard, it is a curious result that Article 1(2) OECD Model does not propose a more equilibrated balance between the interests of residence and source states, appearing, in principle, as an inadequate equation to address all the concerns that arise in this context.[1242] The above idea is reinforced when the text of Article 1(2) OECD Model is simply replicated in Article 3(1) MLI.

A special legal concern regarding Article 1(2) OECD Model is its almost inexistent interplay with the *beneficial ownership* requirement in case of payments of dividends, interest and royalties under Articles 10, 11, and 12 OECD Model. Indeed, the reduced WHT at source in those cases depends not only on the fact that a resident in the other State receives the income but also that this resident is considered the *beneficial owner* of those items of income. In all the illustrations used in this chapter, it was demonstrated that the two provisions are indeed permanently in conflict or not properly aligned. A recent attempt to solve this dichotomy has been elaborated by a group of academics, arguing for a 'deeming rule' to provide who is the *beneficial owner* when Article 1(2) OECD Model does not coincide, giving the same person the benefits of a treaty. However, although the rule initially attends to the fact that no relevant party is acting as an agent, nominee or other intermediary for a third party from the source state's perspective, the proposal seems to be strictly designed to give prevalence to the tax characterisation of the entity in the residence state.[1243] As such, I do not see how source states may fully agree with this pragmatic solution without reservations.

Another concern regarding Article 1(2) OECD Model and Article 3(1) MLI is the interplay between a '*saving clause*', which ensures Contracting States' right to tax their own residents regardless of the application of a treaty. This brings issues on double taxation relief. The solution adopted in paragraph 11.1 to the Commentaries on Articles 23A and 23B is clear in this regard: Contracting States *are not* reciprocally obliged to provide relief for each other's tax levied exclusively on the basis of the residence of the taxpayer. Therefore, relief from double taxation remains only a possibility to the extent that taxation by the other State is in accordance with the provisions of the Convention. This solution is replicated in Article 3(2) and Article 5 – Option C MLI. However, when dealing with the optional *saving clauses* within the MLI, it seems to be that opting for one or the other might not bring the same results. For example, whilst the detailed *saving clause* of Article 11 MLI seems to retain the obligations to provide double

1242. *See also* in this opinion: Nikolakakis et al., *supra* n. 985, pp. 358-359.
1243. *Supra* s. 5.3.1.3.

taxation relief under provisions such as Article 7(3), Article 9, Article 19, Article 20, Article 23A and 23B, Article 24, Article 25 and Article 28 OECD Model, the simplified version of Article 3(3) MLI does not expressly preserve treaty obligations with regard to those articles. Similarly, an approach like the one outlined in paragraph 11.1 of the OECD Commentaries could potentially pose challenges in certain countries. This is either due to specific provisions in tax treaties or a common practice of providing double taxation relief through a broad interpretation of Article 23 in the OECD Model.

All in all, it seems to be that after a deeper look at Article 1(2) OECD Model and Article 3(1) MLI, and the proposed *saving clauses* in Article 1(3) OECD Model and Articles 3, 5 and 11 MLI, all of them are not necessarily the most adequate instruments to address the issues of hybrids and reverse hybrid entities within the treaty context.[1244] It is perhaps time to think of a different solution which truly targets the disparities in the characterisation of entities and which should not necessarily be implemented within tax treaties.[1245] As I propose in Chapter 6, domestic coordination in the tax characterisation of entities may achieve better results by reducing the scope of application of Article 1(2) OECD Model only to those cases in which both the residence and source states treat the entity as fiscally transparent. Similarly, it may provide more consistent tax treaty outcomes, indirectly rebalancing the position between residence and source states, at least when compared with the current application of Article 1(2) OECD Model in the absence of a coordination rule.[1246]

1244. Also in this opinion: Nikolakakis et al., *supra* n. 985, pp. 358 and 360.
1245. *See* the proposal for a '*reactive coordination rule*' at *infra* Chapter 6.
1246. The tax treaty implication of the domestic proposal of coordination (*reactive coordination rule*) is analysed at *infra* Chapter 6, s. 3.

PART III Double Non-taxation and Hybrid Entities: The New Trend of Matching Tax Outcomes

CHAPTER 5

Hybrid Mismatch Arrangements and Linking Rules: Creating Artificial (Mis)Matches

1 INTRODUCTION

The international tax world and the manners to deal with hybrids and reverse hybrid entities have certainly changed after the issuance of the OECD BEPS Project.[1247] Since then, the trend has been especially inclined to match transactions involving hybrid and reverse hybrid entities with the outcomes derived from those transactions, i.e., particularly 'deduction/non-inclusion' (D/NI) outcomes or DNT. This approach has been proposed and designed within the OECD BEPS Action Plan 2 and attempts to recognise a new single category of (international) problems-denominated *hybrid mismatch arrangements* (HMA).[1248] Likewise, and as a remedy to those problems, the OECD proposes the implementation of domestic rules that primarily deny a deduction if the respective income is not included in the hands of the recipient in the other country, i.e., a *primary response*, or to tax the income that originally was not taxed in the hand of the recipient, i.e., a *secondary rule*.[1249] Both rules are recognised under the single denomination of '*linking rules*', as their design also suggests.

This chapter attempts to demonstrate that both the notion of HMA and the solutions created to counteract them ('*linking rules*') are indeed ad hoc constructions that artificially attempt to match transactions involving hybrid entities and reverse

1247. OECD (2013), *supra* n. 2.
1248. OECD (2015), *supra* n. 6, p. 16. However, the OECD already used the concept of HMA in 2012 when it elaborated a report on 'hybrid mismatch arrangements'. This report is with no doubt the anteroom of the proposals included in the OECD BEPS Action Plan 2. *See* OECD (2012), *supra* n. 6.
1249. Chapters 3, 4 and 5 of the OECD Action Plan 2 refer specifically to the recommendations with respect to payments made by a hybrid entity and payments received by a reverse hybrid entity, and which result in D/NI. *See* OECD (2015), *supra* n. 6, pp. 49-66.

hybrids with the DNT outcome (i.e., D/NI), disregarding the core of the issue with respect to hybrids, which is the uncoordinated characterisation of entities by two different countries.[1250] Moreover, this matching practice has the risk of creating a presumption of abusive practices in all those cases in which a transaction involving hybrid entities derives in a D/NI outcome, which certainly deviates from a proper understanding of the notion of DNT and restricts the ability of the taxpayers to efficiently manage their businesses.[1251] Likewise, this chapter suggests that the implementation of domestic *linking rules*, i.e., the domestic remedy suggested by the OECD, might generate important concerns both from a tax policy and from a legal perspective. This latter issue will be particularly tested in light of the application of double tax treaties and the application of Article 24 OECD Model (Non-discrimination) and with EU primary and secondary law.[1252] A similar analysis will be made with respect to the interaction between *linking rules* and interest limitation and CFC rules, respectively.

Section 2 analyses the concept of HMA and the elements required for its formation, specifically referring to the case of hybrid entities and reverse hybrid entities: (i) the '*hybrid element*'; (ii) the existence of a *payment*; and (iii) D/NI outcome (DNT). It also illustrates with examples the cases in which the use of hybrid entities and reverse hybrid entities might derive in a D/NI outcome in order to demonstrate that in both situations, this outcome is more temporal than permanent. The illustration includes the cases of a D/NI outcome using a hybrid entity, a reverse hybrid and the so-called *imported mismatches*. Section 3 turns the analysis into the specific domestic measures recommended by the OECD to counteract HMA, i.e., *linking rules*. This Section also stresses the tax policy and legal concerns associated with the implementation of linking rules, particularly with respect to the application of tax treaties and EU law. Section 4 analyses the interaction between *linking rules* and the application of other domestic anti-abuse and anti-base erosion rules, especially with respect to interest limitation rules and CFC rules that might affect transactions involving hybrid and reverse hybrid entities, respectively. Section 5 provides some final remarks.

1250. *Supra* Chapter 3.
1251. *Supra* Chapter 1.
1252. Testing the implementation of *linking rules* as regards to the non-discrimination clause of Article 24 OECD Model has special relevance because it is indeed the only provision within the OECD Model which could raise concerns with respect to the proposed rules. Likewise, the use of EU law as a subject of analysis is also justified. First, because of the less restrictive notion of 'discrimination' elaborated within the CJEU when compared to the one of Article 24 OECD Model. Second, because the EU has been particularly involved in the implementation of the OECD BEPS measures, including the ones counteracting hybrid mismatches. This task has been materialised with the approval of the EU ATAD, which opted for including *linking rules* to deal with hybrids (both as regards to entities and financial instruments), and the amendments of 2017 (EU ATAD II), which extend the application of the EU ATAD to HMA with third countries. All these developments were previously analysed in this work. *See supra* Chapter 3, s. 5.3.

2 THE CONCEPT OF HYBRID MISMATCH ARRANGEMENTS (HMA)

The final OECD report on Action 2 refers to HMA as arrangements that 'exploit differences in the tax treatment of an entity or instrument under the laws of two or more jurisdictions to achieve double non-taxation, including long-term deferral'.[1253] A similar definition was proposed in the first draft on Action 2 in 2014, which provided that an HMA is 'an arrangement that exploits a difference in the tax treatment of an entity or instrument under the laws of two or more tax jurisdictions to produce a mismatch in tax outcomes where that mismatch has the effect of lowering the aggregate tax burden of the parties to the arrangement'.[1254] Likewise, this work follows the direction already settled in the previous OECD report on hybrid mismatch arrangements (2012), which referred to them as 'arrangements exploiting differences in the tax treatment of instruments, entities or transfers between two or more countries [...] They often lead to 'double non-taxation' that may not be intended by either country, or may alternatively lead to a tax deferral which if maintained over several years is economically similar to double non-taxation'.[1255]

Therefore, exclusively referring to hybrid and reverse hybrid entities, it is possible to argue that, in the OECD view, there will be a '*hybrid entity mismatch arrangement*' when an entity organised in a determined country is regarded either as a transparent or taxable entity in that country, whilst in the other country it is characterised exactly in the opposite manner, the result of which is thus a mismatch in the payments made under that arrangement, which is normally traduced in a D/NI outcome, i.e., DNT or a DD.[1256] In other words, at least three elements will be required in order to determine that a hybrid entity mismatch exists: (i) an '*hybrid element*', i.e., a disparity in the characterisation of the same entity by two or more countries involved in the transactions, (ii) the existence of a '*payment*' between the two parties involving in the hybrid structure, and (iii) a *mismatch* in that payment, namely a D/NI outcome or DNT. These elements are subsequently analysed with regard to hybrid and reverse hybrid entities.

1253. OECD (2015), *supra* n. 6, p. 11.
1254. OECD (2014), *supra* n. 1167, p. 29. Before the issuance of the 2014 Report, the OECD opened the discussion to the public issuing two documents of 19 March 2014: (i) OECD (2014a), Public Discussion Draft, *BEPS Action 2: Neutralize the Effects of Hybrid Mismatch Arrangements (Recommendations for domestic Laws)* and (ii) OECD (2014b), Public Discussion Draft, *BEPS Action 2: Neutralize the Effects of Hybrid Mismatch Arrangements (Treaty Issues)*. The comments received are summarised in a document of 7 May 2014: OECD (2014c), Comments Received on Public Discussion Drafts, *BEPS Action 2: Neutralize the Effects of Hybrid Mismatch Arrangements,* available online at www.oecd.org.
1255. OECD (2012), *supra* n. 6, p. 1.
1256. O. Popa, *Hybrid Entity Payments – Extinct Species after the BEPS Action Plan?*, 59 Eur. Taxn. 9 (2014), Journals IBFD, p. 408.

2.1 The '*Hybrid Element*'

As already stressed in Chapter 3, hybrid entities and reverse hybrids are the result of the different characterisation of entities in two jurisdictions.[1257] In this regard, a *hybrid entity* is an entity regarded as a taxable entity in the country of its organisation, whilst in the other country, the same entity is regarded as fiscally transparent. In other words, the entity under analysis is subject to taxation at the level of the entity in its country of organisation, whilst in the country of the shareholders, it is considered 'tax transparent', i.e., non-taxable at the level of the entity but rather at the level of the shareholders. A *reverse hybrid*, on the contrary, supposes the opposite situation. This is to say, an entity considered a tax-transparent entity in its country of organisation is considered a taxable entity in the other country where the shareholders are residents.[1258]

The 'hybrid element', as described within the OECD BEPS Action 2, seems to be thus a simple recognition of an obvious reality in taxation: domestic rules among different jurisdictions are not necessarily coordinated, let alone harmonised.[1259] Indeed, one should start from the basis that disparities, including disparities in the characterisation of entities, are the general rule and not the exception within cross-border transactions. The above was demonstrated in Chapter 3, where dealing with the domestic rules on characterisation of entities concluded, on the one hand, that there is no perfect system to characterise entities for tax purposes, which can be used homogeneously by States, and, on the other hand, that the distinction of systems to characterise entities, i.e., resemblance test; elective system, etc. do not go beyond of being an interesting academic exercise, although in practice the different systems are normally interconnected; namely, they present elements of each other.[1260] For example, as was already stressed in Chapter 3, the resemblance test applied in the United States before the CTB regulations was not less elective than the current elective system because, in fact, taxpayers could achieve certainty in the characterisation of a foreign entity in advance by acquiring costly tax advisory. This is what I have denominated a de facto elective system.[1261]

Regardless of the above, the 'hybrid element' is indeed a fundamental factor (if not the real reason for the disagreement between States) whose presence determines the first step to confirm the existence of an HMA with respect to entities. On the contrary, the absence of this element also implies the absence of an HMA (or the impossibility of its formation), thus rendering the OECD recommendations inapplicable. The above is especially relevant considering the cases of countries that might remotely or never face issues with respect to hybrid entities or reverse hybrids either because of a coordination in their characterisation of a foreign entity, by statute or administrative practice, as per the rule in the foreign country where the entity is

1257. *Supra* Chapter 3, s. 3.1.
1258. *Ibid.*
1259. *Supra* Chapter 3, s. 6.
1260. *Ibid.*
1261. *Supra* Chapter 3, s. 4.

established,[1262] or simply because they do not provide the alternative for tax transparency within their domestic law or specific rules to characterise a foreign entity as transparent.[1263] Whilst the former, i.e., the coordination in the characterisation of entities as per the foreign rules, reduces the probabilities of originating hybrid entities, the latter reduces the probabilities of reverse hybrid entity mismatches to zero.

Another issue of particular relevance with respect to the 'hybrid element' is the fact that countries might treat some entities as only 'partially' tax transparent, as is the case of some trusts and LLPs.[1264] Although this issue is not directly treated in the OECD report on Action 2 referring to domestic recommendations, it is indeed analysed in the tax treaty recommendations and the access to tax treaty benefits.[1265] As provided in the current paragraph 10 of the commentaries on Article 1(2) OECD Model: 'In the case of an entity or arrangement which is treated as partly fiscally transparent under the domestic law of one of the Contracting States, only part of the income of the entity or arrangement might be taxed at the level of the persons who have an interest in that entity or arrangement [...] whilst the rest would remain taxable at the level of the entity or arrangement.'[1266] In the same order of ideas, therefore, it is possible to conclude that a 'partial hybridity' could exist. In such cases, only the part of the entity treated as tax transparent by one country and taxable by the other country could give rise to the 'hybrid element' that is necessary to originate an HMA. In other words, if the country of establishment of an LLP, e.g., treats the entity as fiscally transparent only with respect to the general partners, whilst the other country considers the LLP as taxable in

1262. *See, e.g.*, the case of Spain with respect to the characterisation of foreign entities for tax purposes. As stressed in Chapter 3, the administrative practice of the DGT (Spanish tax administration) is to follow the characterisation in the foreign country, regardless that by statute the Spanish domestic law provides for a resemblance test. *Supra* Chapter 3, s. 5.1.

1263. Although many developed countries provide the alternatives of tax transparent entities, e.g., partnerships or trusts, this is indeed not the case in developing countries. For example, Brazil and Colombia do not provide for domestic tax transparent partnerships. In Uruguay, a partnership whose partner is a company also resident in Uruguay is not regarded as tax transparent either. Likewise, e.g., Brazil, Colombia, and South Africa do not have rules that allow treating a foreign subsidiary as a tax transparent entity. For a full analysis with respect to problematic of HMA in developing countries (particularly with respect to Brazil, Colombia, Uruguay and South Africa), *see* B. Kuzniacki et al., *Preventing Tax Arbitrage via Hybrid Mismatches: BEPS Action 2 and Developing Countries*, WU International Taxation Research Paper Series No. 2017-03, of 31 March 2017, available online at SSRN.

1264. In the Netherlands, e.g., an *open commanditaire vennootschap* is always transparent for the general partners, whilst it is taxed at the level of the entity with respect to the limited partners. Similarly, the *société en commandite simple* in France, provides for tax transparency with respect to the general partners, whilst the limited partners are not taxed within the regime of transparency. Baker distinguishes at least four levels of transparency: (1) complete transparency, where the entity has no existence, e.g., a contractual joint venture, or where the entity is completely disregarded for tax purposes; (2) transparency with reporting obligations, where the entity has still the obligation to report income or gains, but the tax liability remains on the participants; (3) optional transparency, where the entity or participants may elect for transparency; and (4) partial transparency, where part of the income of the entity is taxed in the hands of the entity and part in the hand of the participants. *See* Baker, *supra* n. 914, pp. 22-23.

1265. OECD (2015), *supra* n. 6, pp. 133 et seq. *See also* the discussion regarding '*wholly and partially*' fiscally transparent, referred to the wording of Article 1(2) OECD Model at *supra* Chapter 4, s. 5.1.4.

1266. OECD Commentary on Article 1, para. 10.

full, only the part of the income or payments associated to the general partners could originate the hybrid element that subsequently might give rise to an HMA.

2.2 The Existence of a '*Payment*'

The second element that constitutes the notion of HMA refers to the existence of a *payment* between the parties involved in the hybrid entity structure.[1267] In this regard, Action 2 of the OECD BEPS Action Plan states that a *payment* means: 'any payment of money (which includes money's worth) made under the financing instrument and includes a distribution, credit or accrual. It includes an amount that is *capable of being paid* and includes any future or contingent obligation to make a payment. The definition of payment includes notional amounts that accrue in respect of a future payment obligation even when the amount accrued does not correspond to any increase in the payment obligation during that period.'[1268] Accordingly, a payment is considered as such when the relevant payment obligation is incurred under the laws of the payer jurisdiction or the payment is derived under the laws of the recipient jurisdiction.[1269] The report, however, expressly excludes a unilateral deduction for invested equity that does not require a payment from the taxpayer, such as the case of 'deemed interest deductions for equity'[1270] and differences in the value with respect to a payment, such as the case of gain or losses from foreign currency fluctuation.[1271]

The concept of *payments* used within the report, however, has not been exempt from criticism.[1272] In fact, if one considers, e.g., an allowance for corporate equity such

1267. As provided within the OECD report: 'The extent of a mismatch is determined by comparing the tax treatment of the payment under the laws of each jurisdiction where the mismatch arises.' *Ibid.*, p. 17.
1268. A payment should also include a part of a payment where the context requires. *Ibid.*, p. 130.
1269. *Ibid.*
1270. These payments would be 'economically closer to a tax exemption or similar taxpayer specific concessions and do not produce a mismatch in tax outcomes in the sense contemplated by Action 2'. *Ibid.*, p. 18.
1271. 'The hybrid mismatch rules are not generally intended to pick-up mismatches that are attributable to differences in the value ascribed to a payment. For example, gain and losses from foreign currency fluctuations on a loan can be said to give rise to mismatches in tax outcomes but these mismatches are attributable to differences in the measurement of the value of payments (rather than its character) and can generally be ignored for the purposes of the hybrid mismatch rules.' *Ibid.*
1272. Cooper, e.g., states that it is interesting that the concept and the rules in question [*linking rules*] refer only to 'payments'. Indeed, he gives the example of a 'double dip' lease where two taxpayers claim the entitlement to depreciation deductions or investment tax credits, and he argues: 'There are certainly "payments" being made, i.e., the price paid by the financier for the equipment and the rent and residual paid by the user, but these are not the same payment, and the tax-relevant item for the user or financier is not itself a "payment", but rather the depreciation deduction created by law. Whilst depreciation is derived from the amount of a payment, it is not itself a payment. What does appear to be clearer is that both parties could claim any additional investment allowance or tax credit that might to be given to the "owners" without being affected by these rules.' In the same order of ideas, Cooper argues that, e.g., a duplication of FTC, i.e., where two parties enjoy the same credit, can occur without the need of a 'payment' between the two claimants. *See*, G. Cooper, *Some Thoughts on the OECD's Recommendations on Hybrid Mismatches*, 69 Bull. Intl. Taxn. 6/7 (2015), Journals IBFD, p.

as a 'deemed interest deduction for equity' (i.e., a fictional deduction), it is clear that this would be immune to the OECD recommendations, although it treats equity like debt in one country[1273] and could perfectly derive in DNT (i.e., the main target of the HMA concept and the proposed *linking rules*), considering that the majority of these notional interest deductions will be regarded as equity in the country of the payee and subject to a participation exemption.[1274] Moreover, if one also considers the differences among the regimes on NID, the determination of what is a 'deemed interest deduction' or whether there was a 'payment' becomes even more complicated. Let us take as an example the *Juros sobre o capital propio* (or *Juros*) in Brazil to illustrate the issue.[1275]

In 1995, Brazil introduced an option for Brazilian companies to deduct from their taxable base the remuneration of net equity as 'notional interest'.[1276] The deduction is

342. The conclusion of Cooper is correct if we consider that the OECD states that 'payments that do not involve the creation of economic rights between the parties' are not regarded as 'payments'. *See* OECD (2015), *supra* n. 6, p. 123, in reference to the definition of 'payment'.

1273. Cooper, *supra* n. 1272.

1274. In Germany, e.g., it is clear that '*interest on equity*' are to be treated as dividends under German Tax Law (DE: s. 20(1) No. 1 of the Income Tax Act [*Einkommensteutergesetz*–EStG]), and thus exempted from taxation in a 95% according to s. 8b(5) of the Corporate Income Tax Act [*Körperschaftsteuergesetz*–KStG]. *See* C. Kahlenberg, *Prevention of Double Non-Taxation: An Analysis of Cross-Border Financing from German Perspective*, 43 Intertax 3, 222 (2015) DOI: 10.54648/taxi2015019. *See also, e.g.*, DE: BFH, 6 June 2012, I R 6, 8/11; Federal Tax Gazette II 2012, 111, which refers specifically to the treatment of the 'Brazilian *juros*' and confirming the application of the participation exemption.

1275. Similar examples of 'fictitious interest deductions for equity' can be found, e.g., in the 'NID regime' under Belgian law. In brief, Belgian law provides the possibility for any company subject to CIT in Belgium, to deduct from its taxable base a so-called notional interest deduction (*deduction pour capital à risqué*). The amount of NID is calculated by multiplying a fictitious interest rate with the relevant equity, which is determined by adjusting certain deductions and based on the nonconsolidated annual accounts of the previous accounting year. Likewise, the interest rate is determined considering the interest rate of medium long-term linear government bonds ('OLO bonds'). For further analysis on the Belgian NID *see, e.g.*, W. Heyvaert and D. Deschrijver, *Belgium Stimulates Equity Financing*, 33 Intertax 10 (2005) DOI: 10.54648/taxi2005072; M. Gérard, *Belgium Moves to Dual Allowance for Corporate Equity*, 46 Eur. Taxn. 4 (2006), Journals IBFD. It is arguable, however, that the Belgian NID is indeed a 'deemed interest deduction' when, on the one hand, it is calculated on a function of net equity invested and, on the other hand, it does not refer at all to effective loan transactions entered into with related or unrelated parties. *See* A. Bax and S. Claes, *The New Belgium-US Tax Treaty-An Analysis*, 47 Eur. Taxn. 7 (2006), Journals IBFD, p. 353. Other European countries have also introduced similar regimes. *See, e.g.*, the cases of Latvia (2008), Portugal (2008), Lichtenstein (2011) and Italy (2011). For further references in the case of Latvia, *see* Z. Kronbergs, *Latvia-2014 Corporate Tax Changes*, 54 Eur. Taxn. 11 (2014), Journals IBFD; in the case of Portugal, *see* G.J. Oliveira Everaert, *Portugal – Corporate Taxation sec. 1.*, Country Surveys IBFD (accessed 31 May 2017), para. 1.7.1.7.; in the case of Lichtenstein, *see* B. Büchel, *Liechtenstein – Corporate Taxation sec. 1.*, Country Surveys IBFD (accessed 31 May 2017), para. 1.3.3. and, finally, in the case of Italy, *see* F. Leone and E. Zanotti, *Notional Interest Deduction Regime Introduced*, 52 Eur. Taxn. 8 (2012), Journals IBFD. A comparative analysis of these regimes can also be found in: F. Massimi and C. Petroni, *Real-World ACE Reforms and the Italian Experience. Towards a General Trend?*, 40 Intertax 11 (2012) DOI: 10.54648/taxi2012065.

1276. BR: Article 9 of Law No. 9.249/95 of 26 December 1995. *See also*, R. Tavares, J. Womack and D. Wilson, *New Brazilian Equity Interest Rules: Efficient Financing for U.S.-Owned Subsidiaries*, Tax Notes Int'l 45 et seq. (6 January 1997); J. Malherbe and G. Vettori, *Deducting Interest on Equity Capital: Brazilian and Belgian Tax Rules Compared*, 1 Eur. Tax Stud. 28 (2010). For

calculated on a daily basis, multiplying relevant net equity by a legal rate of interest: *taxa de juros de longo plazo*, which is published quarterly by the Brazilian Central Bank and whose basis is the inflation rate, increased by a risk premium.[1277] Likewise, the existence of current profits or accumulated earnings of certain amounts is a precondition for the company to make the distribution and to consider the deductibility of those payments.[1278] One of the unique features of the Brazilian notional interest deduction is, however, that they have to be paid or credited to resident and non-resident shareholders.[1279] If thus credited, the interest does not need to be paid to the shareholders in order to be deducted.[1280] Finally, once paid or credited, the notional interest is subject to a 15% WHT,[1281] which is indeed final in case of individuals.[1282]

Considering thus the features of the Brazilian *Juros* and the definition of *payments* provided by the OECD report, one could, in principle, conclude that these amounts are indeed *payments* as they are an amount *capable of being paid*, which also includes 'notional amounts that accrue in respect of a future payment obligation even when the amount accrued does not correspond to any increase in the payment obligation during that period'.[1283] Nevertheless, the special features of the Brazilian *Juros* can also drive us to a different conclusion. Indeed, the precondition of the existence of current profits or accumulated earnings to make the distribution and to consider the deductible amounts, on the one hand, and the fact that a shareholder is not entitled to claim a payment in the same way as in a contractual obligation, i.e., the company is not liable for any payments derived from the equity participation with the shareholders,[1284] on the other hand, reinforces the idea that if a payment is made (or

---

an updated analysis in reference to the conflicts of qualification derived from the Brazilian *juros*, particularly within the context of the tax treaty Brazil-Spain, *see* F. Martlnez Laguna, *Institutional Hybrid Financial Instruments and Double Non-Taxation under Domestic Rules and Tax Treaty Law: The Example of Spain*, 44 Intertax 6/7 (2016) DOI: 10.54648/taxi2016 037.

1277. BR: Law No. 9.365; Law No. 10.183 and Central Bank Resolution No. 2.654/99, cited in: Massimi and Petroni, *supra* n. 1275, pp. 636-637, n. 45; Martinez Laguna, *supra* n. 1276, p. 450.

1278. Martinez Laguna, *supra* n. 1276, p. 451. Originally, the payments were dependent on current benefits or retained earnings in the amount of two times the *juros* paid. However, as noted by Utumi, the limit of 50% of the accumulated profits from previous years no longer exists due to the adoption of IFRS. Thus, profits from previous years must have a specific destination and such accounts do not exist anymore. *See* A. Akie Utumi, *Brazil* in: Cahiers de droit fiscal international Vol. 97b, *The Debt Equity Conundrum* (IFA 2012), p. 140.

1279. Massini and Petroni, *supra* n. 1275, p. 636.

1280. *Ibid.*

1281. The distribution of dividends out of profits to residents and non-residents is not subject to WHT in Brazil. Accordingly, since 2015, dividends are determined based on IFRS rules. *See* E. Salomao and J. Prada, *Corporations and partnerships in Brazil*, Kluwer Law International, Alphen aan den Rijn, 2011, pp. 118-120, s. III.

1282. The WHT tax is final in the case of individuals because the interest received or credited is not included in the payee's taxable income. In contrast, shareholding corporations include the payments in their taxable income, and thus, the WHT is credited against the corporate tax owed by the payee. *Ibid.*, p. 637. The WHT increases to 25% if the payee is resident in a tax heaven. *Ibid.*

1283. OECD (2015), *supra* n. 6, p. 130.

1284. 'The company is not liable for any payment derived from equity participation vis-à-vis any shareholder right.' *See* Martinez Laguna, *supra* n. 1276, p. 451.

accrued), it does not correspond to a future payment obligation, because there is indeed no obligation to pay off interest, but an option to distribute benefits to the shareholders.[1285] This latter feature would situate the Brazilian *Juros* closer to 'a unilateral deduction for invested equity that does not require a payment from the taxpayer',[1286] even though it will most probably generate a conflict of qualification in the country of the shareholder. This issue was not long ago subject to judicial scrutiny in Spain.[1287] In brief, the issue referred to the tax treatment of the Brazilian *Juros* and whether or not they could be subject to the Spanish participation exemption under Article 21 of the Spanish CIT.[1288] In this regard, the Spanish National High Court, on the one hand, stated that the Brazilian *Juros* share the same legal nature as dividends and thus could be perfectly subject to the exemption under Spanish domestic law.[1289] Likewise, the Court dismissed the argument that such an interpretation would result in DNT and considered that the application of a tax benefit in the source country should not denature the Spanish tax benefits once the payment has been considered a dividend both from a Spanish and Brazilian perspective.[1290]

Despite the above, the recognition of the existence of a payment to determine the existence of an HMA may, implicitly, be referring to the fact that in the absence of a payment, the disparity in the characterisation of entities, i.e., the hybrid element, is irrelevant for tax purposes, which indeed makes sense. In fact, the alternative proposal provided by this author also emphasises that the concept of 'tax relevance' is important for the application of the *reactive coordination rule*.[1291] In most of the cases, a payment makes the characterisation of the entity relevant.[1292]

1285. 'The shareholder is not entitled to claim a payment in the same way as it is in a contractual obligation.' *Ibid.*
1286. Indeed, the Brazilian regime appears closer to the Belgian NID which calculates the interest on a function of net equity invested and does not refer at all to effective loan transactions. *See* Bax and Claes, *supra* n. 1275. *See also*, OECD (2015), *supra* n. 6, p. 18.
1287. ES: Judgment of the Spanish High National, SAN 27.2.2014, r. 4. For a more extensive analysis on this matter, *see also* Martínez Laguna, *supra* n. 1276. A Reference can also be found in: M. Cencerrado and M. Soler, *Limit Base Erosion via Interest Deduction and Others*, 43 Intertax 1, 64-65 (2015) DOI: 10.54648/taxi2015005.
1288. Martinez Laguna, *supra* n. 1276, p. 456.
1289. 'The Court focused on the relevant provisions of the relevant Tax Treaty between Brazil and Spain, especially the concept of dividend (Article 10) and interest (Article 11) which, according to the Court shall be interpreted following the rule in Article 3.2, which meant in this case, according to the Brazilian legislation. Following this reasoning, the Court considered that the payments corresponding to the *juros* qualify as dividends and therefore, the exemption granted by Article 21 CTA applied in this case.' *See* Cencerrado and Soler, *supra* n. 1287, p. 64.
1290. ES: Judgment of the Spanish High National, SAN 27.2.2014, r. 6. *See also*, Martinez Laguna, *supra* n. 1276, p. 457. Perhaps it is also interesting to note that the Spanish High National Court referred expressly to the judgment of the German Federal Fiscal Court [*Bundesfinanzhof*] of 6 June 2012, where the German Court also achieved the conclusion that the Brazilian *juros* should be considered in Germany as 'dividends' for purpose of applying the participation exemption. *See* DE: BFH, 6 June 2012, I R 6, 8/11, and Kahlenberg, *supra* n. 1274.
1291. *Infra* Chapter 6, s. 2.2.
1292. For example, a characterisation of a foreign entity under US tax law is relevant when US income was paid to the entity. *See* US: Treas. Reg. s. 301.7701-3(d)(1)(i).

2.3 A D/NI Outcome (Double Non-taxation)

More importantly, however, the existence of a payment is not enough to raise concern or to constitute an HMA that triggers the application of the rules recommended by the OECD.[1293] Indeed, it is necessary that the *payment* is deductible in one country whilst not recognised as income or disregarded in the other country.[1294] In other words, there must be a 'mismatch in the payments', namely, a D/NI, or, which is the same, double non-taxation, in order to trigger the application of the suggested *linking rules*.[1295]

2.3.1 Deduction and Inclusion as Ordinary Income

The OECD BEPS Action 2 states that a: 'Deduction (including deductible payment), in respect to a payment, means that, after a proper determination of the character and treatment under the laws of the payer jurisdiction, the payment is taken into account as a deduction or equivalent tax relief under the laws of that jurisdiction in calculating the taxpayer's net income.'[1296] Therefore, a payment will be taken as a deduction when, under the laws of the payer's jurisdiction, it is part of the calculation of the taxpayer's net income. An immediate question that arises in this regard is that should 'deduction' (or deductible payment) be considered before or after the application of general rules limiting the deductibility of certain payments. In particular, a conflict should arise with respect to domestic rules limiting the deductibility of interest (e.g., interest limitation rules or thin cap rules). The OECD position seems to be clear in this respect when it says: '[...]the jurisdiction specific details of the taxpayer's net income calculation should not generally affect the question of whether a payment is deductible for tax purposes'.[1297] Similarly, the OECD report on Action 2 provides that in the case of concurrent applicability of hybrid mismatch rules (*linking rules*) and interest limitation rules, the former have priority over the latter. Nevertheless, as I argue later in this work, there are strong practical reasons to follow the opposite approach, i.e., applying interest limitation rules first, mostly considering the possibility of solving hybrid mismatches without the need for *linking rules*.[1298]

As regards the inclusion of the payment as *ordinary income* in the country of the payee, the OECD considers that a payment will be treated as 'included in ordinary income' in the country of the recipient 'to the extent that, after a proper determination of the character and treatment of the payment under the laws of the relevant jurisdiction, the payment has been incorporated as ordinary income into a calculation of the payee's income under the law of that jurisdiction'.[1299] Accordingly, *ordinary*

1293. *Infra* s. 3.
1294. 'The hybrid mismatch rule focuses on payments and whether the nature of that payment gives rise to a deduction for the payer and ordinary income for the payee.' OECD (2015), *supra* n. 6, p. 17.
1295. *Infra* s. 3.
1296. OECD (2015), *supra* n. 6, p. 121.
1297. *Ibid.*, p. 125.
1298. *Infra* s. 4.1.
1299. OECD (2015), *supra* n. 6, p. 122.

income, for these purposes, 'means income that is subject to tax at the taxpayer's full marginal rate and does not benefit from any exemption, exclusion, credit or other tax relief applicable to particular categories of payments (such as indirect credits for underlying tax on income of the taxpayer)'.[1300] Moreover, the OECD provides that 'income is considered subject to tax at the taxpayer's full marginal rate notwithstanding that the tax on the inclusion is reduced by a creditor other tax relief granted by the payee jurisdiction for WHT or other taxes imposed by the payer jurisdiction on the payment itself'.[1301]

At least two questions arise with respect to the inclusion of income as 'ordinary income' as per the concept used in the OECD BEPS Action 2 report. The first question refers to the use of losses in the payee jurisdiction, which have been carried forward from previous taxable years. In other words, should the taxpayer entity consider the income as 'included as ordinary income', regardless of the fact that this income has been offset against carried-forward losses? The logical answer should be yes, considering that the use of losses to offset income does not change the fact that a determined taxpayer is subject to tax at the taxpayer's full marginal rate. Indeed, the use of losses to offset the inclusion of income should not vary the conclusion that the income has been indeed included as ordinary income. This position seems to be shared by the OECD when it provides: 'A payment that is offset against deductible expenditure or losses that have been carried-forward, on this definition, should be treated as having been included in income.'[1302]

The second question refers to the role of WHTs at source. Can a WHT vary the conclusion that income is not included in the payee jurisdiction when a WHT precisely affects the creditor of the loan (payee of the interest) and not the payer? Can a WHT indeed accomplish a similar role to that of including income in the corporate tax base of the payee jurisdiction? Should, for example, a denial in the deduction still be necessary as a primary response? The OECD adopts a quite arguable position in this regard where it provides: 'The function of WHTs under the laws of the payer jurisdiction is generally not to address mismatches in the tax outcomes, and a payment should not be treated as included in ordinary income simply because it has been subject to withholding at source.'[1303] Nevertheless, the reality on taxation seems to show the opposite result. As provided by Cooper, e.g., in Australia, a dividend on a non-equity share paid by an Australian company is likely to be subject to WHT at source, which means that the fact the same payment was deductible from the taxable base of the Australian company is to a certain extent offset with the application of the WHT.[1304] In other words, if the final 'evil' is the DNT outcome, the issue seems to be solved with the application of WHTs at source.[1305] This interpretation seems to be also coherent in the case of inbound payments. Indeed, if, due to the different characterisations of the payer entity, the country of the payee disregards a payment (i.e.,

1300. *Ibid.*, p. 123.
1301. *Ibid.*
1302. *Ibid.*, p. 127.
1303. *Ibid.*
1304. Cooper, *supra* n. 1272, p. 348.
1305. *Ibid.*

considers the income as not included as ordinary income) and the payer jurisdiction denies the deduction but applies a WHT, the WHT will most probably not be credited in the payee jurisdiction because of the non-inclusion of income, and will thereby become a real cost for the whole transaction.[1306] The D/NI outcome could be avoided if WHTs are regarded as 'inclusion of income', even though this is not formally made within the tax base of the payee jurisdiction.

Another argument to support this interpretation is the fact that, economically speaking, a WHT refers exclusively to the position of the payee jurisdiction, namely, where, e.g., the creditor of a loan (or the recipient of the interest) is located. In other words, although a WHT is applied at source (payer's jurisdiction), it is the taxpayer in the country of the payee who economically suffers the WHT. Therefore, if a deductible payment is not included in the taxable base of the payee entity but rather is assumed through a WHT on the payment at source, there should not be any difference economically speaking because, in both cases, the payee entity will be the only one economically affected. In other words, the WHT will have the effect of offsetting the non-inclusion of the income at the hands of the payee.

2.3.2 *Is a D/NI Outcome a Presumption of Base Erosion: A Presumption of Abusive Practices or Both?*

As noted already, an important characteristic of the HMA concept is its restricted application, which involves hybrid entity mismatches whose result is a D/NI.[1307] Nevertheless, it is evident that other outcomes can come into play when cross-border transactions are involved, even apart from hybrids. For example, a non-inclusion/non-inclusion outcome could be achieved in case of a sale of shares held in a non-land-rich company made by a resident in a State that applies a participation exemption.[1308] This outcome is, however, outside of the scope of the concept of HMA. Similarly, and as noted already, a deduction might rarely be a presumption of base erosion in the payer jurisdiction when that country also applies a WHT at source.

More arguable, however, is the use of the concept of HMA (limited to D/NI outcomes) and the proposed remedies to counteract them strictly within a context of anti-abuse or anti-avoidance measures. The above can be seen in the recently approved EU ATAD and the inclusion of Article 9 dealing with hybrid mismatches.[1309] As argued somewhere else, however, the absence of a satisfactory explanation to focus an

1306. In Australia, e.g., the fact that a company receives interest on a loan that is equity for Australian tax purposes (not assessable in Australia) changes to the extent a WHT applied at the border, because in such a case the WHT will not be creditable in Australia. *Ibid.*, this is also the reason why denying a deduction and maintaining a WHT at source may transform this WHT into a permanent cost, i.e., as there will be no inclusion of income in the country of the payee, there will be no credit. *See also*, Lüdicke, *supra* n. 870, p. 315, who referring to the explanation of Fig. 4 at p. 314, arrives to the same conclusion.

1307. As already stressed elsewhere in this work, the outcome of DD is also included. However, its analysis is outside of the scope of this work. *Supra* Introduction, s. 2.

1308. Cooper, *supra* n. 1272, p. 339.

1309. Article 9 includes a *primary response* and a *defensive rule* as proposed by the OECD within the Action Plan 2. *See* Council Directive (EU) 2016/1164 of 12 July 2016 (ATAD I).

anti-hybrid rule on the result of a transaction (i.e., D/NI) and not on the purpose of it not only distorts the aim of an 'anti-abuse' measure[1310] but also contradicts the jurisprudence of the CJEU with respect to domestic measures implemented in order to target abusive transactions.[1311] In simple words, the fact of assuming that a transaction involving hybrid entities or reverse hybrid entities should be counteracted just because its outcome is a D/NI (i.e., DNT), regardless of the existence or not of abusive elements in that transaction, creates indeed a true presumption of abuse that might finally negatively impact upon many companies that use legitimate tax planning structures to minimise costs.[1312]

Furthermore, the reference to D/NI outcomes as an exclusive factor to originate an HMA, included as a kind of 'holy grail' in the design of domestic anti-hybrids measures, further increases the abovementioned presumptions when other important factors, which are part of the transaction involving hybrids are not taken into consideration. In particular, the mechanics of group taxation and the consideration of more than a one-year approach should be at least included.[1313] These two factors are analysed in the illustrations below.

2.4 Illustrations of HMAs with Respect to Hybrid Entities and Reverse Hybrid Entities

2.4.1 Example 1: D/NI Using a Hybrid Entity

Let us assume the hypothetical where XCo, a taxable entity incorporated in country X, grants a loan to YSub, an entity organised in country Y. YSub pays back interest in the amount of 100i connected to that loan. Let us preliminarily assume that country Y does not apply a WHT at source. Whilst country X considers YSub as tax transparent, country Y considers the same entity as a taxable entity.

1310. Navarro, Parada and Schwarz, *supra* n. 481, p. 130.
1311. EU: *Cadbury Schweppes* case, *supra* n. 123.
1312. Tax planning is certainly a legitimate practice which ultimate goal is to achieve double non-taxation. *See* Eicke, *supra* n. 188. *See also* OECD (1987), *supra* n. 184. In the United States, e.g., this idea is widely accepted. *See, e.g., Helvering v. Gregory, supra* n. 181. In the same direction *see, e.g., Cadbury Schweppes* case, *supra* n. 123. By other side, there is no doubt that the persons called to manage a company are legally bound to involve in tax planning to minimise costs. As argued by Schön: '[T]he minimization of the corporate tax burden [is] an integral part of the managers' duty of care ... Therefore, they – i.e. the directors themselves – are legally bound to engage in tax strategies.' *See* Schön, *supra* n. 186.
1313. Lüdicke, *supra* n. 870, pp. 313-317.

Figure 76 Example 1: D/NI Using a Hybrid Entity

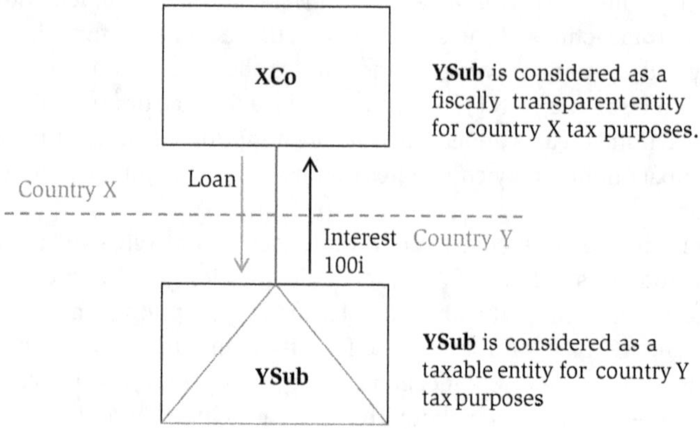

Under this scenario, the interest paid (100i) by YSub can be deducted from the gross income of YSub because YSub is considered as a taxable entity in country Y. Accordingly, the interest paid will not be included as an item of income by XCo because, under the tax law of country X, YSub is considered as a tax transparent entity. In other words, the loan and the interest are completely disregarded for tax purposes. The result is a D/NI derived from the different characterisation of the same entity.

However, let us now include the factors of group taxation and multi-year taxation.[1314] For this purpose, we will assume that YSub also has a subsidiary in country Y (YSub1), which, together with YSub, forms a tax group. We will also assume two different scenarios. The first scenario is that YSub1, in year 1, has an income of 100i, and YSub pays interest of 100i but has no income. In year two, however, YSub has an income of 100i but pays no interest. YSub1 has no income. Thus, in year one and year two together, the combined income of the group is 200i.

1314. *Ibid.*

Figure 77 D/NI Analysis and Group Taxation (First Scenario)

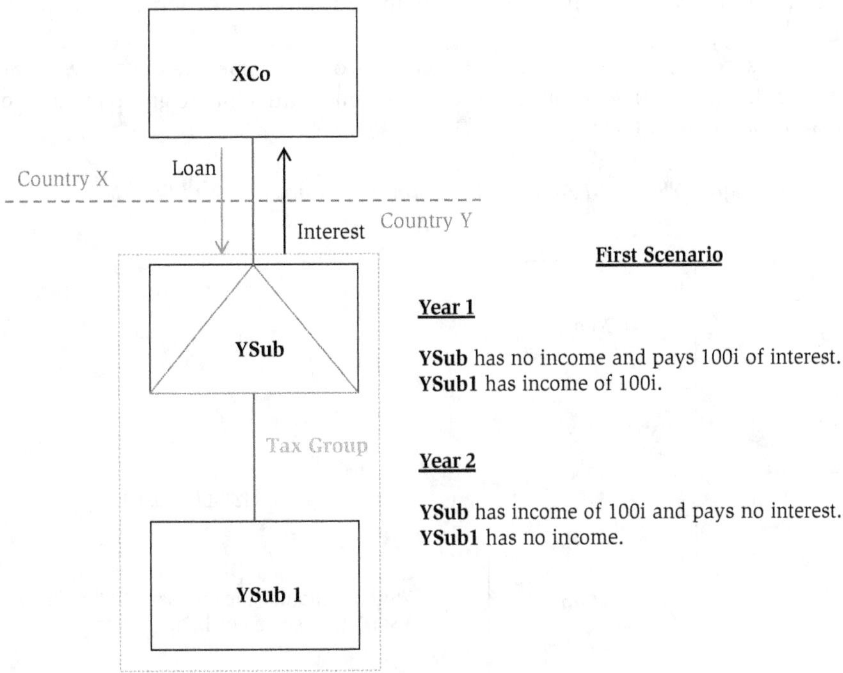

The result in the first scenario, without considering the second year, is exactly as shown in Figure 77. This is to say, the income of the group is offset against the interest deduction, and the interest is not included as income in country X because the loan is disregarded. In other words, we will face a D/NI outcome. This result is obtained by isolating year 1. Nevertheless, if now we consider years one and two together, and we assume that no FTC is granted by country X in year two, then the result in year two is that 100i will be included in the tax base of both countries Y and X, which indeed reflects the combined income of the group.

Two important conclusions can be extracted from the above. First, it demonstrates that if the problem is that income is not taxed at all in year one, this can easily be solved considering the double inclusion of income in year 2, without an FTC in country X. In other words, the fact that the income remains untaxed in year 2 will depend on the design of the FTC in country X. Second, it shows that more than DNT, the real outcome here, when considering the two years together, is a 'one-year deferral', but not properly a permanent DNT outcome.[1315] This coincides with what this author already stated in Chapter 1 of this work: DNT and tax deferral are not equivalent concepts.[1316] Therefore, as stated by Lüdicke, a deduction of a payment

1315. *Ibid.*
1316. *Supra* Chapter 1, s. 2.2.

raises policy concerns only when the income is not included in the tax base of the other country, which only happens in the example above when a single year of taxation is considered. Therefore, a multiyear rather than a one-year period must be considered.[1317]

The second scenario is that YSub has no income or expenses in year two. YSub1 pays dividends of 100i to YSub. Thus, the economic burden of the group in both years taken together is 100i.[1318]

Figure 78 D/NI Analysis and Group Taxation (Second Scenario)

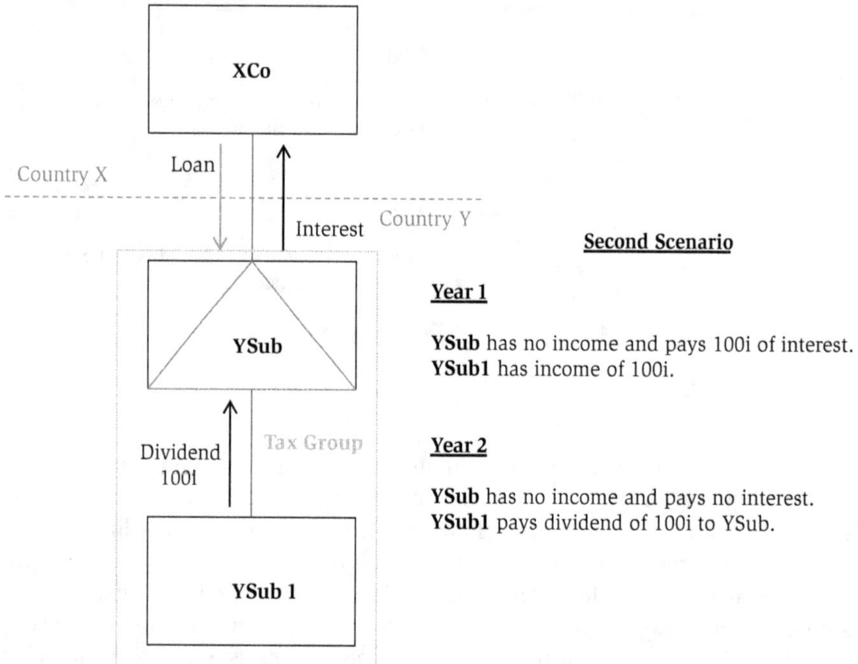

Similarly, in this second scenario, the dividend distributed from YSub1 to YSub will be taxable in country X, but not in country Y, because the underlying income was already attributed to and taxed in country Y in year 1 (i.e., the 100i of income that YSub1 had in year one). There will be no FTC in country X in year 1 because income and expenses were offset due to the group taxation in country Y. Therefore, the overall

1317. Lüdicke, *supra* n. 870, p. 314.
1318. These assumptions are taken from the analysis that Lüdicke makes with respect to hybrid entities and D/NI outcomes to demonstrate that the assumption that a D/NI occurs is indeed relative. *Ibid.*, Fig. 4.

result considering year 1 and year 2 is the taxation of the combined income of the group (100i), although having one year of deferral.[1319]

Some important conclusions derive from the example above. First, and as already stressed, the consideration of the mechanics of group taxation should be considered in order to reflect a consistent result. Second, the D/NI outcome is only temporal, i.e., it is a short-term outcome. Thus, if a rule denying a deduction in country Y applies in year one (primary response), this rule will properly target a one-year deferral but not a true D/NI. Indeed, if, under the circumstances described in the example above, such a rule applies, the outcome will be economic double taxation. Third, if we add to the examples above that a WHT might also be applied in country Y, regardless of the denial of the deduction, such a WHT will not be credited in country X, and it will be a permanent cost for the taxpayer.[1320]

2.4.2 *Example 2: D/NI Using a Reverse Hybrid*

Let us assume the same facts as the first example above, with the difference that YSub is regarded as a reverse hybrid entity. This is to say, under the tax law of country Y, YSub is considered a transparent entity, whilst country X and country Z consider YSub as a taxable entity. Accordingly, we will assume that YSub receives interest from YSub1, which is established in a third country, Z.

Figure 79 D/NI Using a Reverse Hybrid Entity

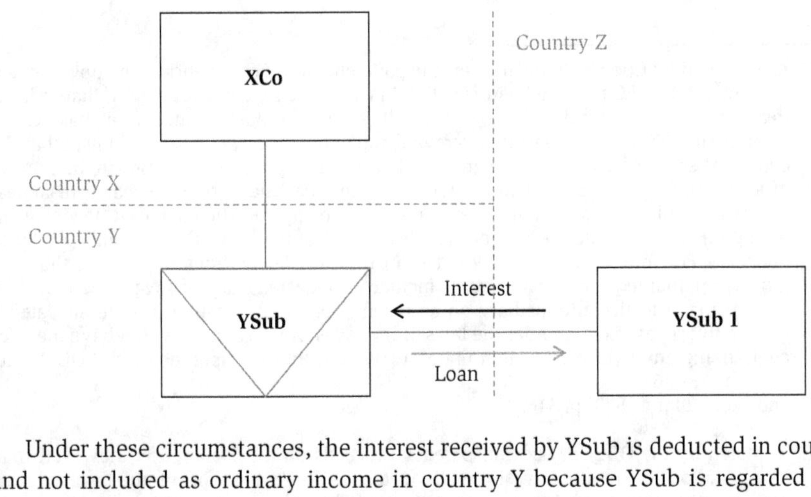

Under these circumstances, the interest received by YSub is deducted in country Z and not included as ordinary income in country Y because YSub is regarded as a

1319. Lüdicke explains that the same is true if, e.g., in the absence of a dividend, a capital gain upon the disposal of the shares in YSub1 in a later year is taxable in country X, at the level of XCo. *Ibid.*

1320. Lüdicke proposes that in the case where a deduction is denied in the country of the payer, the potential WHT that country Y can also apply should be prevented. *Ibid.*, p. 315.

tax-transparent entity there. They are also not included as ordinary income in country X unless dividends are distributed to XCo because country X considers YSub as a taxable entity. In simple words, the interest payments remain untaxed, and the general outcome is a D/NI.

The example above, however, assumes that country X does not have proper CFC rules to tax the interest income received by YSub in country B. Accordingly, it assumes that YSub is indeed a holding company which will never distribute dividends to XCo. If both assumptions are, nevertheless, disregarded, i.e., country X has indeed strong CFC rules, and YSub will eventually distribute dividends, the evil D/NI outcome disappears.[1321] A counterargument thus could be that in the case where YSub is not a controlled company of XCo, e.g., due to a minority of shares owned or because XCo and YSub are indeed unrelated, the CFC rules will be ineffective.[1322] This is indeed correct. However, as it will be explained later, the type of hybrid mismatches that derive from transactions between unrelated parties (not being part of a structured arrangement either) are indeed outside of the international concern.[1323] In addition, it is worth remarking that the OECD proposes, in this case, i.e., payments to reverse hybrid entities, an alternative remedy, which is to 'switch off' the tax transparency treatment in the country of establishment of the reverse hybrid entity, ensuring the taxation in country Y in the example above.[1324]

1321. As provided by Cooper: 'Similarly, for the payments to reverse hybrids, the obvious remedy is to amend the CFC rules in the jurisdiction in which the parent is resident. If that jurisdiction treats the foreign hybrid as an entity and it is deriving passive income or base company income, the CFC rules are a well understood and perfectly acceptable mechanism that should define the scope of tax on the foreign hybrid.' Cooper, *supra* n. 1272, p. 348 In the same order of ideas, the OECD BEPS Action 2 acknowledges that the hybrid mismatch disappears if proper CFC rules or similar anti-deferral regimes are applies when it states: 'Payments made through a reverse structure will not result in D/NI outcomes if the outcome is fully taxed under a CFC, foreign investment fund (FIF) or a similar anti-deferral rule in the investor jurisdiction that requires the investor to include its allocated share of any payment of ordinary income made to the intermediary on a current basis [...] Treating income allocated by a reverse hybrid as taxable under the laws of the investor jurisdiction would have the effect of neutralizing any hybrid mismatch under a payment to a transparent entity.' OECD (2015), *supra* n. 6, p. 64.

1322. Lüdicke, *supra* n. 870, p. 316.

1323. *Infra* s. 3.3.

1324. As stated by the OECD: 'Tax transparency proceeds on the assumption, however, that the income allocated to the investor will be taxable in the hands of the investor. In the cross-border context, this is not always the case.' Thus, the recommendation 5.2 (*Limiting the tax transparency for non-resident investors*) 'encourages jurisdictions to turn off their transparency rules when those rules are primarily used to achieve hybrid mismatches'. OECD (2015), *supra* n. 6, p. 64, Recommendation 5.2. The OECD also states that the recommendation only applies under the following circumstances: (a) a person (entity) is treated as tax transparent under the laws of the country where it is established; (b) that person receives income not subject to tax in that country, and (c) all of part of that income is allocated to non-resident investors that are part of the same control group. *Ibid.*

Finally, and as well as with respect to hybrid entities, two important conclusions can be extracted from this example on reverse hybrids. On the one hand, the D/NI outcome is not necessarily a permanent outcome. The above will rather depend on the design of the CFC rules in country X as well as the fact that YSub distributes dividends to country X. On the other hand, it confirms the fact that in a group transaction (i.e., between related parties) in which a reverse hybrid receives a payment that results in a D/NI outcome, it is presumed that either an abusive practice or base erosion arises.[1325]

2.4.3 *Example 3: Indirect D/NI:* 'Imported Mismatches'

One of the peculiarities of the OECD BEPS proposal on Action 2 refers to the possibility of 'indirectly' achieving a D/NI outcome, namely when a deduction in a certain country is on balance not accompanied by an inclusion of income in another country, using a hybrid arrangement between two other countries.[1326] This is a so-called *imported mismatch*, and the rule proposed to counteract this hybrid structure calls for denying a deduction in the payer jurisdiction to the extent that the payee treats the payment as a set-off against a hybrid deduction in the payee jurisdiction.[1327] As provided by the OECD: 'The policy behind the imported mismatch rule is to prevent taxpayers from entering into structured arrangements or arrangements with group members that shift the effect of an offshore hybrid mismatch into the domestic jurisdiction through the use of a non-hybrid instrument such as an ordinary loan.'[1328] Accordingly, they rely on the absence of rules (i.e., *linking rules*) counteracting the mismatch in the offshore jurisdiction in order to generate the mismatch in tax outcomes, which is later imported into the payer country.[1329] In this sense, some authors consider it justifiable that arrangements producing an 'indirect D/NI outcome' are addressed separately within the OECD BEPS report.[1330]

Although almost all the examples in the OECD report refer to HFI, an illustration of an *imported mismatch* considering exclusively hybrid and reverse hybrid entities could be as follows:

1325. *Supra* s. 2.3.2.
1326. R. De Boer and O. Marres, *BEPS Action 2: Neutralizing the Effects on Hybrid Mismatch Arrangements*, 43 Intertax 1, 29 (2015) DOI: 10.54648/taxi2015003.
1327. OECD (2015), *supra* n. 6, p. 83.
1328. *Ibid.*
1329. *Ibid.*, p. 85.
1330. De Boer and Marres consider that otherwise '[...] they lead to a proliferation of mismatch arrangements'. *See* De Boer and Marres, *supra* n. 1326.

Figure 80 Imported Mismatch

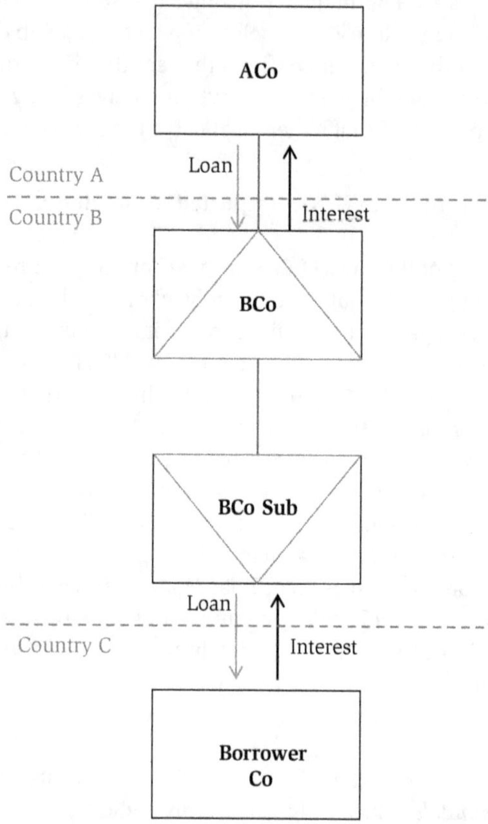

Let us assume three given countries (Figure 80), namely A, B and C. Accordingly, ACo has a subsidiary in country B, BCo, which is for purposes of country A tax transparent, whilst it is a taxable entity in country B (i.e., BCo is a hybrid entity). Consequently, BCo has a subsidiary in the same country, BCoSub. This latter entity is regarded as a tax-transparent entity in country B, but for country A's tax purposes is a taxable entity (i.e., a reverse hybrid). Finally, there is another entity in country C, Borrower Co, which is neither related to BCoSub nor BCo. Likewise, there are two different debtor-creditor relationships. First, Borrower Co borrows money from BCo-Sub and pays interest back to country B. Second, BCo borrows money from ACo and pays interest payments back.[1331]

As for the interest payments from Borrower C to BCoSub, these are not taxed at the level of BCoSub because this is a tax-transparent entity in country B. The interest payments, however, flow through BCoSub and are taxed at the level of BCo. As a result,

1331. Originally, De Boer and Marres provide this example. *Ibid.*, p. 30, Fig. 8.

this loan does not generate an HMA because interest payments are deducted in country C and included as income in country B. On the contrary, the loan and the interest payments between ACo and BCo are disregarded because of the different tax treatment of BCo. In this case, therefore, there is a D/NI outcome.

The example above, however, does not consider two important issues. First, country A might apply its CFC rules and then claim the right to tax the income that, under its view, is attributed to BCoSub as CFC income. If we consider that many countries provide for indirect ownership, BCoSub might perfectly be considered indirectly owned by ACo. In addition, interest paid from Borrower Co to BCoSub will generally be regarded as CFC income. As a result, double taxation might certainly arise because interest might be taxed as CFC income in country A and will definitely be taxed at the level of BCo.[1332] Thus, unless a tax credit is granted in country A, double taxation will be a reality. This situation can be perfectly assumed in the real world. For example, let us assume that ACo is a USCo that owns 100% of BCo, and this latter subsequently owns 100% of BCoSub. ACo would be deemed to own BCoSub because of the indirect ownership rules in the United States.[1333] Accordingly, no tax credit would be granted considering that BCo and not BCoSub paid the respective taxes in country B. The double taxation, in this case, remains a permanent effect.[1334] Second, the example does not consider, e.g., the possibility that BCo and BCoSub are part of a 'tax group'. In such a case, the interest received and paid at the level of the group will be offset. It would be, therefore, arguable that a mismatch is imported to country C.

The justification for *imported mismatches* is rather clear: it pretends to avoid *linking rules* become useless by using countries that do not introduce the OECD recommendations.[1335] Nevertheless, it is undeniable also that they increase the level of complexity in determining cases of HMA. Indeed, they require looking beyond the transaction between two members of a control group (or a structured arrangement) to identify possible mismatches. The above sets up an important burden both to taxpayers and tax administrations, an issue that is in part recognised by the OECD as well.[1336]

3 *LINKING RULES* AND THE NEW ERA OF BEPS

The mechanical process of matching transactions related to the different characterisation of the same entity by two different jurisdictions and the outcome of DNT (i.e., D/NI) – *hybrid mismatch arrangements* – has also certainly given rise to ad hoc or

1332. Although it can be just an interest spread on balance. *Ibid.*
1333. The indirect ownership consists of stock beneficially owned by a US person through a foreign corporation, partnership, trust or state. Thus, ACo would be deemed to indirectly own BCoSub. Bitter and Lokken, *supra* n. 556, pp. 69-10.
1334. An indirect tax credit would not apply either, because the indirect tax credit gives double tax relief for the cases of a US Corp. that owns at least 10% of the foreign subsidiary and receives dividends from this latter. US: IRC s. 902.
1335. 'Imported Mismatches rely on the absence of effective hybrid mismatch rules in offshore jurisdictions in order to generate the mismatch in tax outcomes which can then be imported into the payer jurisdiction.' *See* OECD (2015), *supra* n. 6, p. 85.
1336. As provided by the OECD: 'While these rules involve an unavoidable degree of coordination and complexity [...].' *Ibid.*, p. 84. *See also*, De Boer and Marres, *supra* n. 1326, p. 30.

mechanical solutions. Indeed, Action 2 of the BEPS Action Plan recommends a two-level solution to deal with the issue. On the one hand, a *primary response* is applied at the level of the payer. On the other hand, a *defensive rule* is applied at the level of the recipient of the payment. Both rules are subsequently analysed.

3.1 Primary Response

The *primary response* consists of a recommendation to introduce a rule at a domestic level which denies the deduction of interest payments if these payments are not included as ordinary income in the recipient country.[1337] In other words, and particularly with respect to hybrids and reverse hybrid entities, it implies denying the deductibility of certain payments in all those transactions in which those payments are made by a hybrid entity or received by a reverse hybrid, resulting in a D/NI outcome because of the different characterisation of the same entity.[1338] Therefore, as it may be observed, the domestic deductibility, in this case, is contingent on the inclusion or recognition of income in a foreign country, which in both cases, i.e., hybrid entities and reverse hybrids, will not occur because the two countries involved in the transaction consider the payer (in the case of payments from hybrid entities) or the payee (in the case of payments made to reverse hybrid entities) differently for tax purposes. Consequently, the payment and the whole transaction will either be disregarded, as is the case of payments made by hybrid entities, or simply not recognised in the country of the investors unless and until they are distributed as dividends, as is in the case of reverse hybrids.[1339] Likewise, it is obvious that a payment must originally be allowed as deductible in order to apply the *primary response*.[1340]

Regardless, the primary response remains as a recommendation to be introduced at a domestic level by countries around the globe, and there are countries that have already started introducing it within their domestic legislation, particularly to counteract HMA related to hybrid financial instruments. For example, Section 12(1) No. 10 of the Austrian Corporate Income Tax Law (Austrian CITL) provides for a denial of the

1337. As stated by the OECD: 'Both payments made under hybrid financial instruments and payments made by and to hybrid entities can give rise to D/NI outcomes. In respect of such hybrid mismatch arrangements this report recommends that the response should be to deny the deduction in the payer jurisdiction.' *See* OECD (2015), *supra* n. 6, p. 17.

1338. In reference to the concept of 'deduction' and recognition of income as 'ordinary income', *supra* s. 2.3.1.

1339. The application of the *primary response* with respect to cases of hybrid financial instruments is slightly different because it implies, in most of the cases, the application or not of the exemption system to relieve double taxation in the country of the payee. In most of the countries, the participation exemption will apply regardless of the taxation of the income in the other countries based on a pure interpretation of the exemption system. However, there are countries that have included switchover clauses that allow the non-application of the exemption to the extent the payment was deducted in the country of the payer.

1340. As provided by the OECD: '[...] the disregarded hybrid payments rule should only operate to the extent that the payer is entitled to a deduction for a payment under local law'. OECD (2015), *supra* n. 6, p. 51. The interaction of the primary response and other domestic rules denying the deductibility of interest, in particular 'interest limitation rules', is analysed in *infra* s. 4.

interest paid to a foreign corporation if the receiving corporation belongs to the same group and the payment is exempted at the level of the foreign receiving corporation or the income is subject to an effective tax rate of less than 10%.[1341] Similarly, Article 15(j) of the Spanish Corporate Income Tax Law (Spanish CITL) introduced a rule applicable to hybrid instruments, which provides that expenses of a transaction between related parties will not be considered deductible if, due to a conflict of qualification, they do not generate income or generate exempted income or income subject to a nominal tax rate below 10% at the level of the recipient.[1342] For this provision to apply, therefore, the following three circumstances must be met: (i) the transaction must take place between related parties, as defined by Article 18 Spanish CITL, (ii) the Spanish taxpayer must incur expenses that are, in principle, tax deductible under the Spanish law, and (iii) the expenses do not give rise to corresponding taxable income in the associated non-resident taxpayer due to a conflict in the characterisation of the payment.[1343] Likewise, it was discussed in Germany the introduction of a similar provision disallowing an interest to the extent the recipient does not characterise the income received as interest.[1344] However, this provision has not yet entered into force.[1345]

At the EU law level, a *primary response* was also introduced in the final text of the EU ATAD, which could certainly fill the gap left by the EU countries that have not yet responded to the OECD recommendations.[1346] Indeed, one particular characteristic with respect to the rule introduced in the EU ATAD is that it applies to both hybrid instruments and hybrid entities, which extends the scope of the existing domestic rules that were launched mostly targeting hybrid financial instruments. As read within the text of Article 9 of the EU ATAD: 'To the extent that a hybrid mismatch results in a deduction without inclusion, the Member State of the payer shall deny the deduction of such payment.'[1347] Similarly, the text of the amendment to the EU ATAD (ATAD II), dealing with hybrid mismatch arrangement with third countries, provides that: 'To the extent that a hybrid mismatch results in a deduction without inclusion: a) the

1341. M. Jann, J. Schuch and G. Toifl, *Austria – Corporate Taxation* s. 1., Country Analyses IBFD, s. 1.4.10 (accessed 6 June 2017).
1342. ES: Article 15(j) of the Corporate Income Tax Law [*Ley del Impuesto sobre Sociedades*], as introduced by the Royal Law Decree [*Real Decreto Legislativo]* No. 4/2004 of 5 March 2014. *See also*, Á. de la Cueva González-Cotera and C. Morlán Burgasé, *Spain – Corporate Taxation* s. 1., Country Analyses IBFD (accessed 6 June 2017).
1343. S. López Ribas, *Financing Activities: Hybrid Mismatches and the Tax Deductibility of Interest in Spain*, 70 Bull. Intl. Taxn. 8 (2016), Journals IBFD, p. 455. The provision is written in a neutral way avoiding referring to income received 'by a non-resident'. However, it appears to be clear that this is the only situation in which a different characterisation might arise.
1344. The draft stated that payments should not be deductible if such payments are not included in the tax base of the direct or indirect recipient or subject to an exemption at the level of it due to a qualification mismatch between the two legal systems: the payer and the payee. Accordingly, the payments shall only be deductible as business expenses in Germany, provided they are not deductible from the tax base of the payer in another jurisdiction. *See* D. Gutmann et al., *The Impact of the ATAD on Domestic Systems: A Comparative Survey*, 57 Eur. Taxn. 1 (2017), Journals IBFD, p. 17.
1345. *Ibid*.
1346. *Supra* Chapter 3, s. 5.3.
1347. EU: Council Directive (EU) 2016/1164 of 12 July 2016 (ATAD I).

deduction shall be denied in the Member State that is the payer jurisdiction [...].'[1348] The above, however, does not mean to recognise that the solution adopted is necessarily the correct one. As this author argues further on in this work, a more direct approach to counteract HMA with respect to hybrid entities and reverse hybrids should be constructed to target the real reason for the mismatch, i.e., the disparity in the characterisation of entities, without indirectly affecting the deductibility of payments.[1349] Interestingly, this approach was originally supported by the European Commission but later on abandoned, perhaps due to the political pressure that the whole OECD BEPS proposal involves.[1350]

3.2 Defensive Rule

The *defensive rule* consists of recognising the payment as ordinary income in the country of the recipient, being a mirror image of the primary recommendation abovementioned.[1351] The *defensive rule*, therefore, as its name suggests, applies only to the extent the payer country does not disallow the deduction of the payment, and thus, there is still a risk that this remains untaxed.[1352] From a tax policy perspective, it makes sense to let the source country, i.e., country of the payer, have the first bite at the apple as it is, after all, where the payment is issued and where the mismatch originated based on the characterisation of the entity in its home country (payer country) by the payee country. The above, however, also embodies a practical reason: to avoid the simultaneous application of the proposed countermeasures. Nevertheless, as it will be argued later on in this work, this aim is far from being accomplished, and the circular effect of *linking rules*, i.e., the contingent application of *primary response* and *defensive rule*, is one of the main negative characteristics of the OECD proposals that may lead to confusion among States in terms of which State is entitled to react, which consequently affects the final effectiveness of the rules.[1353] Last but not least, the *defensive rule* applies only with respect to cases involving hybrid entities and not with respect to reverse hybrids where the *primary response*, the improvement of offshore investment regimes (e.g., CFCs) and the restrictions to tax transparency in the country where the reverse hybrid is located, are the proposed countermeasures instead.[1354]

1348. EU: Council Directive (EU) 2017/952 of 28 May 2017 (ATAD II).
1349. *Infra* Chapter 6.
1350. *Supra* Chapter 3, s. 5.3.2.
1351. OECD (2015), *supra* n. 6, p. 52.
1352. The contingent application of the *defensive rule* is clearly stated by the OECD when it provides: '*If the payer jurisdiction does not neutralize the mismatch* then the payee jurisdiction will require such payment to be included in ordinary income to the extent the payment gives rise to a D/NI outcome' (emphasis added). *See* OECD (2015), *supra* n. 6, p. 49.
1353. *Infra* s. 3.4.1.
1354. The exclusion of a *defensive rule* with respect to cases of reverse hybrid receiving payments is, however, very clear. Indeed, in most of those cases the D/NI outcome targeted by the rules can easily be solved with the application of CFC rules in the country of the investors. *See also* with respect to turning off the tax transparency treatment in the country where the reverse hybrid entity is established, *supra* s. 2.4.2. As regards to the interaction between the primary response and the CFC rules, *infra* s. 4.2.

As well as the primary response, some countries have also already introduced a *defensive rule* to apply to cases dealing with HMA derived from hybrid financial instruments. This is, e.g., the case of Austria, which introduced Sections 10(1) and 7 within the CIT, which provides that the general exemption of dividends does not apply if those dividends were treated as tax-deductible expenses at the level of the payer (source State).[1355] Accordingly, Spain introduced Article 21(1)(b) within the Spanish CIT, which provides that dividends received, which are derived from profit participation that has generated a deduction at the level of payer, will not be exempted in Spain.[1356] As noted, therefore, the rule has no other link apart from the deductibility at the level of the payer, without reference, e.g., to the characterisation of the payments.[1357] Likewise, Germany also enacted a provision that intended to deal with the application of the domestic exemption method with respect to payments considered equity in Germany.[1358] The rule states that the domestic exemption of remuneration payments from dividend-generating equity is not granted insofar as the payments are deducted in the country of the payer, demonstrating again that the exemption on dividends is contingent on the tax treatment of those dividends in the foreign country.[1359]

The *defensive rule* has also been introduced within EU law through a series of modifications. In particular, I refer to the modification of the PSD in 2014 that basically provided that MS should refrain from taxing profits to the extent that such profits are not deductible at the level of the subsidiary or to tax them if a deduction was indeed granted.[1360] This provision that, originally applied only with respect to hybrid financial instruments, is now also extended to cover HMA related to hybrid entities and reverse hybrid entities with the introduction of Article 9 of the EU ATAD[1361] and the recent

1355. Jann, Schuch and Toifl, *supra* n. 1341, s. 7.2.6.2.
1356. The Law No. 27/2014 of 27 November 2014 introduced different rules tackling D/NI schemes, including a *defensive rule* with respect to hybrid financial instruments. However, prior to this reform in 2014, the exemption method applied to the extent the following requirements were met: (i) the resident company has, directly or indirectly, maintained for one year a participation of, at least, 5% ownership in the subsidiary; (ii) the subsidiary must have been subject to a tax equivalent to the Spanish CIT, and (iii) the distributed profits derive necessarily from business activities running abroad. The requirement of bullet '(ii)', however, is considered fulfilled if the subsidiary is a resident of a country with which Spain had signed a tax treaty containing an exchange of information provision. *See* Martinez Laguna, *supra* n. 1276, pp. 453 and 458. *See also*, D. Jiménez-Valladolid de L'Hotellerie-Fallois, *Double (no) imposición e híbridos financieros: tendencias internacionales y reforma del Impuesto sobre Sociedades*, in: *La Reforma del Sistema Tributario Español (2a parte), Encuentro de Derecho Financiero y Tributario (3a Ed.), Doc. No. 10/2015*, Institutos de Estudios Fiscales, Madrid, 2015.
1357. Martinez Laguna, *supra* n. 1276, p. 458.
1358. DE: s. 8b(1) of the German CIT. The provision, however, does not deal with the application of the exemption method by reason of a tax treaty. *See* S. Bärsch and C. Spengel, *Hybrid Mismatch Arrangements: OECD Recommendations and German Practice*, 67 Bull Intl. Taxn. 10 (2013), Journals IBFD, p. 526.
1359. *Ibid.*
1360. EU: Council Directive 2014/86/EU of 8 July 2014 amending Directive 2011/96/EU.
1361. EU: Council Directive (EU) 2016/1164 of 12 July 2016 (ATAD I). Also, *supra* Chapter 3, s. 5.3.2. The compatibility of the defensive rule considered before and after the introduction of this directive is discussed in *infra* s. 3.5.2.1.2 of this chapter.

issuance of the ATAD II, applied with respect to the mismatches with third countries outside the EU.[1362]

The mechanic of the *defensive rule* with regard to hybrid entities is quite interesting and deserves special attention. Indeed, if one looks closer into the application of the rule, one could conclude *a priori* that the effect at the level of the payee State is to implicitly recognise the characterisation of the entity given at the level of the payer State. In other words, the *defensive rule* would provide a de facto rule of coordination at source.[1363] Nevertheless, this statement is not entirely correct. First, the *defensive rule* provides that income should be recognised as 'ordinary income' in the State of the payee entity (i.e., taxed there), which is not the same as providing that the characterisation of the entity at source should prevail. In fact, if the rule were to target the HMA considering the different characterisation in both countries, i.e., the core of the issue, neither the *primary response* nor *defensive rule* would be needed. Second, the taxation of income at the level of the payee would never be mandatory if a rule coordinating the characterisation of entities is applied. The above would finally depend on the specific rules in the country of the payee. In other words, the outcome of the transaction (i.e., D/NI) would not be the basis for the application of the rule, as it is in the case of the *defensive rule*, which only applies if an HMA occurs and to the extent the *primary response* did not apply first. On the contrary, the outcome would be relegated to the background, renouncing the consequentialist approach adopted by the OECD.[1364]

3.3 'Limitations' Within the Scope of the *Linking Rules*

The *primary response* and the *defensive rule* apply with certain limitations. This is to say, not every single hybrid entity mismatch giving rise to a D/NI outcome may trigger the application of the rules, but rather only hybrid entity mismatches that are within the context of either a 'control group' or a so-called structured arrangement.[1365]

1362. Following the OECD proposal in terms of having a defensive rule that applies contingently to the prior application of a primary response in the payer country, the final text of the EU ATAD II states: 'To the extent that a hybrid mismatch results in a deduction without inclusion: b) where the deduction is not denied in the payer jurisdiction, the amount of the payment that would otherwise give rise to a mismatch outcome shall be included in income in the Member State that is the payee jurisdiction.' EU: Council Directive (EU) 2017/952 of 29 May 2017 (ATAD II), Article 9.

1363. Accordingly, and with respect to hybrid financial instruments, one could argue that the *defensive rule* acts also in a similar way as a 'switchover clause' that permits switching off the application of the exemption method.

1364. A deeper analysis is developed further on in this work, which finally opts for proposing a domestic rule coordinating the characterisation of entities. *Infra* Chapter 6.

1365. As provided by the OECD with respect to the rules applicable in case of payments made by a hybrid entity: 'This rule only applies if the parties to the mismatch are in the same control group or where the payment is made under a structured arrangement and the taxpayer is a party to that structured arrangement.' OECD, *supra* n. 6, p. 49. In the same order of ideas, and with respect to the recommended rules applied with respect to payments received by reverse hybrid entities, the OECD states: 'The recommendation only applies where the investor, the reverse hybrid and the payer are members of the same control group or if the payment is made under a structured arrangement and the payer is party to that structured arrangement.' *Ibid.*, p. 55. Similarly, hybrid mismatches derived from a HFI and whose outcome is a D/NI, are also

Nevertheless, as demonstrated below, both concepts are not necessarily limitations to the application of *linking rules* but rather an excessive extension of these rules, which leaves almost no space for cases in which they would not be applied.

3.3.1 Control Groups and 'Acting Together' Test

The concept of 'control group', as defined in the OECD BEPS Action Plan 2, is rather wide.[1366] Indeed, it includes at least four different scenarios: (1) when there is a consolidation for accounting purposes under IFRS or local GAAP; (2) when a person can 'effectively control' the second person through an investment in that person, or there is a third person who has a sufficiently significant investment in both persons giving rise to an effective control;[1367] (3) when a person holds, directly or indirectly,[1368] 50% or more of the voting rights or value of equity interests[1369] of a second person or a third person holds 50% or more of the voting rights or value of equity interests in both, and (4) when two persons are regarded, for purposes of Article 9 OECD Model, as 'associated enterprises'.[1370]

---

limited to 'related parties' and 'structured arrangements'. The concept of 'related parties' and 'controlled groups', however, are slightly different, starting from the consideration of different percentages of ownership required.

1366. The final report of the OECD BEPS Action plan 2 states: 'Two persons are in the same control group if: (i) they are consolidated for accounting purposes; (ii) the first person has an investment that provides that person with effective control of the second person or there is a third person that holds the investment which provides that person with effective control over both persons; (iii) the first person has a 50% or greater investment in the second person or there is a third person that holds a 50% or greater investment in both; or (iv) they can be regarded as associated enterprises under Article 9 [OECD Model].' OECD (2015), *supra* n. 6, p. 113.

1367. The OECD gives the example of a substantial shareholder in a widely held company and that participation gives him the effective control over the appointment of directors. *Ibid.*, p. 116.

1368. The understanding of indirect participation is rather clear. The OECD illustrates this giving the example of a person (A), who holds 50% of the shares in BCo, which itself holds also 50% of CCo. Thus, A would be indirect owner of CCo in a 25% share of indirect ownership. *Ibid.*, The concept of indirect ownership coincides with the one used within US law with respect to CFC rules, where the stock held by foreign entities is considered as indirectly owned proportionally by its shareholders or partners. *See* Bitter and Lokken, *supra* n. 556, p. 69-10. *See also* the explanation of 'indirect ownership' under the US tax law at *supra* n. 716.

1369. The reference to voting rights 'or' equity interest has the clear purpose of avoiding the circumvention of the rule, e.g., issuing shares without voting rights. Similar rules are applied, e.g., in the United States with respect to CFC rules. In fact, before 1987 control was measured only by voting power and the alternative of total value was added to avoid manipulation. *See* US: Staff of Joint Committee on Taxation, 99th Cong., 2nd Sess., General Explanation of the Tax Reform Act of 1989, p. 988, cited in: Bittker and Lokken, *supra* n. 556, p. 69-8.

1370. It is not entirely clear the reason of this inclusion, because the meaning of 'control' for the purposes of the application of Article 9 OECD Model is left to the domestic laws of the countries. The OECD Model does not give any hints with respect to thresholds or criteria to consider two enterprises as *associated enterprises*. Nevertheless, the OECD justifies this reference as to clarify that *linking rules* should apply even in the case where a transaction is subject to transfer pricing adjustments. OECD (2015), *supra* n. 6, p. 117. Perhaps it would have been enough to state this reference without complicating the definition of *control group*.

Whilst some authors have argued that the reasons to restrict the scope of HMA are to avoid undue complexity in the application of the linking rules[1371] or to implicitly constrain the application of the rules to transactions that might be abusive,[1372] these aims seem to be contradictory with the extremely wide concept of control group provided by the OECD.[1373] Indeed, what seems to be clear instead is that there is a strong attempt to include as many situations as possible within the concept of control group in order to avoid the manipulation of the rules. For example, if control groups would include only the participation of a person over another in a certain percentage or voting rights or equity interest, as it happens with other tax rules that require control, e.g., CFC rules, it would be very easy to circumvent the application of linking rules by the taxpayers.[1374] Nevertheless, the fear with respect to the circumvention of the rules should not be a basis for an unnecessary extension of concepts that finally increase the level of complexity in the application of the rules rather than reducing it.

The above can especially be seen with respect to the concept of 'Acting Together', which extends further the interpretation of the concept of control group. As provided by the OECD: 'For purposes of the related party rules a person who acts together with another person in respect of ownership or control of any voting rights or equity interests will be treated as owning or controlling all the voting rights and equity interests of that person.'[1375] The purpose of the 'acting together' rule is thus, on the one hand, to prevent taxpayers from avoiding the control group requirement by transferring their voting interest or equity interests to another person who continues to act under their direction.[1376] On the other hand, it aims to prevent, e.g., a group of minority shareholders from entering into an arrangement that allows them to act together and benefit from the outcome of an HMA, avoiding again the application of *linking rules*.[1377] Accordingly, and as well as with the concept of 'control group', the 'acting together' test considers at least the following scenarios with respect to two persons that act together in respect of the ownership or control of any voting right or equity interest: (a) they are member of the same family; (b) one person acts as per the wishes of the other person; (c) they have entered into an arrangement that has materially impacted the value or control of the voting rights or equity interests; or (d) the ownership or

1371. De Boer and Marres, *supra* n. 1326, p. 19.
1372. *See, e.g.*, Cooper, *supra* n. 1272, p. 342.
1373. The intention of the OECD to limit the scope of the rule to *control groups* might be regarded as a small attempt to affect only those hybrid transactions that might be considered *abusive*, presuming that this will happen more likely with transactions within control groups. Nonetheless, the wide construction of the concept of *control groups* is contradictory and it does not give the impression of any limitation within the scope. In contrast, therefore, my proposal does not contemplate the limitation of the *reactive coordination rule* to transactions within control groups. This has to be with the main tax policy reason behind the design of the proposed reactive coordination rule, which is the simplicity in its application. *Infra* Chapter 6, s. 2.2.
1374. De Boer and Marres, *supra* n. 1326, p. 19.
1375. OECD (2015), *supra* n. 6, p. 113.
1376. *Ibid.*, p. 117.
1377. *Ibid.*

control of any such rights or interests are managed by the same person or group of persons.[1378]

With regard to the first scenario, the OECD provides that 'a person will be deemed to hold any equity or voting interests that are held by the members of that person's family'.[1379] This requirement resembles the concept of 'constructive ownership' in the United States, which means that a person is regarded to be the owner of stock owned by certain relatives, e.g., a spouse.[1380] The second scenario includes the situations where a person is required or expected by another person to act in accordance with the wishes of another person in respect of the voting rights or equity interest of the latter.[1381] The OECD clarifies, however, that a person is acting in accordance with the wishes of another only when the person is 'legally bound to act'.[1382] The distinction seems to be very straightforward, although it can represent problems in countries (mostly civil law countries) where indirect representation is possible.[1383] Indeed, in many civil law countries, the concept of '*commissionaire*' implies that a person acts in its own name but on account of the principal.[1384] Therefore, before third parties, the only relationship is with the commissionaire but never with the principal.[1385] Therefore, since the commissionaire acts in his own name, it is difficult to sustain that he acts on behalf of another or that he is 'legally bound to act' by another person when, in fact, the representation is only indirectly with respect to the principal, being perhaps the type of arrangement outside the scope of the concept of 'acting together'. This interpretation, however, could be refuted because of the reference that a person '[...] can be expected to act' and because the contract between the principal and the commissionaire exists regardless of the lack of relationship between a third party and the principal.[1386] The third scenario assumes that the arrangement must have a material impact on the value of those interests or rights. In other words, they must have a material impact on the ability of a holder to exercise control or ownership over its equity or voting rights.[1387] For example, if a shareholder is part of a shareholder's agreement by which he is obliged to offer his shares to the existing shareholders at an FMV before selling them to third parties, this would not generally create a material impact on the value of the shares.[1388] This seems to be a restriction on the test itself,

1378. *Ibid.*, p. 113, Recommendation 11.
1379. *Ibid.*
1380. *See* US: IRC s. 318 and explanation of the concept of '*constructive ownership*' at *supra* n. 717.
1381. OECD (2015), *supra* n. 6, p. 117, para. 370, letter a).
1382. *Ibid.*, I assumes that this would cover basically all the situations in which two parties have, e.g., an agency agreement.
1383. Avery Jones and Ward, *supra* n. 372, p. 345. *See also*, Parada, *supra* n. 372.
1384. This is not the same as the '*undisclosed agency*' in common law countries, where even though the name of the principal is not disclosed, the only relationship is always with the principal because no distinction is made in common law with respect to direct and indirect representation. *See* Parada, *supra* n. 372, p. 63.
1385. The principal is not legally bound with third parties who may, e.g., not initiate a legal action against the principal. *Ibid.*
1386. The commissionaire arrangement is still legally bound for the principal. *Ibid.*, p. 62.
1387. *Ibid.*
1388. OECD (2015), *supra* n. 6, p. 451, Ex. 11.4.

which is also restricted in terms that this is intended to capture only arrangements with other investors, and it does not cover arrangements that are part of the terms of the equity or voting interests or those which operate exclusively between the holder and the issuer, e.g., an arrangement between a partnership and one of the partners would not be included.[1389] Finally, the fourth scenario treats investors as 'acting together' when they are managed by the same person or group of persons, e.g., in the case of a group of partners (investors) within a partnership, who are managed by the general partner.[1390] This element is, however, constrained by the fact that it does not apply to investors that are CIV.[1391]

Despite the above, the 'acting together' test also attempts to catch situations between unrelated parties, even when the common control has not played any role in the transaction, giving rise to the mismatch.[1392] This is illustrated in Example 11.4 of the OECD Action Plan 2, which, in brief, refers to a company (BCo) which is owned by a majority shareholder (ACo), which holds 40% of the shares. The remaining ownership is represented by 55% owned by different shareholders and 5% owned by C, a minority shareholder. C acquires a financial instrument, and even though he is not a 'related party' with BCo (he does not meet the requirement of being in the same control group and does not hold at least 25% of the shares by value or voting rights), the sole fact of being part of an agreement with the other shareholders that provides the majority shareholder with the first right of refusal on any disposal of shares, brings him within the scope of application of the linking rules.[1393] Although the example is not illustrated using the concept of control group but rather the concept of 'related parties' (applicable to hybrid financial instruments), it is interesting to remark that the sole fact that the investor has entered into an agreement with a majority shareholder puts him under the umbrella of the 'acting together test', and therefore, under the application of *linking rules*.[1394] Indeed, in my view, this simply reaffirms what has already been stressed before with respect to the (unnecessary) extension of the concept of 'control group', mostly when other concepts are also coming into play, such as the concept of *structured arrangements* analysed below.

3.3.2 Structured Arrangements

The OECD defines a *structured arrangement* as 'any arrangement where the hybrid mismatch is priced into the terms of the arrangement or the facts and circumstances (including the terms) of the arrangement indicate that it has been designed to produce a hybrid mismatch'.[1395] As such, therefore, a structured arrangement is intended to

1389. *Ibid.*, p. 118.
1390. *Ibid.*
1391. It is important to remark in this case that the 'investors' are those who must rely on the exception for CIV and not, e.g., the partnership which they are investing in, and which is related to the entity with which the mismatch was generated. *Ibid.*, p. 453, Ex. 11.5.
1392. *Ibid.*, p. 118.
1393. *Ibid.*
1394. *Ibid.*
1395. *Ibid.*, p. 105.

capture transactions that are structured or based on hybrid outcomes, e.g., D/NI, or that depend on these outcomes in order to produce a commercial profit.[1396]

As per the definition above, there are at least three main elements that are required to conclude that a *structured arrangement* exists and, thus, to confirm the application of *linking rules*: (i) the existence of an arrangement; (ii) a hybrid mismatch priced into the terms of that arrangement, or facts and circumstances of the arrangement that indicate that the arrangement was designed to produce a hybrid mismatch; and (iii) a person being party to this arrangement.[1397] As regards the existence of an arrangement, the OECD states that an arrangement 'will include a number of separate arrangements that all form part of the same plan or understanding and will include all the steps and transactions by which that plan or understanding is carried into effect'.[1398] The above also confirms the idea that tax administrations should not only look at the specific transaction (or contract) generating the hybrid mismatch, e.g., the loan agreement, but to the whole structure or tax planning in order to determine the existence of a *structured arrangement*. This makes the concept of arrangement certainly very wide.

Accordingly, it is required that the hybrid mismatch is 'priced into the arrangement' or that the 'facts and circumstances' surrounding the arrangement suggest that this was designed to produce a hybrid mismatch. These two requirements represent two different realities. First, the former, i.e., the 'priced into the agreement' test, is the intention to objectivise the test. Indeed, as per the OECD, a hybrid mismatch will be 'priced into the terms of the arrangement if the mismatch has been factored into the calculation of the return under the arrangement'.[1399] The test, therefore, focuses only on the terms of the arrangement itself, without paying attention to other factors, such as the relationship between the parties.[1400] In other words, it represents an honest intention to establish an objective criterion. Second, however, the 'fact and circumstances' test is not only a wider test, as recognised by the OECD,[1401] but certainly a more subjective one.[1402] The OECD provides a non-exhaustive list of facts and circumstances that would suggest that an arrangement should be treated as structured, including, e.g., arrangements designed, or part of a plan, to create hybrid mismatches; arrangements that incorporate a term, step or transaction used to create hybrid mismatches; marketed arrangements where all the advantages, or some of them, are based on the hybrid mismatch, among others.[1403] All these factors, which include

1396. Cooper, *supra* n. 1272, p. 342.
1397. Although the report does not mention it, I believe that these three elements are interconnected, and therefore, the absence of any of them supposes the failure in passing the test to confirm the existence of a structured arrangement, and subsequently, the application of *linking rules*.
1398. OECD (2015), *supra* n. 6, p. 106.
1399. *Ibid.*
1400. *Ibid.*, p. 107.
1401. *Ibid.*
1402. The OECD, however, argues that both tests determining whether a *structured arrangement* exists are indeed 'objective'. *Ibid.*, p. 106, para. 319.
1403. The full non-exhaustive list includes: 'a) an arrangement that is designed, or is part of a plan, to create a hybrid mismatch; b) an arrangement that incorporates a term, step or transaction used in order to create a hybrid mismatch; c) an arrangement that is marketed, in whole or in

looking at, e.g., the relationship between parties, the circumstances under which the arrangement was made, the steps and transactions involved, or the economic and commercial benefits derived from it, must be considered from the view of an 'objective and well-informed observer', who will conclude that the arrangement was designed to produce a hybrid mismatch.[1404] Similarly, for example, an arrangement is considered marketed not only in written or electronic manners but also 'orally'.[1405] However, who else, beyond the persons who were part of a meeting, could certainly prove that the arrangement was indeed marketed in the absence of written and electronic support? And if witnesses attest such, what is the legal value of their statement? After all, what is clear so far is that the *structured arrangement* test, as designed, will generate an important extra burden not only for the tax administrations but also for the taxpayers who decide to counterargue the reasoning of the tax administrations in determining the existence of a structured arrangement, not avoiding but perhaps increasing the complexity for cases involving hybrid mismatches.[1406]

In the same order of ideas, and at least referring exclusively to structures involving hybrid entities and reverse hybrids, it is almost impossible not to consider any arrangement involving these types of structures as *structured arrangements*. Let us assume, e.g., a simple tax planning structure involving the financing of some subsidiaries through simple loans and the use of CTB to avoid CFC rules in the parent companies in the United States due to passive income received at the level of the subsidiaries.[1407] This planning is developed by a law firm, which nevertheless writes a report to the taxpayers in a general manner, i.e., as a type of 'doing business report', that includes a general explanation of the US tax rules, including CFC rules and CTB regulations and the tax treatment of the loan for US tax purposes. Would that be considered as 'marketed' by an 'objective observer'? If not marketed, can it be affirmed by this 'objective observer' that the arrangement was made to create a hybrid mismatch? It is evident that the 'hybrid mismatch' will come up after all because if a parent company in the United States is lending money to a subsidiary in Europe, which for US tax purposes is regarded as tax transparent whilst in Europe is considered as a taxable entity, the interest will end up as a deduction at the level of the payer subsidiary whilst the loan will be treated as a non-recognised loan in the United States. This is indeed publicly known information.[1408] Moreover, if the use of the CTB rules were to

part, as a tax-advantaged product where some or all the tax advantage derives from the hybrid mismatch; d) an arrangement that is primarily marketed to taxpayers in a jurisdiction where the hybrid mismatch arises; e) an arrangement that contains features that alter the terms under the arrangement, including the return, in the event that the hybrid mismatch is no longer available; or f) an arrangement that would produce a negative return absent the hybrid mismatch'. *Ibid.*, p. 105, Recommendation 10.2.

1404. *Ibid.*, p. 107.
1405. *Ibid.*, p. 109.
1406. In this opinion, de Boer and Marres argue: 'This complexity may be mitigated by the limitation in scope, but complexity is not avoided, not in the least because the scope is extended to structured arrangements, which is a rather vague concept.' De Boer and Marres, *supra* n. 1326, p. 40.
1407. For references to the CTB system and its use to avoid Subpart F income in the United States (CFC rule), *supra* Chapter 3, ss 4.4.1. and 4.4.2.
1408. It is within the law and can be consulted by everybody.

avoid CFC legislation and not to disregard the loan,[1409] it is difficult to affirm that the arrangement was directly designed for the purpose of generating a hybrid mismatch. Yet, as the 'facts and circumstances test' also incorporates a term, step or transaction used for the purpose of creating a hybrid mismatch and an arrangement that is 'part of a plan' to create a hybrid mismatch, it could still be possible for an 'objective observer' to consider this planning as a *structured arrangement*.[1410] Therefore, it seems to be, at least *a priori*, impossible that a structure involving hybrid entities or reverse hybrids will not be regarded as a *structured arrangement*. This simply reaffirms an idea already stressed in this work, which is that the concept of *structured arrangement* is more than simply a limitation to the application of linking rules, but indeed an excessive extension of their scope where almost everything can be captured.[1411]

In spite of the above, the presence of a *structured arrangement* lacks importance if taxpayers are not part of that arrangement.[1412] For this purpose, a person is considered to be party to a structured arrangement 'when that person has sufficient involvement in the design of the arrangement to understand how it has been structured and what its tax effects might be'.[1413] In contrast, the OECD clarifies that a person will not be party to a structured arrangement if that person does not benefit from the mismatch. Likewise, the concept excludes a person who could not 'reasonably have been expected to be aware of it'.[1414] According to the OECD, the knowledge test is 'objective', i.e., a taxpayer should not have an obligation to undertake additional due diligence on a commercial transaction beyond what 'would be expected of a reasonable and prudent person'.[1415] It is, however, difficult to agree that a test requiring such a criterion, i.e., the reference to a 'reasonable and prudent person' criterion, can indeed be regarded as objective. On the contrary, it is most likely that the understanding of what is a prudent and reasonable person will vary significantly from country to country, becoming a very subjective rather than objective test, if not completely vague. In addition, and regardless of the absence of reference to this matter, it seems to be logical, at least from a juridical point of view, that the tax administrations have the burden of proof in this case. In simple words, the tax administrations should prove that a taxpayer is sufficiently involved in the design of the arrangement and not otherwise.

Moreover, a person is not regarded as party to the arrangement if this person did not benefit from the mismatch or could not reasonably have been expected to be aware of it.[1416] The reasonable question is, again, who should prove the above? An intuitive answer, at least from a legal point of view, is that the tax administration should prove that the taxpayer benefited from the hybrid mismatch or that this taxpayer was at least

1409. Let us imagine, e.g., that the report was made based on the necessities of the client to simply avoid the anticipation of distributions, and thus recognition of income in the United States due to the application of CFC rules, without any other references to tax benefits.
1410. OECD (2015), *supra* n. 6, p. 108.
1411. This is perhaps given by the vague construction of it. De Boer and Marres, *supra* n. 1326, p. 40.
1412. *Ibid.*, p. 110.
1413. *Ibid.*, p. 106.
1414. *Ibid.*
1415. *Ibid.*, p. 111.
1416. *Ibid.*

aware of it, considering that many jurisdictions do not accept the proof of negative facts, i.e., that the taxpayer was not benefited. Nevertheless, the OECD seems to only partially recognise the above when it states: '[...] a tax administration should not be required to establish that the taxpayer has benefited from the mismatch before requiring that the adjustment be made'.[1417] In other words, a presumption is created since the taxpayer should first neutralise the mismatch, regardless that it was not aware or did not benefit from it, and then the tax administration might prove its involvement.

As a result, it is possible to conclude that the whole design of the concept of *structured arrangements* lacks not only proper objective criteria but is also very risky to apply from a legal point of view, particularly to ensure legal certainty. It is expected that taxpayers involved in transactions with hybrid entities and reverse hybrids will be almost always challenged and, in most cases, will be considered to have been part of a *structured arrangement*, considering the ambiguous nature of this concept. Indeed, if the ultimate intention of the OECD was to reduce the scope of application of *linking rules* in order to more closely target only abusive transactions, it would have been better, at least from a practical point of view, to rely on more accepted concepts, rather than introducing new and more complex ones.[1418] Last but not least, it is expected that the number of complexities arising from the application of this concept will simply increase in practice, generating a further negative effect in terms of administrative efficiency.[1419]

3.4 Tax Policy Concerns

Beyond the limitations in the scope of application of *linking rules,* the design and introduction of the linking rules within domestic laws also raise other important tax policy concerns. The author summarises these general concerns as follows: (i) the 'circular effect'; (ii) dependency on foreign laws; and (iii) economic double taxation issues. All these tax policy concerns are analysed as follows.

3.4.1 Circular Effect

Perhaps the most evident deficiency in the proposed *linking rules* is its 'circular effect'.[1420] Indeed, a payment will not be considered deductible in the country of the payer to the extent that payment is not included as income in the country of the

1417. *Ibid.*

1418. Although this issue exceeds the purpose of this chapter and the whole work, it would have been perhaps more interesting to follow common criteria, generally accepted, such as the concept of 'wholly artificial arrangements' widely recognised by the CJEU in Europe. *Supra* Chapter 1, s. 4.2. *See also*, de Boer and Marres, *supra* n. 1326.

1419. Cooper indirectly refers to this when he says: 'Clearly, there are practical difficulties in applying these rules [*control groups and structured arrangements*] to widely held instruments where the treatment of the payer might be contingent on the treatment of holders in many different states' (emphasis added). Cooper, *supra* n. 1272, p. 342.

1420. *See* K. Dziurdz, *'Circular Linked' Rules Countering Deduction and Non-Inclusion Schemes: Some Thoughts on Tie-Breaker Test*, 67 Bull. Intl. Taxn. 6 (2013), Journals IBFD. *See also*, Marchgraber, *supra* n. 881, pp. 141-142; Lüdicke, *supra* n. 870, p. 313.

recipient, and vice versa. In other words, a payment will be taxed to the extent a deduction on such payment was granted.[1421] Therefore, if two countries decide to include *linking rules* to target hybrid entity mismatches, they will necessarily become circularly linked since the application of the rules will necessarily depend on the tax treatment of the entity in the other country in which the mismatch in the payments originated.[1422] This could drive us to the absurd result that whilst the country of the payer denies the deduction so long as that payment is not exempted in the payee country (or the payment is disregarded in the case of a payment derived from a hybrid entity), the payee country considers that it will not apply the exemption only to the extent that the deduction was granted in the country of the payer, leaving both countries in an undecided position.[1423]

As proposed already in the past, these problems of circularity could be solved using 'tiebreaker rules'.[1424] However, the design of such rules is, again, not an easy task. For example, the OECD BEPS Action Plan 2 provides for a priority in the application of the rules.[1425] In this sense, a *primary response* will apply to deny a deduction to the extent that the corresponding payment is not included as income in the other country, and a defensive rule will apply only to the extent that a primary response was not applied.[1426] This is indeed a tiebreaker rule that provides for the application of the respective rule to counter the hybrid entity mismatch only if the other country does not apply the rule. However, as it can be seen, the tiebreaker rule does not solve the circular problem because the application of the rule depends again on

1421. *Supra* s. 3.1. and s. 3.2.

1422. This issue, however, would not exist if only one of the two approaches is used to counteract D/NI outcomes, i.e., either denying a deduction in the country of the payer or taxing a disregarded payment (or not granting the exemption in the case of HFI) in the country of the payee. *See* Dziurdz, *supra* n. 1420, p. 307.

1423. *Ibid.*, *see also*, N. Schmidt and K. Binder, *Chaos durch doppelten Kampf gegen doppelte Steuervorteile*, Die Presse (14 January 2013), available at www.dipresse.com.

1424. 'It would be hard to say which of the two rules [*primary response* or *defensive rule*] should have priority, whether both rules apply or both do not apply, or whether the only effective solution is to toss a coin. Consequently, a tie-breaker test is needed.' Dziurdz, *supra* n. 1420, p. 310. In 2012 (before the OECD BEPS Project), the OECD also recognised this issue when it stated: '[c]ountry rules linking the domestic tax treatment to the foreign tax treatment do not generally contain a tie-breaker test for cases where the other country involved has similar rules'. OECD (2012), *supra* n. 6, p. 24. *See also*, Marchgraber, *supra* n. 881, p. 142. Nevertheless, the OECD seems to address a different position with respect to tiebreaker rules within the OECD BEPS report: '[...] these recommendations contain an ordering rule so that one rule is turned-off when the counterparty jurisdiction with the same set of rules can neutralize the effect of the hybrid mismatch arrangements in a more effective and practical way. This ordering rule *avoids the need for an express tie-breaker rule* and achieves the necessary degree of co-ordination without resorting to the competent authority procedure' (emphasis added). *Ibid.*, p. 96. However, this would not solve the problem of opportunistic behaviours or who is 'getting in first' in terms of revenue collection.

1425. As regards to the *linking rules*, the OECD states: 'The rules apply automatically and there is a rule order in the form of primary rule and a secondary rule or defensive rule. This prevents more than one country applying the rule to the same arrangement and also avoids double taxation.' OECD (2015), *supra* n. 6, pp. 11-12.

1426. *Ibid.*

whether the other country's corresponding rule is applied.[1427] In other words, the circularity issue is simply moved from the rule counteracting the hybrid mismatch to the tiebreaker rule.[1428]

Commentators have also analysed other approaches that include, on the one hand, the possibility of disregarding the rule in the other country when it includes a 'back link' and, on the other hand, assuming an international meaning of the concept of debt and equity (as regards to HFI).[1429] As for the first approach, it could indeed stop the problem of circularity, although only temporarily and perhaps at a much higher cost. Indeed, if both countries include the tiebreaker rule, they will nullify each other's corresponding anti-hybrid rule, resulting in non-deduction/non-exemption, or which is the same: economic double taxation.[1430] This result is evident in the case of primary response and defensive rule because both rules involve a 'back link' to each other country's rules.[1431] As for the second approach, it seems more logical because it targets the real cause of hybrid mismatch arrangements, namely the divergent characterisation of financial instruments or entities.[1432] Nevertheless, in my opinion, such an approach in the case of hybrid entities and reverse hybrids should not be reduced to a simple tiebreaker rule solving the problems of application of the complex *linking rules* but should rather be applied as a separate standard that simply replaces the proposed OECD rules.[1433]

3.4.2 *Dependency upon Foreign Laws*

Another important feature of the proposed *linking rules* is the high reliance on foreign laws involved in their application.[1434] One could argue that there are plenty of other rules within tax law which refer to foreign laws and impose a certain degree of

1427. As stated by Dziurdz: 'One country's rule countering deduction and non-inclusion schemes would apply only if the other country's corresponding rule did not apply, and the other country's corresponding rule would not apply only if the first-mentioned rule applied. This yet again depends on whether or not the other country's corresponding rule applied, and so on.' Dziurdz, *supra* n. 1420, p. 308.
1428. 'If the tie-breaker test considered the fact of whether or not the other country's corresponding rule applies [...] there would again be a "circular link", but this time at the level of the tie-breaker test.' *Ibid.*
1429. *Ibid.*, pp. 308-309, who proposes a 'solution (2)' and 'solution (3)'.
1430. Although, it appears that countries are more willing to accept this result rather than economic double non-taxation. For example, in 2007 Denmark introduced a provision by which an interest deduction is granted only to the extent that the correspondent interest amount is not exempted in the other country. This rule, or the underlying policy behind it, was widely criticised, because the same precautions (i.e., avoiding the mismatch) are not considered when double taxation, rather double non-taxation, arises. *See, e.g.*, Bundgaard, *supra* n. 823, pp. 202-204. *See also* (from an Austrian perspective): S. Kirchmayr and G. Kofler, *Beteiligungsertragsbefreiung und Internationale Steuerarbitrage, 10* Zeitschrift für Gesellschaftrecht und angrenzendes Steuerrecht 9 (2011); M. Stefaner, *Konsequenzen der Anwendung von § 10 Abs. 7 KStG*, 22 Steuer und Wirtschaft International 8 (2012).
1431. Dziurdz, *supra* n. 1420, p. 308.
1432. *Ibid.*, p. 309.
1433. The author will go back to this proposal at *infra* Chapter 6.
1434. As stressed by Cooper: 'It has been clear for a long time that, if these recommendations [*linking rules*] are pursued and properly implemented, a state's tax law would become much

dependency, e.g., rules on tax credit or CFC rules, and thus, there should not be a problem at all to include rules 'linking' the outcomes of transactions involving hybrids. Nonetheless, there is a huge difference between a certain degree of reliance on foreign laws and a full dependency, the latter of which appears to be proposed under the linking rules.[1435] Indeed, it is difficult to argue that a country could become contingent or structurally dependent on the policies and practices of another country just because the former applies CFC rules or calculates a foreign tax credit relying on the concept of income in the other country. However, the design of the *linking rules* implies a direct connection to the law of the other country, including its further modifications, which demonstrates indeed a much higher degree of dependency.[1436]

A dependency on foreign laws in the case of tax matters should be carefully analysed from a tax policy perspective because one should not forget that countries attempt to accomplish a basic aim when imposing taxes, namely to generate revenues.[1437] Thus, even though countries might sometimes act in the interest of other countries, they will most probably only do so with those countries with which they have a deeper affinity based on cultural, economic or geographical reasons.[1438] In all other cases, it is expected that these countries want to act in their own interest, which could generate new issues that could make these rules destined to fail. For example, if two countries introduce both a *primary response* and a *defensive rule*, will the country of the payee accept that the deduction was denied in the country of the payer, or will it consider a different approach and decide to apply a *defensive rule*? As noted by Cooper already, there is indeed a high risk of 'getting in first', which is, in fact, an

more contingent and structurally dependent on the policies and practices of other governments.' Cooper, *supra* n. 1272, p. 346.

1435. To explain this difference, Lüdicke states: 'The former [CFC rule] seems easier for taxpayers and tax administrations as it requires less technical understanding about foreign tax rules and less factual knowledge about the fact and circumstances.' Lüdicke, *supra* n. 870, p. 313.

1436. An experience from excessive reliance on foreign laws can be taken from the modification to the German DCL regime (Dual Consolidated Losses). The German tax group of companies (*Organgesellschaften*), unlike other countries, is also applicable to dual residence entities, as it does not require that the legal seat of the members of the group to be in Germany. Rather, it only requires that the place of management of the tax group and the controlling company (*Organträger)*'s participation in the tax group is allocated to a German PE. The above implies that, in cases where no double tax treaty is applicable, losses from dual residents of the tax group could be offset against income in Germany and in the country where the relevant legal seat is located. To avoid such an effect, the German law was modified to establish that the negative income of a controlling company (*Organträger*) or a controlled company (*Organgesellschaft*) will be disregarded for German tax purposes to the extent that it is taken also into account by a foreign country in the taxation of the controlling company, the controlled company or any other person. However, as argued by Bärsch and Spengel, the simultaneous application of DCL rules in Germany and other countries and the fact that the rule will apply in cases beyond DCL cases, e.g., negative income generated by a foreign PE where the foreign income is not tax exempt in Germany due to the application of the credit method, might result in no loss set off at all. *See* Bärsch and Spengel, *supra* n. 1358, p. 527. In the same order of ideas, i.e., in reference to the German experience on DCL, Lüdicke argues that collateral damage is unavoidable, and that there is no doubt in German tax literature that the provision is excessive, inappropriately drafted, and not administrable. *See* Lüdicke, *supra* n. 870, p. 313, *also* n. 16.

1437. To give up revenues is not always an easy task. Cooper, *supra* n. 1272, p. 346.

1438. *Ibid.*

expected reaction of countries whose interests are based on the generation of revenues.[1439] Similarly, the risk of extreme dependency cannot only be derived from the law in the other country but also from the facts and circumstances, which puts countries in a more complicated situation.[1440] Following the example of Cooper with respect to HFI, it is clear that if a deduction associated with a payment using an HFI is denied in the country of the payer because this is made to a related party or *structured arrangement*,[1441] but then the instrument is sold to an unrelated party, the deduction should be reinstated.[1442] This demonstrates that the taxpayer's position in the country of the payer is directly linked, in this case, to the behaviour of the foreign taxpayer. In other words, the deduction of the payment will finally depend on the behaviour of the taxpayer in the foreign country.

A different dimension of the same problem is given by the costs associated with the reliance on foreign law, both from taxpayers' and tax administrations' perspectives. In fact, it is undeniable that taxpayers will still attempt to escape the *linking rules* in one way or another. The above could indeed imply an increase in tax planning costs, given by the most complex set of international *linking rules* and foreign laws that should be taken into consideration when tax planning.[1443] Accordingly, tax administrations will need a further and deeper knowledge of foreign laws in order to determine whether a deduction was indeed granted or whether the other country 'included' the payment as income, even though the concepts of deduction, inclusion, and income might certainly vary from each other. In a nutshell, and once again, *linking rules* increase uncertainty and transaction costs, both negative effects from a tax policy perspective. As argued by Lüdicke: 'Legislators should not underestimate the theoretical and the practical difficulties which arise if the application of the domestic taxation is made dependent on the details of foreign tax laws.'[1444]

3.4.3 Economic Double Taxation and Lack of Coherence

Connected to the circularity issues already discussed, it is undeniable that *linking rules* may generate new situations of economic double taxation.[1445] This issue, in principle, should not raise major concerns since there are plenty of examples in which economic double taxation is indeed an accepted or tolerated outcome.[1446] Nevertheless, this potential outcome should be analysed in line with the supposed coherence that Action

1439. *Ibid.*
1440. As stressed by Cooper: 'It is one thing to accept a constrain on sovereignty, as another sovereign state has acted, but it is quite a different matter to accept a constrain on sovereignty based on facts and circumstances happening abroad.' *Ibid.*
1441. *Supra* s. 3.3.2.
1442. Cooper, *supra* n. 1272, p. 347.
1443. The probabilities for complexities increase considering, e.g., *imported mismatches*. *Supra* s. 2.4.3.
1444. Lüdicke, *supra* n. 870, p. 317.
1445. This could perfectly happen when a *primary response*, denying a deduction in the payer country applies simultaneously with a *defensive rule*, which provides for taxation of a disregarded payment made by a hybrid entity.
1446. *Supra* s. 3.4.1.

2 attempts to implement.[1447] Indeed, as noted already in this work, *linking rules* attempt to counteract transactions involving hybrid entities (and hybrid financial instruments) in which the outcome of DNT arises in the form of a D/NI, although without creating new situations of double taxation.[1448] However, the proposed rules demonstrate a sound preference for the avoidance of economic DNT (i.e., D/NI outcome) over the avoidance of economic double taxation (i.e., non-deduction/inclusion).[1449] This idea is reinforced when one sees that there is no rule to solve potential issues of economic double taxation if, e.g., the denial of a deduction (i.e., *primary response*) finally results in the inclusion of income in the other country.[1450]

This situation becomes even clearer when we analyse the interaction of the *linking rules* with other rules denying deductions at a domestic level. Let us assume, for example, the application of *linking rules* and interest limitation rules in a given country.[1451] As a general rule, interest limitation rules, i.e., earning stripping rules, are designed in a way that if a taxpayer (Corporation) is in a situation of excess of indebtedness, i.e., its amount of interest expenses is over the amount of interest income, the amount of deductible interest income is limited according to certain criteria, normally a percentage of the amount of EBITDA (Earnings before Interest, Taxes, Depreciation and Amortization).[1452] The above implies that for that given

1447. As stated by the OECD: 'The recommendations set out in this report are intended to operate as a *comprehensive* and *coherent* package of measures to neutralize mismatches that arise from the use of hybrid instruments and entities without imposing undue burdens on taxpayers and tax administrations.' OECD (2015), *supra* n. 6, p. 94.

1448. *Supra* s. 2.

1449. *Supra* s. 3.4.1.

1450. On the contrary, the pragmatic approach taken by the OECD, in terms of taxing the income 'no matter where' and 'no matter base erosion', can be seen in the wording used to describe the policy behind the anti-hybrid rules [*design principles*], where it clearly says: '[...] hybrid mismatch rules apply automatically and without regard for whether the arrangement has eroded the tax base of the country applying the rule. This approach assures consistency in the application of the rules (and their outcomes) between jurisdictions and also avoids the practical and conceptual difficulties in distinguishing between acceptable and unacceptable mismatches or trying to allocate taxing rights based on the extent to which a country's tax base has been eroded through the hybrid mismatch arrangement'. OECD (2015), *supra* n. 6, p. 95.

1451. Interest limitation rules are also part of the proposal in the BEPS Action 4. *See* OECD, *Limiting Base Erosion Involving Interest Deductions and Other Financial Payments, Action 4 – 2015 Final Report*, OECD Publishing, Paris, 2015. *See also*, OECD, *Limiting Base Erosion Involving Interest Deductions and Other Financial Payments, Action 4 – 2016 Update: Inclusive Framework on BEPS*, OECD Publishing, Paris, 2016.

1452. For example, in Germany, as a general rule, a 'business' [*Betrieb*] is limited to deducting net interest expenses, i.e., the amount after offsetting the interest expenses against the interest earnings of the business as business expenses up to 30% of the amount of the taxable EBITDA. If there is thus an excess of net interest expenses, this is not deductible in the fiscal year, although it can be carried forward indefinitely and deducted in the subsequent fiscal years subject to the same threshold limitation. This general rule, however, has some exceptions. First, it only applies to the extent that the amount of net interest expenses exceeds EUR 3 million ('*de minimis* rule'). This amount was increased in 2009. The original amount was EUR 1 million. *See* DE: Citizen Relief Act [*Bürgerentlastungsgesetz*] of 16 July 2009, BGBl 1, 1959 (2009) and Growth Acceleration Act [*Wachstumsbeschleunigungsgesetz*] of 22 December 2009, BGBl 1, 3950 (2009). Second, it does apply only to the extent a business belongs, even

taxable year, the Corporation will see how its taxable base is increased in the same amount of non-deductible interest expenses, which, nonetheless, will be included in the country of the recipient, thus generating a situation of economic double taxation.[1453] This effect, however, is normally offset with the possibility for the taxpayer to carry forward the non-deductible amount and use those non-deductible expenses as per the same limitations already mentioned.[1454] Now, let us imagine that the payment of interest is connected with HFI, and thus, we should also apply the *primary response*. As per the OECD report on Action 2, the *primary response* has priority over the interest limitation rule and should apply first, whilst the remaining part of the interest expenses not affected by the linking rule will be subject to the interest limitation.[1455] Therefore, the country of the payer will deny the deduction because it considers that the income is not taxed in the other country. The denial of the deduction, in this case, will not generate economic double taxation if the income is not included in the other country. However, if, for any reason, the income is included in the other country (e.g., because the other country applies a different criterion for inclusion or a timing issue), the effect of economic double taxation will not be solved since the *primary response* does not provide for a non-deductible expense to be carried forward. In other words, if this hypothetical situation happens, the part of the interest expenses paid and affected by the *primary response*, i.e., where the interest limitation rule does not apply, will suffer

---

partially, to a tax group ('stand-alone clause'). Third, and finally, even in the case a business belongs to a tax group, the interest limitation rule does not apply if the business's equity ratio does not fall short of the group's equity ratio by more than 1% ('escape clause'). Generally speaking, the German interest barrier is codified in s. 4h of the Income Tax Act [*Einkommensteutergesetz*– EStG], which contains the general rule and the exceptions applicable to this rule. Likewise, §8a(2) and §8a(3) of the Corporate Income Tax Act [*Körperschaftsteuergesetz*– KStG] provides some special rules regarding the exceptions when applied specifically to corporate entities. The German interest limitation rule replaced the former thin capitalisation rule previously applied and it is applicable for accounting periods starting after 25 May 2007 and not ending before 1 January 2008. *See* K. von Brocke and E. Garcia Perez, *Group Financing: From Thin Capitalization to Interest Deduction Limitation Rules*, 16 Intl. Transfer Pricing J. 1 (2009), Journals IBFD, p. 31. *See also* in reference to the German rules, e.g., M. Scheunemann and T. Müller-Duttiné, *New German Tax Rules on Financing Expenses*, 35 Intertax 8/9 (2007) DOI: 10.54648/taxi2007056; A. Fross, *Earnings Stripping and Thin Cap Rules: Maintaining an Arm's Length Distance*, 53 Eur. Taxn. 10 (2013), Journals IBFD.

1453. A very simple example could be the following: let us imagine a company, in year X, with a given taxable EBITDA of 2,000, net interest expenses of 1,000, and taxable profits of 1,000. The amount of interest expenses is, however, limited to 30% of the amount of EBITDA in that year X. Therefore, the company may only deduct 600, being the remaining 400 added back to the taxable income, increasing the tax base of the company. Accordingly, however, the full amount of interest paid (1,000) will be taxable in the payee country. As a result, therefore, the non-deduction of 400, and its inclusion as income in the other country, represents a clear case of economic double taxation.

1454. In some cases, however, although an unlimited carry forward is offered, such an option is limited in practice. In Germany, e.g., in case of the discontinuance of the business or change of control, the non-deductible expenses cannot be used, which in other words implies that the economic double tax effect is permanent. DE: s. 4(h)(5)(1) of the Income Tax Act [*Einkommensteutergesetz*– EStG]. *See also*, C. Knöller, *The Efficacy of thin Capitalization Rules and their Barriers: An Analysis from UK and German Perspective*, 39 Intertax 6/7, 324-325 (2011) DOI: 10.54648/taxi2011037.

1455. For a more complete analysis on the interaction of linking rules and interest limitation rules, *infra* s. 4.1.

economic double taxation if the income is included in the other country, without any chance of turning that back. Therefore, this simply reinforces the idea that when putting together economic double taxation and economic double non-taxation in a balance, there is a certain inclination to opt for counteracting the latter rather than the former, even under the risk of producing new cases of economic double taxation.[1456] This is not only contrary to what the OECD attempts to demonstrate, i.e., the coherence within the application of the rules, but also an evident proof of lack of consistency when applying the rules, at least when the two aims (i.e., double taxation and DNT) are confronted.

3.5 Legal Concerns

Another issue associated with the implementation of the OECD *linking rules* as a manner to deal with the issues of hybrid and reverse hybrid entities refers to the legal compatibility of these rules, especially when they are tested against tax treaties (in particular, Article 24 OECD Model/non-discrimination provision) and EU primary and secondary law. This Section provides some insights with respect to this analysis.

3.5.1 Compatibility with Tax Treaties

Both the *primary response* and the *defensive rule* might *a priori* raise issues with respect to the compatibility between these domestic rules and tax treaties. Specifically, it points to the potential discrimination under Article 24 of the OECD Model when a deduction is denied in one country unless the income is included in another country, or when income is taxed at the recipient's level despite a deduction being granted in another country.

3.5.1.1 General Structure of Article 24 OECD Model: Non-discrimination

Unlike other non-discrimination provisions, Article 24 OECD Model is very straightforward in terms of its application.[1457] Indeed, e.g., it covers only cases of direct or de jure discrimination, excluding indirect, hidden or de facto discrimination.[1458] Indeed,

1456. *Supra* s. 3.4.1.

1457. The above also means that the analysis of discrimination is rather restricted.

1458. *See, e.g.*, A. Rust, in: Reimer and Rust (eds), *Klaus Vogel on Double Taxation Conventions*, 4th ed., 2015, Article 24 at m.no. 5. In a different perspective, e.g., the approach to discrimination under WTO covers both de jure and de facto discrimination, and it also includes possibilities for justification. *See* K. Dziurdz, *Non-Discrimination and Harmful Tax Competition under WTO Law and Article 24 of the OECD Model*, in: D. Weber and P. Pistone (eds), *Non-Discrimination in Tax Treaties: Selected Issues from a Global Perspective*, EC and International Tax Law Series Vol. 14, IBFD, Amsterdam, 2016, p. 210. Similarly, the EU law approach to non-discrimination includes both types of discrimination (direct and indirect) and provides for justification grounds. *See* F. Vanistendael, *Non-Discrimination: Can the EU Learn from the OECD Model Convention and Vice Versa?*, in: D. Weber and P. Pistone (eds), *Non-Discrimination in Tax Treaties: Selected Issues from a Global Perspective*, EC and International Tax Law Series Vol. 14, IBFD, Amsterdam, 2016, p. 227. As Vanistendael explains, however, in order to establish that discrimination occurs, a strict *comparability test* is applied: only those domestic provisions differentiating by reason of nationality or residence might give rise to discrimination.[1459] Therefore, every other relevant difference in circumstance is considered for the purpose of preventing comparability.[1460] Likewise, Article 24 OECD Model gives no space for 'justifications'.[1461] This latter characteristic is, nevertheless, not absolute because where a ground for different treatment acts as a substitute or a proxy for nationality of residence, direct discrimination can still be established.[1462]

The non-discrimination situations within Article 24 OECD Model include, on the one hand, paragraphs 1 and 2 refer to discrimination based on nationality.[1463] On the

---

the difference is basically because the aim of the EU was to achieve a rather stronger level of integration, which included 'the establishment of a common market, which later would develop into the internal market'. *Ibid.*, p. 226. This is certainly not the aim of the OECD Model or the international tax treaty network. *See also* in this opinion, e.g., K. Dziurdz and C. Marchgraber, *Non-Discrimination in European and Tax Treaty Law: An Overview* in: K. Dziurdz and C. Marchgraber (eds) *Non-Discrimination in European and Tax Treaty Law*, Linde, Vienna (2015), p. 10. Accordingly, the OECD Commentaries on Article 24 clearly state: 'The non-discrimination provisions of the Article seek to balance the need to prevent unjustified discrimination with the need to take account of these legitimate distinctions. For that reason, the Article should not be unduly extended to cover so-called indirect discrimination.' *See* OECD Commentary on Article 24 concerning non-discrimination, para. 1.

1459. Rust, *supra* n. 1458, Article 24 at m.no. 35.

1460. For example, residence is a relevant comparability for purposes of Article 24(1) OECD Model, because everything in the circumstances, except for nationality, must be the same. *See* OECD Commentary on Article 24 concerning non-discrimination, paras 7 et seq. *See also* Dziurdz and Marchgraber, *supra* n. 1458.

1461. Rust, *supra* n. 1458, Articles 24 at m.no. 4 and 132. Indeed, as explained by Vanistendael in reference to the fact that the OECD Model does not contain express grounds for justification: 'Unlike in the EU treaties, there are no reasons of public policy to make exceptions to the non-discrimination rule. Since the rules of the Model Convention are to be interpreted by many different national courts, chances that these courts would develop any doctrine resembling the rule of reason doctrine of the ECJ, permitting them to make exceptions to the nondiscrimination principle on the basis of a uniform juridical doctrine, are non-existent.' *See* Vanistendael, *supra* n. 1458, p. 246.

1462. For example, as per the OECD Commentaries on Article 24, the requirement of holding or being entitled to a passport is regarded as substitute for nationality. *See* OECD Commentary on Article 24 concerning non-discrimination, para. 1. *See also*, Dziurdz, *supra* n. 1458, and Dziurdz and Marchgraber, *ibid.*

1463. Article 24(1) OECD Model, on the one hand, prohibits a contracting State from subjecting the nationals of another Contracting State, who find themselves in the same circumstances, in particular with respect to residence, as the nationals of the first State, to a more burdensome tax treatment in comparison with the one imposed on nationals of the first State. *See* Rust, *supra* n. 1458, Article 24 at m.no. 5. The rule applies both to individuals and legal entities. Nevertheless, the importance for individuals is rather reduced, considering that nationality is no longer a proxy used to determine tax liability. *See* Y. van Brussel, *The Relevance of Residence as a Safeguard in Article 24(1) of the OECD Model* in: K. Dziurdz and C. Marchgraber (eds) *Non-Discrimination in European and Tax Treaty Law*, Linde, Vienna (2015), p. 354. As an exception, the United States still uses nationality to determine the worldwide taxation of individuals. This is also stated within the observation made by the United States to the Commentaries on Article 24, where it emphasises that 'its non-resident citizens are not in the same circumstances as other non-residents', precisely because the United States taxes its non-resident citizens on worldwide income. *See* OECD Observations to the Commentary on Article 24 concerning non-discrimination, para. 83. For a critical analysis regarding the use of citizenship in the United States, *see*, e.g., R. Avi-Yonah, *The Case of*

other hand, paragraphs 3, 4 and 5 include discrimination based on residence.[1464] Therefore, and as per the design of the proposed *linking rules*, the analysis will concentrate on paragraphs 4 and 5 of Article 24 OECD Model. Whilst the former refers to a specific non-discrimination rule with respect to the deductibility of expenses paid by an enterprise to a resident of the other Contracting State, the latter prohibits a more burdensome taxation of an enterprise established in a Contracting State by the sole reason of being wholly or partially owned by taxpayers in the other Contracting State.

3.5.1.2 Linking Rules and Article 24(4) OECD Model

Article 24(4) OECD Model provides that 'interest, royalties and other disbursements paid by an enterprise of a Contracting State to a resident of the other Contracting State shall, for the purpose of determining the taxable profits of such enterprise, be deductible under the same conditions as if they had been paid to a resident of the first-mentioned State'.[1465] Therefore, in principle, a rule denying a deduction of certain deductible payments (e.g., interest), which only applies in cross-border situations, might be considered against the non-discrimination provision of Article 24(4) OECD Model. In contrast, however, it could also be argued that if the rule (hypothetically) applies indistinctively to domestic and cross-border situations, and since Article 24(4) OECD Model does not cover cases of indirect or hidden discrimination, *linking rules* would be perfectly compatible with the non-discrimination provision.

The analysis becomes even more complex if we consider the lack of comparability between domestic and cross-border situations. Indeed, as HMA involving hybrid entities and reverse hybrids may only occur in cross-border situations, i.e., a country will never disagree with itself with respect to the characterisation of entities, there is no pure domestic situation to compare with and, in the absence of comparability, there is no discrimination.[1466] Additionally, and as stressed somewhere else already, *linking rules* are not designed based on residence but rather based on the existence of a hybrid

Taxing Citizens, Public Law and Legal Theory Working Paper No. 10-009 (2010), available at Michigan Law ELSC Website. *See also*, R. Mason, *Citizenship Taxation*, 89 Southern California Law Rev. 169 (2016). Accordingly, Article 4 OECD Model uses nationality as a 'tiebreaker' when competing claims over individual taxpayers result in a jurisdictional collision. *See* Article 4, para. 2 d) of the OECD Model Tax Convention (2014). A similar norm is contained in Article 4, para. 3 d) of the US Model Tax Convention (2016). The practical importance of Article 24(1) OECD Model varies with respect to companies, because full tax liability by reason of incorporation under domestic law is often the criterion to determine nationality under Article 3(1)(g) OECD Model. *See* K. van Raad, *Nondiscrimination in International Tax Law*, Series of International Taxation No. 6, Kluwer Law and Taxation Publishers, Deventer, 1986, p. 75. Article 24(2), on the other hand, applies the same rule with respect to discrimination to persons who are regarded as 'stateless' who have no nationality. There is no equivalent provision under EU law. *See* Vanistendael, *supra* n. 1458, p. 243.

1464. The scope of Article 24(3), however, is limited to PEs. According to this article, a PE cannot be taxed worse than a domestic enterprise. For a further analysis, *see*, *e.g.*, H. Bhuta, *Progressive Tax Rates in a Profit or Loss Situation under Article 24(3) of the OECD Model*, in: K. Dziurdz and C. Marchgraber (eds) *Non-Discrimination in European and Tax Treaty Law*, Linde, Vienna (2015), pp. 377 et seq.
1465. Article 24(4) OECD Model Tax Convention (2014).
1466. Dziurdz, *supra* n. 1458, p. 213.

mismatch, i.e., for purposes of this work, a disparity between two countries with respect to the characterisation of the same entity.[1467] All of the above would drive us to conclude *a priori* that a non-deductibility based on the recognition of income in the other Contracting State (i.e., *primary response*) would be a simple additional condition for the deductibility, which may not be regarded as directly discriminatory.

In spite of the above, it is still relevant to question whether the existence of a hybrid entity mismatch that results in a D/NI outcome might be regarded as a substitute proxy for discrimination based on residence or nationality.[1468] Dzuirdz assumes this question in the hypothetical situation of a country without access to the sea, which provides for a less favourable tax treatment to the profits of PEs belonging to non-resident enterprises if the respective enterprise, in its residence country, is located within 50 kilometres of the sea.[1469] According to Dzuirdz, this situation mirrors in part what happens with HMA, where mismatches will not arise in all circumstances but rather only with respect to certain non-residents where the hybrid mismatch results indeed in a D/NI.[1470] In both situations, however, the less favourable treatment might be a relevant criterion for the domestic 'anti-sea access' or the 'anti-HMA' provision, justifying the different treatment.[1471] Therefore, the relevant question is still whether or not sea access or the HMA prevents direct discrimination or whether they are indeed a mere pretext for disadvantaging non-residents.[1472] If the genuine tax policy were to prevent sea access or the occurrence of an HMA, there would be no conflict with Article 24(4) OECD Model because, as stressed already, this article only prevents discrimination based on nationality or residence, i.e., direct discrimination.[1473]

If the question above was analysed in a bilateral context, there would certainly be more possibilities to conclude that a discriminatory treatment occurs.[1474] For example, if Spain provides for a domestic rule denying the deduction of interest paid to a German parent company if, due to the different characterisation of the Spanish entity by Germany, the payment is not recognised as income in Germany, it is evident that the rule will affect all German residents (as non-residents). However, if Germany were to include the same rule, no Spanish parent company with a German subsidiary would be affected, considering the Spanish practice of following the characterisation of foreign

1467. As stated by Rust with respect to the design of *linking rules*: '[...] residence in the other Contracting State is neither necessary nor sufficient condition'. *See* A. Rust, *BEPS Action 2: 2014 Deliverable – Neutralizing the Effects of Hybrid Mismatch Arrangements and its Compatibility with the Non-Discrimination Provisions in Tax Treaties and the Treaty on the Functioning of the European Union*, BTR 3, 312 (2015).
1468. Dziurdz, *supra* n. 1458, p. 215.
1469. The author assumes the case of Austria, which does not have sea borders. *Ibid.*, p. 214.
1470. Nevertheless, Dziurdz explains that the fact that only few non-residents are disadvantaged does not prevent discrimination under Article 24(3) OECD Model. *Ibid.*
1471. *Ibid.*, p. 215.
1472. 'Determining the actual reason for different treatment and the background of a rule is not merely an issue of subjective intent. It is rather necessary to objectively determine the aim of the rule under scrutiny by analyzing its wording, context and systematics as well as the historical background.' *Ibid.*
1473. *Supra* s. 3.5.1.1.
1474. *Ibid.*

entities according to the rules of the foreign country.[1475] This analysis can be compared with the analogy that Dzuirdz makes with respect to sea access.[1476] If the treaty applied were Austria-Malta, then only Maltese companies with PEs in Austria would be affected, but not the other way around.[1477] Nevertheless, avoiding the specific bilateral context, it is clear that a rule such as the one introduced by Spain in the example above, applicable to all countries, would affect some countries and others not. The above, however, would simply mean that an indirect discrimination, not covered by Article 24(4) OECD Model, would arise.

As a result, therefore, it is possible to conclude that a different treatment for non-residents may exist when this different treatment is not necessarily a substitute for residence or nationality. In the same order of ideas, it is arguable that *linking rules* raises *a priori* discriminatory issues, considering mostly the strict comparability set up in Article 24(4) OECD Model.

3.5.1.3 Linking Rules and Article 24(5) OECD Model

Most tax treaties around the globe include a provision like Article 24(5) OECD Model. According to this provision: 'Enterprises of a Contracting State, the capital of which is wholly or partly owned or controlled, directly or indirectly, by one or more residents of the other Contracting State, shall not be subjected in the first-mentioned State to any taxation or any requirement connected therewith which is other or more burdensome than the taxation and connected requirements to which other similar enterprises of the first-mentioned State are or may be subjected.'[1478]

Therefore, the wording of paragraph 5 suggests some minimum requirements for its application.[1479] First, the provision applies only in case of resident subsidiaries, which are treated in a less favourable manner because of being controlled by a non-resident rather than a resident company.[1480] Put simply, this rule seeks to guarantee equal treatment for taxpayers in the same state, preventing a Contracting State from providing less favorable treatment to a resident business owned or controlled by residents of another Contracting State.[1481]

Second, the reason for the discrimination must rely exclusively on the fact that resident enterprises are owned or controlled, directly or indirectly, by a resident

1475. *Supra* Chapter 3, s. 5.1.
1476. Dziurdz, *supra* n. 1458, p. 216.
1477. *Ibid.*
1478. Article 24(5) OECD Model Tax Convention (2014).
1479. B. Da Silva, *Revisiting the Application of the Capital Ownership Non-Discrimination Provision in Tax Treaties* in: D. Weber and P. Pistone (eds) *Non-Discrimination in Tax Treaties: Selected Issues from a Global Perspective*, EC and International Tax Law Series Vol. 14, IBFD, Amsterdam (2016), p. 74.
1480. OECD Commentary on Article 24 concerning non-discrimination, para. 5, m.no. 76.
1481. *See* A. Rust, *International Tax Neutrality and Non-discrimination–Legal Perspective* in: M. Lang, P. Pistone, J. Schuch, C. Staringer, A. Storck and M. Zagler (eds) *Tax Treaties: Building Bridges between Law and Economics*, IBFD, Amsterdam, 2010 p. 641. Article 24(5) OECD Model does not protect the shareholders, resident in the other Contracting State. *See also*, Rust, *supra* n. 1458, Article 24 at m.no. 108.

enterprise in the other Contracting State. In other words, and as stressed already with respect to Article 24 OECD Model in general, this provision covers exclusively cases of direct discrimination.[1482] Third, the discriminatory treatment refers to 'other or more burdensome taxation' or 'connected requirements'. Whilst the reference to a 'more burdensome taxation' clearly requires a comparison of tax burdens, i.e., quantum of tax,[1483] the reference to 'other taxation' is rather unclear.[1484] Nevertheless, the inclination of some scholars to associate the first expression with a comparison of tax rates and the latter as a reference to the tax base, which would include, e.g., limitation in the deductibility of expenses, seems to be a clearer approach to interpretation.[1485] Finally, and as regards the object of comparison, the provision refers to 'similar enterprises'. Despite the unclear wording of Article 24(5) OECD Model to ascertain similarity,[1486] there are no doubts now that the phrase 'similar enterprises' refers to a comparison with domestic entities owned or controlled by residents of the same State of the subsidiary.[1487]

With regard to *linking rules*, however, i.e., rules motivated by the prevention of HMA that result in DNT, the relevant question remains the same, namely, do these rules genuinely aim to prevent DNT resulting from hybrid entity mismatches or do they indeed, by reason of foreign ownership, put the residence enterprise in a more burdensome position? Only in this latter case, i.e., a case of direct discrimination, could the application of Article 24(5) OECD Model be relevant.

As I have stressed already, the design of *linking rules* is rather broad.[1488] In principle, they attempt to cover all situations, domestic and cross-border, that might give rise to D/NI, regardless of the fact that, in practice, hybrid mismatches involving hybrid entities and reverse hybrids are limited or might only arise in cross-border transactions.[1489] One could nevertheless argue as a contrast that *linking rules*, as regards hybrid entity mismatches, apply only in the case of control groups.[1490] The above could give us some hints that the rules provide indeed a limitation based on foreign ownership, which could conflict with Article 24(5) OECD Model. Indeed, a

1482. *Supra* s. 3.5.1.1.
1483. J. Avery Jones et al., *The Non-Discrimination Article in Tax Treaties*, 31 Eur. Taxn. 10 (1991), Journals IBFD, p. 336.
1484. J. Kostohryz, *Ownership Non-Discrimination under Article 24(5) of the OECD Model in the Case of Low-Taxed Payments, Linde*, Vienna, 2015, p. 542.
1485. *See, e.g.*, van Raad, *supra* n. 1463, p. 93. Indeed, disallowing a deduction in one country has the direct effect of increasing the tax base in the country where the restriction is carried out. Therefore, the quantum of the tax is also higher. *See* Da Silva, *supra* n. 1479, p. 76.
1486. The dispute of interpretation referred basically to consider that the comparison should be made either with an enterprise owned by residents of the same State or by residents of a third State. *See* D. Oliver, *Differential Treatment of Discrimination?*, BTR 6, 435-441 (1993).
1487. OECD, *Application and Interpretation of Article 24 (Non-Discrimination)-Public Discussion Draft*, OECD Publishing, Paris, 2007, p. 27. *See also, inter alia*, Rust, *supra* n. 1463, Article 24 at m.no. 114; van Raad, *supra* n. 1463, pp. 188-189; B. Arnold, *Tax Treaty Monitor: Tax Treaty News*, 63 Bull. Intl. Taxn. 7 (2009), Journals IBFD, p. 270; J. Oliver, *Other Similar Enterprises – NEC Semi-Conductors Ltd and others v. Inland Revenue Commissioners*, BTR 2 (2004), pp. 80-83.
1488. *Supra* s. 3.3.
1489. *See* the examples of Spain, Austria and to certain extent Germany at *supra* ss 3.1. and 3.2.
1490. *Supra* s. 3.3.1.

primary response denying the deduction of a payment in the source country will apply only if that payment is not recognised as income (which occurs in the case of hybrid entities because of the tax treatment of the payer under the domestic rules of the payee country) and only to the extent that the transaction is made within a control group.[1491] However, the inclusion of the broader concept of *structured arrangements*, which also triggers the automatic application of the rules together with cases of control groups, might certainly refute this argument.[1492] The broader interpretation of the concept of *structured arrangement* makes, in theory, possible to include all of the other cases that are not strictly within a control group, refuting the idea that the rule is designed to provide a limitation based exclusively on the foreign ownership of entity. Indeed, one should not forget that it is not prima facie relevant for purposes of Article 24(5) OECD Model, whether interests are paid to a resident or non-resident creditor.[1493] The discrimination must be based exclusively on the foreign ownership or control. In other words, paragraph 5 is not concerned about the debtor-creditor relationship unless a different treatment is based on ownership or control.[1494] In this regard, e.g., a *primary response* denying an interest deduction in the case where the payment is not regarded as income because of the different characterisation of the payer entity might be arguably considered discriminatory if the rule would apply, indistinctly, in cases of a resident entity controlled by a foreign parent company (i.e., control groups) and, at the same time, in cases where is considered that an arrangement was marketed in order to produce the hybrid entity mismatch, and the DNT result (i.e., structured arrangement), independently on the ownership or control relationship between debtor and creditor.

Finally, considering that Article 24(5) OECD Model does not prevent discrimination at the level of the resident-shareholders, the taxation at the level of the payee entity by reason of a deducted payment at the level of the payer, i.e., the potential discrimination derived from the application of a *defensive rule*, would not be included within the scope of this article.

3.5.2 *Compatibility with EU Law*

As regards the analysis of the compatibility of *linking rules* and EU law, I will attend to the classic distinction between EU secondary law and EU primary law (fundamental freedoms), as detailed below.

3.5.2.1 *EU Secondary Law*

In the early stage of the BEPS project, scholars discussed the potential introduction of *linking rules* to deny a deduction in the payer MS if the income is not recognised as such and taxed in the other country or taxing the income at the level of the payee MS, i.e.,

1491. *Ibid.*
1492. *Supra* s. 3.3.2 referred to the concept of '*structured arrangements*'.
1493. OECD Commentary on Article 24 concerning non-discrimination, para. 79.
1494. The debtor-creditor relationship might be targeted within the scope of Article 24(4) OECD Model. Rust, *supra* n. 1458, Article 24 at m.no. 107.

not applying an unconditional exemption, if the deduction in the other MS was indeed granted.[1495] The discussion related basically to the compatibility of the proposed *linking rules* with respect to two EU Directives: (i) the I&R Directive 2003/49/EU,[1496] and (ii) the PSD 2011/96/EU,[1497] with regard to the primary response and secondary rule, respectively. Both rules are, nonetheless, included today in the 2016 EU ATAD[1498] and its amendment of 2017 (ATAD II).[1499] Therefore, as such, *linking rules* are indeed in compliance with EU secondary law.

3.5.2.1.1 Primary Response

With regard to the primary response, Article 1(1) of the I & R Directive states that: 'Interest or royalty payments arising in a Member State shall be exempt from any taxes imposed on those payments in that State, whether by deduction at source or by assessment, provided that the beneficial owner of the interest or royalties is a company of another Member State or a permanent establishment situated in another Member State of a company of a Member State.'[1500] As such, it is clear that the rule attempts to prevent the source MS from imposing taxation on those payments when these are received by a recipient in another MS. Therefore, in principle, denying a deduction at the level of the payer MS (i.e., primary response) would not infringe the directive, because the directive does not refer to the taxation of the payer (who owes the interest) but rather to the taxation of the creditor (payee).[1501] This interpretation is based on the decision of the CJEU in *Scheuten Solar Technology GmBH v. Finanzamt Gelsenkirchen-Süd*, which concerned a Dutch parent company (Scheuten Solar System BV), which wholly owned a German LLC (SST).[1502] For a period between August 2003 and December 2004, Scheuten Solar System BV granted a series of loans and received in return payment of interest from SST.[1503] For purposes of the tax assessment in Germany, however, SST was allowed to deduct only 50% of the interest paid, which generated that the other 50% had to be added back to the tax base of the company.[1504] SST initiated thus a proceeding against the decision of the *Finanzamt* in Germany, arguing that the fact of adding back the amount of non-deductible interest expenses was indeed contrary to Article 1(1) of the I&R Directive because it constitutes taxation

1495. Rust, *supra* n. 1467.
1496. EU: Council Directive 2003/49/EC of 3 June 2003.
1497. EU: Council Directive 2011/96/EU of 30 November 2011 on the common system of taxation applicable in the case of parent companies and subsidiaries of different Member States, OJ L345/ 8 (2011), hereinafter]Council Directive 2011/96/EU of 30 November 2011'.
1498. EU: Council Directive (EU) 2016/1164 of 12 July 2016 (ATAD I). *See also, supra* Chapter 3, s. 5.3.2.
1499. EU: Council Directive (EU) 2017/952 of 29 May 2017 (ATAD II).
1500. Article 1(1) of the Council Directive 2003/49/EC of 3 June 2003.
1501. Rust, *supra* n. 1481, p. 312.
1502. EU: Judgment in *Scheuten Solar Technology GmBH v. Finanzamt Gelsenkirchen-Süd*, C-397/09, ECLI:EU:C:2011:499.
1503. *Ibid.*, para. 14.
1504. *Ibid.*, para. 15.

on the amount of non-deductible interest.[1505] The Court, in this regard, was clear and provided that: 'The scope of Directive 2003/49, as defined in Article 1(1) of the directive, thus concerns the exemption of interest and royalty payments arising in their source Member State, provided that the beneficial owner is a company of another Member State or a permanent establishment situated in another Member State of a company of a Member State.'[1506] Accordingly, it stated: 'It follows that Article 1(1) of Directive 2003/49, read in the light of recitals 2-4 in the preamble to the directive, aims to avoid legal double taxation of cross-border payments of interest by prohibiting the taxation of interest in the source Member State to the detriment of the actual beneficial owner. That provision thus concerns solely the tax position of the interest creditor.'[1507] This last statement of the CJEU clarifies, therefore, that denial of a deduction in the source MS do not violate the Directive because, indeed, the scope of the directive only includes the potential legal double taxation that the creditor could suffer, but it cannot be interpreted beyond this scope.[1508] In other words, the domestic rules used to calculate the tax assessment of the taxpayer who paid the interest, e.g., rules denying a deduction under certain circumstances, are out of the scope of Article 1(1) I&R Directive.[1509] Therefore, when applying the reasoning of the Court to the application of a *primary response* denying a deduction at the level of the payer, our conclusion should be similar; namely, it is not an infringement of the directive.

Most of this discussion is, however, completely overcome today due to the approval and entry into force of the EU ATAD.[1510] Indeed, Article 9(2) of the ATAD states: 'To the extent that a hybrid mismatch results in deduction without inclusion, the Member State of the payer shall deny the deduction of such payment.'[1511] In other words, the denial of a deduction in the source MS is allowed under EU secondary law to the extent that this denial attempts to counteract the non-inclusion of income in the other MS, which resulted from the use of a hybrid structure, either through the use of a financial instrument or an entity.[1512] Likewise, considering the latest development with respect to hybrid mismatches in Europe, a similar rule has been extended to situations involving third countries.[1513]

3.5.2.1.2 Defensive Rule

With respect to the *defensive rule*, i.e., the rule imposing that the State receiving a payment involving a hybrid structure where that payment is deductible in the State of source, one should be aware that this rule was already introduced within Article

1505. *Ibid.*, paras 18-19.
1506. *Ibid.*, para. 25.
1507. *Ibid.*, para. 28.
1508. *Ibid.*, para. 34. *See also*, Rust, *supra* n. 1481, p. 312.
1509. *Ibid.*
1510. EU: Council Directive (EU) 2016/1164 of 12 July 2016 (ATAD I).
1511. Article 9(2) of the Council Directive ATAD I.
1512. *Supra* Chapter 3, s. 5.3.2.
1513. EU: Council Directive (EU) 2017/952 of 29 May 2017 (ATAD II).

4(1)(a) of the PSD in 2014.[1514] Indeed, as provided within the updated text of Article 4(1)(a) of the PSD, a parent company will refrain from taxing the profits received by a subsidiary: '[...] to the extent that such profits are not deductible by the subsidiary, and tax such profits to the extent that such profits are deductible by the subsidiary'.[1515] Currently, thus, MS are obliged to tax and not to unconditionally grant the exemption method to relieve double taxation if a distribution of profits were deductible in the source MS.[1516] On the other way around, MS would be prevented from taxing those payments, to the extent that they are not deductible, which includes the possibility that they were not deducted by application of, e.g., a thin cap rule, earning stripping rule (i.e., interest limitation) or any other anti-base erosion provision.[1517]

The introduction of the *secondary rule* within EU law, even before the issuance of the EU ATAD in 2016, explains why it was not originally necessary to include such a rule within the final text of the EU ATAD.[1518] However, the inclusion of a *secondary rule* within the PSD itself limits the application of the rule. First, the PSD only applies to transactions between MSs, excluding, therefore, third countries.[1519] Second, it only applies in case of a 'parent-subsidiary' relationship, with minimum participation and other requirements,[1520] which could, e.g., exclude cases of hybrid mismatches involving *structured arrangements* that are not necessarily related to such relationship.[1521]

Perhaps recognising the limitations stated above, the European Commission launched at the beginning of 2017 a proposal for amending the EU ATAD (2016), which introduces a *secondary rule* but within Article 9 of the ATAD, whose final text was

---

1514. EU: Council Directive 2014/86/EU of 8 July 2014 amending Directive 2011/96/EU.
1515. Article 4(1)(a) of the Council Directive 2011/96/EU as amended by Council Directive 2014/86/EU of 8 July 2014.
1516. Originally, however, the exemption had to be granted without conditions as it can be interpreted from the original text of the PSD, which provided that the parent company should 'refrain from taxing such profits'. Article 4(1)(a) of the Council Directive 2011/96/EU (original text).
1517. In this opinion, *see also* de Boer and Marres, *supra* n. 1326, p. 34. This issue has special importance after the approval of the final text of the ATAD (2016), because indeed this document contains both an interest limitation and a rule dealing with hybrid mismatches, which resembles the proposal of the OECD BEPS Action Plan. The ATAD does not contain any rule of hierarchy to solve this issue. *See* Articles 4 and 9 of the Council Directive (EU) 2016/1164 of 12 July 2016 (ATAD I).
1518. EU: Council Directive 2014/86/EU of 8 July 2014 amending Directive 2011/96/EU, Article 4(1)(a).
1519. Article 1(1), letters (a) to (d) of the Council Directive 2011/96/EU as amended by Council Directive 2014/86/EU of 8 July 2014.
1520. For example, a minimum holding period of two years can be required to apply the PSD. *See* Article 3(2)(b) of the Council Directive 2011/96/EU as amended by Council Directive 2014/86/EU of 8 July 2014.
1521. The proposal for a Directive modifying the Council Directive (EU) 2016/1164 of 12 July 2016 (ATAD I), provides that a *structured arrangement* 'means an arrangement involving a hybrid mismatch where the mismatch outcome is priced into the terms of the arrangement or an arrangement that has been designed to produce a hybrid mismatch outcome, unless the taxpayer or an associated enterprise could not reasonably have been expected to be aware of the hybrid mismatch and did not share in the value of the tax benefit resulting from the hybrid mismatch'. EU: Proposal ATAD II (17 February 2017), p. 17. This text was included also in the finally approved Council Directive EU: Council Directive (EU) 2017/952 of 29 May 2017 (ATAD II).

approved in May 2017.[1522] As regards D/NI outcomes, the new Article 9(2)(b) reads as follows: 'To the extent that a hybrid mismatch results in a deduction without inclusion: [...] (b) where the deduction is not denied in the payer jurisdiction, the amount of the payment that would otherwise give rise to a mismatch outcome shall be included in income in the Member State that is the payee jurisdiction.'[1523] As noted, therefore, the wording and scope of the proposed *secondary rule* included as part of Article 9 of the ATAD is indeed wider than the existing rule within the PSD. First, it refers to 'payments' rather than just 'distribution of profits', as it is the current scope of application of the PSD.[1524] Second, it applies to cases that might include third countries outside the EU, which is indeed prevented under the pure application of the PSD. Therefore, the implementation of a *defensive rule* would not infringe on EU secondary law, whether before the implementation of the ATAD or after it, because it was already part of the PSD since 2014. Nevertheless, in my opinion, the implementation of Council Directives targeting specifically hybrid mismatches both inside and outside the EU (ATAD I and II) will create an overlapping rule with respect to the *defensive rule* included within the PSD, which, unless modified, will become useless.

3.5.2.2 *EU Primary Law: Fundamental Freedoms*

The EU was created with the purpose of economically binding European countries in order to avoid future wars.[1525] This economic integration also supposes the accomplishment of some minimum standards of protection, i.e., fundamental freedoms that include the free movements of goods, persons, services, and capital, which are rigorously enforced before the CJEU.[1526] In other words, unlike direct taxation, which remains a matter of MS sovereignty within the EU, this competence must be exercised in accordance with the fundamental freedoms.[1527] Therefore, every national tax

1522. *Ibid., see also, supra* Chapter 3, s. 5.3.3.
1523. EU: Council Directive (EU) 2017/952 of 29 May 2017 (ATAD II).
1524. Article 4(1) of the PSD provides that: 'Where a parent company or its permanent establishment, by virtue of the association of the parent company with its subsidiary, receives distributed profits [...].' Article 4(1) of the Council Directive 2011/96/EU as amended by Council Directive 2014/86/EU of 8 July 2014.
1525. R. Mason, *A Theory of Tax Discrimination*, NYU Jean Monnet Working Paper No. 09/06 (2006), p. 2.
1526. *Ibid.*
1527. The lack of harmonisation in direct taxes is due to the unanimity requirement, which requires all MS to agree. The above is nonetheless a very difficult aim to achieve. Terra and Wattel, *supra* n. 381, pp. 16-17. There are, however, two possible exceptions to the unanimity requirement in tax matters. The first one stems from Articles 107 and 108(3) last sentence [State Aid rules] of the TFEU, which forbid granting any aid to undertakings without prior Commission approval. The second one is found in Article 116 TFEU, concerning market distortions caused by disparities between national laws or practices, which allows a qualified majority for the adoption of directives counteracting those matters. *Ibid., see also, e.g.*, A.J. Easson, *Taxation in the European Community*, European Community Law Series: 5, The Athlone Press, London, 1993, pp. 15-16.

measure must be reviewed by the CJEU under an infringement procedure or a preliminary ruling.[1528]

To determine whether a national rule creates or not tax discrimination,[1529] the CJEU carries out an analysis involving different phases. In the first place, the CJEU determines which of the fundamental freedoms is indeed potentially infringed. Once this has been done, it proceeds to make a comparability analysis, by which it compares the situation of the complaining taxpayer (normally a non-resident with economic connection with the host country) with a comparable domestic situation in order to determine whether or not these two comparable situations are treated equally.[1530] If the result of this second phase is that the national rule is discriminatory, there must still be justifications for the discrimination.[1531] The analysis between *linking rules* and EU primary law,[1532] therefore, will be made considering this line of analysis. It will also distinguish between *primary response* and *defensive rule*, and it will finally include a separate Section with the analysis regarding proportionality.[1533]

3.5.2.2.1 Primary Response

3.5.2.2.1.1 Analysis of Comparability

As regards the *primary response* and whether this rule would infringe on the non-discrimination principle under the TFEU, it should be noted that the jurisprudence of

1528. EU: Consolidated Version of the Treaty on the Functioning of the European Union (TFEU) of 26 October 2012, OJ C 326/47 (2012). *See* Articles 258 and 267 TFEU. *See also, e.g.*, EU: Judgment in *Wielockx v. Inspecteur der Directe Belastingen*, C-80/94, EU:C:1995:271 and Judgment in *Royal Bank of Scotland plc v. Elliniko Dimosio (Greek State)*, C-311/97, EU:C:1999:216.
1529. Mason and Knoll argue that: '[...] in common markets, like the EU and the United States, the best interpretation of the nondiscrimination principle is that it requires what we call "competitive neutrality", which prevents states from putting residents at a tax-induced competitive advantage or disadvantage relative to nonresidents in securing jobs'. R. Mason and M. Knoll, *What is Discrimination?*, 121 Yale L.J. 1014, 1014 (2012).
1530. Mason, *supra* n. 1525, p. 3.
1531. *See* J. Di Maria, *Comparability in the Case of Hybrid Mismatch: In Search of an Approach Suitable for the Current European Landscape* in: K. Dziurdz and C. Marchgraber (eds) *Non-Discrimination in European and Tax Treaty Law*, Linde, Vienna (2015), p. 70. For purposes of this work, it is interesting to question specifically whether the 'fight against tax abuse' or the DNT outcome itself (i.e., the D/NI outcome) might be used as the justification grounds to allow a different treatment between domestic and cross-border situations.
1532. Some scholars have already expressed their concerns with respect to the compatibility of *linking rules* and EU primary law. *See, e.g.*, Rust, *supra* n. 1481; Marchgraber, *supra* n. 881. *See also*, J. Bundgaard, *Hybrid Financial Instruments and Primary EU law – Part 1*, 53 Eur. Taxn. 11 (2013), Journals IBFD; J. Bundgaard, *Hybrid Financial Instruments and Primary EU law–Part 2*, 53 Eur. Taxn. 12 (2013), Journals IBFD; C. Kahlenberg, *Extension of the Domestic Correspondence Principle*, 54 Eur. Taxn. 1 (2014), Journals IBFD; O. Thömmes and A. Linn, *The New German DCL and Dividends Matching Rules and EU Law*, 42 Intertax 1 (2014) DOI: 10.54648/taxi2014003; J. Becker and T. Loose, *Zur geplanten Ausdehnung des materiellen Korrespondenzprinzips auf hybride Finanzierungen*, 21 Internationales Steuerrecht 19 (2012); O. Dörfler, R. Heurung and G. Adrian, *Korrespondenzprinzip bei verdeckter Gewinnausschüttung und verdeckter Einlage*, 45 Deutsches Steuerrecht 12 (2007).
1533. The analysis of proportionality is important, because even though a national provision is considered discriminatory but justified, it should be tested whether it is proportionate.

the CJEU is, unfortunately, neither consistent nor uniform to provide an unequivocal answer.[1534]

If we consider as a starting point the decision in *Schempp* (Case C-403/03), we can rapidly conclude that rules addressing disparities or inconsistencies between MSs would not infringe the non-discrimination principle under the TFEU because of the lack of comparability between domestic and cross-border situations in those cases.[1535] In *Schempp,* the CJEU linked the deductibility of maintenance payments at the level of the obligor with the payment of taxes at the level of the beneficiary. Therefore, the fact that a deduction was denied because there was no corresponding inclusion of income in the other country was indeed regarded as acceptable.[1536] As provided by the CJEU: 'It follows that, contrary to Mr. Schempp's claims, the payment of maintenance to a recipient resident in Germany cannot be compared to the payment of maintenance to a recipient resident in Austria. The recipient is subject in each of those two cases, as regards taxation of the maintenance payments, to a different tax system. Consequently, the fact that a taxpayer resident in Germany is not able [...] to deduct maintenance paid to his former spouse resident in Austria does not constitute discrimination within the meaning of Article 12 EC.'[1537] Nevertheless, a completely different approach was assumed in *Eurowings* (Case C-294/97).[1538] In this decision, the CJEU concluded that the deductibility of leasing payments for purposes of the German trade tax should not be denied based on the contingency that these payments are subject to trade tax at the level of the recipient, considering that the tax advantage (i.e., the deductibility) and the disadvantage (i.e., the taxation of these payments) concern two different taxpayers.[1539] As stated by the Court: '[...] a merely indirect link between a fiscal advantage accorded

1534. *See, e.g.*, N. Bammens, *The Principle of Non-Discrimination in International and European Tax Law*, IBFD Doctoral Series, Vol. 24, IBFD, Amsterdam, 2012, p. 521.
1535. The case basically referred to a German taxpayer who intended to deduct some maintenance payments paid to his former spouse, an Austrian resident, within the period 1994 and 1997. The German tax authority [*Finanzamt München*] required a certification from the Austrian tax authority demonstrating that the maintenance payments were actually taxable in the hand of his former spouse in Austria. However, considering that these payments are generally excluded from taxation under Austrian law and that this law does not allow the payments to be deducted, such certification was not provided. The German taxpayer was therefore prevented from deducting the maintenance payments in Germany. *See* EU: Judgment in *Egon Schempp v. Finanzamt München V* (C-403/03) [2005] ECLI:EU:C:2005:446, hereinafter '*Schempp* case', paras 7-9. Determining comparable situations is indeed the cornerstone in the CJEU's discrimination analysis. This task, however, is very challenging and there is little guidance on how to choose a comparable. *See* Mason, *supra* n. 1525, p. 22. Likewise, a worse treatment for cross-border situations will be discriminatory only when the cross-border situation is similar to a pure domestic situation, such that there is no justification for treating those situations in a different manner. *Ibid., see also*, EU: Judgment in *Finanzamt Köln-Altsadt v. Schumacker*, C-279/93, ECLI:EU:C:1995:31. For an analysis on *Schumacker*, *see* F.A. Garcia Prats, *Revisiting 'Schumacker': Source, Residence and Citizenship in the ECJ Case Law on Direct Taxation* in: I. Richelle, W. Schön and E. Traversa (eds) *Allocating Taxing Powers Within the European Union*, Springer, Heidelberg (2013), pp. 1-42.
1536. Marchgraber, *supra* n. 881, p. 139. *See also*, Rust, *supra* n. 1481, p. 317.
1537. EU: *Schempp* case, *supra* n. 1535, para. 35. Article 12 EC corresponds to Article 18 TFEU today.
1538. EU: Judgment in *Eurowings Luftverkehrs AG v. Finanzamt Dortmund-Unna*, C-294/97, EU:C:1999:524, hereinafter '*Eurowings* case'.
1539. Rust, *supra* n. 1481, p. 317.

to a taxable person, such as the absence in the case of German undertakings leasing from lessors established in Germany of the obligation to make the add-backs in question, an unfavorable tax treatment of another taxable person, such as the liability of such lessors to pay trade tax, cannot be used to justify the fact that German undertakings are treated differently [...]'.[1540]

As regards to the comparability analysis and the case law of the CJEU, two different approaches can be distinguished.[1541] First, the CJEU applies an 'overall approach', i.e., an analysis considering the overall position of the taxpayer or a group of taxpayers, taking into account the deviating tax advantages in another MS.[1542] This can be seen, e.g., in *Shempp*,[1543] where the Court considered that there could not be a comparable situation and that the discrimination was the result of a disparity between MSs, considering also the deviating tax consequences in the other MS to conclude that

1540. EU: *Eurowings* case, *supra* n. 1538, para. 42.

1541. Therefore, depending on which CJEU's approach is finally adopted; a *primary response* could be (or not) regarded as discriminatory. In addition, however, Mason proposes a third alternative approach, which has never been applied by the CJEU so far: '*the internal consistency test*'. As stated by Mason: 'Under this approach, developed by the U.S. Supreme Court to analyze state tax discrimination claims under the Dormant Commerce Clause, the ECJ would ask: If all twenty-seven Member States enacted the challenged rule, would intra-Community commerce bear a burden that purely domestic commerce would not also bear?' R. Mason, *Made in America for European Tax: The Internal Consistency Test*, 49 Boston College Law Rev. 4, 1277 (2008). According to the author: '[...] the internal consistency test would help prevent two kinds of judicial errors in tax discrimination cases. One type of error occurs when the ECJ fails to recognise that cross-border disadvantages arise from disparities, not discrimination; another type occurs when the ECJ fails to discover discrimination because compensatory taxes in one state obscure the cross-border tax disadvantage caused by another state's discrimination'. *Ibid.*, p. 1325.

1542. In a critical view on the overall approach, Weber states: 'The assumption, which the ECJ accepts, that it is only the Member States that/which have the power to define the criteria for direct taxation means, in my opinion, under Community law, prohibited restrictions of the freedom of movement arise only as the result of the legislation of a single Member State and not the legislation of another Member State. Thus, restrictions do not depend on disparities between Member States [...].' D. Weber, *In Search of a (New) Equilibrium Between Tax Sovereignty and the Freedom of Movement Within the EC*, 34 Intertax 12, 599 (2006) DOI: 10.54648/taxi2006086. *See also*, Di Maria, *supra* n. 1531, p. 76.

1543. This approach has also been applied in other several decisions of the CJEU, starting from the landmark case of *Schumacker* case, *supra* n. 1535. *See also, e.g.*, *Wielockx* case, *supra* n. 1528; EU: Judgment in *P.H. Asscher v. Staatsecretaris van Financiën*, C-107/94,EU:C:1996:251; EU: Judgment in *F.W.L. de Groot v. Staatsecretaris van Financiën*, C-385/00, EU:C:2002:750; EU: Judgment in *Arnoud Gerritse v. Finanzamt Neukölln-Nord*, C-234/01, EU:C:2003:340; EU: Judgment in *Friederike Wallentin-Hermann v. Alitalia*, C-169/03, EU:C:2004:771; EU: Judgment in *Pirkko Marjatta Turpeinen*, C-520/04, EU:C:2006:703; EU: Judgment in *Bosal Holding BV v. Staatsecretaris van Financiën*, C-168/01, EU:C:2003:479; EU: Judgment in *Marks & Spencer plc v. David Halsey (Her Majesty's Inspector of Taxes)*, C-446/03, ECLI:EU:C:2005:763; EU: Judgment in *Test Claimants in the Thin Cap Group Litigation v. Commissioners of Inland Revenue*, C-524/04, EU:C:2007:161 and EU: Judgment in *Columbus Container Services BVBA & Co. v. Finanzamt Bielefeld-Innenstadt*, C-298/05, EU:C:2007:754. *See also, e.g.*, opinions of the Advocate General Geelhoed in EU: *Judgment in Test in Class IV of the ACT Group Litigation v. Commissioners of Inland Revenue*, C-374/04, EU:C:2006:139, point 39; in EU: Judgment in *Denkavit International and Denkavit France*, C-170/05, EU:C:2006:266, points 33-40; in *Thin Cap Group* case, *Ibid.*; in EU: Judgment in *Maragarete Block v. Finanzamt Kaufbeuren*, C-67/08, EU:C:2008:92, para. 31. As noted by Weber: 'It has become clear that Advocate General Geelhoed does not agree with the per-country approach [...] and (thus) is a proponent of the overall approach.' Weber, *supra* n. 1542, p. 600.

a deduction could be denied because there was not a respective inclusion of income in the other MS.[1544] Nevertheless, it is very arguable that the Court had achieved such a conclusion (i.e., lack of comparability) on the basis of differences between tax systems, because disparities are indeed a consequence of the coexistence of discrete national tax systems[1545] and they are not equivalent to prohibited discrimination under EU law.[1546] In this regard, it is always worth remembering that, within the current EU framework, MSs remain free to design their own tax policies and the failure to recognise tax discrimination undermines the economic integration of Europe.[1547] On the contrary, the CJEU has opted for a 'per-country approach', i.e., determining the existence of a discriminatory provision as per the specific jurisdiction under analysis, without considering the offsetting tax advantages that might be independently available for the taxpayer in another MS.[1548] In *Eurowings*, e.g., the CJEU analysed the disadvantage created in isolation, i.e., disregarding the tax burden of the lessor in another MS, and concluding that the leasing payments for purposes of the German trade tax should not be denied based on the contingency that these payments are subject to trade tax at the level of the recipient.[1549] This approach seems, in principle, to be more consistent with the current EU framework where MSs have exclusive competence on matters related to direct taxation and where harmonisation is still not achieved.[1550] In other words, considering the sovereignty of MSs on direct tax matters, MSs' tax systems should not be affected by other MSs' tax systems.[1551] In the same order of ideas, an MS should not

1544. EU: *Schempp* case, *supra* n. 1535.
1545. S. Douma, *The Three Ds of Direct Tax Jurisdiction: Disparity, Discrimination and Double Taxation,* 46 Eur. Taxn. 11 (2006), Journals IBFD, pp. 522-533.
1546. As was provided by Mason: 'Only discriminatory tax law, not disparate ones, violate the EC Treaty.' *See* Mason, *supra* n. 1525, p. 4. In the same order of ideas, Weber argues: '[...] disparities do not result in restriction of the freedom of movement because that would mean that the sovereignty to levy tax would be endangered [...] *inherent* to tax sovereignty to levy taxes is that exercise of this sovereignty does not depend on how another Member State taxes'. *See also*, Weber, *supra* n. 1542, p. 602.
1547. Mason, *supra* n. 1525, p. 1.
1548. Di Maria, *supra* n. 1531, p. 72.
1549. *Eurowings* case, *supra* n. 1538. Other decisions in which the CJEU has applied the 'per-country approach' are, e.g., *Cadbury Schweppes* case, *supra* n. 123; EU: Judgment in *Société de Gestion Industrielle (SGI) v. Belgian State*, C-311/08, ECLI:EU:C:2010:26, hereinafter 'SGI case'; EU: Judgment in *Lankhorst-Hohorst GmbH v. Finanzamt Steinfurt*, C-324/00, ECLI: EU:C:2002:749; EU: Judgment in *X and Y v. Riksskatteverket*, C-436/00, EU:C:2002:704; EU: Judgment in *Deutsche Shell GmbH v. Finanzamt für Dortmund-Unna*, C-294/97, EU:C:1999:524; EU: Judgment in *Finanzamt Offenbach am Main-Land v. Keller Holding GmbH*, C-471/04, EU:C:2006:143; EU: Judgment in *Rewe Zentralfinanz eG v. Finanzamt Köln-Mitte*, C-347/04, EU:C:2007:194, among others.
1550. Weber, *supra* n. 1542, pp. 601-607. Here the author explains his arguments to support the 'per-country approach' over the 'overall approach'. In the same order of ideas, Lang states: 'The ECJ should be consistent in taking into account the legal situation in *one Member State only* when deciding whether a Member State has not complied with the freedoms ("per-country approach"). An "overall approach" makes it difficult to determine responsibility for infringements of the freedoms.' M. Lang, *Recent Case Law of the ECJ in Direct Taxation: Trends, Tensions, and Contradictions*, EC Tax Rev. 3, 113 (2009) DOI: 10.54648/ecta2009015. *See also*, Di Maria, *supra* n. 1531, pp. 81-86.
1551. Mason, *supra* n. 1525, p. 59. Likewise, Weber states: '[...] it is inherent to the sovereignty to tax that MS may limit their tax jurisdiction (in other words, not levy tax) and that taxation in one MS is not linked to taxation in another MS'. Weber, *supra* n. 1542, p. 593.

be obliged to adapt their own tax system to the different systems of tax of the other MS.[1552]

Finally, it is important to remark that HMA creates prohibited discrimination because of its very nature, and as such, the CJEU should not refrain from characterising *linking rules* as discriminatory, regardless of the good intentions behind their proposal.[1553] Nevertheless, and considering the EU framework and the uncoordinated existence of direct taxation, it is important that the determination on whether particular rules violate the TFEU is made independently without regard to any offsetting tax advantage in another MS.[1554] The above might grant not only more consistency to the comparability test but also more clarity to the jurisprudence of the CJEU on these matters.[1555]

3.5.2.2.1.2 Justification Grounds for Discrimination

Assuming that a domestic *primary response* is regarded as discriminatory, there are still grounds for justification for such discrimination.[1556] In this regard, the question is which type of justification must be used to allow a discriminatory rule. As this task has already been assumed somewhere else,[1557] this author will focus only on whether the 'cohesion of tax systems', 'the fight against tax abuse' or the 'DNT outcome itself' might be regarded as justification grounds for the imposition of discriminatory provisions.

3.5.2.2.1.2.1 The Cohesion of Tax Systems

The decision in *Schempp* is not only important to confirm the lack of comparability, as noted above, but also to reinforce the idea of 'cohesion of tax systems' as a justification ground to allow discrimination. The 'cohesion of tax systems' is based on the idea that

1552. *Ibid.*
1553. Beyond technicalities, HMA derived from the use of hybrid and reverse hybrid entities may only appear in cross-border situations. Therefore, a rule denying a deduction because income is not recognised in the other country due to the differences in characterising the same entity will always involve an 'indirect' or 'hidden' discrimination, regardless of the neutral manner in which these rules are drafted. In this opinion: Rust, *supra* n. 1481, pp. 313 and 320. In an analysis exclusively within the EU context, and before the issuance of the BEPS Action Plan in 2013, Fibbe also recognises that conflicts derived from the different classification of an entity are exclusively referred to entities involved in cross-border activities. As provided by Fibbe: 'Classification conflicts due to autonomous classification methods only arise in situations where an entity incorporated under the laws of one state is involved (actively or passively) in cross-border activities and as a consequence is classified for the tax purpose of two or more MSs.' *See* Fibbe, *supra* n. 863, p. 176.
1554. Mason, *supra* n. 1525, p. 59.
1555. *Ibid.*
1556. Di Maria, *supra* n. 1531.
1557. Bundgaard provides a deeper analysis in this regard, which covers different justifications grounds, including: (i) loss of revenues, (ii) the level of taxation and prevention of harmful tax competition, (iii) ensuring the effectiveness of fiscal supervision, (iv) coherence of the tax system, (v) balanced allocation of the power to impose taxes, (vi) prevention of double use of losses and (vii) prevention of tax abuse. This author concludes that, at least in respect of these justification grounds, it is highly expected that none of them will be successfully used considering the case law of the CJEU. *See* Bundgaard, *Hybrid Financial Instruments and Primary EU law–Part 2, supra* n. 1532, pp. 587-594.

a direct link exists between granting a tax advantage and offsetting that tax advantage by a fiscal levy.[1558] This idea was already argued in *Bachmann* (Case C-204/09)[1559] and *Commission v. Belgium* (Case C-300/09).[1560] In *Bachmann*, which in brief referred to the deductibility of contributions in Germany related to the insurance of individuals and the condition of being subject to tax in Belgium, the CJEU sustained: 'The cohesion of such a tax system, the formulation of which is a matter for each Member State, therefore presupposes that, in the event of a State being obliged to allow the deduction of life assurance contributions paid in another Member State, it should be able to tax sums payable by insurers.'[1561] Accordingly, in *Commission v. Belgium*, which also referred to the deductibility of contributions being offset by the taxation of payments made by insurers pursuant to their contracts, the Court stated: 'The cohesion of such a tax system, the formulation of which is a matter for the Belgian State, presupposes, therefore, that in the event of that State being obliged to allow the deduction of life assurance contributions paid in another Member State, it should be able to tax sums payable by insurers.'[1562] In both cases, thus, the CJEU concluded that a link between the deductibility of those payments and the taxation in the other MS would exist, which would also be needed to keep the cohesion of tax systems.[1563] As provided by the Court: 'As regards the need to preserve the cohesion of the tax system at issue, it should be noted that there exists a connection under the Belgian rules between the deductibility of contributions and the liability to tax of sums payable by insurers pursuant to pension or life assurance contracts.'[1564]

The 'cohesion of tax systems', however, has not always been successfully applied, and when it has been, it was only when provisions at issue concerned the same taxpayer and the same tax.[1565] Moreover, the 'coherence of tax systems' as a justification for discriminatory domestic provisions was expressly restricted in *Eurowings*.[1566] In this case law, the Court argued that: '[...] a difference of treatment cannot be justified on grounds linked to the need for coherency of taxation'.[1567] Interestingly also, the Court rejected the idea that the 'difference of treatment can also not be justified by the fact that the lessor established in another Member State is there subject to lower taxation'.[1568] Similarly, the CJEU argued in *Cadbury Schweppes* (Case C-196/04) that any tax advantage given from low taxation to a subsidiary in an MS, different from the MS where the parent company is incorporated, cannot by itself authorise an MS to offset that tax advantage by a less favourable treatment to the

1558. Marchgraber, *supra* n. 881, p. 140.
1559. EU: Judgment in *Hans Martin Bachmann v. Belgian State* (C-204/90) [1992], ECLI: EU:C:1992:35, hereinafter '*Bachmann* case'.
1560. EU: Judgment in *Commission of the European Communities v. Kingdom of Belgium* (C-300/90) [1992], ECLI:EU:C:1992:37, hereinafter '*Commission v. Belgium* case'.
1561. EU: *Bachmann* case, *supra* n. 1559, para. 23.
1562. *Ibid.*, para. 16.
1563. *Ibid.*
1564. Paragraph 14.
1565. Bundgaard, *Hybrid Financial Instruments and Primary EU law–Part 2, supra* n. 1532, p. 589. *See also*, Marchgraber, *supra* n. 881, p. 140.
1566. EU: *Eurowings* case, *supra* n. 1538.
1567. *Ibid.*, para. 41.
1568. *Ibid.*, para. 43. *See also*, de Boer and Marres, *supra* n. 1326, p. 33.

parent company, which could happen, e.g., when a deduction is denied to the extent the income is not recognised in the other MS.[1569] In simple words, a *primary response* at hand could not be justified on the basis of the coherence of the tax systems within the EU.

3.5.2.2.1.2.2 The Fight Against Tax Abuse

As regards the 'fight against tax abuse' as a justification ground for discrimination, it is highly arguable that a rule denying a deduction in all cases involving hybrid entities or reverse hybrids, where the outcome is a D/NI, is indeed justified. This rule, as such, would certainly go beyond preventing tax abuse.[1570] Indeed, the boundaries of tax abuse (avoidance) are well settled both in case law and in the EU law doctrine.[1571] With respect to the former, the CJEU has stated in *Cadbury Schweppes*: '[...] in order for a restriction on the freedom of establishment to be justified on the ground of prevention of abusive practices, the specific objective of such a restriction must be to prevent conduct involving the creation of wholly artificial arrangements which do not reflect economic reality [...].'[1572] The CJEU has already stated that a subjective and an objective test would determine the existence of a wholly artificial arrangement. Whilst the subjective test would require the intention of the taxpayer to obtain a tax advantage, the objective one is determined by the physical existence of an entity in terms of premises, staff, and equipment.[1573] As provided by the Court: 'If checking those factors leads to the finding that the CFC is a fictitious establishment not carrying out any genuine economic activity in the territory of the host Member State, the creation of that CFC must be regarded as having the characteristics of a wholly artificial arrangement. That could be so in the particular case of a 'letterbox' or 'front' subsidiary [...].'[1574] Therefore, provisions as the *primary response*, which contain requirements as regards the level of taxation in the other country, would be beyond the understanding of tax abuse within the EU unless they refer exclusively to wholly artificial arrangements. In other words, and as well settled by the case law of the CJEU, restrictive national provisions that are applicable to every situation and for whatever reason are too general to combat abuse.[1575] Likewise, the CJEU, although with respect to a VAT

1569. As provided by the Court in *Cadbury Schweppes*: 'In that respect, it is settled case-law that any advantage resulting from the low taxation to which a subsidiary established in a Member State other than the one in which the parent company was incorporated is subject cannot by itself authorize that Member State to offset that advantage by less favorable tax treatment of the parent company.' *Cadbury Schweppes, supra* n. 123, para. 49. *See also*, de Boer and Marres, *supra* n. 1326, p. 34.
1570. Rust, *supra* n. 1481, p. 313.
1571. *Supra* Chapter 1, s. 4.2.3.
1572. *Cadbury Schweppes* case, *supra* n. 123, para. 55.
1573. *Ibid.*, para. 67.
1574. EU: *Cadbury Schweppes* case, *supra* n. 123, para. 68.
1575. D. Weber, *Abuse of Law in European Tax Law: An Overview and Some Recent Trends in the Direct and Indirect Tax Case Law of the ECJ–Part 2*, 53 Eur. Taxn. 7 (2013), Journals IBFD, p. 313. *See also, e.g.*, EU: Judgment in *Hughes de Lasteyrie du Saillant v. Ministère de l'Economie des Fianances et de l'Industrie*, C-9/02, ECLI:EU:C:2004:138; Judgment in *Commission of the European Communities v.* Hellenic Republic, C-178/05, ECLI:EU:C:2007:317; EU: *Lankhorst-Hohorst* case, *supra* n. 1549; Judgment in *Jobra Vermögensverwaltungs-Gesellschaft mbH v. Finanzamt Amstetten Melk Scheibbs*, C-330/07, ECLI:EU:C:2008:685.

case, has settled that 'tax arbitrage', i.e., using different VAT rules in two MSs, is not equivalent to tax abuse.[1576]

3.5.2.2.1.2.3 The DNT Outcome

Finally, with respect to the use of DNT (i.e., a D/NI outcome) as a justification ground for discrimination, the jurisprudence of the CJEU is also very ambiguous.[1577] For example, since the landmark decision in *Marks & Spencer* (Case C-446/03), it seems to be accepted that the risk of double utilisation of losses can be a justification for a different treatment between the domestic and cross-border situations.[1578] As stated by the Court: 'As regards the second justification, relating to the danger that losses would be used twice, it must be accepted that Member States must be able to prevent that from occurring.'[1579] Nevertheless, in *Philips Electronics* (Case C-18/11), the CJEU expressed doubts with respect to the double utilisation of losses as an independent justification ground.[1580] This is confirmed in the words of the Court when it says: 'As regards, second, the objective of preventing the double use of losses, it must be observed that even if such a ground, considered independently, could be relied on, it cannot in any event be relied on in circumstances such as those in the main proceedings to justify the national legislation of the host Member State.'[1581] In the same order of ideas, *Philips Electronics* could serve the purpose of confirming, in case of hybrid entity or reverse hybrid transactions, that rules denying a deduction in one country would not be justified unless there is a respective inclusion of income in the other country.[1582]

1576. EU: Judgment in *HMRC v. RBS Deutschland Holding GmbH*, C-277/09, ECLI:EU:2010:810. As provided by Bundgaard as well: 'In light of the Commission's conclusion that new coordinated solutions need to be developed, tax arbitrage does not seem (in view of the EU Commission) to be considered abuse de lege lata.' Bundgaard, *Hybrid Financial Instruments and Primary EU law–Part 2, supra* n. 1532, p. 593. *See also*, Rust, *supra* n. 1481, p. 313.

1577. In this opinion: Marchgraber, *supra* n. 881, p. 141. De Broe also recognises that whether or not an arrangement leading to DNT abuses EU law remains unanswered. *See* L. De Broe, *Some Observations on the 2007 Communication from the Commission: 'The Application of Anti-abuse Measures in the Area of Direct Taxation Within the EU and in Relation to Third Countries'*, 17 EC Tax Rev. 3, 142 et seq. (2008) DOI: 10.54648/ecta2008065. Nonetheless, De Broe also analyses the issue of compensatory taxation and prevention of DNT, concluding that tax jurisdiction shopping is only illegitimate, and thus a compensatory taxation permitted, if a taxpayer has set up a wholly artificial arrangement with the purpose of avoiding taxation. For this purpose, De Broe gives as example *Lasteyrie* (Case C-9/02), emphasising that the CJEU did not suggest in this case that there were abuse when the French resident moved to Belgium and sold his shares to get a tax-free capital gain and then returning to France, but there would be only if that is done in short time frame. *See* De Broe, *supra* n. 255, p. 921; EU: *Lasteyrie* case, *supra* n. 1575.

1578. EU: *Marks & Spencer* case, *supra* n. 1543. The comparability between double utilisation of losses and other situations of double non-taxation is, nevertheless, arguable. *See, e.g.*, M. Lang, *Direct Taxation: Is the ECJ Heading in New Direction?*, 46 Eur. Taxn. 9 (2006), Journals IBFD, p. 426.

1579. EU: *Marks & Spencer* case, *supra* n. 1543, para. 47.

1580. EU: Judgment in *The Commissioners for Her Majesty's Revenue & Customs v. Philips Electronics UK Ltd*, Case C-18/11, ECLI:EU:C:2012:532.

1581. *Ibid.*, para. 28.

1582. 'It follows that the host Member State, on whose territory the economic activity giving rise to the losses of the permanent establishment is carried out, cannot, in a situation such as that at

Likewise, as regards the use of DNT as a justification ground for discrimination, one should ask whether the avoidance of DNT is indeed an obligation under EU law. A good starting point for answering this question could be the opinion of the CJEU with respect to the obligation to prevent double taxation. In this sense, it is worthy to recall what the Court just said in *Kerckhaert and Morres* (Case C-513/04): 'Community law [...] does not lay down any general criteria for the attribution of areas of competence between Member States in relation to the elimination of double taxation within the Community.'[1583] Accordingly, the Court in *CIBA* (Case C-96/08) stated that: 'double taxation [...] does not alone constitute a restriction prohibited by the Treaty'.[1584] Therefore, if EU law does not set up any obligation to prevent double taxation, it seems, at first glance at least, inconsistent to accept the avoidance of DNT as a justification ground for restriction, especially when both double taxation and double non-taxation are identified as incompatible with the internal market.[1585] Also considering the above, this author rejects the idea that ensuring single taxation might serve as a justification ground.[1586]

Therefore, neither the cohesion of tax systems within the EU nor the fight against tax abuse, or DNT itself, could serve the purpose of justifying a discriminatory measure. The spectrum of justification is thus severely reduced, and it opens the door for future issues with respect to the application of the *primary response* and *linking rules* in general.

---

issue in the main proceedings, use the objective of preserving the allocation of the power to impose taxes between the Member States as justification for the fact that, under its national legislation, the possibility of transferring, by means of group relief and to a resident company, losses sustained by the permanent establishment in that Member State of a non-resident company is subject to a condition that those losses cannot be used for the purposes of foreign taxation, whilst the transfer of losses sustained in that Member State by a resident company is not subject to any equivalent condition.' *Ibid.*, para. 27. *See also*, Bundgaard, *Hybrid Financial Instruments and Primary EU law–Part 2, supra* n. 1532, p. 590, who provides a similar conclusion with respect to HFI.

1583. EU: Judgment in *Mark Kerckhaert and Bernadette Morres v. Belgische Staat*, C-513/04, ECLI:EU:C:2006:713, para. 22.

1584. EU: Judgment in *CIBA Speciality Chemicals Central and Eastern Europe Szolgáltató, Tanácsadó és Keresdedelmi kft v. Adó- és Pénzügyi Ellenrzési Hivatal (APEH) Hatósági Fosztály*, C-96/08, ECLI:EU:C:2010:185, para. 28.

1585. Marchgraber, *supra* n. 881, p. 141. As provided also by the European Commission: 'Tax systems must allow cross-border economic activity to develop within the Union. However, at the same time, there is a need to ensure that the increased opportunities for cross-border trade and investment do not lead to an unacceptable loss of tax revenues through tax arbitrage, avoidance or fraud. Just as it is necessary to prevent the double taxation of cross-border income flows, transactions within the Union should not be able to escape tax altogether.' EU: European Commission, *Taxation in European Union, Report on the Development of Tax Systems*, COM (96) 546 final, OJ C 296/43, 22 October 1996.

1586. Bundgaard also recognises this idea when he states: 'Member States may initially argue that any anti-arbitrage measure is being put in place simply to ensure single taxation of income and to prevent white income (i.e., non-taxed income). Ensuring single taxation can thus be said to align the cross-border situation to the domestic situation or to a cross-border situation where no tax benefit can be obtained. However, to date, such a justification has not been seen in the case law [...].' J. Bundgaard, *supra* n. 1532, p. 587. For the analysis of the '*single tax principle*' and the origin of the idea of ensuring single taxation within cross-border transactions, *see supra* Chapter 1, s. 3.

3.5.2.2.2 Defensive Rule

Unlike the case of HFI, the *defensive rule* in case of hybrid entities works in a slightly different manner.[1587] In fact, in case of hybrid entities, there is no discussion with respect to the application or not of the exemption method in the MS of the parent entity with respect to the payment received from the MS of the payee.[1588] Indeed, the issue is with respect to the taxation of such payment in the MS of the parent company when, in principle, the whole transaction between the parent company and the other entity should have been disregarded in the MS of the parent company, because of the characterisation that this country gives to the entity established in the other MS.[1589]

If one considers that MSs have exclusive sovereignty to classify foreign entities for domestic tax purposes, there should not be, in principle, a problem when an MS, as part of its classification rules, provides for some exceptions under which its own classification of the entity will not be taken into account or will be switched in order to follow the one provided in the MS where the entity is established.[1590] In other words, the *defensive rule* has an effect similar to a 'switch-over clause' in the sense that it, to a certain extent, obliges the MS of the parent company to recognise the characterisation of the entity in the other MS when taxing a payment which, in principle, should be disregarded because of its own classification of the entity in the other MS. Indeed, one could conclude that such an exception, i.e., the taxation of the payment, and thus, the recognition of a tax transparent entity as taxable under certain circumstances, is part of the sovereignty of the MS of the parent company to determine who is a taxpayer.[1591]

Nevertheless, the design of the *defensive rule*, as proposed, is rather different. First, it does not refer to the characterisation of the entity at all.[1592] Second, the

1587. The *defensive rule* is not part of the OECD BEPS proposal in the case of payment received by reverse hybrid entities.
1588. On this matter, Rust states that denying the exemption method in case of the application of the defensive rule is equivalent to the application of the indirect credit method. He considers that the non-application of the exemption ensures that domestic and cross-border investments are treated equally. *See* Rust, *supra* n. 1481, p. 321. Nevertheless, he also recognises that a defensive rule in case of HFI might be regarded as a hidden discrimination. *Ibid.*, 320.
1589. *Supra* s. 2.4.1 provides an example of a payment made by a hybrid entity, which results in D/NI. The non-inclusion, in this case, derives exclusively to the non-recognition of the transaction between the payer and the payee due to the different characterisation of the payee entity in both countries.
1590. The CJEU clearly held in *Columbus Container Services* that MS are autonomous in classifying foreign entities for domestic tax purposes. As stated by the Court: 'it must be recalled that the fiscal autonomy referred to in paragraphs 44 and 51 of this judgment also means that the Member States are at liberty to determine the conditions and the level of taxation for different types of establishments chosen by national companies or partnerships operating abroad, on condition that those companies or partnerships are not treated in a manner that is discriminatory in comparison with comparable national establishments'. EU: Judgment in *Columbus Container Services BVBA & Co. v. Finanzamt Bielefeld-Innenstadt*, C-298/05, ECLI: EU:C:2007:754, para. 53. For an analysis on *Columbus Container Services, see* Fibbe, *supra* n. 863, pp. 167-177. Likewise, as provided by Weber: 'In my view, each Member State has the freedom to classify whichever taxpayer in whatever way, on the basis of its own tax rules. If this were not the case, the Member State's sovereignty would be at risk.' Weber, *supra* n. 1542, p. 593.
1591. *Supra* s. 3.2.
1592. *Ibid.*

contingency relates exclusively to the fact that the payment was or was not deducted in the payee MS. Therefore, this author maintains his conclusions with respect to the *primary response*, namely, the tax disadvantage in this case (i.e., the taxation of a payment in the MS of the parent company) should be analysed in isolation and not considering the overall effects in the other MS.[1593] If analysed in isolation, there are indeed more probabilities of finding discriminatory features than applying an overall approach.

As regards the justification grounds for discrimination, the author will refer to the analysis already made with respect to the *primary response*.

3.5.2.2.3 *Primary Response/ Defensive Rule* and the Proportionality Test

The final step that the CJEU conducts to determine the compatibility of a domestic provision with EU law is a test of proportionality. Under the proportionality test, the CJEU carries out an analysis of whether the domestic legislation that applies is broader than its aim and whether its means and ends correspond.[1594] As per the design of the *linking rules*, it is highly expected that they raise EU law issues, especially considering their automatic application[1595] and the fact that they disregard which jurisdiction has the right to tax.[1596]

As already stressed, the proportionality test will depend on the justifications under which the *linking rules* are implemented domestically. In this regard, and if the justification of the rules is, e.g., the balanced allocation of taxing rights, it is clear from the CJEU case law that the rules, as proposed, would not pass the proportionality test. For example, in *National Grid Indus* (Case C-371/10), the Court stated: 'The Member State concerned is exercising its power of taxation solely in relation to the capital gains

1593. *Eurowings* case, *supra* n. 1538.

1594. Bundgaard, *Hybrid Financial Instruments and Primary EU law–Part 2, supra* n. 1532, p. 593. Bundgaard, however, does not carry out the analysis on proportionality, because he considers that none of the justification grounds potentially used to justify a discriminatory measure would be indeed successful. Therefore, the analysis on proportionality would lack real interest.

1595. The OECD states that '[t]he rules apply automatically [...]'. OECD (2015), *supra* n. 6, p. 11.

1596. The whole premise behind the HMA and the *linking rules* is indeed to tax 'somewhere' the income derived from a hybrid mismatch, which does not only deviate from the rest of the BEPS project that attempts to tax income in the jurisdiction where the income is sourced or the activities are conducted, but also to rely on a sort of unproved certainty that income 'should be taxed somewhere'. The OECD Action Plan clearly states: 'Specifically, this Action Plan should provide countries with domestic and international instruments that will better align rights to tax with economic activity.' *See* OECD (2013), *supra* n. 2, p. 11. For a critical analysis of the idea that income should be taxed somewhere, *see supra* Chapter 1, s. 3, referred to the discussion on the 'single tax principle'. In a similar opinion with respect to the issues of proportionality with respect to *linking rules*, *see* P. Benéitez Régil, *BEPS Actions 2, 3 and 4 and the Fundamental Freedoms: Is There a Way Out?*, 56 Eur. Taxn. 6 (2016), Journals IBFD, pp. 242-243. She advocates for the inclusion of a 'valid economic reasons' test within the BEPS measures under analysis, regardless of EU considerations and considering that taxation should aim for neutrality. *Ibid.*, p. 245.

generated in *its territory* […].'[1597] Accordingly, it said: 'Such a measure [tax on capital gains] is intended to prevent situations capable of jeopardizing the right of the Member State of origin to exercise its powers of taxation in relation to activities carried on in its territory, and may therefore be justified on grounds connected with the preservation of the allocation of powers of taxation between the Member States.'[1598] Furthermore, the Court argued: '[…] a Member State is entitled to tax the economic value generated by an unrealized capital gain *in its territory* […] (emphasis added).'[1599] 'It is proportionate for that Member State, for the purpose of safeguarding the exercise of its powers of taxation, to determine the tax due on the unrealized capital gains that have arisen *in its territory* […] (emphasis added).'[1600] Similarly, in *SGI* (Case C-311/08), the Court stated: 'First, as regards the balanced allocation between Member States of the power to tax, it should be recalled that such a justification may be accepted, in particular, where the system in question is designed to prevent conduct capable of jeopardizing the right of a Member State to exercise its tax jurisdiction in relation to activities carried out in *its territory* (emphasis added).'[1601] Accordingly, it provided: '[…] national legislation which is not specifically designed to exclude from the tax advantage it confers such purely artificial arrangements - devoid of economic reality, created with the aim of escaping the tax normally due on the profits generated by activities carried out *on national territory* […] (emphasis added).'[1602] In the same order of ideas, the CJEU in *N* (Case C-470/04) recognised that the existing taxation regime in the Netherlands can be justified by reason of a balanced allocation of the power to tax between MSs, but in order to be proportionate, such system should consider the decrease in value of the assets after the transfer of the residence.[1603] It is arguable, thus, that *linking rules*, i.e., rules attempting to ensure taxation 'somewhere' might be suitable to accomplish the role of balancing the allocation of taxing rights. In fact, those rules do not distinguish between income generated from activities performed in a specific jurisdiction and somewhere. As such, they could rarely be considered proportional.

1597. EU: Judgment in *National Grid Indus BV v. Inspecteur van de Belastingdienst Rijnmond/kantoor Rotterdam*, C-371/10, ECLI:EU:C:2011:785, para. 43.
1598. *Ibid.*, para. 46.
1599. *Ibid.*, para. 49.
1600. *Ibid.*, para. 52.
1601. EU: *SGI* case, *supra* n. 1549, para. 60.
1602. *Ibid.*, para. 66.
1603. The case referred to the transfer of residence from the Netherlands to another MS and the respective application of exit taxation. In this case, the amount of exit tax was calculated without considering the decrease in value occurring after the transfer of the residence. Marchgraber, *supra* n. 881, p. 141. The Court held that such a regime could be justified by reason of a balanced allocation of taxing powers between MSs. However, for it to be considered as proportional, such system should take into consideration this reduction in value of the assets after the transfer, unless such reduction has already been taken into account in the host country. EU: Judgement in *N v. Inspecteur van de Belastingdienst Oost/kantoor Almelo*, C-470/04, ECLI:EU:C:2006:525, para. 54. *See also*, H. van den Broek and G.T.K. Meussen, *Netherlands – National Grid Indus Case: Re-thinking Exit Taxation*, 52 Eur. Taxn. 4 (2012), Journals IBFD, s. 5.5., referred to proportionality and the *N* case.

Similar concerns are raised if other justification grounds are accepted. For instance, if the fight against tax abuse were the justification ground, it is clear that the application of *linking rules* beyond what is properly considered tax abuse would be disproportionate.[1604] Indeed, the rules do not include any element of 'abuse' that should be tested.[1605] On the contrary, and as already stressed in this work, they apply to counteract any D/NI outcome derived from the use of hybrid and reverse hybrid entities no matter what.[1606] The above conclusion does not change with the restriction on '*control groups*' and '*structured arrangements*', which, as analysed already, are either an extension of classic concepts of control or are indeed extremely vague that it is almost impossible to determine their proper extension.[1607] Moreover, if tax avoidance or abuse is accepted and applied as a justification ground, the design of *linking rules* suggests that there is no opportunity for the taxpayer to prove otherwise.[1608] The above would contradict the case law of the CJEU, which has consistently held that for anti-avoidance legislation to be considered proportional, it is necessary that the taxpayer can prove, without administrative concerns, that the arrangement is commercially or economically justified.[1609] The rules apply automatically. Using DNT itself as a justification ground might, on the other hand, change the analysis. After all, HMA does not cover all cases of DNT, but rather specific cases of DNT derived from the use of hybrid entities or HFI, which suppose the deductibility of a payment in one country and the non-inclusion of the respective income in the other country.[1610] However, it is hard to believe that DNT could even be accepted as a justification ground without there being any obligation at the EU law level to prevent DNT.[1611]

All in all, it seems that *linking rules* will suffer serious difficulties when passing the proportionality test, at least in the form they have so far, because, as such, they certainly conflict with most of the case law of the CJEU.

1604. *Cadbury Schweppes* case, *supra* n. 123. *See also*, Rust, *supra* n. 1481, p. 313.
1605. Following Dourado, HMA in absence of artificiality will amount to aggressive tax planning, but not to avoidance of abuse. Dourado, *supra* n. 202, p. 48.
1606. I have already expressed concerns that the limitation of the HMA concept to cases of D/NI exclusively, and the respective automatic application of the countermeasures, creates a presumption of abuse. *Supra* s. 2.3.2.
1607. *Supra* s. 3.3.1 and s. 3.3.2.
1608. Benéitez Régil, *supra* n. 1596, p. 243.
1609. 'National legislation which provides for a consideration of objective and verifiable elements in order to determine whether a transaction represents an artificial arrangement, entered into for tax reasons, is to be regarded as not going beyond what is necessary to attain the objectives relating to the need to maintain the balanced allocation of the power to tax between the Member States and to prevent tax avoidance where, first, on each occasion on which there is a suspicion that a transaction goes beyond what the companies concerned would have agreed under fully competitive conditions, *the taxpayer is given an opportunity, without being subject to undue administrative constraints, to provide evidence of any commercial justification that there may have been for that transaction* (emphasis added).' *See SGI* case, *supra* n. 1549, para. 71.
1610. *Supra* s. 2.
1611. *See* references at *supra* n. 1578.

4 INTERACTIONS BETWEEN *LINKING RULES* AND OTHER DOMESTIC ANTI-AVOIDANCE AND ANTI-BASE EROSION PROVISIONS

This last section analyses the interaction between the recommendation of the OECD Action Plan 2 (*linking rules*) and the application of domestic interest limitation rules and CFC rules that might affect transactions involving hybrid and reverse hybrid entities. The analysis demonstrates that in both cases, the application of interest limitation rules in the case of payments made by a hybrid entity and CFC rules in the case of payments received by a reverse hybrid might be highly efficient in mitigating cases of hybrid mismatches without the need to apply *linking rules*. Similarly, it stresses that for the sake of simplification, domestic interest limitation rules and CFC rules should be applied with priority over *linking rules*.

4.1 *Linking Rules* and Domestic Interest Limitation Rules

Many countries around the globe include within their domestic legislation rules limiting the deductibility of interest expenses involving cross-border financial structures.[1612] The design of these rules is, generally speaking, made either by way of establishing a fixed debt-equity ratio, i.e., thin capitalisation rules, or by way of limiting the excess of interest expenses to a certain percentage of EBITDA, i.e., 'earning stripping rules', the latter being the more widely applied in recent times. Indeed, many countries opt today for a limitation in the deduction of net interest expenses up to 30% of the amount of EBITDA to the extent that the net interest expenses do not exceed a certain threshold in some cases and, in other cases, only if the entity in excess of indebtedness is part of a tax group.[1613] The application of the interest limitation rule implies thus that a certain amount of interest expenses, normally deductible within a taxable year, will not be deductible in this case, although they may, under certain circumstances, be carried forward.[1614] As such, therefore, it is possible to imagine many situations in which a hybrid entity taxpayer paying interest abroad will be subject to both a domestic interest limitation rule and a domestic linking rule, i.e., *primary response*, limiting the deductibility of the same amount of interest. The question is, therefore, which rule should be applied first.

The OECD Action Plan 2 provides that in the case of the concurrent applicability of an interest limitation rule and hybrid mismatch rule, the former has priority because

1612. These rules are also part of the BEPS proposal, included specifically in Action 4, *supra* n. 1451.

1613. *See, e.g.*, the case of Germany and references at *supra* n. 1452. A mirror rule has been also recently introduced as secondary EU law. EU: Council Directive Council Directive (EU) 2016/1164 of 12 July 2016 (ATAD), Article 4.

1614. As noted already, however, even though an unlimited carry forward is offered under the laws of certain countries, its practical application is limited in certain cases. In Germany, e.g., the above happens in case of the discontinuance of the business or change of control. DE: s. 4(h)(5)(1) of the Income Tax Act [*Einkommensteutergesetz*– EStG]. *See also*, Knöller, *supra* n. 1454.

'the hybrid mismatch rule makes adjustments in respect of particular items that are taken into account for the purposes of calculating taxpayer's overall income or expenses and therefore, as a matter of logic, would generally apply before any such general or overall limitation'.[1615] In the same order of ideas, the OECD states: 'Rules to address hybrid mismatch arrangements should be applied by an entity before the fixed ratio rule and group ratio rule to determine an entity's total net interest expense. Once this total net interest expense figure has been determined, the fixed ratio rule and group ratio rule should be applied to establish whether the full amount may be deducted, or to what extent net interest expenses should be disallowed.'[1616]

The position of the OECD is, nevertheless, arguable. First, both rules, i.e., interest limitation rules and hybrid mismatch rules, are used to calculate the taxpayer's overall income and expenses. Indeed, both rules will have the same effect of increasing the taxable base of the payer entity in the amount of non-deductible interest in the country of the payer.[1617] As such, therefore, it is not evident that an interest limitation rule accomplishes a role different than helping to determine the taxpayer's overall income and expenses, as suggested by the OECD.[1618] Second, a *primary response* should be applied only to the extent the taxpayer is effectively entitled to deduct interest in the country of the payer. The above, however, could not be affirmed in the case of an entity that is generally prevented from deducting interest through an interest limitation rule. This latter issue seems to be recognised within the OECD Action Plan 2, which

1615. OECD (2015), *supra* n. 6, p. 97.
1616. *Ibid.*, p. 103.
1617. *See, e.g.*, the EBITDA example at *supra* n. 1453. Now, instead of considering the non-deductibility by an interest limitation rule (400), please consider that the full amount of 1,000 (deductible interest expenses) is disallowed. The effect is exactly as regards the interest limitation rule. In this case, the amount of disallowed interest expenses must be added back to the taxable profits of the payer entity, and therefore, they increase the tax base for that taxable year.
1618. For example, it could also be argued that both interest limitation rules and anti-hybrid rules that attempt to deny deductible payments equally contravene the 'ability-to-pay' principle. This idea is also argued by Lüdicke, who states with respect to *linking rules* that: 'They contravene the ability-to-pay principle and may hit minority shareholders.' Lüdicke, *supra* n. 870, p. 317. Although a deeper analysis as regards to *linking rules* and the ability-to-pay principle certainly exceeds the purpose of this work (mostly considering the lack of a homogeneous concept), it is perhaps interesting to note that issues concerning the limitation in the deductibility of payments and ability-to-pay principle have even achieved the level of judiciary in some countries, e.g., Germany. In this country, the ability-to-pay principle is expressly recognised within Article 3 of the German Constitution granting the equal treatment to taxpayers in similar circumstances, including corporations through the net principle objectives or *objektives Netto Prinzip*, which means that corporations should consider for their calculation of annual taxes all the income and expenses related to the business. Therefore, a limitation in the deductibility of ordinary expenses, regardless of the policy reasons given for their establishment, would be in principle violating the 'ability-to-pay' principle. This important debate has been considered in a recent landmark decision of the German Federal Fiscal Court [*Bundesfinanzhof*], which confirmed most of the constitutional concerns stressed already in the past with respect to the German interest limitation rule [*Zinsschranke*]. DE: BFH, 14 October 2015, I R 20/15. The final decision depends of the German Federal Constitutional Court [*Bundesverfassungsgericht*, BVerfG), which is still pending. For an analysis on the arguments of the BFH, *see*, e.g., S. Lampert, T. Meickmann and M. Reinert, *Article 4 of the EU Anti Tax Avoidance Directive in Light of the Questionable Constitutionality of the German 'Interest Barrier' Rule*, 56 Eur. Taxn. 8 (2016), Journals IBFD, pp. 324-327.

provides: 'The hybrid entity rule (Recommendations 3-7), however, only operate to the extent a taxpayer is actually entitled to a deduction for a payment under local law. Accordingly these rules will not apply to the extent the taxpayer is subject to transaction or entity specific rules under the parent or payer jurisdiction that prevent the payment from being deducted.'[1619] In my view, interest limitation rules accomplish this role of preventing a payment (i.e., interest) from being deducted in the country of the payer and should therefore be considered before applying a different rule, whose aim is also different, but whose result is similar, i.e., limitation in the deductibility of certain payments.

There are also strong practical reasons to support the application of an interest limitation rule before the hybrid mismatch rule. These reasons can be summarised as follows: (i) the possibility of 'carrying forward' the non-deductible expenses if the interest limitation rule is applied first, (ii) the control on the application of the *defensive rule,* which will be applied only on the amount of interest effectively deducted in the payer's country, and, in some cases, (iii) the possibility of indirectly solving the issue of a hybrid mismatch without applying complex *linking rules*.[1620] All these reasons can be illustrated in the following hypothetical. Let us assume a company, ACo, incorporated in country A, with a subsidiary, BCo, incorporated in country B. ACo grants a loan to BCo, and this latter pays interest of 200i back to ACo in year X. Country A considers that BCo is tax transparent, whilst country B regards the same entity as a taxable entity. Accordingly, let us also assume that country B has within its domestic laws both an interest limitation rule and a *primary* response. The domestic interest limitation rule in country B, on the one hand, provides for a limitation in the deductibility of interest up to 30% of the amount of EBITDA without a threshold amount and is applicable both to single entities and entities that are part of the same tax group. The *primary response*, on the other hand, provides for a denial of the deductibility of interest in those cases in which deductible interest is paid by an entity considered taxable in its country of incorporation whilst tax transparent in the country of the recipient of the income, and that transaction gives rise to a D/NI outcome. Finally, let us assume the following given amounts for BCo:

Figure 81 Linking Rules and Interest Limitation Rules

Interest Expenses	200i
Interest Income	0i
Net Interest Expenses	200i
EBITDA	400i

In the first scenario, i.e., applying the *primary response* first, BCo will be denied the deduction of interest expenses in the amount of 200i because the loan and the

1619. OECD (2015), *supra* n. 6, p. 97.
1620. In the same opinion: De Boer and Marres, *supra* n. 1326, pp. 40-41. These authors state that 'the introduction of a more generic interest deduction limitation, such as the limitation of excessive interest deduction through thin cap or earning striping rules, or via global allocation of interest expenses by formulary apportionment' could work.

respective amount of interest are disregarded in the country of the payee, and thus, not included as income by ACo. Likewise, this amount of non-deductible interest will not be carried forward to future years. In addition, the interest limitation rule will not be applicable after all because there is no remaining interest on which to apply the interest limitation rule. Indeed, if applied, it would imply a 'double non-deduction' affecting the same item of expenses, which is an issue that should certainly be avoided.[1621]

On the contrary, in the second scenario, i.e., if the interest limitation rule applies first, the outcome is rather different. In such a case, the deductibility of interest is limited first to an amount of 30% of EBITDA. This is, in our case, the amount of 120i. Likewise, the amount of non-deductible interest is reduced to 80i, which may also be carried forward to further years according to the domestic rules of country B. Therefore, the *primary response* will be applied only to the amount of 'effectively deductible interest', namely, the amount of 120i. This also means that the *defensive rule* in the country of the payee (country A) will be limited to that amount. In other words, the payee could be obliged to include only 120i of interest as income. Second, the amount of 80i of non-deductible expenses can be carried forward and used in future years, subject to the same limitation of 30% of EBITDA.

In principle and pragmatically speaking, the outcome of the first scenario seems to be more effective because it simply denies the full amount of interest expenses just because a hybrid structure is involved. Nonetheless, the above result is indeed disproportionate, mostly considering that the denial of the deduction applies as a presumption of the fact that having a payment involving a hybrid payer is indeed abusive because of the DNT outcome.[1622] Accordingly, the denial of the interest deduction derived from the application of the *primary response* cannot be used in further years, which might conflict with domestic tax principles recognised in some countries, e.g., the ability-to-pay principle.[1623] On the contrary, as noted in the second scenario, if the interest limitation rule is applied first, it guarantees that at least an amount of interest will be effectively deductible in the taxable year in which it arises, giving the possibility to the other country to react and to tax the same amount of income using a *defensive rule*. Accordingly, the amount of non-deductible expenses derived from the application of the interest limitation rule can, in most cases, be carried forward, which would not conflict with, e.g., the ability-to-pay principle.[1624]

There is, however, one criticism that can be made with respect to the application of the interest limitation rule before a hybrid mismatch rule (i.e., *primary response*), which is the ability of the taxpayer to manipulate the amount of EBITDA to obtain a higher amount of deductible expenses. The above is certainly possible if the EBITDA is

1621. The OECD is indeed concerned about denying a deduction twice when it provides: 'The mechanism for coordinating the interaction between the two rules [interest limitation and hybrid mismatch rule] will depend on how the interest limitation rule operates; however, the interaction between these rules should not have the net effect of denying a deduction twice for the same item of expenditure.' OECD (2015), *supra* n. 6, p. 98.
1622. *Supra* s. 2.3.2.
1623. *Supra* n. 1619.
1624. This is, however, relative. *See, e.g.*, the case of the German interest limitation rule, which although provides a carry forward of non-deductible interest, they are indeed lost in the case of a change of control or discontinuance of the business. *supra* n. 1452.

calculated on a whole group of companies. This chance, nevertheless, is diminished if the country of the payee has included a *defensive rule* and taxes the amount of interest on which deduction was granted. Therefore, if the final aim of the BEPS Action Plan 2 is to ensure single taxation, this aim could anyway be accomplished by giving priority to the interest limitation rule over the primary response.[1625]

4.2 *Linking Rules* and CFC Rules

As well as in the case of interest limitation rules, countries around the world normally include rules to anticipate the taxation in the shareholders' country of undistributed profits generated at the level of the subsidiary, thus avoiding a long-term deferral.[1626] These rules, known as 'CFC rules', generally operate in the same manner all around the world;[1627] namely, they require control from the shareholders, and they are applied on undistributed passive income generated at the level of the foreign-controlled subsidiary.[1628] In other words, a 'deemed dividend' is calculated on the profits of a foreign subsidiary, and it is taxed then in the country of residence of the shareholders controlling the company, or a regime of full transparency applies.

When analysing the application of linking rules, especially in transactions involving deductible payments to reverse hybrids, it is easy to figure out that CFC rules can be very effective in accomplishing a role similar to that provided under a *defensive rule*.[1629] Let us assume the following hypothetical. ACo is a corporation incorporated in country A, which wholly owns BCo, an entity established in country B. This latter entity receives deductible interest from a subsidiary established in country C, CCo. Likewise, BCo is regarded as tax transparent in its country of establishment whilst as an opaque entity in countries A and C. We will also assume that interest payments are fully deductible in country C and that country A possesses CFC rules, which apply to passive income held by foreign subsidiaries. The transaction, therefore, gives rise to a deduction in country C without inclusion of income in countries B and A.

1625. The above, however, does not mean to recognise that the aim pursued by the OECD is correct. It simply means that, having 'coherence' in mind, it would not really matter to apply the interest limitation rule with priority over the anti-hybrid rule proposed (i.e., *primary response*), giving the taxpayer also a fairer result.

1626. *See, e.g.*, the reference to CFC rules in the United States, *supra* Chapter 3, s. 4.4.1, which was also the pioneer country to introduce these types of rules in 1962. *See* Parada, *supra* n. 276, p. 958.

1627. Perhaps one interesting exception is Brazil, where, e.g., the CFC rules apply both to passive and active income, not following the international standard of taxing only passive income. BR: Article 74 of the Provisional Measure No. 2158-35/2011. *See also* Parada, *supra* n. 276, p. 964; Freita de Moraes e Castro (2010), *supra* n. 276, p. 13.

1628. Bittker and Lokken, *supra* n. 556, p. 69-3.

1629. This is reinforced and recognised by the OECD BEPS Report on Action 2, where it says: 'A payment to a reverse hybrid will not be treated as giving rise to a D/NI outcome if the mismatch is neutralized by the investor or the establishment jurisdiction adopting a specific rule designed to bring into account items of ordinary income paid to a reverse hybrid. This includes any rules [...] (including under a CFC regime) [...].' OECD (2015), *supra* n. 6, p. 57.

Figure 82 Linking Rules and CFC Legislation, Example 1

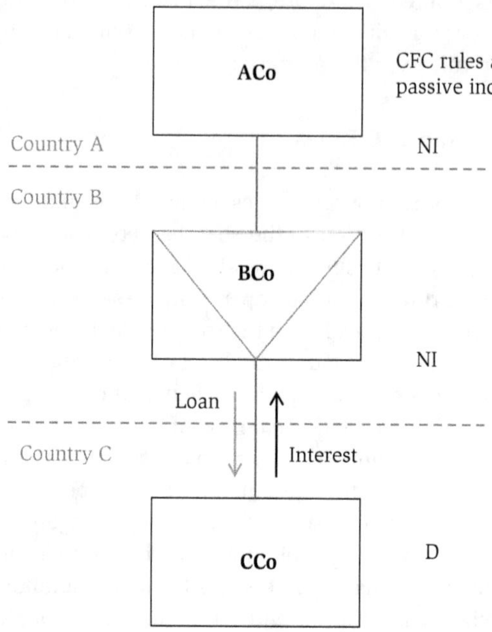

If we also assume that all the countries introduced *linking rules*, the question is: should country C apply first a *primary response* denying the deduction of interest, or will it be equally as effective to just let country A apply its CFC rules instead?

In my view, a coherent and coordinated application of the rules is a key issue to avoid compliance costs and extra administrative burdens.[1630] Having this in mind, it seems to be rather clear that in a triangular situation such as the one described above, it would be a simpler solution to let country A tax the income according to its own CFC rules rather than obliging country C to deny a legitimate deduction. In other words, a *primary response* in country C should be relegated to the background if country A possesses strong CFC rules that may guarantee that the income does not remain untaxed, which is again the goal of the OECD BEPS Action 2. These ideas are indeed recognised by the OECD BEPS Action Plan, which provides: 'Payments made through

1630. As stated by the OECD as well: 'The recommendations set out in this report are intended to operate as a comprehensive and coherent package of measures to neutralize mismatches that arise from the use of hybrid instruments and entities without imposing undue burdens on taxpayers and tax administrations.' *Ibid.*, p. 94.

a reverse hybrid structure will not result in D/NI outcomes if the income is fully taxed under a CFC, foreign investment fund (FIF) or a similar anti-deferral rule in the investor jurisdiction that requires the investor to include its allocated share of any payment of ordinary income made to the intermediary on a current basis.'[1631] Moreover, the final report on Action 2 states: 'Treating income allocated by a reverse hybrid as taxable under the laws of the investor jurisdiction would have the effect of neutralizing any hybrid mismatch under a payment to a transparent entity.'[1632] Finally, and recognising that a proper application of CFC rules in the investor country (country A in our case) could solve the hybrid mismatch, the OECD proposes that 'the payer jurisdiction could suspend the application of the hybrid mismatch rule insofar as payments were allocated to the investor in the investor jurisdiction'.[1633] Accordingly, the report clearly states that a *defensive rule* in country B, in our example, is unnecessary given the fact that a CFC rule will apply in country A. As provided by the OECD: 'A defensive rule is unnecessary given the specific recommendations in Chapter 5 for changes in CFC rules and other offshore investment regimes that would require payments to a reverse hybrid to be included in income in the investor jurisdiction.'[1634]

Yet, special attention should be given to the design of the domestic CFC legislation that might allow an easy circumvention of the rules. The above can be illustrated with the application of the 'same-country exception' in the United States.[1635] This exception states that Subpart F income (CFC income) will not include dividends, interest, rents, and royalties received by a related corporation organised under the same laws of the CFC and which has a substantial part of its assets used in its trade or business located in that country.[1636] Therefore, in our example above, if we assume that country A is the United States and CCo was established in country B instead of country C, the same-country exception would most probably apply in order to exclude the interest received by BCo as CFC income.

1631. *Ibid.*, p. 64.
1632. *Ibid.*
1633. *Ibid.*
1634. *Ibid.*, p. 56.
1635. US: IRC s. 954(c)(3). Also, *supra* Chapter 3, s. 4.4.1.
1636. *Ibid.*

Figure 83 Linking Rules and CFC Legislation, Example 2

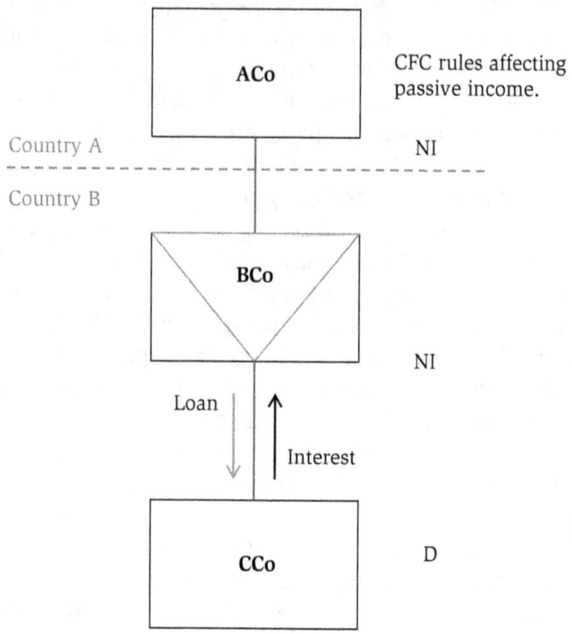

In addition, and contrary to the argument that this result might also be achieved through the elective characterisation of entities in the United States treating BCo as tax transparent in this case, what this example demonstrates is that, regardless the tax characterisation in the United States, the avoidance of the rule had nothing to do with the possibility of ACo to elect how to treat the BCo for tax purposes, but mostly with the design of the CFC rules, in particular, with the existence of the *same-country exception* under US tax law. The above reaffirms what this author already stated in Chapter 3 when referring to the CTB rules and CFC legislation.[1637]

Finally, one should also consider that if countries start implementing CFC rules around the world, some conflicts might arise with respect to 'who is entitled' to apply their CFC rules. The OECD opts for giving priority to the country where the shareholder chain has the closest relationship with the CFC in question.[1638] Nevertheless, it is possible that issues will still exist.[1639] For this purpose, it would be perhaps a most interesting and direct solution to truly solve the hybrid entity mismatch (indirectly helping also to achieve the aim of taxing the income 'somewhere') by providing a rule in the country of the investor which allows the investor in these reverse hybrid

1637. *Supra* Chapter 3, s. 4.4.1.
1638. OECD, *Designing Effective Controlled Foreign Company Rules, Action 3 – 2015 Final Report*, OECD Publishing, Paris, 2015, p. 67, rec. 130, Fig. 7.1.
1639. C. Kahlenberg, *The Interplay Between OECD Recommendations of Action 2 and 3 Regarding Hybrid Structures*, 44 Intertax 4, 320-322 (2016) DOI: 10.54648/taxi2016024.

mismatch situations, to follow the characterisation of the country where the entity is established (i.e., to treat the entity as tax transparent). In such a case, income would flow through to the level of the final investor, where it will be recognised as income without the need to rely on CFC rules, avoiding potential conflicts of application of these rules.[1640]

5 FINAL REMARKS

There is no doubt that HMA is an ad hoc tax notion, as many other ad hoc tax notions internationally used within the international tax context, including, e.g., the concepts of residence and source. Nevertheless, its problem relies particularly on the exacerbated attempt to match transactions involving hybrids and reverse hybrid entities with the outcomes derived from those transactions, under the assumption that income should be taxed 'somewhere', no matter where. The above does not only deviate from the problem of hybrid entity mismatches itself, i.e., the different characterisation of the same entity by two jurisdictions, but it also creates new presumptions of base erosion and potentially abusive transactions just because they involve the DNT outcome. This idea is certainly reinforced when the concept of *imported mismatches*, as regards hybrid entities, comes into play.

Linking rules follow a similar pattern. This is to say, once the problem is created (i.e., an HMA is recognised), the rules to solve it indeed make sense in such a context, i.e., where everything must be matched, and income should be taxed somewhere. Nonetheless, none of these rules truly solve the true hybrid entity mismatch. On the contrary, they assume a *consequentialist role* based exclusively on the outcome that the hybrid entity transactions generate, i.e., a D/NI outcome (or DNT), targeting just the hybrid entity mismatch indirectly.[1641] It is precisely this consequentialist design of *linking rules* which generates important issues both from a tax policy and a legal perspective. From a tax policy perspective, *linking rules* tend to be circular; namely, if implemented by all countries, they will have no other effect apart from nullifying each other, even if a tiebreaker rule comes into force. More importantly, perhaps, an uncoordinated application of a *primary response* and a *defensive rule*, i.e., a circular application, might give rise to a new issue of economic double taxation, which did not exist before the application of these rules. Accordingly, it should not be underestimated that *linking rules* are extremely dependent on the functioning and application of foreign laws, which, without broader and efficient access to information between tax administrations, especially between developing countries, might raise serious concerns with respect to their effectiveness.

As regards the legal concerns, it is true, on the one hand, that *linking rules* do not raise many concerns with respect to Article 24 OECD Model (non-discrimination) due to the restrictive approach that the non-discrimination provision within the OECD

1640. I will get back to this proposal at *infra* Chapter 6.
1641. Nevertheless, neither the *primary response* nor the *defensive rule* solves the hybrid mismatch, they simply make income to be taxed, which is arguable the true reason for the existence of HMA.

Model has in comparison, e.g., with EU law. On the other hand, issues with respect to EU law are restricted to primary law, especially after the inclusion of *linking rules* targeting hybrid entity mismatches within the 2016 EU ATAD and its 2017 amendment (ATAD II), which make these rules applicable to both EU and non-EU mismatches. Unfortunately, however, the jurisprudence of the CJEU is neither unequivocal nor consistent in providing a concrete answer with respect to the compatibility between *linking rules* and EU primary law. The above, however, as presented in the Chapter, should not prevent us from arguing that some issues could still raise concerns. For this reason, *linking rules* and fundamental freedoms should be thoroughly analysed with respect to the non-discrimination principle within the TFEU, at least, as stated by other authors, 'before all Member States fall completely in love with such provisions in the global battle against tax arbitrage'.[1642]

All in all, it seems to be clearer now that the idea of 'coordination' with respect to the characterisation of entities for tax purposes seems to be not only a more direct approach to deal with hybrid and reverse hybrid entities but may also provide a more efficient (and manageable) approach to deal with perhaps the only real problem arising from hybrid entity mismatches, namely the disparate tax characterisation of entities.

1642. Bundgaard, *Hybrid Financial Instruments and Primary EU law–Part 2, supra* n. 1532, p. 594.

CHAPTER 6

Hybrid Entities Without Double Non-taxation: An Alternative Approach

1 INTRODUCTION

The assumed interconnection between the use of hybrid and reverse hybrid entities and the DNT outcome has produced a complex set of rules to be implemented both at a domestic and tax treaty level, even though their true efficacy is still incognito.[1643] Indeed, this set of rules not only imposes problems of potential extra burden for tax administrations and taxpayers but also, and perhaps more importantly, does not truly solve the hybrid entity mismatch, i.e., the different tax characterisation of the same entity by two or more jurisdictions.

This chapter follows a different path and proposes a domestic *reactive coordination rule*, which aims to be a domestic alternative to coordinate the characterisation of entities following the tax characterisation of the entity given in the *home country*, i.e., the country where the entity is formally and legally organised. Likewise, the proposal is based on three main tax policy aims that support its whole design, namely simplicity, coherence, and administrability, and it is completely agnostic with regard to the DNT outcome derived from the hybrid entity structure.

Section 2 describes the mechanics of the proposal, including its scope of application and the tax policy ideas behind it, i.e., simplicity, coherence, and administrability. Likewise, it explains with concrete examples, both with regard to hybrids and reverse hybrid entities, the functioning of the proposal, also detailing its advantages and disadvantages, especially when compared with other current proposals on hybrid entity mismatches. It finally provides a comparison between the proposed rule and other existing rules addressing the same path of coordination to clearly set up the common points and deviations that make the proposed rule in this chapter any way preferable. Section 3 analyses the implications of the domestic *reactive coordination*

1643. *Supra* Chapter 4 and Chapter 5.

rule at a tax treaty level, particularly with regard to the application of Article 1(2) OECD Model. As recognised in Chapter 4, the inclusion of Article 1(2) OECD Model solves many issues regarding the proper allocation of tax treaty benefits when tax-transparent entities are involved. However, this article is far from being a fair solution for developing (source) countries. This issue could, nevertheless, be mitigated in the hypothetical that the domestic *reactive coordination rule* is applied worldwide. Indeed, if that occurs, the scope of application of Article 1(2) OECD Model will be automatically reduced, providing more consistent tax treaty outcomes and indirectly enhancing the position of source countries in those cases where the application of Article 1(2) OECD Model leads to unfair results.

2 *REACTIVE COORDINATION RULE:* A DOMESTIC ALTERNATIVE

This section describes the domestic proposal to coordinate the characterisation of entities according to the legal characterisation of the entity in the home country, i.e., the country where the entity whose characterisation is under debate is legally and formally established, organised, or incorporated. It also provides an analysis of the general tax policy justifications and describes the advantages and disadvantages of its application, especially when compared with the existing OECD *linking rules.*[1644]

2.1 General Description of the Proposal

Despite the suggestive wording of this proposal, it is important to remark that the proposal has nothing to do with an unrealistic attempt to harmonise the characterisation of entities all around the world. This idea, which would theoretically eliminate the mismatches derived from the different characterisation of entities, cannot be feasibly implemented on a worldwide basis and would not perform any function beyond being a very optimistic academic approach with no practical consequence.[1645]

On the contrary, the current proposal attempts a more realistic approach, which consists of establishing a *reactive coordination* rule that aligns the characterisation of foreign entities for domestic tax purposes according to the characterisation given in the country where the entity is established or incorporated, i.e., the 'home country'.

A general wording for this rule could be as follows:

> Where according to the rules of a State, a different tax characterisation is given to the same entity, the tax characterisation given to the entity by the State where the entity is organized, shall be followed by the other State.

1644. *See* analysis at *supra* Chapter 5.

1645. Although the idea of harmonisation at a regional level, e.g., within the European Union, might be indeed an attractive solution. For a proposal to harmonise the characterisation of entities in the EU through a mutual recognition of entities in the internal market, *see* Fibbe, *supra* n. 863.

2.1.1 'Entity' *Understood in a Broad Sense*

As stressed already in Chapter 3,[1646] this work uses the term *entity* as including any other arrangement, regardless of the legal position taken by a country regarding who derives the income from that entity/arrangement and whether or not the entity or arrangement has legal personality according to the rules of a specific jurisdiction. Similarly, the proposed wording of the *reactive coordination rule* does not refer to 'entity' as limited to a *legal entity*, i.e., a body having legal existence separate from its owners or participants and having its own rights and liabilities, but rather to *entities* in a broad sense including legal entities and other arrangements. Therefore, no interpretation issues should arise simply because of the fact that one of the States considers an entity as tax transparent and, therefore, not as a legal entity in the strict sense.[1647]

2.1.2 *Home Country: Where the Entity Is Formally/Legally Organised*

As the wording of the proposed rule suggests, the coordination in the characterisation of the entity should be done according to the tax characterisation given in the country where the entity is organised. For this purpose, the reference to *where the entity is organised* should be understood as the country where all the necessary formalities required for its establishment are fulfilled. For example, if a taxpayer decides to carry out a business through an LLC in the United States, he will have to comply with all the formalities required by the specific state governing the constitution of the LLC, e.g., Delaware, Florida, etc. Accordingly, if a taxpayer wanted to establish a silent partnership in Germany (*stille Gesellschaft*), he would have to meet the formal requirements required under German law. Accordingly, it may be observed that in all such cases, there will always be only one jurisdiction governing the formalities of the constitution of an entity.[1648]

The reference to the *country where the entity is formally and legally organised* should not represent a problem even in cases of legal entities organised at a supranational level because even in those cases, there is still a reference to one jurisdiction in the end. For example, the European Company (SE),[1649] the European Cooperative Society (SCE)[1650] or the European Economic Interest Grouping (EEIG)[1651] are legal

1646. *Supra* Chapter 3, s. 2.1.
1647. Alternatively, the wording may include a specific reference to *'entity or arrangement.'* However, the author considers that the above inclusion might create more interpretation problems than limiting the wording to entities and explaining that the concept is used in a boarder way. The above does not prevent countries from including such a reference to 'arrangements' if, in the country's view, such would avoid further interpretation conflicts of the rule. The wording 'entity or arrangement' is also used within the proposed Article 1(2) OECD Model. For a critical view on the reference to 'arrangements' in the context of Article 1(2) OECD Model, *see supra* Chapter 4, s. 5.1.3.
1648. This differs from the criteria to determine the tax residence of entities, in which case there may be more than one jurisdiction claiming that an entity is resident in its jurisdiction.
1649. EU: EC Regulation 2157/2001, Official Journal L 204/01.
1650. EU: EC Regulation 1435/2003, Official Journal L 207/03.
1651. EU: EEC Regulation 2137/1985.

forms that, to a large extent, are governed by uniform EU law but which are still partly regulated by the national provisions of the MS of incorporation.[1652]

2.1.3 Home Country v. Source Country

The reference to 'home country' instead of 'source country' has the purpose of covering both the cases of hybrid and reverse hybrid entities without providing different rules that might complicate the wording and the application of the proposal.[1653]

As stressed already in this work, most of the cases of hybrid entities that are relevant for tax purposes, i.e., where a cross-border payment comes into play, imply that a hybrid entity is an entity making such a payment. In other words, in all those cases, the source country will coincide with the home country of the hybrid entity.[1654] The above does not mean to disregard the fact that, in some cases, a hybrid entity could receive a payment, the source country thereby being different from the home country. However, such cases are generally not relevant from the OECD perspective and the application of *linking rules* because such payments will be taxed at the level of the hybrid entity or at the level of the investors, ensuring, in both cases, the single taxation policy behind the proposed *linking rules*.[1655] In my perspective, therefore, the application of the *reactive coordination rule* in those cases would be relevant only where the rule refers to the source country instead of the home country and the source country is a third country that also considers the entity as tax transparent. In such a case, the hybrid mismatch rule proposed in this chapter would not be effective in solving the

1652. *See* Cerioni, *supra* n. 549. *See also*, Korving and Wijtvliet, *ibid*.
1653. However, a different wording could read as follows: 'Where according to the rules of a State, a different legal characterisation is given to the same entity taxpayer, the legal characterisation given to the entity by the State *where the payment is sourced, in the case of hybrid entities, or where the entity is organized or incorporated, in the case of reverse hybrids*, shall be followed by the other State' (emphasis added).
1654. This idea is implicitly recognised within the OECD BEPS Action Plan 2, which only considers cases of payments made by a hybrid payer and which result in a D/NI outcome (or DD). OECD, *supra* n. 6, p. 49, Recommendation 3(3). Similarly, the EU proposals to deal with hybrid mismatches, both inside and outside the internal market (i.e., EU ATAD I and EU ATAD II), also consider only cases of payments made by a hybrid entity. *See* EU: Council Directive (EU) 2016/1164 of 12 July 2016 (ATAD I) and Council Directive (EU) 2017/952 of 29 May 2017 (ATAD II). The above has to be with the design of the countermeasures. In simple words, as *linking rules* start from the assumption that a mismatch in the tax outcomes is what finally determines the application of the rules, the payments received by an entity considered as a taxable entity in its country of organisation and as tax transparent in the country of the investors, would, most probably, not generate a D/NI outcome because the income would be taxed either in the country of the hybrid entity or in the country of the investors, or both. Therefore, such payment is irrelevant for purposes of the rules, even though potential double taxation might occur and that the true mismatch, i.e., the different characterisation of the same entity, remains. For the analysis of HMA and linking rules, *see supra* Chapter 5, ss 2 and 3.
1655. *Ibid*.

mismatch at all.[1656] This concern disappears, however, if the third country (i.e., source country) also treats the entity as opaque.[1657]

Similarly, in most of the cases involving reverse hybrid entities, it is assumed that the reverse hybrid entity receives the payment, normally from a third country.[1658] In this case, the source country of the payment and the home country of the reverse hybrid do not coincide at all. Moreover, in most of those cases, the country of the investors and the source country normally characterise the entity in the same manner, i.e., as a taxable entity. Therefore, in such a case, the disparity emerges from the different characterisation of the entity in comparison to that in the home country.[1659] However, this does not mean to recognise that payments from a reverse hybrid might also occur. They may, but once again, they would not be relevant from an OECD perspective and the application of *linking rules* because, in such a case, the payment will be recognised as income in the country of the investor (i.e., if the payee is there), ensuring single taxation.[1660] For the purpose of the application of the *reactive coordination rule* to cases involving payments from a reverse hybrid, the distinction between source and home country would be irrelevant because the home and source country in those cases will be the same.

All in all, for purposes of simplicity and as per the arguments already stressed, the proposed *reactive coordination rule* will refer to the characterisation of the entity in the *home country*.

2.2 Scope of the Rule

As stressed in the OECD BEPS Action Plan 2, most of the concerns derived from the potential abuse of hybrid and reverse hybrid entities are given within the context of 'control groups', being thus the scope of the OECD proposed rule reduced to those cases.[1661] The above, however, does not coincide with the rather wide concept of 'control groups'[1662] and 'acting together' and the vague concept of 'structured arrangements'.[1663] Rather, all these concepts demonstrate the opposite, i.e., the OECD proposed rules attempt to apply to a wider range of possible situations. Needless to say,

1656. Because the home country would keep considering the entity as opaque and the country of the investors would 'follow' the characterisation of the source country (a third country), which also treats the entity as tax transparent.
1657. In such a case the only concern would be to ensure a double taxation relief for the potential double taxation of the income both in the home country of the hybrid entity and in the country of the final investors.
1658. OECD (2015), *supra* n. 6, pp. 55 et seq.
1659. *Supra* Chapter 5, s. 2.4.2.
1660. The same would occur if the payments were made to a third country with which the reverse hybrid has, e.g., a loan transaction, that gives rise to the payment. In such a case, however, as the entity is transparent in its home country, the payments made are never deductible. In other words, even today would be considered an HMA.
1661. *Supra* Chapter 5, s. 3.3.1.
1662. *Ibid.*
1663. For a deeper analysis of the concept of '*structured arrangements*,' *see supra* Chapter 5, s. 3.3.2.

the use of these concepts certainly makes the application of the OECD rules very complex.

The *reactive coordination rule* assumes a simplified and more honest approach instead. It proposes an application of the rule to all those cases where there are disparities between two countries with respect to the tax characterisation of the same entity. This is, on the one hand, in line with the three main policy reasons that sustain this proposal, namely simplicity, coherence, and administrability of the rule,[1664] and, on the other hand, with the idea of designing rules targeting the core of the issue regarding hybrids and reverse hybrid entities, i.e., the different characterisation of entities for tax purposes. However, this does not mean that the rule attempts to harmonise the domestic characterisation of foreign entities for domestic tax purposes at all. On the contrary, it attempts to be an alternative that raises more coherent results and avoids unnecessary complexities in its design.

Another issue with respect to the scope of the proposed rule is the fact that the rule aims to apply only to the extent that the disparity in the characterisation of entities is 'tax relevant', i.e., if there is a transaction that originates a payment that makes the disparity relevant for tax purposes. This idea mirrors a US tax rule that applies in the case where an eligible entity elects to treat a foreign entity in a manner different from the one provided by the US default classification rules.[1665] For this purpose, the US tax law provides that 'a foreign entity's classification would be relevant if US income was paid to the entity [...]'.[1666] The reference to 'tax relevance', therefore, ensures that the rule does not apply automatically but only when a relevant tax payment has been made. A similar idea is behind the construction of the concept of HMA, which includes the existence of a payment as a necessary element to determine the existence of an HMA.[1667]

2.3 Tax Policy Justifications

As noted already, the proposed *reactive coordination rule* is based on three main tax policy justification grounds: (i) simplicity, (ii) coherence, and (iii) administrability, which are explained below.

2.3.1 Simplicity

Simplicity should be the basis of any tax rule, mostly when it implies the regulation of transactions that involve the interaction of tax laws from many different jurisdictions. For that reason, the proposed *reactive coordination rule* attempts to be designed and applied in a very simple manner. This is to say, the rule will provide a simple exception to be implemented within domestic laws with respect to the rules used to characterise foreign entities for tax purposes. When a country does not contemplate these rules, it

1664. *Infra* s. 2.3.
1665. *Supra* Chapter 3, s. 4.3.
1666. US: Treas. Reg. s. 301.7701-3(d)(1)(i).
1667. *Supra* Chapter 5, s. 2.2.

will directly apply as a specific anti-hybrid measure added to the domestic legislation. And when the country provides for a similar measure, it will apply to the extent not covered by that rule. For example, the Danish anti-hybrid rules (or anti-CTB regulations) attempt to re-characterise a Danish domestic entity when the majority of the foreign shareholders consider the entity in a different manner than the tax characterisation given under Danish tax law.[1668] These rules could co-exist with a rule that provides that when Denmark characterises a foreign entity differently than the foreign country, Denmark should follow the characterisation of the foreign entity given in its foreign country of organisation. Similarly, e.g., a *reactive coordination rule* could be perfectly compatible with the administrative practice in Spain, which interprets the domestic law as following the tax characterisation of the entity given in the other country.[1669]

Contrary to the proposed OECD *linking rules*, therefore, the *reactive coordination rule* does not look at the tax outcomes in one or the other country, but rather, it focuses directly on the origin and cause of the mismatch, i.e., the different characterisation of foreign entities for domestic tax purposes.[1670] The above does not only avoid complexity, but it also prevents presumptions of abusive practices.[1671]

2.3.2 *Coherence*

From a strict tax policy perspective, results at least curious that all the proposals to counteract the use (or misuse) of hybrid entities and reverse hybrid entities so far either target only the outcome of the transactions, i.e., D/NI outcome (e.g., OECD linking rules),[1672] or provide for the country where the entity is established to reaccommodate the tax characterisation of the entity to the one provided in the country of the investors.[1673]

In a coherent tax policy approach, however, it should be the country that creates the hybrid entity mismatch, i.e., the country that characterises the entity in a manner different from that of the home country, which should initially react in this situation. As well stressed by Lüdicke: 'It is primarily for the state which qualifies foreign entities differently from their home state to introduce anti-hybrid mismatch rules […].'[1674] Following this idea, the design of the *reactive coordination rule* calls for the country generating the hybrid mismatch to react by accommodating the tax characterisation of the entity to the one provided in the country where the relevant entity is legally

1668. For the Danish anti-hybrid rules, *see supra* Chapter 3, s. 5.2.
1669. Nevertheless, in this case an express inclusion of the rule within Spanish domestic law would be more recommendable to avoid contradictory interpretations. For the Spanish administrative practice, *see supra* Chapter 3, s. 5.1.
1670. Interestingly, however, as demonstrated later in the application of the rule to cases involving hybrids and reverse hybrid entities, it also solves issues of DNT and do not generate cases of double taxation. As such, the rule should also be well received by those supporting the idea that single taxation in cross-border transactions. *Infra* ss 2.4.1 and 2.4.2.
1671. *Supra* Chapter 5, s. 2.3.2.
1672. *Supra* Chapter 5, s. 3.
1673. For example, Article 9a EU ATAD II *Supra* Chapter 3, s. 5.3.3.2.
1674. Lüdicke, *supra* n. 870, p. 317.

organised. In other words, the rule makes it unnecessary for the home country of the hybrid entity or reverse hybrid to change its own characterisation of a domestic entity just because of a legal fiction in another country. The above also avoids an excessive reliance upon foreign laws and contingencies that are based on whether that income is deductible in one country or is included as income in the other country.

2.3.3 *Administrability*

Finally, a rule coordinating the characterisation of entities is indeed easier to administer than one providing for more complex contingencies, such as deductibility in one country or inclusion as income in the other country. It is evident that under the proposed *reactive coordination rule*, a contingency still exists; that is, a country should follow the characterisation of the entity in the other country. However, this contingency is kind of inherent to the hybrid mismatch itself,[1675] resulting, therefore, in a more beneficial scenario both for tax administrations and taxpayers.

For tax administrations, the rule will reduce the complexities of determining whether, under foreign laws, an income was deducted or included as income, thus reducing to a certain extent the uncertainty on whether taxing rights should be given up or not.[1676] Similarly, a rule providing for coordination as per the home country of the entity seems to be more in line with other tax rules relying on what happens offshore,[1677] although without a sequence framework as the one proposed with the OECD *linking rules*. In other words, the proposed *reactive coordination rule* applies more as a unilateral measure that considers the treatment of the entity offshore but without excessively relying on all the movements in foreign laws.

For taxpayers, a rule providing for coordination in the characterisation of entities will allow them to be less concerned about foreign laws, ultimately reducing the costs related to tax planning and tax compliance.

2.4 Application of the *Reactive Coordination Rule*

Some illustrations might be helpful to understand the application of the proposed rule. As follows, some examples are given with regard to hybrid and reverse hybrid entities.

2.4.1 *Application to Cases Concerning Payments Made by* Hybrid Entities

With regard to hybrid entities, the application of the rule can be illustrated in the following hypothetical: XCo is a taxable entity incorporated in country X, which grants

1675. For example, a tax authority in the country of the shareholder will only have to determine what is the characterisation of the entity in its home country, which is a rather clear issue, since domestic laws generally provide certainty on whether an entity is tax transparent or tax opaque.

1676. 'Surrendering sovereignty over tax matters to other states is not something governments are used to or are likely to enjoy.' Cooper, *supra* n. 1272, p. 346.

1677. For example, rules on foreign tax credit.

a loan to YSub, an entity organised in country Y. YSub pays back interest in the amount of 100i. Whilst country X considers YSub as tax transparent, country Y considers the same entity as a taxable entity.

Figure 84 Reactive Coordination Rule and Payments Made by Hybrid Entities

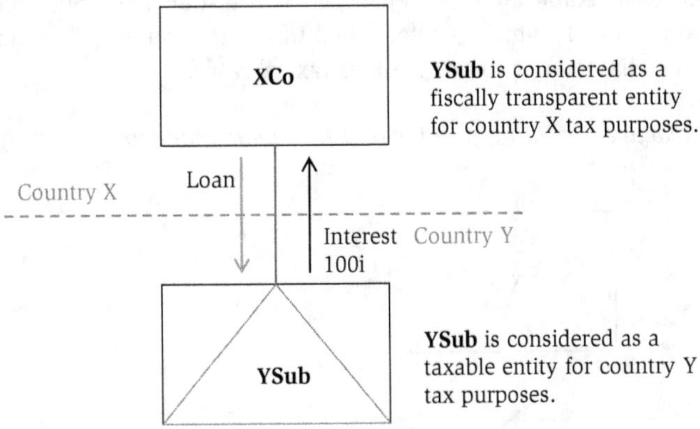

In this scenario, the amount of interest paid (100i) by YSub can be deducted from the gross income of YSub because YSub is considered a taxable entity in country Y. Accordingly, the interest paid will not be included as ordinary income in country X, because under the tax laws of country X, YSub is considered a tax transparent entity. In other words, the loan and the interest are completely disregarded for tax purposes.

If we now consider that all countries have introduced the proposed *reactive coordination* rule, it would imply, in the example above, that once a disparity exists with respect to the characterisation of YSub, which is tax relevant since there is a payment of interest and a loan between YSub (country Y) and XCo (country X), the taxpayer in country X (XCo) should follow the characterisation of the entity in the home (also source) country, i.e., country Y. Therefore, once the rule is applied, the loan and the interest payments between XCo and YCo must be recognised in both countries. This means that there will be no need to limit the deductibility of interest in country Y, as the interest will (most probably) be taxed in country X.[1678] More importantly, there will be no hybrid entity mismatch anymore. That is, the potential disparity in the characterisation of YSub is sorted.

1678. The risk of economic double taxation is also reduced, because of the non-deductibility in country Y when income is included in country X. In contrast, this is likely to occur with the application of the OECD *linking rules*, despite the existence of a hierarchy in the application of those rules. This is discussed in more detail at *supra* Chapter 5, ss 3.4.1 and 3.4.3 referred to the circular effect of *linking rules* and economic double taxation.

2.4.2 *Application to Cases Concerning Payments Made to* Reverse Hybrid Entities

Let us assume the same facts as the example using hybrid entities, with the only difference that YSub is regarded as a reverse hybrid entity, i.e., under the tax law of country Y, YSub is considered as a transparent entity whilst country X and country Z consider YSub as a taxable entity. Likewise, we will assume that YSub receives interest payments from YSub 1, which is established in a third country, Z, which makes the disparity in the characterisation of YSub as tax relevant.

Figure 85 Reactive Coordination Rule and Payments Made to Reverse Hybrid Entities

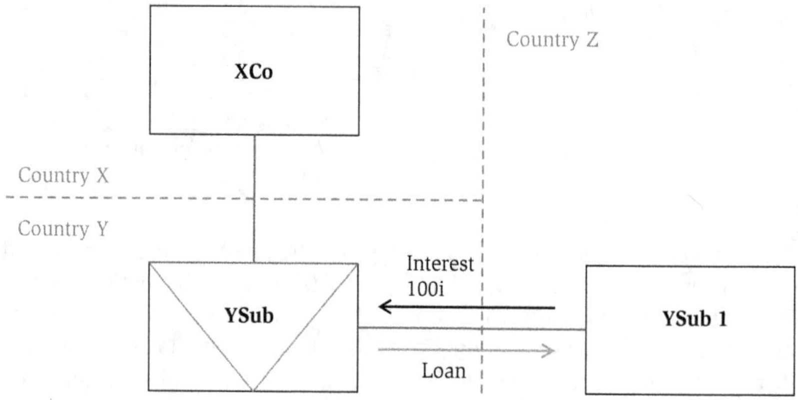

The interest payments received by YSub are deductible in country Z but not included as ordinary income in country Y, where YSub is considered a tax-transparent entity. They are also not included as ordinary income in country X because country X considers YSub as a taxable entity.[1679]

If we now consider the application of the proposed *reactive coordination* rule, country X shall follow the characterisation of YSub in country Y, the home country. Country Y treats YSub as tax transparent. Therefore, the income might be taxed in the hands of the investors, i.e., country X. More importantly, it would not be necessary to establish a limitation in the deductibility of the interest payments in country Z to the extent that income is not included in country Y or to rely on the effective application of the CFC legislation in country X. On the contrary, under the proposed *reactive coordination rule*, the right to tax is finally granted at the level of the investors and the hybrid mismatch is solved through the coordination in the characterisation of YSub.

1679. Unless, of course, dividends are distributed from YSub to XCo or country X effectively applies CFC rules.

2.4.3 *Advantages*

The *reactive coordination rule* has some evident advantages, which are mostly related to the simple and direct functioning of the proposed rule when compared to the proposed OECD *linking rules*. These advantages are analysed as follows.

2.4.3.1 *Non-contingent Application*

The proposed *reactive coordination rule* supposes the reaction of only one country without the contingency of what is going to happen in the other country.[1680] This is to say, if all countries introduced the rule, it is only the country that originates the mismatch, i.e., the country that characterises the entity differently than the home country, which should react by aligning its characterisation of the foreign entity according to the rules in the home country of the entity. This will eliminate the sequence mechanic between *primary response* and *defensive rule*, avoiding circularity and the potential economic double taxation issues that might arise. Similarly, it will avoid the unnecessary dependency on foreign laws that the application of OECD *linking rules* suggests.[1681]

2.4.3.2 *Disparities over Outcomes*

As stressed already, there is a sound criticism with respect to the proposed OECD *linking rules*, which is their excessive focus on the outcomes of the hybrid transactions rather than on the core of the disparities, i.e., the different characterisation of entities by two or more countries.[1682]

The proposed *reactive coordination rule* provides a more direct approach, which privileges the origin of the disparities, i.e., the different characterisation of the same entity, over the tax outcome of the transaction to design the rule. The above also brings to the front the core of the problem, which was relegated to the background under the proposed OECD *linking rules*. This is also coherent with one of the main conclusions of

1680. As stressed already in this work, one of the main critics to the OECD *linking rules* is their sequencing application. A *primary response* applies denying a deduction in the country of the payer to the extent that income has not been included in the country of the payee. Accordingly, a *defensive rule* depends exclusively on the application of the primary response, i.e., it applies only to the extent a deduction was granted in the country of the payer. *Supra* Chapter 5, ss 3.1 and 3.2.
1681. *Supra* Chapter 5, s. 3.4.
1682. As Cooper well explains: '[...] there is a sense in which constructing the rules around outcomes clouds as much as it reveals. The rules for situations (1) to (3) involving hybrid entities are all separately constructed, i.e. they have distinct preconditions, only one involves changes to domestic law, the exceptions are different and for one there is no secondary defensive rule. And yet all the situations identified have the same problem at their core, i.e. *the states do not agree whether there is an entity*' (emphasis added). Cooper, *supra* n. 1272, p. 339.

this work, which is that DNT should not be used as a proxy to determine the existence of abusive practices through the use of hybrids and reverse hybrid entities.[1683]

2.4.3.3 *Complexity Is Reduced*

This is perhaps the most important advantage of the proposed *reactive coordination rule*, being also in line with one of its main tax policy aims, namely simplicity.[1684]

The application of the rule is rather simple because it attempts to coordinate the tax characterisation of the entity according to the one given in the country where the entity is formally and legally organised, thus avoiding unnecessary complexities, such as having to establish whether or not a payment was deducted in one country or included in the other country, or relying excessively on foreign laws.[1685] Likewise, the rule is easy to administer both for taxpayers and tax administrations.[1686]

2.4.4 *Disadvantages*

The proposed reactive coordination rule is, however, far from being perfect and might result in a series of potential disadvantages, which are explained below.

2.4.4.1 *Legal Certainty*

Legal certainty might be affected because of the application of the *reactive coordination rule.* Indeed, taxpayers in the investor country might feel prejudiced by the application of a domestic rule that aims to coordinate the characterisation of entities according to the one given in a different country.

Nevertheless, the legal certainty issue might be more illusory than real because where the rule is implemented, taxpayers will know with certainty that in all cases involving hybrid and reverse hybrid entities, the rule will apply to follow the tax characterisation of the entity in the *home country*. Therefore, it could be arguably sustained that the principle of legal certainty is affected. A different situation could be the case in which the rule provides for a re-characterisation of domestic entities as per the characterisation of the entity in a foreign country, such as the case of the Danish anti-hybrid rule. In such a case, there could be more arguments to sustain that legal certainty is affected.[1687]

1683. *Supra* Chapter 1, s. 6 and *infra* Chapter 7, s. 2.
1684. *Supra* s. 2.3.1.
1685. *Supra* s. 2.3.3.
1686. *Ibid.*
1687. For example, a taxpayer might rightfully complain that the fact of electing to do business in this country through a partnership (tax transparent entity) does not guarantee that in the future, and due to the tax characterisation in another country, the partnership will be treated as a taxable entity.

2.4.4.2 Tax Sovereignty

Some commentators may argue that tax sovereignty, as an inherent element of any tax system, could be affected by the introduction and application of the proposed *reactive coordination rule*. The argument is basically that countries are free to choose the elements of their tax systems, including the determination of when an entity or arrangement is tax transparent or opaque, regardless of where that entity is legally formed. Therefore, a rule such as the *reactive coordination rule* could limit such freedom, forcing a country to adapt its domestic rules of characterisation of entities to that of a foreign country, ultimately ceding tax sovereignty.[1688]

The argument is sound, but it is also misleading. First, it distorts the idea of tax sovereignty, presenting it as an absolute feature of tax systems when, in fact, tax sovereignty has never been conceived in absolute terms.[1689] Indeed, countries constantly adapt their sovereignty to tax to that of other countries, and the best example of this is bilateral tax treaties, which limit the sovereignty of two countries to tax certain items of income, avoiding double taxation.[1690] Other examples can also be found at a domestic level. For instance, countries normally cede tax sovereignty when the application of an FTC comes into play.[1691] In fact, an FTC is granted domestically only to the extent that taxes are effectively paid in another country but under the rules of that other country. In other words, granting or denying a credit is a domestic exercise generally limited by the understanding of what other country considers a payment of taxes. Similarly, CFC rules work in a way by which the sovereignty of country X is given up partially, allowing a different state Y to tax the profits of a subsidiary in country X, although no distribution of profits has taken place yet. This proves again that the limits of sovereignty are always permeable, and an absolute idea of tax sovereignty is simply erroneous.

Second, the argument misinterprets the scope of the *reactive coordination rule*. Indeed, the application of the *reactive coordination rule* does not affect the sovereignty of a country to decide the tax characterisation of its own domestic companies. In contrast, it reinforces it since the proposed rule ensures that other countries follow the

1688. *See, e.g.*, McGowan, *supra* n. 541, pp. 256-258 (who argues that 'As part of its tax sovereignty, a jurisdiction must also be free to decide when and how to treat an entity or arrangement as 'transparent', whether formed under the laws of that jurisdiction or elsewhere'). *Ibid.*, p. 164 (where McGowan argues that in a triangular case, and in reference to the *proposed reactive coordination rule* in this book, that countries would not 'want to delegate to a third country… control over what entities it treats as opaque or transparent).

1689. As argued by D. Ring: 'Obviously states do not exercise unimpeded control over tax policy choices – they are influenced and constrained by the political economy within their own domestic system (e.g., pressure from powerful taxpayers) and by the need to account for the implications of their tax rules globally (e.g., will the state's new tax be deemed a creditable foreign tax by other countries)'. D. Ring, *Democracy, Sovereignty and Tax Competition: The Role of Tax Sovereignty in Shaping Tax Cooperation*, Fl. Tax Rev. 9 (2009), SSRN draft, p. 4.

1690. *See supra* Chapter 4.

1691. This can also be seen when a new tax is imposed, and other countries need to determine whether that tax is creditable. *See* Ring, *supra* n. 1689.

tax characterisation given in the country where the entity is legally organised.[1692] In other words, the coordination of the legal characterisation of a foreign entity as per the given characterisation in its country of legal formation supposes a recognition of the sovereignty of countries to characterise their own domestic entities or arrangements, limiting this capacity only when it comes to the characterisation of foreign entities, and even in those cases, that limitation is only partial since it is triggered exclusively when a hybrid transaction is relevant for tax purposes.[1693]

Third, and finally, the *reactive coordination rule* is a rule of coordination and not a rule of harmonisation.[1694] Therefore, tax sovereignty is not more limited than in cases that are found already in the practice of states, such as the case of Spain, Denmark, or South Africa, which coordinate the domestic tax characterisation of foreign entities to that in a foreign country.[1695] This demonstrates one more time that arguments of loss of sovereignty or legislative control seem to be more an overreaction than a proper reflection of the reality of taxation around the world.

In sum, therefore, tax sovereignty appears, in principle, as a disadvantage for the application of the *reactive coordination rule*. However, this argument is rapidly discarded since it proves to be true only to the extent that one understands tax sovereignty in absolute terms. As noted already, this is not only misleading but also far from the practice of states in tax matters around the world.

2.4.4.3 Some Undesirable Effects

Another potential disadvantage of the rule comes from some undesired effects which are derived exclusively from the application of the rule. As follows, three situations are analysed: (i) potential double taxation, (ii) tax benefits not granted in the absence of the rule, and (iii) disregarded transactions due to the sole application of the rule.

2.4.4.3.1 Potential Double Taxation

Although less likely to happen and excluded from the OECD BEPS Action Plan 2, a hybrid entity might also receive some payments.[1696] In such a case, the sole application of the *reactive coordination rule* might result in cases of double taxation.

1692. *Supra* s. 2.2.
1693. This comes from the idea that a hybrid entity structure should not be relevant for tax purposes but only when there is a payment associated to that structure. This payment makes the whole transaction tax relevant and triggers the application of the reactive coordination rule domestically.
1694. For an example of harmonisation, *see* the proposal of Fibbe at *supra* n. 863.
1695. For Spain and Denmark, *see supra* Chapter 3, sections 5.1 and 5.2. For the case of South Africa, *see* McGowan, *supra* n. 541, p. 257 (referring to Article 1 of the South African Income Tax Act, which provides for a tax transparency treatment of foreign tax transparent partnerships, regardless of their legal personality).
1696. This case is, however, not included within the OECD BEPS Action Plan 2 because it does not generate a D/NI outcome. As the entity receiving the income is considered as tax transparent in the country of the investors, it is assumed that the income will be taxed in that country. OECD (2015), *supra* n. 6, pp. 49 et seq. Likewise, this case is excluded from the EU ATAD I and

Let us assume the same example in section 2.4.1 with the difference that YSub has a subsidiary in country Z, and it receives interest payments associated with a loan granted by YSub to YSub 1.

Figure 86 Potential Double Taxation

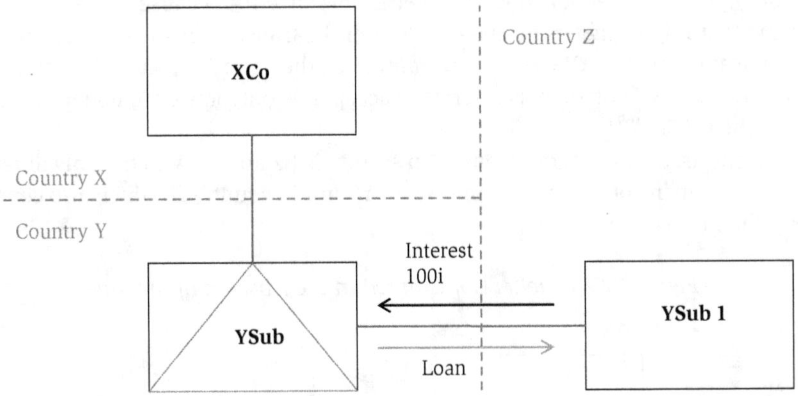

In the absence of the rule, this situation would not raise much concern following the OECD tax policy behind the *linking rules*, i.e., single taxation, because the interest payments would flow through YSub and would be most likely taxed at the level of the investor (XCo). Nevertheless, the hybrid mismatch remains.

Applying the *reactive coordination rule*, however, country X would also consider YSub as an opaque entity. The above means that country X would no longer be able to tax the interest payments (100i) unless CFC rules apply. If that happens, however, income might be taxed twice, i.e., once at the level of YSub in country Y because the entity is taxable and once at the level of XCo in country X because of the application of CFC rules. Therefore, to avoid such a result, it is recommendable that together with the implementation of the *reactive coordination rule*, CFC rules guarantee a tax credit for the taxes already paid in country Y.

2.4.4.3.2 Tax Benefits Not Granted in Absence of the Rule

Another good example of cases in which the pure application of the *reactive coordination rule* might bring undesirable results is the case of payments made from a reverse hybrid entity.

EU ATAD II. *See* EU: Council Directive (EU) 2016/1164 of 12 July 2016 (ATAD I) and Council Directive (EU) 2017/952 of 29 May 2017 (ATAD II). However, this case might generate double taxation if the country of investors does not grant double taxation relief for the taxes paid in the country where the entity is organised, i.e., where the entity is indeed a taxable entity. The proposed *reactive coordination rule*, on the contrary, does not start from the assumption of matching tax outcomes to avoid DNT, but rather of matching the characterisation of entities, which is the true core of the issue regarding hybrid and reverse hybrid entities.

If an interest payment is made from a reverse hybrid entity to a third country that also considers the entity as tax transparent,[1697] the outcome of that transaction would be a non-deductible interest payment in the payer country, whose income will also not be recognised in the country of the payee, which considers the payer as tax transparent. Accordingly, since the country of the investors considers the payer as a separate entity, it has no impact on the transaction between payer and payee. As per the state-of-the-art, this hybrid transaction does not generate concerns because there is no D/NI outcome that might trigger the classification of the transaction as an HMA and, thus, the application of the OECD *linking rules*. In other words, a non-deduction/non-inclusion, i.e., DNT outcome, is a perfectly acceptable outcome even under the current view of the OECD.[1698]

Let me assume the same example in section 2.4.2 above, with the only difference being that YSub in country Y pays interest to YSub 1 in country Z, which also considers YSub as tax transparent.

Figure 87 Benefits Not Granted in the Absence of the Rule

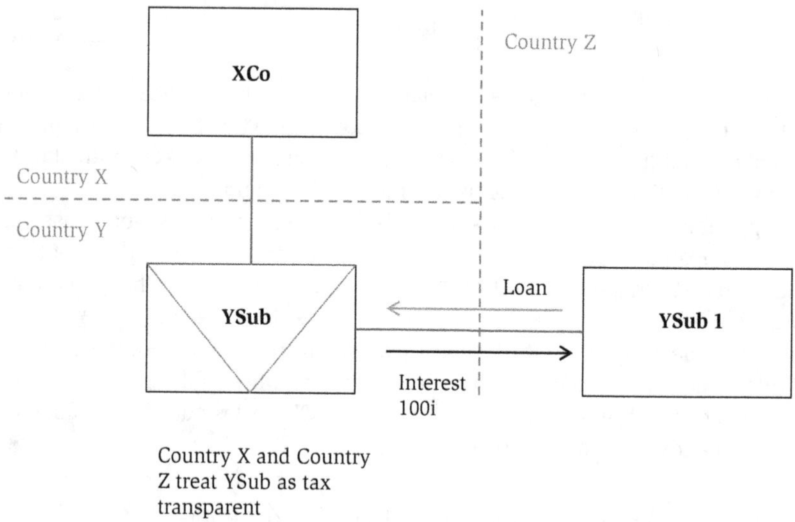

1697. The country of the investors considers the entity as opaque, which makes the entity a reverse hybrid entity. *Supra* Chapter 3, s. 3.1.

1698. Because the disparity does not originate a D/NI outcome. *See* OECD (2015), *supra* n. 6, pp. 55 et seq. It is also not included within the EU ATAD I and II. *See* EU: Council Directive (EU) 2016/1164 of 12 July 2016 (ATAD I) and Council Directive (EU) 2017/952 of 29 May 2017 (ATAD II).

In this scenario, the outcome is a non-deduction/non-inclusion, which is certainly out of the scope of BEPS and the concept of HMA.

However, if we now consider the application of the *reactive coordination rule* to this transaction, it will imply that the country of the investors (country X) shall follow the characterisation of the entity in the country where this is legally organised (country Y). Thus, a deduction might be created in the country of the investors only because of the application of the rule, which could give rise to future abusive situations. Such a result seems to be inappropriate, considering that it grants a tax benefit that did not exist before the application of the *reactive coordination rule* and which may be an open door for abusive practices. Therefore, in order to avoid this potential negative effect, I propose that in those triangular cases in which both the payer country (country Y) and the payee country (country Z) treat the reverse hybrid as tax transparent, the *reactive coordination rule* be 'switched-off' or unapplied.[1699] As the outcome without the application of the proposed rule did not generate any international tax policy concerns before the application of the rule, it might be a perfectly acceptable result if the *reactive coordination rule* is not applied in these cases.

2.4.4.3.3 Disregarded Transactions for the Sole Application of the Rule

Another example might be given when the reverse hybrid entity is making a payment to the investors,[1700] which, by the sole application of the *reactive coordination rule*, might be disregarded for tax purposes.

Let me assume the example in section 2.4.2 with the sole difference that XCo grants a loan to YSub, and the latter pays interest back. In such a case, and only due to the application of the *reactive coordination rule* that provides for the coordination in the characterisation of YSub as per its characterisation in country Y (i.e., as a tax transparent entity), the outcome will be that the whole transaction between XCo and YSub is disregarded. This outcome is the direct result of the application of the *reactive coordination rule*.

1699. The 'switch-off' of the rule does not require a deeper explanation, because it only implies that countries might opt to include in their domestic laws, together with the suggested wording of the *reactive coordination rule*, an exception for the application of the rule in cases as the one described above, i.e., where a reverse hybrid entity makes a payment to a payee in a third country different from the country of the investors.

1700. This scheme is also outside of the scope of the OECD *linking rules* because it does not generate a D/NI outcome, and thus, no HMA concern exists.

Figure 88 Disregarded Transaction for the Sole Application of the Rule

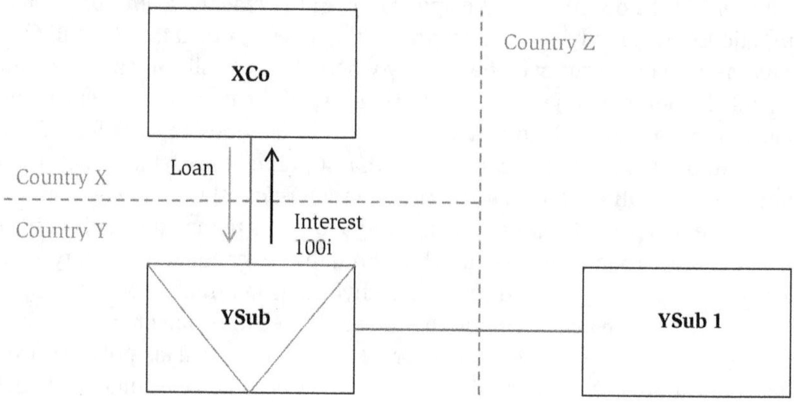

In order to avoid then on-recognition of the loan and the interest payments as a result of the application of the *reactive coordination rule*, the rule will be switched-off in this case.

The possibility of disregarding the whole transaction just because of the application of the *reactive coordination rule* may, however, give rise to abusive practices. Therefore, I consider, once again, that a 'switch-off' rule with respect to the *reactive coordination rule* may be applied here.

In general terms, the possibility of 'switching off' the application of the *reactive coordination rule* should be interpreted neither as a contradiction nor a defect of the proposed rule. On the contrary, as stressed already, the tax policy behind the proposed rule is not to achieve full harmonisation in the rules used by countries to characterise foreign entities for tax purposes but rather to create a more direct and simple manner to tackle the potential misuse of hybrid and reverse hybrid entities, especially when compared to the existing OECD *linking rules*. Likewise, and as its name suggests, a 'reactive' rule necessarily implies that some cases will remain outside its scope, including, for example, all those cases in which the different characterisation of the same entity by two States does not become relevant for tax purposes.

2.5 Similarities and Differences with Other Examples of Coordination

At first glance, the proposal of this chapter mirrors perhaps other existing proposals of coordination already studied in Chapter 3.[1701] This statement is indeed correct since those proposals and the one developed in this chapter attempt to coordinate the tax characterisation of entities rather than the tax outcomes of transactions involving hybrid or reverse hybrid entities. In other words, they all target the core of the hybrid

1701. *Supra* Chapter 3, s. 5.

entity mismatch. However, there are still substantial differences among them. Both similitudes and differences are analysed in the following subsections.

2.5.1 *The Spanish Example of Coordination and the* Reactive Coordination Rule

The Spanish example of coordination is perhaps not the strictest point of comparison since the Spanish coordination outcome is exclusively the result of the interpretation of the Spanish law, repeatedly used by the Spanish tax administration, rather than the result of the specific wording of a tax provision.[1702] Nonetheless, more similarities than differences can be found when the outcomes of both, i.e., the Spanish administrative practice and the proposed rule, are put together.

As stressed already in Chapter 3,[1703] Article 37 of the Spanish NRITL provides for a resemblance test with regard to the tax characterisation of foreign entities.[1704] In particular, Spanish law attempts to treat foreign entities whose juridical nature is identical or analogous to those of the entities subject to the income attribution regime in Spain, i.e., a tax treatment in which the income of the entity is taxed only in the hands of the owners as if they were subject to that income attribution regime in Spain.[1705] Although the wording of the Spanish law is not entirely clear, many Spanish scholars agree that, as per the Spanish tax administration's practice, the tax treatment given in the foreign country is the central element to determining the legal characterisation of the foreign entity.[1706] Like the *reactive coordination rule*, therefore, the Spanish tax administration practice tends to respect the tax characterisation of the entity in the country in which it is organised, i.e., the home country.

Nevertheless, the Spanish rule can neither be interpreted from the strict wording of the rule nor can one be sure that the same interpretation will always be sustained. Thus, a proper rule within the Spanish statute, which recognises the long-standing tax administration practice in Spain, is definitely recommendable. In this regard, the *reactive coordination rule* may replace such a gap, also ensuring through its implementation by other countries that the Spanish characterisation of its own entities will be respected, and solving thus those cases of hybrid entity mismatches that the current administrative practice has not been able to resolve until this point.[1707]

1702. *Supra* Chapter 3, s. 5.1.
1703. *Supra* Chapter 3, s. 5.1.
1704. *Supra* Chapter 3, s. 5.1.2. *See also*, ES: Article 37 of the Spanish Non-Resident Income Tax Law–NRITL, Royal Legislative Decree No. 5/2004 of 5 March 2004.
1705. For the different binding rulings issues by the DGT (Spanish tax administration), *see supra* Chapter 3, s. 5.1.3.
1706. *See, e.g.*, Jiménez-Valladolid de L'Hotellerie-Fallois and Vega Borrego, *supra* n. 803. *See also*, Mosquera Mouriño, *ibid*.
1707. As stated in Chapter 3, there is no rule in Spain that guarantees that a Spanish entity is considered either transparent or opaque under the laws of a foreign country, which might certainly generate a hybrid entity mismatch. *Supra* Chapter 3, s. 5.1.

2.5.2 *The Danish Rule and the* Reactive Coordination Rule

In 2004 and 2008, the Danish tax law was modified in order to include some rules to counteract the influence and the use of the US CTB regulations with respect to Danish entities.[1708] In brief, the Danish rules provide that if certain requirements are met, a domestic Danish taxable entity, considered tax transparent by a foreign country, can also be re-characterised as a transparent entity in Denmark.[1709] Likewise, a Danish transparent entity can be re-characterised as a taxable entity if the foreign country also considers it a taxable entity.[1710] To a certain extent, therefore, one might argue that the Danish rules represent an attempt to solve hybrid entity mismatches coordinating the characterisation of their own domestic entities as per the one provided in the country of the investors, or the majority shareholders, at least.

Based on their design, though, the Danish rules represent exactly the opposite of what is proposed in this chapter. This does not diminish the importance of the Danish rules. On the contrary, they make complete sense in the context where the rules were launched, i.e., to limit the scope of application of the CTB regulations in the United States through a unilateral response from Denmark. Indeed, a 'coordination rule' in the country of the investors (i.e., the US) would have been simply impracticable.[1711]

Another characteristic of the Danish rules is that they attempt to apply within a limited scope. For example, one of the requirements under the Danish rules refers to hybrid entities in which more than 50% of the ownership, by value or votes, is in the hands of a foreign entity.[1712] Similarly, the rules preventing reverse hybrid entity mismatches provide that the direct owners/partners holding more than 50% of the capital or voting rights must be tax residents in one or more foreign jurisdictions, including the Faroe Islands or Greenland.[1713] The above does not coincide with the attempt of the *reactive coordination rule*, which is to apply the rule to all hybrid entity mismatches, regardless of whether or not they originated within control groups.

There are, however, other substantial differences between the Danish rule and the proposed *reactive coordinate rule*. For example, the anti-hybrid entity rule in Denmark applies to the extent the foreign country is a member of the EEA or a tax treaty partner with Denmark.[1714] This regional limitation is not contemplated in the proposal for a *reactive coordination rule*. Accordingly, e.g., the Danish anti-reverse hybrid rule applies not only in case the jurisdiction where the owners are tax resident considers the Danish entity to be a separate taxable entity but also in case this country does not exchange information with the Danish tax authorities.[1715] The above certainly extends the scope of the rule beyond cases of disparities in the characterisation of entities, or at

1708. *Supra* Chapter 3, s. 5.2.
1709. A detailed analysis in *supra* Chapter 3, s. 5.2.1.
1710. A detailed analysis in *supra* Chapter 3, s. 5.2.2.
1711. In this opinion, e.g., Dell'Anese, *supra* n. 4, p. 254. *See also*, Møllin Ottosen and Nørremark, *supra* n. 823, p. 513; Bundgaard, *ibid.*, pp. 200-201. All these authors coincide that the target of the 2004 and 2008 rules was exclusively the negative impact of the US CTB regulations.
1712. This is referred as the 'controlled foreign legal entity'. *Supra* Chapter 3, s. 5.2.1.
1713. *Supra* Chapter 3, s. 5.2.2.
1714. *Supra* Chapter 3, s. 5.2.1.
1715. *Supra* Chapter 3, s. 5.2.2.

least presumes that the foreign characterisation of Danish transparent entities is opaque by the sole reason that information is not available. Although this rule might be practical in terms of avoiding uncertainty when information is not available, I consider that such a rule would not be necessary for purposes of the *reactive coordination rule*, mostly in light of the ongoing international scenario in which the automatic exchange of information seems to prevail.[1716]

2.5.3 *The EU ATAD I and II and the* Reactive Coordination Rule

As noted already in Chapter 3, the reactive coordination rule might also be compared with the original proposal for an EU ATAD and the current Article 9a of the EU ATAD.

2.5.3.1 *The Proposal on EU ATAD and the Reactive Coordination Rule*

With regard to the original proposal for EU ATAD, it indeed attempted to solve the hybrid entity mismatch by making the residence country follow the characterisation of the 'source country'.[1717] Nonetheless, the rule maintained the reference to D/NI outcomes in order to determine the existence of a mismatch.[1718] In other words, the matching of tax outcomes seems to be the final aim rather than the hybrid entity mismatch itself. This, for example, excludes cases in which a hybrid entity is receiving interest rather than paying them or cases where a reverse hybrid is making a payment rather than receiving it because, in both cases, there is no D/NI concern.

Contrary to the above, however, the *reactive coordination rule* attempts exclusively and directly to solve the hybrid entity mismatch, taking into consideration even those situations excluded from the proposal for EU ATAD.[1719] For example, since the rule attempts to simply respect the characterisation of the entity in its home country, it could also avoid mismatches in which a hybrid entity is receiving a payment from a third country, i.e., a country that is different from the investors' country where the entity is treated as tax transparent and from the home country where it is considered tax opaque.

Despite the above, the proposed *reactive coordination rule* must be carefully and restrictively applied in cases where: (i) a payment is made to a hybrid entity from a third country; or (ii) a reverse hybrid entity makes a payment to (a) a third country which also treats the entity as tax transparent, or (b) the country of the investors. The idea behind this is to avoid potential double taxation situations or the creation of tax benefits by the sole application of the reactive coordination rule.[1720] For the first case, i.e., a hybrid entity receiving a payment from a third country, I have proposed to contemplate in the CFC rules of the country of the investors' specific rules that grant

1716. For a reference on the global tendency towards transparency and automatic exchange of information, *see supra* Chapter 1, s. 4.1.2.
1717. *Supra* Chapter 3, s. 5.3.1.
1718. EU: Article 10 of the Proposal for EU ATAD.
1719. *Supra* s. 2.4.
1720. *Supra* ss 2.4.4.2.1, 2.4.4.2.2 and 2.4.4.2.3.

double taxation relief for the taxes paid in the country of the hybrid entity. As for the cases of reverse hybrid entities making a payment, a 'switch-off' rule has already been proposed and explained.[1721]

2.5.3.2 *Article 9a EU ATAD and the Reactive Coordination Rule*

As stressed already in this work, Article 9a of the EU ATAD II resembles the Danish anti-reverse hybrid rule, providing for a re-characterisation of a reverse hybrid entity in cases where 50% or more of the voting rights, capital interests or rights to a share of profit in that entity is maintained by shareholders located in a jurisdiction or jurisdictions that regard the entity as a taxable person.[1722] In such a case, the reverse hybrid entity will also be treated as a taxable entity.[1723] Accordingly, the rule contained within the EU ATAD applies with priority over *linking rules*.[1724]

Although there are elements of connection with respect to the proposed *reactive coordination rule*, e.g., the fact that it does not make any reference to tax outcomes but rather to the disparities in the characterisation of the same entity, the EU ATAD rule works exactly in the opposite direction. In other words, it attempts to coordinate via re-characterisation in the home country, i.e., forcing the reverse hybrid to change its own domestic characterisation. This, as argued already, might be justified from a policy perspective, i.e., in order to keep the revenues within the EU.[1725] However, re-characterising an entity in the MS where the entity is organised might also increase uncertainty for those taxpayers who originally decided to opt to carry out businesses using a certain legal form rather than the other.[1726] Moreover, the rule within the EU ATAD is still ineffective in targeting payments made to a reverse hybrid entity in all those cases when the reverse hybrid is incorporated in a third country outside the EU.[1727]

The *reactive coordination rule* works in a different manner because it assumes as a primary tax policy aim that the country that generates the mismatch should react by coordinating its characterisation as per the one provided in the country where the entity is formally and legally organised.[1728] The above, on the one hand, grants legal certainty for those who originally decided to carry out businesses using tax-transparent forms and, on the other hand, may also be more effective in targeting cases where a

1721. *Ibid.*
1722. EU: Article 9a(1) of the Council Directive (EU) 2017/952 of 29 May 2017 (ATAD II). For further details, *supra* Chapter 3, s. 5.3.3.2.
1723. *Ibid.*
1724. EU: Council Directive (EU) 2017/952 of 29 May 29 2017 (ATAD II), rec. 29.
1725. *Supra* Chapter 3, s. 5.3.3.2.
1726. *See, e.g.*, McDaniel, McMahon and Simmons at *supra* n. 563 to *see, e.g.*, why in the US taxpayer prefers transparency rather than opacity.
1727. This is further explained with examples in *supra* Chapter 3, s. 5.3.3.2.
1728. *Supra* s. 2.3.2.

reverse hybrid is not organised within the EU because it simply provides for coordination in the home country regardless of where this is located. Moreover, the disadvantages derived from the application of the proposed *reactive coordination rule* may be mitigated with the proposed solution already explained in this work.[1729]

3 IMPLICATIONS OF THE *REACTIVE COORDINATION RULE* WITHIN TAX TREATIES

As recognised in Chapter 4, the inclusion of Article 1(2) OECD Model solves many issues regarding the proper allocation of tax treaty benefits when tax-transparent entities are involved, avoiding conflicts of allocation of income. However, this provision is far from being a completely fair solution, especially for developing (source) countries.[1730]

Nevertheless, the negative impact of Article 1(2) OECD Model as regards source countries might be indirectly mitigated by the application of the domestic *reactive coordination rule*. In other words, once domestic coordination in the characterisation of entities has been achieved, the application of Article 1(2) OECD Model might be restricted exclusively to those cases in which the source or residence country, in a bilateral context, treats their own domestic entities as tax transparent.

The analysis of the implications of the application of the *reactive coordination rule* with regard to tax treaties will be performed using case studies of hybrids and reverse hybrid entities and involving both bilateral and triangular situations. These case studies are inspired by the illustrations already analysed in Chapter 4 with respect to the application of Articles 1(6) US Model[1731] and Article 1(2) OECD Model,[1732] and all of them assume that there is no PE in the source state. Accordingly, all the examples also assume that all the anti-abuse restrictions within domestic law and tax treaties were overcome.

3.1 Bilateral Cases Using *Hybrid Entities* and *Reverse Hybrid Entities*

This section contains four case studies analysing the implications of the *reactive coordination rule* within the tax treaty context. Whilst Cases A and B refer to income received by or through a hybrid entity, Cases C and D refer to income received through a reverse hybrid entity. All cases assume strict bilateral situations where interest payments are paid from one Contracting State to the other Contracting State.

1729. *Supra* s. 2.4.4.
1730. *Supra* Chapter 4.
1731. *Supra* Chapter 4, s. 4.2.
1732. *Supra* Chapter 4, s. 5.2.

3.1.1 *Case A*

Entity P is organised and resident in State P and has two owners, A and B, who are residents of State R. Accordingly, entity P receives interest payments from a debtor in State P. Whilst State P considers the entity as a taxable entity, State R considers the same entity as fiscally transparent, and thus, the income is allocated to partners A and B. State P has a general WHT on interest paid abroad of 30%, calculated on the gross amount of payments.

Figure 89 Case A

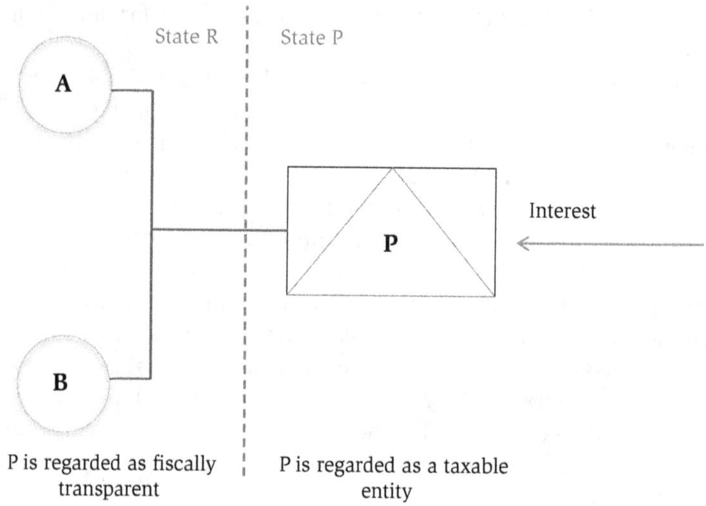

Let me first analyse the solution given by Article 1(2) OECD Model without considering the application of the domestic *reactive coordination rule*.

As stressed in Chapter 4, the preconditions of Article 1(2) OECD Model are met since there is an entity considered fiscally transparent by one of the Contracting States, which is receiving income from the other Contracting State, and that income is allocated to the partners, who are residents of the State that considers the entity as tax transparent. Therefore, according to Article 1(2) of the treaty R-P, partners A and B should be granted the benefits of the tax treaty R-P. This brings us to the specific allocative rule, i.e., Article 11 OECD Model. According to Article 11 of the treaty R-P, State P should apply a reduced WHT of 10% on the gross amount of interest, but only to the extent that partners A and B are regarded as the beneficial owners of the interest. The conflict between the two provisions is thus evident.[1733] In simple words, if State P limits its taxing rights in application of Article 1(2) of the treaty R-P, it would be only

1733. *Supra* Chapter 4, s. 5.3.1.

because State R characterises the entity (legally organised in State P) in a different manner.[1734]

The result is certainly unfair from the source state's perspective. If one assumes that neither Article 1(2) OECD Model nor the principles of the OECD Partnership Report apply, the transaction above should remain as a domestic transaction because, for State P purposes, the payment is being made to a domestic entity, which is considered as taxable in its country of organisation. Nevertheless, the characterisation of the entity by State R is the sole factor that determines the application of the treaty R-P and, thus, the limitation of taxing rights in the source state. In simple words, it is the characterisation in State R that makes the transaction relevant for tax purposes.

Let me now assume that the *reactive coordination rule* has been implemented domestically, both in State R and State P.

Figure 90 Case A after the Application of the Reactive Coordination Rule

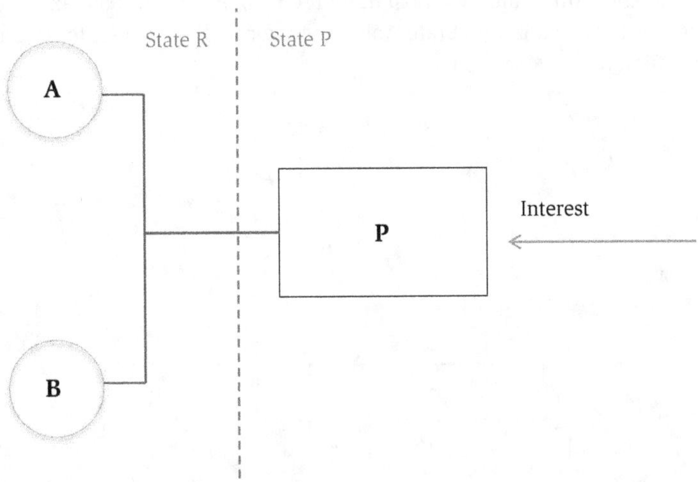

State R and State P consider Entity P as tax opaque because of the application of the *reactive coordination rule.*

In such a case, the hybrid entity mismatch would have been solved even before the application of the R-P treaty. Indeed, according to the *reactive coordination rule,* State R should follow the characterisation of the entity in its country of organisation, i.e., State P in our case. That is, State P and State R will treat the entity as tax opaque. Therefore,

1734. *See* as an alternative to the dichotomy between the solution of Article 1(2) OECD Model and the beneficial ownership requirement of Article 11, the 'deemed' *beneficial owner* proposed by some scholars. *Supra* Chapter 4, s. 5.3.1.1. When applying the solution to this hypothetical, the conflict is pragmatically solved deeming A and B as the *beneficial owners*, although it does not justify why the characterisation in the State of source, i.e., where the entity is legally organised, should be completely disregarded. *Supra* Chapter 4, s. 5.3.1.2. For additional comments from the author to this proposal, *see supra* Chapter 4, s. 5.3.1.3.

Article 1 (2) and the treaty R-P is no longer applicable. In other words, the interest payments to entity P revert to being a purely domestic concern, which seems to be at least a fairer position from the source state's perspective since the treaty R-P applies only due to the different tax characterisation of entity P given in the residence state of its partners.

Nevertheless, the application of the *reactive coordination rule*, in this case, might potentially generate double taxation if the income is also taxed as undistributed profits at the level of the partners of entity P, now regarded by States R and P as a taxable entity. For this purpose, it will be necessary that the domestic design of the CFC rules in State R ensures a tax credit for the taxes already paid in State P[1735] or that CFC rules are simply not applied in this case.

3.1.2 Case B

Let me assume now that entity R is organised and resident in State R and has two owners, A and B, who are also residents of State R. Accordingly, some interest payments are paid from State P. Whilst State R considers entity R as tax opaque, State P considers it as tax transparent. State P also has a general WHT on interest paid abroad of 30 %, calculated on a gross basis.

Figure 91 Case B

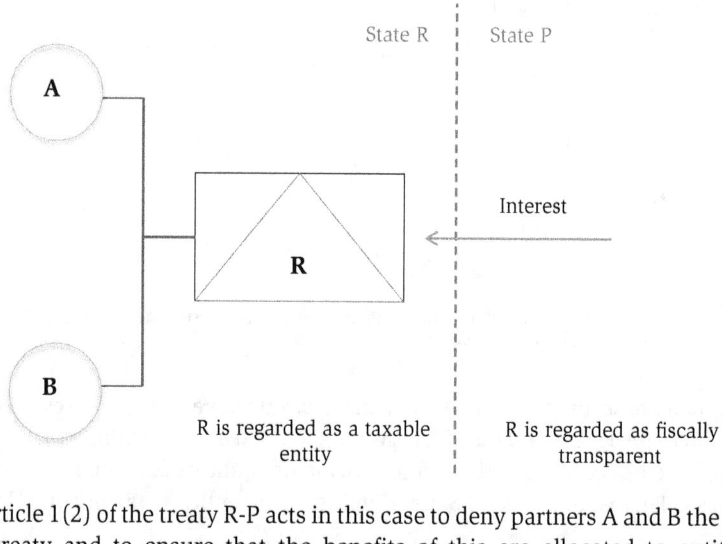

Article 1 (2) of the treaty R-P acts in this case to deny partners A and B the benefits of the treaty and to ensure that the benefits of this are allocated to entity R.[1736] Accordingly, Article 1 (2) of the treaty R-P clarifies who is entitled to claim the double

1735. For example, I.R.C. s. 960 provides for an FTC with respect to the taxes paid at the level of the foreign subsidiaries. If the credit is claim by corporations, the applicable provision is I.R.C. s. 902. Likewise, the deemed FTC under s. 960 is available for taxes paid by subsidiaries until the sixth tier. US: I.R.C. s. 960 and I.R.C. s. 902.

1736. *Supra* Chapter 4, s. 5.2.1.2.

tax relief in the State of residence under Article 23 of the same treaty.[1737] However, State P will, most probably, not consider entity R as the beneficial owner of the interest for purposes of Article 11 of the treaty R-P, denying thus the reduced WHT at source.[1738]

Let me now assume the application of the proposed *reactive coordination rule* at a domestic level first. According to the rule, State P should follow the characterisation of the entity R in its country of organisation, i.e., State R. As State R considers the entity as opaque, State P, by its own domestic law, will consider it also as opaque. Therefore, because of the pre-coordination in the characterisation of entity R at the domestic level, Article 1(2) becomes irrelevant because none of the Contracting States will treat the entity as tax transparent.

Figure 92 Case B after the Application of the Reactive Coordination Rule

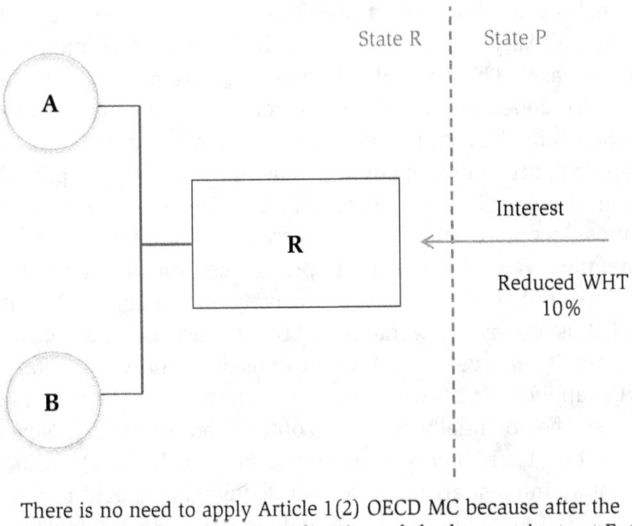

There is no need to apply Article 1(2) OECD MC because after the application of the *reactive coordination rule* both countries treat Entity R as tax opaque

1737. *Ibid.*
1738. The alternative 'deemed' *beneficial owner* rule analysed in *supra* Chapter 4, s. 5.3.1.1, applies in this case distinguishing two situations: (1) if entity R is not considered as a nominee, agent or other intermediary as per the analysis of State P, entity R is 'deemed' as the beneficial owner, (2) however, if entity R is a nominee, agent or other intermediary as per the analysis of State P, the rule states that State P should look at the members A and B. As both are individuals (not fiscally transparent), Article 1(2) *is not in play.* I understand, therefore, that Article 11 should apply to reduce the WHT at source with respect to A and B, who are the beneficial owners, regardless of the tax characterisation of entity R in State R. In other words, Article 1(2) might not apply as to deny the benefits of the treaty to partners A and B. The solution is pragmatic and deals in such a manner with the conflict between the two provisions, i.e., Article 1(2) and 11 OECD Model.

The application of the *reactive coordination rule* at a domestic level provides similar results as that at the tax treaty level if Article 1(2) had been applied, although without conflicting with the *beneficial ownership* requirement of Article 11 of the treaty R-P. Indeed, State P will grant a reduced WHT of 10% in this case because it considers entity R as tax opaque and the beneficial owner of that income.[1739] Similarly, State R will most likely tax the interest at the level of entity R, but at the same time, it will grant a relief of double taxation according to Article 23 of the treaty R-P.[1740]

Although the outcomes of the hypothetical are practically the same either by application of Article 1(2) OECD Model (without considering the *reactive coordination rule*) or after the domestic application of the *reactive coordination rule*, because in both cases, the characterisation of the entity in its country of organisation is followed,[1741] there are still reasons to prefer the *reactive coordination rule*. First, the pre-coordination of the characterisation of the entity provides, to a certain extent, more certainty with regard to the application of the treaty R-P and the allocation of taxing rights. This is because the analysis of the treaty provisions will start from the basis that both Contracting States already agreed domestically in the characterisation of the entity (as tax opaque in our case). Therefore, the discussion will remain only on the application of Article 11 OECD Model, being perhaps the determination of the beneficial owner is the only real issue. Still, the common practice of having the source state treat the payee entity as a taxable entity under its domestic law may certainly simplify the answer of who the beneficial owner is in that case. If not, a deeming rule might apply, which should have the effect of switching off the *reactive coordination rule*.[1742]

There are, however, other reasons to prefer a coordinated solution applying first at a domestic level rather than relying exclusively on the application of Article 1(2) OECD Model. Let us assume, e.g., that A and B in the original example of Case B were residents of State P (source state), which considers entity R as tax transparent. According to the application of Article 1(2) of the treaty R-P, the owners of entities R, A and B might now be potentially entitled to obtain a reduced WHT. Nevertheless, this result seems to be absurd because according to Article 11(1) OECD Model, the requirement that an interest arising in a Contracting State is paid to a resident of the other Contracting State would not be met, making the treaty inapplicable anyway.[1743] The interest payments, in this case, would arise in the same State where the recipients of the payments are residents. Therefore, this situation would not go beyond being a domestic concern. However, nothing would prevent State R from taxing the interest

1739. If for any reason, State P considers that entity R is a nominee, agent or other intermediary, a rule 'deeming' A and B as the *beneficial owners* would be necessary. In such a case, Article 11 should apply to reduce the WHT at source with respect to A and B, regardless of the tax characterisation of entity R in State R. This might be another case of 'switch-off' of the *reactive coordination rule*. For a rule deeming the beneficial owners, *see supra* Chapter 4, s. 5.3.1.1.

1740. This result is achieved even without the proposed *reactive coordination rule* and by the sole application of Article 1(2) of the treaty R-P.

1741. The home country and the country of residence coincide in this case.

1742. *Supra* Chapter 4, s. 4.2.

1743. Article 11(1) OECD Model states: 'Interest *arising in* a Contracting State and *paid to* a resident of the other Contracting State may be taxed in that other State' (emphasis added).

because entity R is indeed a taxable entity there. The double taxation outcome in this case seems to be unavoidable.

Figure 93 Case B (Variation)

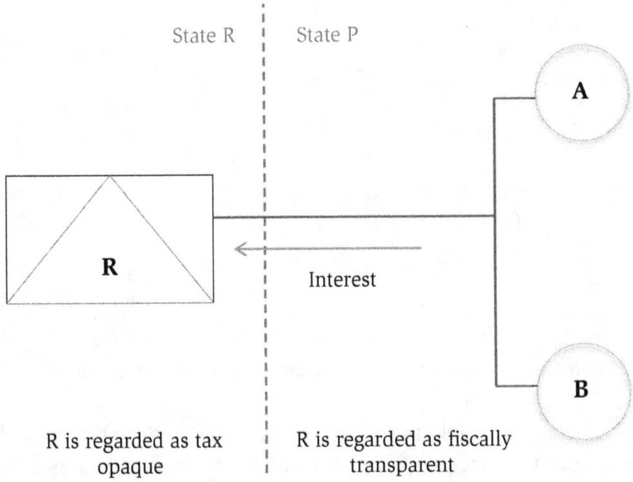

The risk disappears, however, considering the application of the *reactive coordination rule*. Since the rule applies domestically and prior to the application of the treaty, there will be no country treating the entity as tax transparent, and thus, there would not be the need to apply Article 1(2) OECD Model. This ensures a consistent result, exactly as if the Article 1(2) OECD Model was applied, and avoids potential conflicts, too.

3.1.3 Case C

Entity P is organised and resident in State P and has two owners, A and B, who are residents of State R. Accordingly, entity P receives interest payments from a debtor in State P. Whilst State R considers the entity as tax opaque, State P considers the same entity as fiscally transparent, and therefore, the income is allocated to partners A and B. Entity P is thus a reverse hybrid entity. State P applies a 30% WHT on interest paid abroad, which is calculated on a gross basis.

Figure 94 Case C

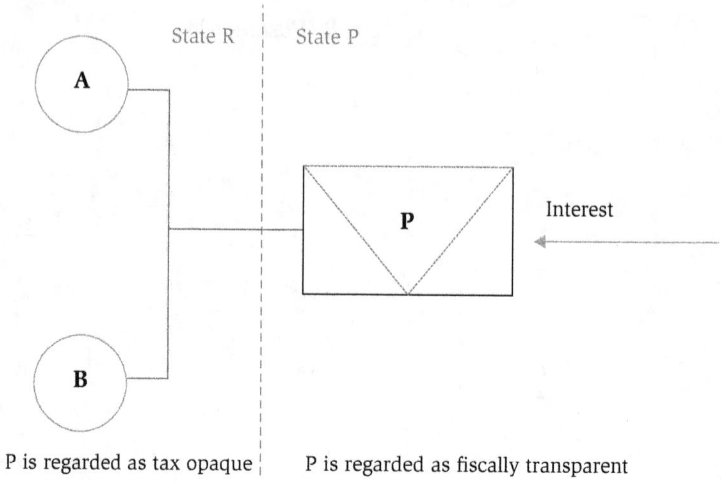

Article 1(2) OECD Model applies in this case to deny the benefits of the treaty to A and B and to confirm that the payments of interest in this case is a mere domestic situation. Therefore, the solution of Article 1(2) OECD Model maintains the transaction as a domestic one, which, however, does not prevent A and B from potentially recognising undistributed profits generated at the level of entity P and taxed in country R as CFC income. Likewise, the solution of Article 1(2) does not prevent that State P still considers A and B as the beneficial owners of the income.[1744]

1744. *Supra* Chapter 4, s. 5.2.1.3.

Figure 95 Case C Before the Application of the Reactive Coordination Rule

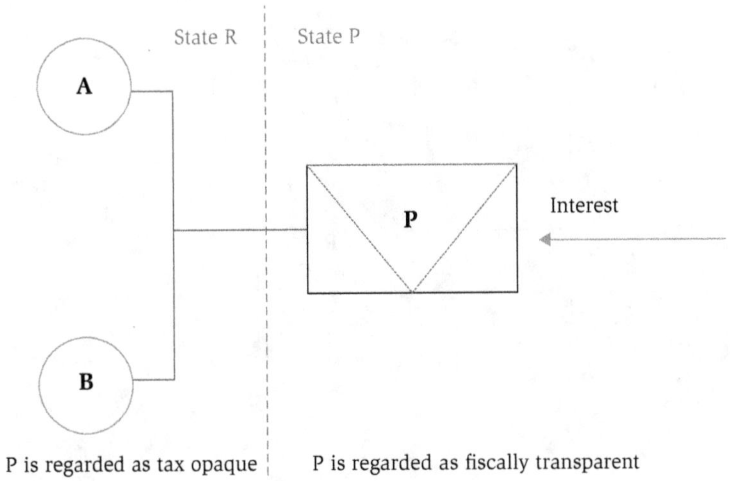

According to Article 1(2) OECD Model, the interest payments are not allocated to A and B. The transaction remains as a domestic one. The characterisation in State R prevails

If we now consider that State R and P introduced the *reactive coordination rule* at a domestic level, and thus, that the characterisation of the entity is coordinated before the application of the tax treaty between R-P, the solution to the case might be slightly different.

Figure 96 Case C after the Application of the Reactive Coordination Rule

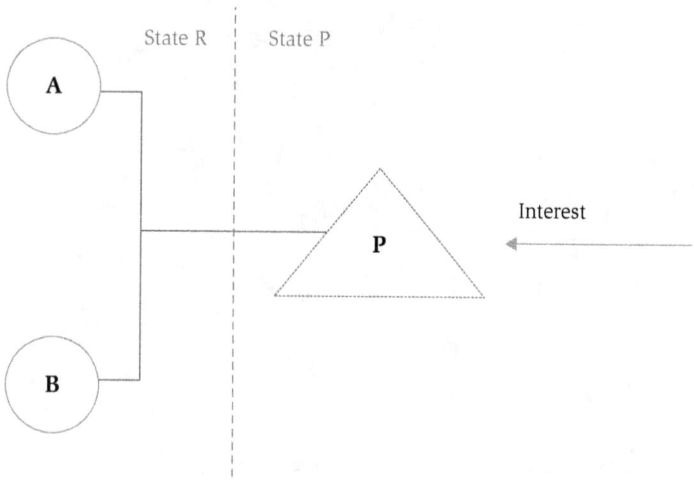

State R and State P consider Entity P as fiscally transparent because of the application of the *reactive coordination rule.* Article 1(2) OECD Model is anyway applied and allocates the interest payments to A and B. Both receive the benefits of the treaty between R-P.

First, the *reactive coordination rule* attempts to coordinate following the characterisation rules of the entity in its home country, i.e., where the entity is legally organised. Therefore, in this case, entity P is organised in State P, where the entity is originally characterised as tax transparent. Therefore, State R should also treat entity P as tax transparent. This implies that both countries will consider that income flows through entity P and is finally allocated to partners A and B. Second, the tax treaty between R-P will come into play. For this purpose, and considering that both countries will treat entity P as tax transparent, Article 1(2) of the treaty R-P should apply. The solution of Article 1(2) in this case will be to grant A and B the benefits of the treaty R-P, which in this case consists of a reduced WHT of 10% applied on the gross amount of interest paid.

As noted, therefore, the solutions of Article 1(2) OECD Model *ex ante* and *ex post* of the application of the *reactive coordination rule* at a domestic level are different. Whilst the solution of Article 1(2) OECD Model *ex ante* is to deny the benefits of the treaty to A and B, thus allowing the characterisation of the entity in the residence state to prevail, keeping the transaction as a domestic one, the solution *ex post* goes in the opposite direction, i.e., it allocates the income to A and B and thus grants them the benefits of the treaty between R-P. In other words, it reduces the WHT that A and B might suffer in the source state and grants double taxation relief in the country of their residence.[1745]

The solution of Article 1(2) OECD Model *ex post* the application of the proposed *reactive coordination rule* seems, therefore, to be preferable. First, it solves the disparity in the characterisation of the entity, which is the core of the issue regarding hybrid and reverse hybrid entities. This is made at a domestic level, which, to a certain extent, allows the application of the treaty in a more consistent manner. Indeed, Article 1(2) OECD Model is not a provision created to deal with hybrid and reverse hybrid entities purely. On the contrary, it deals with items of income received by or through an entity that is considered fiscally transparent by at least one of the Contracting States to avoid conflicts of allocation of income in the tax treaty context. That is its original intent. Indirectly, however, and when hybrid or reverse hybrid entities are involved, it enables the characterisation of the residence state to prevail. Nevertheless, when the solution to the disparities in the characterisation of entities is already provided in the domestic laws, i.e., when both countries previously agree on the characterisation of the entity as tax transparent, the results of the application of Article 1(2) OECD Model is more directly connected with the aim of preventing conflicts of allocation of income.

Second, allocating the income to partners A and B seems to be more logical from the perspective of State P, the source state, because A and B will most likely be regarded as the *beneficial owners* of the interest instead of entity P, which is initially viewed as fiscally transparent in State P. In other words, coordinating the characterisation of the entity as per the one given in its home country, which coincides with the source state in this case, and then applying the treaty R-P, i.e., Article 1(2), brings a more coherent solution from the perspective of the source state. This is because, from State P's perspective, the transaction was never purely domestic but rather a bilateral one. The reason is simple: entity P was, from the time of its organisation in State P, regarded as fiscally transparent, and its income was considered to be allocated to A and B.[1746]

Finally, although less relevant from my perspective, it might be interesting to note that the solution of Article 1(2) OECD Model *ex-post* the application of the *reactive coordination rule* may be relevant to ensure taxation in at least one country. Indeed, if we consider the application of Article 1(2) OECD Model without the proposed *reactive coordination rule*, it will imply that the interest payments are not taxed either in State P (entity P is tax transparent) or in State R (Article 1(2) OECD Model considers that income is not allocated to A and B). The only option to ensure taxation somewhere in this case would be to rely on the application of CFC rules in State R. Nevertheless, once Article 1(2) OECD Model is applied after the coordination of the characterisation of entity P at a domestic level in this case, i.e., *ex-post* the application of the domestic *reactive coordination rule*, income is immediately allocated to A and B, which, to a certain extent, ensures taxation in State R without relying exclusively upon the

1745. As both countries are considering entity P as tax transparent, even though the entity withheld the tax and paid it, that WHT would be understood as flowing to the partners A and B as if they directly paid that tax. This is indeed the basic principle of tax transparency. Therefore, the tax credit or exemption in the country of residence should be granted on the WHT paid.

1746. This solution is also clearly more consistent and less arbitrary than simply deeming entity P as the *beneficial owner*. *See* the solution to example 3, *supra* Chapter 4, s. 5.3.1.2.

application of CFC rules. Therefore, the outcome of the *reactive coordination rule* in the tax treaty context should equally satisfy sceptics and less sceptics on single taxation.

3.1.4 Case D

Let us assume now that entity R is organised in State R and has two owners, A and B, who are also residents of State R. Accordingly, some interest payments are paid from State P. Whilst State R considers entity R as tax transparent, State P considers it a taxable entity. State P also applies a 30% WHT on interest paid abroad, which is calculated on a gross basis.

Figure 97 Case D

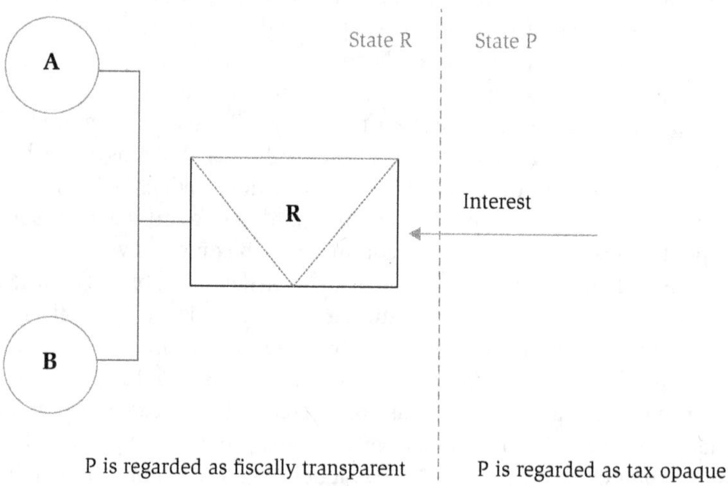

Article 1(2) of the treaty R-P clarifies that the partners A and B are the ones who should claim the benefits of the treaty R-P. However, the application of Article 1(2) of the treaty R-P might still leave open some uncertainty with regard to the application of the treaty between State R and State P because A and B are not regarded as the beneficial owners of the payments.[1747]

Nevertheless, if the domestic *reactive coordination rule* is applied first, both State R and State P will agree with the tax treatment given to entity R as per the characterisation in its home country, i.e., State R. This will not prevent Article 1(2) from applying, but it will ensure that the benefits of the treaty are allocated to A and B, who should now be also regarded as the beneficial owners under State P's perspective.[1748]

1747. *Supra* Chapter 4, s. 5.2.1.4.
1748. Since State P will domestically consider entity R as fiscally transparent, it will most likely look at the owners A and B as the beneficial owners of the interest payments. This solution

Figure 98 Case D after the Application of the Reactive Coordination Rule

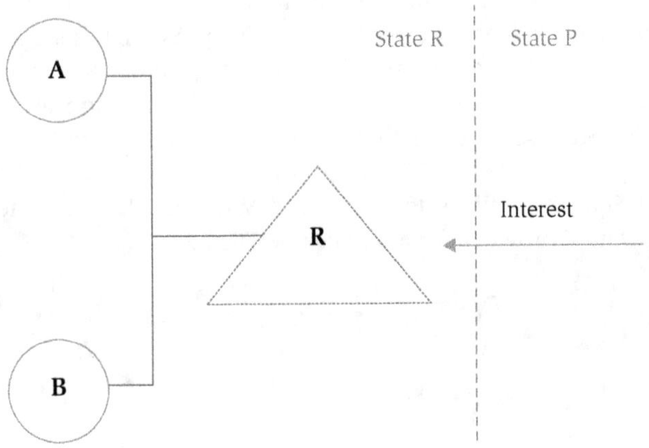

P is regarded as fiscally transparent in State R and State P after the application of the *reactive coordination rule.* The solution of Article 1(2) OECD Model should therefore not conflict with any of the countries involved since they all have agreed in the coordination the characterisation of entity R according to the rules of its home country.

In addition, if A or B, or both, were residents of State P, however, the treaty R-P would not be applicable because, in such a case, the requirement of Article 11(1), which applies to interest arising in a Contracting State and paid to a resident of the other Contracting State, would not be met. This result should, nevertheless, be considered irrelevant for both States R and P since entity R is considered tax transparent.[1749]

3.2 Triangular Cases Using *Hybrid Entities* and *Reverse Hybrid Entities*

This section contains three case studies analysing the implications of the *reactive coordination rule* within tax treaties, but assuming now exclusively triangular situations involving three countries, namely countries X, Y, and Z. Cases E, F, and G of this section demonstrate that the effects of the application of the *reactive coordination rule* may bring more positive outcomes by increasing the simplicity and consistency in the application of tax treaties in triangular situations. Likewise, it has an indirect positive impact with respect to the position of source states when compared with the solutions granted by Article 1(2) OECD Model in the absence of a previous domestic coordination rule.

---

coincides with the outcome in cases where a 'deemed' *beneficial ownership* rule is applied. *Supra* Chapter 4, s. 5.3.1.2, Ex. 4.

1749. Entity R is just a pass-through entity. Interest payments will not be subject to tax in State R, and State P will apply a WHT with respect to the partners A and B. Therefore, there is not even a risk of double taxation.

3.2.1 *Case E*

Let us assume that YCo is an entity incorporated and resident in State Y, which has two partners, A and B, who are residents of State X. Accordingly, YCo has a subsidiary in State Z (ZCo), which is financed by a loan from YCo, resulting in YCo receiving interest payments back from State Z.[1750] YCo is considered as a taxable entity in State Y and in State Z. However, it is regarded as a fiscally transparent entity in State X. Likewise, although Country Z applies a 30% WHT on gross interest paid abroad, the treaty between State X and State Z provides for a reduced WHT of 10%, and the treaty between State Y and State Z provides for a reduced WHT of 5%.

Figure 99 Case E

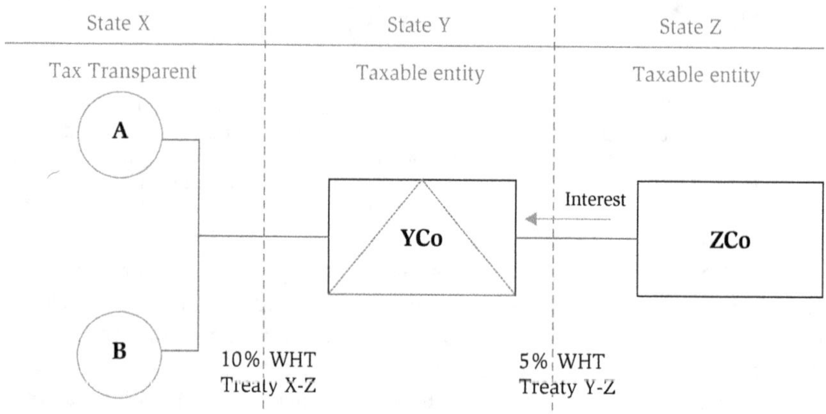

Whilst YCo is regarded as tax transparent in State X, State Y and Z consider it as tax opaque. Likewise, State Z applies a general 30% WHT on the gross payments of interest abroad. The treaty between State X/State Z provides for a reduced 10% WHT, whilst the treaty between State Y/State Z provide for a reduced 5% WHT.

As stressed in Chapter 4,[1751] according to the treaty Y-Z, State Z should reduce its WHT to 5% according to Article 11, and State Y should grant a relief of double taxation as per Article 23. In this case, there is also no conflict as to whom the benefits of the treaty shall be allocated since YCo is considered a taxable entity in both Contracting States.[1752] In other words, Article 1(2) treaty Y-Z does not apply. As for the treaty X-Z, this is also applicable. According to Article 1(2) of the treaty X-Z, income is being received by or through an entity or arrangement considered as fiscally transparent by

1750. The example assumes that the loan and interest are arm's length.
1751. *Supra* Chapter 4, s. 5.2.2.1.
1752. *Ibid.*

one of the Contracting States and which is allocated to the partners A and B, who are also residents of the State treating the entity as tax transparent, i.e., State X. Therefore, State Z must reduce its WHT at source. However, considering that the two treaties are potentially applicable and that they provide different WHT rates, State Z must apply the lower WHT rate of 5%. This is at least the solution suggested by the OECD Partnership report.[1753] Yet, this solution is not only in conflict with the beneficial ownership requirement of Article 11, but it seems to be completely arbitrary and unfair to the source state.[1754]

Let us now assume the application of the *reactive coordination rule*. According to the proposed rule, State X will apply the same characterisation that YCo has in its country of organisation, i.e., State Y. Therefore, the analysis regarding which tax treaty is applicable in this case will start from the basis that all three States involved agree to the fact that YCo must be treated as a taxable entity.

Figure 100 Case E after the Application of the Reactive Coordination Rule

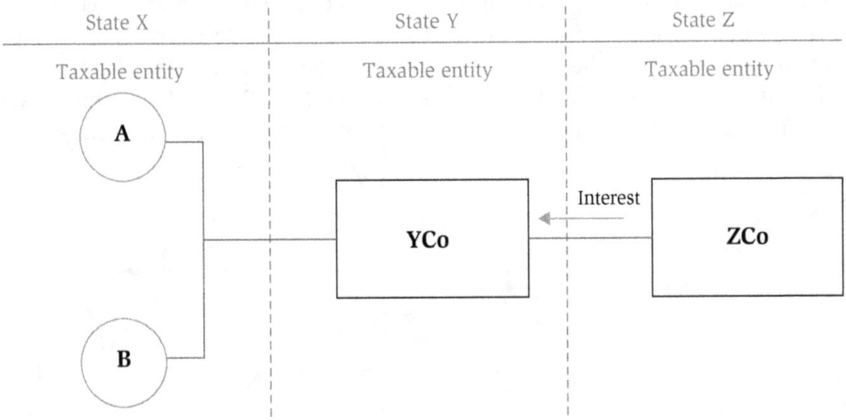

The effect of the *reactive coordination rule* is that all three States in this hypothetical consider now YCo as a taxable entity, which is the original characterisation given in its country of organisation. As a consequence of the above, Article 1(2) OECD Model is no longer applicable.

1753. OECD Commentary on Article 1 concerning the persons covered by the Convention, para. 6.5.
1754. *Supra* Chapter 4, s. 5.2.2.1 and ss 5.3.1 and 5.3.3.

Therefore, the application of the *reactive coordination rule* solves the disparity in the characterisation of entities before the tax treaty is applied, bringing simplicity to the application of tax treaties themselves. For example, after the application of the *reactive coordination rule*, Article 1(2) OECD Model is no longer relevant because all three countries involved have previously agreed that YCo is a taxable entity. Consequently, Article 11 of the treaty Y-Z, the only treaty applicable now, will determine the allocation of taxing rights. In this case, there is almost complete certainty that the *beneficial owner* is YCo.[1755] Accordingly, the non-application of the X-Z treaty is coherent with the object and purpose of tax treaties because since State X no longer considers BCo as tax transparent, it will not consider that any income is allocated to A and B, residents of State X, and thus, there will be no longer a risk of double taxation. The *reactive coordination rule* thus helps clarify the application of tax treaties in this triangular case.[1756]

The solution given by the *reactive coordination rule* is also fairer with the position of State Z, i.e., the source state, when tax treaties come into play. Indeed, State Z will no longer be obliged to limit its taxing rights at source just because a third country's characterisation of an entity differs from the characterisation given to that entity where this is organised and with whom the source State does not disagree in the characterisation of that entity. In other words, the domestic coordination in the characterisation of the entity (YCo) helps avoid the results of Article 1(2) OECD Model, which, solely due to the tax transparent treatment in State X, makes the treaty X-Z applicable.

1755. In this regard, this solution seems to be preferable than applying a 'deemed' *beneficial ownership*. *Supra* Chapter 4, s. 5.3.1.2, Ex. 5. This author does not even see the need of a 'deeming rule' in the case where State Z considers the entity as a nominee, agent or other intermediary. This is because if State Z considers YCo as a nominee, agent or other intermediary (i.e., not as the beneficial owner), the treaty Y-Z would be simply not applicable. The determination of the *beneficial owner* is a rather exclusive task of the State of source.

1756. The solution in light of the *reactive coordination rule* also resembles the US tax treaty practice in the treaty US/Poland, analysed in *supra* Chapter 4, s. 4.3.1.1.1.

Figure 101 Case E and Another Effect of the Reactive Coordination Rule

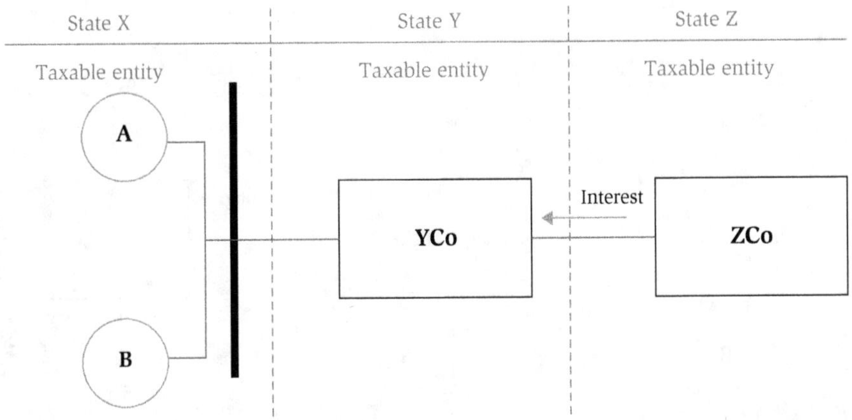

The only relevant applicable tax treaty in this case, after the *reactive coordination rule*, is the tax treaty between Y-Z, which originally should have been the only treaty applicable since Y-Z never disagreed in the tax characterisation of YCo. The solution given by Article 1(2) OECD Model, in absence of the *domestic coordination rule*, obliges State Z to limit also its taxing rights with respect to State X by the sole reason that this country treats YCo differently. After the application of the *reactive coordination rule*, this outcome is avoided and the treaty between X-Z is no longer applicable.

Regardless of the above, the result after the application of the *reactive coordination rule*, in this case, might, however, potentially generate double taxation if the income is also taxed as undistributed profits at the level of the partners of YCo, which is now regarded by States X, Y, and Z as a taxable entity. For this purpose, it will be necessary that the domestic design of the CFC rules in State X ensures a tax credit for the taxes already paid in State P.[1757]

3.2.2 Case F

Case F considers the same facts as Case E, with the only difference that YCo is treated as fiscally transparent in State Z whilst it is regarded as a taxable entity in States X and Y. Likewise, this hypothetical case also assumes that all applicable treaties provide similar reductions of WHT of 10% at source.

1757. *See also* the analysis with regard to Case A at *supra* s. 3.1.1, and the example at *supra* n. 1662.

Figure 102 Case F

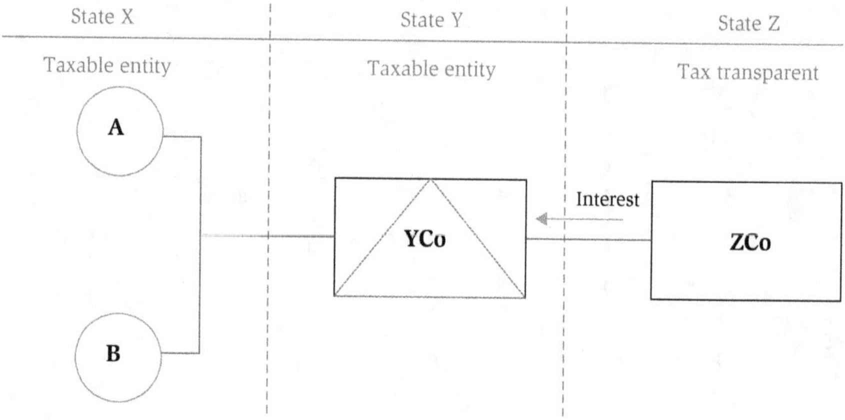

Whilst State X and Y consider YCo as a taxable entity, State Z considers it as fiscally transparent.

With regard to the treaties Y-Z and X-Z, Article 1(2) acts to deny A and B the benefits of the treaties and to ensure that these benefits are allocated to YCo. Nevertheless, in both cases, Article 1(2) does not solve the dichotomy with the *beneficial ownership* requirement of Article 11. In other words, whilst Article 1(2) grants in both cases the benefits of the treaty to YCo, Article 11, in both treaties, considers A and B as the beneficial owners.[1758]

If we now assume the application of the domestic *reactive coordination rule*, the results seem to be more consistent from a tax treaty perspective. Indeed, as noted below, the immediate effect of the application of the rule is that State Z would respect the characterisation of YCo according to the domestic law of State Y, i.e., the home country of the entity. This is to say that YCo would be regarded as a taxable entity for the three States involved in this hypothetical case. Therefore, there are no doubts now that the treaty Y-Z will be fully applied in this case. The above means that State Z will apply a reduced WHT to YCo, and State Y, subsequently, will tax the interest payments but will also apply a relief of double taxation for the full amount of WHT.[1759] Similarly, it confirms that the treaty X-Z will no longer be applicable.

1758. *Supra* Chapter 4, s. 5.2.2.2.

1759. YCo will most likely be the beneficial owner from State Z's perspective. In addition, no 'deemed' *beneficial owner* rules would be needed, because even if State Z considers YCo as a nominee, agent or other intermediary (i.e., not as the beneficial owner), then the treaty Y-Z would be simply not applicable. The determination of the beneficial owner is a rather exclusive task of the State of source. Compare the solution of the 'deemed' *beneficial owner* rule in *supra* Chapter 4, s. 5.3.1.2, Ex. 6.

Figure 103 Case F after the Application of the Reactive Coordination Rule

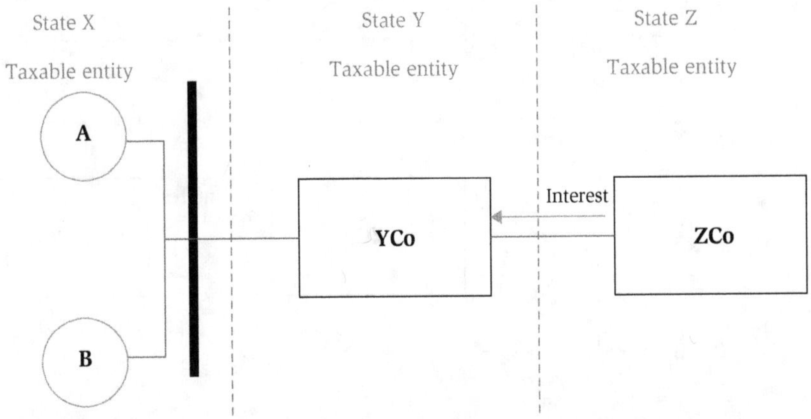

The application of the *reactive coordination rule* does not only eliminate the hybrid entity mismatch, but it clarifies the doubts with respect to which tax treaty is applicable in this case. Since State Z recognises the tax characterisation of YCo given in its country or organisation, the interest payments are allocated to YCo and the treaty between Y-Z is the only one applicable.

As it may be observed, after the application of the *reactive coordination rule* domestically, Article 1(2) OECD Model is no longer needed. Thus, the scope of the provision is again restricted, although justified in the simplicity and consistency of the application of tax treaties. As we have seen before, Article 1(2) OECD Model was not able to solve in this hypothetical the disparity in the characterisation of YCo, which was derived through an improper or incomplete application of the Y-Z tax treaty. This issue is, however, immediately disregarded with the application of the *reactive coordination rule*, which not only solves the disparity *ex ante* but also clarifies the bilateral situation and the tax treaty applicable in this case.

Finally, and as well as in Case E, the result after the application of the *reactive coordination rule* might generate double taxation of income, i.e., once by State Y on the interest received and once by State X on the attributed amount of undistributed profits at the level of partners A and B (i.e., by the application of CFC rules). For this purpose, it will be necessary that the domestic design of the CFC rules in State X ensures a tax credit for the taxes already paid in State P.[1760]

3.2.3 *Case G*

Case G considers the same facts as Case E, with the only difference being that YCo is regarded as a tax-transparent entity in State Y, its country of legal organisation, whilst as a taxable or tax opaque entity for States X and Z tax purposes.

1760. *Supra* n. 1662, as regards to Case A at *supra* s. 3.1.1.

Figure 104 Case G

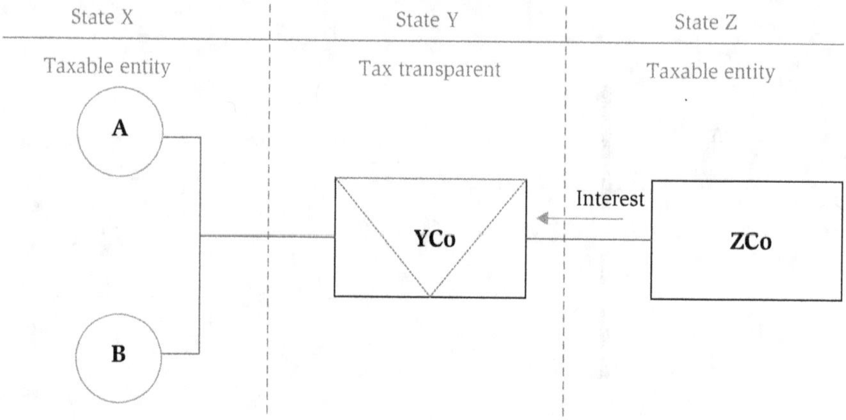

Whilst State Y considers YCo as a fiscally transparent entity, States X and Z consider it as a taxable or tax opaque one. YCo is thus a *reverse hybrid entity*.

Once again, the solution to this case, without considering the impact of the proposed *reactive coordination rule*, must be analysed, considering first the application of the treaty Y-Z. In this regard, as per Article 11 of the Y-Z tax treaty, State Z will consider that interest is being paid to a resident of State Y. Therefore, State Z will, in principle, restrict its WHT from 30% to 10% as per the treaty between Y-Z. State Y, on the other hand, will not consider that interest has been received by YCo because this is indeed a tax-transparent entity in this country. Therefore, it will rarely grant the benefit of the treaty Y-Z to YCo, a non-taxable entity. Article 1(2) of the treaty Y-Z works thus to deny the benefits of the treaty to A and B, who are not considered residents of State Y.

Figure 105 Case G and Its Solution Before the Application Reactive Coordination Rule

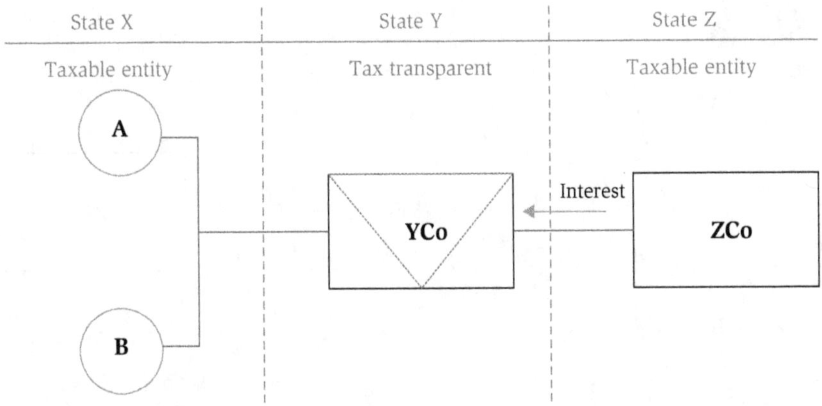

The treaty between Y-Z applies in the perspective of State Z. Therefore, this country would, in principle, limits its taxation rights. However, from the perspective of State Y, there is no interest payment received by a resident of State Y, which means that the benefits of the treaty should not be granted to YCo. Likewise, Article 1(2) OECD Model would grant the benefits the treaty between Y-Z to A and/or B only if they were residents of State Y. Nevertheless, that does not occur in this hypothetical.

As for the treaty X-Z, it is very clear that this treaty does not apply at all because both State Z and State X consider that the interest payments are paid to YCo, which is a resident of State Y.

Let us now consider that the domestic *reactive coordination rule* applies first to coordinate the characterisation of YCo in the three countries involved, according to its original characterisation in the country of its legal organisation, namely State Y.

Figure 106 Case G after the Application of the Reactive Coordination Rule

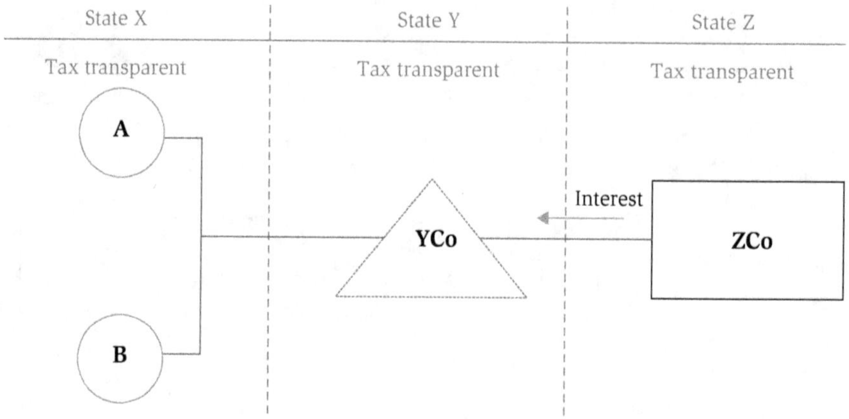

Scenario after the application of the *reactive coordination rule.*

Because of the coordination in the characterisation of YCo according to State Y's domestic rules, the treaty Y-Z is no longer applicable. The reason for this is that now both States Y and Z consider YCo as fiscally transparent and, therefore, not a resident for purposes of the treaty. Therefore, both countries consider that the income flows through YCo directly to partners A and B, who are residents in State X. The only relevant treaty is, therefore, the one between X and Z.

Accordingly, the requirements of Article 11 of the treaty X-Z, in terms of the existence of income arising in one Contracting State and paid to a resident of the other Contracting State, are met in this case. Likewise, State Z considers the reduction of WHT at source proceeds because interest payments are paid to the *beneficial owners* of them.[1761] The application of Article 1(2) of the X-Z treaty is also consistent with the above, allocating the benefits of the treaty between X and Z to partners A and B, who are residents of State X and the beneficial owners of the income from State Z's perspective.

1761. YCo is considered as a fiscally transparent entity in the source state, and thus, most likely as a simple intermediary (not as the beneficial owner). However, A and B, who are individual residents in State X, will most likely be considered as the beneficial owners of the income.

Figure 107 A More Consistent Tax Treaty Outcome

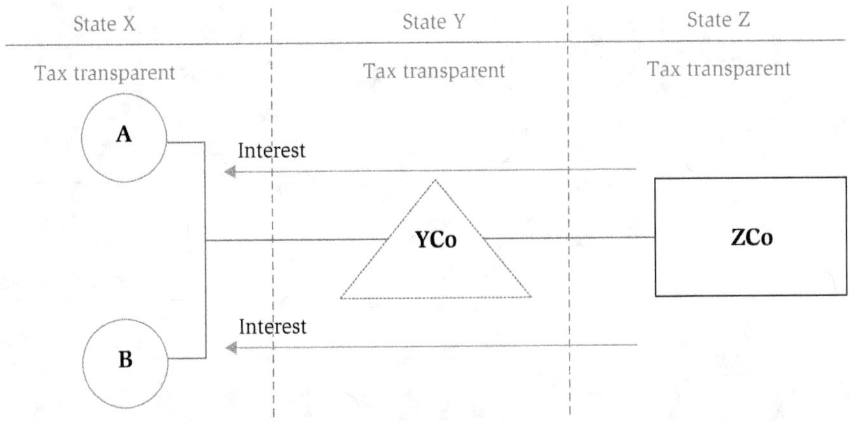

The only relevant tax treaty applicable is between X-Z. The solution of Article 1(2) OECD Model in this case is consistent with the tax characterisation that all countries give to the entity, allocating the benefits of the treaty between X-Z to A and B, residents of State X.

Although the solution after the application of the *reactive coordination rule* seems to be, in principle, a simple switch in the applicable treaty in comparison to the solution without the proposed rule, it certainly brings a more coherent result from a tax treaty perspective. This can be seen, e.g., in the fact that State Z (source state) limits its taxation rights only with respect to the State of the final beneficiary of the income, namely A and B, the partners of YCo. This idea may coincide with the fact that, under State Z's perspective, partners A and B are the beneficial owners of the interest payments since State Z now considers YCo as fiscally transparent.[1762]

If we assume for a moment that A is a resident of State Y whilst B is a resident of State X, then both treaties Y-Z and X-Z would be applicable.

1762. YCo acts in the hypothetical case as a simple conduit company, i.e., the money is just flowing through the entity to the final beneficiaries.

Figure 108 Case G (Variation)

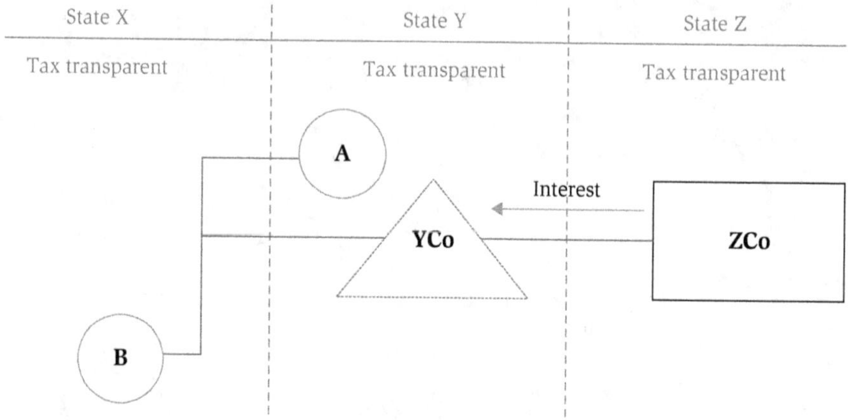

Due to the application of Article 1(2) OECD Model, part of the income would be allocated to A, who could claim the benefits of the treaty between Y-Z. Likewise, the other part of the income would allocated to B, who could claim the benefits of the treaty between X-Z. The source State X shall thus limit its taxing rights as regards to States Y and X.

Although this solution is legally consistent with the fiscally transparent treatment of YCo in all States involved, it might be arguable from a purely economic perspective in the source state. However, the *reactive coordination rule* does not attempt the switch the preferences between residence and source states but rather to achieve more balanced outcomes. In this case, therefore, this result should be assumed as a simple sunk cost since, from a global perspective, there are other cases in which the source state's position is certainly improved.

3.3 The 'Switch-Off' and Article 1(2) OECD Model

As already stressed in this work, there might be cases in which tax benefits or disregarded transactions might result exclusively from the application of the *reactive coordination rule.*[1763]

A tax benefit might arise when an entity considered fiscally transparent in its country of organisation pays interest to a payee located in another country, and both this country and the country of the investors (which are different ones) consider the payer entity as non-transparent or tax opaque.[1764] Since the proposed rule attempts to coordinate the tax characterisation according to the rule in its home country, resulting in all countries involved treating the entity as fiscally transparent, a deduction might be created in the country of the investors only because of the application of the proposed

1763. A 'switch-off' the rule was also discussed as regards to Case B, *supra* s. 3.1.2 of this Chapter.

1764. *See* the example in *supra* s. 2.4.4.2.2.

rule.[1765] Similarly, a transaction might be disregarded by the sole application of the proposed rule in case, e.g., a *reverse hybrid entity* pays interest to its sole investors, which, after the application of the proposed rule, should also consider the entity as tax transparent, and thus, disregards the payment and the loan associated to it.[1766] As the situations described above arise from the sole application of the proposed rule and may give rise to abusive situations, I propose a 'switch-off' in the application of the *reactive coordination rule*. In simple words, the rule will be unapplied in those cases.

A 'switch-off' of the proposed rule might, however, negatively impact the positive results that the rule brings within tax treaties, especially with regard to restricting the application of Article 1(2) OECD Model. Indeed, as noted already, once the domestic coordination in the characterisation of entities has been achieved, the application of Article 1(2) OECD Model is restricted exclusively to those cases in which the source or residence states, in a bilateral context, treats their own domestic entities as tax transparent, which could also, indirectly, result in better solutions for the source state. Nevertheless, this concern lacks practical considerations due to the reduced scope of Article 1(2) OECD Model.

As argued in this work already, the scope of Article 1(2) Model is limited to cases in which an entity or arrangement is treated by one or both Contracting States as fiscally transparent and which has 'income derived by or through' that entity or arrangement. In other words, Article 1(2) OECD Model appears not to cover cases in which a tax-transparent entity, either *hybrid* or *reverse hybrid*, does not receive income. These are exactly the cases in which the author has proposed a 'switch-off' in the *reactive coordination rule*, i.e., cases in which a *reverse hybrid entity* pays but does not receive income. Therefore, even though the switch-off of the *reactive coordination rule* results in keeping the disparity in the characterisation of the entity, its application does not affect tax treaties because Article 1(2) OECD Model does not apply to those cases in which the switch-off can be turned on either.

As a result, in all those cases in which the switch-off might be used, Article 1(2) OECD Model is also inapplicable. Therefore, the hybrid mismatch remains. This outcome is, however, perfectly acceptable since the proposed rule does not attempt to be a rule that harmonises the characterisation of entities for tax purposes. This means that there will be cases which will not be covered by the proposed rule. Likewise, one could argue that the outcome of the transactions in which the switch off of the proposed rule applies does not generate any international tax policy concern before the application of the *reactive coordination rule* either.[1767] Therefore, they could rarely be a cause of concern now.

1765. *Ibid*.

1766. *See* the example at *supra* s. 2.4.4.2.3.

1767. Those international concerns, represented in the OECD BEPS Action Plan 2, are focused on the outcome of the hybrid transaction rather than in the different characterisation of the same entity. Therefore, since no D/NI outcome is generated from the cases in which the switch-off of the proposed rule applies, one can fairly conclude that no concerns should exist when the reactive coordination rule is unapplied in certain cases.

4 FINAL REMARKS

The *reactive coordination rule* appears as an interesting alternative to refocus the discussion regarding the design of rules counteracting the potential misuse of hybrid and reverse hybrid entities. Indeed, and unlike other proposals discussed in a global context thus far, the *reactive coordination rule* is a unique example of a rule that does not only target the core of the issue regarding hybrid and reverse hybrid entities, i.e., the disparate characterisation of an entity by two or more jurisdictions, but also it provides a simple application, avoiding unnecessary contingencies related to the outcomes of transactions.

The above, however, does not make the proposed *reactive coordination rule* a perfect solution either. On the contrary, as demonstrated in this chapter, there are still open questions as regards its application, which are mostly related to some undesirable effects that the application of the proposed rule may originate. These cases refer to the potential double taxation issues in cases where a hybrid entity receives a payment, and the cases in which a tax benefit is granted or a disregarded transaction results solely from the application of the proposed rule. Nevertheless, and to mitigate such results, I have proposed a coordinated application of the rule with other tax measures, such as CFC rules, with regard to the potential double taxation cases involving hybrid entities receiving payments and even a 'switch off' of the proposed rule in cases of tax benefits or disregarded transactions resulting exclusively from the application of the rule. Yet, it is still evident that an impartial implementation of the rule around the world would mitigate its effectiveness.[1768]

The *reactive coordination rule* has also been demonstrated to have a positive impact in the tax treaty context. First, it solves the disparities with respect to the characterisation of an entity before a tax treaty comes into play, which makes the application of the treaty more straightforward. In other words, hybrid and reverse hybrid entities will not be a tax treaty concern anymore, at least not to the extent known before the application of the proposed rule.[1769] Second, it restricts the application of Article 1(2) OECD Model to those cases where the country in which the entity under analysis is legally organised treats the entity as fiscally transparent. This is evident since only in those cases the other countries will follow the tax transparent treatment of the entity if the *reactive coordination rule* was also implemented. A similar

1768. There is, however, no need to be completely pessimistic in this regard. On the contrary, in many of the latest global tax reforms leaded by the OECD, it has been demonstrated that the will of countries is to work together, even though some of those proposals lack a correct design and focus. Therefore, if a rule attempts to counteract the core and not the boundaries regarding issues related to hybrids and reverse hybrid entities, it might be expected at least that the proposed rule will be received positively.

1769. Some could argue that hybrids and reverse hybrid entities were never a tax treaty concern, at least not directly, since domestic laws and not tax treaties govern the characterisation of entities for tax purposes. That statement is, in principle, correct, but it forgets that the sole existence of the disparity in the characterisation of an entity, and the absence of a rule within tax treaties dealing with such disparity, might impact the proper allocation of taxing rights according to a specific tax treaty. Therefore, a coordinated solution at a domestic level is of great relevance for tax treaty purposes as well.

conclusion might be achieved with regard to Article 3(1) MLI, the text of which mirrors Article 1(2) OECD Model.[1770]

Similarly, the restriction in the application of Article 1(2) OECD Model, indirectly achieved through the domestic coordination in the entity's characterisation (i.e., through the *reactive coordination rule*), has a positive impact on source states normally affected by the straightforward application of Article 1(2) OECD Model. As analysed already in Chapter 4 and demonstrated in the case studies used in Chapter 6, Article 1(2) OECD Model gives prevalence to the characterisation of the entity in the residence state, indirectly affecting the position of source states. However, this effect is partially mitigated by the application of the *reactive coordination rule*, as noted in Cases E, F, and G. Yet, in Case G, it might be arguable that the economic position of the source state is better in cases where the partners of the entity are residents in two different countries with a treaty with the source state. Still, this should not be taken as a negative outcome but as a simple demonstration that the *reactive coordination rule* was not created to simply alter the results of Article 1(2) OECD Model now in favour of the position of source states. Instead, it aims to eliminate the disparities in the characterisation of entities at a domestic level, which may indirectly generate a positive outcome in the tax treaty context, including better outcomes for source states when compared to the application of Article 1(2) OECD Model in the absence of the *reactive coordination rule*.

1770. *Supra* Chapter 4, s. 6.1.

CHAPTER 7

Summary and Conclusions

1 INTRODUCTION

As stressed in the beginning of this work, the present research has intended to answer the following research questions:

(1) Is there necessarily an interconnection between the use of hybrid and reverse hybrid entities and the DNT outcome? Should the rules targeting the use (or misuse) of hybrid and reverse hybrid entities be designed based exclusively on the DNT outcome?
(2) Is there an alternative approach to deal more directly with the use (or misuse) of disparities in the characterisation of entities for tax purposes, which does not consider the DNT outcome, or should the current *consequentialist approach* prevail?

In answering these questions, some preliminary assumptions have been taken into consideration:

(a) The sole result of a D/NI outcome, i.e., DNT, should not be considered per se a matter of concern in any cross-border transaction. Likewise, the use of the DNT outcome as an immediate proxy to determine the existence of practices that might be considered abusive when they derive exclusively from the use of hybrids or reverse hybrid entities should be prevented.
(b) *Linking rules*, i.e., rules matching deductions of payments with the respective inclusion of income in the other country, as the ones part of the OECD BEPS Action Plan 2, have the risk of setting up strong presumptions of abusive practices by the sole reason that the outcome of DNT is achieved. Likewise, these rules are highly complex to administer, and they do not target the core

issue with respect to hybrids and reverse hybrid entities, i.e., the different tax characterisation of entities. An alternative should thus be evaluated.

(c) Rules regulating the use of *transparent entities* at the level of tax treaties to prevent access to the benefits of a bilateral tax treaty by third countries out of that treaty are, in principle, recommendable. Nevertheless, the inclusion of Article 1(2) within the OECD Model, resembling Article 1(6) US Model, might generate important issues with respect to developing countries, mostly considering that these countries generally rely on source taxation. Similar concerns are shared with regard to Article 3(1) MLI, which mirrors Article 1(2) of the OECD Model. Alternative solutions, including domestic ones, should be analysed.

As follows, therefore, the author presents the main findings with regard to the research questions and hypotheses surrounding this work.

2 THE UNNECESSARY INTERNATIONAL CONCERN ON DNT

A major part of the debate regarding DNT and the use of hybrid and reverse hybrid entities has been contaminated with some assumptions given by granted. This is due to the generalised idea that income should be taxed at least once in any cross-border transaction, which *a priori* rejects the DNT outcome in any form.

It is undeniable that the idea of tax systems around the world working in a manner to ensure single taxation is attractive. Nevertheless, it is also very risky. As stressed in Chapter 1, the above can be seen, e.g., in the common confusion between DNT and other traditional and undesired legal consequences, such as tax evasion or tax avoidance. However, and perhaps more importantly, it can be noted in the appearance of new pseudo-legal concepts, such as the notion of ATP, whose *consequentialist approach* has only contributed to increasing the level of uncertainty among taxpayers. A similar path can be noticed in the design of specific anti-hybrid rules (i.e., *linking rules*), which assume as a starting point the matching of tax outcomes to ensure single taxation as their central point, disregarding the origin of the issue regarding hybrid and reverse hybrid entities, i.e., the disparate characterisation of entities for tax purposes. Nevertheless, there is one thing that one should not forget in this whole debate regarding DNT, and this is that DNT is an outcome which, absent of any subjective interpretations, should not be regarded per se as a cause of concern.

In the same order of ideas, after analysing the OECD Model provisions and the international tax practice, it is possible to conclude that double taxation treaties do not aim to prevent DNT either. This conclusion, as demonstrated in Chapter 2, remains even after the inclusion of a reference to tax avoidance and tax evasion within the title of some tax treaties. Indeed, what the tax treaty practice demonstrates is something completely different; namely, both pursuing and avoiding (or preventing) DNT are indeed exceptional aims of tax treaties. Therefore, no general tax policy can be interpreted to argue that tax treaties aim to prevent or eliminate DNT. On the contrary, both the prevention and the conscious seek for the DNT outcome are given under very specific circumstances within tax treaties. For example, the DNT outcome arises, and it is tolerated (if not consciously intended) when tax treaties include *tax sparing* or *matching credit* clauses. On the other way around, tax treaties aim to specifically avoid the DNT outcome when *subject-to-tax* or *switch-over* clauses are introduced within a specific tax treaty. This conclusion remains valid even after the implementation of the new OECD interpretation of Article 23A and 23 B OECD Model in the OECD Commentaries, as well as the inclusion of a new Article 23A(4) OECD Model. None of the above-mentioned provisions are effective enough to solve all situations of DNT derived from either conflicts of qualification or interpretation.

A different approach could, however, be suggested after the OECD BEPS Action Plan 6, which includes the modification of the title and preamble of the OECD Model and the inclusion of the STR rule, both referred specifically to the avoidance of DNT. However, the inexact wording of the modified OECD Model preamble could only suggest that the aim to prevent DNT is reserved exclusively for cases where this is the result of tax evasion or tax avoidance. Likewise, the STR rule in the case of Articles 11, 12 and 21 OECD Model does not suggest any obligation to the source State to tax the item of income. On the contrary, it is still facultative for this State to exercise its taxing rights, as demonstrated in the use of the word 'may be' instead of 'is' or 'must be', which could suggest otherwise. Therefore, an interpretation of such a rule as preventing that interest, royalties or other income remain untaxed because of being subject to a STR would be simply imprecise.

As a result, in the current international scenario in which no obligation exists to prevent or to eliminate DNT, or, which is the same, to ensure single taxation, both at a domestic and at a tax treaty level, I conclude that the outcome of DNT should remain as such, i.e., as an outcome, neither being used as proxy to determine the existence of abusive practices through the use of hybrids and reverse hybrid entities nor to assume a crucial role in the design of anti-hybrid provisions.

3 HYBRID ENTITIES: DISPARITIES AS THE TRUE CORE OF THE ISSUE

As stressed in this work already, hybrid and reverse hybrid entities are the result of domestic and sovereign tax policy decisions. This outcome, which is not surprising at all considering that tax systems around the world are neither uniform nor consistent in their tax policies and they normally differ from each other in many aspects, simply confirms that the core issue regarding hybrid and reverse hybrid entities is no other than the disparities in the tax characterisation made by two or more jurisdictions on the same entity. This issue is of fundamental importance regarding the design of potential proposals dealing with hybrid and reverse hybrid entities.

With respect to the rules used to characterise foreign entities for domestic tax purposes, one can conclude that there are no rules that fit all the requirements to be completely inviolable. Therefore, the discussion should not be focused on whether a system is elective or not in comparison to others. Indeed, as demonstrated in Chapter

3, resemblance or comparative tests normally fail in creating consistent characterisations of foreign entities due most of the time to the incompatible characteristics between foreign and domestic entities. Likewise, these tests tend to be generally not less elective than a formally elective system that relies completely on the taxpayer's election. A good example of the above is the *Kintner* test in the United States, which was in force before the CTB regulations were launched. This system allowed sophisticated taxpayers, after proper legal advice, to set up the structures that most accurately fit their pretensions, predicting thus in advance the desired tax treatment of those entities. The above, however, does not mean to recognise the influence of the elective US CTB system to circumvent Subpart F Income and to inappropriately claim an FTC. In those cases, however, the circumvention does not necessarily attend to the electivity of the system used to characterise entities for tax purposes but rather to the poor design of domestic anti-deferral and FTC rules. It is thus necessary that the debate regarding systems to characterise entities for tax purposes does not dismiss this issue.

Another important finding regarding the discussion of hybrid and reverse hybrid entities referred to the existence of concrete examples of coordination in the characterisation of entities around the world. The above demonstrates that the whole idea of coordination is more than an academic optimistic postulate and could certainly serve to concretely redirect the debate regarding the design of anti-hybrid rules. Chapter 3 analysed three specific cases in this regard: (1) the Spanish administrative practice; (2) Denmark rules to deal with hybrid and reverse hybrid entities; and (3) the proposal for EU ATAD (original text) and the specific anti-reverse hybrid rule within the EU ATAD. All these measures and practices showed one thing in common: they are all designed starting from the core of the issue regarding hybrid and reverse hybrid entities, i.e., the different characterisation of entities, also being very effective in solving the real entity mismatch.

In Spain, e.g., the administrative interpretation of the statute (i.e., Article 37 of the Spanish NRIT – *Income Attribution Regime*) is as to follow the characterisation of the entity given in the foreign country. Therefore, even though this interpretation might be subject to criticism, mostly considering the complete deviation from the strict text of the law, its practical implication demonstrates the opposite. Indeed, as per the Spanish administrative practice, the probabilities of disparities in all those cases in which Spain is the country characterising a foreign entity for tax purposes are reduced to zero. Accordingly, in Denmark, there are rules that allow re-characterising domestic entities in cases of disparities with the characterisation given by the majority shareholders owning the entity and located outside Denmark. Unlike interesting in terms of coordination, this approach has also been criticised for relying excessively on foreign laws, also increasing the levels of uncertainty for taxpayers due to the re-characterisation. Finally, a special reference should be made with respect to the Proposal for EU ATAD (2016), which in its original text provided for coordination in the characterisation of entities where the resident MS should follow the characterisation given in the source MS. Unfortunately, this rule was not included in the final text of the EU ATAD launched in 2016. Nonetheless, it is important to note that the modifications to the EU ATAD in 2017 (ATAD II) included a rule dealing specifically with reverse hybrid entities and third countries (Article 9a), which provides for a re-characterisation of a fiscally transparent entity when the entity is regarded by the majority shareholders, residents in a third country, as a taxable entity. This rule resembles the Danish rule also analysed in this work.

The above-mentioned experiences are indeed a very optimistic precedent which allows this author to conclude that the coordination in the characterisation of entities is indeed a more direct and effective manner to deal with hybrid and reverse hybrid entities, at least when compared with the indirect attempt to simply match tax outcomes derived from these hybrid transactions.

4 HYBRID ENTITIES AND THE ENTITLEMENT TO TAX TREATY BENEFITS

The different tax characterisation of entities by two Contracting States might generate problems in determining to whom income should be allocated and, therefore, the benefits of a tax treaty finally granted. In other words, hybrid entities and reverse hybrid entities are indeed a tax treaty concern since tax treaties are applicable to persons who are also considered residents for tax treaty purposes, i.e., as *liable to tax* or subject to full tax liability based on worldwide taxation, regardless the effective payment of taxes. The issue is, however, that most of the non-corporate entities, e.g., partnerships and other disregarded entities, are granted full or partial tax transparency, which is indeed inconsistent with the assertion of full tax liability based on worldwide taxation. In principle, therefore, rules dealing with the allocation of income received through a fiscally transparent entity, considered as such by at least one of the Contracting States, are desirable.

A preliminary look at the principles of the OECD Partnership Report recognised in Article 1(6) US Model, which is also the precedent of Article 1(2) OECD Model and Article 3(1) MLI, gives us the impression of providing a practical solution to the issue, which is that the source state should follow the attribution principles of the residence state, and attribute the income accordingly. In other words, the tax characterisation of the entity in the State of residence prevails, although the above-mentioned provisions do not refer at all, at least not directly, to the prevalence of the tax characterisation in one Contracting State over the other, less to a potential coordination in the tax characterisation of the entity.

The pragmatic solution offered by the provisions analysed in Chapter 4, especially as regards Article 1(2) OECD Model and Article 3(1) MLI, has, nevertheless, important inconsistencies. One of the most notorious inconsistencies is the complete absence of a proper interplay between Article 1(2) OECD Model and the *beneficial ownership* requirement of Articles 10, 11 and 12 OECD Model. Curiously, however, this issue was neither addressed within the 1999 OECD Partnership Report nor within the normative precedent of Article 1(2) OECD Model, i.e., Article 1(6) US Model. Regardless of the above, one should not rest merits to some interesting, isolated examples of rules dealing with this issue, which can be found both in the tax treaties between the United States/Poland and the United States/Canada. This latter example is indeed a direct rule dealing with the conflict between the provision on transparent entities and the *beneficial ownership* requirement, being also the inspiration for a recent academic proposal based on a 'deeming rule' (i.e., deemed *beneficial owner*). Although I recognise that the proposal initially attends to the fact that no relevant party is acting as an agent, nominee, or other intermediary for a third party from the source state's perspective, which would demonstrate a more balanced provision, it rapidly turns to give prevalence to the tax characterisation of the entity in the residence state as a way to solve the conflict. In other words, the conflict between the rule on transparent entities (tax treaty entitlement) and that of the *beneficial ownership* requirement (allocative rule) finally depends on deeming a resident in the residence state as the *beneficial owner*. In other words, the source state, once again, must limit its right to determine, exclusively and based on its domestic laws, to whom dividends, interest and royalties are ultimately paid. As such, therefore, I do not see how source states might fully agree with this pragmatic proposal without at least a minimum degree of hesitation.

Another issue regarding Article 1(2) OECD Model and Article 3(1) MLI is the interplay between the *saving clause*, which ensures Contracting States taxation of their own residents regardless of the application of a treaty, and the relief of double taxation's obligations under a treaty. In this regard, the solution adopted by paragraph 64 of the OECD BEPS Action 6, introducing paragraph 11.1 to the Commentaries on Article 23A and 23B, is rather clear and straightforward, providing that the Contracting States *are not* reciprocally obliged to relieve the double taxation caused for each other's tax levied exclusively on the residence of the taxpayer. In other words, relief of double taxation remains available *only* to the extent that taxation by the other state is in accordance with provisions of the Convention that allow taxation of the relevant income as the source state or as a state where there is a PE to which that income is attributable. This solution is replicated in Article 3(2) and Article 5-Option C MLI. Both Articles refer expressly to paragraph 64 of the OECD BEPS Action 6. However, when dealing with the optional *saving clauses* within the MLI, it seems to be that opting for one or another might not necessarily bring the same results. For example, whilst the detailed *saving clause* of Article 11 MLI seems to retain the obligations to provide double taxation relief under provisions such as Article 7(3), Article 9, Article 19, Article 20, Article 23A and 23B, Article 24, Article 25, and Article 28 OECD Model, the simplified version of Article 3(3) MLI does not expressly preserve treaty obligations as regards to those articles. Similarly, a solution such as the one proposed in paragraph 64 of the OECD BEPS Action 6 might still create issues in some countries where, based on specific tax treaty provisions or the tax treaty practice, used to grant double taxation relief in those and other analogous cases by an extensive interpretation of Article 23 OECD Model.

As concluded in Chapter 4, therefore, Article 1(2) OECD Model and 3(1) MLI, together with the proposed *saving clauses*, might not necessarily be the adequate manner to address the issue of hybrids and reverse hybrid entities within the treaty context. In this regard, the idea of a domestic coordination rule, which should not necessarily imply a modification of the proposed Article 1(2) OECD Model but rather a restriction of its scope, gains strength.

5 AVOIDING THE ARTIFICIAL LINK BETWEEN DNT AND THE USE OF HYBRID ENTITIES

The attempt to create a direct link between the DNT outcome and the use of hybrid and reverse hybrid entities has derived from the elusive notion of HMA. This notion, whose construction is also based on the assumption that income should be taxed somewhere, no matter where, does not only deviate from the problem of hybrid entity mismatches itself, i.e., the different tax characterisation of the same entity by two jurisdictions, but also creates new presumptions of base erosion and abusive transactions just because the outcome of DNT arises. Similarly, *linking rules*, i.e., the rules created to counteract such arrangements, follow the same pattern, although none of these rules solve the true hybrid entity mismatch. On the contrary, they assume a *consequentialist role* based exclusively on the outcome that the hybrid entity transactions generate, i.e., a D/NI outcome (or DNT), targeting just indirectly the hybrid entity mismatch.

The approach adopted in the design of anti-hybrid rules, as demonstrated in Chapter 5, raises important questions both from a tax policy and from a legal perspective. From a tax policy perspective, *linking rules* tend to be circular; namely, if implemented by all countries, they will have no other effect than nullifying each other, even if a tiebreaker rule gets into force. More importantly, perhaps, an uncoordinated application of a *primary response* and a *defensive rule* might give rise to new issues of economic double taxation, which did not exist before the application of these rules. Accordingly, it should not be underestimated the fact that these rules are extremely dependent on the functioning and application of foreign laws, which, unless a broader and more efficient access to information between tax administrations, especially between developing countries, might raise serious concerns with respect to their real effectiveness. Likewise, although *linking rules* do not raise many concerns with respect to Article 24 OECD Model (non-discrimination), mostly derived from the restrictive approach adopted within that non-discrimination provision, there are still serious doubts regarding their compatibility with EU law, especially EU primary law or fundamental freedoms. Unfortunately, however, the jurisprudence of the CJEU is neither unequivocal nor consistent in providing a concrete answer with respect to such issue.

For all the above, I conclude that a different approach should be taken, which not only targets in a more direct manner the issues regarding hybrid and reverse hybrid entities but also provides for a simpler and more efficient design of anti-hybrid provisions.

6 THE ALTERNATIVE: THE *REACTIVE COORDINATION RULE*

Against those who argue for a necessary interconnection between DNT and the use of hybrid and reverse hybrid entities, this work proposes a different approach. This approach is based on two fundamental ideas. First, to propose a simple rule that avoids the complex set of OECD recommendations (*linking rules*), also serving as a valid and more administrable alternative both at a domestic and a tax treaty level. Second, to propose a rule whose design focuses on the real issue involving hybrid and reverse hybrid entities, i.e., the different characterisation of entities by two or more jurisdictions, rather than on the outcomes derived from these transactions.

Chapter 6 presented in detail a proposed *reactive coordination rule* whose mechanic is simple and consists of aligning the characterisation of foreign entities for domestic tax purposes according to the characterisation given in the country where the entity is legally and formally organised, i.e., the home country. The use of the 'home country' as an aligning factor is justified because although it is true that the home and source country will coincide in all those cases in which a payment is made from a hybrid entity, they will certainly not coincide in all those cases in which a payment is received by a reverse hybrid entity. Therefore, having in mind the simplicity of the rule, I have opted for using a more proper connection, i.e., the home country. This is also related to the coherence that this rule looks for. Indeed, hybrid entity mismatches are the result of a different characterisation of an entity when compared to the characterisation given in its country of legal or formal organisation, i.e., the home country. Therefore, and at least from a tax policy perspective, the design of a rule aligning the characterisation of the entity in its home country is at least more coherent in terms of forcing the State producing the mismatch, i.e., the State that applies a characterisation of an entity different from the one given domestically where the entity is legally organised, to react. Similarly, the *reactive coordination rule* assumes a more honest approach in its scope since it applies to all those cases where there are disparities between two or more countries with respect to the characterisation of the same entity. The above is aligned to the three main tax policy reasons sustaining the proposal, namely simplicity, coherence, and administrability of the rule,[1771] first, and second, it accomplishes the idea of targeting the core of the issue regarding hybrids and reverse hybrid entities, that is, the different characterisation of entities for tax purposes.

As stressed in Chapter 6, the proposed rule has the positive impact of truly solving the hybrid entity mismatch, avoiding unnecessary contingencies related to the outcomes of the transactions involved. In simple words, the proposed rule brings disparities back into the front of the discussion regarding hybrid and reverse hybrid entities. However, the rule is not exempt from further improvement. Indeed, the proposed design of the rule leaves open questions regarding its application, which are mostly related to some undesirable effects that the application of the proposed rule might generate. These cases refer to the potential double taxation issues in case a hybrid entity receives a payment and where a tax benefit is granted or a disregarded transaction results solely because of the application of the proposed rule. Yet, in order to mitigate such results, I have proposed a coordinated application of the rule with other tax measures, such as CFC rules, regarding the potential double taxation cases involving hybrid entities receiving payments and, particularly, a 'switch off' of the proposed rule in cases of tax benefits or disregarded transactions resulting exclusively from the application of it. Still, a worldwide and uniform implementation of the proposed rule continues to be a fundamental issue to ensure its real practical impact.

1771. Chapter 6, *supra* s. 2.3.

It is also interesting to note that the *reactive coordination rule* may be an efficient solution from a tax treaty perspective. In fact, the coordination in the characterisation of entities at a domestic level ensures a more proper application of Article 1(2) OECD Model, restricting its scope exclusively to cases in which the home country treats the entity under analysis as tax transparent. The above also indirectly brings fairer results for the source state when compared with the current application of Article 1(2) OECD Model. However, this is not always the case. As analysed in the examples of Chapter VI, the results derived from the application of the proposed reactive coordination rule and its interaction with Article 1(2) OECD Model are not always favourable to the source state. The above is, however, far from being a negative characteristic of the rule. On the contrary, it is the best demonstration that the proposed rule aims to eliminate the disparities in the characterisation of entities at a domestic level, indirectly generating more consistent outcomes in the tax treaty context. However, the proposed rule does not aim to be a rule that switches the balance between the residence and the source states within the tax treaty equation.

All in all, the use and misuse of hybrid and reverse hybrid entities is a challenge that should be adequately addressed, and this should start by assuming a less consequentialist approach. At present, we have just witnessed an attempt to present issues in a different costume, whose pragmatism is sometimes difficult to argue against, too. However, the above should not prevent us from re-orientating the discussion to what really matters in the debate regarding hybrid entity mismatches. This challenge should be assumed before all countries get truly convinced of who is evil and that matching tax outcomes is indeed a preferable path. As proven in this work, alternatives are still possible.

List of References

1. OFFICIAL DOCUMENTATION

BE: 1992 Belgian Income Tax Code.

BR: Law No. 9.249/95 of 26 December 1995.

BR: Provisional Measure No. 2158-35/2011.

CH: DBG (Federal Law on Direct Federal Tax) of 14 December 1990.

CH: StHG (Federal Law on Harmonization of Direct Taxes of the Cantons and Municipalities) of 14 December 1990.

CH: Federal Direct Tax Act [Bundesgesetz vom 18. Dezember 1987 über das international Privatrecht, SR 291].

CH/U.S.: Protocol 2009 amending the Convention between the United States and the Swiss Confederation for the avoidance of double taxation with respect to taxes on income signed at Washington on 2 October 1996, Swiss Federal Gazette 27 November 2010.

CH/U.S.: Convention between the United States of America and the Swiss Confederation for the avoidance of double taxation and the prevention of fiscal evasion with respect to taxes on income, signed at Washington on 2 October 1996 as amended by the Protocol signed on 2 October 1996.

CH/U.S.: Technical Explanations of the Convention between the United States of America and the Swiss Confederation for the avoidance of double taxation and the prevention of fiscal evasion with respect to taxes on income, signed at Washington on 2 October 1996 as amended by the Protocol signed on 2 October 1996.

DE: Income Tax Act [*Einkommensteuergesetz*–EStG]).

DE: Corporate Income Tax Act [*Körperschaftsteuergesetz*–KStG].

DE: Citizen Relief Act [*Bürgerentlastungsgesetz*] of 16 July 2009, BGBl 1, 1959 (2009).

DE: Growth Acceleration Act [*Wachstumsbeschleunigungsgesetz*] of 22 December 2009, BGBl 1, 3950 (2009).

DE: Federal Ministry of Finance [Bundesfinanzministerium], 19 March 2004, IV B4-S1301 USA- 22/04, Schreiben betr. steuerliche Einordnung der nach dem

Recht der Bundesstaaten der USA gegründeten Limited Liability Company, BStBl I 2004.

DE: GmbHG -German Limited Liability Company Act.

DE: AktG – German Stock Corporation Act.

DK: Corporate Income Tax Law [SEL–*Selskabsskatteloven*], adopted by the Bill 119 of 17 December 2003.

ES: Corporate Income Tax Law [*Ley del Impuesto sobre las Sociedades*], Law 27/2014 (consolidated text) of 27 November 2014, BOE No. 288 of 28 November 2014.

ES: Corporate Income Tax Law [*Ley del Impuesto sobre Sociedades*], as introduced by the Royal Law Decree [*Real Decreto Legislativo*] No. 4/2004 of 5 March 2014.

ES: Corporate Income Tax Law [*Ley del Impuesto sobre las Sociedades*], Law 27/2014 (consolidated text) of 27 November 2014, BOE No. 288 of 28 November 2014.

ES: Personal Income Tax Law, Law 35/2006 of 28 November 2006 [*Ley de Impuesto a la Renta sobre las Personas Físicas (LIRPF)*].

ES: Spanish Non-resident Income Tax Law – NRITL, Royal Legislative Decree No. 5/2004 of 5 March 2004.

ES: General Taxation Law [*Ley General Tributaria*], Law No. 58/2003 of 17 December 2003.

ES: Law No. 12/1991 of 29 April 1991 on Economics Interest Groups, and Law No. 18/1982 of 26 May 1982 on Temporary Business Associations.

ES: Royal Decree of 24 July 1889 that publishes the Civil Code.

ES: Royal Decree of 22 August 1885 that publishes the Commercial Code.

EU: Council Directive 2018/822/EU of 25 May 2018 amending Directive 2011/16/EU as regards mandatory automatic exchange of information in the field of taxation in relation to reportable cross-border arrangements, OJ L139 (2018).

EU: Proposal for a Council Directive on the common system of a digital services tax on revenues resulting from the provision of certain digital services, COM (2018) 148 final.

EU: Council Directive (EU) 2017/952 of 29 May 2017 amending Directive (EU) 2016/1164 as regards hybrid mismatches with third countries, OJ L144/1 (2017).

EU: Proposal for a Council Directive amending Directive (EU) 2016/1164 as regards hybrid mismatches with third countries, 6333/17 FISC 46 ECOFIN 95, 17 February 2017.

EU: Proposal for a Council Directive (EU) 2016/0337 of 25 October 2016 on a Common Corporate Tax Base, COM (2016) 685 final.

EU: Proposal for a Council Directive amending Directive (EU) 2016/1164 as regards hybrid mismatches with third countries, COM (2016) 687 final, 25 October 2016.

EU: Council Directive (EU) 2016/1164 of 12 July 2016 laying down rules against tax avoidance practices that directly affect the functioning of the internal market, OJ L193, (2016).

EU: Proposal for a Council Directive laying down rules against tax avoidance practices that directly affect the functioning of the internal market, COM (2016) 26 final.

EU: Proposal for a Council Directive repealing Council Directive 2003/48/EC, COM (2015) 129 final, 18 March 2015.

EU: Commission Communication, A Fair and Efficient Corporate Tax System in the European Union: 5 Key Areas for Action, COM (2015) 302 final, 17/6/2015.

EU: Council Directive 2014/86/EU of 8 July 2014 amending Directive 2011/96/EU on the common system of taxation applicable in the case of parent companies and subsidiaries of different Member States, OJ 219/40 (2014).

EU: Report of the Code of Conduct Group (Business Taxation), 16553/114 Rev. 1, FISC 225, ECOFIN 1166, Brussels (11 December 2014).

EU: Council Directive 2014/86/EU of 8 July 2014 amending Directive 2011/96/EU.

EU: Council Directive 2014/107/EU of 9 December 2014 amending Directive 2011/16/EU as regards mandatory automatic exchange of information in the field of taxation, OJ L359 (2014).

EU: Proposal for a Council Regulation on the Statute for a European Foundation (FE), COM(2012) 35 final, 2012/0022 (AP), 8 February 2012, EU law IBFD.

EU: European Commission Recommendation of 6 December 2012 on aggressive tax planning, COM (2012), 8806 final.

EU: Consolidated Version of the Treaty on the Functioning of the European Union (TFEU) of 26 October 2012, OJ C 326/47 (2012).

EU: Council Directive 2011/96/EU of 30 November 2011 on the common system of taxation applicable in the case of parent companies and subsidiaries of different Member States, OJ L345/ 8 (2011).

EU: Council Directive 2011/16/EU of 15 February 2011 on administrative cooperation in the field of taxation and repealing Directive 77/799/EEC, OJ L64 (2011).

EU: Council Directive 2009/133/EC of 19 October 2009 on the common system of taxation applicable to mergers, divisions, transfer of assets and exchanges of shares concerning companies of different Member States and to the transfer of the registered office of an SE or SCE between Member States.

EU: Council Directive 2003/48/EC of 3 June 2003 on Taxation of Saving Income in the Form on Interest Payments, OJ L157 (2003) as amended through 2006.

EU: Council Directive 2003/49/EC of 3 June 2003 on a common system of taxation applicable to interest and royalty payments made between associated companies of different Member States, OJ L 157/49 (2003).

EU: EC Regulation 1435/2003, Official Journal L 207/03.

EU: EC Regulation 2157/2001, Official Journal L 204/01.

EU: European Commission, *Taxation in European Union, Report on the Development of Tax Systems*, COM (96) 546 final, OJ C 296/43, 22 October 1996.

EU: Council Regulation (EEC) No. 2137/85 of 25 July 1985 on the European Economic Interest Grouping - EEIG - (OJ L 199, 31 July 1985).

EU: EEC Regulation 2137/1985.

International: Vienna Convention on the Law of Treaties (VCLT) of 23 May 1969, United Nations, Treaty Series, Vol. 1155, I-18232.

IT: Corporate Income Tax Act [*Imposta sul reddito d'impresa*], Official Journal [*Gazzetta Ufficiale*] No. 301 of 31 December 1986.

NL: Decree of the State Secretary of Finance, CPP2009/519M of 11 December 2009.

NL: Decrees of 18 December 2004, Nos CPP 2004/2730M and CPP 2004/1304M.

NL: Decree of 18 September 1997, No. DGO 97-00417.

NL: Corporate Income Tax Act 1969.

OECD, *Challenges Arising from the Digitalisation of the Economy: Commentary to the Global Anti-base Erosion Model Rules (Pillar Two)*, OECD Publishing, 2022.

OECD, *Statement on a Two-Pillar Solution to Address the Tax Challenges Arising from the Digitalisation of the Economy,* OECD Publishing, 8 October 2021.

OECD, *Statement on a Two-Pillar Solution to Address the Tax Challenges Arising from the Digitalisation of the Economy,* OECD Publishing, 1 July 2021.

OECD Model Tax Convention on Income and Capital: Condensed Version 2017.

OECD, *Draft Contents of the 2017 Update to the OECD Model Convention*, OECD Publishing, Paris, 2017.

OECD, *Draft Contents of the 2017 Update to the OECD Model Convention, Comments received on the 11 July public release,* OECD Publishing, Paris, 2017a.

OECD, *Neutralizing the Effects of Branch Mismatch Arrangements, Action 2: Inclusive Framework on BEPS*, OECD Publishing, Paris, 2017.

OECD, *Limiting Base Erosion Involving Interest Deductions and Other Financial Payments, Action 4 – 2016 Update: Inclusive Framework on BEPS*, OECD Publishing, Paris, 2016.

OECD, *Explanatory Statement to the Multilateral Convention to Implement Tax Treaty Related Measures to Prevent Base Erosion and Profit Shifting*, OECD Publishing, Paris, 2016.

OECD, *Public Discussion Draft: BEPS Action 2 Branch Mismatch Structures*, OECD Publishing, Paris, 2016.

OECD, *Neutralizing the Effects of Hybrid Mismatch Arrangements, Action 2-2015 Final Report*, OECD Publishing, Paris, 2015.

OECD, *Transfer Pricing Documentation and Country-by-Country Reporting, Action 13 – 2015 Final Report*, OECD Publishing, Paris, 2015.

OECD, *Mandatory Disclosure Rules, Action 12 – 2015 Final Report*, OECD Publishing, Paris, 2015.

OECD, *Comments Received on Revised Public Discussion Draft, Follow-up Work on BEPS Action 6: Prevent Treaty Abuse*, OECD Publishing, Paris, 2015.

OECD, *Preventing the Granting of Treaty Benefits in Inappropriate Circumstances*, Action 6 – 2015 Final Report, OECD Publishing, Paris, 2015.

OECD, *Limiting Base Erosion Involving Interest Deductions and Other Financial Payments, Action 4 – 2015 Final Report*, OECD Publishing, Paris, 2015.

OECD, *Public Discussion Draft, BEPS Action 2: Neutralize the Effects of Hybrid Mismatch Arrangements (Recommendations for domestic Laws)*, OECD Publishing, Paris, 2014a.

OECD, *Public Discussion Draft, BEPS Action 2: Neutralize the Effects of Hybrid Mismatch Arrangements (Treaty Issues)*, OECD Publishing, Paris, 2014b.

OECD, *Comments Received on Public Discussion Drafts, BEPS Action 2: Neutralize the Effects of Hybrid Mismatch Arrangements,* OECD Publishing, Paris, 2014c.

OECD, *Model Tax Convention*, OECD Publishing, Paris, 2014.

OECD, *Commentaries on the OECD Model Tax Convention*, OECD Publishing, Paris, 2014.

OECD, *Preventing the Granting of Treaty Benefits in Inappropriate Circumstances, OECD/G20 Base Erosion and Profit Shifting Project*, OECD Publishing, Paris, 2014.

OECD, *Neutralizing the Effects of Hybrid Mismatch Arrangements*, OECD Publishing, Paris, 2014.

OECD, *Standard for Automatic Exchange of Financial Account Information: Common Reporting Standard*, OECD Publishing, Paris, 2014.

OECD, *Action Plan on Base Erosion and Profit Shifting*, OECD Publishing, Paris, 2013.

OECD, *Addressing Base Erosion and Profit Shifting*, OECD Publishing, Paris, 2013.

OECD, *Report on Hybrid Mismatch Arrangements*, OECD Publishing, Paris, 2012.

OECD, *OECD Model Tax Convention: Revised Proposals Concerning the Meaning of 'Beneficial Owner' in Articles 10, 11 and 12*, OECD Publishing, Paris, 2012.

OECD, *Clarification of the Meaning of 'Beneficial Owner' in the OECD Model Convention. Discussion Draft*, OECD Publishing, Paris, 2011.

OECD, *Tackling Aggressive Tax Planning through Improve Transparency and Disclosure*, OECD Publishing, Paris, 2011.

OECD, *Corporate Loss Utilization through Aggressive Tax Planning*, OECD Publishing, Paris, 2011.

OECD/EU, *Convention on Mutual Administrative Assistance in Tax Matter of 1 June 2011*, OECD Publishing, Paris, 2011.

OECD, *Application and Interpretation of Article 24 (Non-discrimination)-Public Discussion Draft*, OECD Publishing, Paris, 2007.

OECD, *The Application of the OECD Model Tax Convention to Partnerships*, Issues in International Taxation No. 6, OECD Publishing, Paris, 1999.

OECD, *Tax Sparing – A Reconsideration*, OECD Publishing, Paris, 1997.

OECD, *International Tax Avoidance and Evasion, Double Taxation Conventions and the Use of Conduit Companies*, Issues in International Taxation No. 1, OECD Publishing, Paris, 1987.

OECD, *Working Party No. 1 of the Committee on Fiscal Affairs on Double Taxation, Working Group No. 23 (Germany-Belgium), Revision of Article 10 of the 1963 Model Convention and Commentary Thereon*, CFA/WP1(73)2, Paris, 1973, available at www.taxtreatieshistory.org.

OECD, *Working Party No. 27 of the Fiscal Committee (Luxembourg-France-The Netherlands), Report on Suggested Amendments to Articles 11 and 12 of the Draft Convention, Relating to Interest and Royalties Respectively*, FC/WP27(70)1, Paris, 1970, available at www.taxtreatieshistory.org.

OECD, *Observations of Member Countries on Difficulties Raised by the OECD Draft Convention on Income and Capital*, Fiscal Committee TFD/FC/216, Paris, 1967, available at www.taxtreatieshistory.org.

U.K.: HMRC, INTM 180010.

U.K.: HMRC, INTM 180030.

UN: Committee of Experts on International Cooperation in Tax Matters, 11th session, Item 3 (a)(i) of the provisional agenda, Application of treaty rules to hybrid entities, New provision for the United Nations Model Double Taxation Convention between Developed and Developing Countries to address the application of tax treaties to payments made through hybrid entities, Geneva 11–14 October

2016, Annex I: United Nations Model Double Taxation Convention between Developed and Developing Countries: proposed changes to address the application of tax treaties to payments made through hybrid entities.

UN: United Nations Model Tax Convention between Developed and Developing Countries, UN: New York, 2011.

U.S.: Preamble to US Model Income Tax Convention of 17 February 2016.

U.S.: US Model Income Tax Convention of 17 February 2016.

U.S.: Proposed Limitation on Benefits Article, Select Draft Provisions of the US Model Income Tax Convention, 20 May 2015.

U.S.: Proposed Treaty Rules Addressing *'Special Tax Regimes'*, Select Draft Provisions of the US Model Income Tax Convention, 20 May 2015.

U.S.: Final FATCA Regulations (2014), available at http://www.irs.gov/PUP/businesses/corporations/TD9610.pdf.

U.S.: Permanent Subcommittee on Investigations of the Committee of Homeland Security and Governmental Affairs of the United States Senate, Offshore Profit Shifting and the U. S. Tax Code - Part 2 (Apple Inc.), S. Hrg.113-90, U.S. Government Printing Office, Washington (2013).

U.S.: Proposed FATCA Regulations (2012), available at http://www.irs.gov/pub/newsroom/reg-121647-10.pdf.

U.S.: Hiring Incentives to Restore Employment Act, Pub. L. No. 111-147, 124 Stat. 71 (2010).

U.S.: Staff of the Joint Committee on Taxation, Technical Explanations of the Revenue Provisions of the Senate Amendment to the House Amendment to the Senate Amendment to the H.R. 1586, Scheduled for Consideration by the House of Representatives on 10 August 2010, (JCX-46-10).

U.S.: U.S. Joint Committee on Taxation, *Present Law and Background Related to Possible Income Shifting and Transfer Pricing* (JCX-37-10), 20 July 2010.

U.S.: IRS Rev. Proc. 2009-41 of 28 September 2009.

U.S.: US Model Income Tax Convention of 15 November 2006.

U.S.: Technical Explanation of the United States Model Income Tax Convention of 15 November 2006.

U.S.: United States response to United Kingdom note setting forth additional agreements regarding the U.S.-U.K Double Taxation Convention, signed 24 July 2001, London.

U.S.: IRS Notice 2000-7, 2000-4 IRB 49.

U.S.: T.D. 8767, 63 Fed. Reg. 14613, 26 March 1998.

U.S.: Notice 98-35, 1998-27 I.R.B.

U.S.: Notice 98-11, 1998-6 I.R.B.

U.S.: Staff of the Joint Committee on Taxation, *Review of Selected Entity Classification and Partnership Tax Issues*, U.S. Government Printing Office, Washington D.C. (1997).

U.S.: T.D. 8697, 61 Fed. Reg. 66584 of 18 December 1996.

U.S.: United States Model Income Tax Convention of 20 September 1996.

U.S.: Technical Explanation of the United States Model Income Tax Convention of 20 September 1996.

U.S.: IRS Rev. Rul. 93-4, 1993-1 C.B. 225.

U.S.: Staff of Joint Committee on Taxation, 99th Cong., 2nd Sess., General Explanation of the Tax Reform Act of 1989.

U.S.: Restatement (Third) of Foreign Relations Law of the United States (1987).

U.S.: United States Model Income Tax Convention of 16 June 1981.

U.S.: IRS Rev. Rul. 77-214, 1977-1 C.B. 408.

U.S.: IRS General Counsel Memorandum 39.610 of 4 November 1976.

U.S.: IRS General Counsel Memorandum 35.294 of 6 April 1973.

U.S.: Rev. Rul. 73-254, 1973-1 C.B. 613.

U.S.: Treas. Reg. Section 301.7701-1 to 11, T.D. 6503, 1960-2 C.B. 409.

U.S./PL: Convention between the United States of America and the Republic of Poland for the Avoidance of Double Taxation and the Prevention of Fiscal Evasion with respect to Taxes on Income of 13 February 2013.

U.S./PL: Department of the Treasury Technical Explanation of the Convention Between the United States of America and the Republic of Poland for the Avoidance of Double Taxation and the Prevention of Fiscal Evasion with respect to Taxes on Income of 13 February 2013.

U.S./IN: Tax Convention between the Government of the United States of America and the Government of the Republic of India on 1 January 1991.

U.S./CA: Convention between Canada and the United States of America with respect to Taxes on Income and on Capital of 26 September 1980 (as amended through 2007).

U.S./CA: Technical Explanation of the Protocol done at Chelsea on 26 September 2007 amending the Convention between the United States of America and Canada with respect to Taxes on Income and on Capital done at Washington on 26 September 1980, as amended by the Protocols of 14 June 1983, 28 March 1994, 17 March 1995 and 29 July 1997.

2. BOOKS AND CHAPTERS OF BOOKS

Akie Utumi A., *Brazil* in: Cahiers de droit fiscal international Vol. 97b, *The Debt Equity Conundrum*, IFA (2012).

Almudi J., *Avoidance of Double Non-taxation in Spain* in: M. Lang (ed.) *Avoidance of Double Non-taxation*, Linde, Vienna (2003).

Ault H. and Arnold B., *Protecting the Tax Base of Developing Countries: An Overview*, Paper on Selected Topics in Protecting the Tax Base of Developing Countries (UN), Draft Paper No. 1, United Nations, New York (2013).

Avery Jones J., *Tax Treaty Interpretation in the United Kingdom* in: M. Lang (ed.) *Tax Treaty Interpretation*, Linde, Vienna (2001).

Avery Jones J., *The Interaction Between Tax Treaty Provisions and Domestic Law* in: G. Maisto, *Tax Treaties and Domestic Law*, EC and International Tax Law Series Vol. 2, IBFD (2006).

Avi-Yonah R., *International Tax as International Law: An Analysis of the International Tax Regime*, Cambridge University Press, New York, 2007.

Baker P., *Double Taxation Conventions*, Sweet & Maxwell, London, 2014.

Baker P., *The United Nations Model Double Taxation Convention Between Developed and Developing Countries: Possible Extension of the Beneficial Owner Concept* in: Committee of Experts on International Cooperation in Tax Matters: Fourth Session, Geneva (20-24 October 2008).

Balco T. and Skalicka H., *Czech Republic* in: Cahiers de droit fiscal international Vol. 99B, *Qualification of Taxable Entities and Tax Treaty Protection,* IFA (2014).

Baldwin M. and Kiranoglu T., *United Kingdom* in: Cahiers de droit fiscal international Vol. 99B, *Qualification of Taxable Entities and Tax Treaty Protection,* IFA (2014).

Bammens N. and De Broe L., *Treaty Shopping and Avoidance of Abuse in Tax Treaties: Building Bridges Between Law and Economics* in: M. Lang et al. (eds) IBFD 2010, Online Books IBFD.

Bammens N., *The Principle of Non-discrimination in International and European Tax Law*, IBFD Doctoral Series, Vol. 24, IBFD, Amsterdam, 2012.

Barenfeld J., *Taxation of Cross-Border Partnerships, Double Tax Relief in Hybrid and Reserve Hybrid Situations,* Vol. 9 IBFD Doctoral Series, Amsterdam (2005), Section 2.3.2.2, Online Books IBFD.

Berna P., Mischo P. and van Kuij F., *Luxembourg* in: Cahiers de droit fiscal international Vol. 99B, *Qualification of Taxable Entities and Tax Treaty Protection,* IFA (2014).

Bhuta H., *Progressive Tax Rates in a Profit or Loss Situation under Article 24(3) of the OECD Model* in: K. Dziurdz and C. Marchgraber (eds) *Non-discrimination in European and Tax Treaty Law*, Linde, Vienna, 2015.

Bittker B. and Lokken L., *Fundamentals of International Taxation, US Taxation of Foreign Income and Foreign Taxpayers*, Thomson Reuters, Valhala NY, 2011.

Bizioli G., *Comparative Analysis of the Causes of Double (Non-) Taxation in the Income and VAT/GST Contexts* in: M. Lang, P. Melz and E. Krostoffersson (eds) *Value Added Tax and Direct Taxation: Similarities and Differences,* IBFD, Amsterdam (2009).

Bjørnholm N. and Obery Hansen A., *Denmark in International Tax Planning,* Online Books IBFD, 2005.

Brabazon M., *International Taxation of Trust Income: Principles, Planning, and Design*, Cambridge University Press, 2019.

Brauner Y., *Beneficial Owner In and Outside US Tax Treaties* in: M. Lang et.al. (eds) *Beneficial Ownership: Recent Trends*, IBFD, Amsterdam (2013).

Brauner Y., *Chapter 23: United States* in: G. Maisto (ed.) *Residence of Companies under Tax Treaties and EC Law*, EC and International Tax Law Series Vol. 5, IBFD, Amsterdam (2009).

Brownlie I., *Principles of Public International Law*, 4th ed., Clarendon Press, Oxford, 1990.

Bunn D., *A Summary of Criticisms of the EU Digital Tax*, Tax Foundation, 22 October 2018.

Bundgaard J., *Hybrid Financial Instruments in International Tax Law*, Wolters Kluwer, BV The Netherlands, 2017.

Chen H., *Interpretation of Subject-to-Tax Clauses* in: M. Schilcher and P. Weninger (eds) *Fundamental Issues and Practical Problems in Tax Treaty Interpretation*, Linde, Vienna (2008).

Christians A., *Tax Activists and the Global Movement for Development Through Transparency in Tax* in: M. Stewart and Y. Brauner (eds) *Law and Development*, Edward Elgar Publishing (2013).

Coustel A., *France* in: Cahiers de droit fiscal international Vol. 99B, *Qualification of Taxable Entities and Tax Treaty Protection*, IFA (2014).

Crazzolara A., *Italy* in: Cahiers de droit fiscal international Vol. 99B, *Qualification of Taxable Entities and Tax Treaty Protection*, IFA (2014).

Cunningham L. and Cunningham N., *The logic of Subchapter K, A Conceptual Guide to the Taxation of Partnerships*, 4th ed., West, United States, 2011.

Da Silva B., *Revisiting the Application of the Capital Ownership Non-discrimination Provision in Tax Treaties* in: D. Weber and P. Pistone (eds) *Non-discrimination in Tax Treaties: Selected Issues from a Global Perspective*, EC and International Tax Law Series Vol. 14, IBFD, Amsterdam (2016).

Da Silveira R., *Case Eagle II: Tributação de auferidos no exterior em virtude de participação societária* in: L. Freitas de Moraes e Castro and A. Ribeiro (eds) *Tributação Internacional: análise de casos*, MP Editora, São Paulo (2010).

Danon R., *General Report* in: Cahiers de droit fiscal international Vol. 100A- *Tax Incentives for R&D*, IFA (2015).

De Broe L., *International Tax Planning and Prevention of Abuse*, Doctoral Series IBFD, Vol. 14, Amsterdam, 2008.

De Graaf M. and Gooijer J., *Netherlands* in: Cahiers de droit fiscal international Vol. 99B, *Qualification of Taxable Entities and Tax Treaty Protection*, IFA (2014).

Dell'Anese L., *Tax Arbitrage and the Changing Structure of International Tax Law*, Egea, Milan, 2006.

De la Feria R. and Vogenauer S. (eds), *Prohibition of Abuse of Law, A New General Principle of Law?*, Hart Publishing, 2011.

Di Maria J., *Comparability in the Case of Hybrid Mismatch: In Search of an Approach Suitable for the Current European Landscape* in: K. Dziurdz and C. Marchgraber (eds) *Non-discrimination in European and Tax Treaty Law*, Linde, Vienna (2015).

Dorfmüller P., *Germany* in: Cahiers de droit fiscal international Vol. 99B, *Qualification of Taxable Entities and Tax Treaty Protection*, IFA (2014).

du Toit C., *Beneficial Ownership of Royalties in Bilateral Tax Treaties*, IBFD, Amsterdam, 1999.

Dziurdz K. and Marchgraber C., *Non-discrimination in European and Tax Treaty Law: An Overview* in: K. Dziurdz and C. Marchgraber (eds) *Non-discrimination in European and Tax Treaty Law*, Linde, Vienna (2015).

Dziurdz K., *Non-discrimination and Harmful Tax Competition under WTO Law and Article 24 of the OECD Model* in: D. Weber and P. Pistone (eds) *Non-discrimination in Tax Treaties: Selected Issues from a Global Perspective*, EC and International Tax Law Series Vol. 14, IBFD, Amsterdam (2016).

Easson A. J., *Taxation in the European Community*, European Community Law Series: 5, The Athlone Press, London, 1993.

Eicke R., *Tax Planning with Holding Companies – Repatriation of U.S. Profits from Europe,* Kluwer Law International, BV The Netherlands, 2009.

Engelen F., *Interpretation of Tax Treaties under International Law,* Doctoral Series No. 7, IBFD, 2005.

Faes P., *Belgium* in: Cahiers de droit fiscal international Vol. 99B, *Qualification of Taxable Entities and Tax Treaty Protection,* IFA (2014).

Fibbe G., *EC Law Aspects of Hybrid Entities*, Vol. 15, Doctoral Series IBFD, Amsterdam, 2009.

García Prats F. A., *Los Nuevos Estándares Internacionales de Intercambio de Información: FATCA o el fin del Secreto Bancario* in *Intercambio de Información, Blanqueo de Capitales y Lucha contra el Fraude Fiscal* (Dir. F.A. García Prats), Instituto de Estudios Fiscales, Madrid (2014).

Garcia Prats F. A., *Revisiting 'Schumacker': Source, Residence and Citizenship in the ECJ Case Law on Direct Taxation* in: I. Richelle, W. Schön and E. Traversa (eds) *Allocating Taxing Powers Within the European Union*, Springer, Heidelberg (2013).

Garcia Prats F.A., *The 'Abuse of Tax Law': Prospects and Analysis* in: G. Bizioli (ed.) *Essays in International and European Tax Law,* Jovene Editore, Napoli (2010).

Gozdziowska P., Kuzniacki B. and Wickel T., *Poland* in: Cahiers de droit fiscal international Vol. 99B, *Qualification of Taxable Entities and Tax Treaty Protection,* IFA (2014).

Grandinetti M., *Italy* in: D. Gutmann (ed.) *Corporate Income Tax Subjects,* EATLP International Tax Series, Vol. 12, IBFD, Amsterdam (2015).

Gutmann D., *Avoidance of Double Non-taxation in France* in: M. Lang (ed.) *Avoidance of Double Non-taxation*, Linde, Vienna (2003).

Gutmann D., *Tax Treaty Interpretation in France* in: M. Lang (ed.) *Tax Treaty Interpretation*, Linde, Vienna (2001).

Haslehner W., Pantazatou K., Kofler G., and Rust A. (eds), *A Guide to the Anti-tax Avoidance Directive*, Edward Elgar Publishing, 2020.

Haslehner W., *Double Taxation Relief, Transfer Pricing Adjustments and State Aid Law* in: I. Richelle, W. Schön and E. Traversa (eds) *State Aid Law and Business Taxation*, Springer, Heidelberg (2016).

Heber C. and Sternberg C., *Chapter 6: Germany* in: R. van Brederode and R. Krever (eds) *Legal Interpretation of Tax Law,* Kluwer Law International, BV the Netherlands (2014).

Helminen M., *Tax Treaty Interpretation in Finland* in: M. Lang (ed.) *Tax Treaty Interpretation*, Linde, Vienna (2001).

Hernández González-Barreda P., *Beneficial Owner in Tax Law and Tax Treaties,* Bloomsbury Publishing, 2021.

International Law Association, *Statement of Principles Applicable to the Formation of General Customary International Law,* adopted by Resolution No. 16/2000, London Conference (2000).

Ismer/Blank A. in: Reimer and Rust (eds) *Klaus Vogel on Double Taxation Conventions,* Article 2.

Jiménez-Valladolid de L'Hotellerie-Fallois D. and Vega Borrego F., *Chapter 29: Spain* in *Corporate Income Tax Subjects* (ed. D. Gutmann), EATLP International Tax Series, Vol. 12 (2016).

Jiménez-Valladolid de L'Hotellerie-Fallois D., *Double (no) imposición e híbridos financieros: tendencias internacionales y reforma del Impuesto sobre Sociedades* in: *La Reforma del Sistema Tributario Español (2a parte), Encuentro de Derecho Financiero y Tributario (3a Ed.), Doc. No. 10/2015*, Institutos de Estudios Fiscales, Madrid, 2015.

Júnior A., *Caso Eagle 1: Interpretação das Normas Brasileiras de Tributação de Lucros e Rendimentos oriundos do exterior pelo CARF* in: L. Freitas de Moraes e Castro und A. Ribeiro (eds) *Tributação Internacional: análise de casos*, MP Editora, São Paulo (2010).

Kardachaki A. and Psaroulis S., *Greece* in: Cahiers de droit fiscal international Vol. 99B, *Qualification of Taxable Entities and Tax Treaty Protection,* IFA (2014).

Kelsen H., *Principles of International Tax Law*, 2nd ed., Holt, Rinehart &Winston Inc., New York, 1967.

Kemmeren E. in: Reimer and Rust (eds) *Klaus Vogel on Double Taxation Conventions*, 4th edn (2015), Pre Articles 10–12.

Kim S. and Yoon J., *Republic of Korea* in: Cahiers de droit fiscal international Vol. 99B, *Qualification of Taxable Entities and Tax Treaty Protection,* IFA (2014).

Kokott J. and Pistone P., *Taxpayers in International Law: International Minimum Standards for the Protection of Taxpayers' Rights*, Bloomsbury, 2022.

Kollmann J., Roncarati A. and Staringer C., *Treaty Entitlement for Fiscally Transparent Entities: Article 1(2) of the OECD Model Convention* in: M. Lang, P. Pistone, S. Staringer (eds) *Base Erosion and Profit Shifting (BEPS). The Proposal to Revise the OECD Model Convention*, Linde, Vienna (2016).

Kostohryz J., *Ownership Non-discrimination under Article 24(5) of the OECD Model in the Case of Low-Taxed Payments, Linde*, Vienna, 2015.

Krever R. and Mellor P, *Chapter 2: Australia* in: R. van Brederode and R. Krever (eds) *Legal Interpretation of Tax Law*, Kluwer Law International, BV the Netherlands (2014).

Kumar V., *Conflicts of Qualification and Conflicts of Allocation of Income* in: E. Burgstaller and K. Haslinger (eds) *Conflicts of Qualification in Tax Treaty Law*, Linde (2007).

Kuźniacki B., *Beneficial Ownership in International Taxation*, Edward Elgar, 2022.

Lang M. and Staringer C., *General Report* in: Cahiers de droit fiscal international Vol. 99B, *Qualification of Taxable Entities and Tax Treaty Protection,* IFA (2014).

Lang M. et al. (eds) *Beneficial Ownership: Recent Trends*, IBFD, Amsterdam, 2013.

Lang M., *General Report* in: Cahiers de droit fiscal international - Vol. 89a, *Double Non-taxation,* IFA (2004).

Lang M., *Introduction to the Law of Double Taxation Conventions*, 2nd. Ed., Linde Vienna, 2013.

Lang M., *Introduction to the Law of Double Taxation Conventions*, 2nd. ed., Linde, Vienna, 2013.

Lang M., *The Application of the OECD Model Tax Convention to Partnerships, A Critical Analysis of the Report Prepared by the OECD*, Wolters Kluwer, Alphen aan den Rijn, 2000.

Levey M. and Wrappe S., *Transfer Pricing: Rules, Compliance and Controversy*, 3rd ed., Wolters Kluwer Business, Chicago, 2010.

López Roriguez J. and Kofler G., *Beneficial Ownership and EU Law* in: M. Lang et.al. (eds) *Beneficial Ownership: Recent Trends*, IBFD, Amsterdam (2013).

Lüdicke J., *Exemption and Tax Credit in German Tax Treaties–Policy and Reality* in: P. Baker and C. Bobbett (eds) *Tax Policy Math*, Essays in honour of John F. Avery Jones, IBFD (2010).

Maisto G. (ed.), *Multilingual Texts and Interpretation of Tax Treaties and EC Tax Law*, Amsterdam, IBFD, 2005.

Maisto G., *Credit Versus Exemption under Domestic Tax Law and Treaties* in: M. Lang et al., *Tax Treaties: Building Bridges Between Law and Economics*, IBFD (2010).

Martín Jiménez A., *Controversial Issues About the Concept of Tax in Income and Capital Tax Treaties and the post-BEPS World*, in *Tax Treaties After the BEPS Project: A tribute to Jacques Sasseville* (B. Arnold and A. Parollini (eds) (Canadian Tax Foundation 2018).

Masui Y., *Chapter 9: Japan* in: R. van Brederode and R. Krever R. van Brederode and R. Krever (eds) *Legal Interpretation of Tax Law*, Kluwer Law International, BV The Netherlands (2014).

McGowan M., *Classifying Entities and the Meaning of 'Tax Transparency': The UK Perspective*, Wolters Kluwer, 2023.

Matteotti R. and Roth P., *Tax Incentives on Research and Development*, Archives de droit fiscal Suisse May/June 2015, Special issue IFA Basel 2015, available at www.asa.online, acceded on 11 January 2017.

McDaniel P., Ault H. and Repetti J., *Introduction to United States International Taxation*, 5th Ed., Wolters and Kluwer, New York, 2005.

McDaniel P., McMahon M., Jr. and Simmons D., *Federal Income Taxation of Partnerships and S Corporations*, 4th Ed., Foundation Press, New York, 2006.

Menuchin S. and Baram N., *Israel* in: Cahiers de droit fiscal international – Vol. 89a, *Double Non-taxation*, IFA (2004).

Millar R., *Intentional and Unintentional Double Non-taxation* in: M. Lang, P. Melz and E. Kristofferson (eds) *Value Added Tax and Direct Taxation: Similarities and Differences*, IBFD (2009).

Müller J.P. and Cottier T., *Acquiescence* in: R. Bernhardt (ed.) *Encyclopedia of Public International Law*, Volume I (1992).

Navarro A., 'The Allocation of Taxing Rights under Pillar One of the OECD Proposal', in: F. Hasse and G Kofler (eds), *The Oxford Handbook of International Tax Law*, Oxford University Press, 2023.

Ng R., *The Concept of Beneficial Owner* in: T. Ecker and G. Ressler (eds) *History of Tax Treaties. The Relevance of the OECD Documents for the Interpretation of Tax Treaties*, Linde, Vienna (2011).

Oesterhelt S. and Schreiber S. in: Zweifel/Beusch (eds) *Art. 49 of the Swiss Federal Law on Direct Taxation* [Bundesgesetz über die direkte Bundessteuer], 3rd ed., Helbling Lichtenhahn, Basel (2017).

Olenik K., *Tax Treaties and the Recourse to Historical Interpretation under the Vienna Convention on the Law of Treaties* in: T. Ecker and G. Ressler (eds) *History of Tax Treaties. The Relevance of the OECD Documents for the Interpretation of Tax Treaties*, Linde, Vienna (2011).

Palazzi P., *Taxation and Innovation*, OECD Taxation Working Paper No. 9, OECD Publishing, Paris, 2011.

Parada L., 'Tax Neutrality Regimes and GloBE' In W. Haslehner, K, Pantazatou, G, Kofler and A. Rust (eds) *The Pillar 2 Global Minimum Tax*, Edward Elgar Publishing, 2022-23.

Pires M., *International Juridical Double Taxation of Income*, Kluwer Law and Taxation Publishers, Boston, 1989.

Pistone P., *Italy: Beneficial Ownership as Anti-abuse Provision in International Taxation* in: M. Lang et al. (eds) *Beneficial Ownership: Recent Trends*, IBFD, Amsterdam (2013).

Pistor K., *The Code of Capital: How the Law Creates Wealth and Inequality*, Princeton University Press, 2019.

Pulido S., *Avoidance of Double Non-taxation in Portugal* in: M. Lang (ed.) *Avoidance of Double Non-taxation*, Linde, Vienna (2003).

Rasmussen M., *International Double Taxation*, Wolters Kluwer, New York, 2011.

Reimer E., *Tax Treaty Interpretation in Germany* in: M. Lang (ed.) *Tax Treaty Interpretation*, Linde, Vienna (2005).

Ring D., *United States* in: Cahiers de droit fiscal international - Vol. 89a, *Double Non-taxation*, IFA (2004).

Rust A. in: Reimer and Rust (eds) *Klaus Vogel on Double Taxation Conventions*, 4th ed. (2015), Article 24.

Rust A. in: Reimer and Rust (eds) *Klaus Vogel on Double Taxation Conventions*, 4th edn (2015), Article 23.

Rust A., *International Tax Neutrality and Non-discrimination – Legal Perspective* in: M. Lang, P. Pistone, J. Schuch, C. Staringer, A. Storck and M. Zagler (eds) *Tax Treaties: Building Bridges Between Law and Economics*, IBFD, Amsterdam (2010).

Sasseville J., *A Tax Treaty Perspective: Special Issues*, in: G. Maisto (ed.), *Tax Treaties and Domestic Law*, EC and International Tax Law Series, Vol. 2, IBFD, Amsterdam (2006).

Salom J. and Salomé H., *Switzerland* in: Cahiers de droit fiscal international Vol. 99B, *Qualification of Taxable Entities and Tax Treaty Protection*, IFA (2014).

Salomao E. and Prada J., *Corporations and Partnerships in Brazil*, Kluwer Law International, Alphen aan den Rijn, 2011.

Schaffer E., *Chapter 5: Implications of BEPS Action 2 and its Relevance for the Application of Article 17 of the OECD Model* in: *Domestic Attribution of Income and Taxation of International Entertainers and Sportspersons: Theory and Practice of Art. 17 OECD Model Convention* (M. Lang ed., IBFD 2017), Online Books IBFD.

Schön W., *Tax and Corporate Governance: A Legal Approach* in: W. Schön (ed.) *Tax and Corporate Governance*, MPI Studies on Intellectual Property, Competition and Tax Law, Springer, Heidelberg (2008).

Schoueri L., *Chapter 3: Brazil* in: R. van Brederode and R. Krever (eds) *Legal Interpretation of Tax Law*, Kluwer Law International, BV The Netherlands (2014).

Schoueri L., *Tax Sparing: uma reconsideração da reconsideração* in: R. Mariz de Oliveira at al. (eds) *Direito Tributário Atual*, Dialética/IBDT (2011).

Schwarz P., *IP Box Regime im Europäischen Steuerrecht*, Nomos Verlagsgesellschaft, 2017.

Schwarzenberger G., *A Manual of International Law*, 5th ed., Steven & Sons Limited, London, 1967.

Shelton N., *Interpretation and Application of Tax Treaties*, Lexis Nexis, London, 2004.

Spies K., 'Hybrid Entities and Anti-hybrid Rules in the EU ATAD (Article 9 and 9A ATAD)' in W. Haslehner, K. Pantazatou, G. Kofler, and A. Rust (eds), *A Guide to the Anti-tax Avoidance Directive*, Edward Elgar Publishing, 2020.

Terra B. and Wattel P., *European Tax Law*, Kluwer Law International, BV The Netherlands, 2012.

Texeira De Abreu M., Portugal in: Cahiers de droit fiscal international Vol. 99B, *Qualification of Taxable Entities and Tax Treaty Protection*, IFA (2014).

Traversa E. and Hellepute C., *Double (Non-) Taxation in VAT and Direct Taxes: How to Achieve Some Convergence Within a Summa Divisio? A European Perspective* in: M. Lang, P. Melz and E. Kristofferson (eds) *Value Added Tax and Direct Taxation: Similarities and Differences*, IBFD (2009).

Ullah M., *Avoidance of Double Non-taxation in the United Kingdom* in: M. Lang (ed.) *Avoidance of Double Non-taxation*, Linde, Vienna (2003).

United Nations, *Yearbook of the International Law Commission, Vol.* II, New York, 1967.

van Brussel Y., *The Relevance of Residence as a Safeguard in Article 24(1) of the OECD Model* in: K. Dziurdz and C. Marchgraber (eds) *Non-discrimination in European and Tax Treaty Law*, Linde, Vienna (2015).

van Raad K., *Non-discrimination in International Tax Law*, Series of International Taxation No. 6, Kluwer Law and Taxation Publishers, Deventer, 1986.

Vanhaute P., *Belgium in International Tax Planning*, 2nd revised ed., IBFD, Amsterdam, 2008, Chapter 7.10, Online Books IBFD.

Vanistendael F., *Non-discrimination: Can the EU Learn from the OECD Model Convention and Vice Versa?* in: D. Weber and P. Pistone (eds) *Non-discrimination in Tax Treaties: Selected Issues from a Global Perspective*, EC and International Tax Law Series Vol. 14, IBFD, Amsterdam (2016).

Vann R., *Beneficial Ownership: What Does History (and Maybe Policy) Tell Us* in: M. Lang et al. (eds) *Beneficial Ownership: Recent Trends*, IBFD, Amsterdam (2013).

Vann R., *Chapter 18: International Aspects of Income Tax* in: V. Thuronyi (ed.) *Tax Law Design and Drafting*, Vol. II, International Monetary Fund (1998).

Vega Borrego F., *Limitation of Benefits Clauses in Double Tax Conventions*, Kluwer Law International, 2006.

Verstraeten A., *Double (Non)Taxation in VAT and Direct Taxes: Which Tax is better for Developing Countries?* in: M. Lang, P. Melz and E. Krostoffersson (eds) *Value Added Tax and Direct Taxation: Similarities and Differences*, IBFD (2009).

Villar M., *Spain* in: Cahiers de droit fiscal international Vol. 99B, *Qualification of Taxable Entities and Tax Treaty Protection*, IFA (2014).

Vogel K. and Prokisch R., *General Report* in: Cahiers de droit fiscal international - Vol. LXXVIIa, *Interpretation of Double Taxation Conventions*, IFA (1993).

Vogel K. and Rust A. in: Reimer and Rust (eds) *Klaus Vogel on Double Taxation Conventions*, 4th ed., 2015, Introduction.

Ward D. et al., *The Interpretation of Income Tax Treaties with Particular Reference to the Commentaries on the OECD Model*, IBFD, Amsterdam, 2005.

Wassermeyer F., *Doppelbesteuerung (OECD-Musterabkommen* 2010 *Kommentar)* in: F. Wassermeyer, C. Kaeser, M. Lang and J. Schuch (eds) Linde, Vienna, (2015), Article 12, m.no. 33.

Yañez F., Chile in: Cahiers de droit fiscal international Vol. 99B, *Qualification of Taxable Entities and Tax Treaty Protection*, IFA, 2014.

3. JOURNALS

Achatz M, Gröhs B. and Weninger R., *Taxation of Non-resident Individuals in Austria*, 58 Bull. Intl. Taxn. 11 (2004), Journals IBFD.

Allison C., *How Starbucks Lost Its Social License – And Paid 20 Million Pounds to Get It Back*, 71 Tax Notes Int'l 7 (2013).

Alves C., *Preventing Tax Avoidance: Is There Convergence in the Way Countries Counter Tax Avoidance?*, 67 Bull. Intl. Taxn. 7 (2013), Journals IBFD.

Ambagtsheer-Pakarinen L., *Commission*, 56 Eur. Taxn. 1 (2016), Journals IBFD.

Amico J., *Brazil: Developing and Implementing Tax Treaty Policy: The Tax Sparing Clause*, 43 Bull. Intl. Fisc. Doc. 8/9 (1989).

Arnold B., *Tax Treaties and Tax Avoidance: The 2003 Revisions to the Commentary to the OECD Model*, 58 Bull. Intl. Taxn. 6, (2004), Journals IBFD.

Arnold B., *Tax Treaty Case Law News*, 66 Bull. Intl. Taxn. 1 (2012), Journals IBFD.

Arnold B., *Tax Treaty News*, 64 Bull. Intl. Taxn. 10 (2010), Journals IBFD.

Arnold B., *The Interpretation of Tax Treaties: Myth and Reality*, 64 Bull Intl. Taxn. 1 (2010), Journals IBFD.

Arnold B., *Tax Treaty Monitor: Tax Treaty News*, 63 Bull. Intl. Taxn. 7 (2009), Journals IBFD.

Arora J. et al., *U.S. releases Final FATCA Regulations*, 69 Tax Notes Int'l 4 (2013).

Arruda V. and Trindade A., *Tax Sparing and Matching Credit: From an Unclear Concept to an Uncertain Regime*, 67 Bull. Intl. Taxn. 8 (2013), Journals IBFD.

Ault H., *Issues Related to the Identification and Characteristics of the Taxpayer*, 56 Bull. Intl. Taxn. 6 (2002), Journals IBFD.

Ault H., *Some Reflections on the OECD and the Sources of International Tax Principles*, 70 Tax Notes Int'l 12 (2013).

Ault H., *The importance of International Cooperation in Forging Tax Policy*, 26 Brook. J. Int'l L. 1693 (2001).

Ault H., *The Role of the OECD Commentaries in the Interpretation of Tax Treaties*, 4 Intertax 144-148 (1994).

Avery Jones J. and Ward D., *Agents as Permanent Establishments under the OECD Model Tax Convention*, 1 BTR 346 (1993).

Avery Jones J. et al., *Characterization of Other States' Partnerships for Income Tax*, 56 Bull. Intl. Fisc. Doc. 7 (2001), Journals IBFD.

Avery Jones J. et al., *The Non-discrimination Article in Tax Treaties*, 31 Eur. Taxn. 10 (1991), Journals IBFD.

Avery Jones J. et al., *The Origin of the Concepts and Expressions Used in the OECD Model and Their Adoption by States*, 60 Bull. Int'l. Taxn. 6 (2006), Journals IBFD.

Avery Jones J., *Avoiding Double Taxation: Credit Versus Exemption – The Origins*, 66 Bull. Intl. Taxn. 2 (2012), Journals IBFD.

Avery Jones J., *Conflicts of Qualification: Comments on Prof. Vogel's and Alexander Rust's Articles*, 57 Bull. Intl. Taxn. 5 (2003), Journals IBFD.

Avi-Yonah R. and Halabi O., *US Treaty Anti-avoidance Rules: An Overview and Assessment*, 66 Bull. Intl. Taxn. 4/5 (2012), Journals IBFD.

Avi-Yonah R. and Tittle M., *The United States Model Income Tax Convention*, 61 Bull. Int'l Taxn. 224 (2007), Journals IBFD.

Avi-Yonah R., *Commentary (Response to Article by H. David Rosenbloom)*, 53 Tax L. Rev. 167 (2000).

Avi-Yonah R., *International Taxation of Electronic Commerce*, 52 Tax L. Rev. 507 (1997).

Avi-Yonah R., *Tax Competition, Tax Arbitrage and the International Tax Regime*, 61 Bull. Int'l Taxn. 4 (2007), Journals IBFD.

Avi-Yonah R., *The Case of Taxing Citizens*, Public Law and Legal Theory Working Paper No. 10-009 (2010), available at Michigan Law ELSC Website.

Avi-Yonah R., *The International Tax Regime: A Centennial Reconsideration*, University of Michigan Public Law Research Paper No. 462 (2015), full text available at SSRN.

Avi-Yonah R., *Who Invented the Single Tax Principle? An Essay on the History of U.S. Treaty Policy*, 59 N.Y.L. Sch. L. Rev. 309 (2014).

Baker P., *The BEPS Action Plan in the Light of EU Law: Treaty Abuse*, British Tax Review 3 (2015).

Baker P., *Some Recent Decisions of the European Court of Human Rights in Tax Matters*, 55 Eur. Taxn. 2/3 (2015), Journals IBFD.

Baker P., *The Application of the Convention to Partnerships, Trusts and Other, Non-corporate Entities*, 2 GITC Rev. 1 (2002).

Bammens N., *Subject-to-Tax Clauses in Belgian Tax Treaties–'Exemption Vaut Impôt' Doctrine Rejected Again in Case Law*, 68 Bull. Intl. Taxn. 8 (2014), Journals IBFD.

Barenfeld J., *A Common Consolidated Corporate Tax Base in the European Union – A Beauty or a Beast in the Quest for Tax Simplicity*, 61 Bull. Intl. Taxn. 7 (2007), Journals IBFD.

Bärsch S. and Spengel C., *Hybrid Mismatch Arrangements: OECD Recommendations and German Practice,* 67 Bull Intl. Taxn. 10 (2013), Journals IBFD.

Bates J. et al., *Limitation on Benefits Articles in Income Tax Treaties: The current State of Play*, 41 Intertax 7 (2013).

Bates J., *Nature Abhors a Splitter: The FTC Splitter and Indirect FTC Rules*, 61 Tax Notes Int'l 7 (2011).

Bavila A., *Taxation of Trusts in Italy: Capital Gains on Trust Assets and Transparent Trusts*, 64 Bull. Intl. Taxn. 8/9 (2010), Journals IBFD.

Bax A. and Claes S., *The New Belgium-US Tax Treaty-an Analysis*, 47 Eur. Taxn. 7 (2006), Journals IBFD.

Becker J. and Loose T., *Zur geplanten Ausdehnung des materiellen Korrespondenzprinzips auf hybride Finanzierungen*, 21 Internationales Steuerrecht 19 (2012).

Benamran J., *France-Corporate Taxation* section 11, Country Analyses (accessed 1 February 2017).

Benéitez Régil P., *BEPS Actions 2, 3 and 4 and the Fundamental Freedoms: Is There a Way Out?*, 56 Eur. Taxn. 6 (2016), Journals IBFD.

Bernstein J., *Beneficial Ownership: An International Perspective*, 45 Tax Notes Int'l 12 (2007).

Boise C., *Breaking Open Offshore Piggybanks: Deferral and the Utility of Amnesty*, 14 Geo. Mason L. Rev. 667 (2007).

Bosman A., *Casualty under Tax Treaties*, 44 Intertax 5 (2016).

Braidi G. and Cousinou L., *Swiss Banking Secrecy: A Heaven of Peace in Distress for US Taxpayers*, Quid? Fribourg L. Rev. 2 (2014).

Braun J. and Zagler M., *An Economic Perspective on Double Tax Treaties With(in) Developing Countries*, 6 World Tax J. (2014), Journals IBFD.

Brauner Y., *An International Tax Regime in Crystallization*, 56 Tax L. Rev. 259 (2003).

Brauner Y., *BEPS: An Interim Evaluation*, 6 World Tax J.1 (2014), Journals IBFD.

Brauner Y., *Integration in an Integrated World,* 2 N.Y.U. J. L. & Bus. 51 (2005).

Büchel B., *Liechtenstein – Corporate Taxation sec. 1.*, Country Surveys IBFD (accessed 31 May 2017).

Bundgaard J., *Coordination Rules as a Weapon in the War Against Cross-Border Tax Arbitrage–The Case of Hybrid Entities and Hybrid Financial Instruments*, 67 Bull. Intl. Taxn. 4/5 (2013), Journals IBFD.

Bundgaard J., *Hybrid Financial Instruments and Primary EU Law–Part 1,* 53 Eur. Taxn. 11 (2013), Journals IBFD.

Bundgaard J., *Hybrid Financial Instruments and Primary EU Law–Part 2,* 53 Eur. Taxn. 12 (2013), Journals IBFD.

Calderón Carrero J. and Quintas Seara A., *The Concept of 'Aggressive Tax Planning' Launched by the OECD and the EU Commission in the BEPS Era: Redefining the Border Between Legitimate and Illegitimate Tax Planning*, 44 Intertax 3, (2016).

Calderón Carrero J. and Quintas Seara A., *The Taxpayer's Right of Defense in Cross-Border Exchange of Information Procedures*, 68 Bull. Int'l. Taxn. 9 (2014), Journals IBFD.

Camacho Palma R., *An Overview of the Protection of Taxpayer Rights in Portugal*, 50 Eur. Taxn. 1 (2010), Journals IBFD.

Carey K., *Stateless Income's Agency Problem: Are Multinationals Acting in the Best Interest of Shareholders Through the Creation of Stateless Income?* (14 May 2012), full text available at SSRN.

Carman P., *Final FATCA Regulations Provide Certainty, Flexibility*, 15 Derivs. & Fin. Instrums. 2 (2013), Journals IBFD.

Cavelti L., *Automatic Information Exchange Versus the WHT Regime Globalization and Increasing Sovereignty Conflicts in International Taxation*, 5 World Tax J. 2 (2013), Journals IBFD.

Celine A., Desbordes R. and Mucchielli J., *Do Tax Sparing Agreements Contribute to the Attraction of FDI in Developing Countries*, 14 Intl. Tax and Pub. Fin. 5 (2007).

Cencerrado M. and Soler M., *Limit Base Erosion Via Interest Deduction and Others*, 43 Intertax 1 (2015).

Cerioni L., *Cross-Border Mobility of Companies in the European Union: Tax Competition and Increased Scope for the CCCTB Following Cartesio*, 64 Bull. Intl. Taxn. 12 (2010), Journals IBFD.

Cerioni L., *The Commission's Proposal for a CCCTB Directive: Analysis and Comment*, 65 Bull. Intl. Taxn. 9 (2011), Journals IBFD.

Chand V., *Should States Opt for the Saving Clause in the Multilateral Instrument?*, 86 Tax Notes Int'l. 8 (2017).

Christians A., *Avoidance, Evasion and Taxpayer Morality*, 44 Wash. U. J. L. & Pol'y 39 (2014).

Ciro T. and Mascitelli B, *Machinations in the Global Automotive Industry: The Fiat and Chrysler Deal Examined*, 12 Derivs. & Fin. Instrums. 2 (2010), Journals IBFD.

Cleave B., *The Bayfine Case, Elaborate Tax Avoidance Scheme Using Tax Treaty Fails in Court of Appeal of England and Wales*, 65 Bull. Intl. Taxn. 11 (2011), Journals IBFD.

Cleave B., *The Smallwood Case: Dual Residence of Trustees*, 65 Bull. Intl. Taxn. 8 (2011), Journals IBFD.

Cleave B., *The Weiser Case: UK Pension Income Not Subject to Tax in Israel under the Israel-United Kingdom Income Tax Treaty (1962)*, 67 Bull. Intl. Taxn. 6 (2013), Journals IBFD.

Cooper G., *Some Thoughts on the OECD's Recommendations on Hybrid Mismatches*, 69 Bull. Intl. Taxn. 6/7 (2015), Journals IBFD.

Corsini L., *The Taxation of Trusts in Italy*, 53 Bull. Intl. Taxn. 3 (1999), Journals IBFD.

Cui W., *The Digital Services Tax: A Conceptual Defense*, Tax Law Rev 73 (2019).

Cui W., *Passthru Payments and the Fantastic World of FATCA*, 13 Derivs. & Fin. Instrums. 4 (2011), Journals IBFD.

Dagan T., *The Tax Treaty Myth*, 32 N.Y.U. J. Int'l L. Pol. 939 (2000).

Danon R., *Qualification of Taxable Entities and Treaty Protection*, 68 Bull. Intl. Taxn. 4/5 (2014), Journals IBFD.

De Boer R. and Marres O., *BEPS Action 2: Neutralizing the Effects on Hybrid Mismatch Arrangements*, 43 Intertax 1 (2015).

De Broe L. and Bammens N., *Interpretation of Subject-to-Tax Clauses in Belgium's Tax Treaties: Critical Analysis of the 'exemption vaut impôt' Doctrine*, 63 Bull. Intl. Taxn. 2 (2009), Journals IBFD.

De Broe L., *Some Observations on the 2007 Communication from the Commission: 'The Application of Anti-abuse Measures in the Area of Direct Taxation Within the EU and in Relation to Third Countries'*, 17 EC Tax Rev. 3 (2008).

De la Cueva González-Cotera Á. and Morlán Burgasé C., *Spain – Corporate Taxation sec. 1.*, Country Analyses IBFD (accessed 6 June 2017).

De la Feria R., *Tax Fraud and Selective Law Enforcement*, 47 J.L. & Soc'y 240 (2020).

De la Feria R., *Prohibition of Abuse of (Community) Law: The Creation of a New General Principle of EC Law through Tax*, 45 Com. Mkt. L. Rev. 395 (2008).

De Zeeuw M., *The Formulation of Taxpayer Rights and Obligations in a Developing Country*, 14 Asia-Pacific Tax Bull. 1 (2008), Journals IBFD.

Dean S., *Attractive Complexity: Tax Deregulation, the Check-the-Box Election, and the Future of Tax Simplification*, 35 Hofstra L. Rev. 405 (2005).

Desai M. and Hines J. Jr., *Old Rules and New Realities: Corporate Tax Policy in a Global Setting*, 57 Nat'l Tax J. 937 (2004).

Desai M. and Hines J., *Evaluating International Tax Reform*, 56 Nat'l Tax J. 487 (2003).

Desax M., *The Swiss Perspective of Information Exchange*, 58 Tax Notes Int'l 12 (2010).

Desax R., *Practical Protection of Fundamental Rights of Taxpayers*, 69 Bull. Int'l Taxn. 4/5 (2015), Journals IBFD.

Devereux M. et al, *The OECD Global Anti-base Erosion Proposal*, Oxford University Centre for Business Taxation (2020).

Dibout P., *L'inapplicabilité de l'article 209 B du CGI face à la convention fiscal franco-suisse du septembre 1966*, 36 Revue de Droit Fiscal (2000).

Dirkis M., *The 'Lyon's Mouth' Post-Box: A Comparative Review of the Limitations on the Use by Revenue Authorities of Leaked and Stolen Information*, Working Paper University of Sydney, presented at the Tax Research Conference organized by the Ross Parson Centre for Commercial, Corporate and Taxation Law (Sydney) and the Max Planck Institute for Tax Law and Public Finance (Munich), 28–29 November 2016.

Distaso M. and Russo R., *The EC Interest and Royalty Directive- A Comment*, 44 Eur. Taxn. 4 (2004), Journals IBFD.

Doernberg R. and van Raad K., *Hybrid Entities and the U.S. Model Income Tax Treaty*, 19 Tax Notes Int'l 8 (1999).

Dörfler O., Heurung R. and Adrian G., *Korrespondenzprinzip bei verdeckter Gewinnausschüttung und verdeckter Einlage*, 45 Deutsches Steuerrecht 12 (2007).

Douma S., *The Three Ds of Direct Tax Jurisdiction: Disparity, Discrimination and Double Taxation*, 46 Eur. Taxn. 11 (2006), Journals IBFD.

Dourado A. P., *Aggressive Tax Planning in EU Law and in the Light of BEPS: The EC Recommendation on Aggressive Tax Planning and BEPS Action 2 and 6*, 43(1) Intertax 42 (2015).

Dziurdz K., *'Circular Linked' Rules Countering Deduction and Non-inclusion Schemes: Some Thoughts on Tie-Breaker Test*, 67 Bull. Intl. Taxn. 6 (2013), Journals IBFD.

Dziurdz K., Fuentes D. and Pinetz E., *Case Studies on Partnerships and Other Hybrid Entities*, 68 Bull. Intl. Taxn. 3 (2014), Journals IBFD.

Easson A., *Tax Incentives for Foreign Direct Investment, Part I: Recent Trends and Countertrends*, 55 Bull. Intl. Taxn. 7 (2001), Journals IBFD.

Edgar T., *Corporate Income Tax Coordination as a Response to International Tax Competition and International Tax Arbitrage*, 51 Can. Tax J. 3 (2003).

Engelen F. and P. Pötgens, *Report on 'The Application of the OECD Model Tax Convention to Partnerships' and the Interpretation of Tax Treaties*, 40 Eur. Taxn. 7 (2000), Journals IBFD.

Engelen F., *Some Observations on the Legal Status of the Commentaries on the OECD Model*, 60 Bull. Intl. Taxn. 3 (2006), Journals IBFD.

Essers P., *International Tax Justice Between Machiavelli and Habermas*, 68 Bull. Int'l Taxn. 2 (2014), Journals IBFD.

Englisch J., *GloBE Rules and Tax Competition*, Intertax 48(12) (2022).

Eynatten W., De Haen K. and Hostyn N., *The Concept of 'Beneficial Owner' under Belgian Tax Law: Legal Interpretation is Maintained*, 31 Intertax 12 (2003).

Fibbe G. and Stevens A.J.A., *Hybrid Mismatches under the ATAD I and ATAD II*, 26 EC Tax Rev. 3 (2017).

Forcada C., *The Economic Effect of Taxation on the Flow of Software Copyright Royalties in MERCOSUR*, 65 Bull. Intl. Taxn. 7 (2011), Journals IBFD.

Forst D., *Recently Enacted Code Sec. 909 Targets 'Splitter' Transactions (Part 1)*, 14 J. Passthrough Entities 1 (2011).

Freitas de Moraes e Castro L., *Brazil's Anti-treaty Shopping Measures: Current and Future Developments Regarding Beneficial Ownership and Limitation on Benefits Clauses in Tax Treaties*, 65 Bull. Intl. Taxn. 12 (2011), Journals IBFD.

Fraser R. and Oliver J., *Beneficial Ownership: HMRC's Draft Guidance on Interpretation of the Indofood Decision*, BTR 1 (2007).

Freitas de Moraes e Castro L., *Brazilian CFC Rules: Background and Status After Eagle II Case*, 18 Latin Am. L. & Bus. Rep. 3 (2010).

Frisch D., *The Economics of International Tax Policy: Some Old and New Approaches*, 47 Tax Notes 5 (1990).

Fross A., *Earnings Stripping and Thin Cap Rules: Maintaining an Arm's Length Distance*, 53 Eur. Taxn. 10 (2013), Journals IBFD.

Fuest C. et al., *Profit Shifting and 'Aggressive' Tax Planning by Multinationals Firms: Issues and Options for Reform*, 5 World Tax J. 3 (2013), Journals IBFD.

García Prats F. A., *Los límities a la planificación fiscal agresiva y el abuso de las normas tributaries*, at AEDAF, X Congreso Tributario. La Justicia: ¿Garantía del Estado de Derecho? AEDAF, 2015.

Gérard M., *Belgium Moves to Dual Allowance for Corporate Equity*, 46 Eur. Taxn. 4 (2006), Journals IBFD.

Geys B. and Konrad K., *Patriotism and Taxation*, Working Paper of the Max Planck Institute for Tax Law and Public Finance No. 2016-11 (2016).

Gianni M., *International Tax Planning After Check-the-Box*, 2 J. Passthrough Entities 39 (1999).

Gomez A., *Rationalizing the Taxation of Business Entities*, 49 Tax Lawyer 2 (1995).

Graetz M. and O'Hear M., *The 'Original Intent' of U.S. International Taxation*, 46 Duke Law J. 1021 (1997).

Graetz M., *The David R. Tillinghast Lecture, Taxing International Income: Inadequate Principles, Outdated Concepts and Unsatisfactory Policies*, 54 Tax L. Rev. 261 (2001).

Gresik T., *The Taxing Task of Taxing Transnationals*, 39 J. Econ. Lit. 3 (2001).

Gribnau H., *Legislative Instrumentalism vs. Legal Principles in Tax Law*, International Tax Law Review 3 (2012).

Grinberg I., *The New International Tax Diplomacy*, The Georgetown Law Journal 102:1137 (2016).

Grinberg I., *Taxing Capital Income in Emerging Countries: Will FATCA Open the Door?*, 5 World Tax J. 3 (2013), Journals IBFD.

Grubert H. and Altshuler R., *Corporate Taxes in the World Economy: Reforming Taxation of Cross-Border Income*, Working Papers, Department of Economics, Rutgers, the State University of New Jersey No. 2006, 26 (2006).

Gutmann D. et al., *The Impact of the ATAD on Domestic Systems: A Comparative Survey*, 57 Eur. Taxn. 1 (2017), Journals IBFD.

Hammer V., *US Update*, 66 Bull. Intl. Taxn. 6 (2012), Journals IBFD.

Hansson Å. and Brokelind C., *Tax Incentives, Tax Expenditures Theories in R&D: The Case of Sweden*, 6 World Tax J. 2 (2014), Journals IBFD.

Helminen M., *The Problem of Double Non-taxation in the European Union – To What Extent Could This Be Resolved through a Multilateral EU Tax Treaty Based on the Nordic Convention?*, 53 Eur. Taxn. 7, 309 (2013), Journals IBFD.

Henkel U., *Subjektfähigkeit grenzüberschreitender Kapitalgesellschaften*, RIW 7 (1991).

Heyvaert W. and Deschrijver D., *Belgium Stimulates Equity Financing*, 33 Intertax 10 (2005).

Hobbs P., *Entity Classification: The One Hundred-Year Debate*, 44 Cath. U.L. Rev. 437 (1995).

Hohenwarter D., Kofler G., Mayr G. and Sinnig J., *Qualification of the Digital Service Tax Under Tax Treaties*, 47 Intertax 2 (2019).

Hongler P., *Swiss Tax Authorities Clarify Treatment of a Shareholding in a U.S. LLC*, 65 Tax Notes Int'l 8 (2012).

Ismer R. and Jescheck C., *Taxes on Digital Services and the Substantive Scope of Application of Tax Treaties: Pushing the Boundaries of Article 2 of the OECD Model*, 46 Intertax 6/7 (2018).

Jacob F. and Hagena A., *The Germany-Luxembourg Income and Capital Tax Treaty (2012)*, 66 Bull. Intl. Taxn.10 (2012), Journals IBFD.

Jann M., Schuch J. and Toifl G., *Austria – Corporate Taxation sec. 1*, Country Analyses IBFD, section 1.4.10 (accessed 6 June 2017).

Johnston S., *State Court Rejects Challenge Against Use of Stolen Bank Data*, 73 Tax Notes Int'l 876 (2014).

Kahlenberg C., *Classification of Foreign Entities for German Tax Purposes*, 54 Eur. Taxn. 4 (2014), Journals IBFD.

Kahlenberg C., *Extension of the Domestic Correspondence Principle*, 54 Eur. Taxn. 1 (2014), Journals IBFD.

Kahlenberg C., *Prevention of Double Non-taxation: An Analysis of Cross-Border Financing from German Perspective*, 43 Intertax 3 (2015).

Kahlenberg C., *The Interplay Between OECD Recommendations of Action 2 and 3 Regarding Hybrid Structures*, 44 Intertax 4 (2016).

Kane M., *Strategy and Cooperation in International Responses to International Tax Arbitrage*, 53 Emory L.J. 89 (2004).

Kim Y.R.(Christine), *Digital Services Tax: A Cross-Border Variation of the Consumption Tax Debate*, Alabama Law Review 71:1 (2020).

Kirchmayr S. and Kofler G., *Beteiligungsertragsbefreiung und Internationale Steuerarbitrage, 10* Zeitschrift für Gesellschaftrecht und angrenzendes Steuerrecht 9 (2011).

Kleinbard E., *Stateless Income*, 11 Florida Tax Review 699 (2011).

Kleinbard E., *Stateless Income's Challenge to Tax Policy*, USC Center in Law, Economics and Organization, Research Paper No. C11-8, USC Legal Studies Research Paper No. 11-13 (2011).

Kleinbard E., *The Lessons of Stateless Income*, 65 Tax Law Review 99 (2011).

Kleinbard E., *Through a Latte, Darkly: Starbucks's Stateless Income Planning*, Tax Notes 1515-1535 (24 June 2013).

Knöller C., *The Efficacy of Thin Capitalization Rules and Their Barriers: An Analysis from UK and German Perspective,* 39 Intertax 6/7 (2011).

Kofler G and Sinnig J., *Equalization Taxes and the EU's 'Digital Service Tax'*, 47 Intertax 2 (2019).

Kofler G., *Indirect Credit Versus Exemption: Double Taxation Relief for Intercompany Distributions*, 66 Bull. Intl. Taxn. 2, 89 (2012), Journals IBFD.

Kofler G., *Some Reflections on the 'Saving Clause'*, 44 Intertax 8/9 (2016).

Korving J.J.A.M. and Wijtvliet L.W.D., *A Consideration of the European Foundation: Alle Menschen werden Spender,* 67 Bull. Intl. Taxn. 9 (2013), Journals IBFD.

Krauß S., *EU-BEPS? Aktionsplan für eine faire und effiziente Unternehmensbesteuerung in der EU*, Internationales Steuerrecht 2 (2016).

Kronbergs Z., *Latvia-2014 Corporate Tax Changes*, 54 Eur. Taxn. 11 (2014), Journals IBFD.

Kuzniacki B. et al., *Preventing Tax Arbitrage via Hybrid Mismatches: BEPS Action 2 and Developing Countries*, WU International Taxation Research Paper Series No. 2017-03, of 31 March 2017, available online at www.ssrn.org.

Laghmouchi S., *Netherlands: Issues Arising under the Decrees on the Tax Treatment of Foreign (Hybrid) Entities*, 60 Bull. Intl. Taxn. 2 (2006), Journals IBFD.

Lamers A. and J. Stevens, *Classification Conflicts: The Cross-Border Tax Treatment of the Profit Share of Limited Partners*, 44 Eur. Taxn. 4 (2004), Journals IBFD.

Lamers A.W.G., *Classification of Foreign Entities in the Netherlands: Recent Developments*, 38 Intertax 12 (2010).

Lampreave P., *An Assessment of the Anti-tax Avoidance Doctrines in the United States and the European Union*, 66 Bull. Intl. Taxn. 3 (2012), Journals IBFD.

Lang M., *2008 OECD Model: Conflicts of Qualification and Double Non-taxation*, 63 Bull. Intl. Taxn. 5 (2009), Journals IBFD.

Lang M., *Direct Taxation: Is the ECJ Heading in New Direction?*, 46 Eur. Taxn. 9 (2006), Journals IBFD.

Lang M., *Dreifache Nichtbesteuerung als Ergebnis der Anwendung von Doppelbesteuerungsabkommen*, 25 SWI 5 (2015).

Lang M., *Recent Case Law of the ECJ in Direct Taxation: Trends, Tensions, and Contradictions*, 18 EC Tax Rev. 3 (2009).

Lang M., *Tendenzen in der Rechtsprechung des österreichischen Verwaltungsgerichtshofs zu den Doppelbesteuerungsabkomme*, IFF Forum für Steuerrecht 2012.

Lederman L., *The Fraud Triangle and Tax Evasion*, 106 Iowa L. Rev. 1153 (2021).

Lederman L., *The Use of Voluntary Disclosure Initiatives in the Battles Against Offshore Tax Evasion*, 57 Vill. L. Rev. 499 (2012).

Lemos M., *'Non-transparent': The Court of Appeal's Decision on the Delaware LLC in HMRC v. Anson*, XII GITC Rev. 2 (2014).

Leone F. and Zanotti E., *Notional Interest Deduction Regime Introduced*, 52 Eur. Taxn. 8 (2012), Journals IBFD.

Lepard B., *The Necessity of Opinio Juris in the Formation of Customary International Law*, Discussion Paper for Panel on 'Does Customary International Law Need *Opinio Juris?*', available at SSRN.

Levine H. and Miller M., *Proposed Regulations 'Clarifying' the Technical Taxpayer Rule Don't Pass the Giggle Test*, 33 Int'l Tax J. 5 (2007).

Li J., *The Great Fiscal Wall of China: Tax Treaties and Their Role in Defining and Defending China's Tax Base*, 66 Bull. Intl. Taxn. 9 (2012), Journals IBFD.

López Ribas S., *Financing Activities: Hybrid Mismatches and the Tax Deductibility of Interest in Spain*, 70 Bull. Intl. Taxn. 8 (2016), Journals IBFD.

Lüdicke J., *'Tax Arbitrage' with Hybrid Entities: Challenges and Responses*, 68 Bull. Intl. Taxn. 6/7 (2014), Journals IBFD.

Lüdicke J., *Exemption and Tax Credit in German Tax Treaties: Policy and Reality*, 64 Bull. Intl. Taxn. 12 (2010), Journals IBFD.

Mahboob A., *FATCA and the Fat Cats: Foreign Pass-through Payments and the Blocker Problem*, 71 Tax Notes Int'l 12 (2013).

Malherbe J. and Vettori G., *Deducting Interest on Equity Capital: Brazilian and Belgian Tax Rules Compared*, 1 Eur. Tax Stud. 28 (2010).

Marchgraber C., *Conflicts of Qualification and Interpretation: How Should Developing Countries React?*, 44 Intertax 4 (2016).

Marchgraber C., *Tackling Deduction and Non-inclusion Schemes – The Proposal of the European Commission*, 54 Eur. Taxn. 4 (2014), Journals IBFD.

Martin J., *Amazon Fighting IRS Over Cost-Sharing Agreements*, Tax Analyst, Featured Articles, posted online on 21 January 2013.

Martin J., *Lawmakers Seek New Code of Conduct for Tax Accountants*, 70 Tax Notes Int'l 6 (2013).

Martin J., *UK Lawmakers Lambaste Big 4 Accounting Firms*, 69 Tax Notes Int'l 518 (2013).

Martín Jiménez A., *BEPS, the Digital(ized) Economy and the Taxation of Services and Royalties*, 46 Intertax 8/9 (2018).

Martín Jiménez A., *Beneficial Ownership: Current Trends*, 2 World Tax J. (2010).

Martin Jiménez A., *Domestic-Anti Abuse Rules and Double Taxation Treaties: A Spanish Perspective–Part I*, 56 Bull. Intl. Taxn. 11 (2002).

Martinez Laguna F., *Abuse and Aggressive Tax Planning: Between OECD and EU Initiatives–The Dividing Line Between Intended and Unintended Double Non-taxation*, 9 World Tax J. 2 (2017), Journals IBFD.

Martinez Laguna F., *Institutional Hybrid Financial Instruments and Double Non-taxation under Domestic Rules and Tax Treaty Law: The Example of Spain*, 44 Intertax 6/7 (2016).

Mason R. and Parada L., *The Legality of Digital Taxes in Europe*, 40 Va. Tax Rev. 175 (2020).

Mason R. and Daly S., *State Aid: The General Court Decision in Apple*, 99 Tax Notes Int'l 1317 (2020).

Mason R., *The Transformation of International Tax*, 114(3) Am. J. Int'l Law 353 (2020).

Mason R. and Parada L., *Digital Battlefront in the Tax Wars*, 92 Tax Notes Int'l 12, (2018).

Mason R., *Citizenship Taxation*, Southern California Law Rev. 89, Virginia Law and Economics Research Paper No. 2015-07, available at SSRN.

Mason R. and Knoll M., *What is Discrimination?*, 121 Yale L.J. 1014 (2012).

Mason R., *A Theory of Tax Discrimination*, NYU Jean Monnet Working Paper No. 09/06 (2006).

Mason R., *Tax Discrimination and Capital Neutrality*, 2 World Tax J. 2 (2010), Journals IBFD.

Mason R., *Made in America for European Tax: The Internal Consistency Test*, 49 B.C. L. Rev. 4 (2008).

Massimi F. and Petroni C., *Real-World ACE Reforms and the Italian Experience. Towards a General Trend?*, 40 Intertax 11 (2012).

McLure Jr. C., *Substituting Consumption-Based Direct Taxation for Income Taxes as the International Norm*, 45 Nat'l Tax J. 145 (1992).

Mendelson M., *The Subjective Element in Customary International Law*, 66 Brit. Y.B. Int'l L. 1, 208 (1995).

Moyal S., *Back to Basics: Rethinking Normative Principles in International Tax*, 73 Tax Lawyer 1(2019).

Møllin Ottosen A. and Nørremark M., *New Anti-avoidance Rules in Denmark Targets Reverse Hybrids and Convertible Bonds*, 68 Bull. Intl. Taxn. 11 (2008), Journals IBFD.

Moore A., *Ireland-Corporate Taxation sec. 1*, Country Analyses IBFD (accessed 1 February 2017).

Mullis K., *Check-the-Box and Hybrids: A Second Look at Elective U.S. Tax Classification for Foreign Entities*, 64 Tax Notes Int'l 5 (2011).

Navarro A., *Jurisdiction Not to Tax, Tax Sparing Clauses, and the OECD Minimum Taxation (GloBE) Proposal*, Nordic Tax Law Journal 1 (2021).

Navarro A., *International Tax Soft Law Instruments: The Futility of the Static v. Dynamic Interpretation Debate*, 48 Intertax 10 (2020).

Navarro A., Parada L. and Schwarz P., *The Proposal for an EU Anti-avoidance Directive: Some Preliminary Thoughts*, 25 EC Tax Rev. 3 (2016).

Nikolakakis A. et al., *Some Reflections on the Proposed Revision to the OECD Model and Commentaries, and on the Multilateral Instrument, with Respect to Fiscally Transparent Entities*, BTR 3 (2017).

Noked N., *Defense of Primary Taxing Rights* 40 Va. Tax Rev. 341 (2020).

Oliveira Everaert G. J., *Portugal – Corporate Taxation sec. 1.*, Country Surveys IBFD (accessed 31 May 2017).

Oliver D., *Differential Treatment of Discrimination?*, BTR 6 (1993).

Oliver J. D. et al., *Beneficial Owner*, 54 Bull. Int. Taxn. 7, 322 (2000), Journals IBFD.

Oliver J., *Other Similar Enterprises –NEC Semi-Conductors Ltd and Others v. Inland Revenue Commissioners*, BTR 2 (2004).

Oliver S., *The Parent-Subsidiary of 23 July 1990: A United Kingdom Perspective*, 10 EC Tax Rev. 211 (2001).

Parada L., *Full Taxation: The Single Tax Emperor's New Clothes*, Fl. Tax Rev. 24:2 (2021).

Parada L., *Hybrid Entity Mismatches and the MLI: A Tax Policy Assessment*, 49 Intertax 10 (2021).

Parada L., *Between Apple and Oranges: The EU General Court's Decision in the 'Apple Case'*, EC Tax Rev. 2 (2021).

Parada L., *The OECD 'Saving Clause': An American Tailored Provision Made to Measure the World*, Rivista di diritto finanziario e scienza delle finanze, LXXVIII, 1, I, 13-52 (2019).

Parada L., *The Unified Approach Under Pillar 1: An Early Analysis*, 96 Tax Notes Int'l 11 (2019).

Parada L., *Hybrid Entities and Conflicts of Allocation of Income Within Tax Treaties: Is New Article 1(2) of the OECD Model (Article 3(1) of the MLI) the Best Solution Available?* British Tax Rev. 3(2018).

Parada L., *Intergovernmental Agreements and the Implementation of FATCA in Europe*, 7 World Tax J. 2 (2015), Journals IBFD.

Parada L., *Lessons Learned from the Swiss Julius Baer Case*, 74 Tax Notes Int'l 13 (2014).

Parada L., *Agents v. Commissionaires: A Comparison in Light of the OECD Model Convention*, 72 Tax Notes Int'l. 1 (2013).

Parada L., *A Comparative Analysis of CFC Regimes in Latin America*, 68 Tax Notes Int'l 10 (2012).

Parillo K., *German Court Permit Used of Stolen Data in Tax Probes*, 60 Tax Notes Int'l 10, (2010).

Parisi F., *The Formation of Customary Law*, George Mason Law & Economics Research Paper No. 01-06, available at SSRN, p. 5.

Pasculli L. and MacLennan S., *'The Producers' of Tax Abuse: The Corrupting Effects of Tax Law and Tax Reliefs in the U.K. Film Industry*, Law and Contemporary Problems 85:101(2022).

Perdelwitz A., *Treaty Override–Revival of the Debate over the Constitutionality of Domestic Treaty Override Provisions in Germany*, 53 Eur. Taxn. 9/Special Issue (2013), Journals IBFD.

Peters C., *Critical Analysis of the General Court's 'EU Arm's Length Tool': Beware of the Reflexivity of Transfer Pricing Law!* EC Tax Rev. 1 (2022).

Piantavigna P., *Tax Abuse and Aggressive Tax Planning in the BEPS Era: How EU Law and the OECD are Establishing a Unifying Conceptual Framework in International Tax Law, Despite Linguistic Discrepancies*, 9 World Tax J. 1 (2017), Journals IBFD.

Pijl H., *Beneficial Ownership and Second Tier Beneficial Owners in Tax Treaties of the Netherlands*, 31 Intertax 10 (2003).

Pijl H., *The OECD Commentary as a Source of International Law and the Role of the Judiciary*, 46 EU Taxn. 5 (2006), Journals IBFD.

Pinto D., *Exclusive Source or Residence-Based Taxation–Is a New and Simpler World Tax Order Possible?,* 61 Bull. Intl. Taxn. 7 (2007), Journals IBFD.

Pistone P., *La Planificación Fiscal Agresiva y las Categorías Conceptuales del Derecho Tributario Global,* Revista Española de Derecho Financiero 170, Abril-Junio 2016.

Popa O., *Hybrid Entity Payments–Extinct Species after the BEPS Action Plan?,* 59 Eur. Taxn. 9 (2014), Journals IBFD.

Popa O., *UK Investors in US LLCs Exposed to Double Taxation–Is This the End of the Story?,* 53 Eur. Taxn. 6 (2013), Journals IBFD.

Prebble J., *Exploiting Form in Avoidance by International Tax Arbitrage–Arguments Towards a Unifying Hypothesis of Taxation Law*, 17 Asia-Pac. Tax Bull. 1 (2011), Journals IBFD.

Prest C., *French Tax Authorities Lose Battle on Stolen Data*, 62 Tax Notes Int'l 3 (2011).

Prokisch R., *Fragen der Auslegung von Doppelbesteuerungsabkommen*, 4 SWI 52 (1994).

Reinhold S., *Good Faith in International Law*, Bonn Research Paper on International Law, Paper No. 2 (2013).

Resch R., *The New German Unilateral Switch-Over and Subject-to-Tax Rule*, 47 Eur. Taxn. 10 (2007), Journals IBFD.

Riedy J., *IRS Uses Voluntary Payment Rule to Challenge Foreign Tax Credits Separated from the Income Base*, 34 Int'l. Tax J. 3 (2008).

Riedy J., *Proposed Code Sec. 901 Regulations Revise the Technical Taxpayer Rule*, 6 J. Tax'n Global Transactions 19 (2006).

Riis A. and Lytken P.E., *Denmark-Corporate Taxation sec. 10*, Country Analyses IBFD (accessed 6 February 2017).

Ring D., *Democracy, Sovereignty and Tax Competition: The Role of Tax Sovereignty in Shaping Tax Cooperation*, 9 Fl. Tax Rev. (2009).

Ring D., *One Nation among Many: Policy Implications of Cross-Border Tax Arbitrage*, 44 B.C. L. Rev. 1 (2002).

Rogers S., Cassidy D. and Mace J., *U.K. Tax Treatment of U.S. LLCs Post-Anson*, 82 Tax Notes Int'l 4 (2016).

Roin J., *Competition and Evasion: Another Perspective on International Tax Competition*, 89 Geo. L. J. 543 (2001).

Roin J., *Taxation Without Coordination*, 31 J. Leg. Stud. 1, Part 2 (2002).

Ronco S., *Scambio di informazioni tra Stati Uniti e Svizzera: il caso Julius Baer*, Rassegna Tributaria 6, (2014).

Rosembuj T., *International Tax Arbitrage*, 39 Intertax 4 (2011).

Rosenberg R., *New Foreign Tax Credit Anti-splitting Rule*, 129 Tax Notes 6 (2007).

Rosenbloom H.D., *Cross-Border Arbitrage: The Good, The Bad and the Ugly*, 85 Taxes – The Tax Mag. (2007).

Rosenbloom H.D., *Current Developments in Regard to Tax Treaties*, 40 N.Y.U. Inst. on Fed. Tax'n §31 (1982).

Rosenbloom H.D., *Tax Treaty Abuse: Policies and Issues*, 15 Law & Pol'y Int'l Bus. 763 (1983).

Rosenbloom H.D., *The David R. Tillinghast Lecture: International Tax Arbitrage and the 'International Tax System'*, 53 Tax L. Rev. 137 (2000).

Rust A., *BEPS Action 2: 2014 Deliverable–Neutralizing the Effects of Hybrid Mismatch Arrangements and Its Compatibility with the Non-discrimination Provisions in Tax Treaties and the Treaty on the Functioning of the European Union*, BTR 3 (2015).

Sanghavi D., *BEPS Hybrid Entities Proposal: A Slippery Slope, Especially for Developing Countries*, 85 Tax Notes Int'l 4 (2017).

Scheunemann M. and Müller-Duttiné T., *New German Tax Rules on Financing Expenses*, 35 Intertax 8/9 (2007).

Schnitger A. and Oskamp M., *Empfehlungen der OECD zur Neutralisierung von 'Hybrid Mismatches' auf Abkommensebene*, 23 IStR 11 (2014).

Schön W., *International Tax Coordination for a Second-Best World (Part II)*, 2 World Tax J. 1 (2010), Journals IBFD.

Schön W., *Neutrality and Territoriality–Competing or Converging Concepts in European Tax Law?*, 69 Bull Intl. Taxn. 4/5 (2015), Journals IBFD.

Schön W., *Tax Competition in Europe – The National Perspective*, 42 E.U. Taxn. 12, 495 (2002).

Schön W., *Transfer Pricing Issues of BEPS in the Light of EU Law*, 3 Brit. Tax Rev. 417 (2015).

Selig M., *Half Trust, Half Company, All Anstalt: The History and Possible Tax Consequences of the Liechtenstein Anstalt Down Under*, 53 Intl. Fisc. Docn. 8/9 (1999), Journals IBFD.

Serim N., *Taxpayers' Rights–The Turkish Model*, 48 Eur. Taxn. 4 (2008), Journals IBFD.

Shaviro D., *The Two Faces of the Single Tax Principle*, New York University Law and Economics Working Papers, Paper 419 (2015).

Shepard L., *Don't Ask, Don't Tell: Swiss Behavioral Patterns*, 66 Tax Notes Int'l 1 (2012).

Sheppard L., *Apple's Tax Magic*, Worldwide Tax Daily (26 May 2013).

Sheppard L., *Machiavellian Pragmatism in Tax Enforcement*, 77 Tax Notes Int'l 11 (2015).

Sicular D., *The New Look-Through Rule: W(h)ither Subpart F?*, 46 Tax Notes Int'l 6 (2007).

Soled J., *Use of Judicial Doctrines in Resolving Transfer Tax Controversies*, 42 Bos. College L. Rev. 3 (2001).

Soler M. and Gil E., *Encouraging Research and Development (and Innovation) in the Spanish Tax System*, 70 Bull. Intl. Taxn. 8 (2016), Journals IBFD.

Soong Johnston S., *State Court Rejects Challenge Against Use of Stolen Bank Data*, 73 Tax Notes Int'l 9 (2014).

Spudis B. and Wilczynski M., *Entity Classification Update: Rev. Rul. 93-4*, 71 Taxes 164 (1993).

Staigner J. and Köth V., *Abkommensberechtigung einer französischen SICAV sowie des deutschen REIT*, BB 47 (2012).

Stefaner M., *Konsequenzen der Anwendung von § 10 Abs. 7 KStG*, 22 Steuer und Wirtschaft International 8 (2012).

Steindl M. and Stiastny M., *The Impact of the OECD Partnership Report (1999) on Tax Avoidance in Outbound Cases*, 68 Bull. Int'l. Taxn. 2 (2014), Journals IBFD.

Stewart D., *Ireland Targets 'Stateless' Companies in 2014 Budget*, 72 Tax Notes Int'l 3 (2013).

Stewart M., *Transnational Tax Information Exchange Networks: Steps Towards a Globalized, Legitimate Tax Administration*, 4 World Tax J. 2 (2012), Journals IBFD.

Tavares R., Womack J. and Wilson D., *New Brazilian Equity Interest Rules: Efficient Financing for U.S.-Owned Subsidiaries*, Tax Notes Int'l (6 January 1997).

Suzuki Y., *Principle or Clause of 'Saving' in Tax Conventions: Introduction and Analysis of One Japanese Case*, WU International Taxation Research Paper Series No. 2015-07.

Thömmes O. and Linn A., *The New German DCL and Dividends Matching Rules and EU Law*, 42 Intertax 1 (2014).

Ting A., *iTax–Apple's International Tax Structure and the Double Non-taxation Issue*, BTR 1 (2014).

Ting A., *The Politics of BEPS – Apple's International Tax Structure and the US Attitude towards BEPS*, 69 Bull. Intl. Taxn. 6/7 (2015), Journals IBFD.

Traversa E., *Tax Incentives and Territoriality Within the European Union: Balancing the Internal Market with the Tax Sovereignty of Member States*, 6 World Tax J. 3 (2014), Journals IBFD.

Van den Broek H. and Meussen G.T.K., *Netherlands- National Grid Indus Case: Re-thinking Exit Taxation*, 52 Eur. Taxn. 4 (2012), Journals IBFD.

Van den Hurk H., *Starbucks Versus the People*, 68 Bull. Intl. Taxn. 1 (2014), Journals IBFD.

Vogel K., *Conflicts of Qualification: The Discussion Is Not Finished*, 57 Bull. Intl. Taxn. 2 (2003), Journals IBFD.

Vogel K., *Worldwide v. Source Taxation of Income – A Review and Re-evaluation of Arguments (Part II)* 16 Intertax 10 (1988).

Von Brocke K. and Garcia Perez E., *Group Financing: From Thin Capitalization to Interest Deduction Limitation Rules*, 16 Intl. Transfer Pricing J. 1 (2009), Journals IBFD.

Weber D., *Abuse of Law in European Tax Law: An Overview and Some Recent Trends in the Direct and Indirect Tax Case Law of the ECJ–Part 2*, 53 Eur. Taxn. 7 (2013), Journals IBFD.

Weber D., *In Search of a (New) Equilibrium Between Tax Sovereignty and the Freedom of Movement Within the EC*, 34 Intertax 12 (2006).

Weisbach D., *The Use of Neutralities in International Tax Policy*, 68 Nat'l Tax J. 635 (2015).

West C., *References to the OECD Commentaries in Tax Treaties: A Steady March from 'Soft' Law to 'Hard' Law?*, 9 World Tax J. 1 (2017).

Wheeler J., *The Attribution of Income to a Person for Tax Treaty Purposes*, 59 Bull. Intl. Fisc. Doc. 11 (2005), Journals IBFD.

Wheeler J., The *Missing Keystone of Income Tax Treaties*, 3 World Tax J. (2011), Journals IBFD.

Wittendorff J., *Danish Parliament Enacts Transparent Entity Legislation*, 34 Tax Notes Int'l 1 (2004).

Wittendorff J., *Denmark's Hovmand Clarifies Pending Transparent Entities Legislation*, 33 Tax Notes Int'l 9 (2004).

Zammit I., *Centralized Intellectual Property Business Models–Tax Implications of EU Patent Box Regimes*, 69 Bull Intl. Taxn. 9 (2015), Journals IBFD.

4. JURISPRUDENCE AND ADMINISTRATIVE DECISIONS

AUS: *Thiel v. Federal Commissioner of Taxation* [1990] HCA 37; 171 CLR 338.

BE: Mons., 11 September 2013, No. 11/1078/A.

BE: Court of Appeals of Brussels, 30 April 1998, AFT, 1999, 119–125.

BE: Brussels Court of Appeals, 28 May 1969, *Rev. Fisc.* 81 (1970).

BR: Administrative Council of Administrative Appeals, Judgment No. 101-95.802 – *Eagle I.*

BR: Administrative Council of Administrative Appeals, Judgment No. 101-97.070 – *Eagle II.*

CH: Federal Administrative Court [*Bundesverwaltungsgericht*–BVGer], Urteil A-6843/2014 of 15 September 2015.

CH: Bundesverwaltungsgericht: Medienmitteilung v. 24 September 2015, *Keine Amtshilfe bei gestohlenen Daten,* Urteil A-6843/2014 v. 15 September 2015.

CH: *X. v. Federal Tax Administration,* A-5390/2013, Swiss Federal Administrative Court [*Bundesverwaltungsgericht*], 6 January 2014 in: P. Baker (ed.), 17 ITLR, Lexis Nexis, London (2014).

CH: Decision of the Swiss Federal Administrative Court [*Bundesverwaltungsgericht*] A-737/2012 of 5 April 2012.

DE: BVerfG, Beschl. 15.12.2015 – 2 BvL 1/2, URL: http://www.bverfg.de/e/ls20151215_2bvl000112.html.

DE: BFH, 14 October 2015, I R 20/15.
DE: VGH Urteil v. 24 February 2014 [VGH B 26/13] Steuk 2014, 106.
DE: BFH, 6 June 2012, I R 6, 8/11; Federal Tax Gazette II 2012, 111.
DE: BVerfG Beschl. v. 9 November 2010 [2 BvR 2101/09] – DStR 2010, 2512.
DE: BFH 17.02.2003. 1 R 14/02. BStBl II 2004.
DE: BFH of 13 June 1992, IX R 182/87, BStBl. 1992 II, 972.
DE: BFH of 29 October 1974, I R 240/72, BStBl. 1975 II, 126 and BFH of 7 December 1994, I K 1/93, BStBl. 1995 II, 175.
DE: 1965 BStBl III 258 (BFH 1965).
ES: Judgment of the Spanish High National Court, SAN 27.2.2014.
ES: DGT, Consulta Vinculante No. V1398-16 of 5 April 2016.
ES: DGT, Consulta Vinculante No. V3319-16 of 17 July 2016.
ES: DGT, Consulta Vinculante V2378-15 of 28 July 2015.
ES: DGT, Consulta Vinculante No. V3836-15 of 2 December 2015.
ES: DGT, Consulta Vinculante No. V036-14 of 10 February 2014.
ES: DGT, Consulta Vinculante No. V1631-14 of 25 June 2014.
ES: DGT, Consulta Vinculante No. V0012-11 of 11 January 2011.
ES: DGT, Consulta General No. 0024-07 of 1 July 2007.
ES: DGT, Consulta General No. 0196-05 of 1 June 2005.
ES: DGT, Consulta General No. 2110-04 of 30 December 2004.
EU: Judgment in *Sabou v. The Czech Republic*, Case C-276/12, ECLI:EU:C:2013:678.
EU: Judgment in *The Commissioners for Her Majesty's Revenue & Customs v. Philips Electronics UK Ltd*, Case C-18/11, ECLI:EU:C:2012:532.
EU: Judgment in *Société d'investissement pour l'agriculture tropicale S.A. (SIAT) v. Belgian State*, C-318/10, EU:C:2012:415.
EU: Judgment in *Scheuten Solar Technology GmBH v. Finanzamt Gelsenkirchen-Süd*, C-397/09, ECLI:EU:C:2011:499.
EU. Judgment in *National Grid Indus BV v. Inspecteur van de Belastingdienst Rijnmond/kantoor Rotterdam*, C-371/10, ECLI:EU:C:2011:785.
EU: Judgment in *Société de Gestion Industrielle (SGI) v. Belgian State*, C-311/08, ECLI:EU:C:2010:26.
EU: Judgment in *HMRC v. RBS Deutschland Holding GmbH*, C-277/09, ECLI: EU:2010:810.
EU: Judgment in *CIBA Speciality Chemicals Central and Eastern Europe Szolgáltató, Tanácsadó és Keresdedelmi kft v. Adó- és Pénzügyi Ellenrzési Hivatal (APEH) Hatósági Fosztály*, C-96/08, ECLI:EU:C:2010:185.
EU: Joined Judgments *X and Passenheim-van Schoot*, C-155/08 and C-157/08, ECLI: EU:C:2009:368.
EU: Judgment in *Maragarete Block v. Finanzamt Kaufbeuren*, C-67/08, EU:C:2008:92.
EU: Judgment in *Jobra Vermögensverwaltungs-Gesellschaft mbH v. Finanzamt Amstetten Melk Scheibbs*, C-330/07, ECLI:EU:C:2008:685.
EU: Judgment in *Commission of the European Communities v.* Hellenic Republic, C-178/05, ECLI:EU:C:2007:317.
EU: Judgment in *Test Claimants in the Thin Cap Group Litigation v. Commissioners of Inland Revenue*, C-524/04, EU:C:2007:161.

EU: Judgment in *Columbus Container Services BVBA & Co. v. Finanzamt Bielefeld-Innenstadt*, C-298/05, EU:C:2007:754.

EU: Judgment in *Rewe Zentralfinanz eG v. Finanzamt Köln-Mitte*, C-347/04, EU:C:2007:194.

EU: Judgment in *Finanzamt Offenbach am Main-Land v. Keller Holding GmbH*, C-471/04, EU:C:2006:143.

EU: Judgment in *Cadbury Schweppes and Cadbury Schweppes Overseas Ltd v Commissioners of Inland Revenue*, C-196/04, EU:C:2006:544.

EU: Judgment in *N v. Inspecteur van de Belastingdienst Oost/kantoor Almelo*, C-470/04, ECLI:EU:C:2006:525.

EU: Judgment in *Halifax plc., Leeds Permanent Development Services Ltd., County Wide Property Investments Ltd. v. Commissioners of Custom and Excise*, C-255/02, ECLI:EU:C:2006:121.

EU: Judgment in *Pirkko Marjatta Turpeinen*, C-520/04, EU:C:2006:703.

EU: *Judgment in Test in Class IV of the ACT Group Litigation v. Commissioners of Inland Revenue*, C-374/04, EU:C:2006:139.

EU: *Judgment in Test in Class IV of the ACT Group Litigation v. Commissioners of Inland Revenue*, C-374/04, EU:C:2006:139.

EU: Judgment in *Denkavit International and Denkavit France*, C-170/05, EU:C:2006:266.

EU: Judgment in *Mark Kerckhaert and Bernadette Morres v. Belgische Staat*, C-513/04, ECLI:EU:C:2006:713.

EU: Judgment in *Marks & Spencer plc v. David Halsey (Her Majesty's Inspector of Taxes)*, C-446/03, ECLI:EU:C:2005:763.

EU: Judgment in *Marks & Spencer plc v. David Halsey (Her Majesty's Inspector of Taxes)*, C-446/03, ECLI:EU:C:2005:763.

EU: Judgment in *Egon Schempp v. Finanzamt München V*, C-403/03, ECLI: EU:C:2005:446.

EU: Judgment in *Friederike Wallentin-Hermann v. Alitalia*, C-169/03, EU:C:2004:771.

EU: Judgment in *Hughes de Lasteyrie du Saillant v. Ministère de l'Economie des Fianances. et de l'Industrie*, C-9/02, ECLI:EU:C:2004:138.

EU: Judgment in *Arnoud Gerritse v. Finanzamt Neukölln-Nord*, C-234/01, EU:C:2003:340.

EU: Judgment in *Bosal Holding BV v. Staatsecretaris van Financiën*, C-168/01, EU:C:2003:479.

EU: Judgment in *F.W.L. de Groot v. Staatsecretaris van Financiën*, C-385/00, EU:C:2002:750.

EU: Judgment in *Lankhorst-Hohorst GmbH v. Finanzamt Steinfurt*, C-324/00, ECLI: EU:C:2002:749.

EU: Judgment in *X and Y v. Riksskatteverket*, C-436/00, EU:C:2002:704.

EU: Judgment in *Eurowings Luftverkehrs AG v. Finanzamt Dortmund-Unna*, C-294/97, EU:C:1999:524.

EU: Judgment in *Royal Bank of Scotland plc v. Elliniko Dimosio (Greek State)*, C-311/97, EU:C:1999:216.

EU: Judgment in *Deutsche Shell GmbH v. Finanzamt für Dortmund-Unna*, C-294/97, EU:C:1999:524.

EU: Judgment in *P.H. Asscher v. Staatsecretaris van Financiën*, C-107/94,EU:C:1996:251.

EU: Judgment in *Finanzamt Köln-Altsadt v. Schumacker*, C-279/93, ECLI: EU:C:1995:31.

EU: Judgment in *Wielockx v. Inspecteur der Directe Belastingen*, C-80/94, EU:C:1995:271.

EU: Judgment in *Hans Martin Bachmann v. Belgian State*, C-204/90, ECLI: EU:C:1992:35.

EU: Judgment in *Commission of the European Communities v. Kingdom of Belgium*, C-300/90, ECLI:EU:C:1992:37.

EU: Judgment in *Columbus Container Services BVBA & Co. v. Finanzamt Bielefeld-Innenstadt*, C-298/05, ECLI:EU:C:2007:754.

EU: Judgment in *Costa v. E.N.E.L.*, C-6/64, EU:C:1964:66.

FR: Conseil d' État, 28 June 2002, Case No. 232276, *Schneider Electric*, RJF 10/02, no. 1080.

FR: CE, 3rd and 8th s.-s., 24 May 2000, req. no. 209 699 et rec. no. 209 891, CRCAM *Normand (Concl.), DF* no. 48, 2000, comm. 943, concl. Touvet.

International: *Case Concerning the Gabcikovo-Nagymaros Project (Hungary/Slovakia)*, Judgment of 25 September 1997, I.C.J. Reports 1997.

International: *Case Concerning the Delimitation of the Maritime Boundary in the Gulf of Maine Area (Canada v United States of America)* (Merits), Judgment of 12 October 1984, I.C.J. Rep 305.

International: *The case of the S.S. 'Lotus'*, Collection of Judgments, Publications of the Permanent Court of International Justice, Series A-No. 10, 7 September 1927.

LU: Cour adm., 27 juillet 2011, n 28115C du role.

NL: Decision of the Dutch Supreme Court *Hoge Raad*, 1 December 2006, BNB 2007/75-79.

NL: Decision of Amsterdam Tax Court of Appeal of 4 January 1995, No. 93/1467, Infobulletin, 95/315.

NL: Supreme Court 16 March 1994, no. 27.764, BNB 1994/191.

JP: Supreme Court, 29 October 2009, Glaxo, Minshu, Vol. 63 No. 8, 1881.

U.K.: *Anson (Appellant) v. Commissioners for Her Majesty's Revenue and Customs (Respondent) [2015] UKSC 44 on appeal from [2013] EWCA Civ 63*, 1 July 2015.

U.K.: FTT, 10 August 2012, *Paul Weiser v. Commissioner for Her Majesty's Revenue and Customs*, [2012] UKFTT 501 (TC), [2012] SFTD 1381, Tax Treaty Case Law IBFD.

U.K.: CA, 23 March 2011, *Bayfine UK v. Commissioner for H M Revenue and Customs*, [2011] EWCA Civ 304, Tax Treaty Case Law IBFD.

U.K.: First-tier Tribunal, 22 February 2010, Case TC00399, Appeal No. SC/3106/08, *Swift v. Commissioners for HM Revenue and Customs*, Tax Treaty Case Law IBFD.

U.K.: Upper Tribunal, 3 August 2011, FTC/39/2010, [2011] UKUT 318 (TCC), Tax Treaty Case Law IBFD.

U.K.: CA, 8 July 2010, *Smallwood (Trevor Smallwood and Mary Caroline Smallwood, Trustees of the Trevor Smallwood Trust) v. Commissioners for the H M Revenue and Customs*, [2010] EWCA Civ 778, Tax Treaty Case Law IBFD.

U.K.: CA, 9 June 1998, *Memec Plc. v. Commissionaire of Inland Revenue*, Tax Treaty Case Law IBFD.

U.K.: *Padmore v. IRC* [1989] STC 493.

U.K.: *Duke of Westminster v. IRC*, [1936] 19 D.T.C. 490, 520 (Can.).

U.S.: US Tax Court of 11 April 1983, No. 20766-81, *Estate of Burghardt v. Commissioner*, 80 T.C. 705 (1983).

U.S.: *Guardian Industries Corp v. Unites States,* 477 f. 3d 1368, 1371 (Fed. Cir. 2007).

U.S.: USTC, 5 August 1971, *Aiken Industries Inc. v. Commissioner of Internal Revenue*, 56 T.C. 925.

U.S.: *Kholer Co. v. US*, 124 F3d 1451 (Fed. Cir. 1997).

U.S.: *United States v. Kintner*, 216 F2d 418 (9th Cir. 1954).

U.S.: *Pelton v. Commissioner*, 82 F. 2d 473 (7th Cir. 1937).

U.S.: *Morrissey v. Commissioner*, 296 U.S. 344 (1935).

U.S.: *Helvering v. Gregory,* 69 F.2d 809, 810 (2d Cir. 1934).

U.S.: *Cook v. United States*, 288 US 102 (1933).

5. OTHER SOURCES

CH: Press release, Media Relations A-5390/2013 and A-5540/2013, Swiss Federal Administrative Court, St. Gallen (8 January 2014).

EU: European Commission Press release, *Fair Taxation: Commission welcomes new rules to prevent tax avoidance through non-EU countries,* 21 February 2017.

EU: European Commission Press release, *State aid: Commission opens formal investigation into Luxembourg's tax treatment of McDonald's,* 3 December 2015.

EU: European Commission Press Release IP/15/5043, *Fighting tax evasion: EU and Switzerland sign historic tax transparency agreement*, 27 May 2015.

Höltschi R., *Automatischer Informationsaustausch, Schweiz und EU unterzeichnen AIA*, Neue Zürcher Zeitung (27 May 2015).

IBFD Glossary, available online at the IBFD Tax Research Platform.

International: Tax Justice (ONG) www.taxjustice.net.

International: Mansour B., OECD breaks silence on lobbying – Tax Justice Network Response, Press Office, 9 July 2023.

International: Agyemang E. and Fildes N., *OECD pressed Australia to drop plan to reveal where multinational pay tax*, Financial Times, 7 July 2023.

OECD, Glossary of Tax Terms, available at www.oecd.org.

Schmidt N. and Binder K., Chaos durch doppelten Kampf gegen doppelte Steuervorteile, Die Presse (14 January 2013), available at www.dipresse.com.

Index

SERIES ON INTERNATIONAL TAXATION

1. Alberto Xavier, *The Taxation of Foreign Investment in Brazil,* 1980 (ISBN 90-200-0582-0).
2. Hugh J. Ault & Albert J. Rädler, *The German Corporation Tax Law with 1980 Amendments,* 1981 (ISBN 90-200-0642-8).
3. Paul R. McDaniel & Hugh J. Ault, *Introduction to United States International Taxation,* 1981 (ISBN 90-6544-004-6).
4. Albert J. Rädler, *German Transfer Pricing/Prix de Transfer en Allemagne,* 1984 (ISBN 90-6544-143-3).
5. Paul R. McDaniel & Stanley S. Surrey, *International Aspects of Tax Expenditures: A Comparative Study,* 1985 (ISBN 90-654-4163-8).
6. Kees van Raad, *Nondiscrimination in International Tax Law,* 1986 (ISBN 90-6544-266-9).
7. Sijbren Cnossen (ed.), *Tax Coordination in the European Community,* 1987 (ISBN 90-6544-272-3).
8. Ben Terra, *Sales Taxation. The Case of Value Added Tax in the European Community,* 1989 (ISBN 90-6544-381-9).
9. Rutsel S.J. Martha, *The Jurisdiction to Tax in International Law: Theory and Practice of Legislative Fiscal Jurisdiction,* 1989 (ISBN 90-654-4416-5).
10. Paul R. McDaniel & Hugh J. Ault, *Introduction to United States International Taxation* (3rd revised edition), 1989 (ISBN 90-6544-423-8).
11. Manuel Pires, *International Juridicial Double Taxation of Income,* 1989 (ISBN 90-6544-426-2).
12. A.H.M. Daniels, *Issues in International Partnership Taxation,* 1991 (ISBN 90-654-4577-3).
13. Arvid A. Skaar, *Permanent Establishment: Erosion of a Tax Treaty Principle,* 1992 (ISBN 90-6544-594-3).
14. Cyrille David & Geerten M.M. Michielse (eds), *Tax Treatment of Financial Instruments,* 1996 (ISBN 90-654-4666-4).
15. Herbert H. Alpert & Kees van Raad (eds), *Essays on International Taxation,* 1993 (ISBN 90-654-4781-4).
16. Wolfgang Gassner, Michael Lang & Eduard Lechner (eds), *Tax Treaties and EC Law,* 1997 (ISBN 90-411-0680-4).
17. Glória Teixeira, *Taxing Corporate Profits in the EU,* 1997 (ISBN 90-411-0703-7).
18. Michael Lang et al. (eds), *Multilateral Tax Treaties,* 1998 (ISBN 90-411-0704-5).
19. Stef van Weeghel, *The Improper Use of Tax Treaties,* 1998 (ISBN 90-411-0737-1).

20. Klaus Vogel (ed.), *Interpretation of Tax Law and Treaties and Transfer Pricing in Japan and Germany*, 1998 (ISBN 90-411-9655-2).
21. Bertil Wiman (ed.), *International Studies in Taxation: Law and Economics; Liber Amicorum Leif Mutén*, 1999 (ISBN 90-411-9692-7).
22. Alfonso J. Martín Jiménez, *Towards Corporate Tax Harmonization in the European Community*, 1999 (ISBN 90-411-9690-0).
23. Ramon J. Jeffery, *The Impact of State Sovereignty on Global Trade and International Taxation*, 1999 (ISBN 90-411-9703-6).
24. A.J. Easson, *Taxation of Foreign Direct Investment*, 1999 (ISBN 90-411-9741-9).
25. Marjaana Helminen, *The Dividend Concept in International Tax Law: Dividend Payments Between Corporate Entities*, 1999 (ISBN 90-411-9765-6).
26. Paul Kirchhof, Moris Lehner, Kees van Raad, Arndt Raupach & Michael-Rodi (eds), *International and Comparative Taxation: Essays in Honour of Klaus Vogel*, 2002 (ISBN 90-411-9841-5).
27. Krister Andersson, Peter Melz & Christer Silfverberg (eds), *Liber Amicorum Sven-Olof Lodin*, 2001 (ISBN 90-411-9850-4).
28. Juan Martín Jovanovich, *Customs Valuation and Transfer Pricing: Is It Possible to Harmonize Customs and Tax Rules?*, Second Edition, 2018 (ISBN 978-90-411-6134-5).
29. Stefano Simontacchi, *Taxation of Capital Gains under the OECD Model Convention: With Special Regard to Immovable Property*, 2007 (ISBN 978-90-411-2549-1).
30. Michael Lang, Josef Schuch, & Claus Staringer (eds), *Tax Treaty Law and EC Law*, 2007 (ISBN 978-90-411-2629-0).
31. Duncan Bentley, *Taxpayers' Rights: Theory Origin and Implementation*, 2007 (ISBN 978-90-411-2650-4).
32. Sergio André Rocha, *Interpretation of Double Taxation Conventions: General Theory and Brazilian Perspective*, 2008 (ISBN 978-90-411-2822-5).
33. Robert F. van Brederode, *Systems of General Sales Taxation: Theory, Policy and Practice*, 2009 (ISBN 978-90-411-2832-4).
34. John G. Head & Richard Krever (eds), *Tax Reform in the 21st Century: A Volume in Memory of Richard Musgrave*, 2009 (ISBN 978-90-411-2829-4).
35. Jens Wittendorff, *Transfer Pricing and the Arm's Length Principle in International Tax Law*, 2010 (ISBN 978-90-411-3270-3).
36. Marjaana Helminen, *The International Tax Law Concept of Dividend*, Second Edition, 2017 (ISBN 978-90-411-8394-1).
37. Robert F. van Brederode (ed.), *Immovable Property under VAT: A Comparative Global Analysis*, 2011 (ISBN 978-90-411-3126-3).
38. Dennis Weber & Stef van Weeghel, *The 2010 OECD Updates: Model Tax Convention & Transfer Pricing Guidelines - A Critical Review*, 2011 (ISBN 978-90-411-3812-5).
39. Yariv Brauner & Martin James McMahon, Jr. (eds), *The Proper Tax Base: Structural Fairness from an International and Comparative Perspective— Essays in Honour of Paul McDaniel*, 2012 (ISBN 978-90-411-3286-4).
40. Robert F. van Brederode (ed.), *Science, Technology and Taxation*, 2012 (ISBN 978-90-411-3125-6).

41. Oskar Henkow, *The VAT/GST Treatment of Public Bodies*, 2013 (ISBN 978-90-411-4663-2).
42. Jean Schaffner, *How Fixed Is a Permanent Establishment?*, 2013 (ISBN 978-90-411-4662-5).
43. Miguel Correia, *Taxation of Corporate Groups*, 2013 (ISBN 978-90-411-4841-4).
44. Veronika Daurer, *Tax Treaties and Developing Countries*, 2014 (ISBN 978-90-411-4982-4).
45. Claire Micheau, *State Aid, Subsidy and Tax Incentives under EU and WTO Law*, 2014 (ISBN 978-90-411-4555-0).
46. Robert F. van Brederode & Richard Krever (eds), *Legal Interpretation of Tax Law*, 2014 (ISBN 978-90-411-4945-9).
47. Radhakishan Rawal, *Taxation of Cross-border Services*, 2014 (ISBN 978-90-411-4947-3).
48. João Dácio Rolim, *Proportionality and Fair Taxation*, 2014 (ISBN 978-90-411-5838-3).
49. Paulo Rosenblatt, *General Anti-avoidance Rules for Major Developing Countries*, 2015 (ISBN 978-90-411-5839-0).
50. Gaspar Lopes Dias V.S., *Tax Arbitrage through Cross-Border Financial Engineering*, 2015 (ISBN 978-90-411-5875-8).
51. Geerten M.M. Michielse & Victor Thuronyi (eds), *Tax Design Issues Worldwide*, 2015 (ISBN 978-90-411-5610-5).
52. Oktavia Weidmann, *Taxation of Derivatives and Cryptoassets*, Second Edition, 2024 (ISBN 978-94-035-2383-5).
53. Chris Evans, Richard Krever & Peter Mellor (eds), *Tax Simplification*, 2015 (ISBN 978-90-411-5976-2).
54. Reuven Avi-Yonah & Joel Slemrod (eds), *Taxation and Migration*, 2015 (ISBN 978-90-411-6136-9).
55. Alexander Bosman, *Other Income under Tax Treaties: An Analysis of Article 21 of the OECD Model Convention*, 2015 (ISBN 978-90-411-6610-4).
56. John Abrahamson, *International Taxation of Manufacturing and Distribution*, 2016 (ISBN 978-90-411-6664-7).
57. Frederik Boulogne, *Shortcomings in the EU Merger Directive*, 2016 (ISBN 978-90-411-6713-2).
58. Angelika Meindl-Ringler, *Beneficial Ownership in International Tax Law*, 2016 (ISBN 978-90-411-6833-7).
59. Andreas Waltrich, *Cross-Border Taxation of Permanent Establishments: An International Comparison*, 2016 (ISBN 978-90-411-6832-0).
60. Sergio André Rocha & Allison Christians (eds), *Tax Sovereignty in the BEPS Era*, 2017 (ISBN 978-90-411-6707-1).
61. Peter Antony Wilson, *BRICS and International Tax Law*, 2018 (ISBN 978-90-411-9435-0).
62. Louise Otis, Brigitte Alepin & Blanca Moreno-Dodson (eds), *Winning the Tax Wars: Tax Competition and Cooperation*, 2018 (ISBN 978-90-411-9460-2).

63. Marta Castelon, *International Taxation of Income from Services under Double Taxation Conventions: Development, Practice and Policy*, 2018 (ISBN 978-90-411-9594-4).
64. D.M. Broekhuijsen, *A Multilateral Tax Treaty: Designing an Instrument to Modernise International Tax Law*, 2018 (ISBN 978-90-411-9872-3).
65. John Abrahamson, *International Taxation of Energy Production and Distribution*, 2018 (ISBN 978-90-411-9101-4).
66. Leopoldo Parada, *Double Non-taxation and the Use of Hybrid Entities*, Second Edition, 2024 (ISBN 978-94-035-4666-7).
67. Richard Snoeij, *International Tax Aspects of Sovereign Wealth Investors: A Source State Perspective*, 2018 (ISBN 978-90-411-9431-2).
68. Aleksandra Bal, *Taxation, Virtual Currency and Blockchain*, 2019 (ISBN 978-94-035-0103-1).
69. Werner Haslehner, Georg Kofler, Katerina Pantazatou & Alexander Rust (eds), *Tax and the Digital Economy: Challenges and Proposals for Reform*, 2019 (ISBN 978-94-035-0361-5).
70. Eva Escribano, *Jurisdiction to Tax Corporate Income Pursuant to the Presumptive Benefit Principle: A Critical Analysis of Structural Paradigms Underlying Corporate Income Taxation and Proposals for Reform*, 2019 (ISBN 978-94-035-0640-1).
71. Jérôme Monsenego & Jan Bjuvberg (eds), *International Taxation in a Changing Landscape: Liber Amicorum in Honour of Bertil Wiman*, 2019 (ISBN 978-90-411-9234-9).
72. Kasper Dziurdź, *Non-discrimination in Tax Treaty Law and World Trade Law: The Impact of Formal, Substantive and Subjective Approaches*, 2019 (ISBN 978-94-035-0904-4).
73. Félix Daniel Martínez Laguna, *Hybrid Financial Instruments, Double Nontaxation and Linking Rules*, 2019 (ISBN 978-94-035-1074-3).
74. Jan Gooijer, *Tax Treaty Residence of Entities*, 2019 (ISBN 978-94-035-1301-0).
75. John Abrahamson, *International Taxation of Banking*, 2020 (ISBN 978-94-035-1094-1).
76. Richard Krever & François Vaillancourt (eds), *The Allocation of Multinational Business Income: Reassessing the Formulary Apportionment Option*, 2020 (ISBN 978-94-035-0614-2).
77. Ajit Kumar Singh, *Exploring the Nexus Doctrine in International Tax Law*, 2021 (ISBN 978-94-035-3363-6).
78. Galya Savir, *Regulation and Tax in Space*, 2021 (ISBN 978-94-035-3393-3).
79. Rita Julien, *Credit Method Compatibility and Constraints under EU Law: An Analysis of the Case Law of the CJEU*, 2022 (ISBN 978-94-035-2363-7).
80. Sergio André Rocha & Allison Christians (eds), *A Multilateral Convention for Tax: From Theory to Implementation*, 2022 (ISBN 978-90-411-9428-2).
81. Brigitte Alepin, Lyne Latulippe & Louise Otis (eds), *Coordination and Cooperation: Tax Policy in the 21st Century*, 2022 (ISBN 978-94-035-3740-5).
82. Chunyang Zhang, *The Role of Tax Law in Mergers and Acquisitions: A Chinese Perspective*, 2022 (ISBN 978-94-035-3741-2).

83. Florian Navisotschnigg, *Substance in International Tax Law: DEMPE Approach, Substantial Activity Requirement and Beneficial Ownership*, 2022 (ISBN 978-94-035-4895-1).
84. Mees Vergouwen, *The Effect of Directives Within the Area of Direct Taxation on the Interpretation and Application of Tax Treaties*, 2023 (ISBN 978-94-035-0907-5).
85. Rachna Matabudul, *Tax Treaty Dispute Resolution: Lessons from the Law of the Sea*, 2023 (ISNB 978-94-035-3407-7).